AF413575

KNOWING AND SEEING
REFLECTIONS ON FIFTY YEARS OF DRAWING CITIES

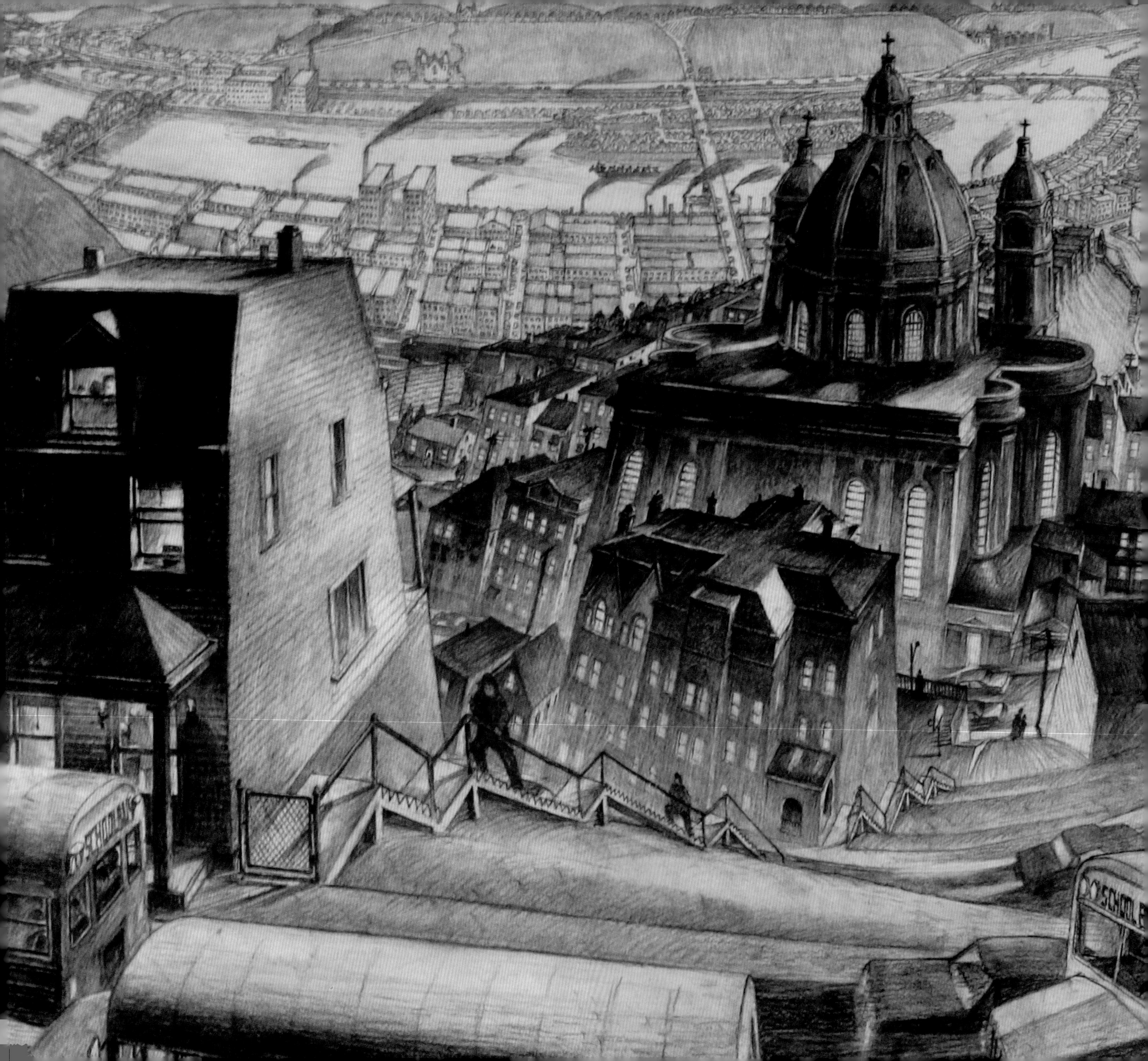
SCHOOL BUS
SCHOOL B

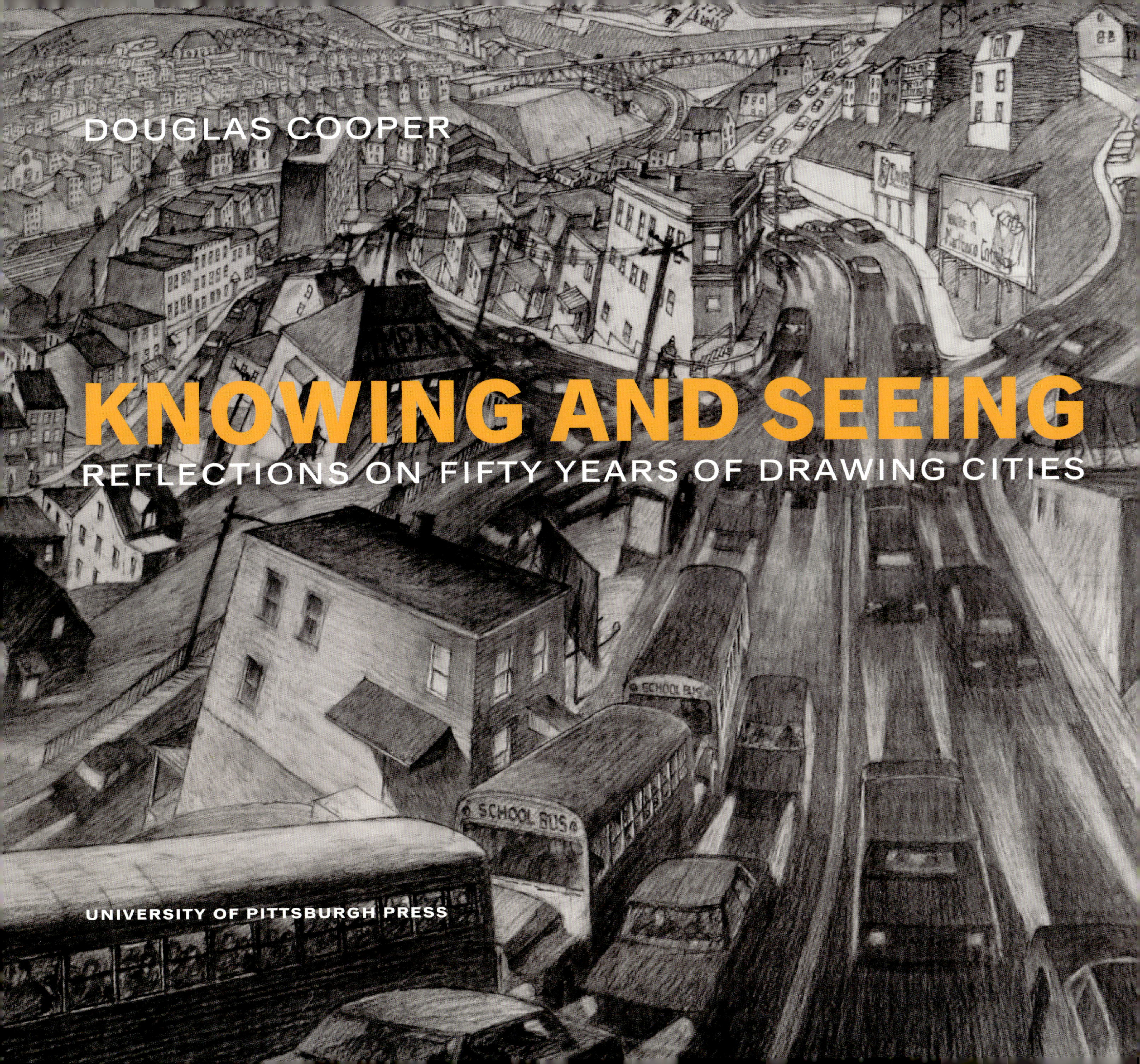

DOUGLAS COOPER
KNOWING AND SEEING
REFLECTIONS ON FIFTY YEARS OF DRAWING CITIES
UNIVERSITY OF PITTSBURGH PRESS
SCHOOL BUS
SCHOOL BUS

Published by the University of Pittsburgh Press, Pittsburgh, Pa., 15260
Copyright © 2019, University of Pittsburgh Press
All rights reserved
Printed in China

10 9 8 7 6 5 4 3 2 1

Cataloging-in-Publication data is available from the Library of Congress

ISBN 13: 978-0-8229-4570-3
ISBN 10: 0-8229-4570-3

Cover art: *City Church City*, Doug Cooper and Stefani Danes, 2018.
Charcoal on paper on board, fabric mounted around board, 80 × 216 inches.
East Liberty Presbyterian Church, Pittsburgh.

Cover and text design: Counterpunch Inc./ Linda Gustafson

Caption for title spread: *The School Outing*, Doug Cooper, 2013.
Charcoal on paper on board, 48 × 96 inches. Private collection.

FOR STEFANI

CONTENTS

FOREWORD

The spectacles presented in Doug Cooper's drawings include Pittsburgh as though it were perceived all at once in its entirety. His drawings realize an urban immensity that is neither the product of a meticulous portrait nor a sensational creation of an imaginary abstraction of specific buildings and people moving about in a fictional landscape. His details are grounded in the mundane realities of actual things and places.

A first read, upon seeing his compositions, is one of familiarity. However, upon closer inspection, you may find yourself viewing a city from above the cottony clouds of the atmosphere, while simultaneously looking at inhabitants conversing inside their apartments. Yet the two locations in space seem attached to one another. In another drawing you may find yourself standing in a group of rooms in which up and down, left and right, inside and outside, and behind are simultaneously visible without your head being spun around. The passage of time is collapsed into a concrete form.

Obviously, our minds know how to do all that or we would be lost in our own back yards! Thus Cooper's procedure may be understood as an exploration of workings of the mind in the medium of dots, lines, and patches of vine charcoal work. That exploration reveals Cooper's logical strategy to materially combine disparate things and events and thus to choreograph *moments of difference* into a majestic spatial unity. To achieve this he had to discover,

formulate, and shape patterns of complex fluid motions into networks dedicated entirely to a continuous connection of differences. Yet the "networks" themselves appear to be conventional and natural frameworks. Certainly, he is devoted to presenting actual and memorable places, rather than inventing esoteric mechanisms or imagining worlds for their own artistic shape and sake. Cooper succeeds in presenting a way of visual thinking about the fragmented details and events of a particular place without recourse to a cinematic or sequential system of presentation.

Like myself, Cooper selected an institute of technology as his home for higher education. I can understand that sentiment. He possesses the soul of a scientist, albeit a scientist capable of solving problems by thinking visually, rather than numerically or verbally. Despite presenting a robust dynamic of human and mechanical activity, his fundamental worldview contains a vision of repose, of life being completely natural and ordered.

His "scientific," scholarly, and artistic journey is described and illustrated in the following chapters. A purpose of this foreword is to alert the reader to the added joy of exploring Cooper's precise line work with an eye toward detecting some of the visual pyrotechnics that achieve a complex unity of differences

The final reward will be an intimate inspection of Cooper's material techniques of drawing per se, which display the actions of an artist making something. You will see up close that he works in what I call the "Z-dimension"; that is, the dimension that pushes into the material surface away from the planar right-left or up-down. It is the dimension of touch we associate with sculpture, manual drawing, and relief in which three-dimensionality is actual, rather than virtual (as on a computer screen). The millions of charcoal marks congeal into an intricate earthbound terrain that cement and sensualize the realities of Doug Cooper's visionary project. You will see the scientist and the visual artist performing as one authority.

Kent Bloomer
Yale University
November 2018

PREFACE AND ACKNOWLEDGMENTS

I don't remember a time when I have not made drawings. During childhood it was the one thing I knew I could do well, and I was passionate about it. One of my most vivid childhood memories is of an argument in my second-grade classroom with my best friend, Toby, about the two airplanes we had drawn. It was just after the Korean War, and we'd drawn military airplanes. His was drawn from above and from the side in a composite view. He'd drawn all four wings in true proportion, shown all four engines with propellers, and had multiple turrets spraying bullets in all directions. Mine was drawn in an eye-level perspective—my older sister had shown me how to do it just days before. We each thought our own drawing was better. My airplane felt so real to me it seemed ready for flight, and my sense of its physical presence thrilled me. Toby thought my drawing was simply wrong. For him it was essential that all the parts would be shown in their true relationships to each other. My plane had a foreshortened body. Only one wing and one engine were fully visible. His drawing might not look like an airplane in flight, he argued, but at least all of it was there. On and on our argument went, from his desk at one end of the row to mine at the other. He was trying to make something that was present, and I was trying to make something that felt present: conception versus perception, knowing versus seeing, and the subject of this book.

My career-long focus on drawing cities has stemmed from a drawing assignment from 1965, when I was a freshman studying architecture at Carnegie Tech in Pittsburgh. In its way it joined the same issue that Toby and I had years before. It was a kind of contrarian assignment given by the sculptor Kent Bloomer, and it undermined everything I thought I knew about drawing at the time. Bloomer asked us to draw both the insides and outsides of the places we were studying. As clues to what he wanted us to explore, he pointed to illuminated manuscripts and paintings by proto-Renaissance masters, and he often expressed a deep distrust of perspective as a representation of how we see and understand the world around us. He somehow wanted us to go beyond just showing what we might see of a subject at any one point in time and instead use drawing to address our experience of it over time as well: to see it, but also to know it.

I've worked on Bloomer's assignment for more than fifty years now, and have written about it in articles and books; most notably, *Steel Shadows*, which addresses my Pittsburgh drawings. I discuss Bloomer's assignment here in this book as well, with new interpretations about its meaning. But the purpose of this book is to address that assignment within the broader framework of this set of questions:

Many landscape paintings have addressed the insides and outsides of places. What can they tell us about the underlying meaning of Bloomer's assignment?

Historically, mapmaking has addressed perceptual and conceptual understandings of our surroundings. How might that tradition relate to my landscape drawings?

Embodied cognition offers important insights into connections between mind and body. How might the act of drawing, the movement of the hand itself, become a source of perceptual and conceptual content?

Pittsburgh is blessed with a singular topography and industrial history, and many talented painters and photographers have been inspired by it. How does the spirit of this place emerge in their work and mine?

Dating back to the caves of southern France, murals have always been understood as integral parts of the architecture of their settings. How do murals contribute to the sense of place of those buildings in which they are placed?

In making murals I've worked with residents of cities around the world and with numerous fellow artists. What content has that collaboration brought to my work?

I write this book at age seventy-two as a road map through my experience of drawing the urban landscape. I offer it as a scaffold of questions and example answers for others who might at some time wish to pursue such work in the future.

After a good foundation with a wonderful art teacher, Don Hickman at the Choate School in Wallingford, Connecticut, the key mentors for my work have been two of my teachers from Carnegie Tech's (now Carnegie Mellon's) architecture school: Kent Bloomer and his good friend David Lewis—Bloomer for the assignment itself and Lewis for helping me to understand what it might ultimately mean. Jimmy Goldman played a key role in my choice to focus my senior thesis on my drawings of Pittsburgh. Much of that work owed to two professors from prior years, Ray Gindroz and Troy West. At the end of that thesis, Leon Arkus, then director of the Carnegie Museum of Art, came by to see my work at the invitation of my professor, Chin Pai. Leon saw something

in this work and on the spur of the moment bought several drawings for the Carnegie Museum of Art's permanent collection. That encouraging development was key in leading me away from practicing architecture and into a career of drawing cities.

Soon thereafter, architect Herbert Ohl hired me to come work for him in Germany on the basis of the four or five slides I sent him. In his enthusiasm for my quirky way of drawing, I found confirmation of the career direction I was taking. Others have jumped in to help at fateful junctures as well. During my years teaching drawing at Carnegie Mellon University in Pittsburgh, Omer Akin, Vivian Loftness, Laura Lee, and Steve Lee have been wonderfully supportive department heads; Laura Lee in particular helped me secure the commission for the mural in Qatar. Richard Armstrong, former director of the Carnegie Museum, helped with my being able to show the complete *Visible Cities* mural at the Carnegie Museum during the summer of 1993. Todd Hunt later pushed for that work's purchase by the Senator John Heinz History Center. Martin Prekop, former dean of the College of Fine Arts at Carnegie Mellon University, was the person who cemented my focus on civic murals by offering me the opportunity to create a mural for the CMU university center. Nino Saggio set up all the early contacts that enabled me to do the mural in Rome. Dean of CFA Dan Martin and Ralph Horgan were tremendously helpful in moving the Tepper mural forward. Architect Andy Tesoro has helped with commissions in New York and has provided a home away from home for me and my family on gallery visits there. Sam Berkowitz and Alison Brand Oehler and all the people at Concept Gallery have been wonderful advocates for my work in Pittsburgh. Syl Damianos has been a huge help at various points in my career as well. I've been so very lucky with the people I've bumped into by chance.

I've always had a supportive home life, beginning with constant encouragement from my parents and three wonderful sisters. My oldest sister, Carolyn, was an inspiration to me with all of the exquisite maps she drew, and it was my pursuit of her advice on how to draw airplanes in perspective that led me into that argument with my friend Toby. Barbie and Pam have come to exhibitions of mine—and it was Pam's son Grégoire, along with John Trivelli and my former student Patty Culley, who became my key colleagues on so many murals. My former wife, Meg, was a patient participant in many of the formative travels and travel drawings that I describe in these pages. And her gregarious nature (and that of her family) was an encouragement to go out and engage the many stories from other people that became a significant part of the way I've approached drawing cities. There were times when our house seemed to be made of wall-sized charcoal drawings, and I got only the warmest response from Meg and our two daughters, Laura and Sarah. Laura and Sarah often helped me with the drawing, when these started to become murals. The times of working with them in my studio have been among the happiest of my life. Their enthusiasm for the work I did in Bryce Canyon in 1989 played a big role in the most important midcourse shift in my work. I remember a critique with my then colleague Bruce Lindsey being a big help at that juncture as well.

The last chapter of this book is about the collaboration that is necessary to make murals, and in it I mention the roles that others have played. But I particularly want to emphasize the contributions that Ross Kronenbitter and more recently my stepson, Ben Ledewitz, have made. They've both been so generous with their time and spirit in working through the many problems that come up unexpectedly with mural installations. And Ben has a whole cadre of friends he can draw upon to help out when needed.

The writing itself has also drawn in people to help. Judith Lesniewicz, Don Carter, David Lewis, Kent Bloomer, and my mother-in-law, Lois Danes, read early drafts. Meg Taylor edited an early draft and has been a great supporter of the idea of this book. She put me in contact with Linda Gustafson at the Toronto-based design firm Counterpunch, who did a first mockup and finally the design for this book. Laura and Sarah looked at a draft as well at a midway point when I was in Seattle to see Sarah and Nina Gorfer's wonderful photographs on view out there. During that time, I had a chance to talk at length with Laura about some of the ideas about landscape I was getting into, and it was she who suggested I read up on Jay Appleton's prospect-refuge theory.

The really intense period of writing has been the past two years. And in that time the book has evolved from a fairly shallow description of the murals themselves—and how I made them—into a much deeper investigation into the underlying ideas behind them. For that I have my dear wife and now mural collaborator Stefani to thank. Over the years she's been my loving companion in that difficult role of supporter and honest critic of my work in progress and now of this book. She has pushed and pushed hard in getting me to go deeper into the intellectual foundation of the work and then to organize it in such a way that that foundation can be made clear to the reader.

Doug Cooper
March 25, 2019

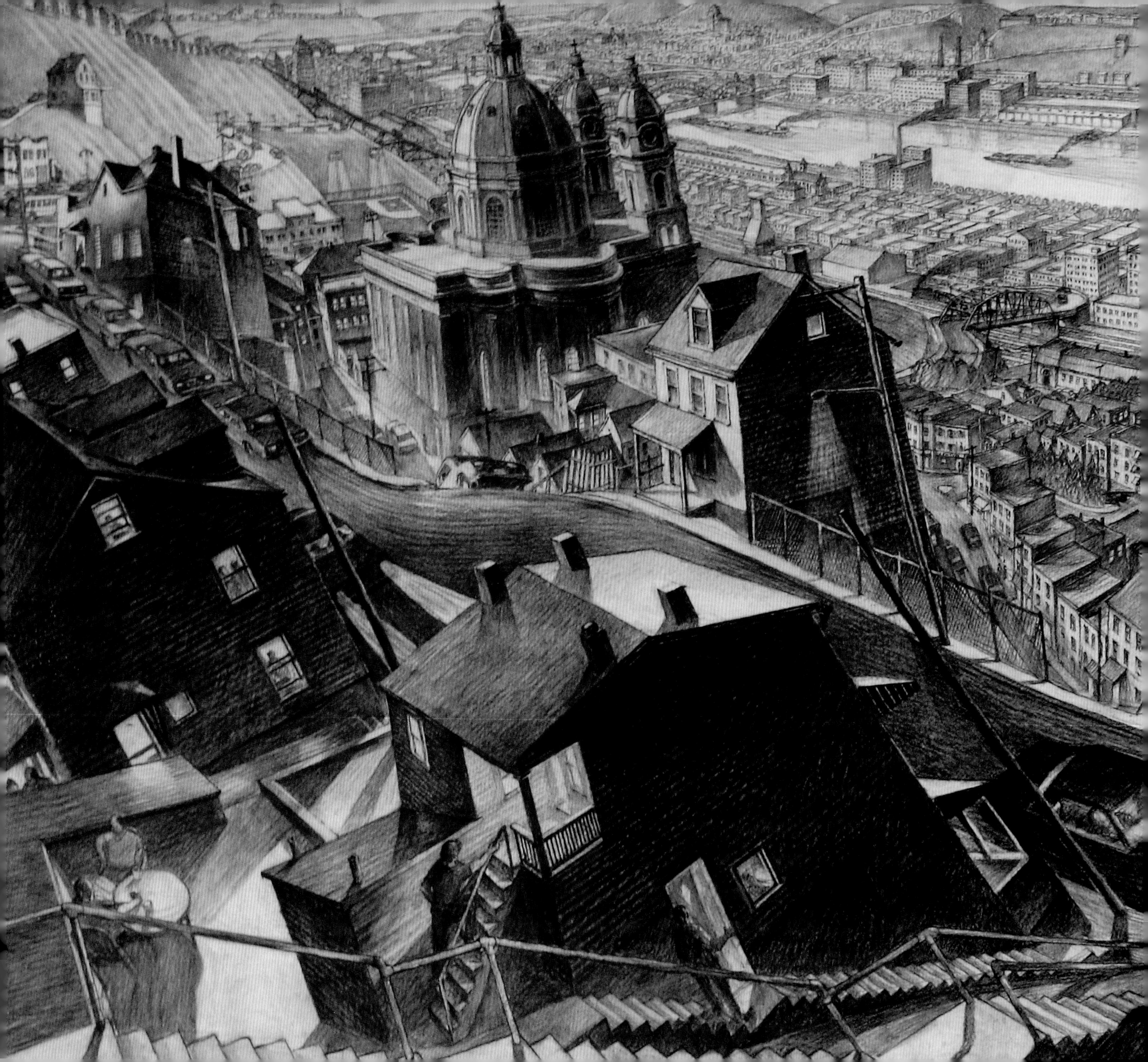

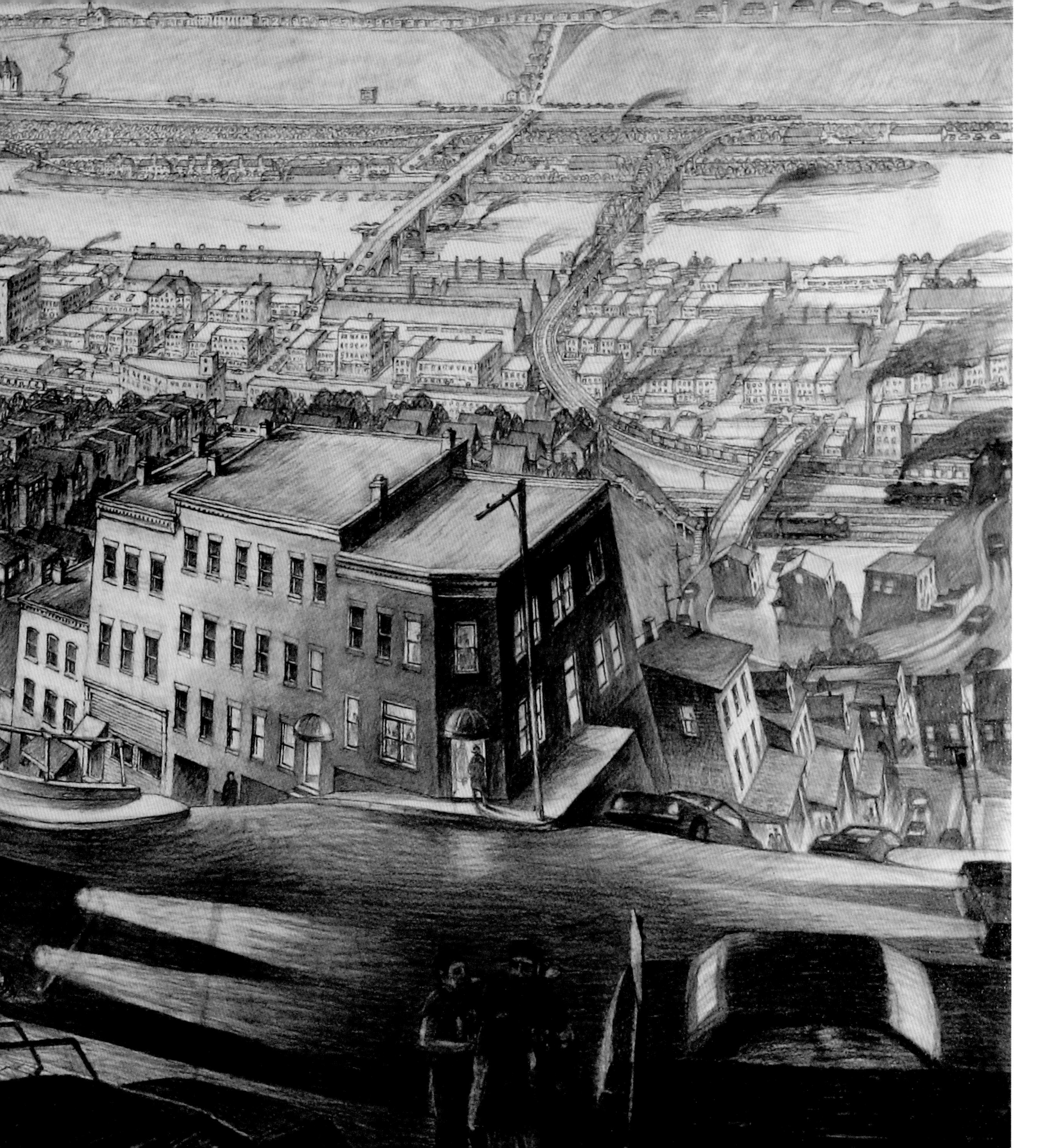

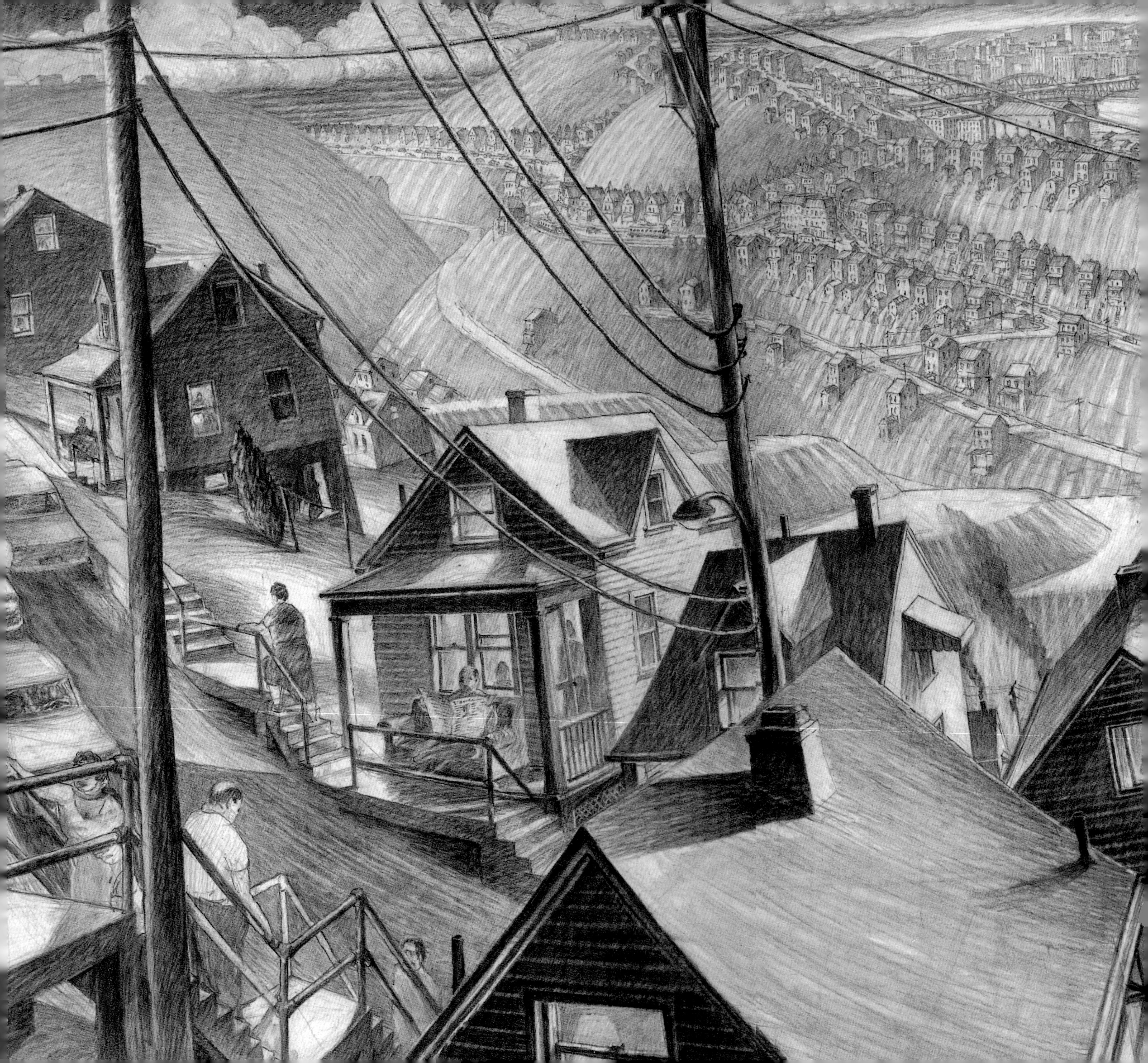

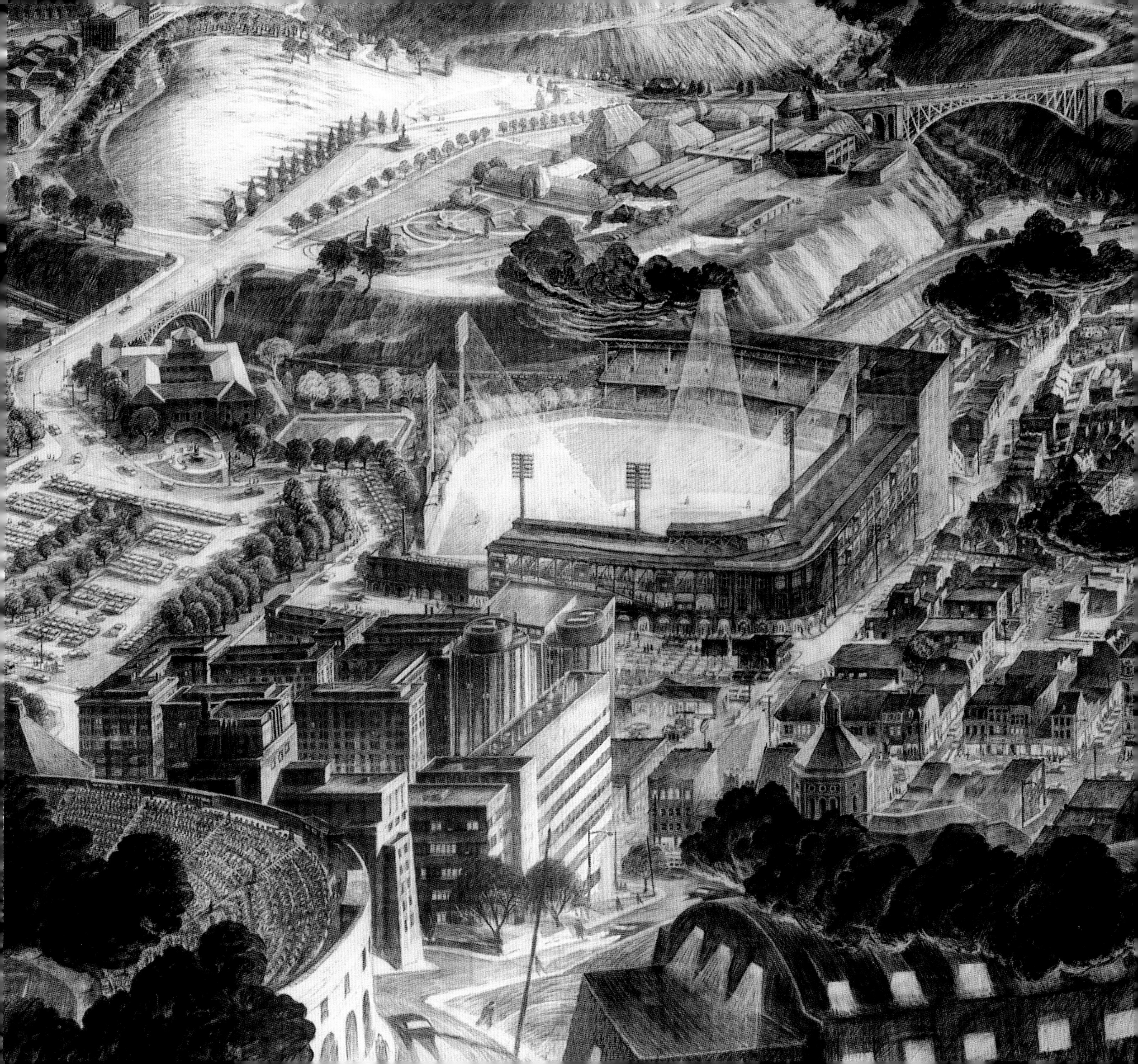

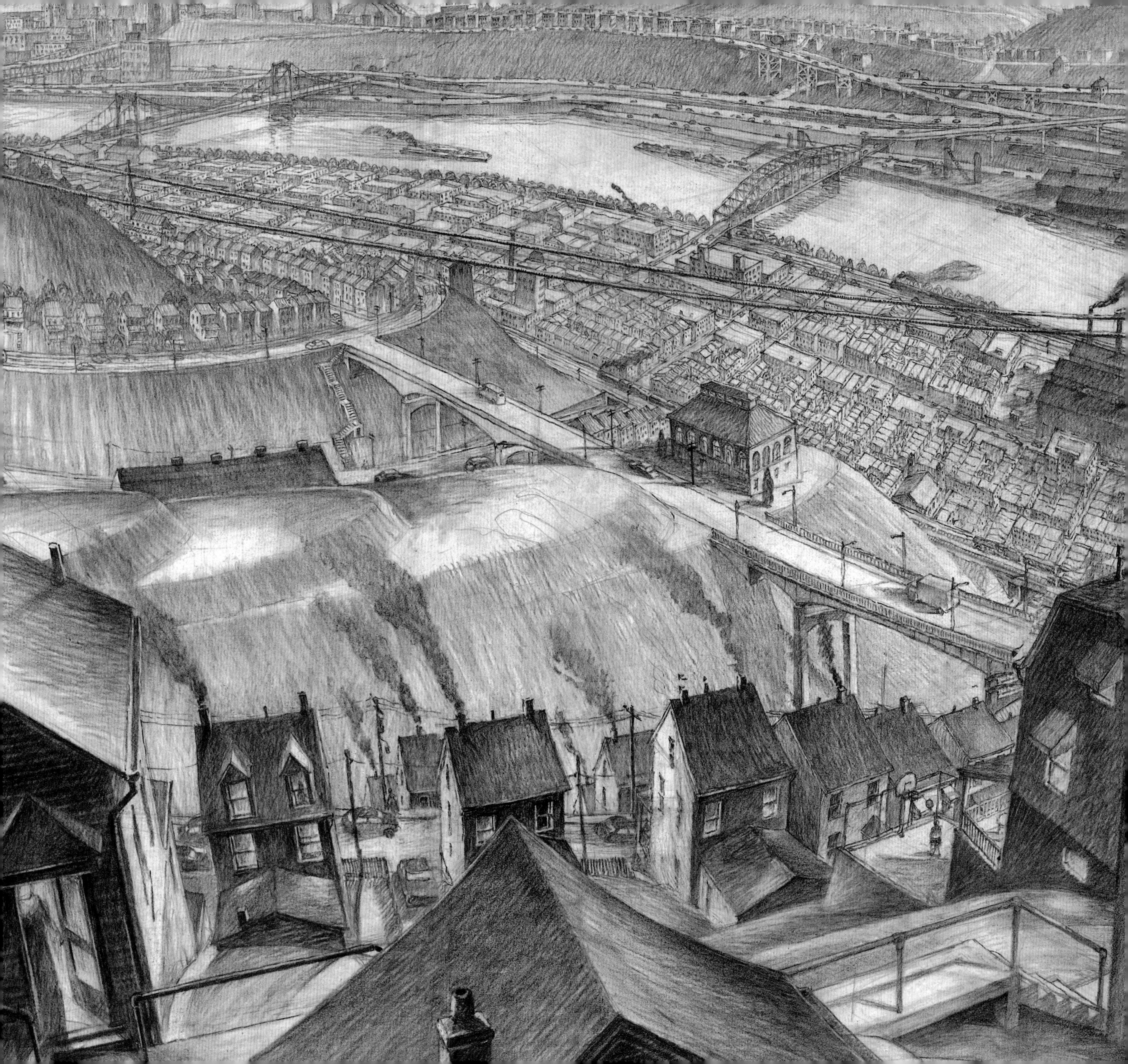

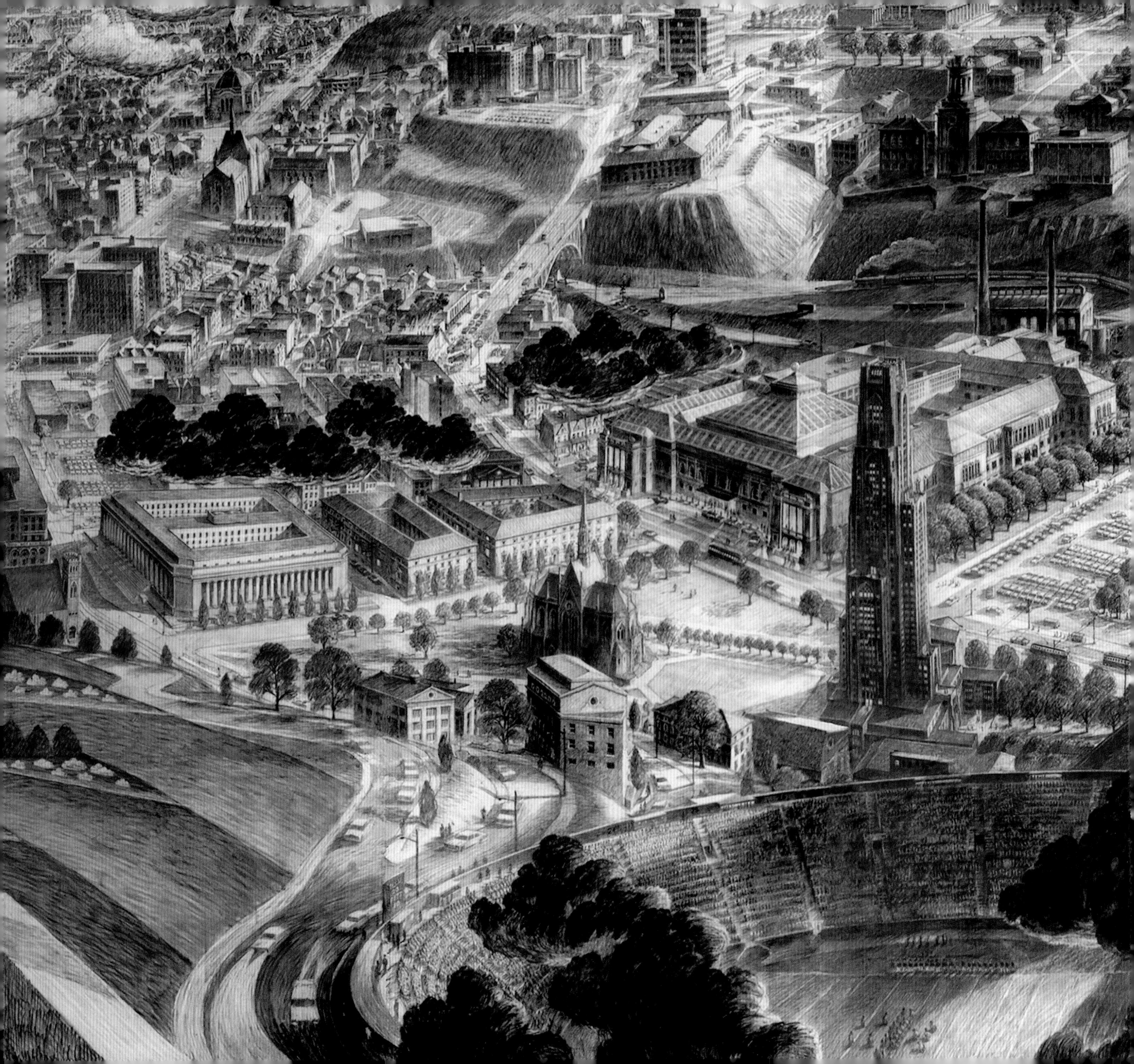

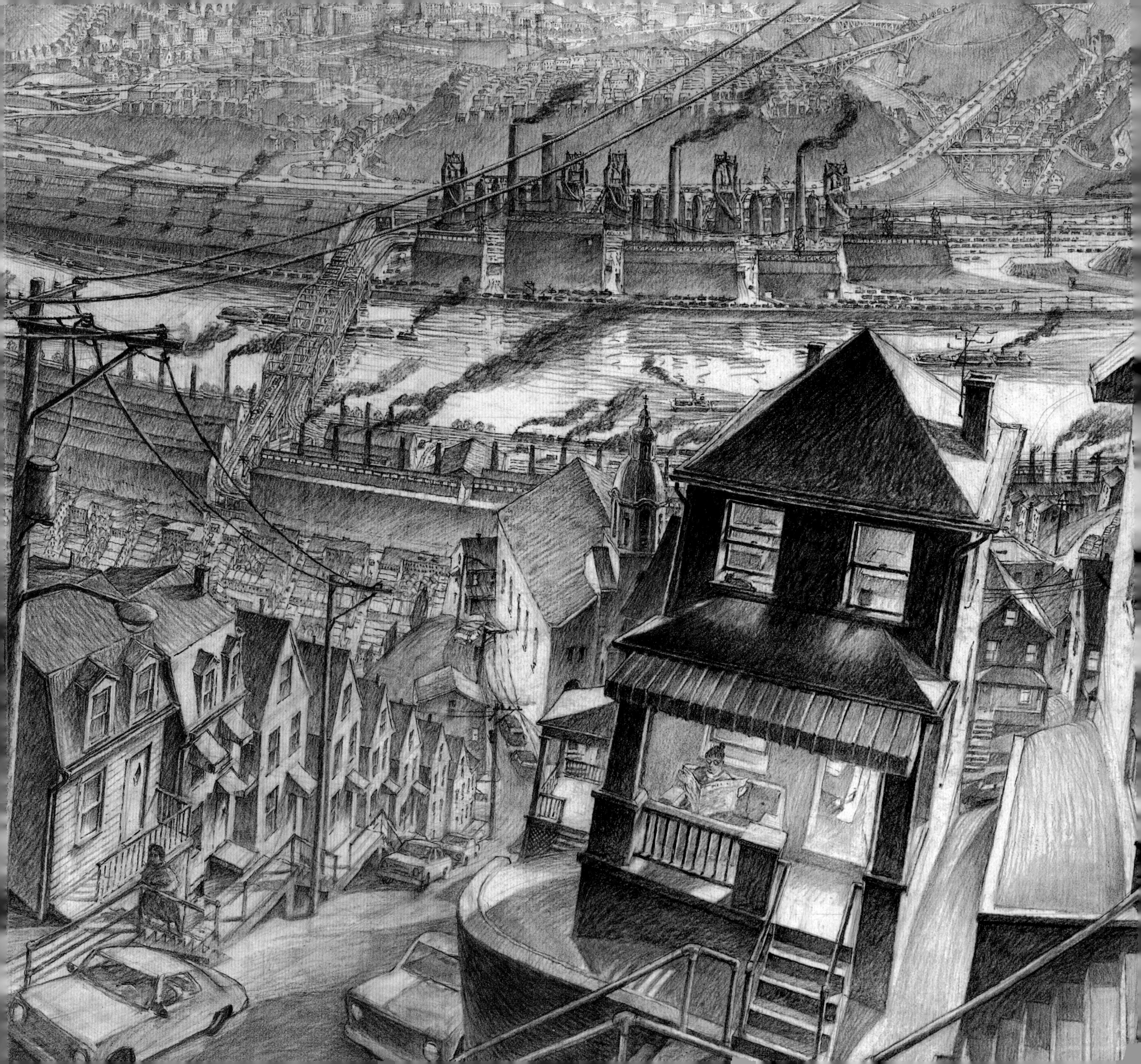

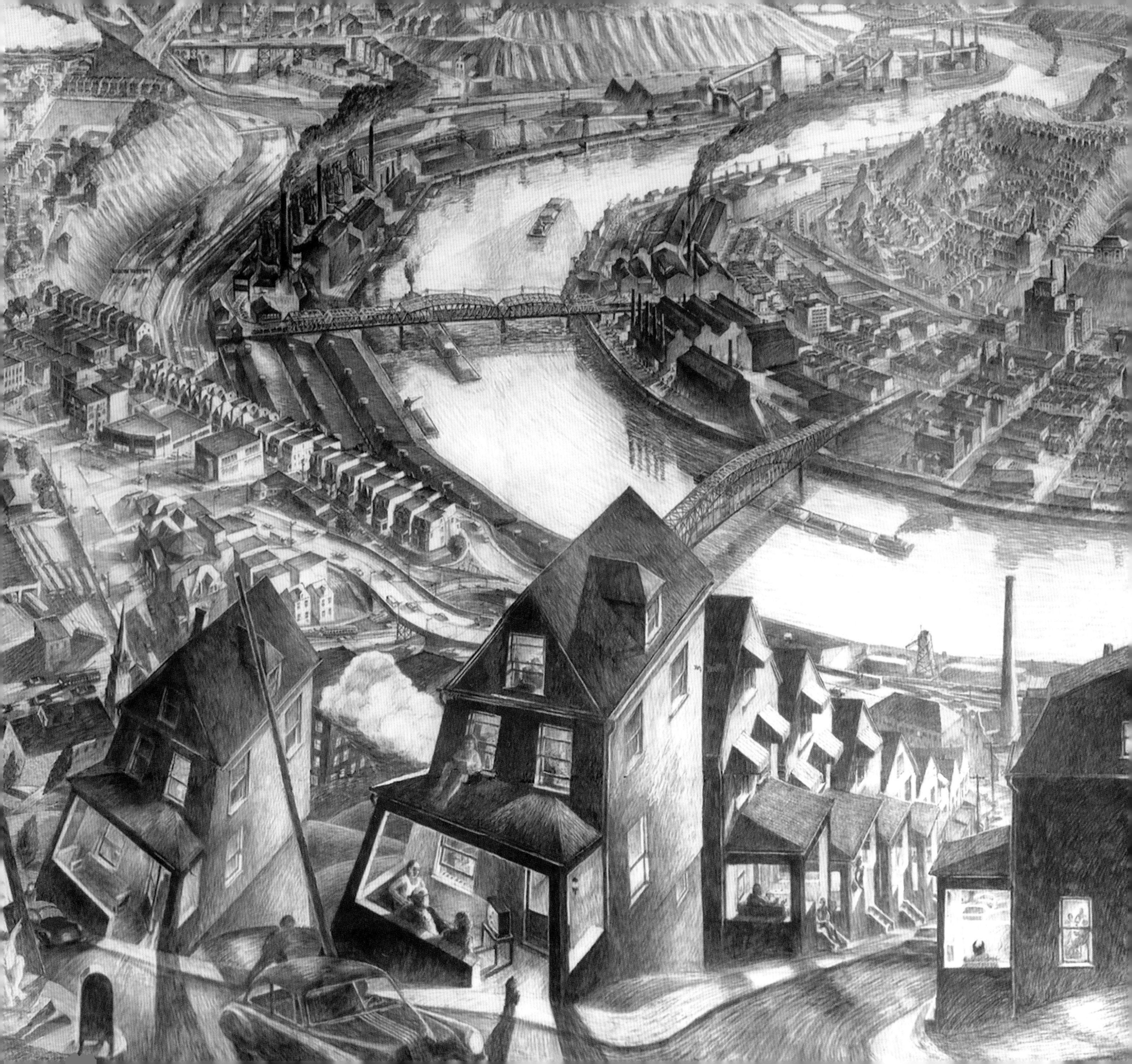

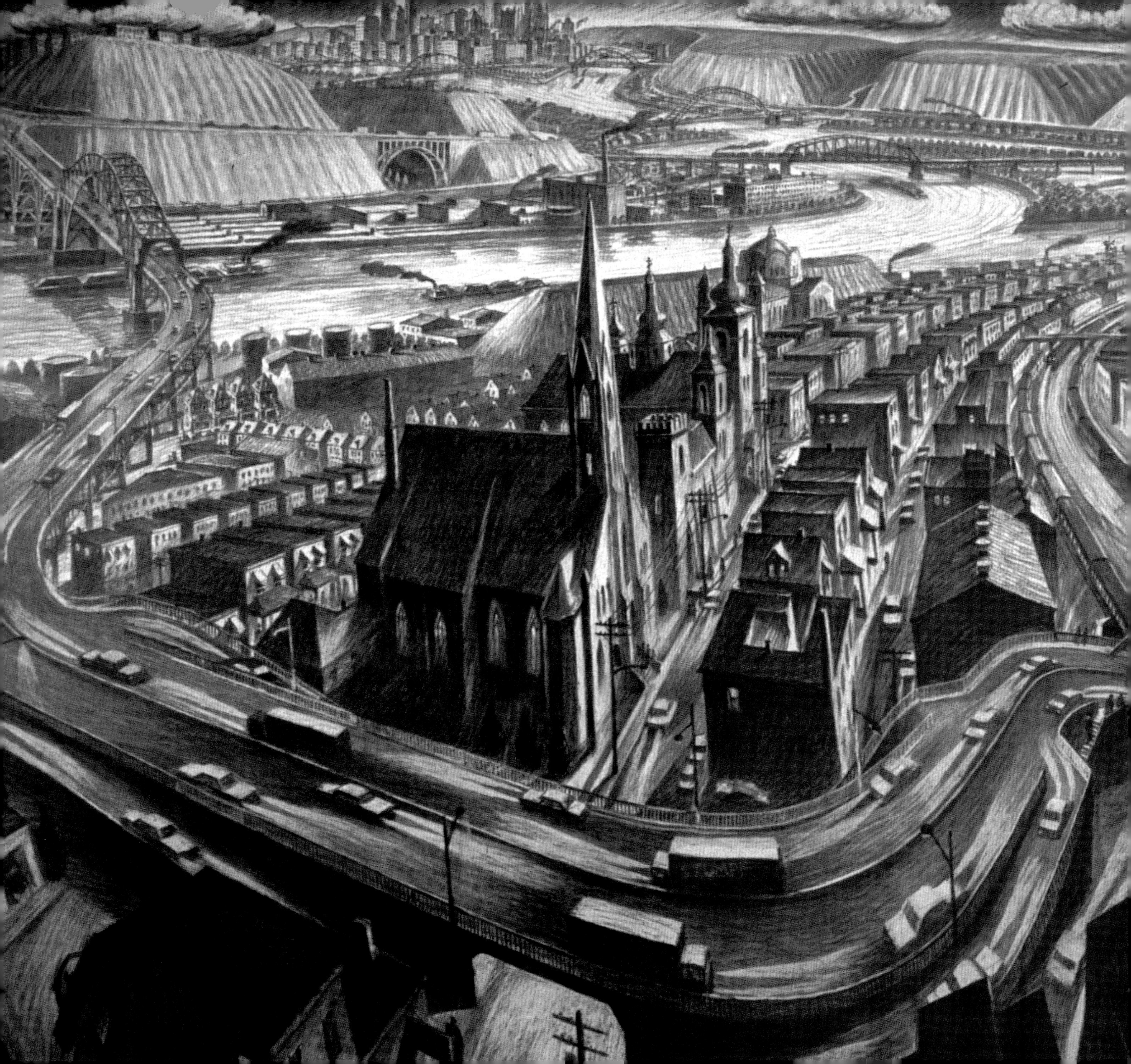

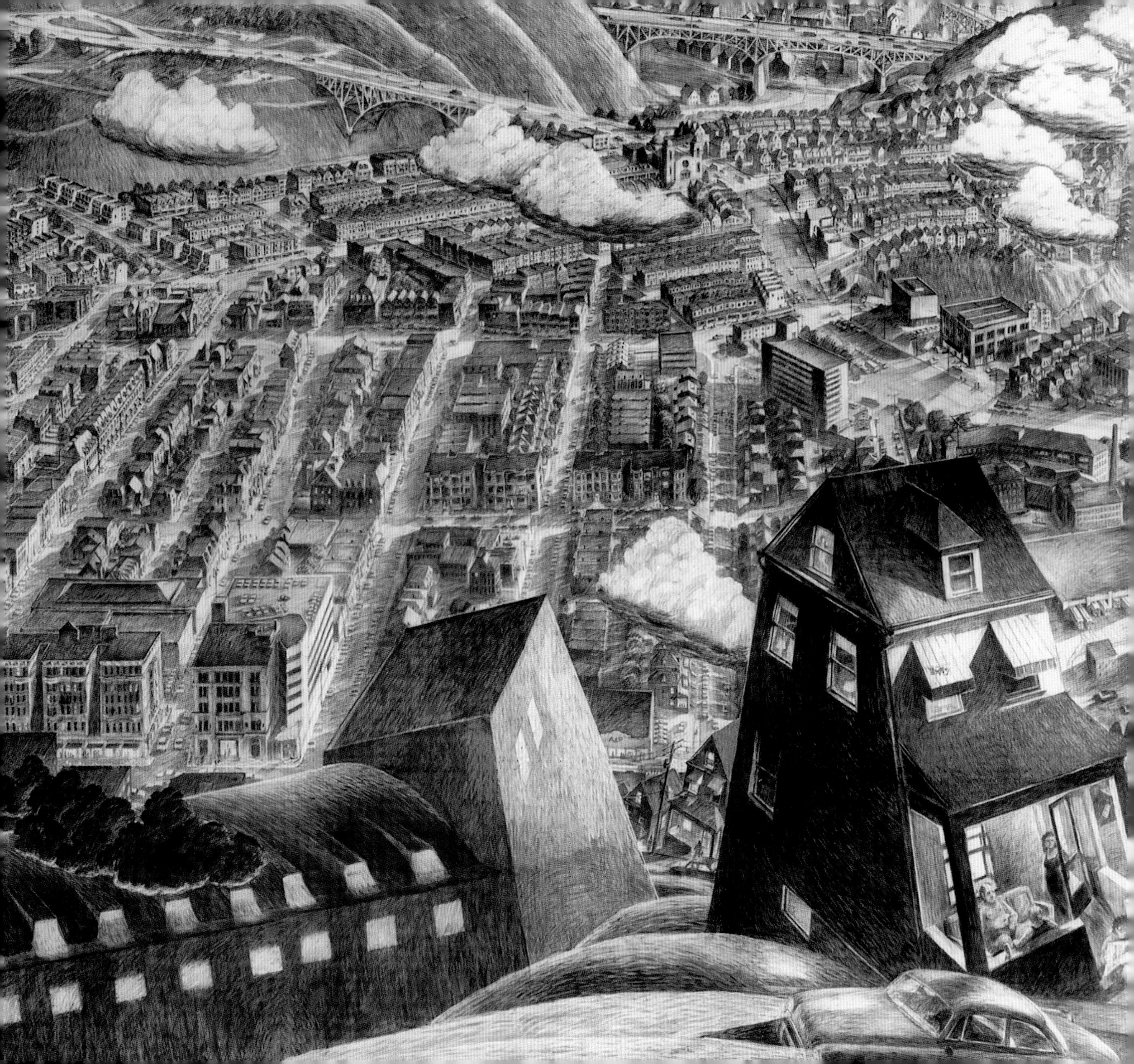

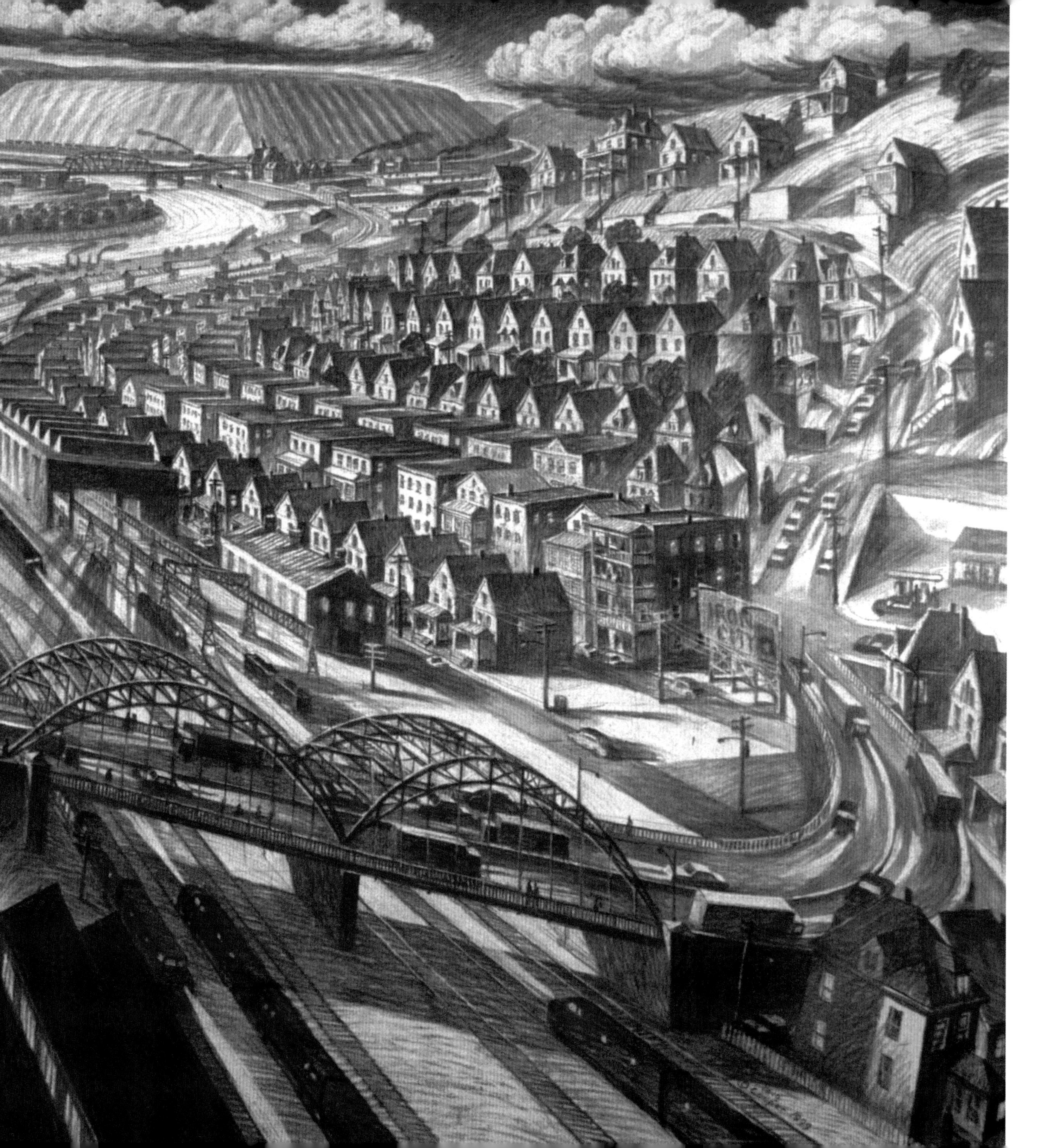

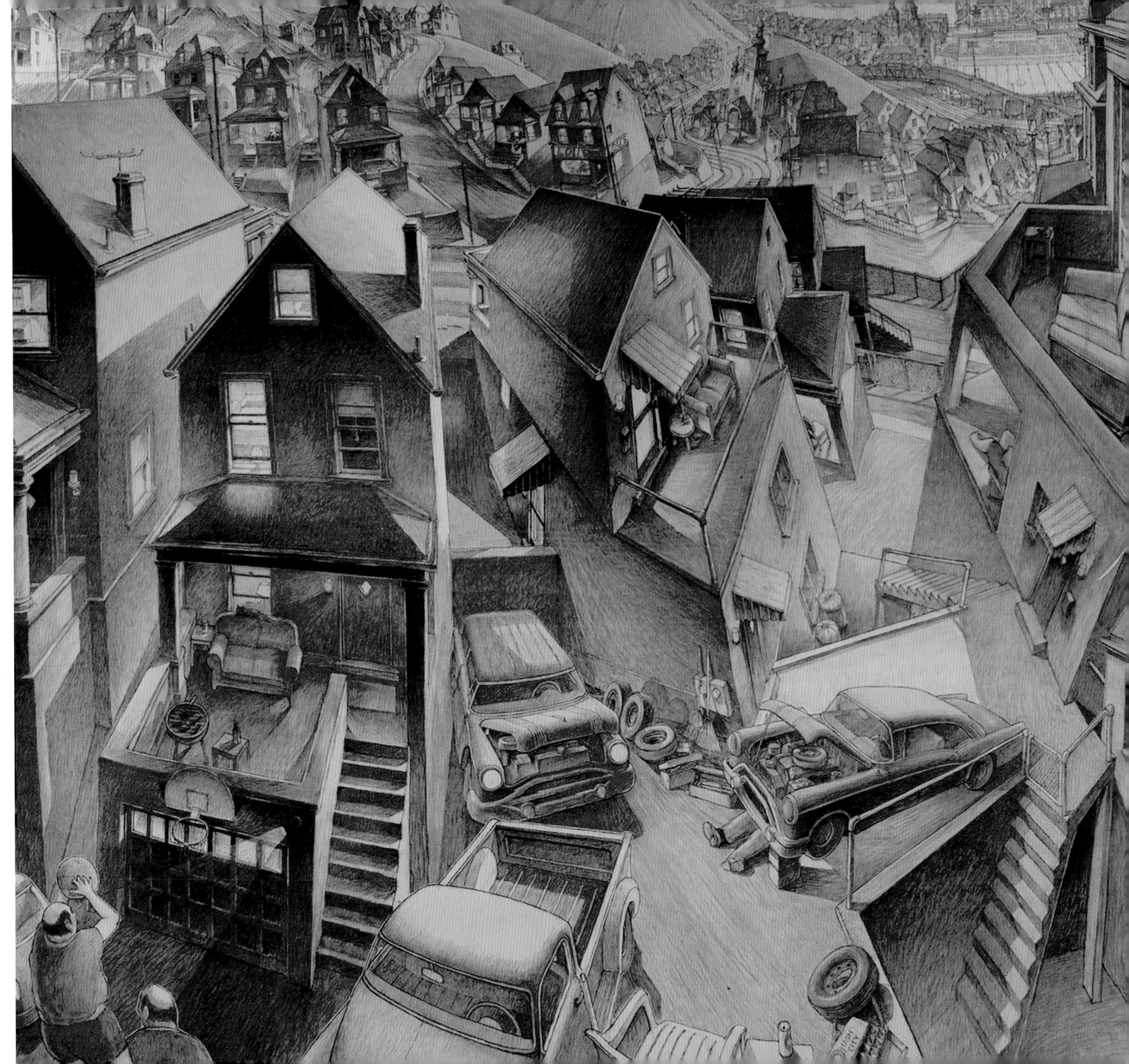

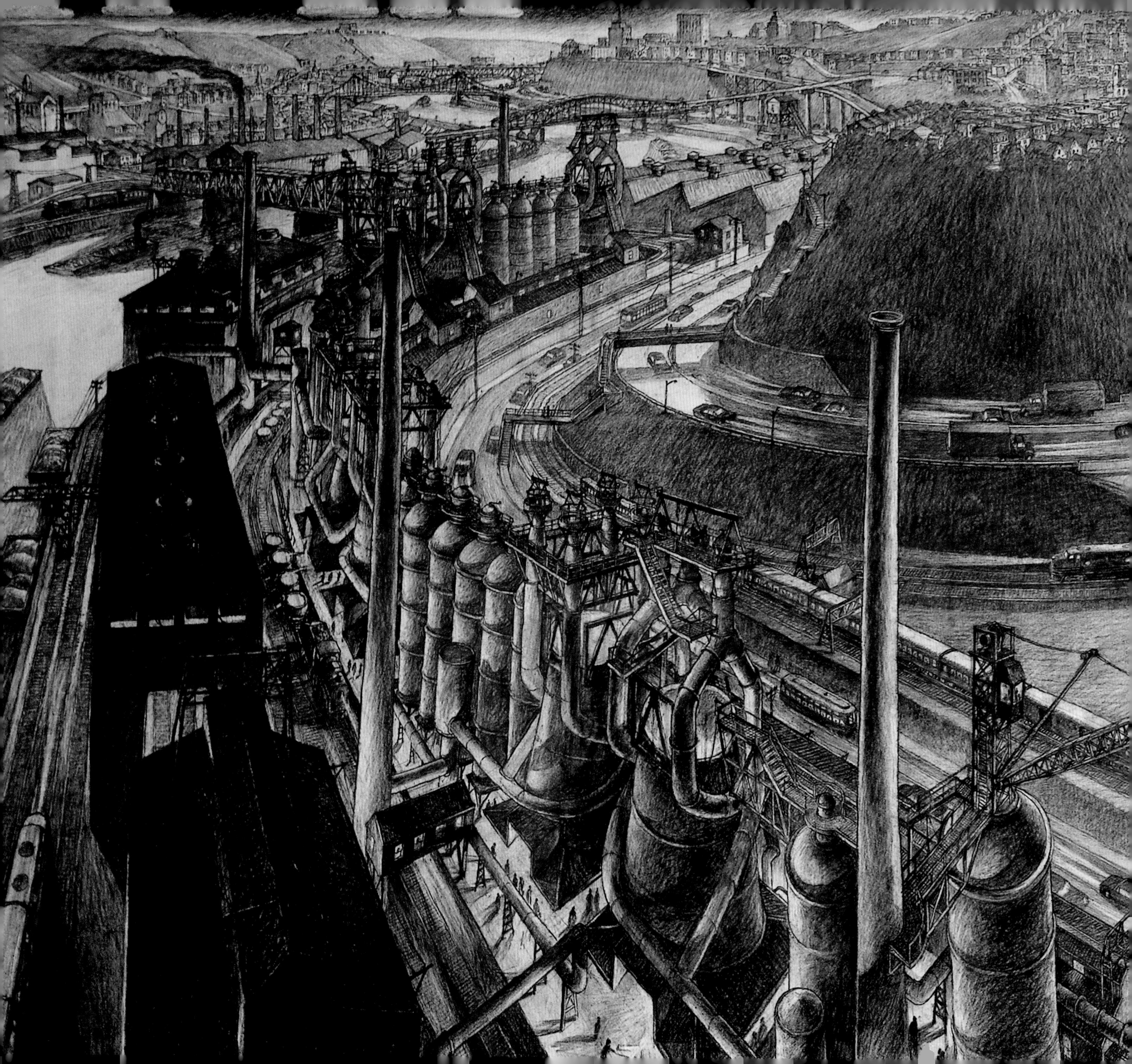

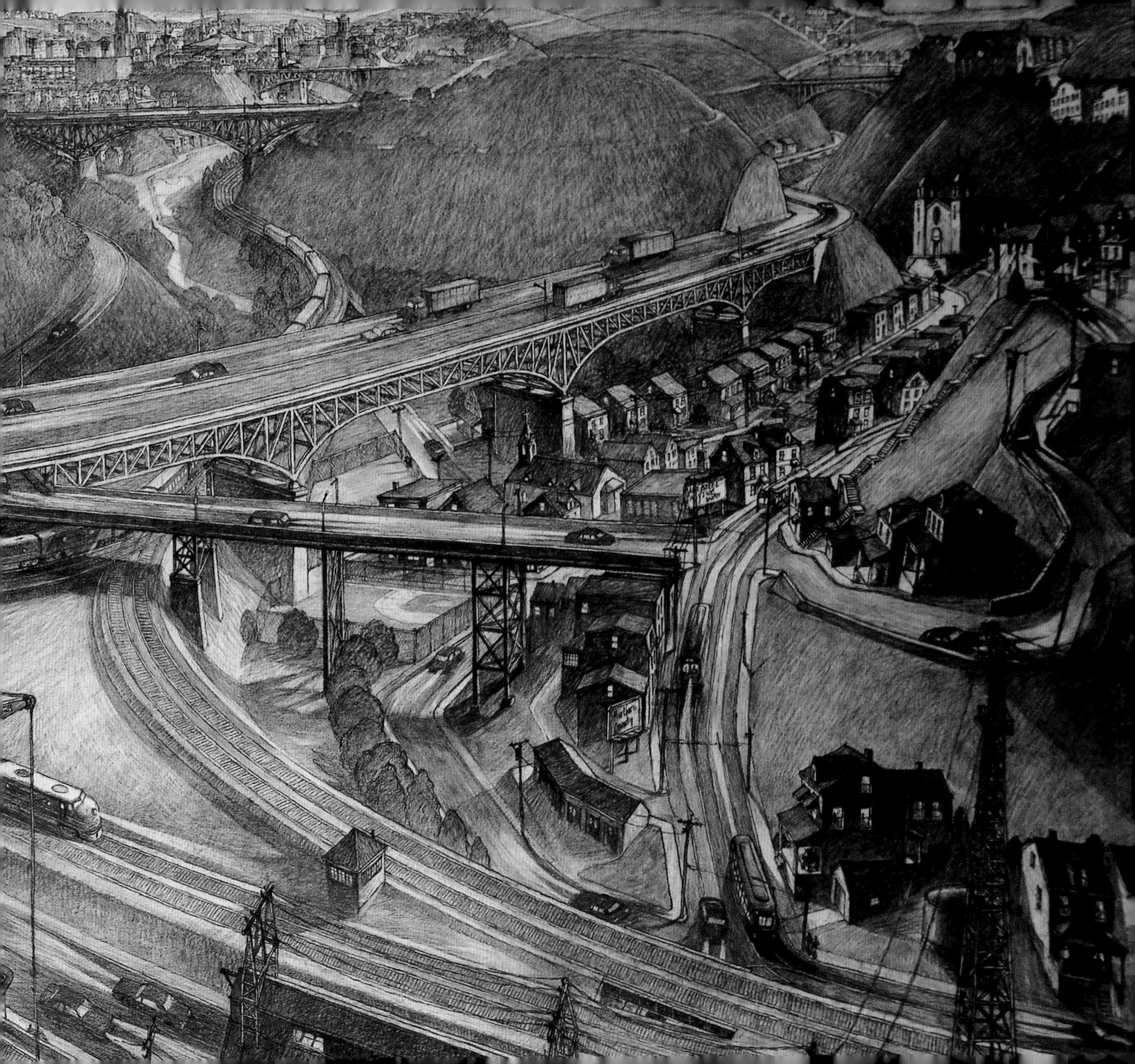

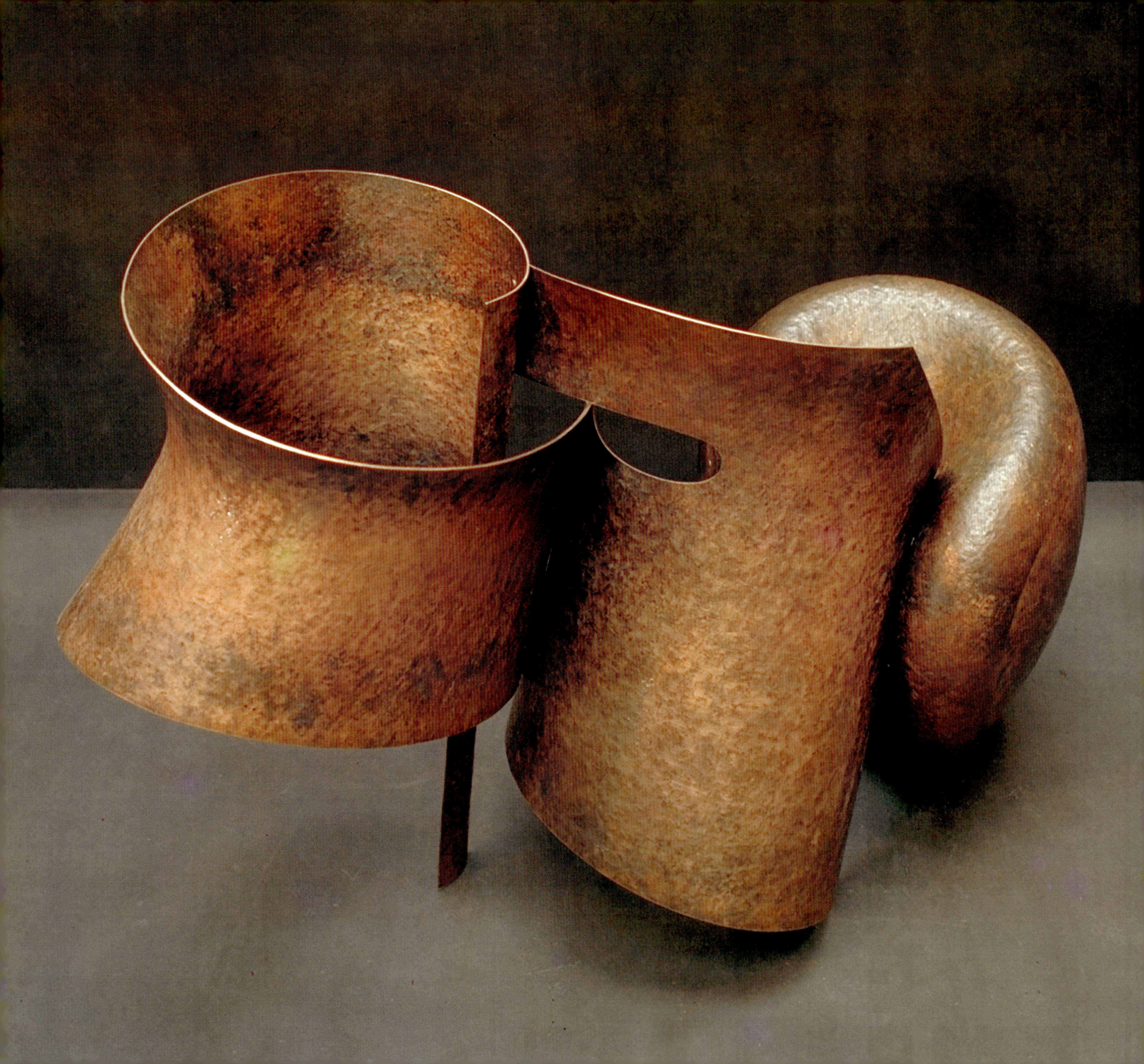

CHAPTER 1

INSIDE AND OUTSIDE

Professor Kent Bloomer was an unusual choice to teach drawing during our first-year in the architecture program at Carnegie Tech in Pittsburgh in the fall of 1965. He is a sculptor (fig. 1.1) who had earned degrees in physics and architecture at MIT. In the first class he gave us what seemed an impossible assignment: *Make a drawing that shows the inside of our studio and the space outside as well.* Then he left the room, saying he'd be back in a week to have a look. Inside and outside? More than one place in one drawing? We were dumbfounded. But the assignment would continue for the rest of the semester and eventually into my career drawing urban landscapes.

Bloomer's assignment had a lot to do with his practice as a sculptor. Accustomed to working in three dimensions, he was suspicious of the fundamental illusion of drawing: two dimensions representing three. In particular he questioned linear perspective because of its limitation to one viewpoint. For me this was particularly jarring because so much of my use and understanding of drawing had grown out of my facility in perspective from an early age. He somehow wanted to free us from the limitation of describing only what we might see at any one point in time and instead use drawing to represent our experience of a subject over time: to see it but also to know it.

For models, Bloomer showed us images created before the rediscovery of linear perspective in the Renaissance: illuminated manuscripts (fig. 1.2)—one showed a duke conferring with his ministers inside a castle and then outside leading his troops into battle—and the work of proto-Renaissance painters such as Giotto, Ambrogio Lorenzetti, and Simone Martini. He showed us how their paintings combined multiple views (looking upward at ceilings and downward at floors), and he pointed out their insides and outsides. The one I remember most is *The Effects of Good Government in the City and in the Country*, one of a series of three frescos painted by Lorenzetti (ca. 1290–1348) in Siena's Palazzo Pubblico (town hall). It is centered on the marketplace inside the city, but also incorporates the fields and hills outside its walls (fig. 1.3). The rolling Tuscan hills in the fresco inspired me to try a new approach to drawing the city outside our studio, where I found many of the same visual properties Bloomer had pointed out in the paintings. One drawing showed the Carnegie Tech campus in a wide-angle view in the foreground and the rest of the city uplifted in the background and viewed maplike from above (fig. 1.4).

1.1. *Brass Sculpture*, Kent Bloomer, 1968. Brass, 19 × 19 × 31 inches. Private collection.

1.2 (*right*). Pliny the Elder writing in his study beside a natural landscape
populated with animals at the beginning of Pliny's *Historia Naturalis*,
ca. 1457–58. 16¼ × 11 inches. Harley 2677, f. 1, British Library Catalogue
of Illuminated Manuscripts.

1.3 (*below*). *The Effects of Good Government in the City and in the Country*,
Ambrogio Lorenzetti, 1337–1339. Fresco. Palazzo Pubblico, Siena, Italy.
Scala/Art Resource, NY.

1.4 (*facing page*). *Carnegie Tech Campus and Surrounding City*, Doug
Cooper, 1966. Pencil on paper, 54 × 120 inches. Collection of the artist.

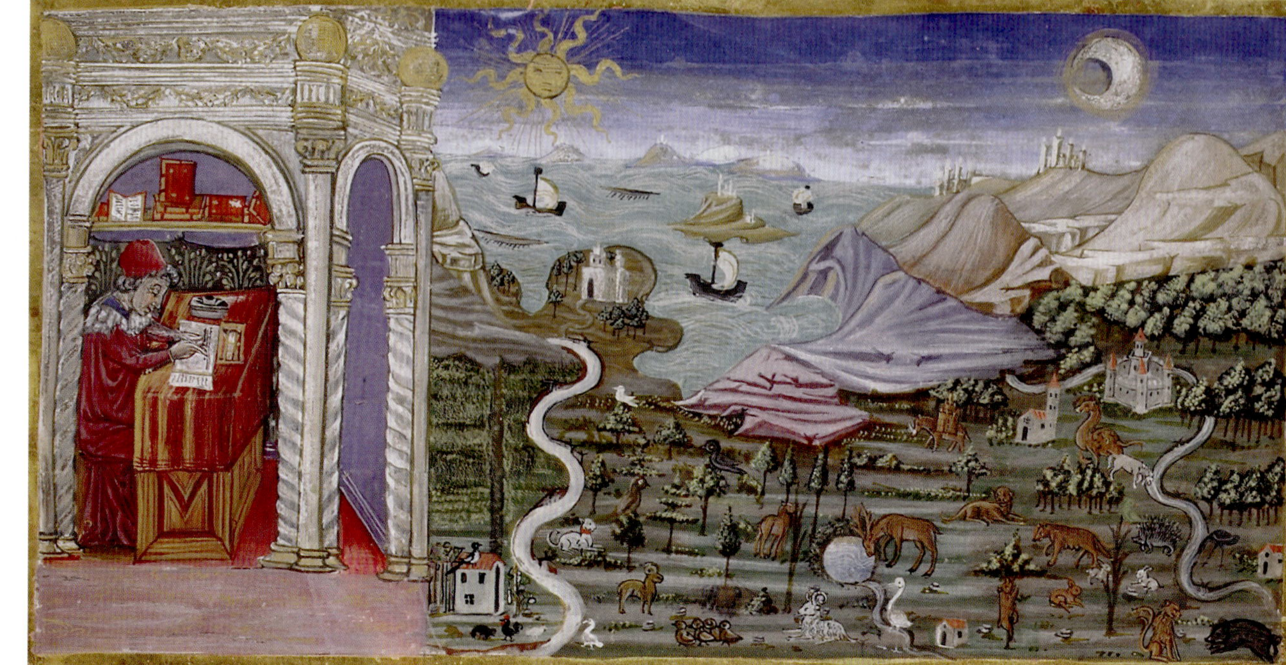

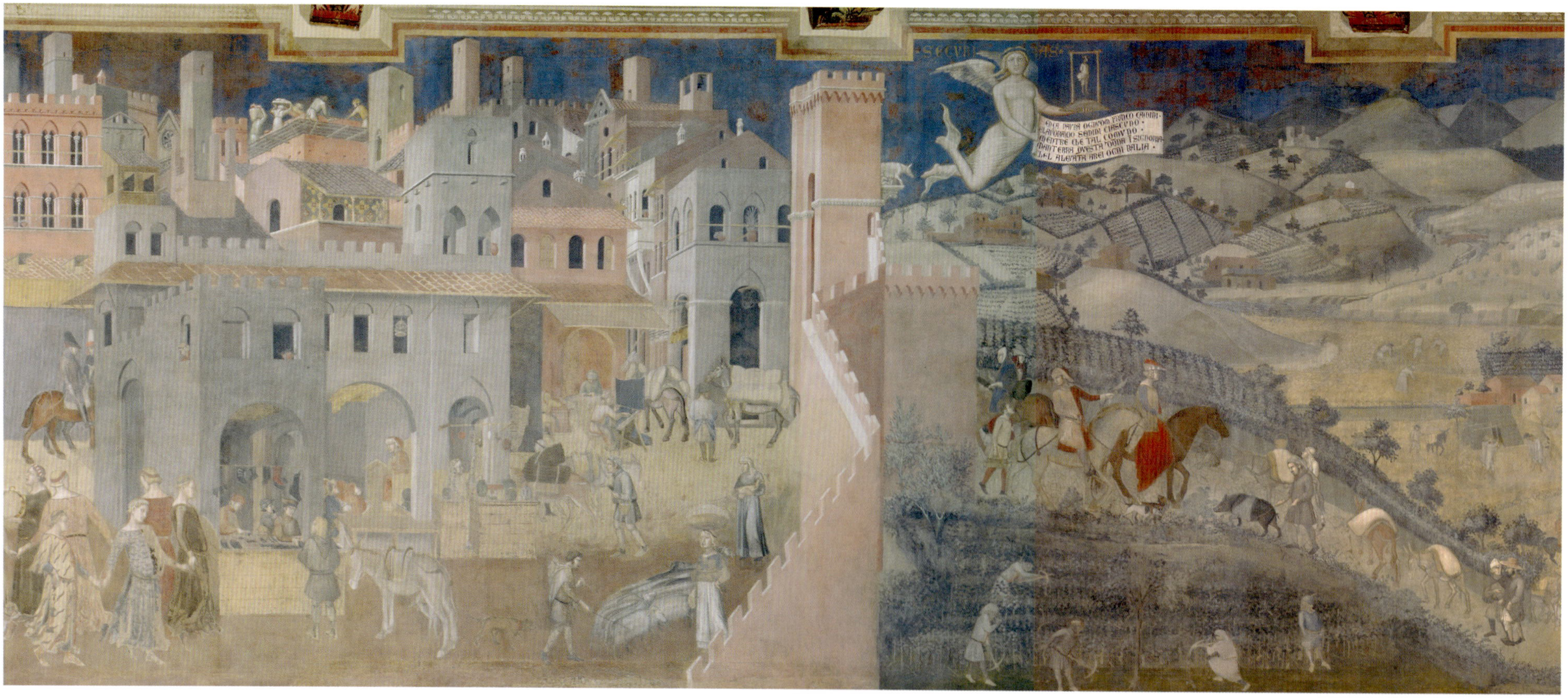

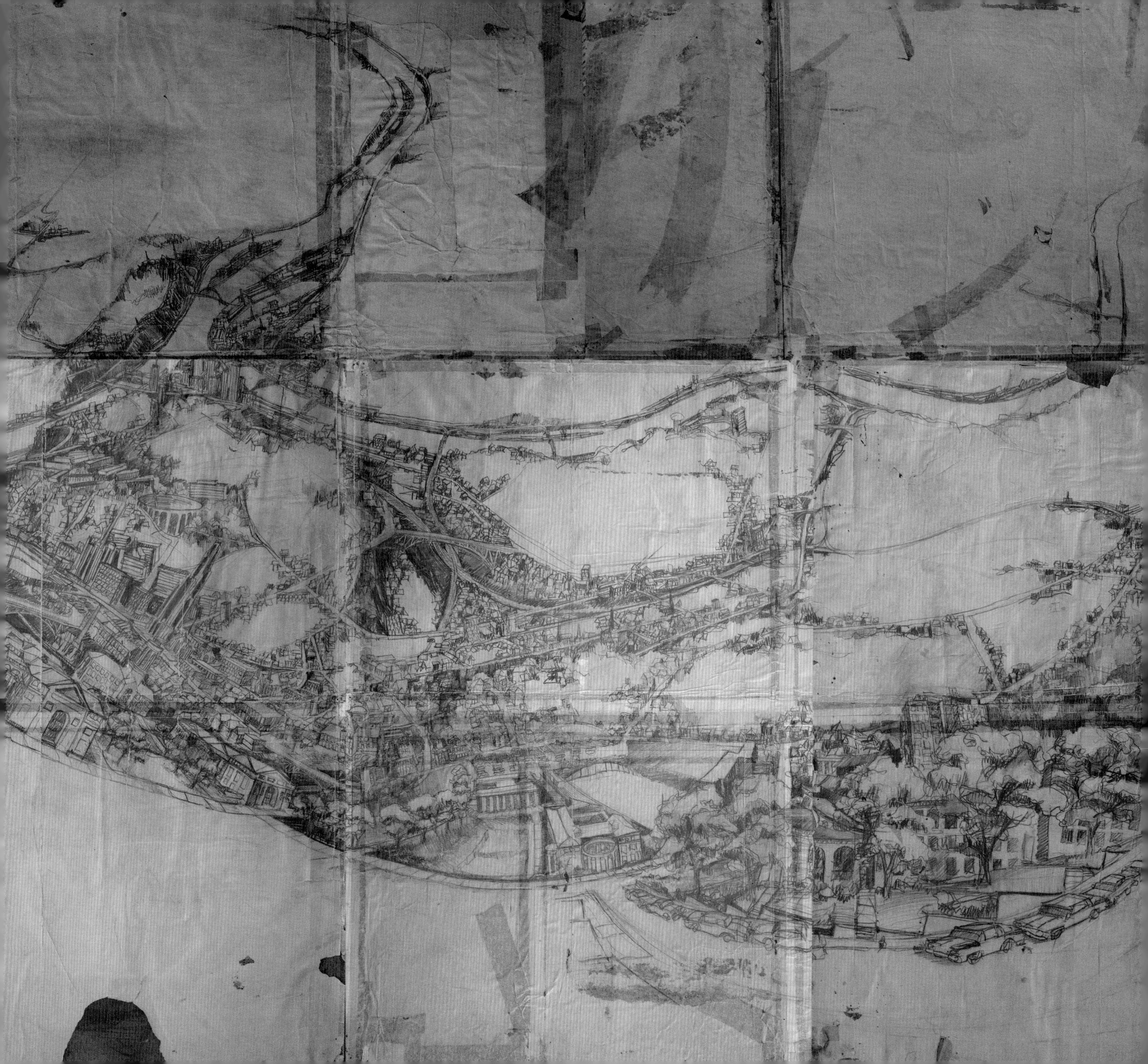

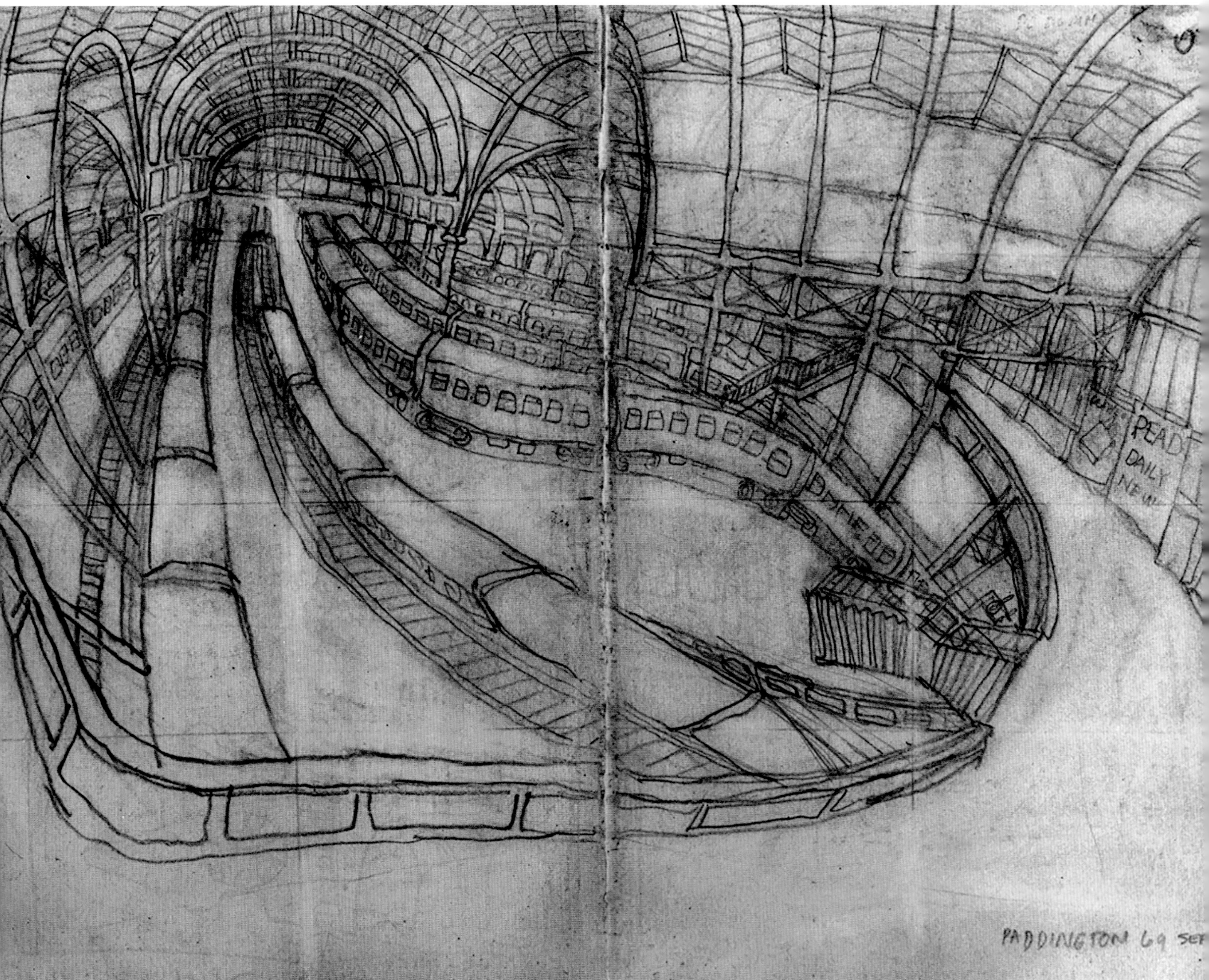
READ
DAILY
NEW
PADDINGTON 69 SEP

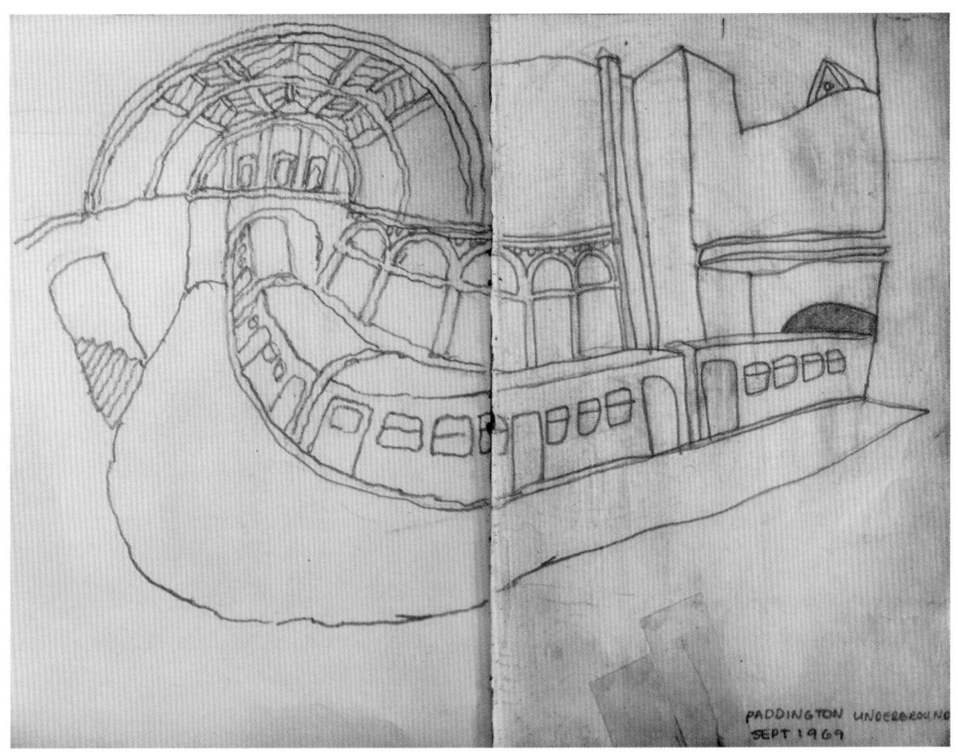

1.6. *Paddington Station, Circle Line Station*, Doug Cooper, 1969. Pencil on paper, 8 × 10½ inches. Collection of the artist.

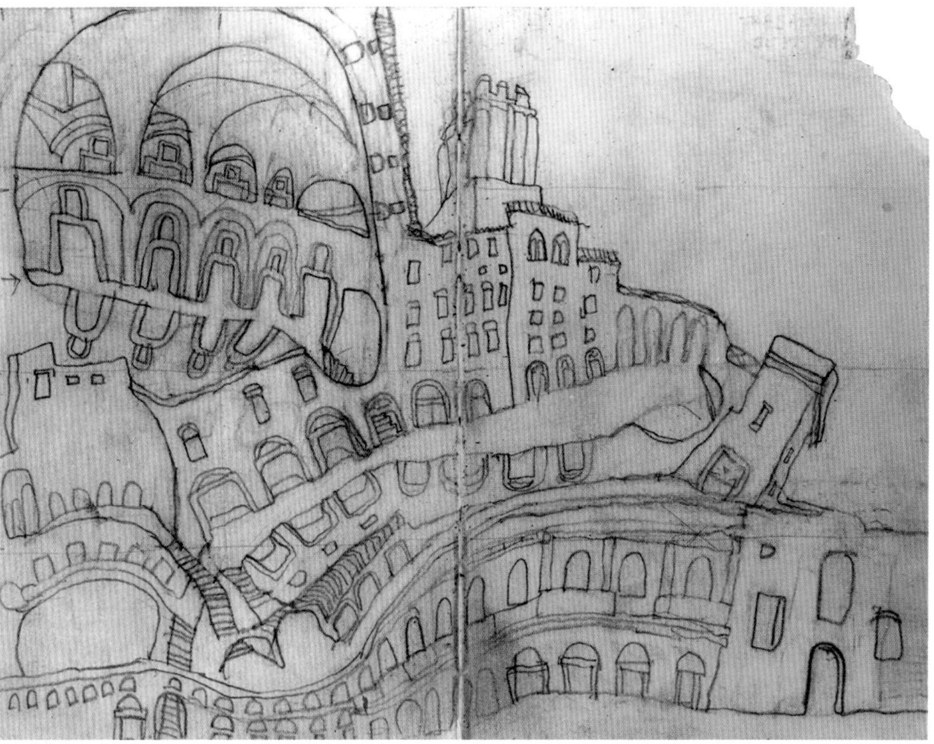

1.7. *Trajan's Market*, Doug Cooper, 1969. Pencil on paper, 8 × 10½ inches. Collection of the artist.

London, Rome, Pittsburgh, 1969

It was four years after Kent Bloomer's course that I first made real progress with his assignment. My former wife, Meg, and I were on a whirlwind trip through Europe—I had won a stipend to study and sketch architecture. When we reached London I found that by taking the Circle Line, the oldest section of the Underground, I could visit most of the city's late nineteenth-century iron-and-glass railroad stations. Over the years they had been expanded with additional bays, and so, no matter where I stood to draw them, their interior spatial boundaries extended beyond the foreground bay where I had begun drawing. I was excited by the serial character of the visual experience—each interior space unfolding into another. These stations (with their spatial complexity) seemed an ideal place to revisit Bloomer's assignment.

As a traveler, I was limited to a small sketchbook, but one day in Paddington Station, I found a helpful improvisational strategy: drawing small in one corner of my sketchbook at the outset (fig. 1.5). I began with a small view, looking down the length of one bay from a walkway overlooking the tracks. Then I moved downstairs to the platform below, where I let the drawing expand and distort to include what I discovered from this new location. I returned the next day to draw Paddington's connection to the Circle Line (fig. 1.6).

A drawing from later in the trip at Trajan's Market in Rome showed me a way to combine multiple interiors in one drawing. It was near closing time as we entered, so each of us explored different routes to double the information we could gather. Then, after leaving, while I sat and drew, Meg told me where she had gone and what she had seen. And then I fit her descriptions into the drawing I had already begun. Half life drawing and half mnemonic drawing, it seemed I'd stumbled on a way to combine ongoing visual experience with memory (fig. 1.7).

1.5. *Paddington Station*, Doug Cooper, 1969. Pencil on paper, 8 × 10½ inches. Collection of the artist.

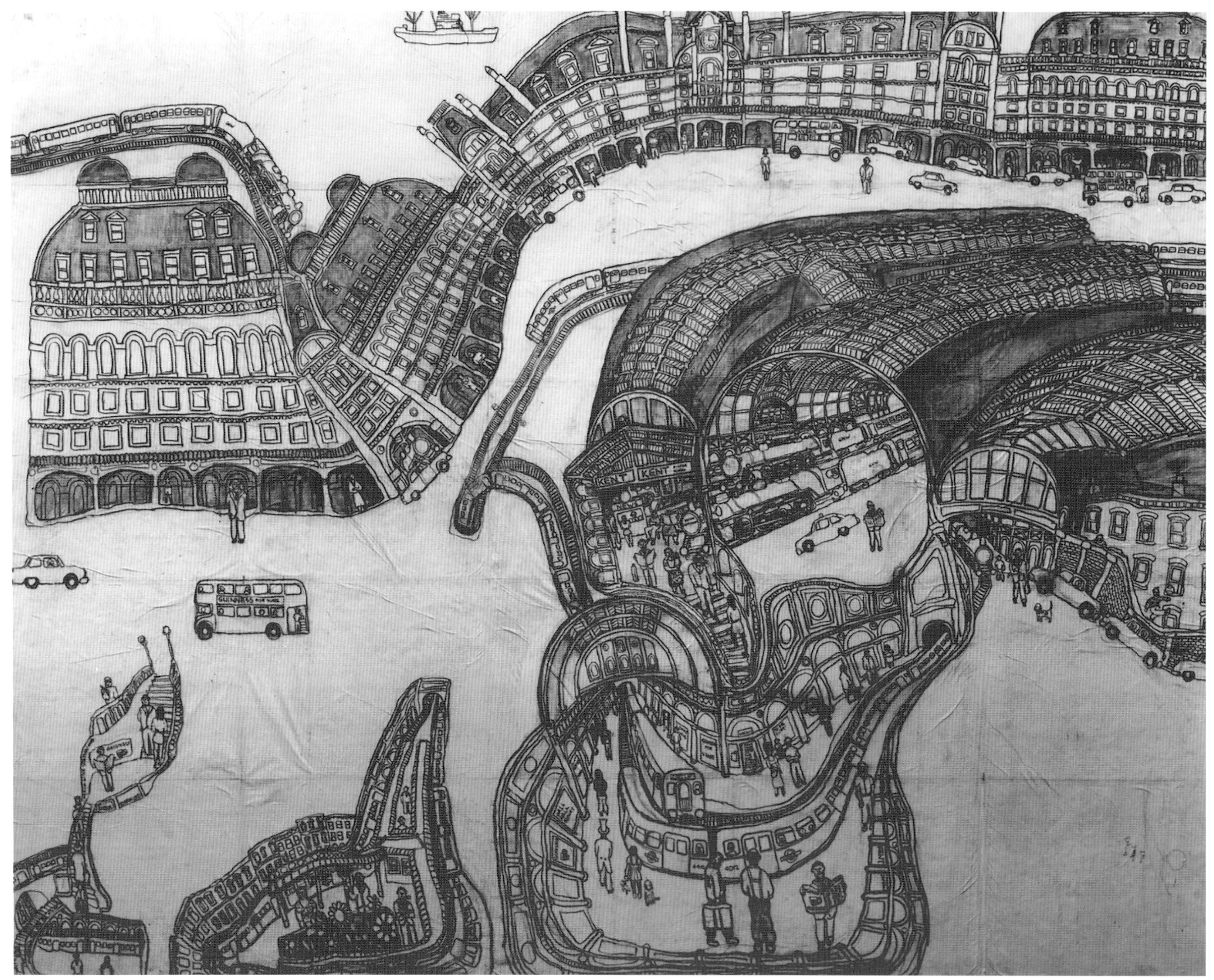

1.8. *Going from Paddington to Victoria on the Circle Line*, Doug Cooper, 1969. Charcoal on paper, 90 × 110 inches. Carnegie Museum of Art, Pittsburgh.

After returning to Pittsburgh, I began a drawing that would combine the two sketches I had done at Paddington by using the same cutaway technique I'd found useful at Trajan's Market. I was looking for a way to reconstruct my experiences of both the station's multiple interior spaces and my numerous trips on the Circle Line: a kind of pictorial map of memories (fig. 1.8).

I worked on our dining room wall while listening to the New York Mets beat the Baltimore Orioles in an improbable World Series outcome. Like the Mets that October, or so it seemed at the time, the drawing progressed like a force of nature, and I just tried to keep out of its way. I started with a version of the sketch I had drawn on site at Paddington's Circle Line stop, and then proceeded upward into a cutaway view of the station hall itself. Eventually, the drawing went outside to include various stops I remembered from trips along the Circle Line—one had flowers along its platforms—and finally reached Victoria Station in the south of London and the channel ferry to France as its final destination at the drawing's top. I gave the drawing a name I thought captured its sense of travel: *Going from Paddington to Victoria on the Circle Line*. I felt it was my first successful response to Bloomer's assignment to combine insides with outsides.

Drawing Pittsburgh

With Pittsburgh as my primary subject, I've come to understand why Bloomer wanted us to use multiple viewing angles. The city's landscape invited me to look up at the undersides of porches, down steps, and left and right with bending roads (fig. 1.9). Over years of drawing the city's steep terrain, I've tilted viewing angles, moved vanishing points, rotated coordinates, and uplifted neighborhoods below so I could reveal the layout of their streets and houses (fig. 1.10). This way of drawing seemed to be a natural extension of the experience of vision itself in Pittsburgh. All of that happened as a matter of course.

However, I have puzzled more deeply over the core element of Bloomer's assignment: that we address both the inside and outside spaces of our subjects. It's easy to focus on the directional attributes of vision reflected in Lorenzetti's fresco, but miss the larger issue of its meaning. After all, the view is directed not only at the interior of Siena, but also at the surrounding countryside, and the point of the mural is the relationship between the two. Bloomer's assignment seemed to point to a deeper understanding of how we think about the world around us: some fundamental cognitive map arising from pairing inside and outside.

Inside and Outside Space

There is a scene in Tom Wolfe's book *The Right Stuff* (1979)—about the Project Mercury space program—that demonstrates the interdependence of our concepts of inside and outside space. When the scientists directing the project presented the prototype orbital capsule to the Project Mercury astronauts for the first time, the astronauts balked; they insisted on a window and threatened to call in the press until the directors agreed to add one. They simply refused to be inactive passengers in the windowless capsule the directors were proposing. "Spam in a can" was what the famed test pilot Chuck Yeager called them. The Mercury Seven were all ex-fighter-pilot jocks, accustomed to (and thrilled by) the kind of extreme flying that was fully engaged with the dangerous world outside an aircraft. Several had been pilots of the first experimental high-performance piloted rockets. And pilots they wanted to remain.

Eventually they were given a pitch/yaw/roll control. They wanted the vehicle to have an escape hatch with explosive bolts they could activate to get outside quickly in an emergency. This they also got. They even objected to the word the scientists were using for the vehicle, "capsule," insisting it be called a spacecraft.

There was something existential about the astronauts' argument. For them the capsule's interior was simply not viable without physical knowledge of the outside: no outside, no inside, and vice versa. Taking their point more generally and applying it to the architecture of landscapes, we might ask whether inside space is comprehensible at all without the parallel existence of outside space. For the perception of an urban landscape, it suggests that we can only understand the domain of any place within a city—our room, our house, our neighborhood, or our borough—if each is somehow distinguishable from a larger outside. And further, it seems the presence of an outside is also necessary to define the boundaries of any of these places.

As a fundamental law, our sorting of the world into insides and outsides seems akin to the figures and grounds of Gestalt psychology, and yet different in that we also reside and move within the perceptual field we are considering. So in the more complicated condition of the cityscape or the landscape more generally, how are insides perceived as separate from outsides: distinguished, that is, by means beyond just a simple boundary wall?

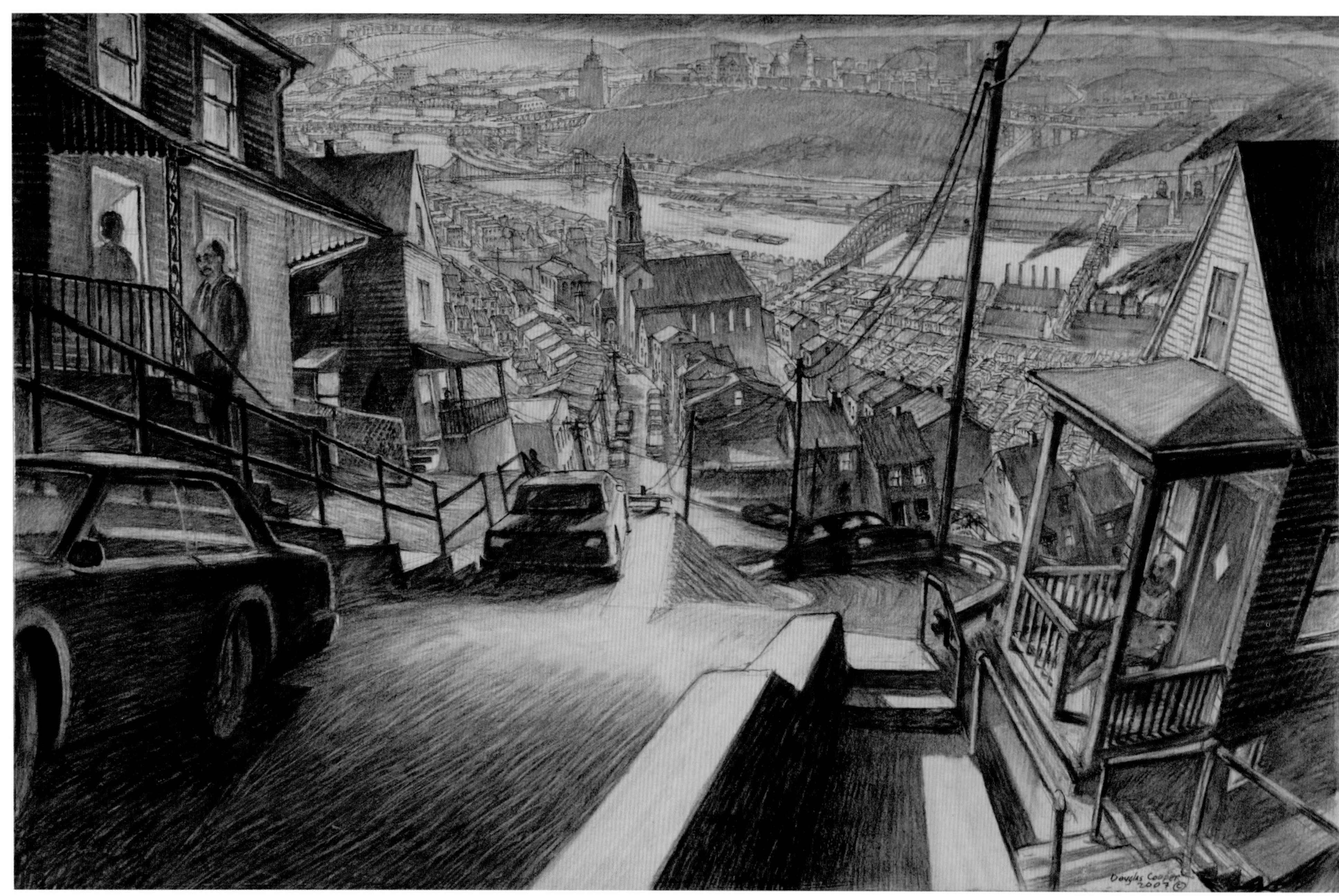

1.9. *Return from Evening Mass*, Doug Cooper, 2007. Charcoal on paper on board, 36 × 48 inches. Private collection.

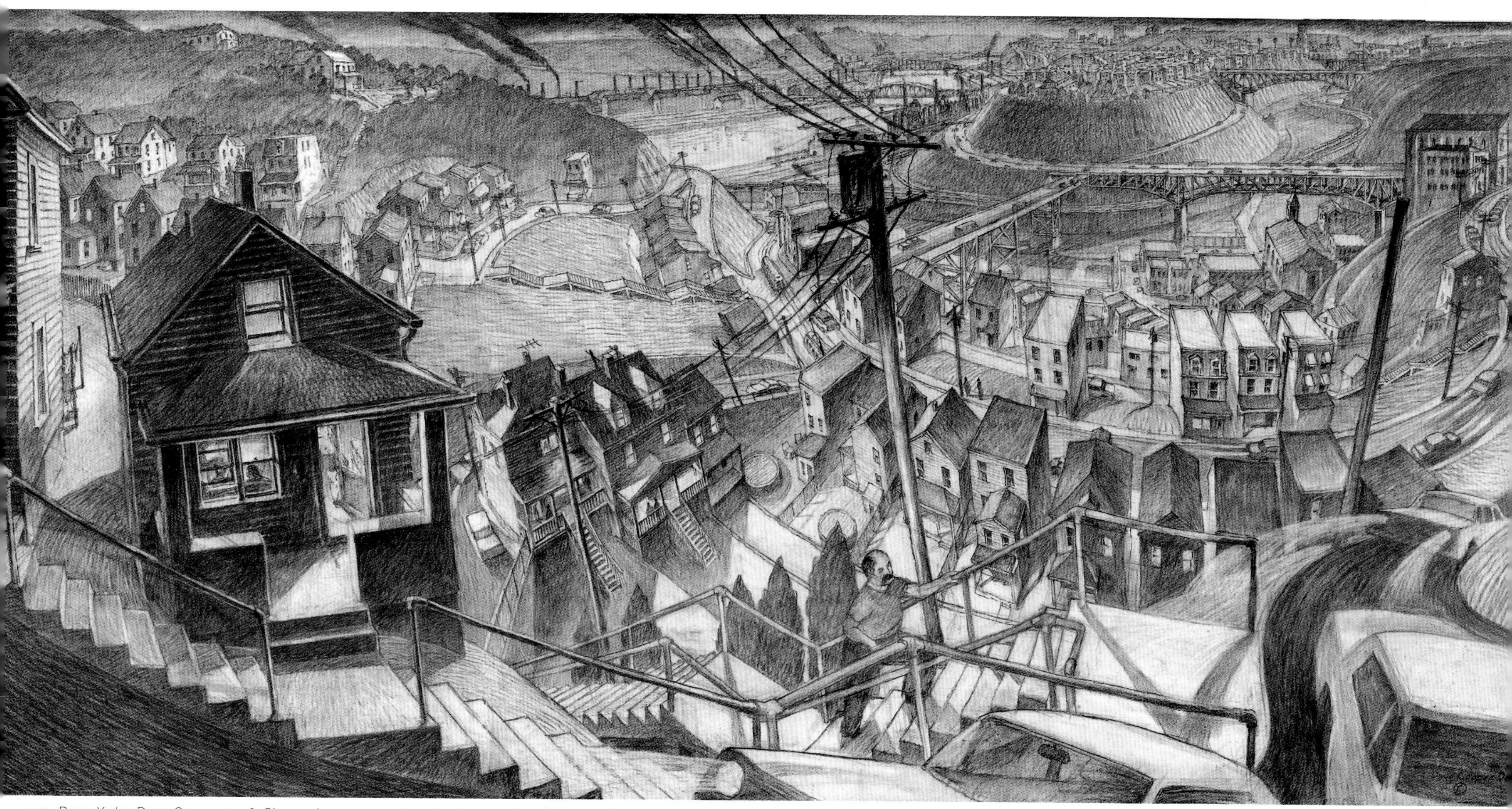

1.10. *Down Yoder*, Doug Cooper, 2006. Charcoal on paper on board, 36 × 72 inches. Private collection.

Insights from Kevin Lynch

In his landmark book, *The Image of the City* (1960), Kevin Lynch did much to clarify how we understand the cities in which we live. "Mental map" is the term he used for our conceptual understanding: how we know where we are in a city and how we find our way around in it. Using cities as diverse as Boston, Jersey City, and Los Angeles, and using drawings by subjects he interviewed, Lynch distilled five elements we use in forming our images of cities. These are:

(1) Paths, the linear routes along which we move;

(2) Edges, the linear boundaries that define recognized areas such as neighborhoods;

(3) Nodes, points of convergence, such as important street corners;

(4) Landmarks, another kind of point we recognize, but different from a node in that we do not need to personally use it (such as a courthouse we've never visited or a church we do not attend); and

(5) Districts and neighborhoods, the medium-to-large areas we recognize as having a common, identifying character.

The most relevant of these for our discussion of insides and outsides in the city are edges and landmarks.

Edges

Linear geographical features such as rivers or streams or shorelines along a lake form some of the more obvious spatial boundaries. Even a fairly narrow waterway can provide a sufficient break in the urban fabric so that one neighborhood can seem to end and another begin when we cross it. Other geographical boundaries are ravines or steep slopes. In my hometown, Pittsburgh, these offer one of the principal ways neighborhoods are defined. Major streets, divided highways, and rail lines also create boundaries. Phrases such as "the other side of the tracks" suggest just how deeply felt these neighborhood edges can be.

Boundaries can also reflect more qualitative distinctions such as class divides. Although lacking any literal physical barrier, such boundaries can be read through differences in house size (the smaller houses of a working-class neighborhood versus the larger houses of a more affluent one), lot size and openness (a densely packed neighborhood abutting a zone of strip malls), or differences in maintenance (a neighborhood with run-down and boarded-up properties versus one in which buildings are well maintained).

Landmarks, Centers, and Spines

Insides have implied centers, and proximity to these is part of the identification we feel with an inside. The hearth—analogous to the heart of a body—is the center of the home. A central piazza, with its church and civic buildings, forms the center of most Italian towns. The same is true for the village green in New England. Central Park serves as the center of the island of Manhattan.

Landmark buildings, in Lynch's parlance, are often understood as centers. Much of the strong sense of belonging felt by residents of Pittsburgh's Polish Hill arises in the presence of the Immaculate Heart of Mary church, completed in 1896 (fig. 1.11). Reputedly, members of the parish built it largely in the time they could spare away from work. But even present-day residents of the neighborhood, who share none of that history, who are not Catholic, and do not attend the church, still consider the Immaculate Heart of Mary the center of their neighborhood, for the simple reason that the building looms over the neighborhood, dwarfing the houses that surround it, and its presence is felt throughout.

Linear elements such as rivers and roadways can also serve as centers. The strong identification inhabitants of a river valley feel with their place is surely due in part to the hills that flank its edges, but equally to the river that forms their valley's spine. And they understand locations within their valley relative to that river.

Insides and Outsides in Pictures

If we construct a mental map of the city from the perceptual markers of insides and outsides that Lynch has outlined, how might these same elements be evident in pictures? For insides and outsides to be recognized in an essential way (insideness versus outsideness), a distinction between the two must be perceivable: there must be a boundary, and both must be present.

Sometimes that boundary can be literal. In Lorenzetti's *Effects of Good Government*, Siena's fortifications divide the city from its surrounding countryside. Sometimes the boundary can be more qualitative. In *The Newborn Child*, a painting by Georges de La Tour (1593–1652), the bond so apparent

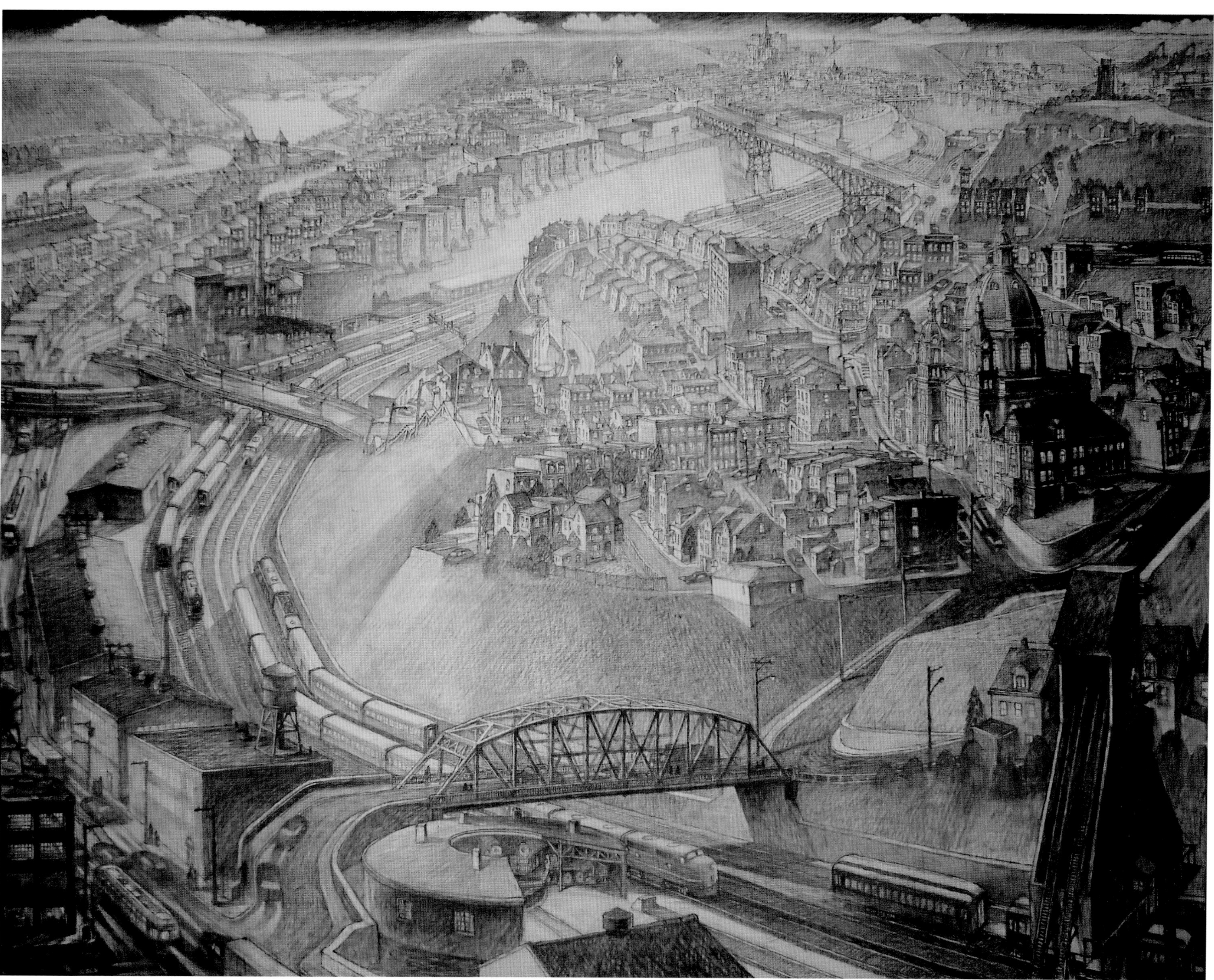

1.11. *Polish Hill*, Doug Cooper, 2013. Charcoal on paper on board, 48 × 60 inches. Private collection.

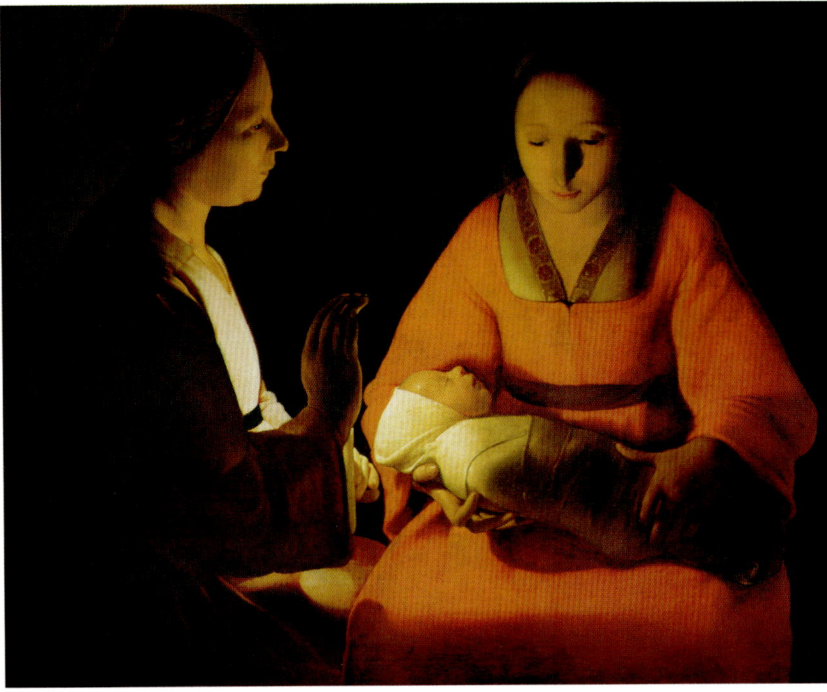

1.12. *The Newborn Child (Nativity)*, Georges de La Tour, ca. 1645. Oil on canvas, 30 × 36 inches. Musée des Beaux-Arts de Rennes, France. Erich Lessing/Art Resource, NY.

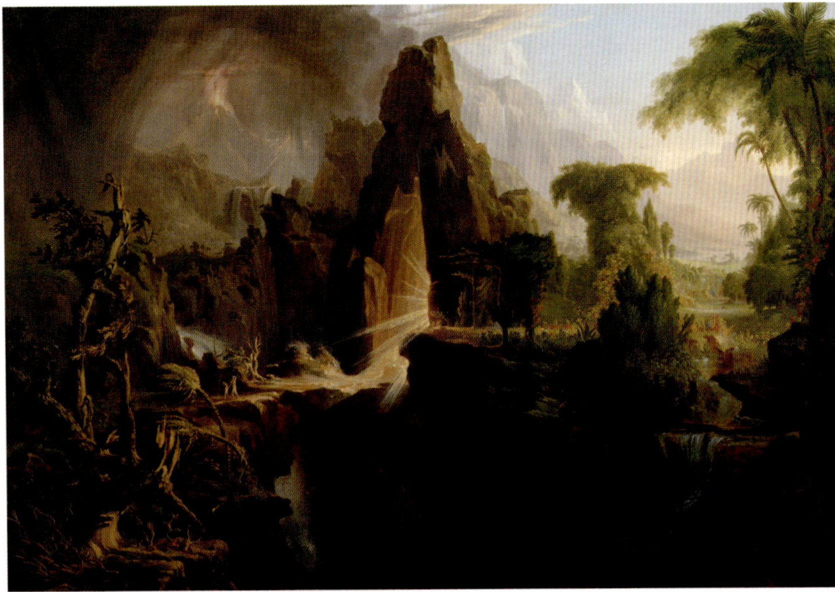

1.13. *Expulsion from the Garden of Eden*, Thomas Cole, 1828. Oil on canvas, 39¾ × 54½ inches. Gift of Martha C. Karolik for the M. and M. Karolik Collection of Paintings, 1815–1865, Museum of Fine Arts, Boston.

between the infant Jesus, Mary, and her attendant (the painting's insideness) arises in their shared center of light (fig. 1.12). At the same time, that bond depends upon the dark that surrounds the figures. In this case, contrast of value between outside and inside is key.

Just how important the presence of both elements, inside and outside, might become for the meaning of a work can be seen by looking at *The Expulsion from the Garden of Eden*, a painting by Thomas Cole (1801–1848) (fig. 1.13). Here we have merely to remove the outside from view and note how the meaning of the work changes (fig. 1.14). Our perception of the painting's inside, Eden, and our sense of it as a paradise lost is only possible with the contrasting presence of the adjacent and distinctly hellish exterior to which Adam and Eve are forever banished.

I feel certain that Bloomer intended us to get into such rich territory as this by pairing inside and outside. After all, when he taught Basic Design to architecture students in prior years, he had always addressed properties of interior and exterior architectural space through three-dimensional projects. In the fall of 1965, his final year at Carnegie Tech (he was leaving for Yale), when he was asked to teach drawing, he remained determined to address the spatial issues that were so central to his teaching. How do these core issues of insideness and outsideness continue to inform the urban landscapes I have chosen to focus upon ever since his class?

Two Compositional Approaches

Because they make up the bulk of my life's work, drawings of Pittsburgh offer the best examples of compositional approaches I have found useful in drawing urban landscapes. I've discovered that the city's terrain has created two kinds of places: nested and layered. Nested places have an inside within an outside. Like my sketch of the Woods Run Valley (fig. 1.15), my nested drawings tend to have a strong sense of plan in order to reflect their strong unifiers—a railroad line, a streambed, or a church, and their strong boundaries—the slopes or houses that define them. I've experienced other neighborhoods as layered places. I draw them as visual journeys from foreground to background (bottom to top) to reveal their sequences of interior and exterior spaces. *Memories of the Valley* (fig. 1.16) shows a steep and bending foreground descent to an uplifted middle-ground valley leading to a set of distant hills.

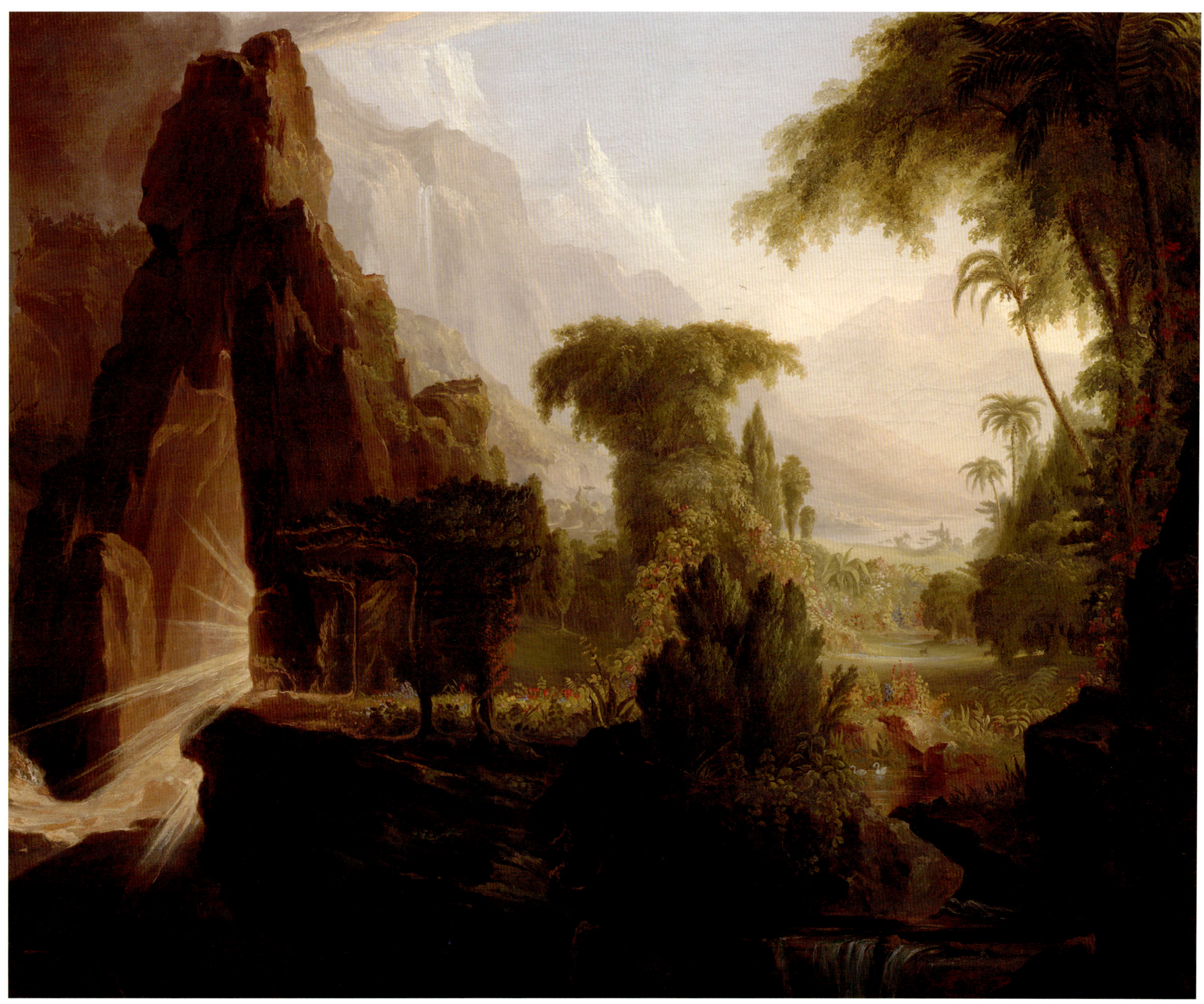

1.14. Detail, *Expulsion from the Garden of Eden*, Thomas Cole, 1828. Oil on canvas, 39¾ × 54½ inches. Gift of Martha C. Karolik for the M. and M. Karolik Collection of Paintings, 1815–1865, Museum of Fine Arts, Boston.

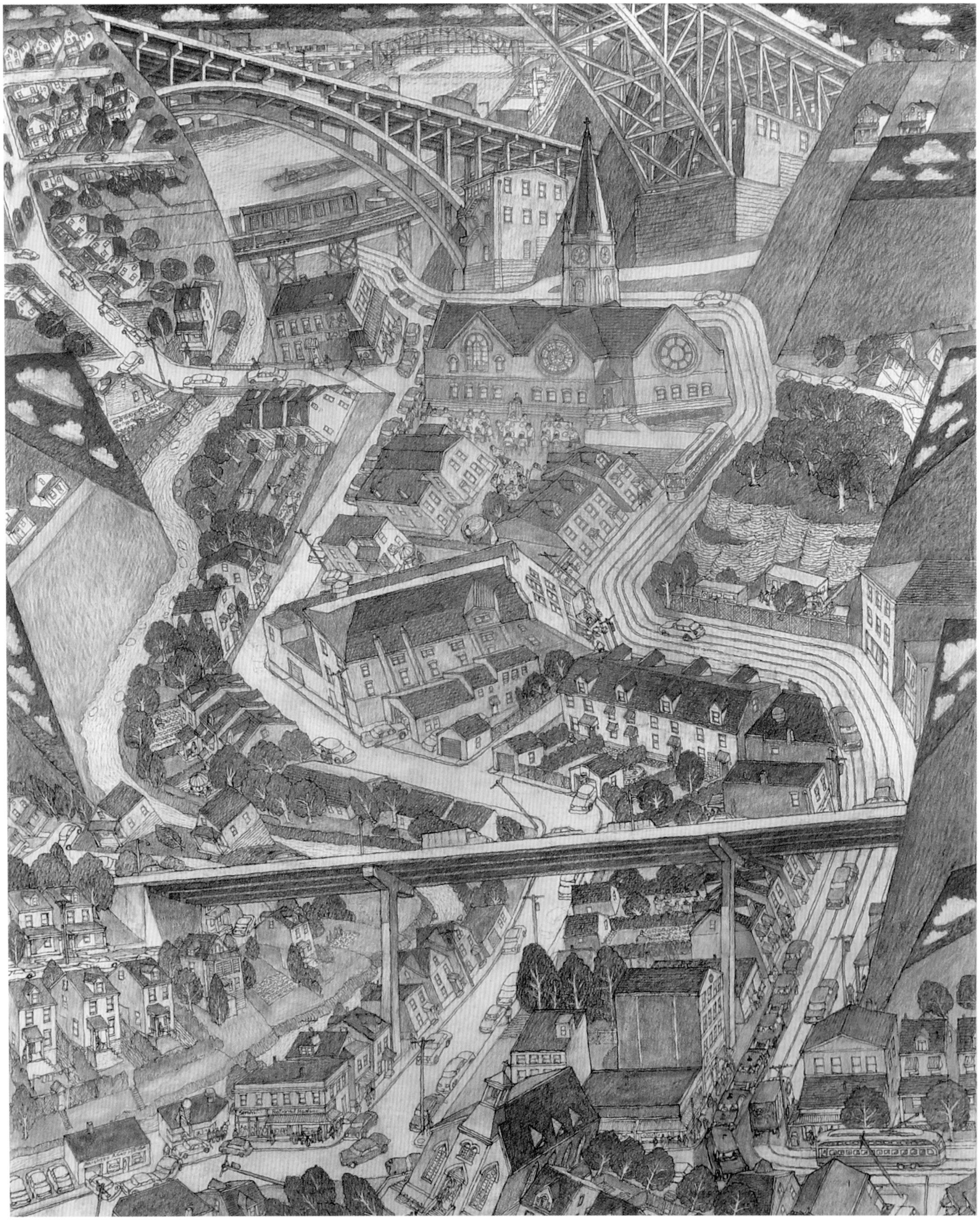

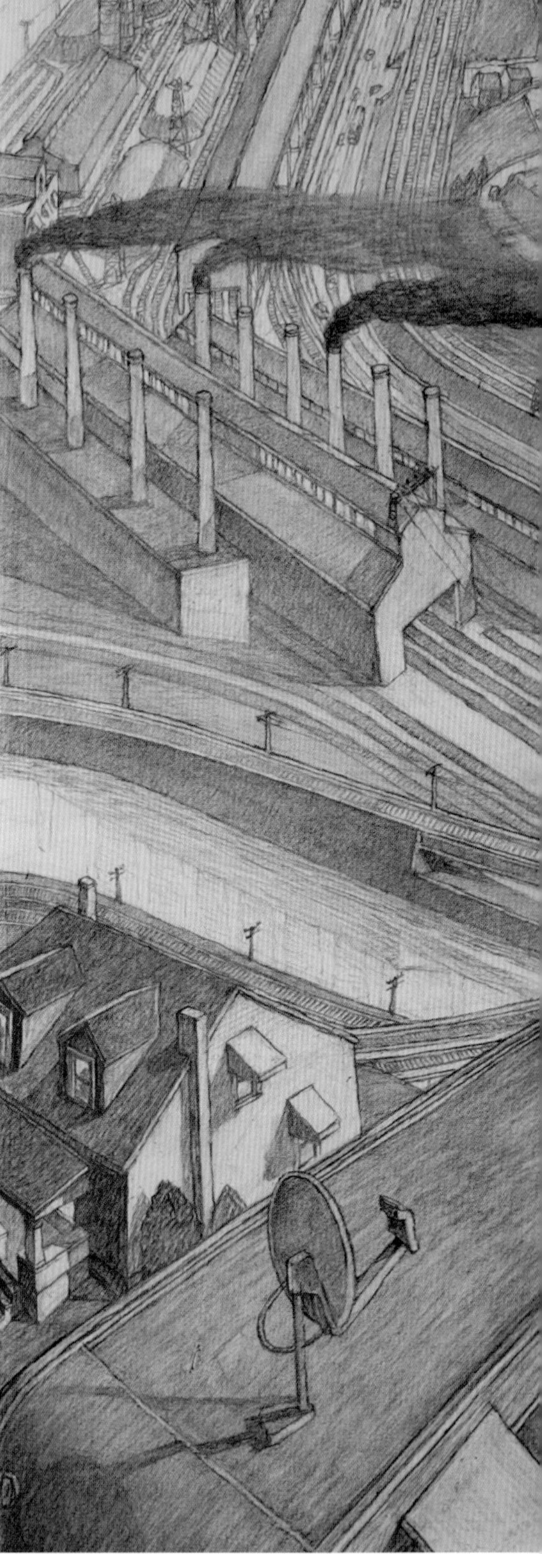

1.15 (*left*). *Woods Run*, Doug Cooper, 2018. Charcoal on paper on board, 72 × 48 inches. Collection of the artist.

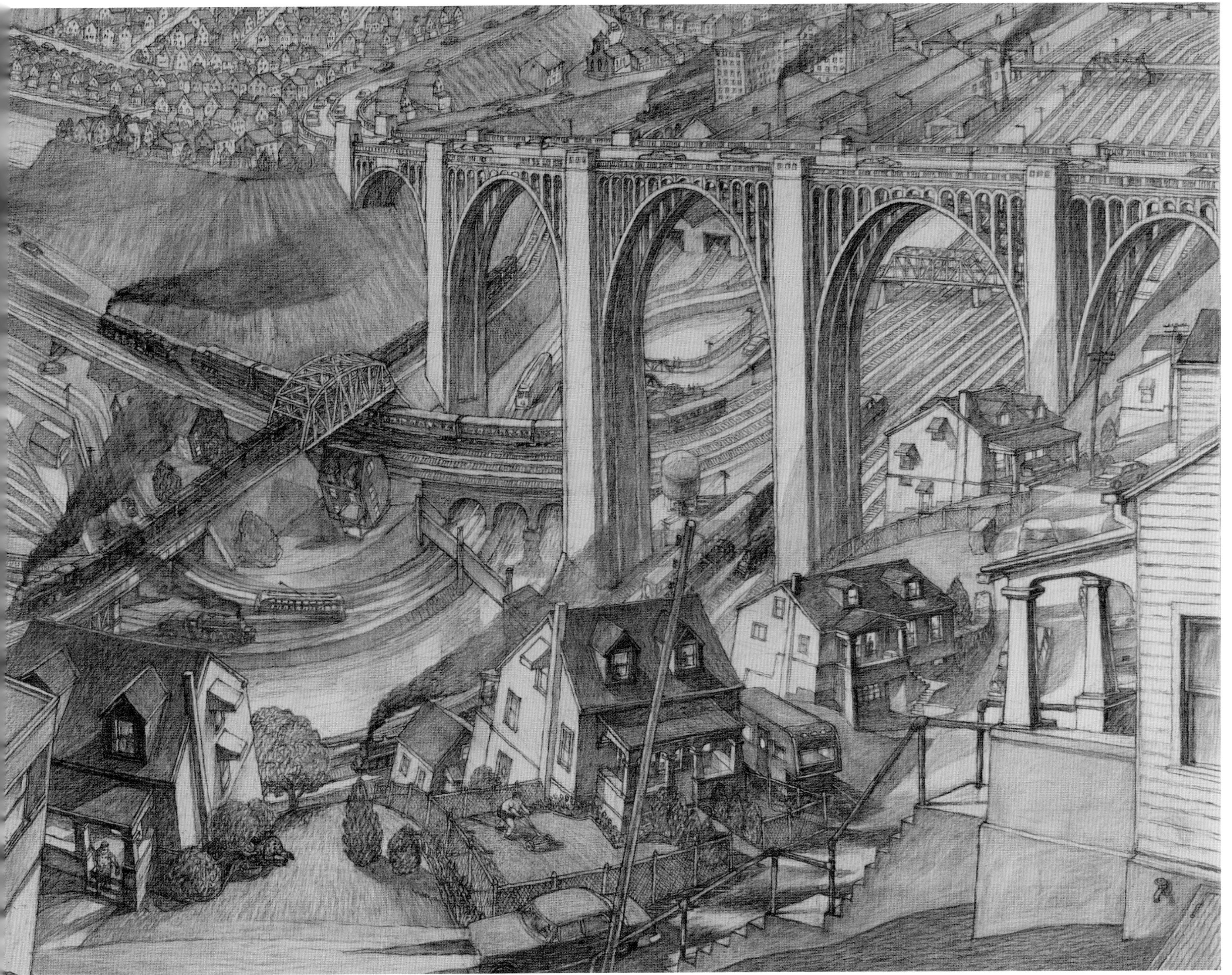

1.16. *Memories of the Valley*, Doug Cooper, 2015. Charcoal on paper on board, 36 × 48 inches. Private collection.

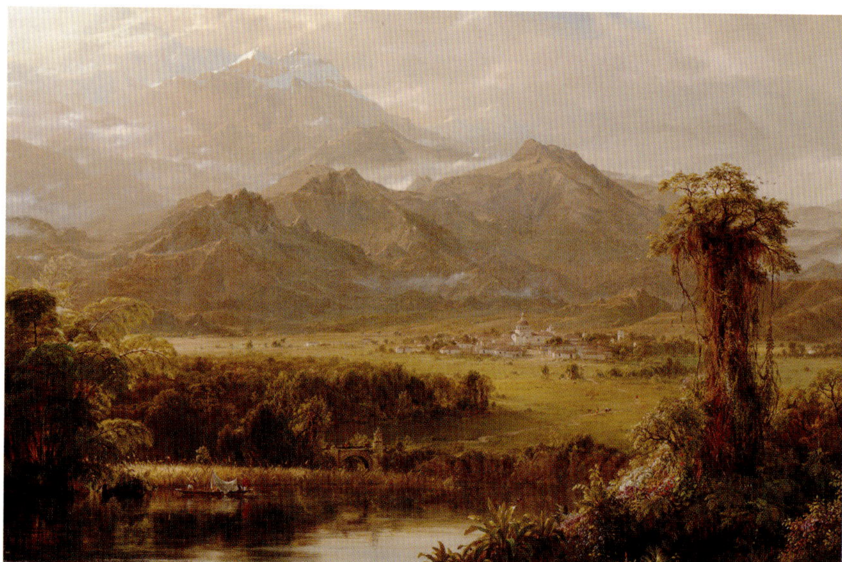

1.17. *Mountains of Ecuador*, Frederic Church, 1855. Oil on canvas, 24 × 36¼ inches. Wadsworth Atheneum Museum of Art, Hartford, CT.

Layered Compositions

In *The Experience of Landscape* (1975), British geographer Jay Appleton proposed the prospect-refuge theory as a way of explaining preferences people seem to have for some landscapes over others. The archetypal condition he identified through empirical research (largely into landscape paintings) is one in which people find sheltered refuge at forest edges from which they can emerge into more open areas, such as clearings and meadows. He and others have speculated that this preference arose out of our early existence as hunter-gatherers on the African savannah—the preference being for safe, sheltered areas from which prospective game or potential danger could be observed and plans of attack or flight considered.

Appleton was from England, and many of his examples are from British Romantic landscape painters. But we can find these same properties in paintings of the Hudson River school in the United States in the mid-nineteenth century. Many of them favored layered compositions that used physical boundaries supplemented by light to distinguish foregrounds, middle grounds, and backgrounds along an upward visual journey: near to far.

Mountains of Ecuador, by Frederic Church (1826–1900), is a fine example of this composition type (fig. 1.17). Its foreground is centered on a lazy river leading to a distant stone bridge; a boat drifts in the middle. A stand of trees on the opposite bank beyond the bridge marks the edge of its foreground interior, and the cooler and darker quality of its light lends it a sense of sheltered repose. A narrow path then leads the eye to a second interior: a broad plain with a town and prominent church at its center. This is distinguished from the foreground by its warmer and brighter light and more open prospect. A darker range of foothills defines its far edge. Finally, far in the distance and made distinct from the foothills by a brighter, almost heavenly light, are the mountain peaks that mark the painting's climax.

In drawing Pittsburgh, I have often used a similar layered composition, aligning multiple insides vertically from bottom to top, and, like Church, I have defined the boundaries of these spaces with light and dark. *Iroquois to Forbes Field* has a bright foreground streetscape of automobiles, streetcars, and lighted apartment windows looking out from the Iroquois Building. I bordered that with a darkened roofscape; above that I set a floodlit baseball game at Forbes Field. Finally, I contrasted that with a daytime ascent into the hills of the distant neighborhoods of Squirrel Hill and Bellefield (fig. 1.18).

The sense of foreground definition in Church's *Mountains of Ecuador* in a stand of darkened trees on the river's opposite bank has a counterpart in my use of accelerated perspective to enclose foreground spaces. The mural I completed for Carnegie Mellon University's Jared L. Cohon University Center has examples of this approach. Looking at one of its foregrounds, we see a set of houses creating a neighborhood pocket at an intersection high up a slope overlooking the city (fig. 1.19). The houses are skewed toward each other to add spatial definition to the foreground. Throughout this scene, I switched time of day from day to night and back, to create boundaries within its narrative. The nighttime foreground scene contrasts with a maplike daytime view over South Oakland below, which in turn overlooks a nighttime view of the Jones & Laughlin blast furnaces along the banks of the Monongahela River further below. That river then leads the eye to the hills of Greenfield and Homestead in the far distance. Though the composition's mood is markedly different from Church's painting, it shares its same underlying structure and uses light, albeit of a different character, to set its boundaries.

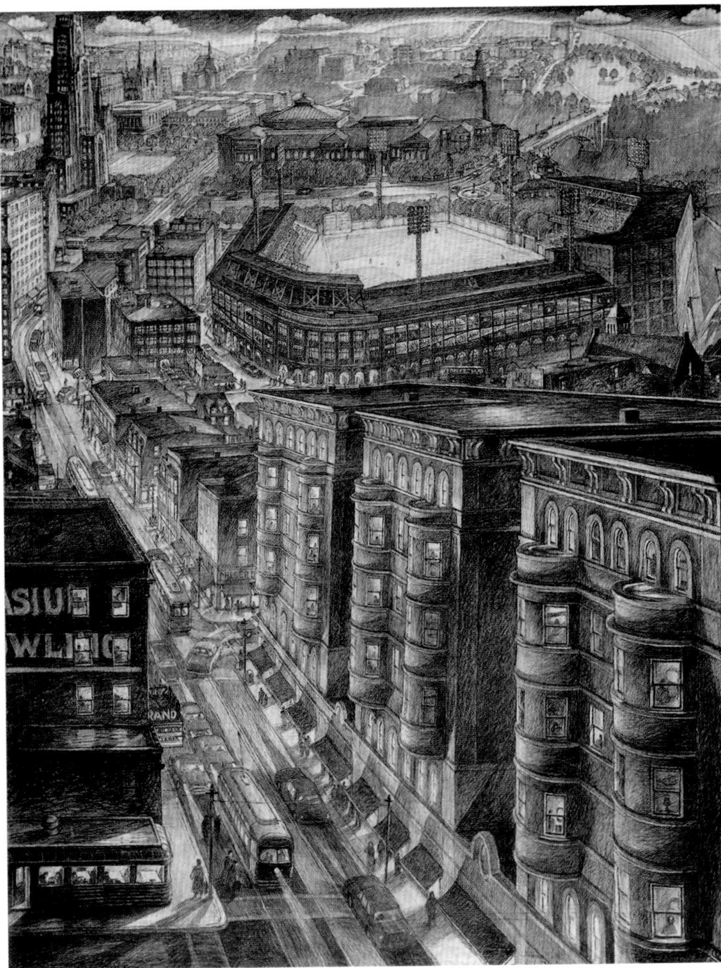

1.18. *Iroquois to Forbes Field*, Doug Cooper, 2013. Charcoal on paper on board, 60 × 48 inches. Private collection.

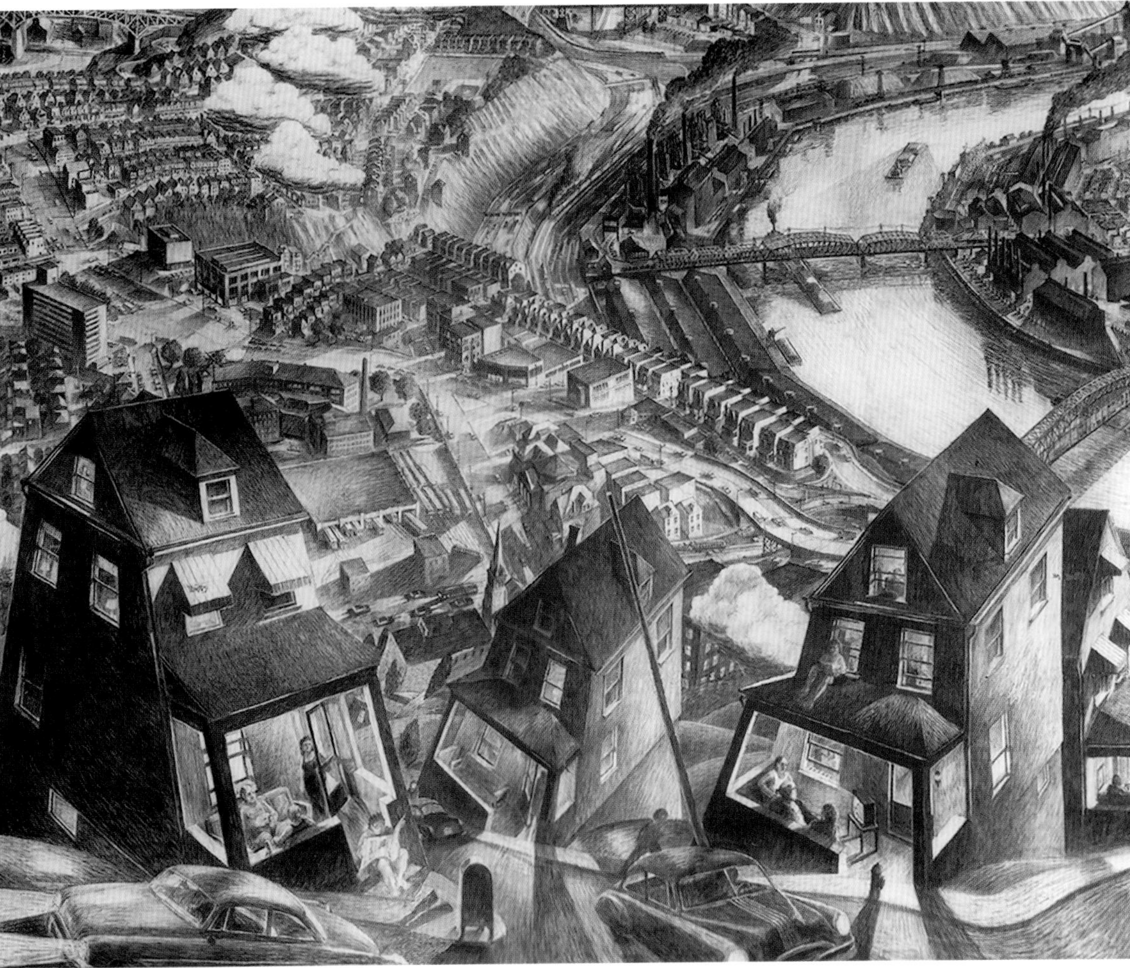

1.19. East wall showing Aliquippa and Robinson Streets, Jared L. Cohon University Center mural, Doug Cooper with John Trivelli and Jonathan Kline, 1996. Charcoal on paper on board, approx. 10 × 150 feet. Carnegie Mellon University, Pittsburgh.

Nested Compositions

As I described earlier, a nested composition is one in which an inside is within an outside. A painting we have already discussed, Thomas Cole's *Expulsion from the Garden of Eden*, is an example. Cole composed it as four quadrants, with the one in the upper right assigned to Eden and the three remaining given over to the hellish outside. He separated inside from outside with value contrast and an overall change of mood, notably the weather.

During Bloomer's class I learned of an unusual nested composition, one with a planlike progression of spaces. One day Bloomer invited his friend and colleague David Lewis in for a look at the drawing I was creating of the Carnegie Tech campus and the surrounding city. Lewis is an urban designer, but he had spent several years in the 1950s in Saint Ives, Cornwall, where he knew several now well-known artists: sculptor Barbara Hepworth, painter Ben Nicholson, and potter Bernard Leach. He considered my drawing through the experience of those years and saw similarities with the work of the painter Alfred Wallis (1855–1942). Wallis had been a seaman all his life and lived near the harbor in Saint Ives. He had begun painting at seventy-five, using bits of old cardboard and ship's paint.

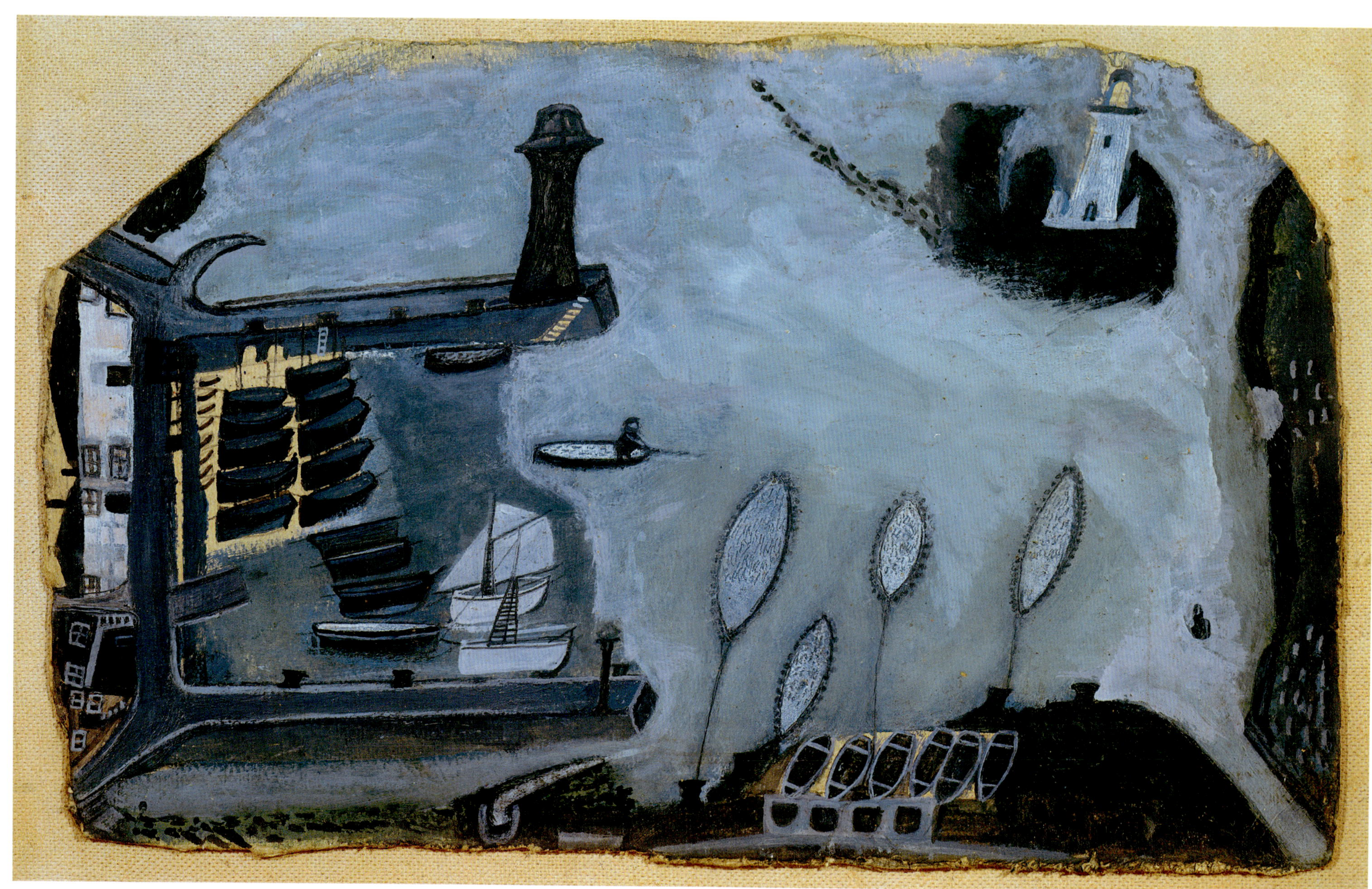

1.20. *This Is Sain Fishery That Used to Be*, Alfred Wallis, ca. 1935. Oil on board. Barbara Hepworth Museum and Sculpture Garden, Saint Ives, UK.

One of Wallis's paintings pictures a harbor and its surrounding village (fig. 1.20). Lewis is an unusually animated person, and he described the painting in the Cornwall dialect as if he were the artist and the painting were there in front of him. As he spoke, he pointed at things in the phantom painting. "This 'ere is William Cocking's boat. The sea's rough and the harbor do keep'n boats safe from they big waves. This 'ere is Wally Stevens's house. The hill do climb up 'ere an' go over top an' come down 'ere to lighthouse. Under the sea is fishing nets, full o' pilchards." I later tracked down the painting and have used it ever since as a guide for understanding insideness.

Why do so many—myself included—find this painting so compelling? Wallis's painting is maplike in the way it depicts the harbor. It shows its shape as a body of water, and, as a map would, addresses questions of location. Indeed , in a pinch, we can imagine a fisherman using a copy of it to steer his boat into the harbor, avoid shoals, and find a berth.

Yet it's clearly more than a standard map. In what Wallis included or left out, made larger or made smaller, it gives enactment, form and relative importance to the particulars of his daily life as a fisherman. The nets full of fish are oversized, and so is a fisherman's boat—presumably William Cocking's. The individual houses are small and fundamentally background. The two light-houses are enlarged.

The painting's interior spaces are set in a Russian-doll-like progression of entrance spaces (one inside the other), each serving as a threshold for the next in sequence. Outside the harbor is a roiling and dangerous sea. The outer harbor has its dangers too, along the dark shoals beneath the far lighthouse, and its currents appear difficult to navigate. The waters look calmer near the shore. The inner harbor is a good anchorage, and safest of all and away from danger on the warm strand, the boats are finally brought to rest. The painting captures the fullness of a fisherman's life—its dangers and moments of calm—and stages their relationship to one another in creating that life.

Backyard Auto Repair uses a similar maplike nested composition to create an inside (fig. 1.21). Its boundary is established mostly with the abrupt shift in size between the houses bordering the backyard and the houses of the surrounding neighborhood. Its center is the shared center of a set three automobiles in various states of repair. Though less obvious as a nested composition than either Wallis's harbor or *Backyard Auto Repair*, *Bigelow Boulevard* nestles

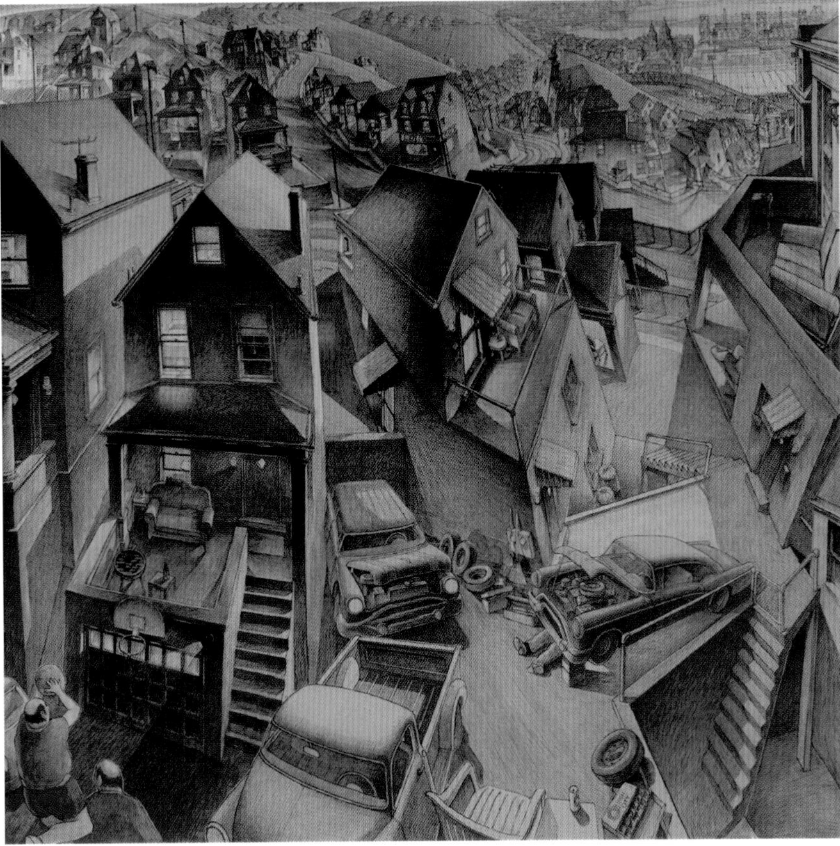

1.21. *Backyard Auto Repair*, Doug Cooper, 2011. Charcoal on paper on board, 96 × 96 × 5 inches. Private collection.

the Polish Hill neighborhood onto a Pittsburgh plateau shelf (fig. 1.22). As I described earlier, it is a neighborhood with a strong center: the Immaculate Heart of Mary Church, with its imposing cupola and twin bell towers. And it has strong edges. Along its northern and eastern edges the ground slopes steeply down uninhabited slopes to the railroad below. To the west is a steeply sloping scrub forest. At the south is the heavily traveled Bigelow Boulevard. As we've seen in previous examples, boundaries are largely a matter of emphasis in landscapes. In this case I used exaggeration: making the boulevard seem impassable by filling it with rushing automobiles and school buses and in the background by lifting the slope of its northern edge to highlight its shape.

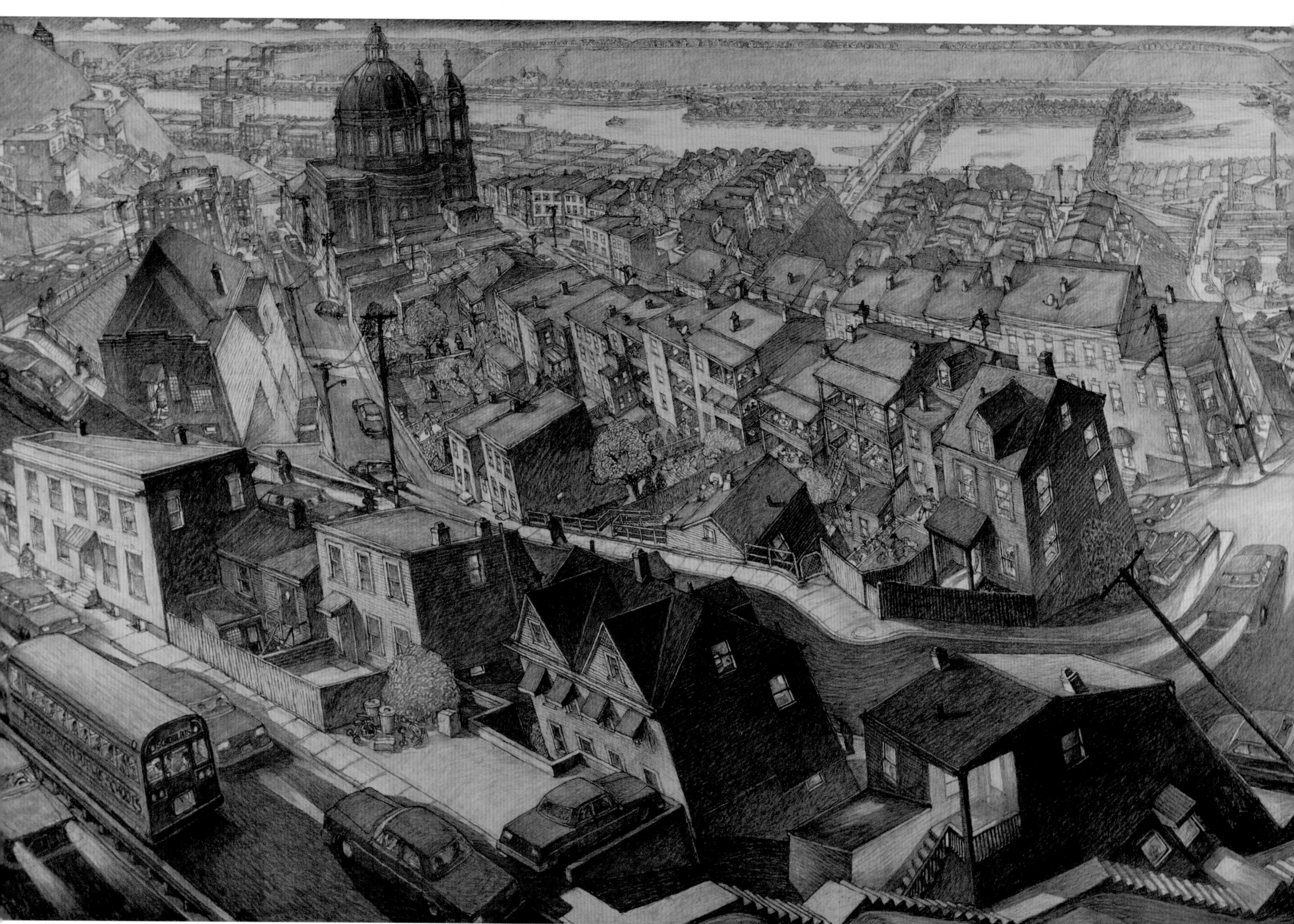

1.22. *Bigelow Boulevard*, Doug Cooper, 2015. Charcoal on paper on board, 48 × 72 inches. Private collection.

Why Bring Insides and Outsides Together?

So, why bring insides and outsides together within one image, as Bloomer had assigned? What foundational spatial meaning might it lead us to discover?

Nude in Bathtub, a much-loved painting by Pierre Bonnard (1867–1947) in Pittsburgh's Carnegie Museum, uses a nested composition: a woman in a tub inside a bathroom (fig. 1.23). Although the painting has a strong boundary defining its inside—the tub's rim—its mood and color temperature are the same across the whole of the work. And yet, despite this lack of contrast, when we view this painting we feel a profound sense of insideness. It feels cozy and intimate. So is contrast between inside and outside—just recognizing a distinction between the one and the other—the principal issue?

I submit that contrast is but one instance of a larger idea: reciprocity between the inside and outside of a composition such that a greater whole is created—one plus one adding up to more than two. The two must have boundaries and thresholds between them, and the parts may differ from or be similar to one other, as we've just seen; but above all they must engage each other. They must *talk* to each other. The parts may be in opposition, as in Cole's *Expulsion*; or they might form a progression, as in Wallis's harbor; or be sympathetic to each other, as in Bonnard's *Nude in Bathtub*. But *wholeness* is ultimately the objective. In *Expulsion* wholeness is found in the larger idea for which the landscape stands as a metaphor: mankind's fall from grace. With Wallis's harbor it is the wholeness of a fisherman's life. And with Bonnard's bathtub it is the wholeness of a feeling, one with which all of us might easily identify: the warm, relaxing, and consummate joy of a warm bath.

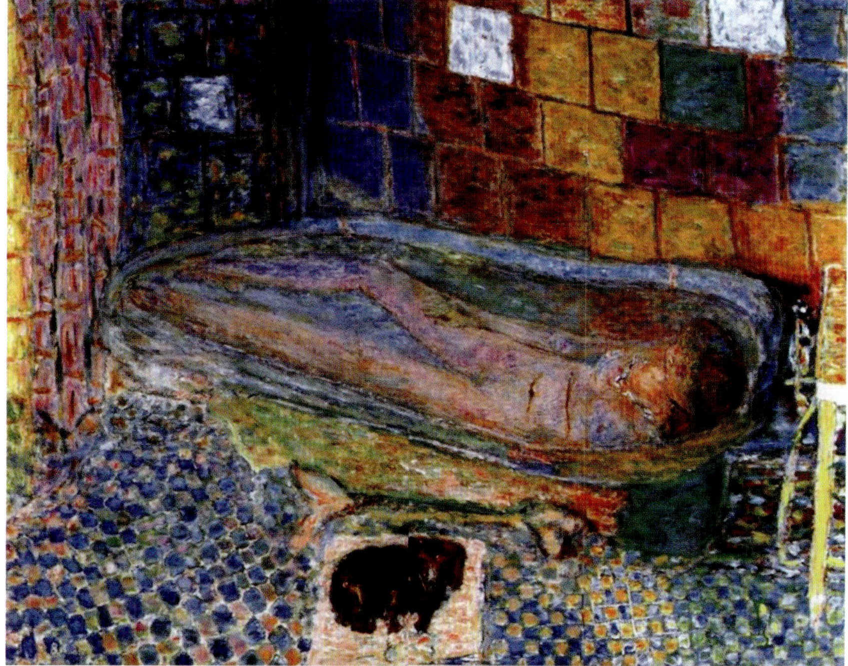

1.23. *Nude in Bathtub*, Pierre Bonnard, ca. 1940–1946. Oil on canvas, 48¼ × 59¼ inches. Carnegie Museum of Art, Pittsburgh.

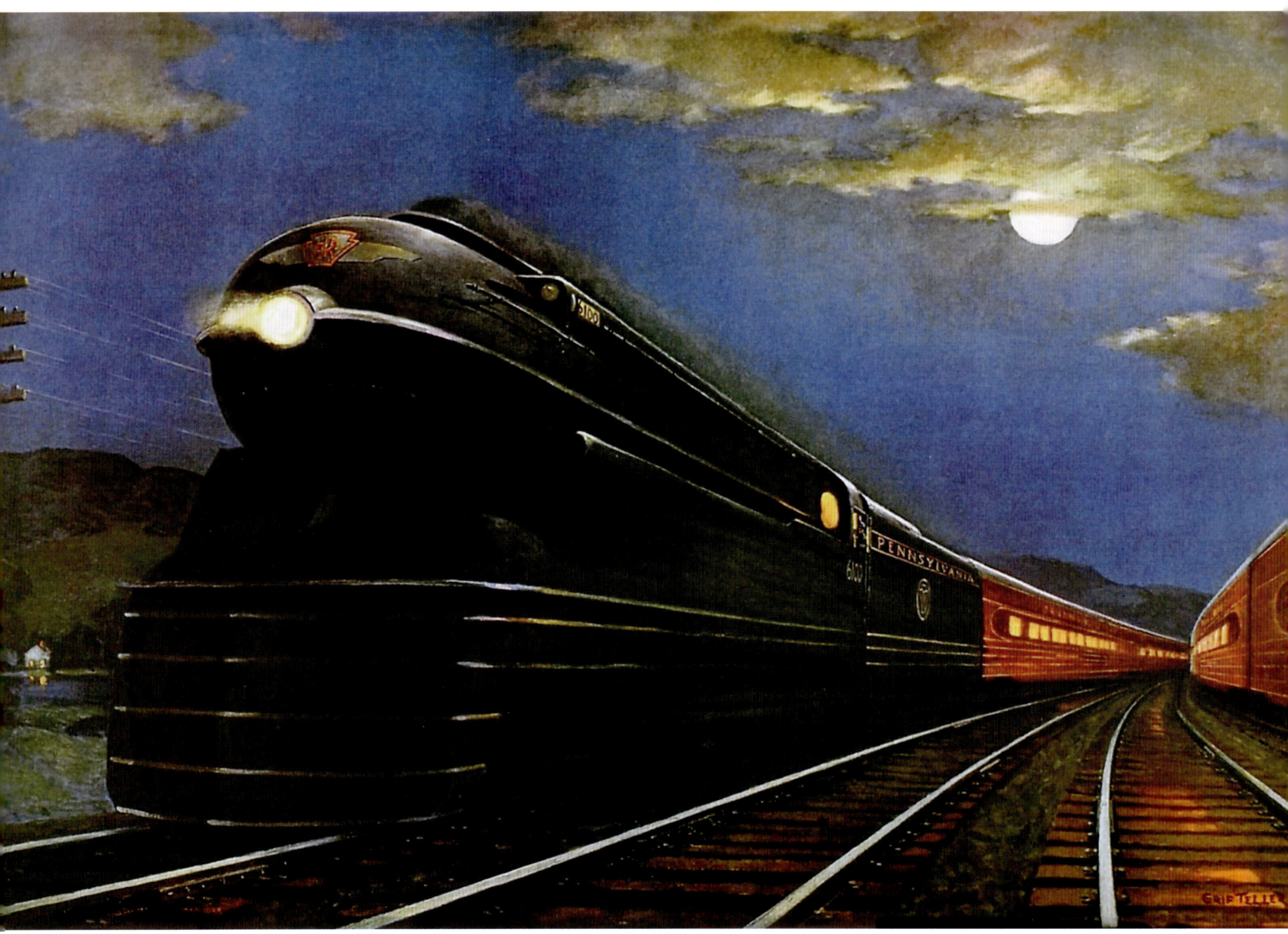

2.1. *Leaders of the Fleet of Modernism*, Grif Teller, 1939. Pennsylvania Railroad Calendar.

THE MAP IN THE IMAGE

I lay awake most of that late summer night watching the world rush by the sleeper's lower-berth window. It was August 1953; I was almost six, and my father was bringing me on the night train to Pittsburgh to visit my grandmother, who lived outside the city (fig. 2.1). The first hint of our destination came with the many steam engines that began passing us in the opposite direction once we'd climbed over the first ridge of the Allegheny Mountains at the Horseshoe Curve. These rushed out of a night of reflected moons and luminous clouds that followed us all the way down the Conemaugh River to the steel mills at Johnstown.

We passed under the Westinghouse Bridge when we were in the dining car. Below us and alongside the Westinghouse Plant, Turtle Creek flowed a color yellow I'd never seen before (fig. 2.2). "There's a story about this bridge," my father said suddenly over his coffee. "When they were pouring the concrete, a worker fell into the form. You can't get them out during a pour. They leave them in. He's still in there." I imagined him still in there: still drowning in the concrete, still trying to swim to the top of the pour.

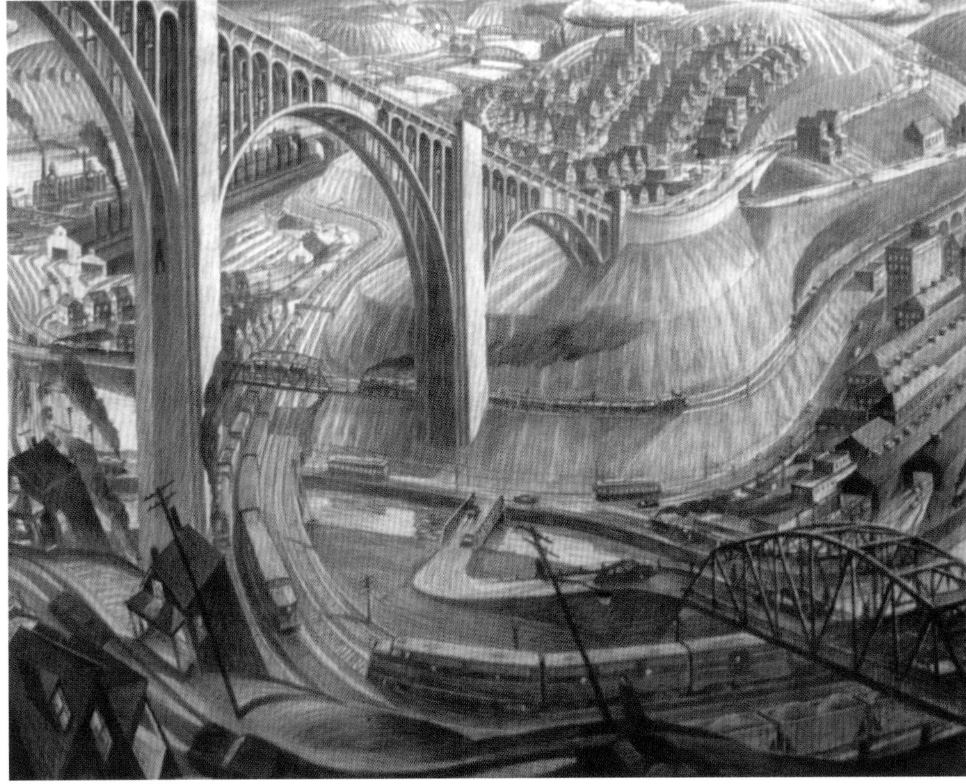

2.2. Detail, *Morning Arrivals in Turtle Creek*, Doug Cooper, 1999. Charcoal on paper on board, 48 × 96 inches. Private collection.

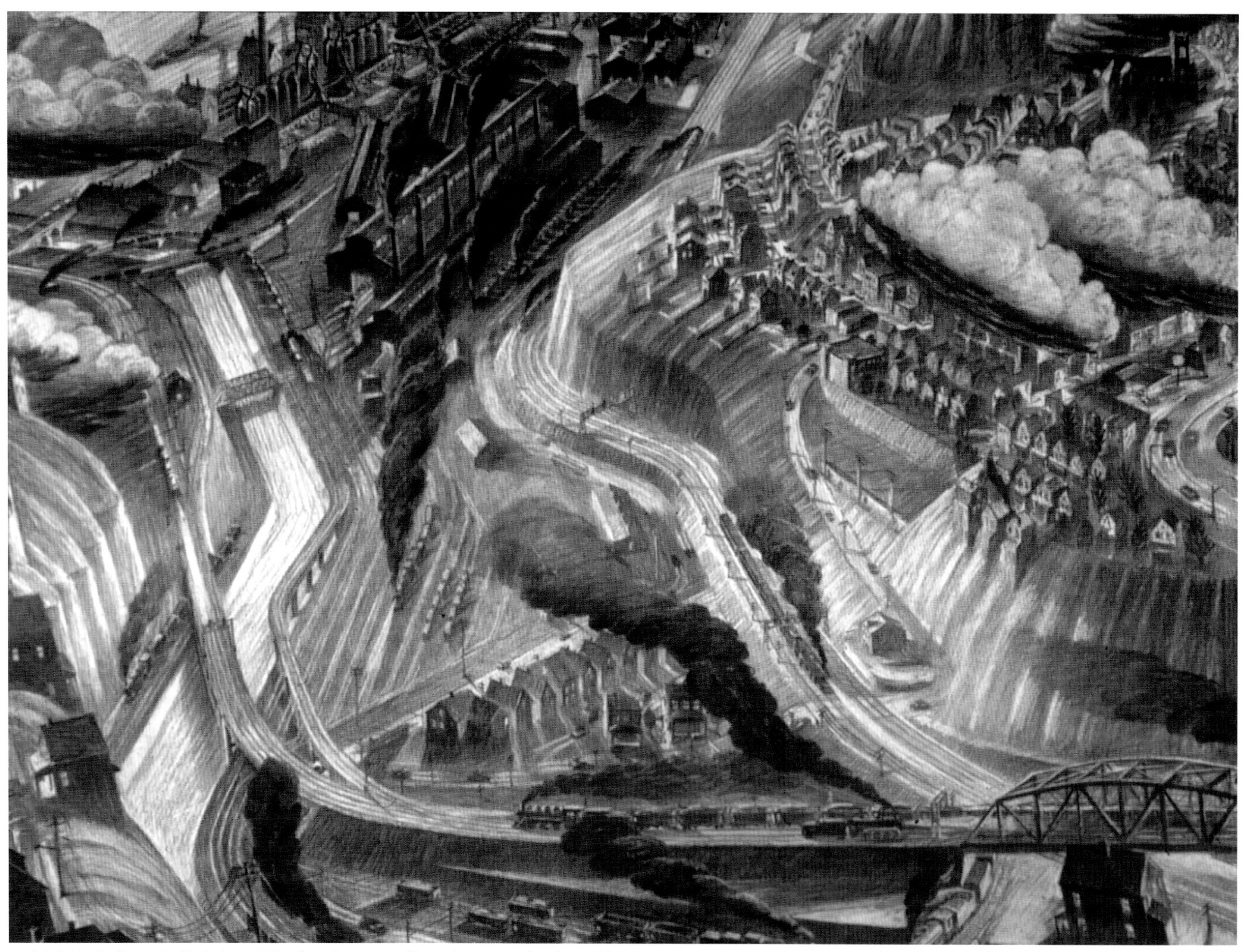

2.3. Detail, *Morning Train under Westinghouse Bridge*, Doug Cooper, 1999. Charcoal on paper on board, 72 × 96 inches. Private collection.

Then the valley opened, and while the train rounded the bend overlooking Braddock, the smoke and fire plumes of the Edgar Thomson Steel Works rose beside us (fig. 2.3). It would have been a layered scene as I imagine it now: all red heat in the foreground and hazy dark profiles of sheds and furnaces behind. Peekaboo morning light reflected past them from the distant Monongahela River. Gas jets fired overhead. Then the view closed again as the train turned into the cut through Swissvale. House-house-house-house-house—street! House-house-house-house-house—street! The train gained speed on the long straightaway through Wilkinsburg and all the way to Pittsburgh.

My father stayed in town for work. I was picked up at Pennsylvania Station by my aunt Mary and taken to my grandmother's. She lived in a big white clapboard house with a hipped roof and a Palladian window in the upstairs bathroom. I called my grandmother Mema. Afternoons we spent on her porch under green canvas awnings.

Mema had scrapbooks from a trip she had taken with my grandfather to Eastern Europe during the 1930s, and she brought these out to the porch to show me. It was in a mine on this trip in Bulgaria, Mema told me, that my grandfather had "caught" the cancer that would kill him years later.

But that afternoon, looking at the scrapbook, Mema was remembering only the romance of their trip. She had difficulty seeing, so she used a large rectangular magnifying glass held close to her face to view the pictures. The bridge at Budapest, she was telling me, connects two cities, Buda and Pest, on opposite banks of the Danube, and she turned the scrapbook so I could see her postcard picture of the Chain Bridge that crosses from Buda to Pest across the river (fig. 2.4). The postcard showed enough of Buda to give a sense of its presence: some houses below and towers to the side. Pest, with its domes and spires, loomed off in the distance, a mysterious and alluring destination behind the great stone piers carrying the catenary chains. The postcard image was at once picture and map—two places, Buda and Pest, and a journey between them.

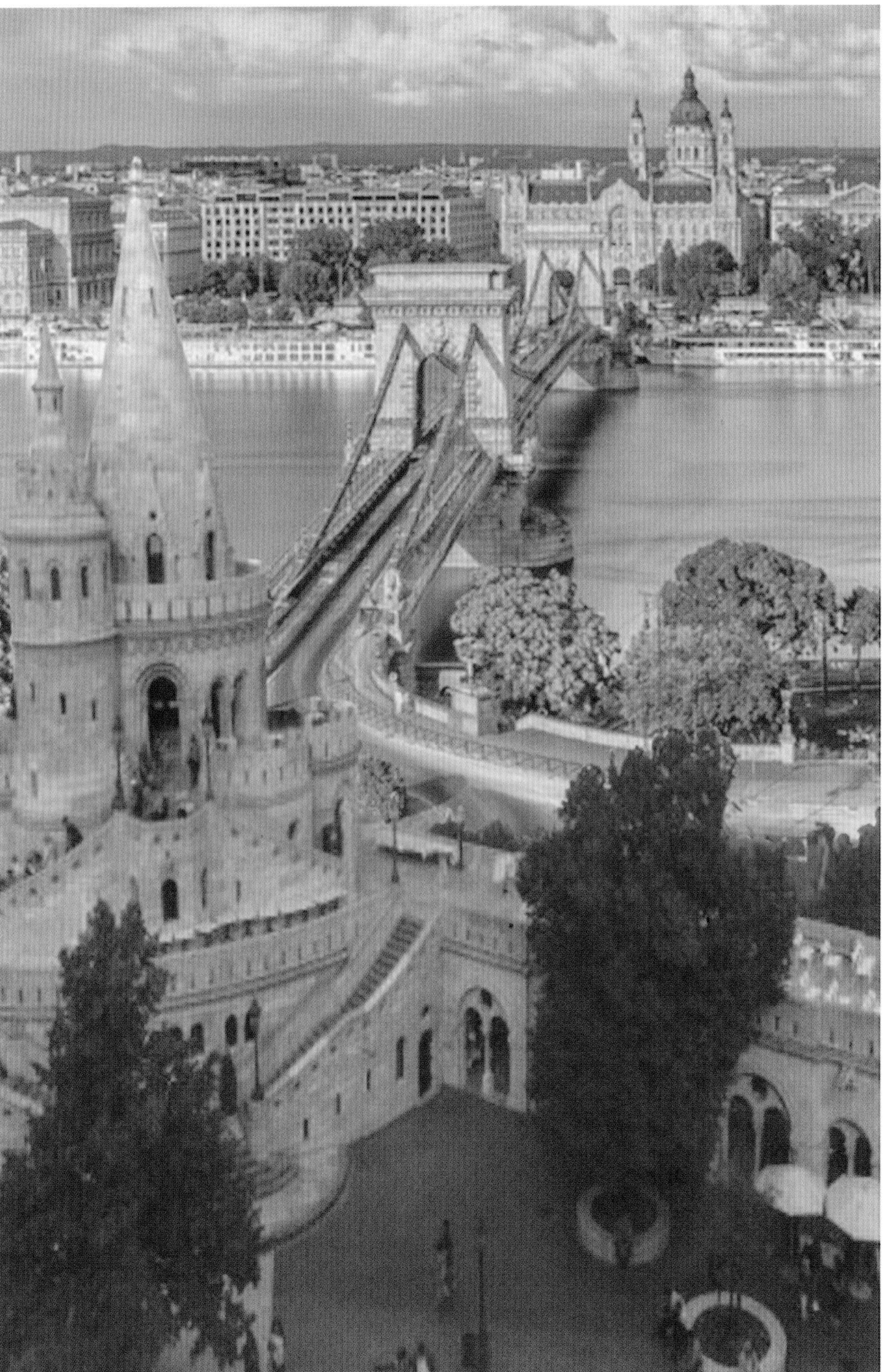

2.4. Chain Bridge, Budapest.

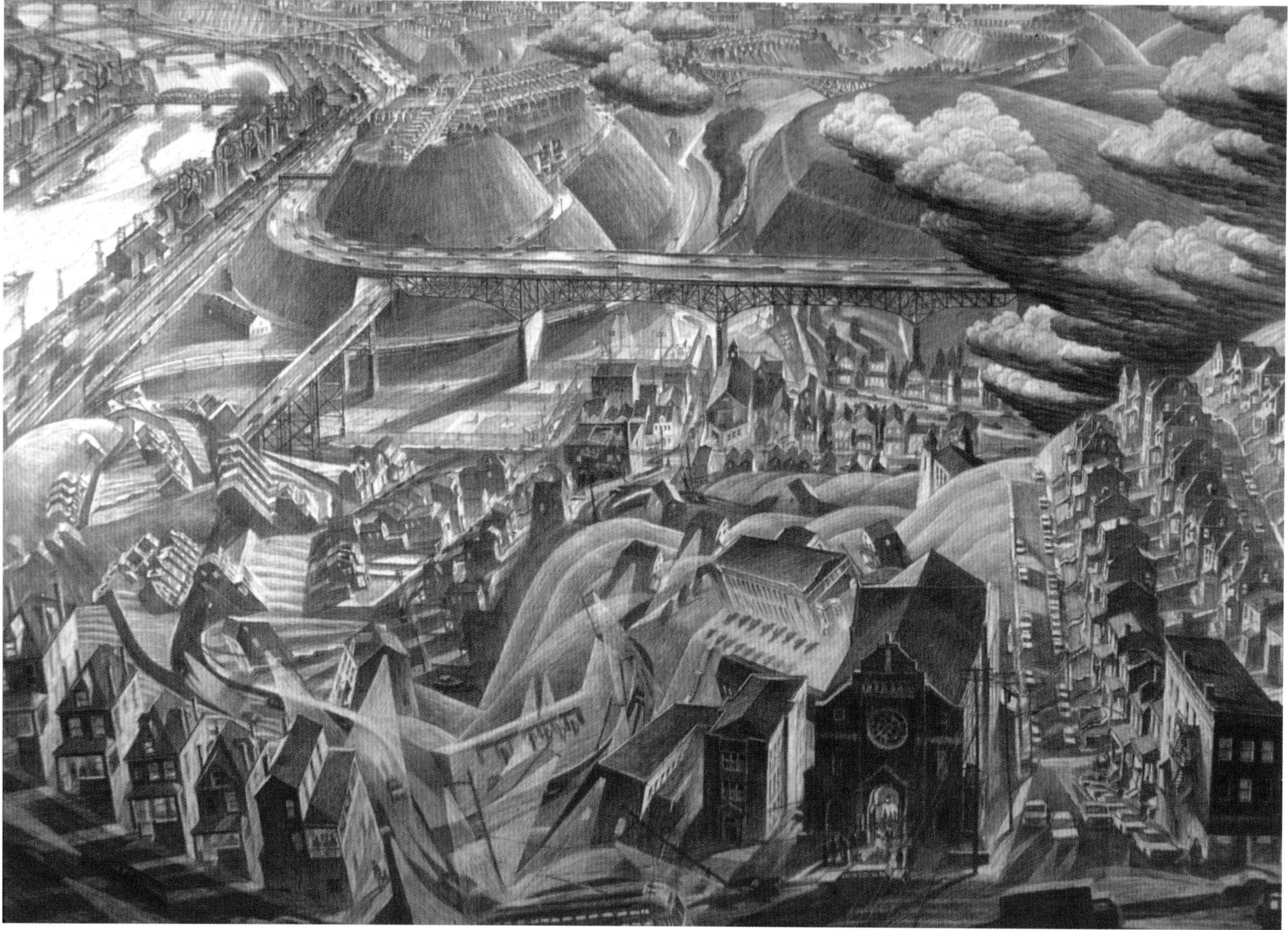

Drawings as Maps

Like the views above and at right, (figs. 2.5, 2.6) most of the cityscapes I've drawn over the last fifty-plus years could be mapped into the underlying structure of either the first or second half of the story I just told about my childhood trip: either the journey by train through Turtle Creek Valley and under the Westinghouse Bridge or the one I imagined crossing the Chain Bridge from Buda to Pest while looking at my grandmother's postcard. I say *mapped* because more and more I've come to think of these landscape drawings fundamentally as maps.

One type, matching the valley trip, uses the same nested structure I discussed in chapter 1 in reference to paintings by Thomas Cole and Alfred Wallis. In my work, these show valleys with spines (railroads, streets, rivers, etc.) running their lengths (fig. 2.7) or they show neighborhoods with landmarks at their centers (fig. 2.8). Another, matching the story's second half, uses a layered vertical composition that I attributed to Romantic landscape painting in the previous chapter. These show journeys moving upward from places of origin at the picture's base to destinations at the top, and show something of the experience of the journey along the way (fig. 2.9).

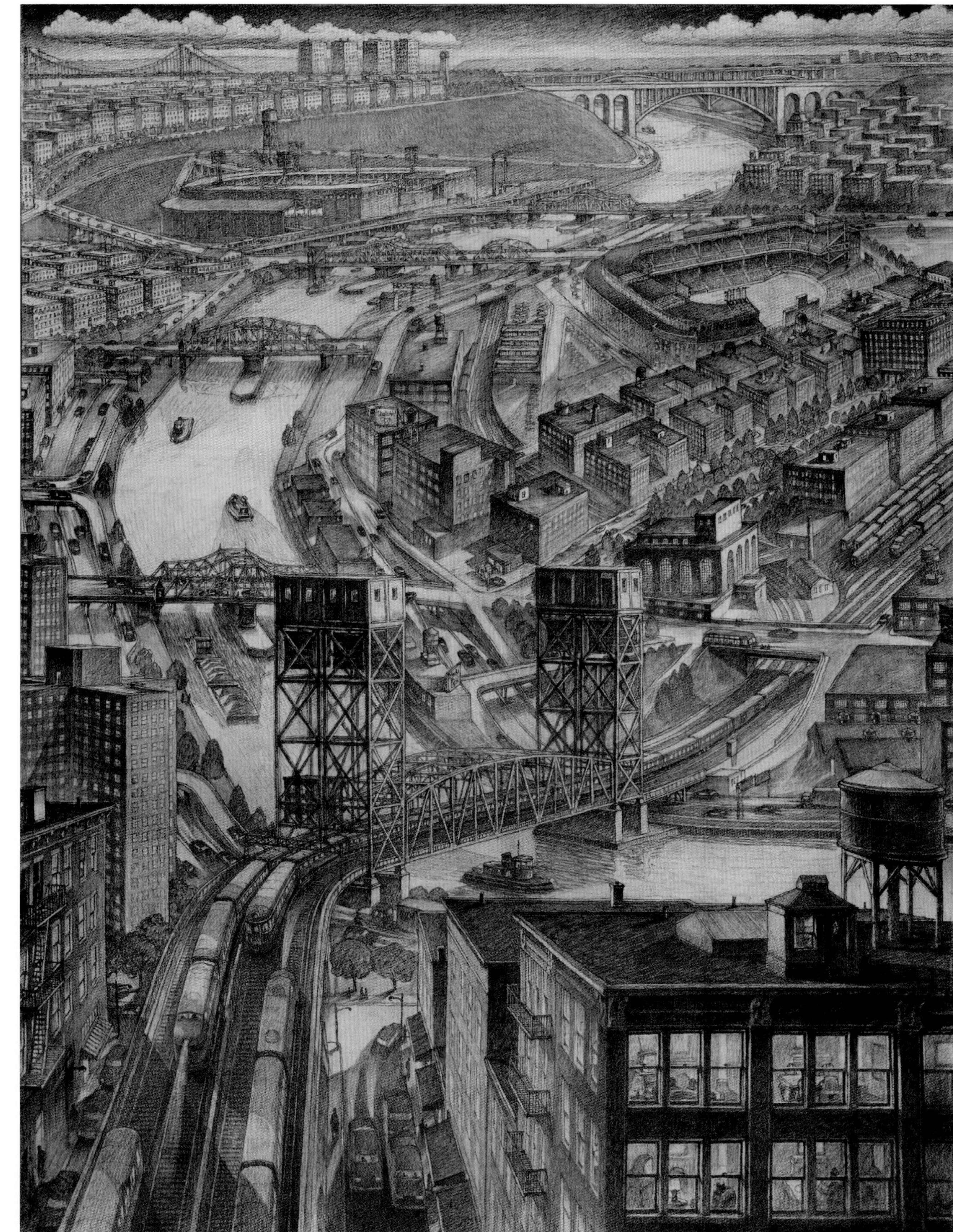

2.5 (*facing page*). *St. Roselia Saturday*, Doug Cooper, 1999. Charcoal on paper on board, 72 × 96 inches. Private collection.
2.6 (*right*). *Evening Arrivals in Harlem*, Doug Cooper, 2012. Charcoal on paper on board, 60 × 48 inches. Private collection.

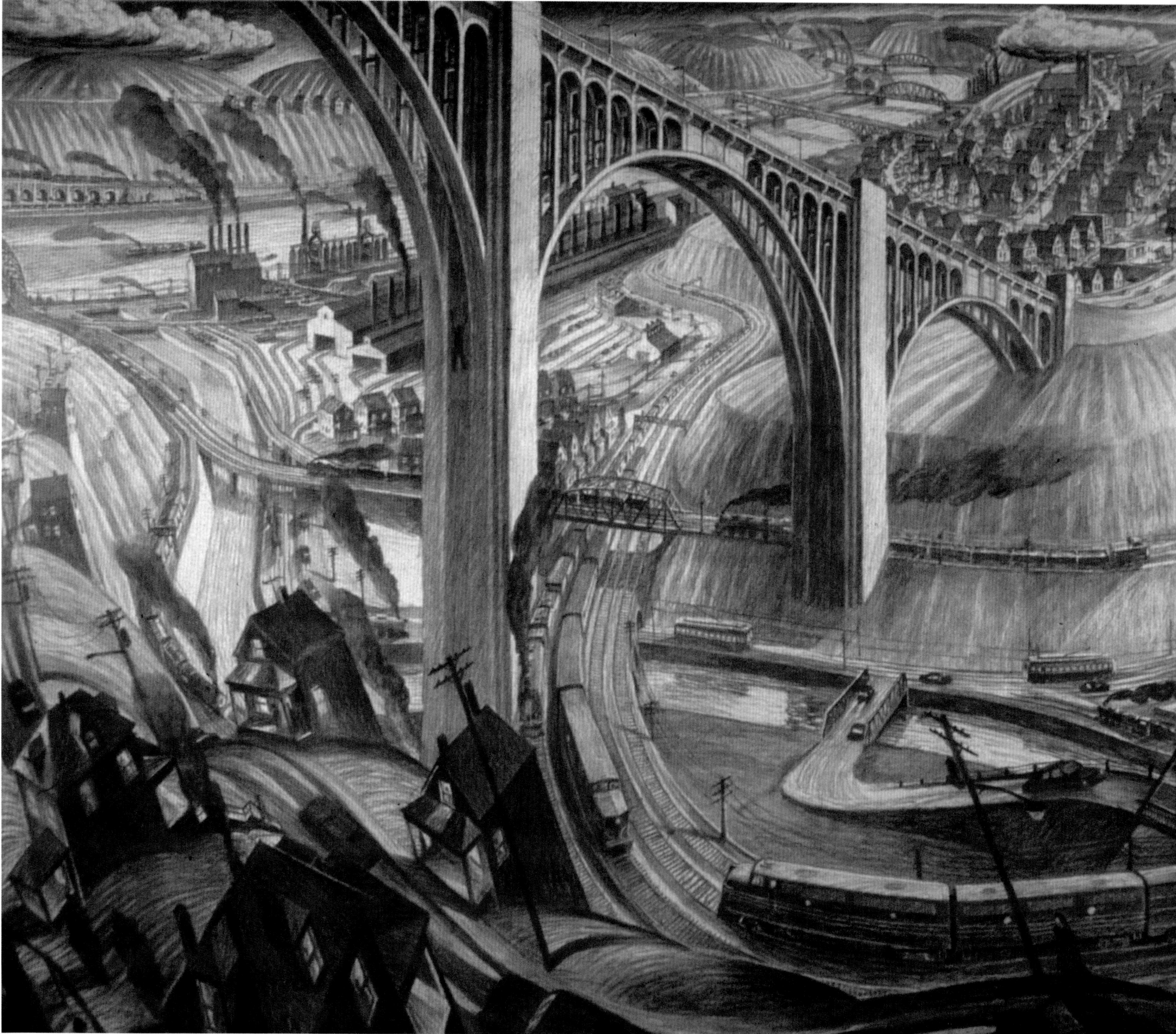

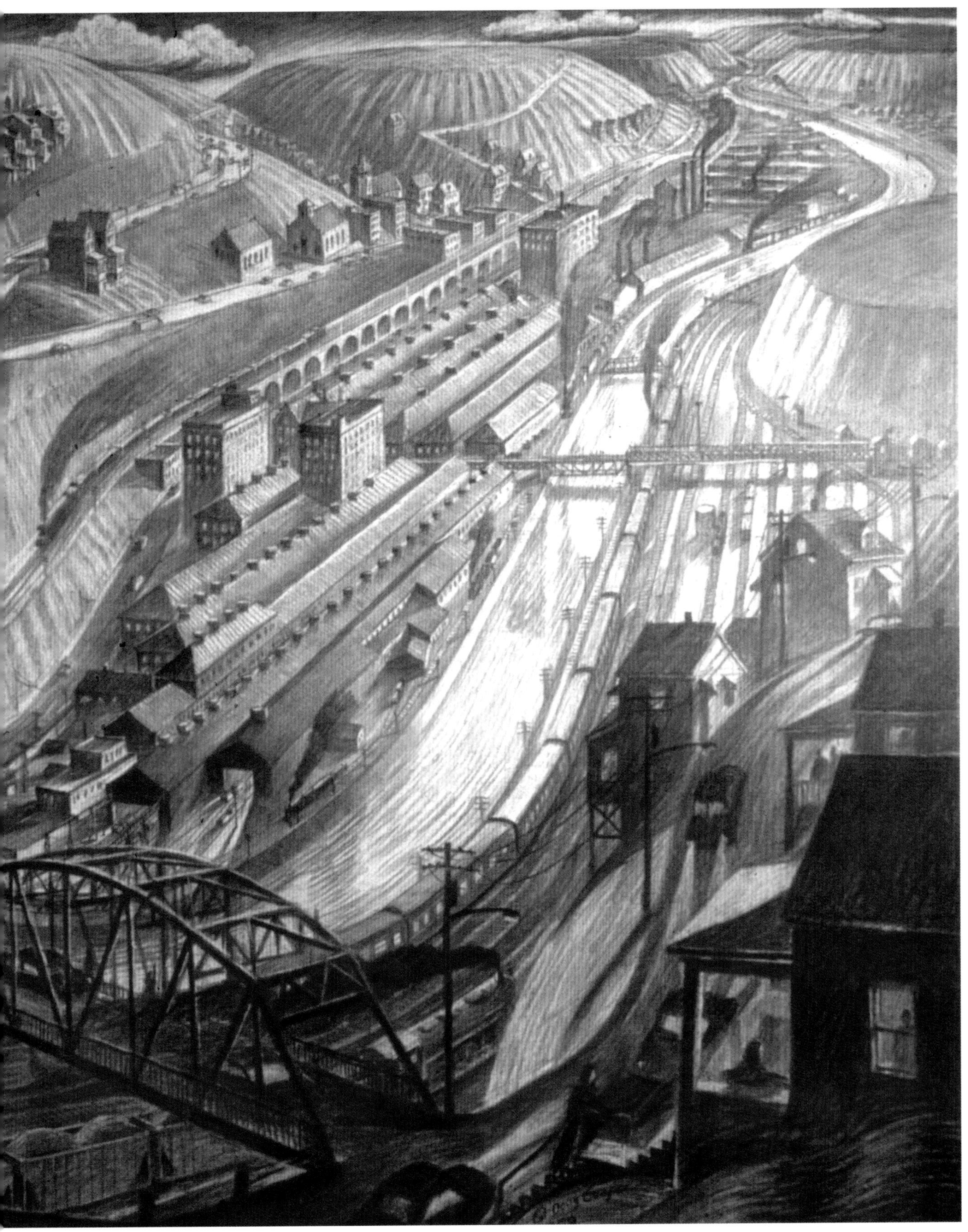

2.7. *Morning Arrivals in Turtle Creek*, Doug Cooper, 1999.
Charcoal on paper on board, 48 × 96 inches. Private collection.

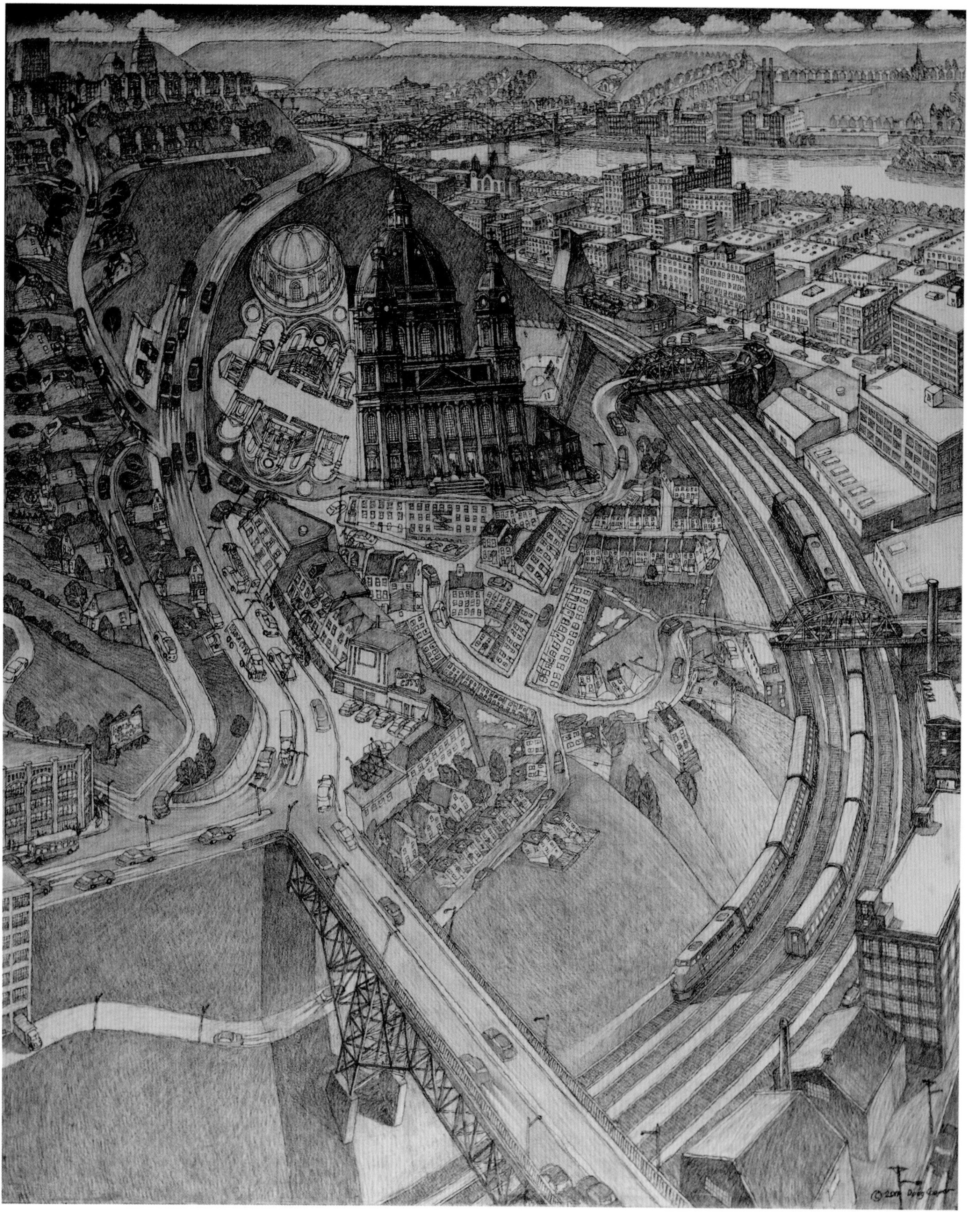

2.8. *On the Way to Immaculate Heart of Mary*, Doug Cooper, 2018. Charcoal on paper on board, 60 × 48 inches. Collection of the artist.

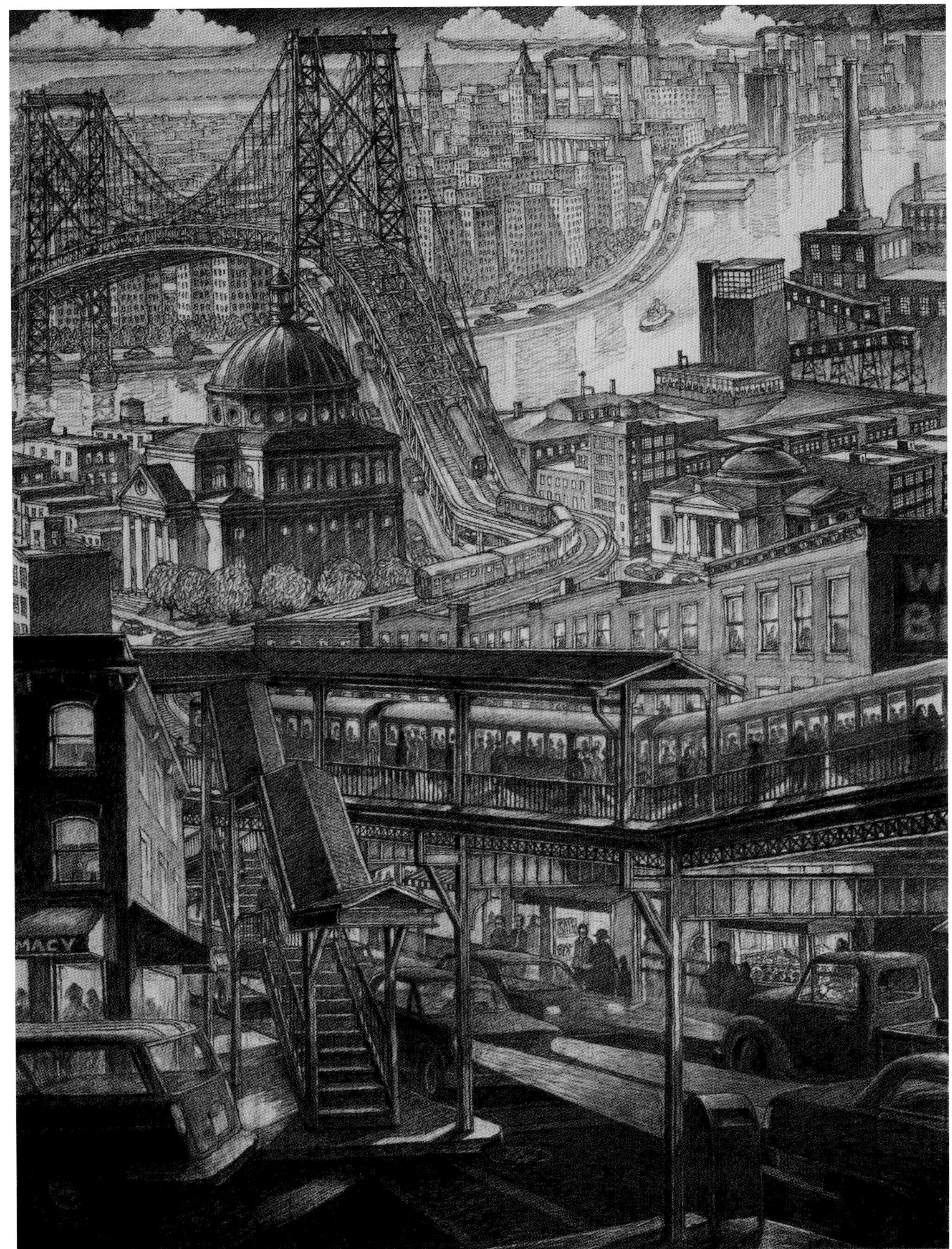

2.9. *Broadway Elevated*, Doug Cooper, 2014.
Charcoal on paper on board, 48 × 36 inches.

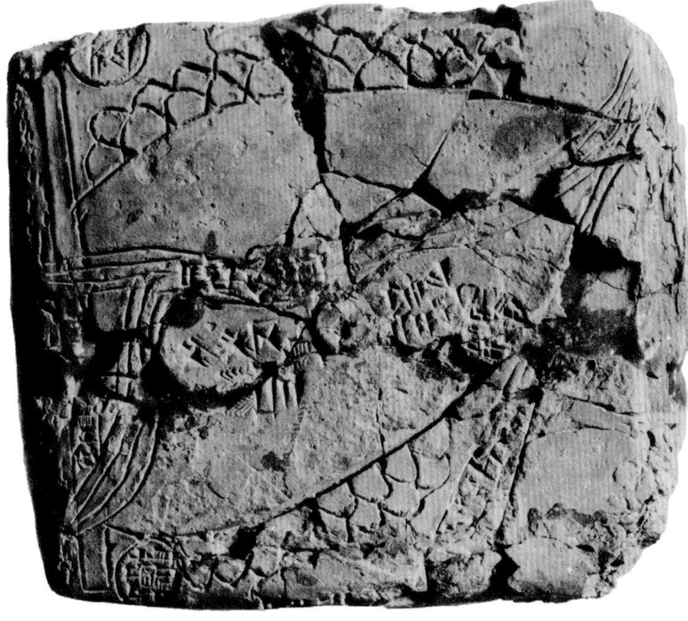

2.10. GA.SUR ("Nuzi"), clay tablet map of Nuzi, third millennium BC. Courtesy of the Harvard Semitic Museum, Harvard University, Cambridge, MA.

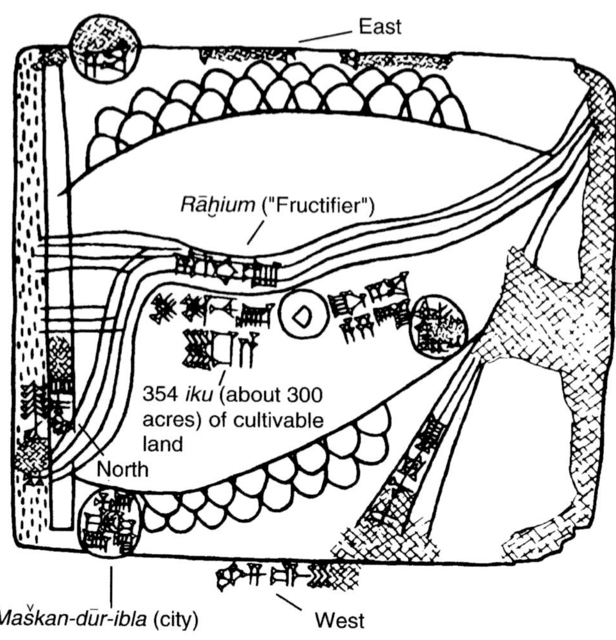

2.11. GA.SUR ("Nuzi"), drawing of clay tablet map of Nuzi. Courtesy of the Harvard Semitic Museum, Harvard University, Cambridge, MA.

The question I have in mind is this: in what ways are these landscapes really maps? First, we'll consider maps through history. Most will be pictorial maps. We'll look at how their creators conceived of landscape and how they represented the experience of it. I'll position my drawings in the context of that history both to understand them anew and perhaps to recognize some things I might have done differently were I to draw them now. We'll consider three types of maps, nested place maps, journey maps, and finally cosmic maps. We'll start with the two basic questions that maps have always addressed: Where are we, and how do we get to where we're going?

Where Are We?

Many historic maps have embraced pictorial content. Many have also used the same sort of bounded spatial composition seen in some of the paintings shown in the previous chapter: Wallis's harbor painting and Pierre Bonnard's *Nude in Bathtub*. These are nested images, which center on places.

The earliest such map we have is a clay tablet from Nuzi, in northeast Iraq, from the third millennium BC—here shown also in a drawn version (figs. 2.10, 2.11). It maps a land set between two ranges of hills flanking rivers. In *Topographical Maps* the noted historian of geography P. D. A. Harvey points to the "dome-like" shape of the hills in characterizing the tablet as a combination of map and picture. We can almost imagine the inhabitant of this river valley making such a map after a lifetime of first looking one way and then in the opposite direction at the hills that bounded a life lived within their confines. Noteworthy is the way the profiles of these hills are shown relative to the valley they define—from the center of the valley outward as we might face them.

A compelling instance of inside-outward generation of boundaries in a pictorial map is one of Rome from the late thirteenth century (fig. 2.12). Many major interior landmarks, such as the aqueducts and the Pantheon, are recognizable, and Rome's famed hills are shown in stylized elevations. An important point of comparison between this map and the Nuzi map is the way the city wall defines its inside. Rome is wrapped by it: crenellation by crenellation and watchtower by watchtower. The subject of the map is decidedly Rome from the inside looking out, not from the outside looking in.

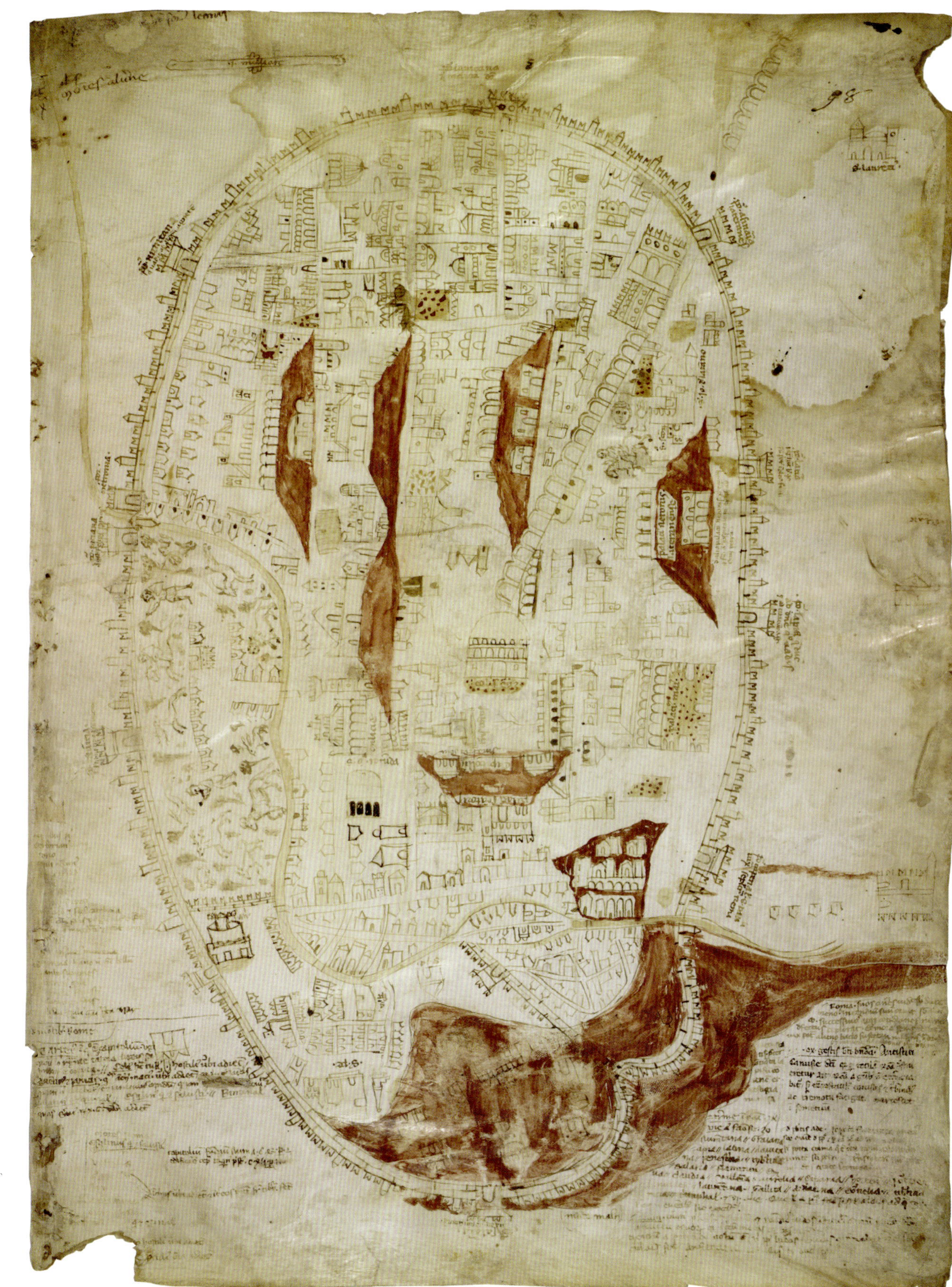

2.12. Plan of Rome, from Paolino Veneto, *Magna chronologica*, ca. 1320. MS. Lat. Z-399, no. 1610, f. 98r, Biblioteca Nazionale Marciana, Venice.

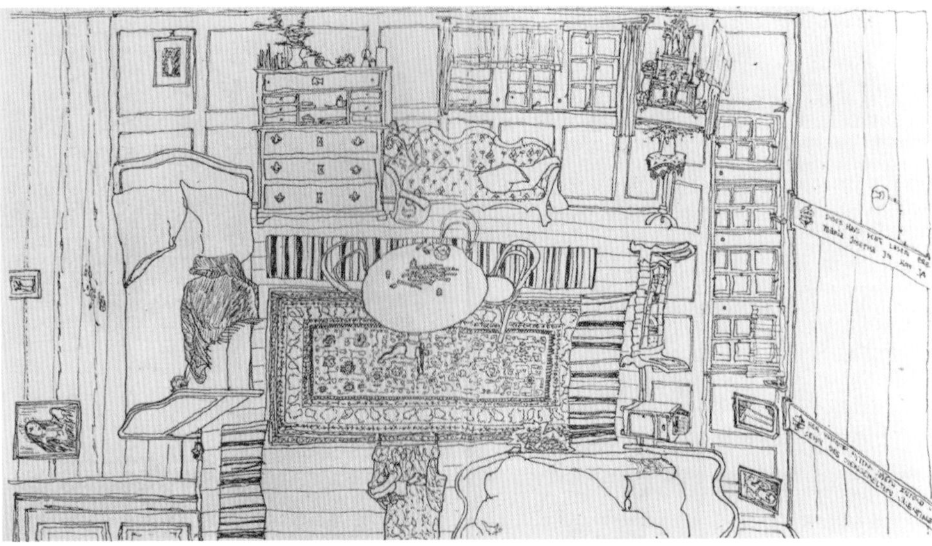

2.13. *Room in Switzerland*, Joerk Haberman, ca. 1979. Private collection.

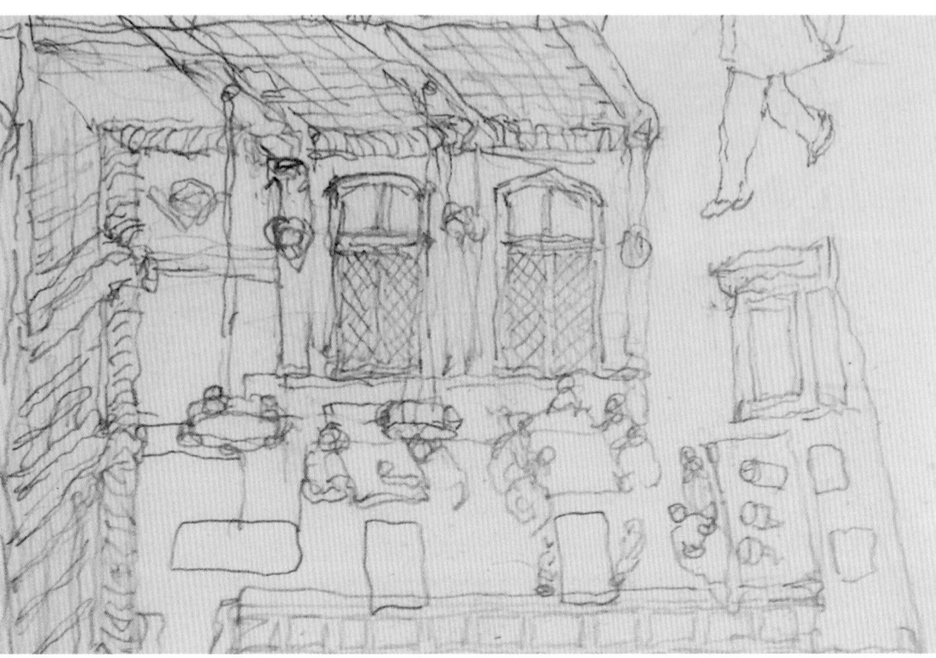

2.14. Detail, *Liverpool Station*, Doug Cooper, 2017. Pencil on paper, 36 × 45 inches. Collection of the artist.

The visual sense of looking in an outward direction from an interior seems to be part of the very experience of interior space. Over many years my friend Joerk Haberman and I used to trade drawings of interiors. He was my best friend when I lived in Frankfurt, Germany, years ago. My favorite of his has always been an ink drawing he made of a room in a house in Switzerland where our families had both vacationed (fig. 2.13). We both knew we'd never see the room again—the house was being sold—but because we liked the room so much, he had decided to draw it while he still could. And so, in a manner comparable to the map of Rome described earlier, his drawing grew as a continuous record, while he did a 360-degree turn around the room.

Mapping Liverpool Station

On a recent sketching trip in Europe, I made a drawing quite similar in spirit to Joerk's, but with a more complex subject. I visited Liverpool Station, one of the terminals I had not drawn when I was in London in September 1969. The terminal has a light-filled interior concourse that opens to two major thoroughfares along its eastern and southern faces. Like so many London stations, it incorporates the remains of a hotel, which in this case forms the corner of the station at the intersection of the two streets. It was there that I began the drawing in a pub, starting with people seated at tables with pints of beer and then detailing the woodwork of the Victorian interior around me (fig. 2.14).

Over the course of the next several days on additional sheets of paper added around my original pub drawing, I built the interior of the station, drawing each of its interior faces, left, right, front, and back, and then filling the interior with trains. Then I went outside, including the streets east and south of the station and adding drawings of other pubs and restaurants that I visited on subsequent days. With the addition of the streets surrounding the station, the drawing became a kind of Nuzi map inside a Nuzi map (fig. 2.15).

Portolan Charts versus Mercator Maps

Beyond just documenting a place—what Joerk did with the room in Switzerland and I did at Liverpool station—what might maps portray about

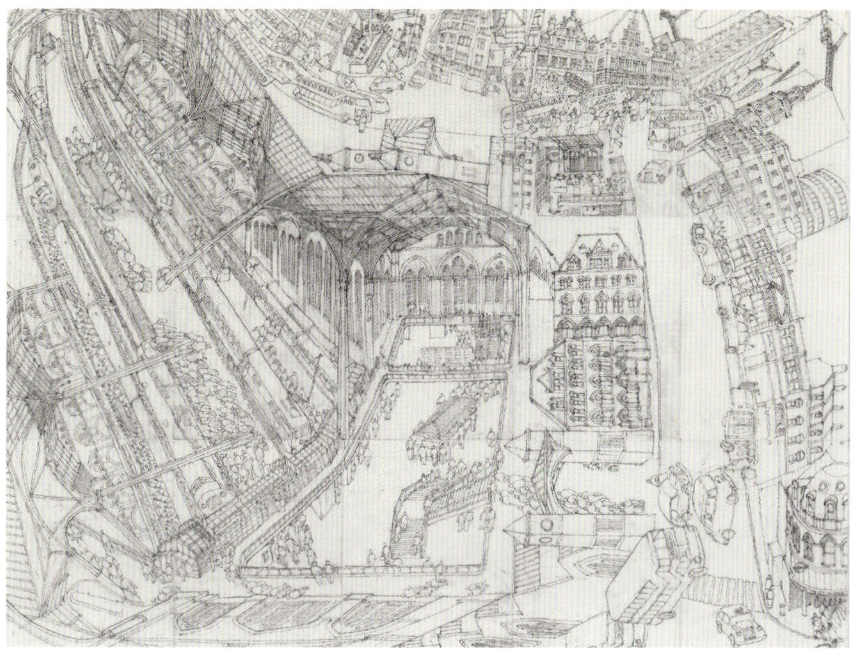

2.15. *Liverpool Station*, Doug Cooper, 2017. Pencil on paper, 36 × 45 inches. Collection of the artist.

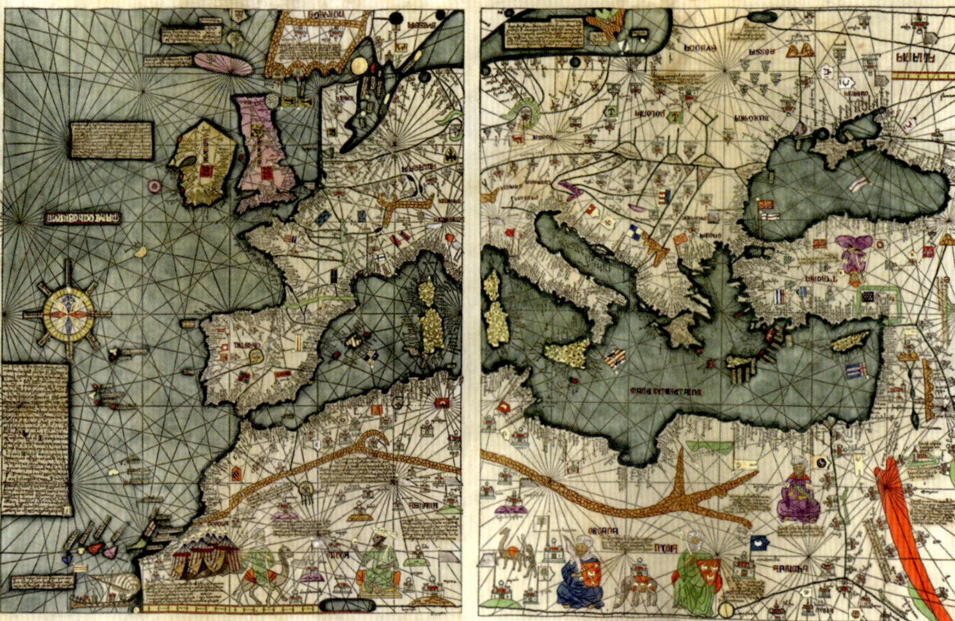

2.16. *Catalan Atlas*, Abraham Cresques, 1375. Bibliothèque nationale de France. Science Source Images.

the *experience* of being somewhere? In considering the Nuzi clay tablet map, I hinted at a possible relationship of the map to the mapmaker's life experience. Whether true or not about that particular map, are there historical maps where a clear relationship between people's experience of a landscape and the map itself can be established?

Portolan charts originated from late twelfth-century practices of navigating the bounded waters of the Mediterranean and its many subparts: the Adriatic, the Aegean, and so on. To my eye they are among the most beautiful of all maps, with their compass roses and their lines tracking every which way from port to port across the various bodies of water that make up the Mediterranean Sea. Called *portolan charts* from the Italian *portolano*, meaning "related to ports," they drew from an interesting mix of scientific and empirical knowledge (fig. 2.16). They were used for navigation beginning in the late Middle Ages and into the age of exploration.

What is so compelling about portolan charts is how much their method of generation and graphic display reflected the experience of sailing the

Mediterranean, where they were first used. By that time magnetic compasses, which had been invented by the Chinese, were in use by Europeans. To generate an accurate map of those contained waters, navigators needed only to combine accurate measures of compass headings, called rhumb lines (the source of the many lines crisscrossing the charts), with accurate measures of the distances needed to reach an opposite shore on those same headings.

Many were drawn by sailors, and sometimes they were team efforts with artists and writers who were taken along on voyages to generate accurate pictures and detailed descriptions of coastal conditions from which the shorelines of bodies of water were then drawn. Some, such as the beautifully illustrated Portuguese Cantino planisphere (1502), showed trees and exotic birds and animals along these coasts (figs. 2.17, 2.18). Although they were eventually used for depicting parts of the world outside their place of origin—Brazil and Africa in the map just mentioned—portolan charts have to be considered in relation to the conditions within which they were first

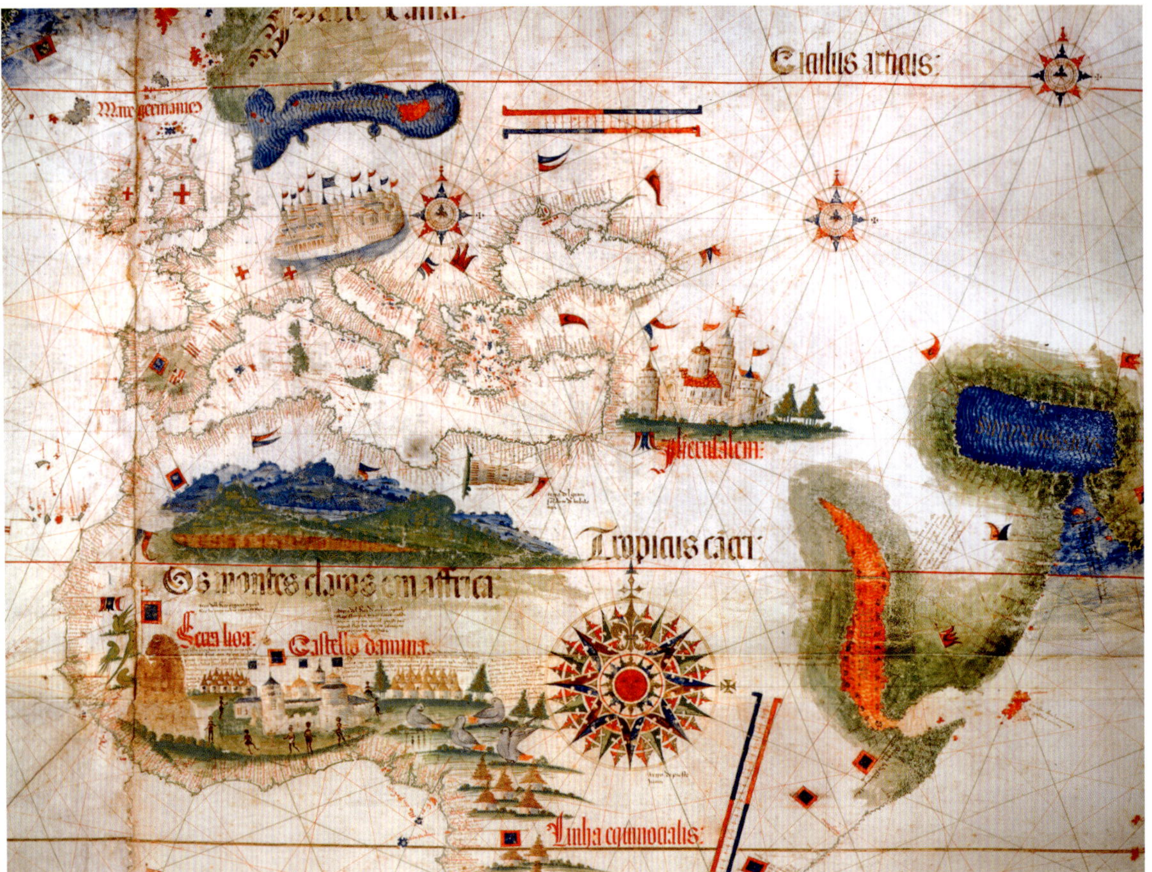

2.17. Europa, Africa, and the Middle East, detail from the "Cantino Map." *Carta del nevechar per le isole novamente trovate in parte dell'India*. Planisphere illuminated in Portugal in 1952, after the voyages of Christopher Columbus and Amerigo Vespucci Portuguese origin, 105 × 220 centimeters. Biblioteca Estense, Alfredo Dagli Orti/Art Resource, NY.

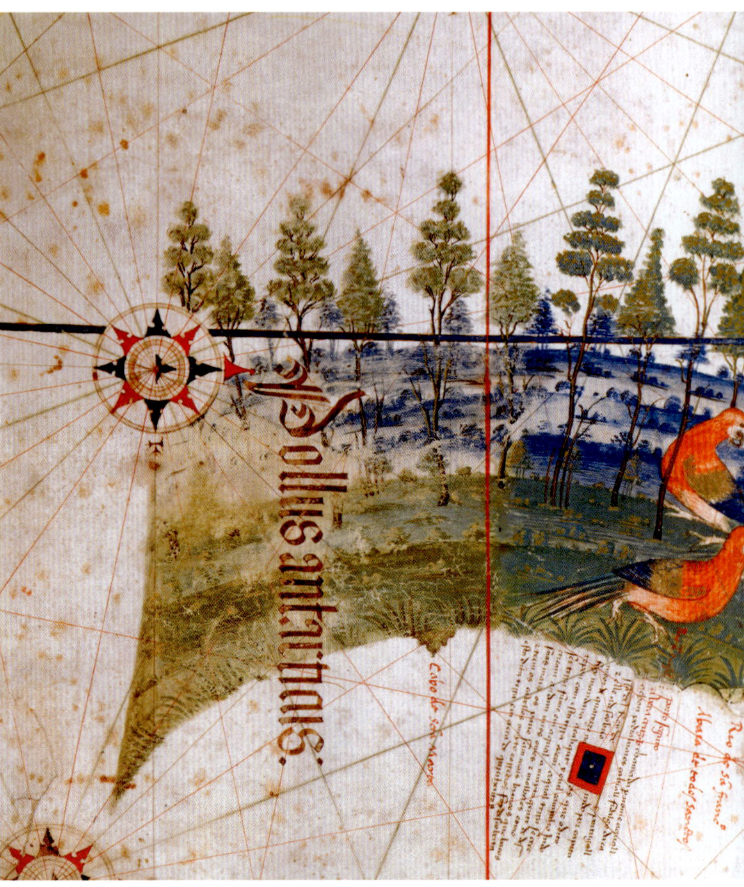

2.18. Coast of Brazil with exotic birds living in the forests, detail from the "Cantino Map." *Carta del nevechar per le isole novamente trovate in parte dell'India*. Planisphere illuminated in Portugal in 1952, after the voyages of Christopher Columbus and Amerigo Vespucci Portuguese origin, 105 × 220 centimeters. Biblioteca Estense, Alfredo Dagli Orti/Art Resource, NY.

generated—the enclosed waters of the Mediterranean—one in which sailors could always rely upon eventually bumping into an opposing shore. They are part and parcel of the experience of travel within an interior rather than exterior space.

Although portolan charts represented the experience of navigating the interior space of the Mediterranean very well, once Europeans ventured out into the more open waters of the Atlantic and then the Pacific beginning in the sixteenth century, the maps of Gerardus Mercator (1512–1594) and

others gradually supplanted them (fig. 2.19). The distances involved and the unbounded character of these new conditions simply did not relate well to the methods and foundational understanding of portolan charts: relying on the knowledge that there was land at the other end of whatever course would be followed. Moreover, portolan charts did not account for the curvature of the earth, a problem of negligible consequence for smaller bodies of water but of greater importance over the vast distances that were being newly explored. Mercator maps, on the other hand, had the great advantage of maintaining

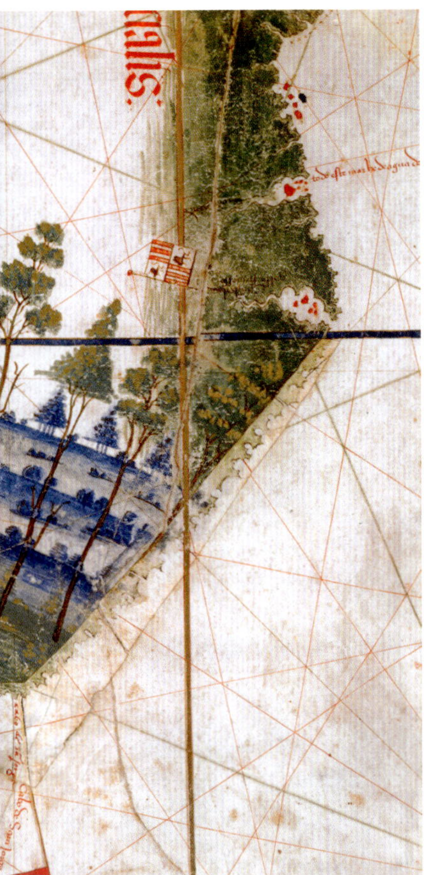

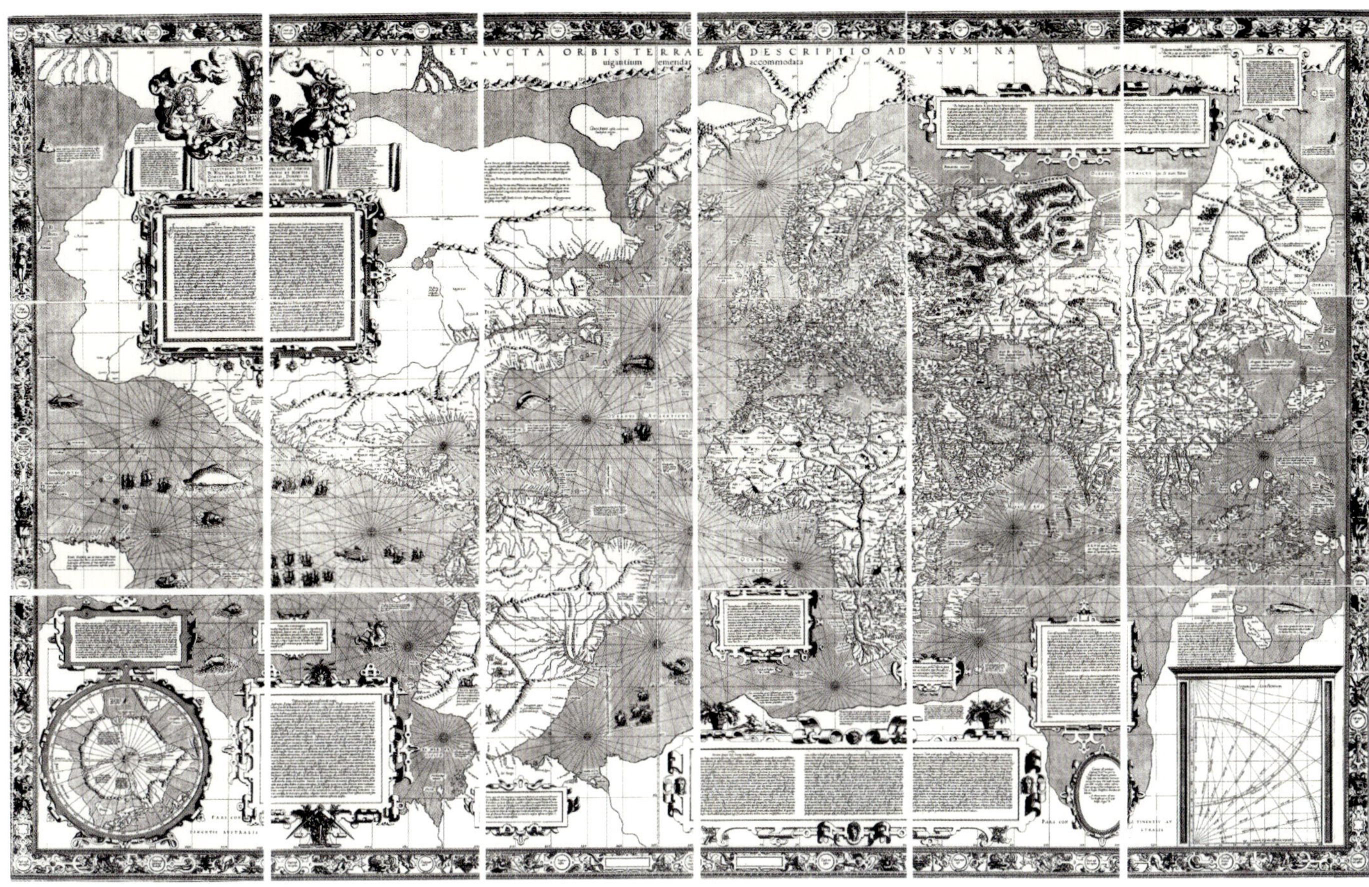

2.19. World map, Gerardus Mercator, 1569. From Wikipedia Commons.

true compass readings. No matter where they were on the globe, navigators could lay out compass headings, draw lines along those headings, and know exactly where in the world they would end up and what they would encounter along the way. The distortion of land and water shapes in latitudes near polar zones that the projection generated was a small matter when compared to this critical benefit. In a sense they brought a kind of scientific knowing to mapping: knowing at a distance through the utility of their gridwork projected out over the globe.

Inside versus Outside

With these two map types, we see that the task of mapping interior space can be fundamentally different than the task of mapping exterior space. Further these differences reflect differences between our *experience* of the one versus the other. How might this distinction be reflected in drawings I have made?

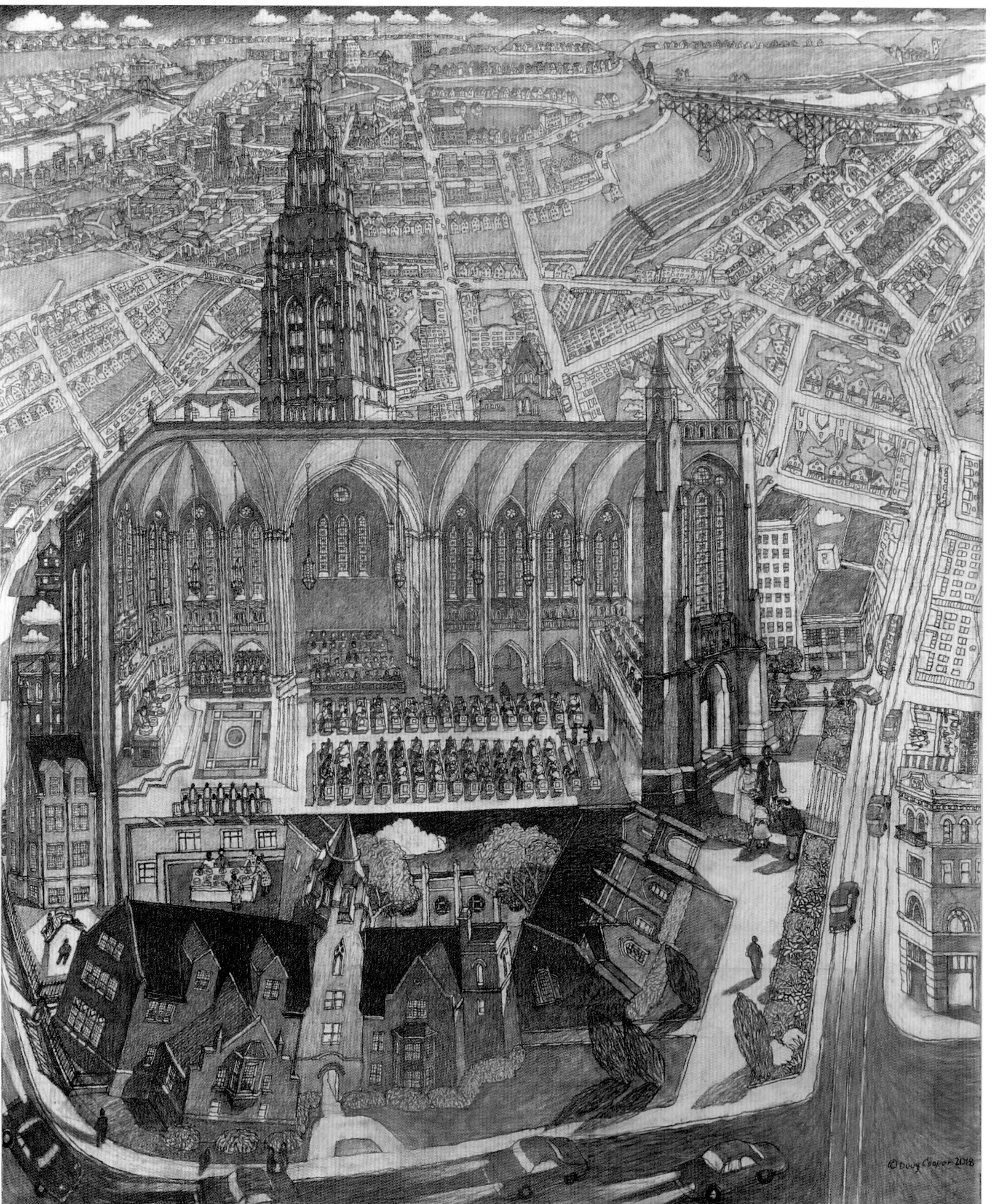

2.20. *East Liberty Presbyterian Church*, Doug Cooper, 2018. Charcoal on paper on board, 60 × 48 inches.

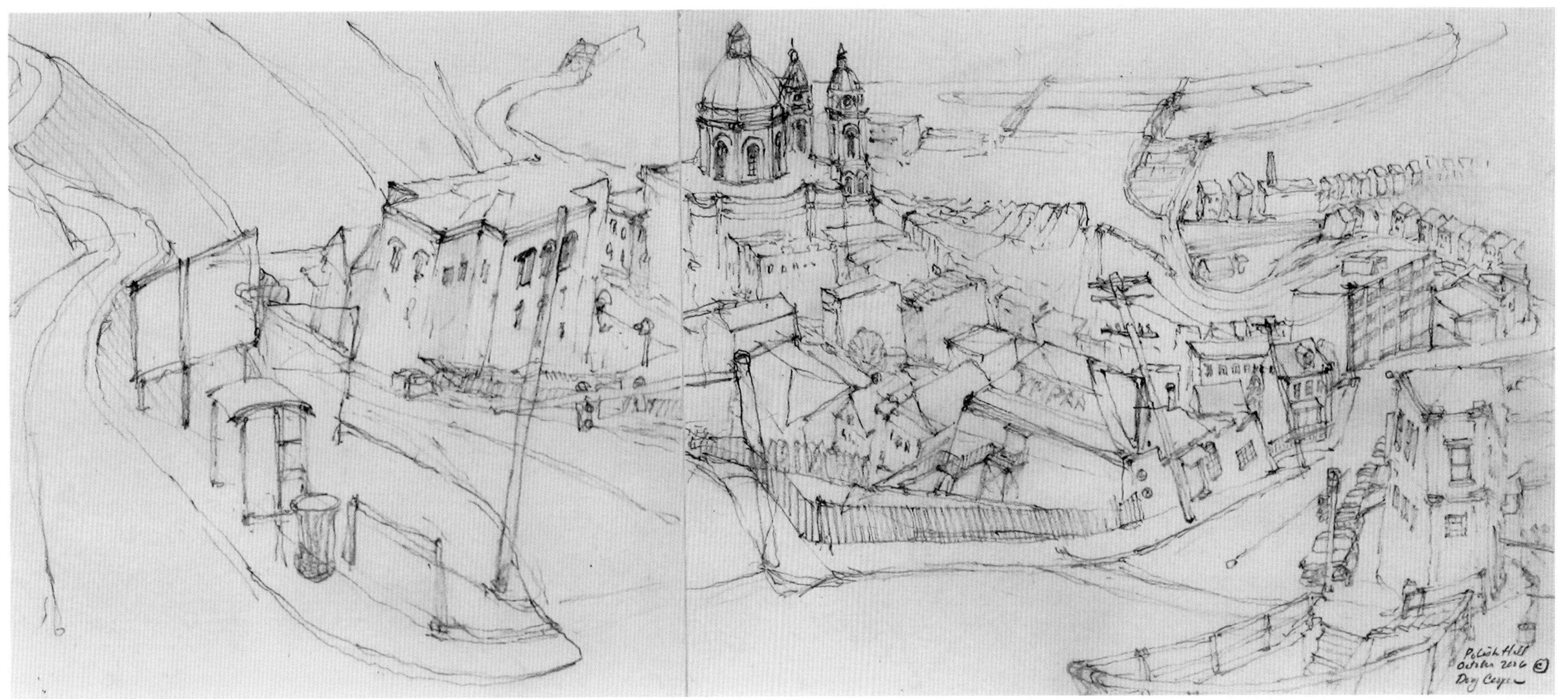

2.21. *Bigelow and Herron*, Doug Cooper, 2006. Pencil on paper, 10 × 14 inches. Private collection.

East Liberty Presbyterian Church is a good example of a drawing that contrasts inside and outside. It shows the church my wife Stefani and I attend, and I drew it as part of a series of works on the subject of sacred space. Inside, order and calm prevail. Outside, streets race every which way. The contrast is partly an issue of style. The inside is rendered in tones, and the outside is drawn more with lines (fig. 2.20).

Other drawings have represented movement within an interior—what portolan charts show so well with their rhumb lines. One, a drawing of Polish Hill, started with an on-site sketch. On the last warm October day in 2006 I visited the corner of Herron Avenue where it crosses Bigelow Boulevard above Polish Hill. I began with foreground elements: the triangular building at my right, then the Young Men's Polish American Association across the street (with its distinctive YMPAA block letters printed on the roof), and then turning more to the left, the bus stop. It amounted to a kind of scan of the foreground. Then I expanded the drawing's scope beyond these nearer elements to show routes to places I knew I could reach if I went beyond the immediate foreground: Polish Hill's landmark Immaculate Heart of Mary church, and two streets: Paulowna Street descending behind the church, and Herron Avenue descending and following a switchback to reach the base of the hill where it bridged over the railroad (fig. 2.21).

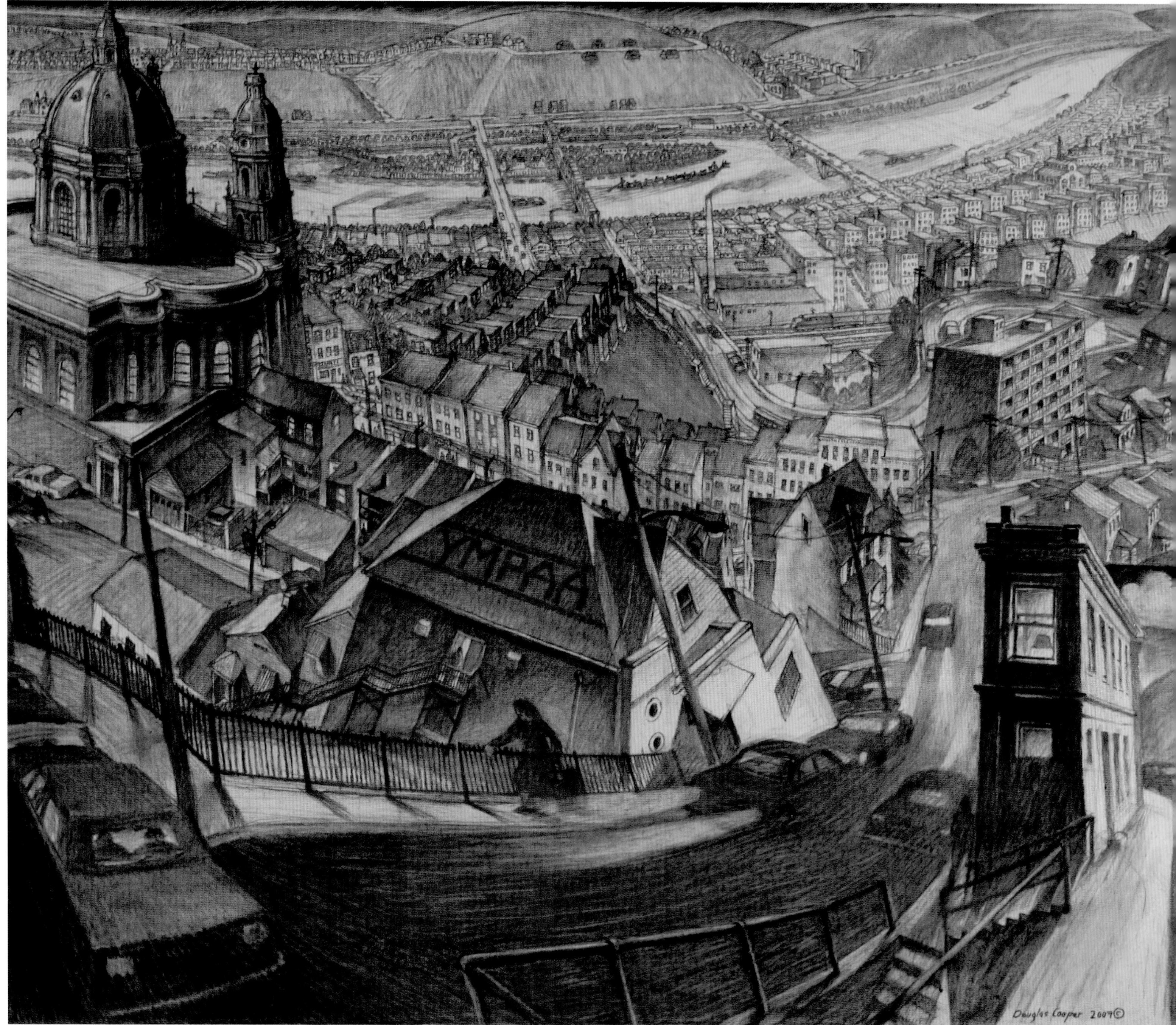
YMPAA
Douglas Cooper 2009

As I look at this sketch now and consider the more elaborately rendered drawing that I later completed based upon it, I recognize something of the distinction the makers of portolan charts must have experienced when, after sailing the enclosed waters of the Mediterranean Sea, they passed through the Strait of Gibraltar into the open waters beyond (fig. 2.22). So long as my drawing remains within the confines of Polish Hill, the marks reflect one character of experience, but once the drawing arrives at the base of Herron Hill and crosses the bridge across the railroad, a different order prevails: one that reflects Mercator's extended grid. *Evening Corners* (fig. 2.23) makes this distinction between foreground movement and a background grid even more extreme.

2.22 (*facing page*). Detail, *Bigelow and Herron*, Doug Cooper, 2006. Pencil on paper, 10 × 14 inches. Private collection.

2.23 (*below*). *Evening Corners*, Doug Cooper, 2012. Charcoal on paper on board, 48 × 60 × 5 inches. Collection of Deborah Battistone and Gerard Damiani.

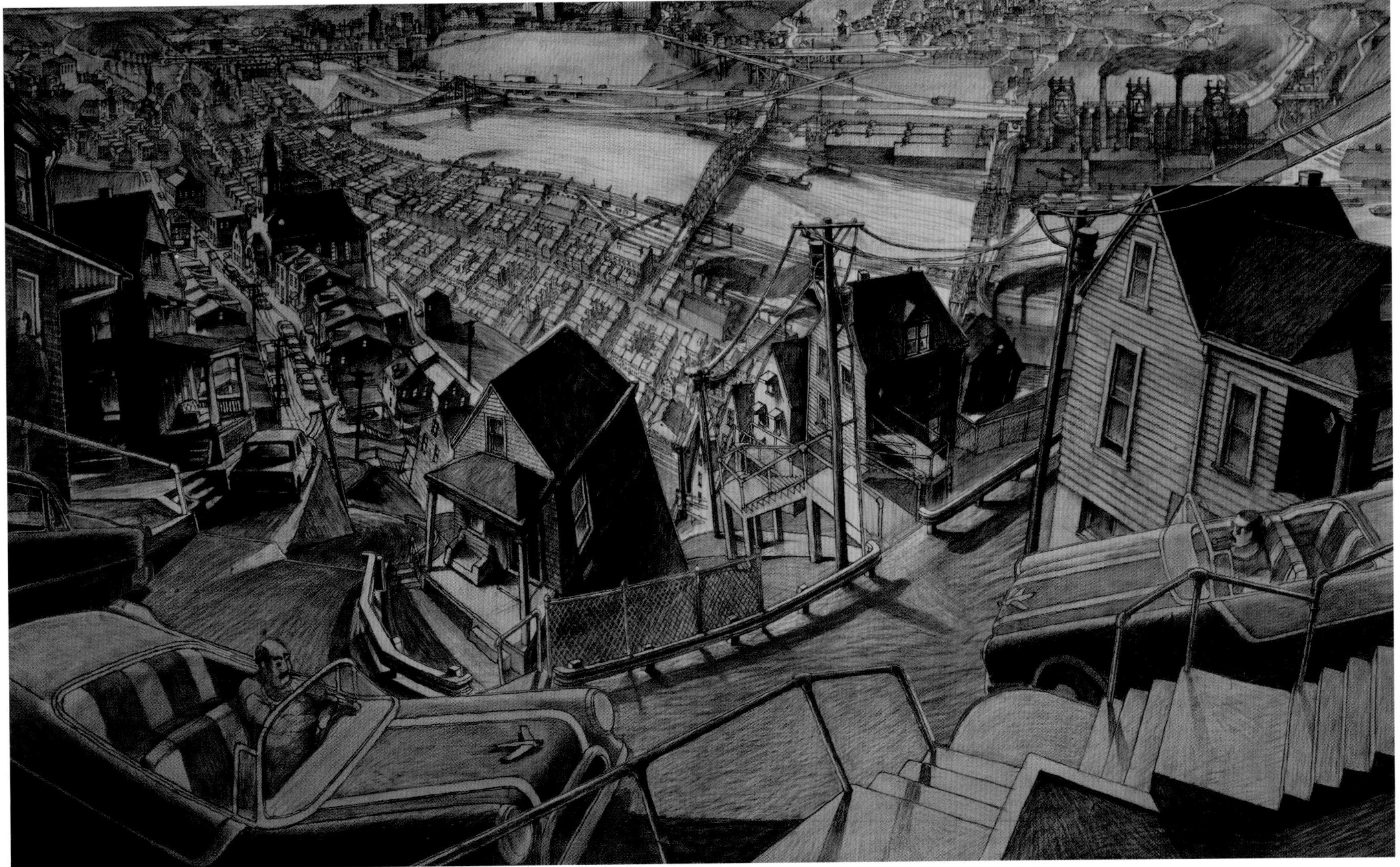

Where Are We Going?

Now let's turn from nested maps to another tradition of pictorial mapmaking: the itinerary maps used by pilgrims throughout the Middle Ages. These showed (bottom to top) what travelers might expect to see along their routes to faraway destinations: journeys to locations like Santiago de Compostela in Spain or the Holy Land. The map shown here, from the mid-thirteenth century, shows a portion of a larger journey from London to the Holy Land. It begins in the lower left just over the Alps and then travels upward to Modena and Bologna, then returns to the map's base and moves upward again past Florence and Rome, and eventually reaches the island of Sicily (fig. 2.24).

As Harvey points out, we find this same bottom-to-top structure in a wider tradition of pictorial maps across multiple cultures from East Asia to Mexico, in addition to Europe. Typically, these arrange profiles of buildings (and other features) with multiple horizons from bottom to top. Usually their scale is maintained consistently throughout with no particular representation of depth—foreground to background—other than the common pictorial convention that lower in the picture is closer and higher farther away. One example is the Japanese seventeenth-to-eighteenth-century woodcut *Map of Kuon-ji Temple.* A common scale is maintained throughout the foreground and middle ground and then the map's ultimate spiritual destination, Mount Fuji, is shown smaller in the faraway distance (fig. 2.25).

However, one pictorial map that Harvey shows *does* magnify the sizes of foreground elements. It's a woodcut of the Holy Land published in 1486 with an account by Bernhard von Breidenbach of his visit there (fig. 2.26). It was drawn by Erhard Reuwich, an artist from Utrecht whom Breidenbach took to the Holy Land to record his travels in drawings. The drawing greatly exaggerates the size of the journey's destination: Jerusalem—the Dome of the Rock is clearly visible. Nothing new in that, many maps did much the same. But Reuwich's foreground coastline view is different. It used a significantly lower viewing angle, and greatly enlarged sizes at dockside—note the size of the ship in the lower left corner (fig. 2.27). This enlarged foreground gives the dockside a *presence* we can share as viewers. Part of it is detail—we are able to feel present simply by knowing more about the scene. But the angle of view plays a role too. With a near-eye-level view, we feel as if we are there in the scene: with the voyagers who are now finally disembarking their ship after a

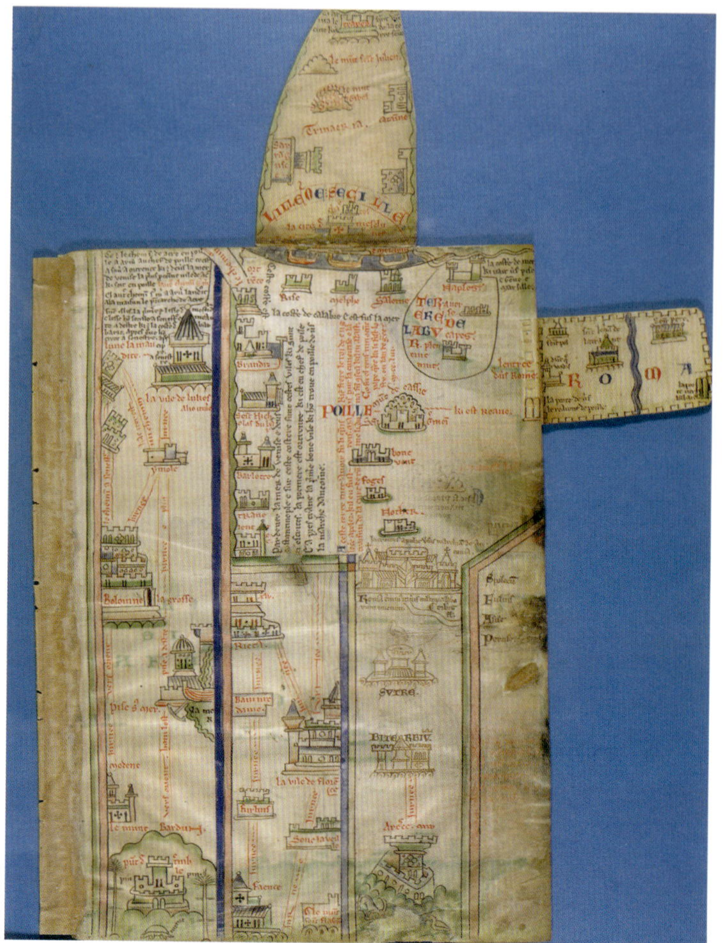

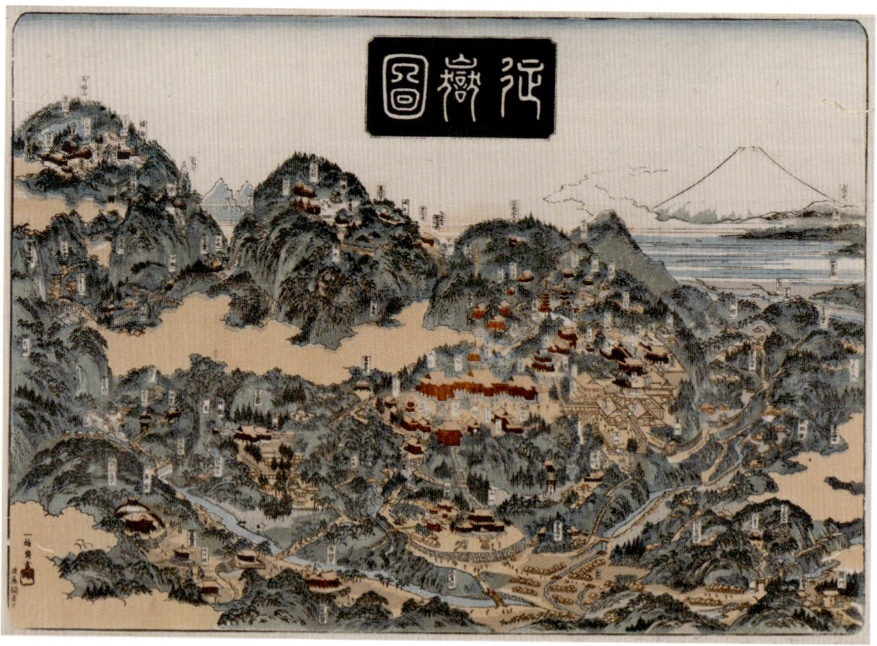

2.24 (*facing page, top*). Itinerary, London to Jerusalem (whole folio), part of the itinerary from London to Jerusalem, including the city of Rome. From *Historia Anglorum*, originally published/produced in England, Saint Albans, 1250–1259. British Library. Copyright British Library Board/Robana/Art Resource, NY.

2.25 (*facing page, bottom*). *Map of Kuon-ji Temple*, Utagawa Kunisada I (Toyokuni III), Edo period. Woodblock print (*nishiki-e*) ink and color on paper, 14 ¾ × 20 ⅞ inches. William Sturgis Bigelow Collection, Museum of Fine Arts, Boston.

2.26 (*below*). Map of Holy Land, published with Bernhard von Breidenbach's account of his travels, Erhard Reuwich, 1486. Woodcut, Courtesy of the Metropolitan Museum of Art, New York.

2.27 (*right*). Detail, map of the Holy Land, published with Bernhard von Breidenbach's account of his travels, Erhard Reuwich, 1486. Woodcut. Courtesy of the Metropolitan Museum of Art, New York.

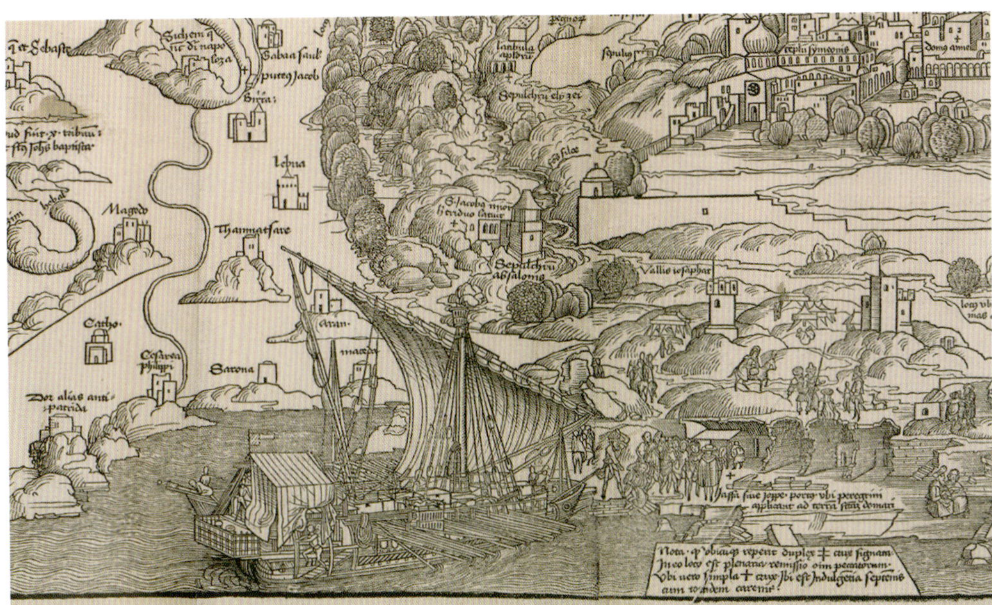

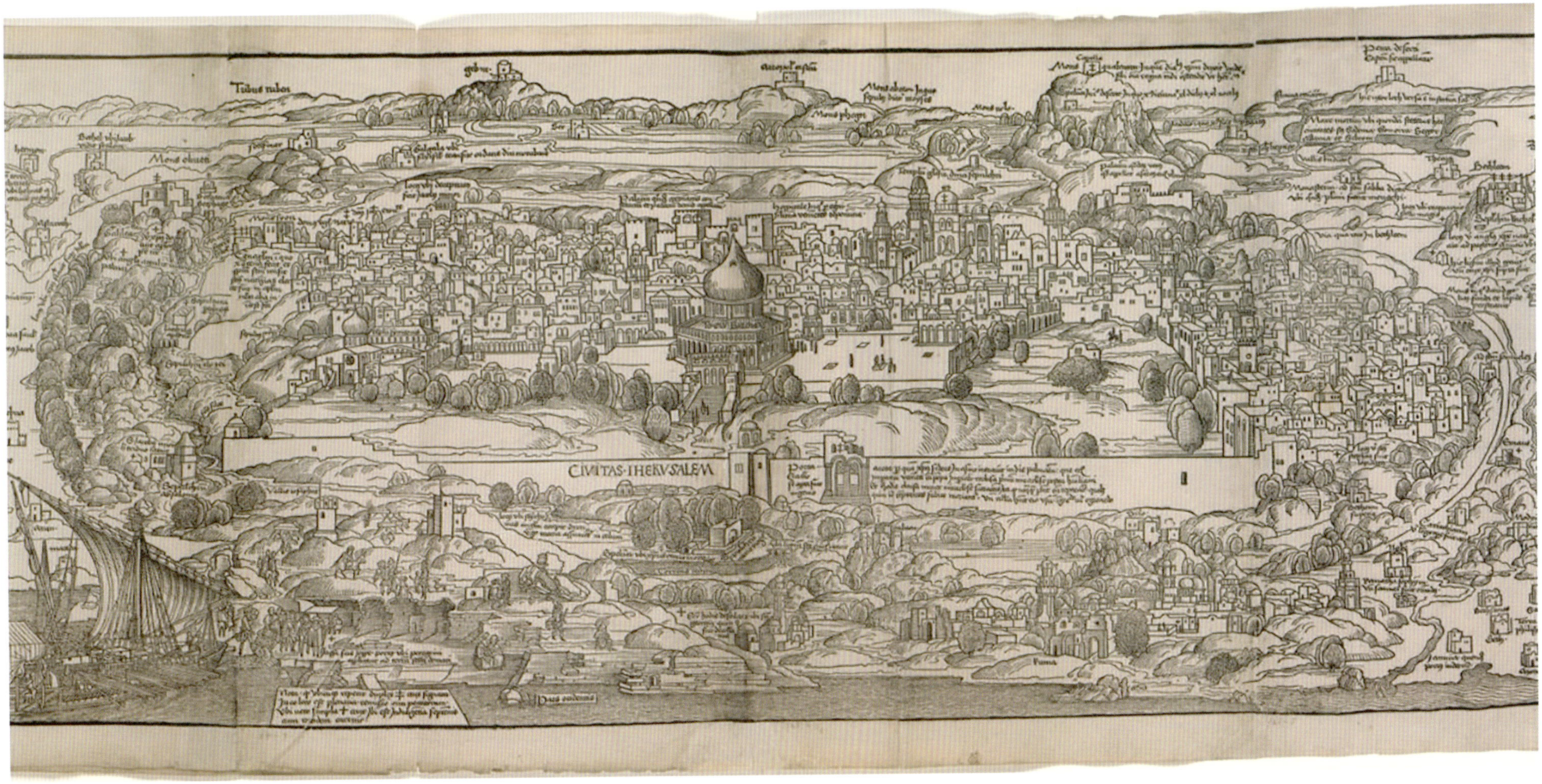

long voyage—remember, the purpose of the drawing was illustrating the *story* of Breidenbach's journey. So, the drawing is about the *experience* of traveling (as well as a map of the journey), and the enlarged foreground is what makes the experiential part vivid.

The timing of this illustrative map of Breidenbach's journey and its use of a magnified eye-level foreground is interesting in relation to what is going on elsewhere in Europe at the same time. In his thought-provoking book *The Renaissance Rediscovery of Linear Perspective* (1975), Samuel Edgerton referenced two images of Florence, the background in *Madonna della Misericordia* (mid-1300s, anonymous) and the *View of Florence with the Chain* (1480s, Francesco Rosselli), that bracketed the Renaissance rediscovery of linear perspective (figs. 2.28, 2.29). Edgerton used these two images to advance a number of theories about how our sense of the world might have changed with perspective's reemergence—suggesting a relationship to the 1492 voyage of Christopher Columbus, and to the maps designed for navigation that came thereafter (Mercator and others). But more importantly for our understanding of maps and pictures together, these two views give us a sense of what is changing in pictorial space as the Renaissance unfolds.

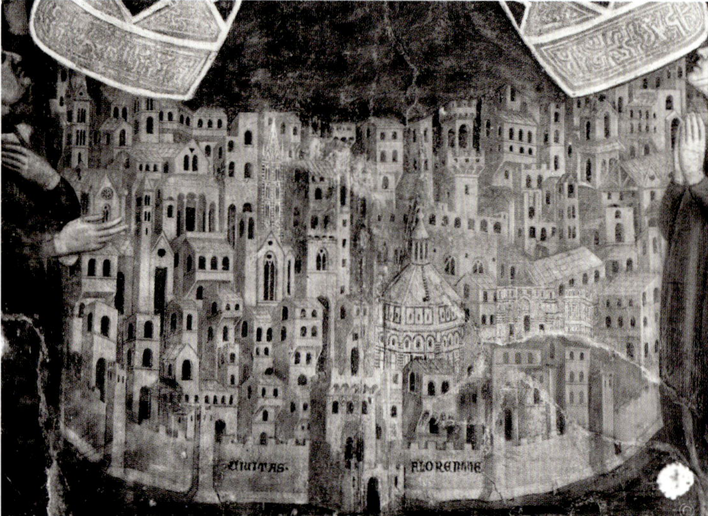

2.28. Detail from the Madonna della Misericordia fresco. *Panorama of Florence.* Loggia del Bigallo, Florence, Italy. Alinari/Art Resource, NY.

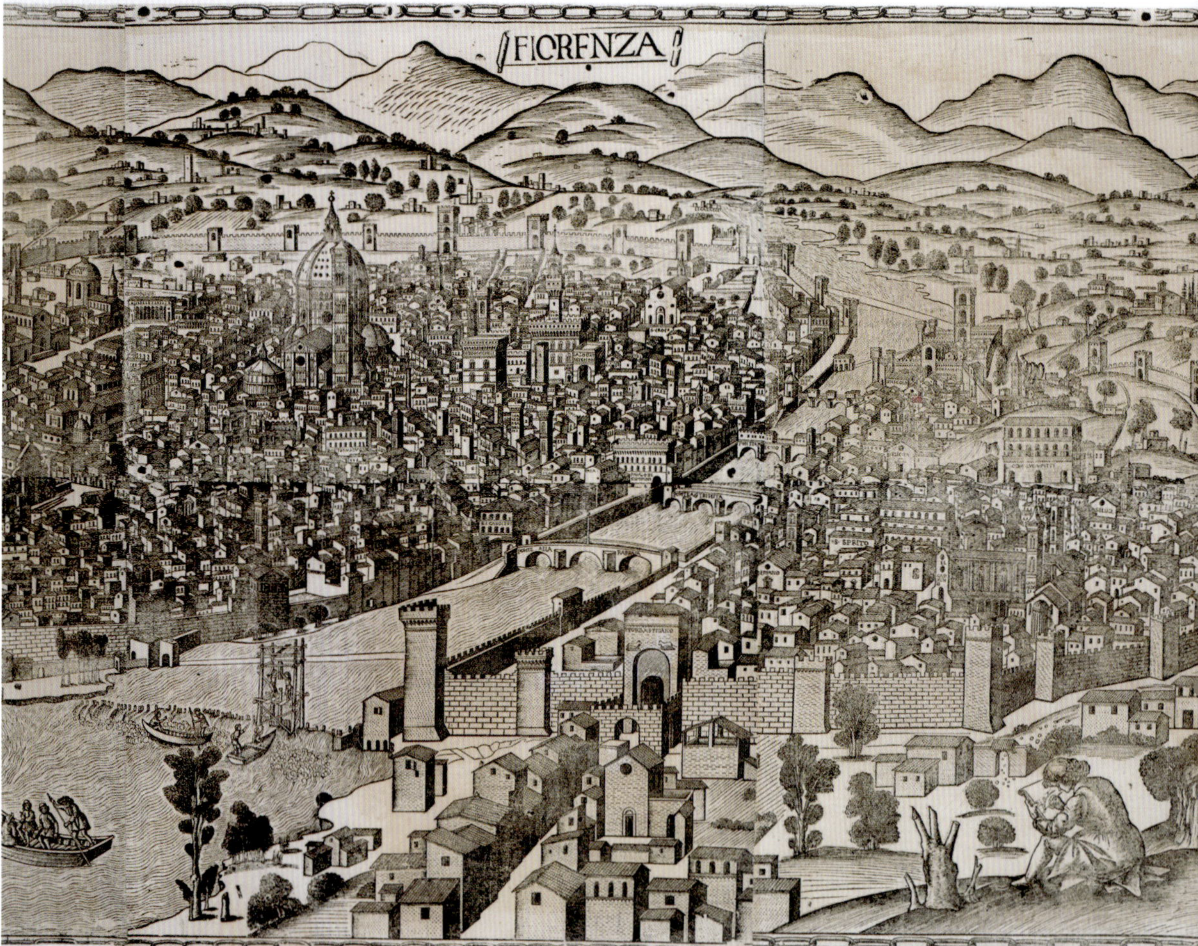

2.29. Large view of Florence, Mappa della Catena [Chain map], Lucantonio degli Uberti?, ca. 1500–1510. Woodcut on eight blocks (no. 2), 57.8 × 131.6 centimeters. Jörg P. Anders Alinari/Art Resource, NY.

Proto-Renaissance and Renaissance Space

As with most transitional views, in both of the images that Edgerton discussed, there are elements of the period that came before and the one that would follow. The fresco is a composite view: some elements are viewed frontally, some from the side, some upward, and some downward. Convergent perspective is absent. In this it reflects the kind of projection typically used by proto-Renaissance masters. However, the fresco also has a vivid presence. With its hurly-burly and density of shapes, it *feels* like a city. For Edgerton it seems to capture the sense of a city a visitor might feel upon arriving there for the first time.

Rosselli's Florence is more obviously a map. It shows the city and its surrounding hills and shares characteristics with the bird's-eye views of Matthäus Merian (1593–1650) and others who followed him: maps whose steep viewing angles offered a clear sense of the layout of a whole series of cities across Europe.

However, lower in the view and in front of the city wall, the image is more perspectival. It drops the angle of view and shows men fishing with nets in the Arno. It seems to invite the viewer into the scene, perhaps to join the man we see in the lower right-hand corner seated on a knoll with a sketchbook on his lap while drawing a view out over the city (fig. 2.30).

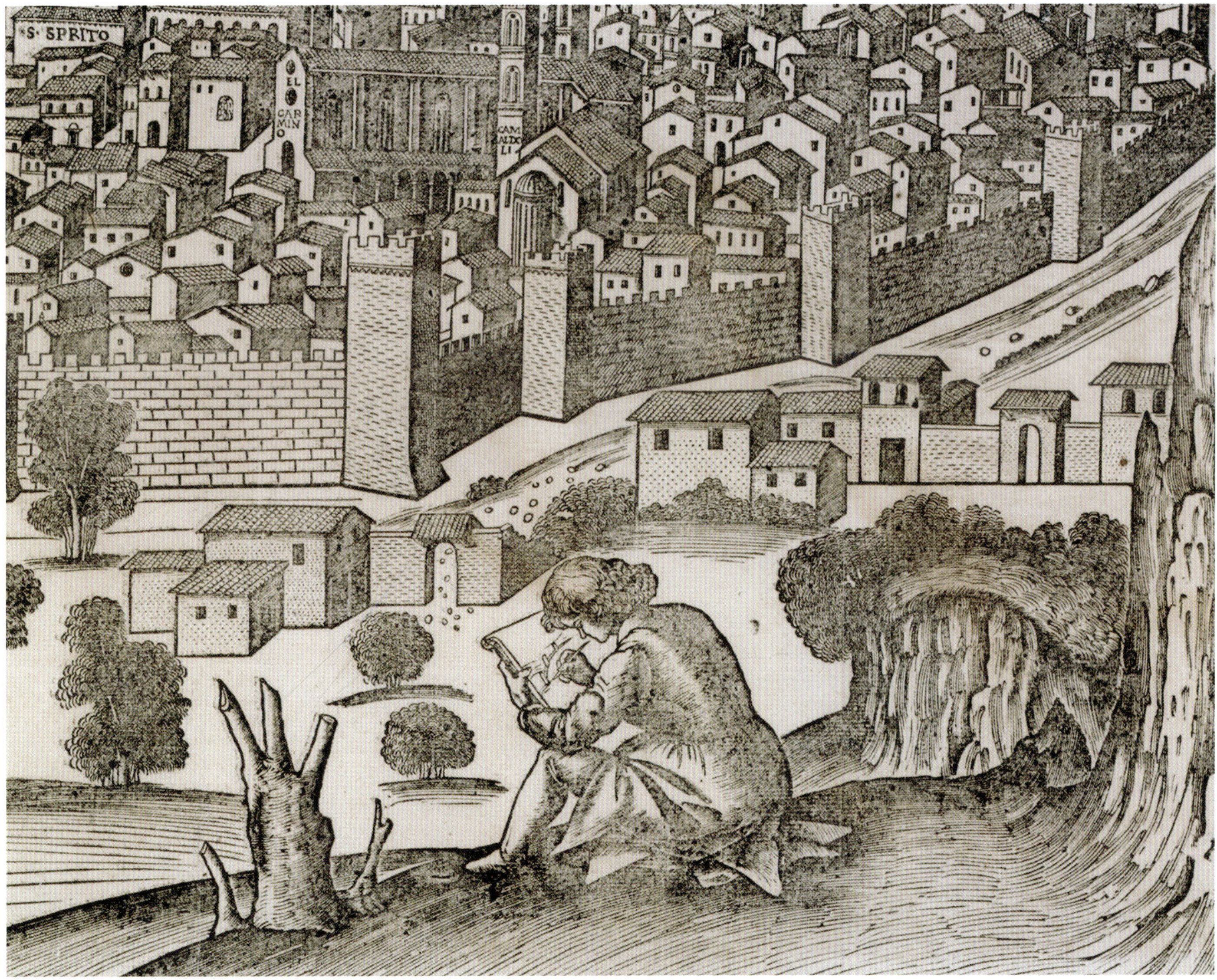

2.30. Detail, large view of Florence, Mappa della Catena [Chain map], Lucantonio degli Uberti?, ca. 1500–1510. Woodcut on eight blocks (no. 2), 57.8 × 131.6 centimeters. Jörg P. Anders Alinari/Art Resource, NY.

We find this same transitional character of map combined with picture—of knowing combined with seeing—in the work of Paolo Uccello (1397–1475). Uccello was widely known for his fascination with perspective (contemporaries thought him obsessed with the subject). And yet in some of his best-known images, a series of paintings depicting the battle at San Romano between Florence and Siena, he seems to rely equally on pictorial conventions of the proto-Renaissance (fig. 2.31). Though his foreground is dominated by linear perspective—indeed, some of the soldiers within it seem to have cast away their weapons and died in perfect perspectival convergence (fig. 2.32)—the background landscape is uplifted and flattened in a way that would fit right into Lorenzetti's fresco in Siena.

It has been within this transitional period, the proto-Renaissance and early Renaissance, that I have found the most useful spatial models for my drawings. They offer a sense of overview and prospect throughout, even as they use the emerging knowledge of perspective to enliven the foregrounds. They follow the familiar structure of beginning, middle, and end that is common to landscape and story narratives alike. This was the sense of narrative that inspired me in the photograph my grandmother showed me of Budapest's Chain Bridge. The foregrounds have presence (I accelerate the perspective), and the middle grounds are uplifted and have interesting paths and intermediate places of refuge. There is always at least one destination (a Pest for a Buda), and sometimes two, and like the drawing shown at the beginning of this chapter, bridges have been a constant theme. I refer to this as the *bottom-to-top journey structure.*

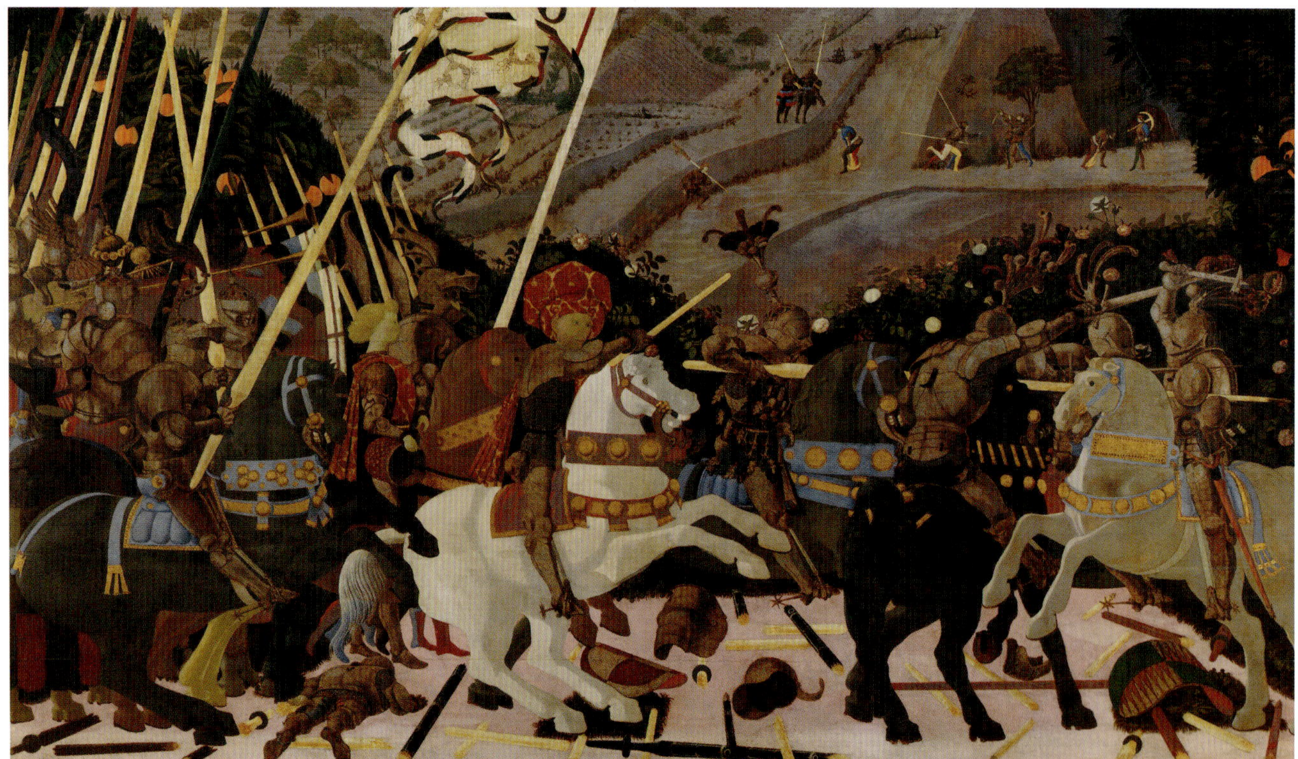

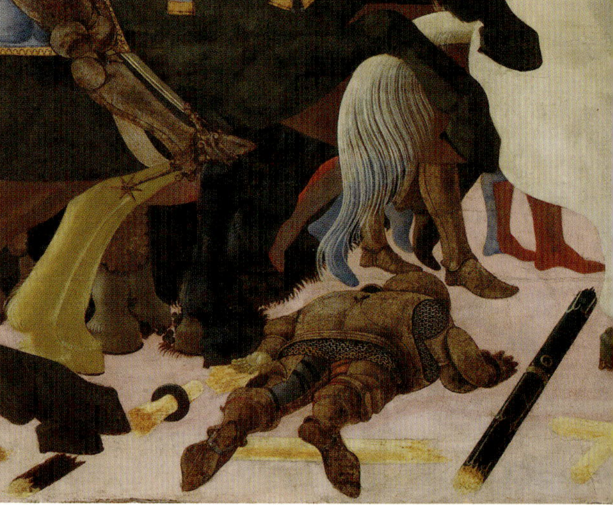

2.31 (*above*). *The Rout of San Romano*, Paolo Uccello, ca. 1450. National Gallery, London.
2.32 (*above right*). Detail, Paolo Uccello, ca. 1450. National Gallery, London.

2.33 (*right*). Jared L. Cohon University Center mural, Doug Cooper with Sarah Cooper, Jonathan Kline, and John Trivelli, 1996. Charcoal on paper on board, approx. 10 × 150 feet. Carnegie Mellon University, Pittsburgh.

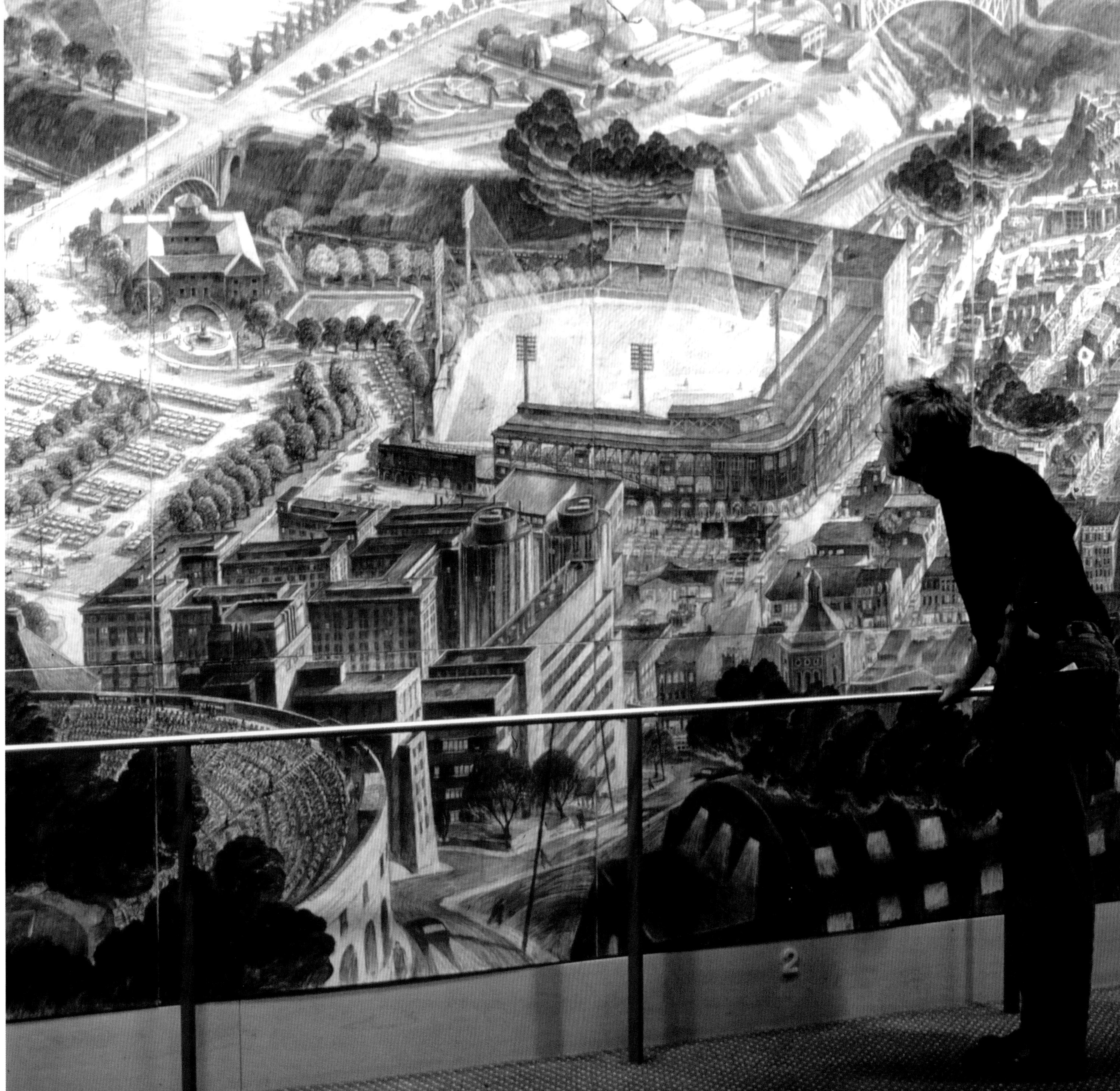

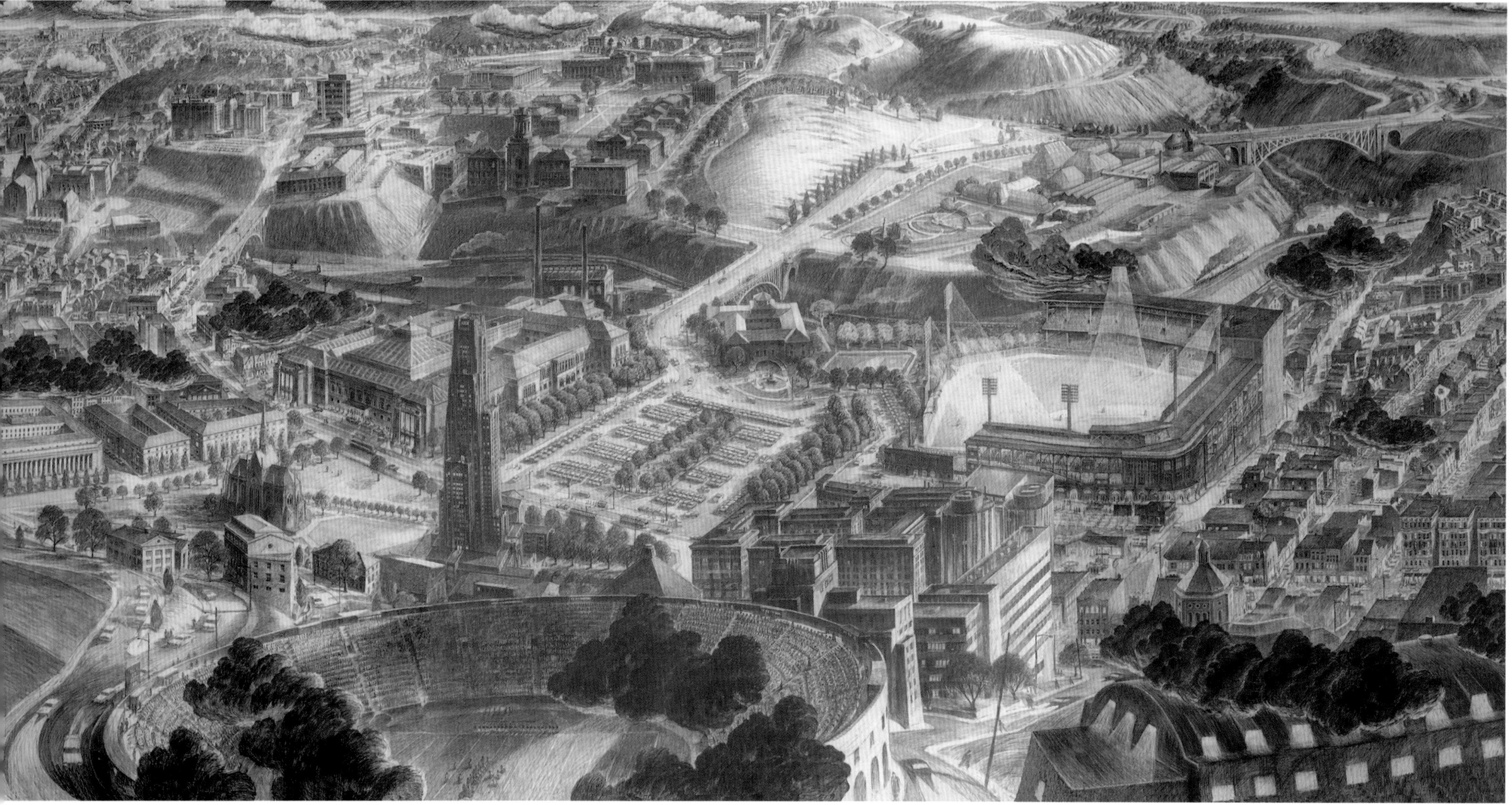

2.34. East wall right, Jared L. Cohon University Center mural, Doug Cooper with Sarah Cooper, Jonathan Kline, and John Trivelli, 1996. Charcoal on paper on board, approx. 10 × 150 feet. Carnegie Mellon University, Pittsburgh

A Map for Carnegie Mellon

The first opportunity I found to pursue the bottom-to-top journey structure was a mural I completed for Carnegie Mellon University (CMU)'s Jared L. Cohon University Center in 1995–1996. The idea for the mural had originated with Martin Prekop, then dean of CMU's College of Fine Arts, where I teach. He was thinking of a work for one of the meeting rooms in the center, but when I met with architect Michael Dennis to find a suitable location and saw the large entrance hall in the architect's plans, a two-story rotunda, I knew I wanted to do the mural for the mezzanine that surrounds it (fig. 2.33). With its walls aligning with the cardinal orientations of the campus as a whole, I thought I could use the mural to welcome visitors to the university and the city.

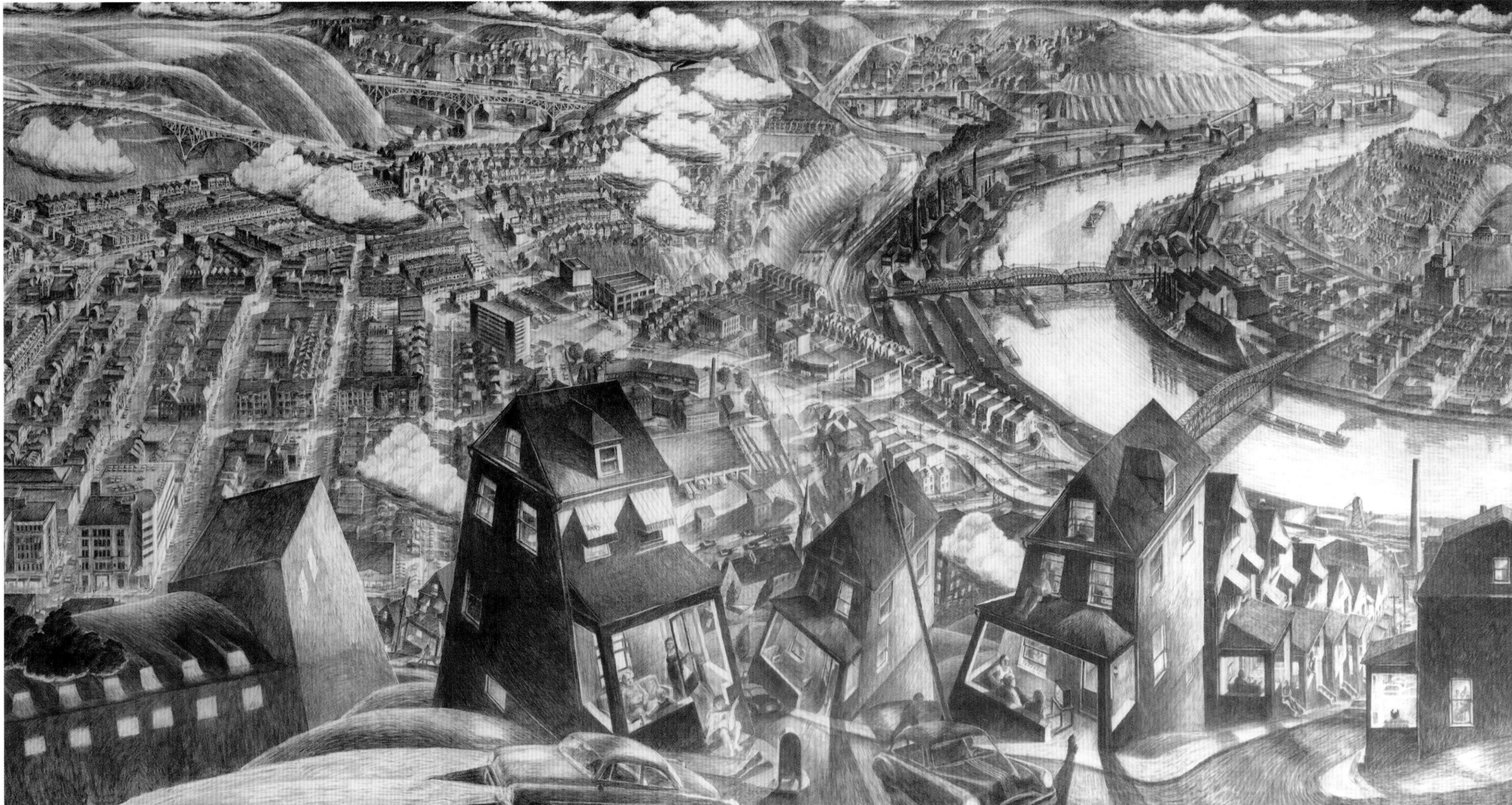

2.35. East wall middle, Jared L. Cohon University Center mural, Doug Cooper with Sarah Cooper, Jonathan Kline, and John Trivelli, 1996.
Charcoal on paper on board, approx. 10 × 150 feet. Carnegie Mellon University, Pittsburgh.

From the start, I conceived of the mural's east wall as a series of fore-grounds overlooking an uplifted middle-ground map (figs. 2.34, 2.35). In the backgrounds of this map, I positioned views that extended far up Pittsburgh's ravines and river valleys as visual destinations.

The university center would be one of the first locations both pro-spective students and returning alumni would visit when they arrived on campus, and I thought this wall would serve both groups well. For those who would be seeing the campus and the city for the first time, the maplike middle ground would help orient them in the city and acquaint them with a bit of its history as well. I imagined them find-ing their way around it and learning about some of its landmarks and unique history: Forbes Field (former home of the Pirates, Pittsburgh's baseball team); the Carnegie Museum, with its signature glass roof; the Jones & Laughlin Mill below South Oakland; and, along other walls, a plane crashing mysteriously into the Monongahela River in 1956 (the plane was never found) (fig. 2.36); and changes over time to the city's downtown (fig. 2.37). For returning alumni, many of whom had rented apartments in the areas pictured below, the maplike portions would provide a mnemonic landscape. I asked the students who assisted me on the mural, Jonathan Kline and John Trivelli, to research the neighborhoods below the overlooks, and together we managed to include almost every house in some areas. I imagined alumni using the map as a prod of sorts, one that would unlock the experiences they had shared many years before with their classmates— they might even find the houses in which they had once lived.

Very quickly I found reason to distort sizes in these maplike areas—enlarging landmarks such as Forbes Field and the Cathedral of Learning (the University of Pittsburgh's forty-two-story gothic revival tower). Oversizing them accomplished two goals: helping the mural project over greater distances and aligning it more closely with the *conceptual* map of the city all visitors, new ones and old ones alike, might eventually bring to it.

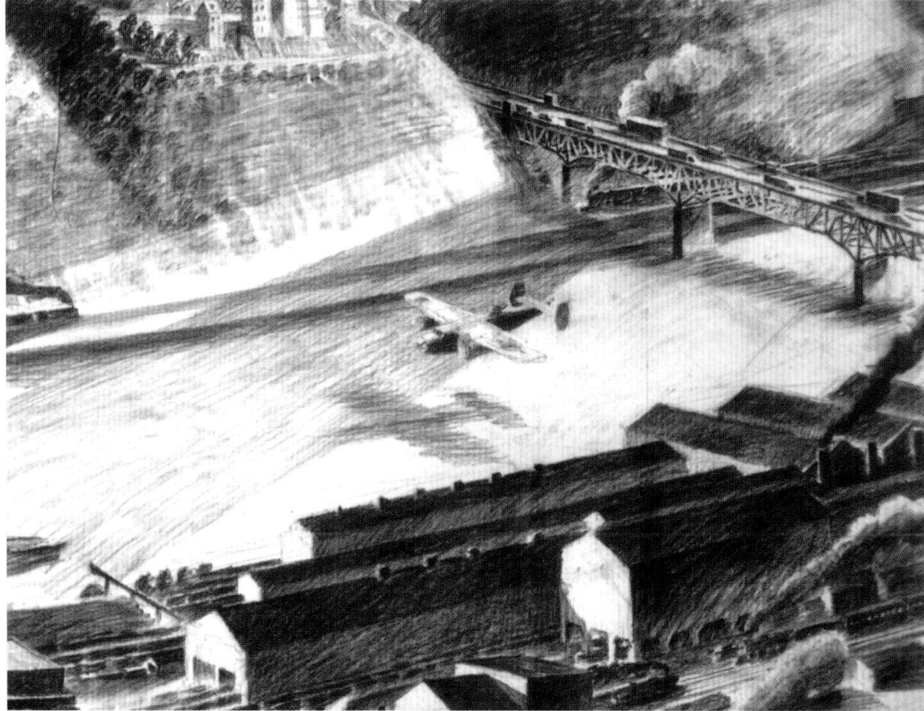

2.36 (*above*). North wall detail showing airplane crash. Jared L. Cohon University Center mural, Doug Cooper with Sarah Cooper, Jonathan Kline, and John Trivelli, 1996. Charcoal on paper on board, approx. 10 × 150 feet. Carnegie Mellon University, Pittsburgh.

2.37 (*right*). North wall detail showing foreground overlooking downtown. Jared L. Cohon University Center mural, Doug Cooper with Sarah Cooper, Jonathan Kline, and John Trivelli, 1996. Charcoal on paper on board, approx. 10 × 150 feet. Carnegie Mellon University, Pittsburgh.

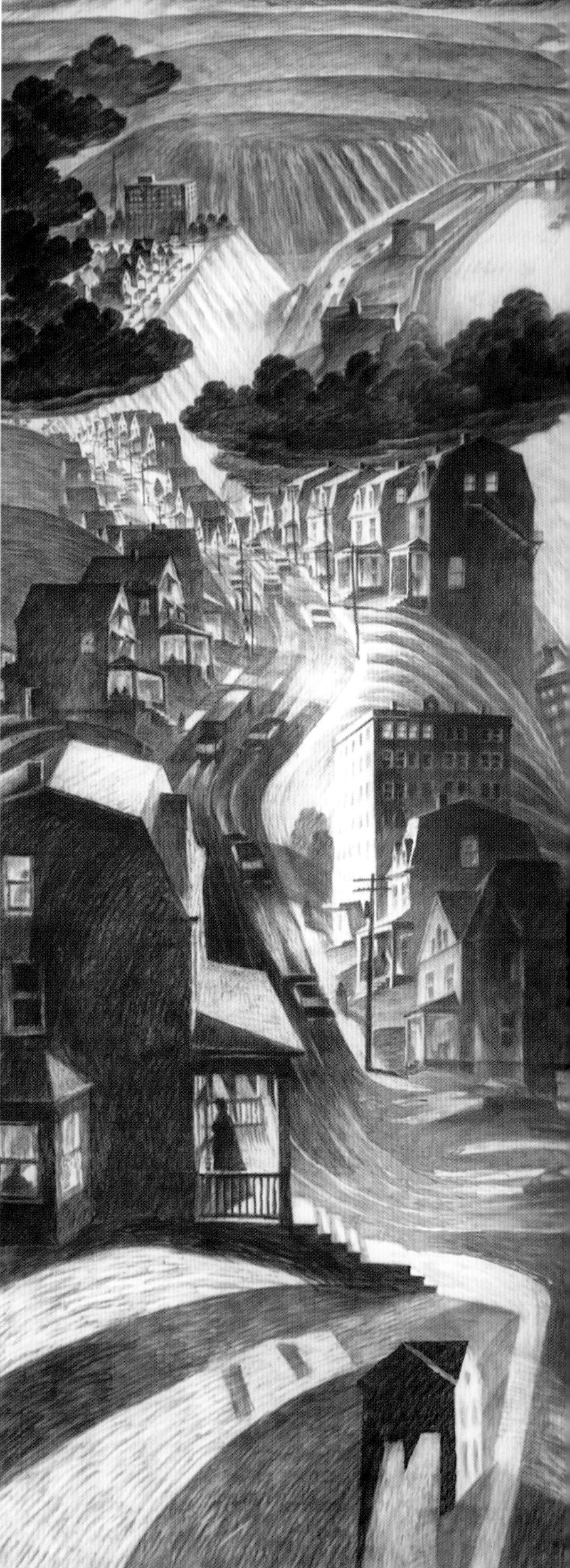

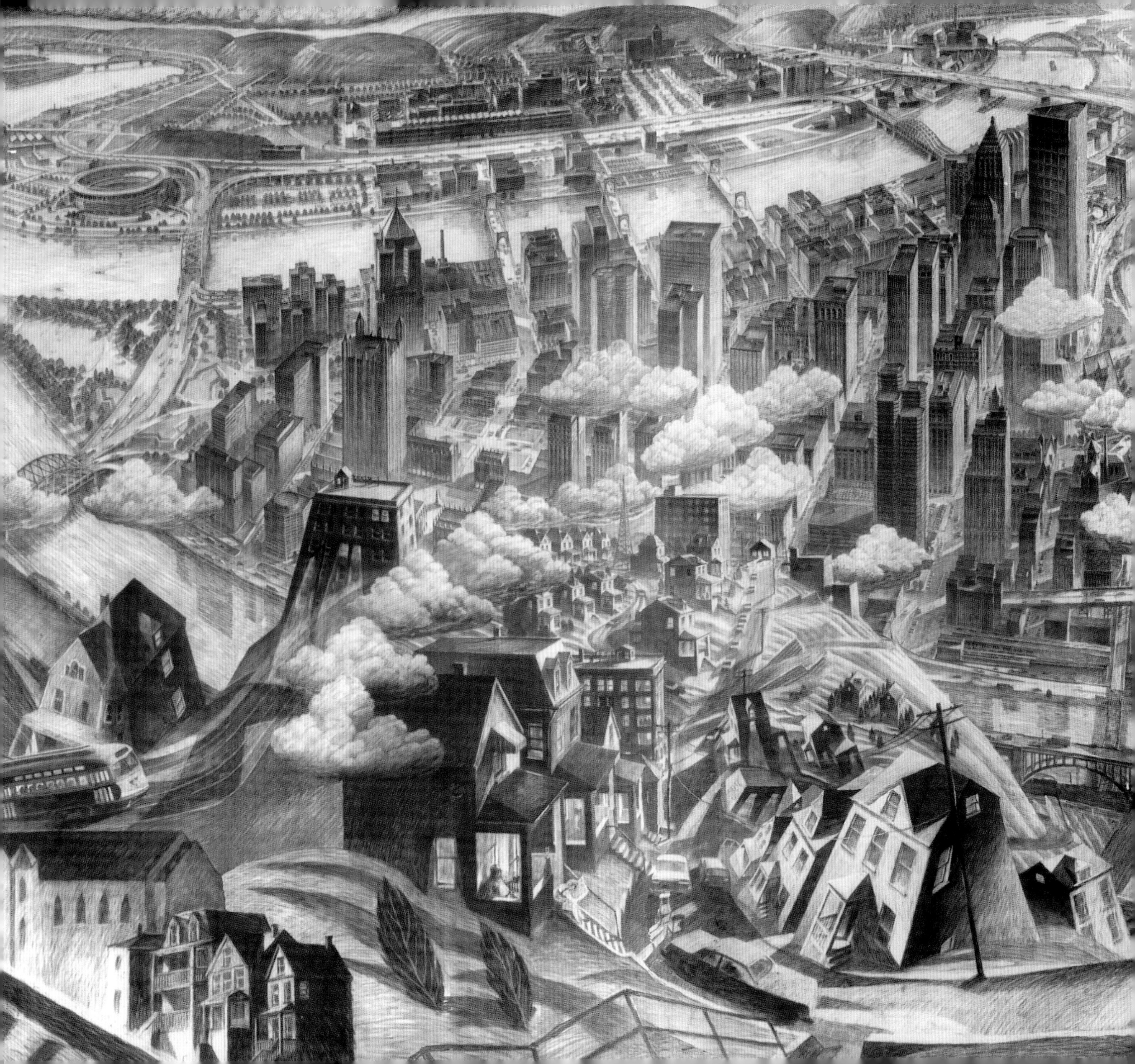

I'd compare these middle-ground maps to the paintings of Grandma Moses (1860–1961), whose work was centered on the region of her home in eastern New York state, near the town of Hoosick Falls. The layouts of a particular town or farm or grouping of houses all convey the sense that we could use them to find our way around. *Country Fair* (1950) is a good example (fig. 2.38). As in her other paintings, Gandma Moses used no atmospheric perspective. Each house is painted with equal attention to its detail whether it is near or far from the viewer. In viewing the painting we feel as if we have equal access to all its parts.

If the middle grounds share something with Grandma Moses, the fore-grounds are a different matter. For them I used an accelerated perspective to locate and enclose viewers in a small neighborhood surrounded by houses. Into this east wall foreground I set personal vignettes with people enjoying life on porches: a guy drinking a beer, his wife set apart and reading the newspaper on a front stoop; an older daughter, who cannot wait to leave town, looking wist-fully out an open screen door; a woman escaping the heat of a summer by read-ing a book on a porch roof (fig. 2.39). These were directed at people with greater familiarity with the city: longtime residents who might find resonance between this imagery and their personal experience of their own neighborhood.

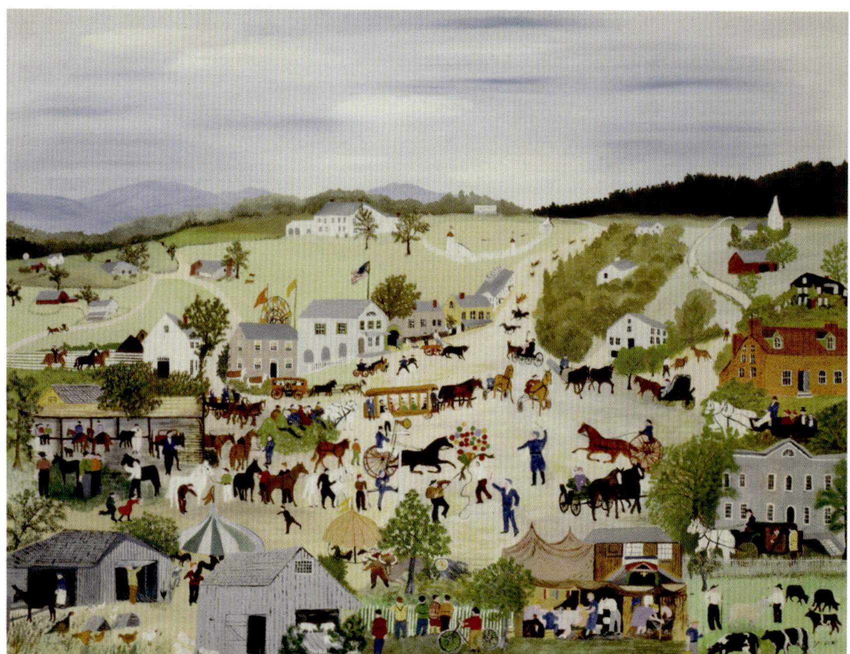

2.38. *Country Fair*, Anna Mary (Grandma) Moses, 1950. Oil on canvas, 35 × 45 inches. Kallir 921. Copyright ©1950 (renewed 1978), Grandma Moses Properties Co., New York. By permission of Grandma Moses Properties, Kallir 921, c/o Galerie St. Etienne, New York.

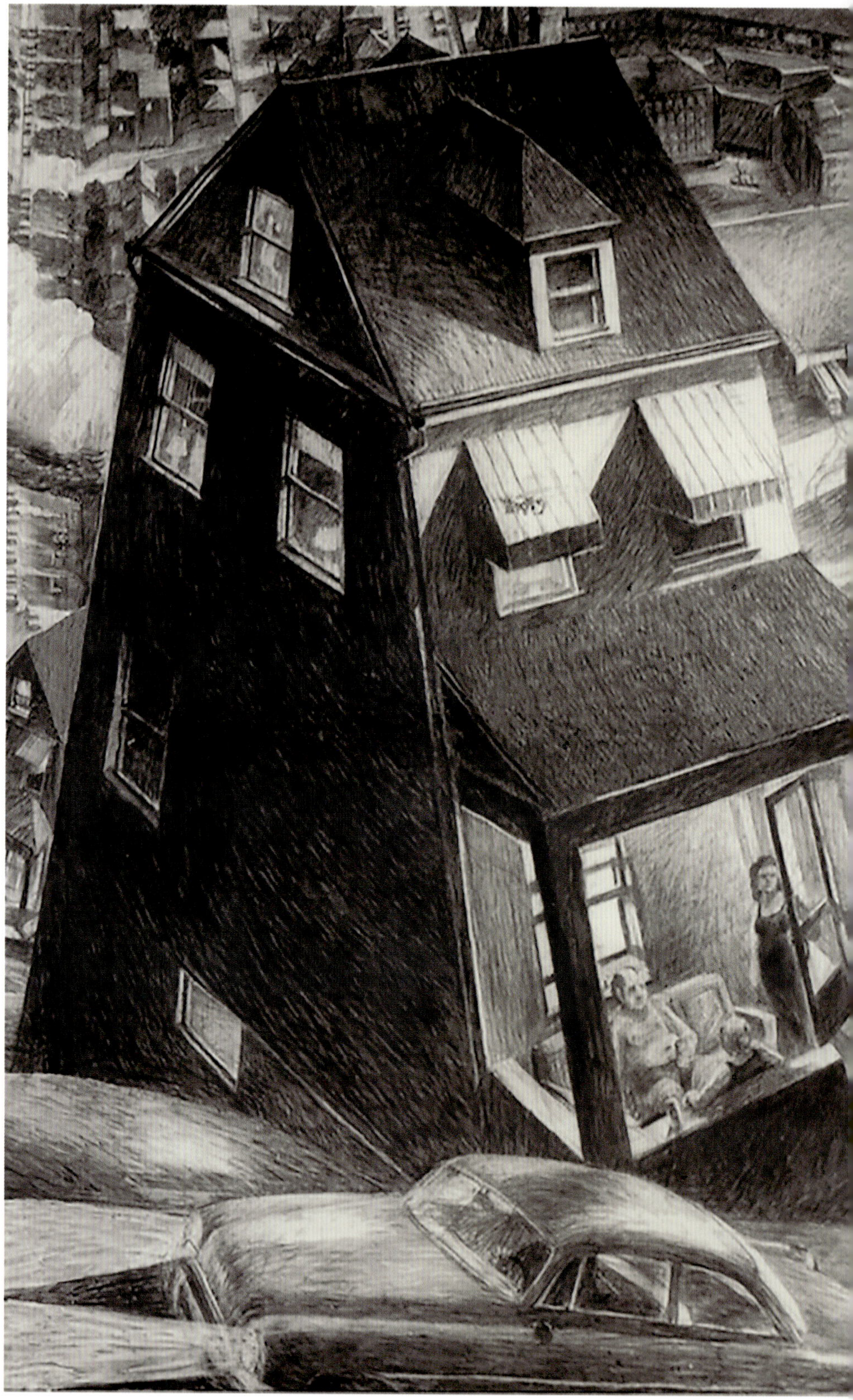

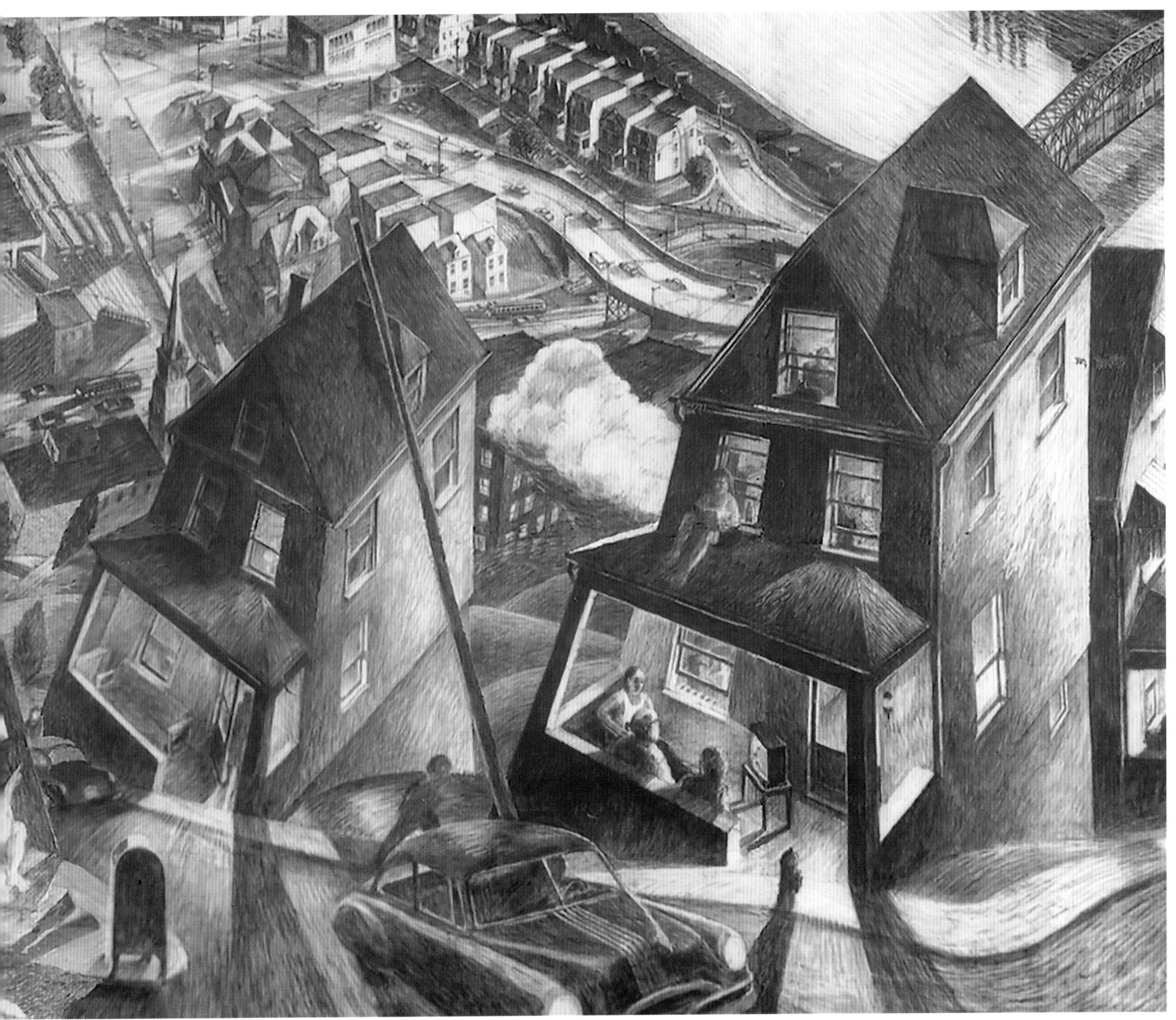

2.39. East wall, right detail, showing porches. Jared L. Cohon University Center mural, Doug Cooper with Sarah Cooper, Jonathan Kline, and John Trivelli, 1996. Charcoal on paper on board, approx. 10 × 150 feet. Carnegie Mellon University, Pittsburgh.

Hill District Map

A journey map that has substantial stylistic differentiation over its height is one I created as part of a larger mural. That mural is now housed at Pittsburgh's Senator John Heinz History Center, and the part shown here shows Pittsburgh's Hill District (fig. 2.40). It was based on a map I had drawn with the assistance of others when I was a student at Carnegie Tech and working in professor Troy West's advocacy planning group, Architecture 2001. Through that work experience I had gotten to know the Hill well.

In this newer work I wanted to differentiate the sources of the information the drawing was mapping. Its upper part was built around drawings made by residents and former residents of the Hill whom I met at Vintage, a senior center in Pittsburgh's East End. My collaborators made drawings of places they remembered on sheets of paper, which I then glued directly into a street map of the Hill.

But the foreground at the map's base represented my own experience of the city. It looks down the South Side Slope and across the Monongahela River to the Hill District, and it has a very different character than the Hill District map above (fig. 2.41).

I love the twisting descents of the South Side Slopes along 18th Street, the city steps on Sterling Street, and the houses that seem ready at any moment to let hold of their moorings and slide on down the hillside. And so, as I developed this view, I let my hand skitter down those same steps as I drew them—steps drawn with the memory of having descended them and slopes shaped with the memory of the water that once eroded them.

With these two different parts, the drawing joined two distinct ways of knowing into one vision of the city. At the top there is historical knowledge of the Hill: stories and memories gathered from current and former residents and compiled street by street. And at the base there is a more haptic way of knowing: a knowledge of the South Side Slopes that came largely through my feet and legs, climbing up and down its hundreds of steps.

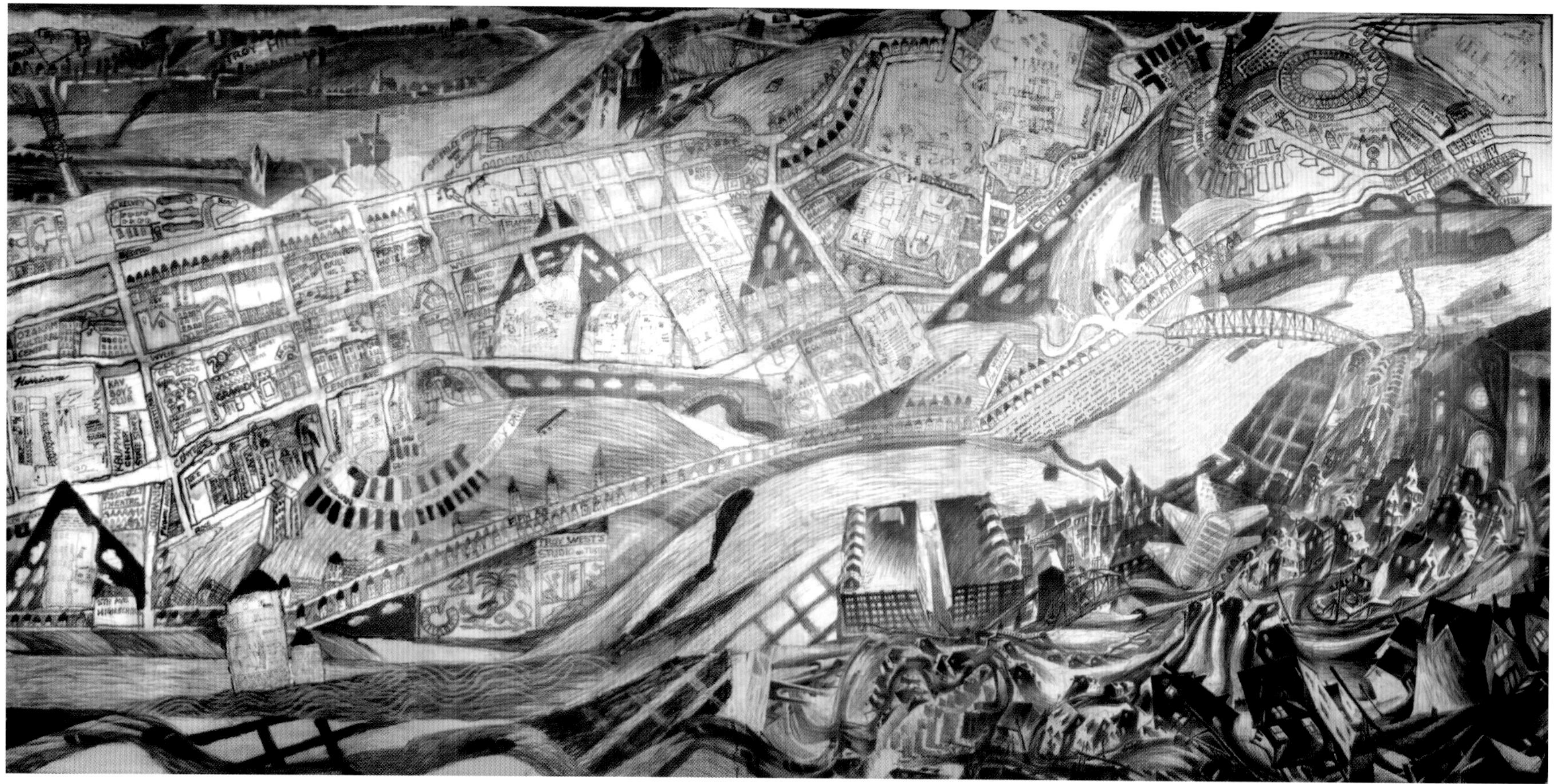

2.40. *Hill District Map*, Doug Cooper, 1992. Charcoal on paper on canvas, 80 × 162 inches. Senator John Heinz History Center, Pittsburgh.

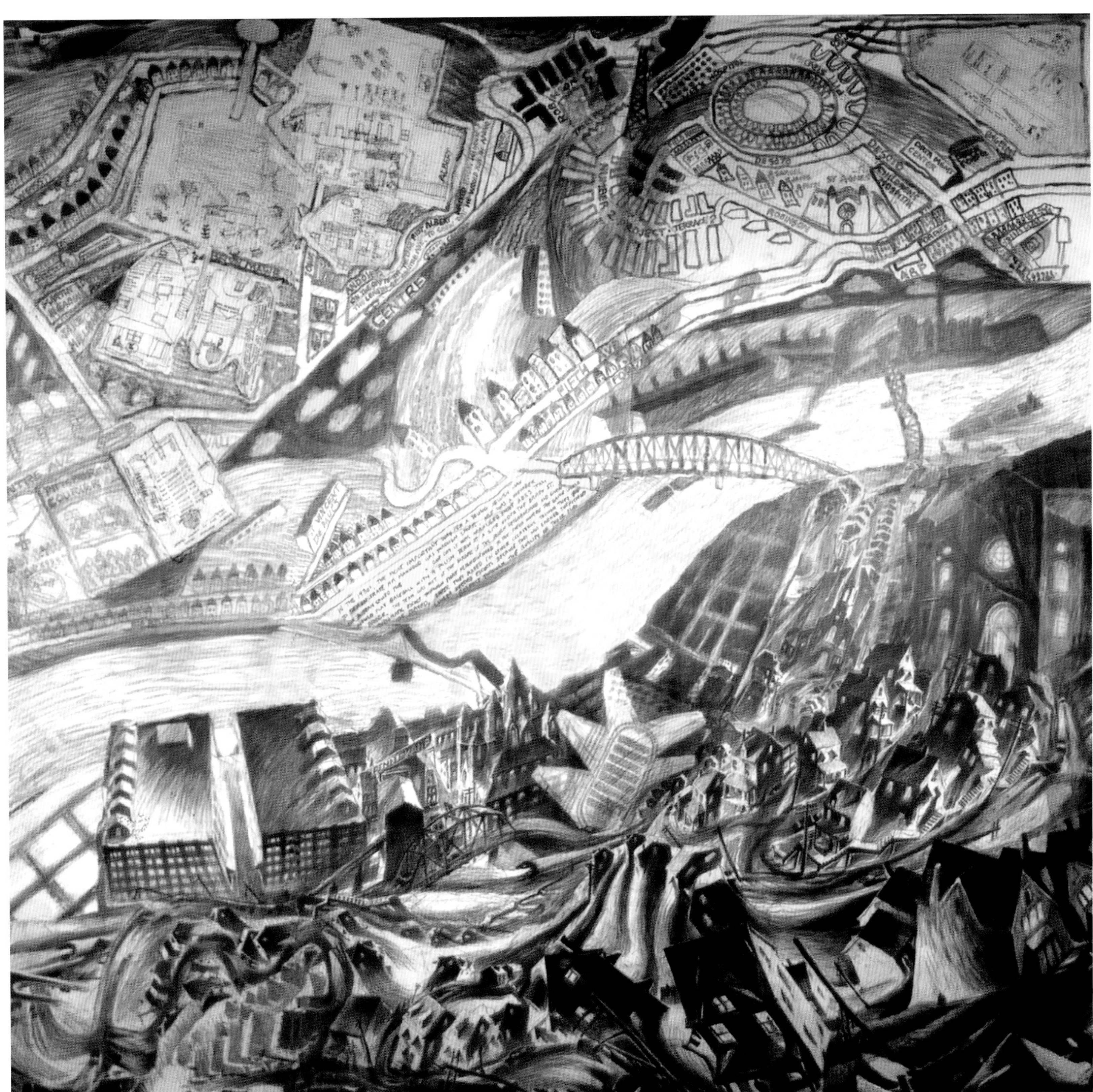

2.41. Detail, lower right. *Hill District Map*, Doug Cooper, 1992. Charcoal on paper on canvas, 80 × 162 inches. Senator John Heinz History Center, Pittsburgh.

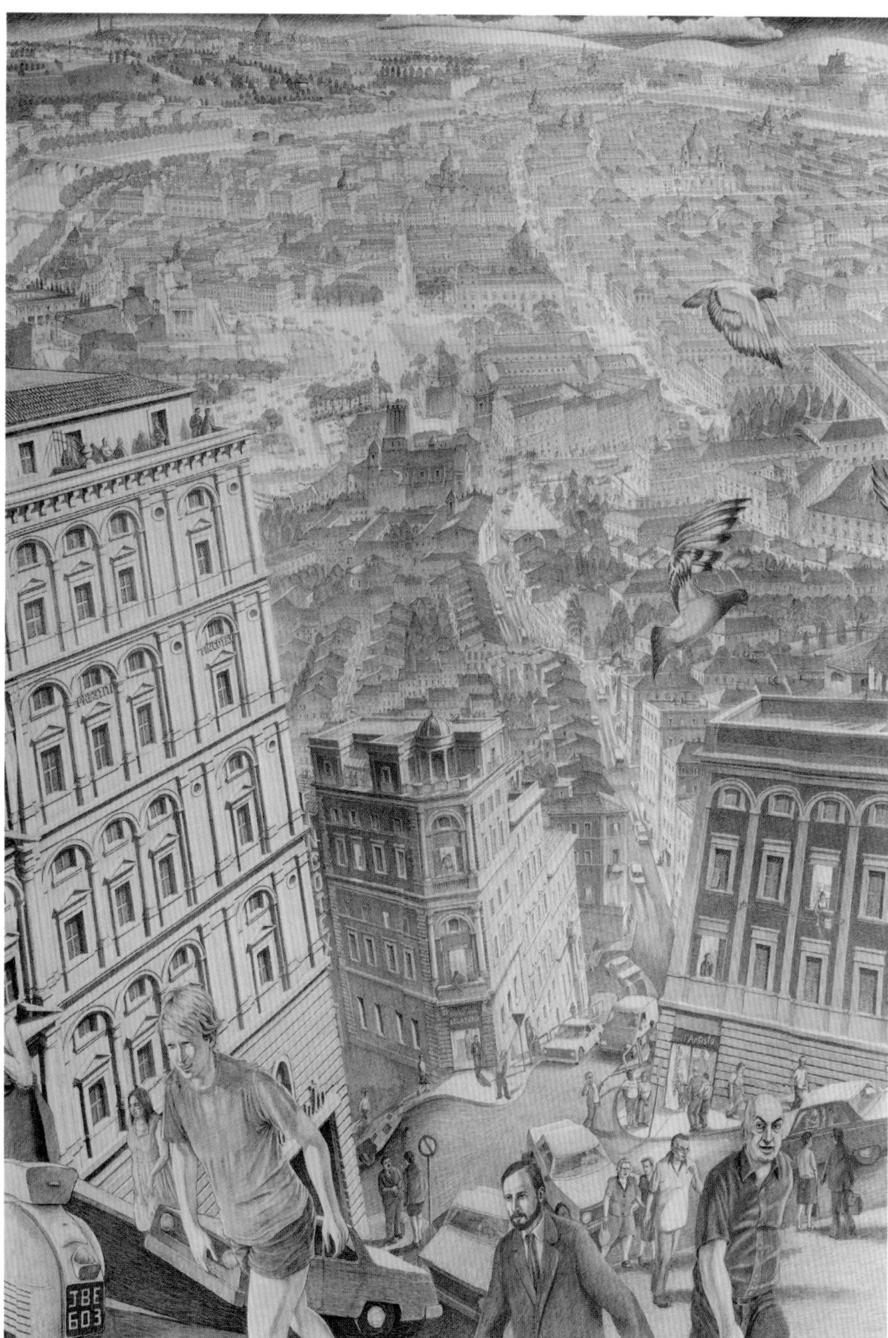

2.42. West wall detail looking toward Saint Peter's. Aula Magna, Ex Caserma Sani mural, Doug Cooper with Grégoire Picher and Patty Culley, assisted by Ross Christy, Carla Collada, Lara Hoke, Ashok Kanagasundram, and Jan Vairo, 2005. Charcoal on paper on board, approx. 16 × 200 feet. Università Roma Tre, Rome.

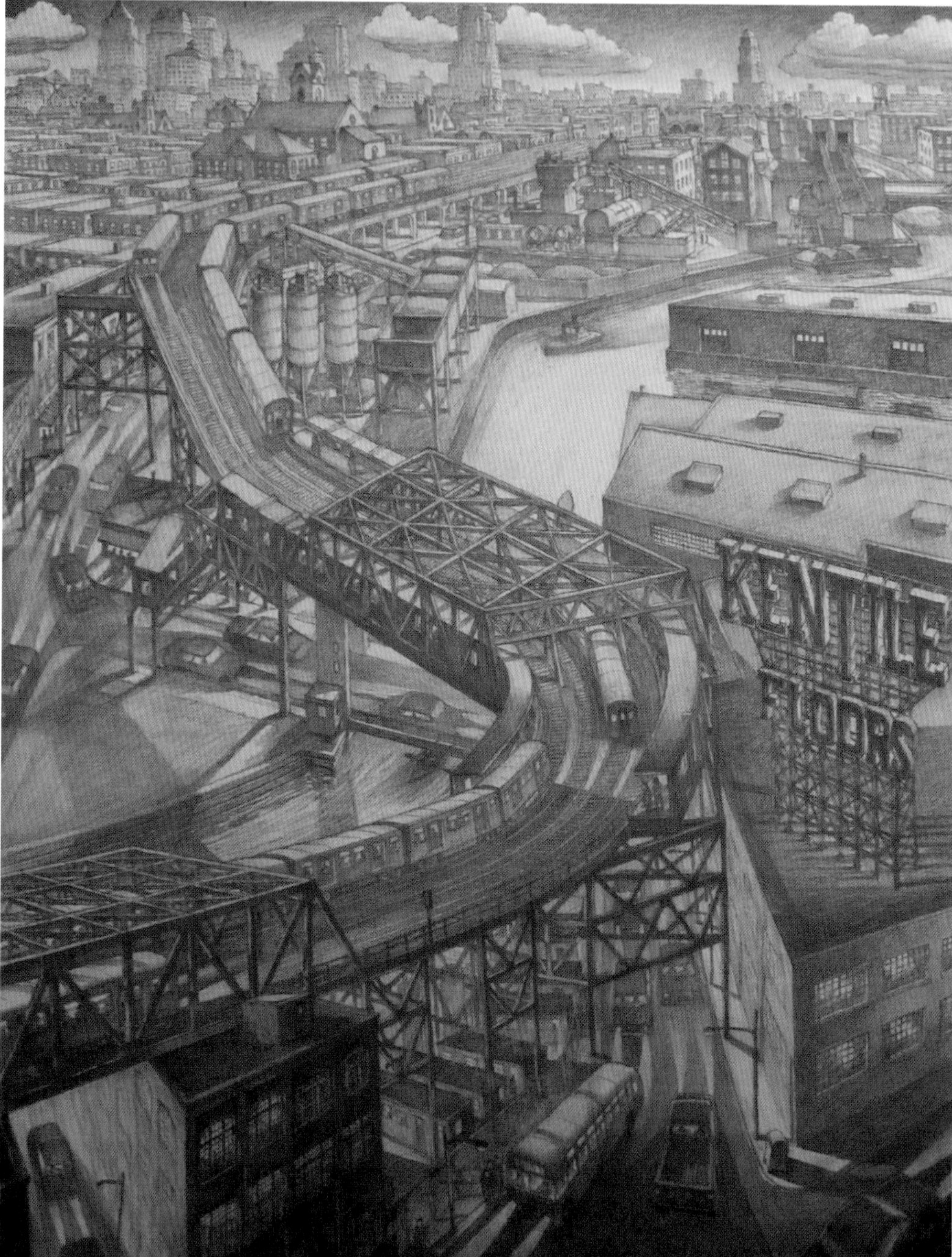

2.43. *Crossing the Gowanus*, Doug Cooper, 2014. Charcoal on paper on board, 48 × 36 inches.

Bridges and Viaducts

Very early on I recognized that much of the allure of mapping Pittsburgh came from the sense of overview characteristic of its terrain. Views from its plateau tops and midslope overlooks offer easy visual connections to other locations in the city: point to point. In subsequent years, I sought mural commissions in other cities where I knew I would find similar conditions: San Francisco, Rome, and Seattle. Rome is a prime example, with its long and hilly point-to-point connections such as the view showing a continuous path from Piazza dell'Esquilino behind Santa Maria Maggiore all the way to Saint Peter's by way of Via Panisperna and Corso Vittorio Emanuele II (fig. 2.42).

When I have taken on flatter landscapes, it has been to return to the subject originally awakened by my grandmother years ago: bridges. They are interesting subjects to draw in Pittsburgh, of course, but ever since reading David McCullough's book about the construction of the Brooklyn Bridge, the bridges in and around New York have held a particular fascination for me.

Below the joining of the Harlem and East Rivers, where the waterborne traffic historically shifted from barges to high-masted oceangoing vessels, the only bridge types that could span the great width of the East River with sufficient clearance were steel suspension bridges (Triboro, Bronx-Whitestone, Williamsburg, Manhattan, and Brooklyn Bridges), bowstring trusses (Hellgate), or cantilevered steel trusses (Queensboro).

In all these instances, because of the lowness of the banks on either side of the river and the high clearances required for their spans, the bridges needed long viaducts that would carry vehicular traffic up to the considerable height of the main span. As with all bridges, there is a strong sense of connection, place to place (what I remembered from Budapest), that makes them an ideal mapping subject. I've found that emphasizing the viaduct, as much as the main span, has lengthened the sense of path in the drawings and made them stronger as journey maps as a result.

All these drawings have strongly articulated foregrounds where I try to emphasize a character of insideness. *Crossing the Gowanus Canal* has a foreground defined by the shadowy space beneath the transit truss and the well-known (and since removed) Kentile Tile sign above (fig. 2.43). While the rest of the scene is shown in daylight, the foreground is shown at night. In *Forsyth and Division Streets*, it is the area beside and underneath the viaduct leading up to the Manhattan Bridge and over the East River (fig. 2.44). Both have strong spines—the viaducts themselves and the main spans—and strong destinations: Brooklyn.

Seattle is another city with interesting bridges, in Seattle's case because the waterways the bridges cross are flanked by high bluffs. This circumstance creates a condition where two bridges are sometimes built at the same location—one high and one low—such that there are two alternative bridge routes to the same place (fig. 2.45). Occasionally in New York I have found a similar pairing wherever bridges have been located close to one another (fig. 2.46).

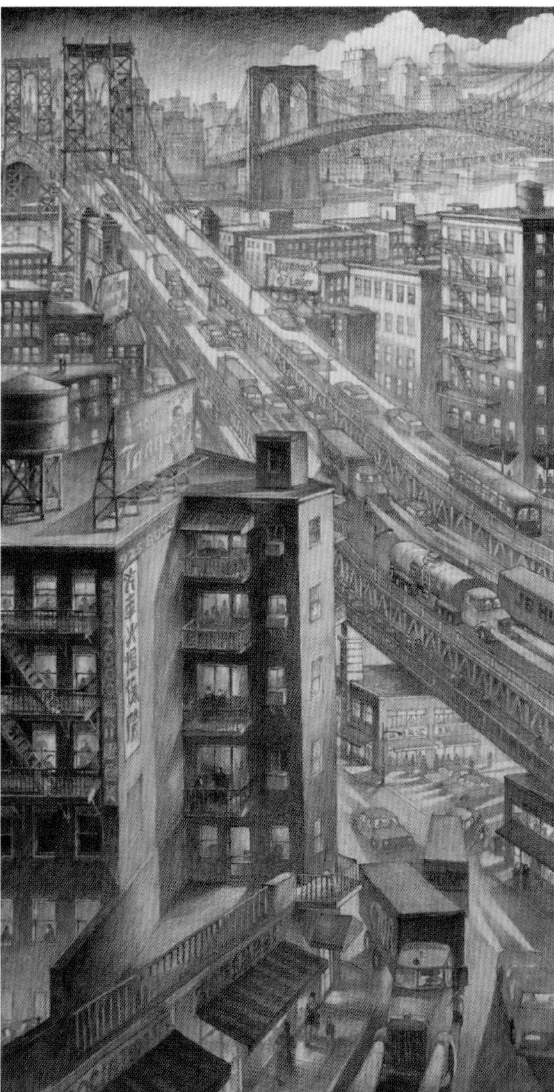

2.44. *Forsyth and Division Streets*, Doug Cooper, 2014. Charcoal on paper on board, 48 × 36 inches.

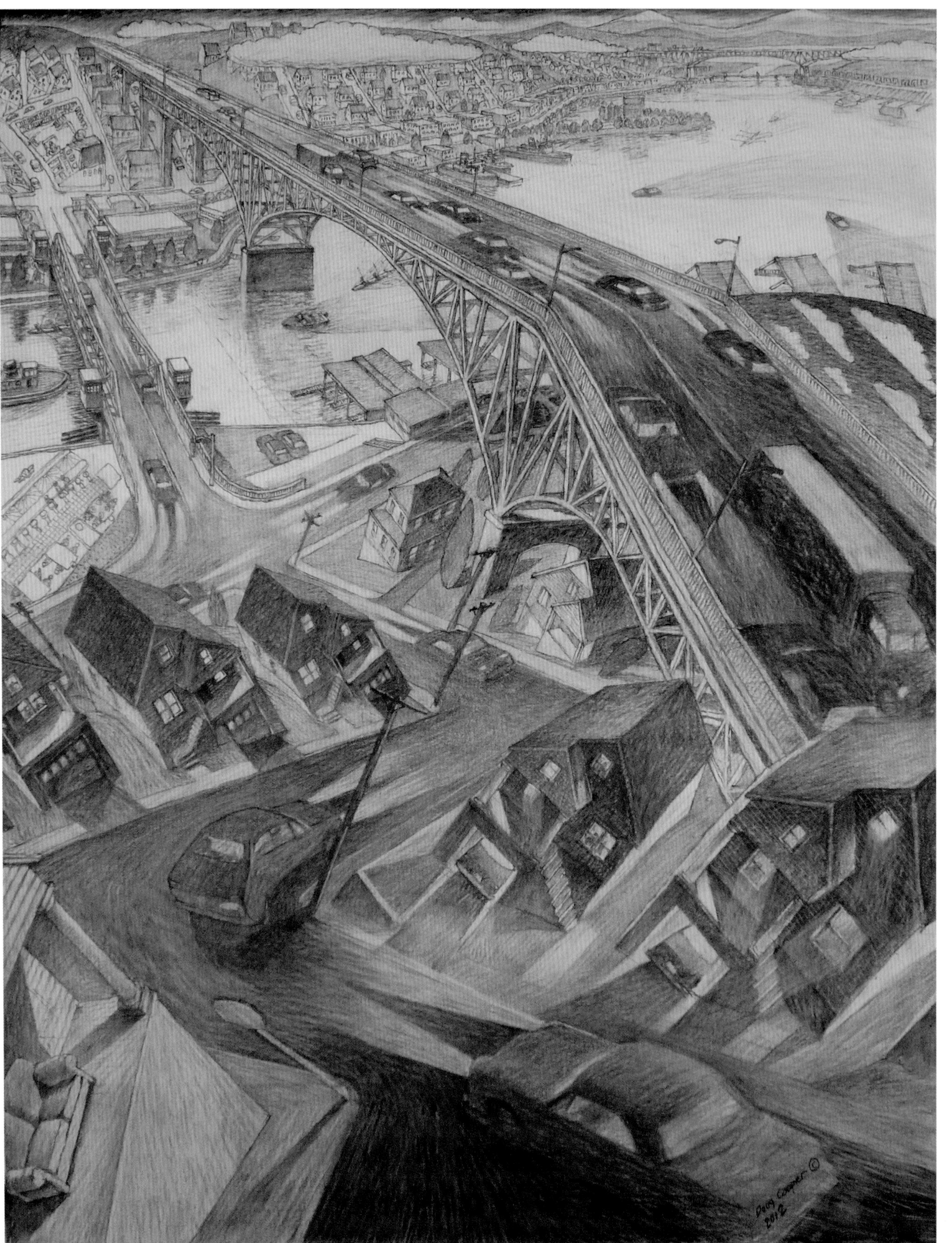

2.45. *Two Routes Across*, Doug Cooper, 2012.
Charcoal on paper on board, 48 × 36 inches.

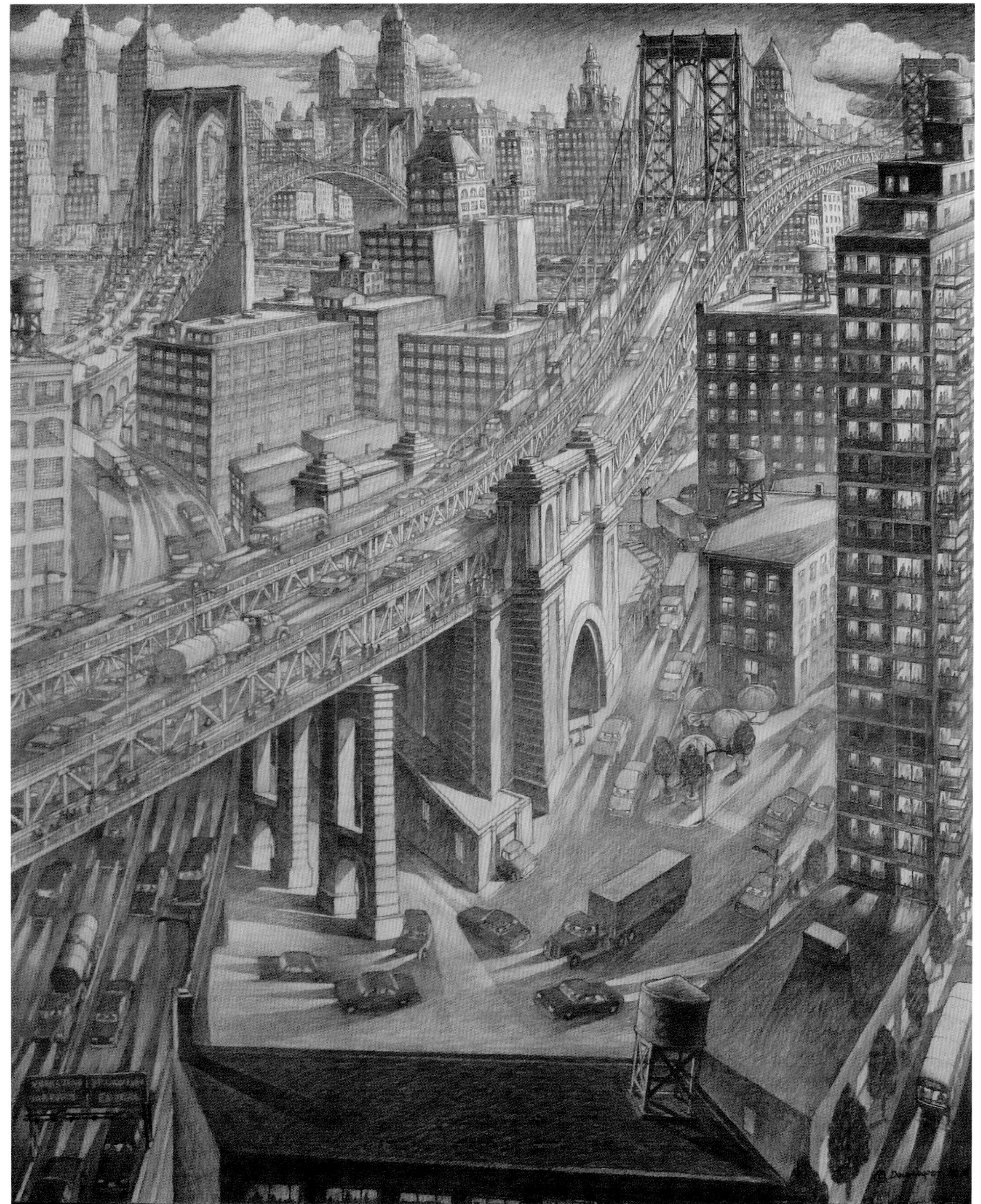

2.46. *DUMBO*, Doug Cooper, 2014. Charcoal on paper on board, 60 × 48 inches.

Maps of the Cosmos

At the beginning of this chapter I mentioned a third tradition of mapmaking: cosmic maps. Their purpose is to depict something beyond the questions of where we are or where we are going. The word *cosmos* comes from Greek and refers to an ordered universe. In this tradition, there is the intention to show *all that there is* or could be within such a universe.

If we stretch our use of the term a bit, a map of a cosmos might show an entire system such as the well-known map of the London Underground. Or it might show a small world such as *Winnie-the-Pooh*'s Hundred Acre Wood. Or in the normal use of the term, it might be a mandala, a spiritual symbol of the universe within Buddhism and Hinduism.

What are some of the specific characteristics of cosmic maps? One that is common is distortion, whether of size or shape, in the service of their central intention: showing relationships within a whole system. One of the earliest intentionally distorted maps is the *Tabula Peutingeriana*, reputedly prepared by Agrippa during the reign of Augustus (fig. 2.47). The version shown here is a thirteenth-century copy of an earlier, fourth-century copy. Rome and the Italian peninsula are large and located at the map's center. Distortions of shape are extreme in order to fit the map into the proportion dictated by the vast width of its scroll format (it measures 33 centimeters high by 6 meters wide). The map is about topological relationships, pure and simple; it is a system map showing what roads connect which city to which and how in the end they all lead to Rome.

The so-called *mappae mundi* of the Middle Ages also freely distorted land areas in an effort to depict the relative importance of places in relationship to the spiritual needs of their Christian users. These used what historians call the "T-O" format because of the way they shaped the Mediterranean Sea, Black Sea, Don River, and the Nile into a *T* shape within a circle in order to divide the world into its known continents: Europe, Africa, and Asia.

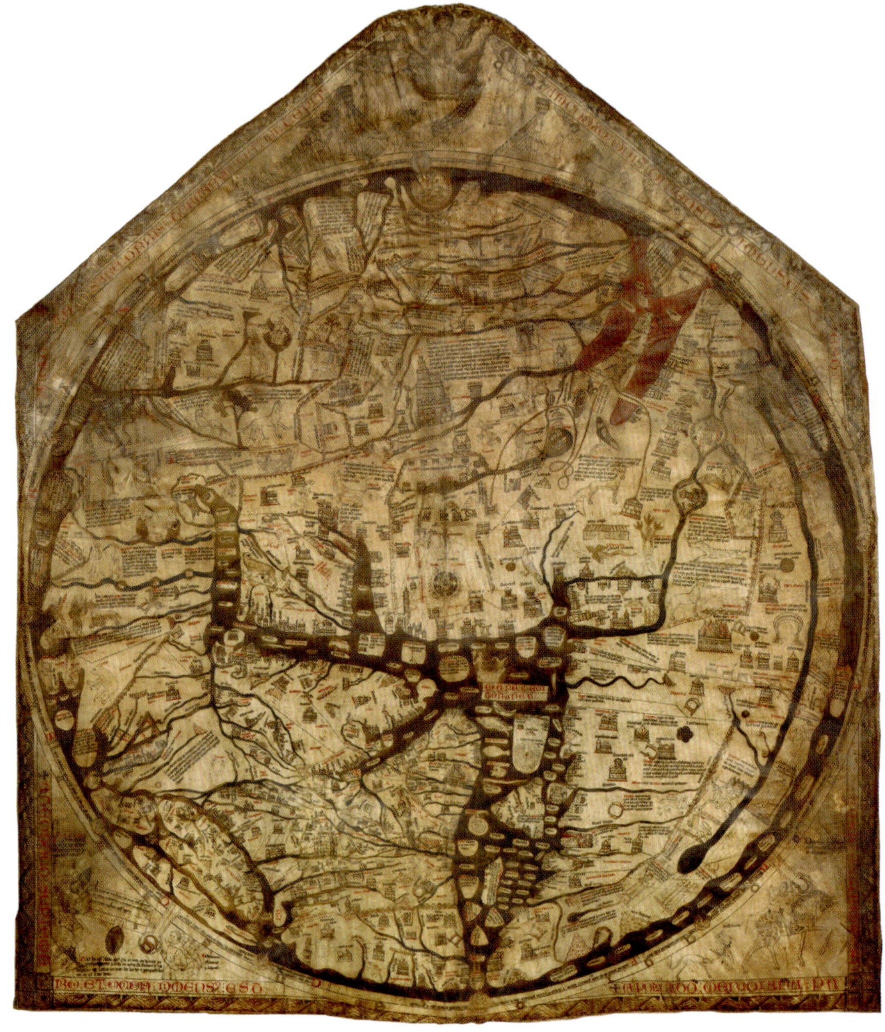

2.48 (*above*). *Hereford Mappa Mundi*, ca. 1300.
2.49 (*right*). Detail of Holy Land, *Hereford Mappa Mundi*, ca. 1300.

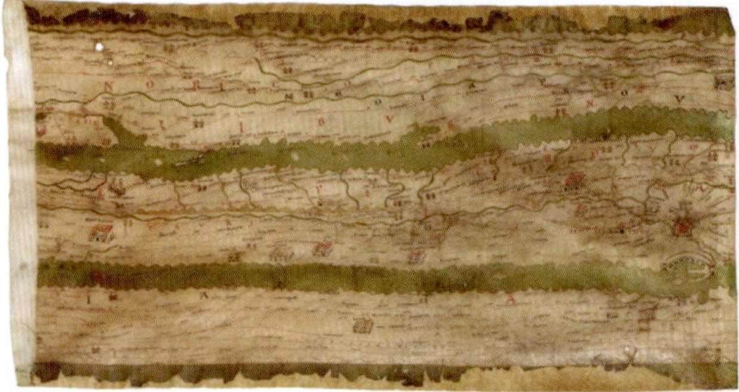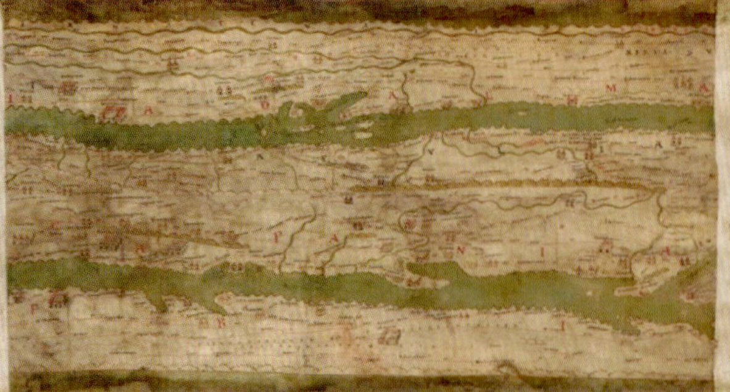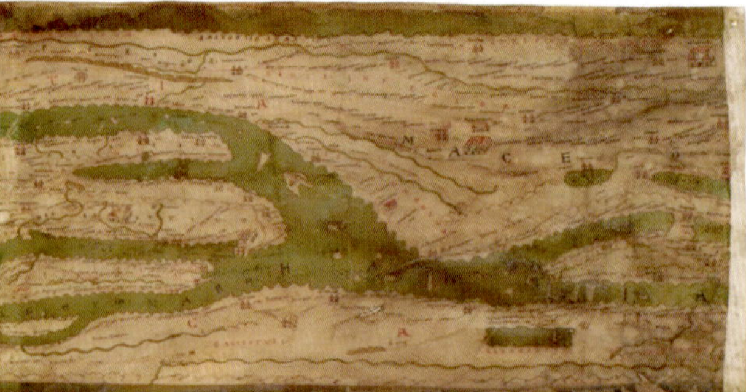

2.47. Detail showing Italy, *Tabula Peutingeriana*. Nineteenth-century facsimile of thirteenth-century version of fourth-century original, ca. 1300. Cod. 324. Courtesy of the Austrian National Library, Vienna.

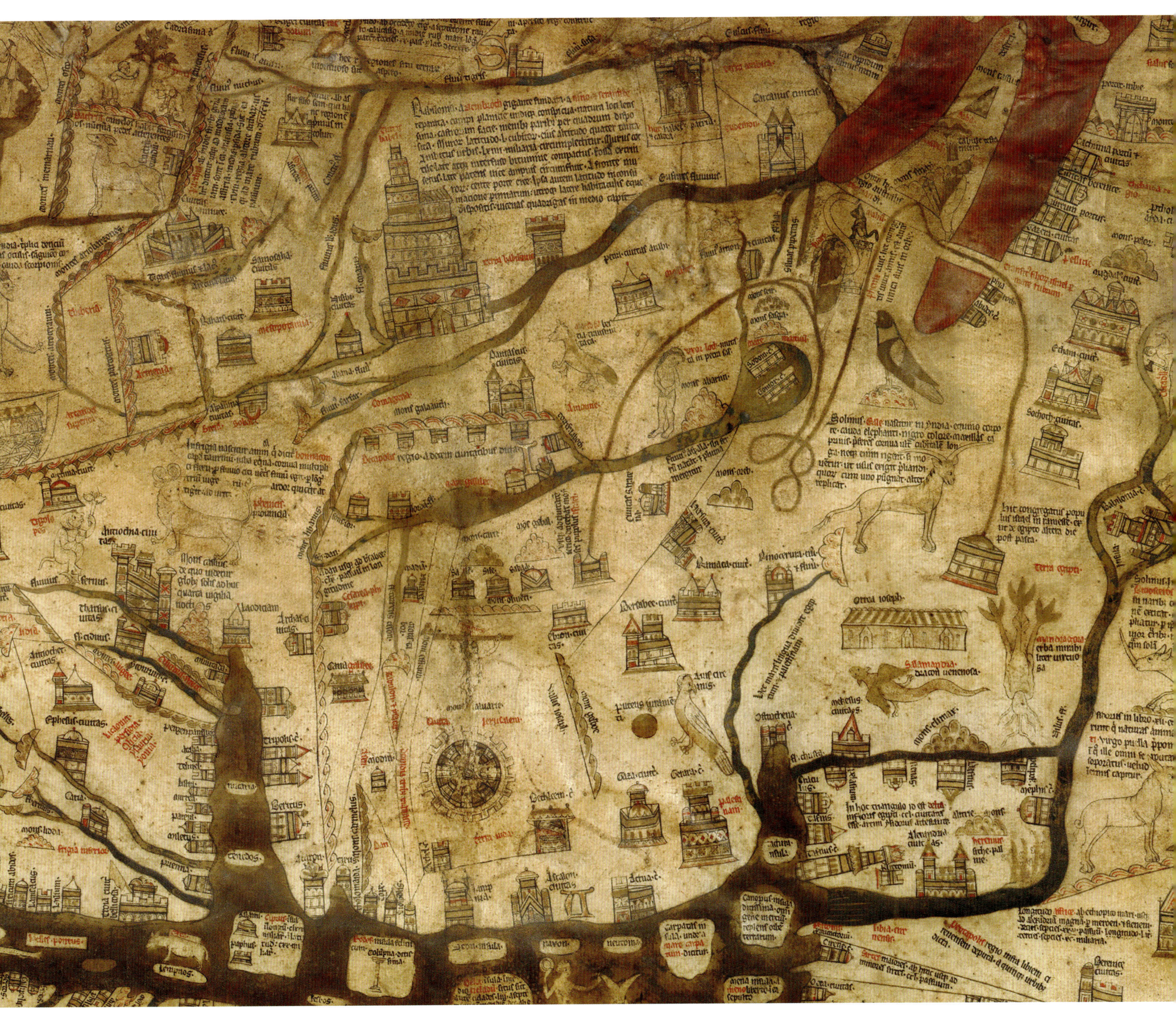

One of the most famous of these is the Hereford Mappa Mundi (ca. 1300), which is housed in the Cathedral Annex in the village of Hereford along England's border with Wales (fig. 2.48). It was drawn on parchment—an animal skin—and retains the animal's shape. The map represents the world as it might have seemed to a Christian at the time (hence east is at its top as a spiritual destination). The British Isles appear as a small set of odd shapes in the lower left quadrant, whereas the Holy Land with Jerusalem at its center dominates almost one half of the map (fig. 2.49).

So, in a cosmic map, relationships to an outside are not the issue. In a sense there is no outside. The intent is oneness, and there is a conceptual issue at the heart of these maps. It arises in that moment in which we *recognize* oneness: smaller moments of recognition, such the oneness of the neighborhood in which we live, or larger spiritual ones, such as perceiving the oneness of ourselves with the world around us or with God.

The World of the Snoqualmie

I've ventured into this area of pictorial maps only rarely. Possibly it is because maps of this type are less purely geographic in intent. However, in 2003–2005 I completed a mural series for the entrance lobby of the King County Courthouse in Seattle, Washington, in which I did use this form. I collaborated with my nephew Grégoire Picher, who was responsible for the figures, and my former student Patty Culley. The entire work comprises a set of more than sixteen walls—some as tall as fourteen feet. The scope of the mural commission was regional: the county, not just Seattle. It included areas from Puget Sound to the Cascades and well south of Mount Rainier. While researching content for the mural, I uncovered an intractable dispute: the disposition of Snoqualmie Falls. Because the home of the mural would be a courthouse, I thought I should address this dispute in the mural.

There were (and still are) competing claims over the falls from three groups: (1) the Snoqualmie Tribe, for whom the site is sacred; (2) Puget Sound Energy, which operates a hydroelectric plant at the falls; and (3) various businesses operating below the falls—primarily hop growers, dairy farmers, and recreational boating companies. I chose to represent this conflict in a section of the mural that extends partly over a doorway—hence the rectangular bite taken out of the image (figs. 2.50, 2.51).

The legal issues were and still are complicated, but here's a summary: The promoters of recreational boating, local farmers, and Puget Sound Energy desire a regulated flow of water, to have a reliable and safe water supply for boating and farming downriver and to maintain power generation for the turbines. Oppositely, the Snoqualmie require a free flow of water over the falls. Their tribal spokeswoman, Lois Sweet Dorman, explained to me why that is. In their creation story the moon mother's son created the falls out of a fish weir to give the Snoqualmie people a place of life-sustaining abundance. In their tradition, the falls are the place of birth and burial of the Snoqualmie (their vertical axis), and the souls of their dead are carried to their creator by the mists that form when the water of the falls is flowing freely.

As I look at this portion of the mural today, I find I had mapped these two parts—the areas above and below the falls—into a kind of world map, a mappa mundi of the Snoqualmie Tribe centered on the falls. The area above the door presents the Sky World of the Snoqualmie Tribe: Mount Si, where in the creation story the mother of Moon gave birth to him and where his body now lies; the falls pouring over top of the door form a threshold into the world below. In the foreground of the mural at the base of the falls, the lower world begins. References to the conflict surrounding the falls—the power plant, cows, and boaters—are set about what becomes an extended view of the Snoqualmie River heading northward toward Puget Sound.

Between these two worlds stands Dorman, who is still the spokeswoman for the tribe concerning the falls. I was not seeking to resolve the dispute with this composition, only to show that the one unifying element in it was the river itself and that in consideration of the river's long-term health might be found its one viable solution.

I had not thought of this portion of the courthouse mural as a cosmic map when I composed it. Rather, it is in the retrospective spirit of this book that I'm looking at this and other works through a different lens than I did when I completed them. If I were to make the panel today, I would compose it differently and add additional elements, among them the origin story of the falls and the presence of rainfall to complete the water cycle of the river. But I do recognize the wholeness of the panel's intent. The subject was Snoqualmie Falls, the watershed itself, and the people whose lives had always been sustained by it.

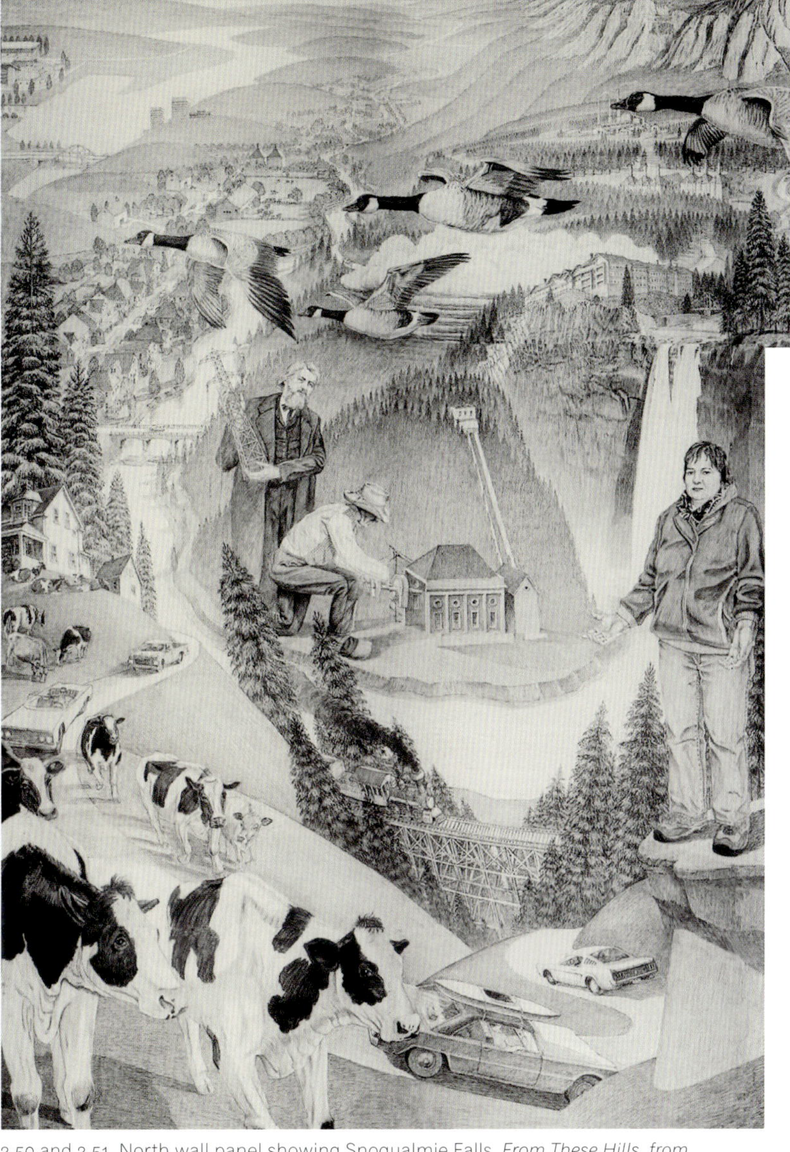

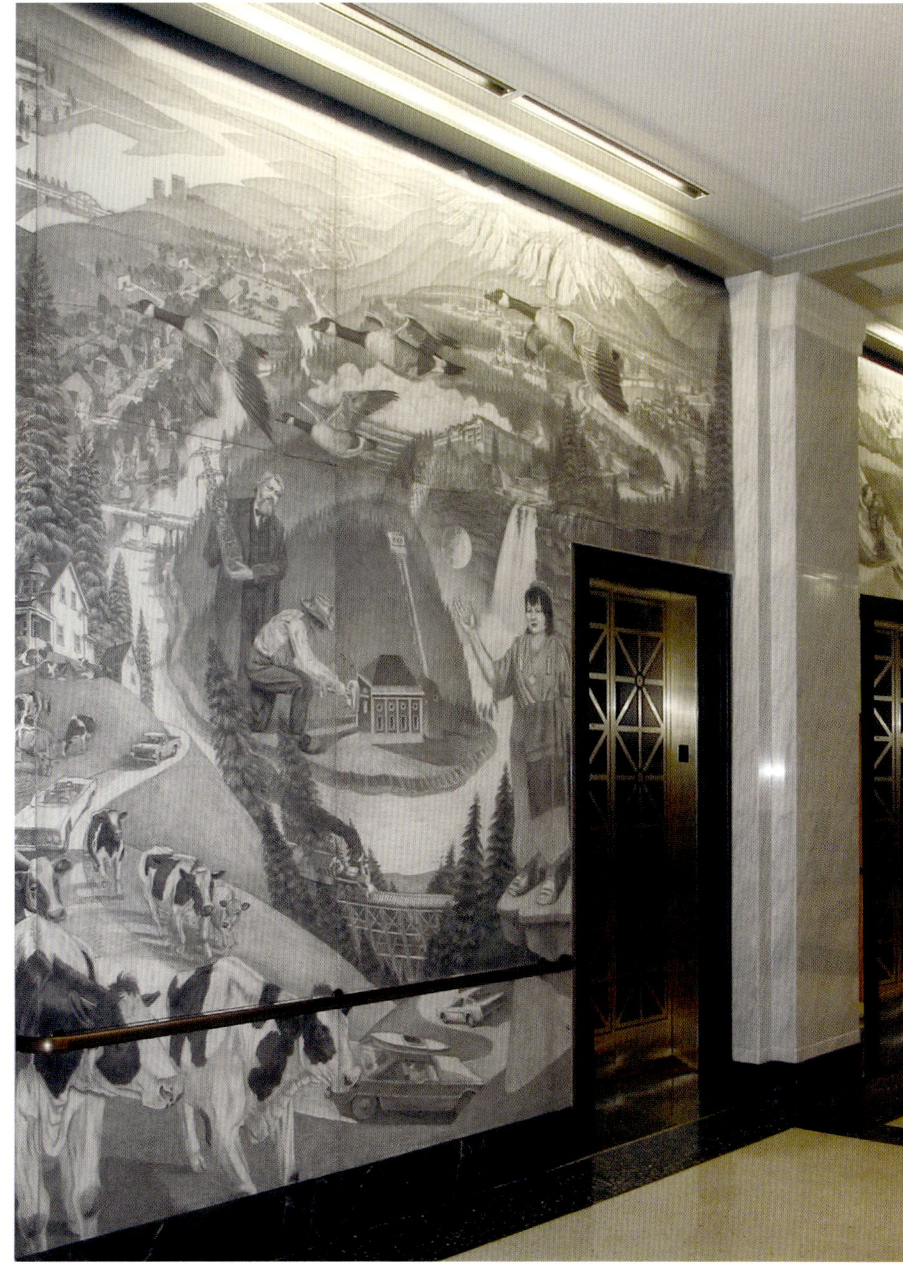

2.50 and 2.51. North wall panel showing Snoqualmie Falls. *From These Hills, from These Valleys*, mural series, Doug Cooper with Grégoire Picher and Patty Culley, 2005. Charcoal on paper on board. King County Courthouse, Seattle.

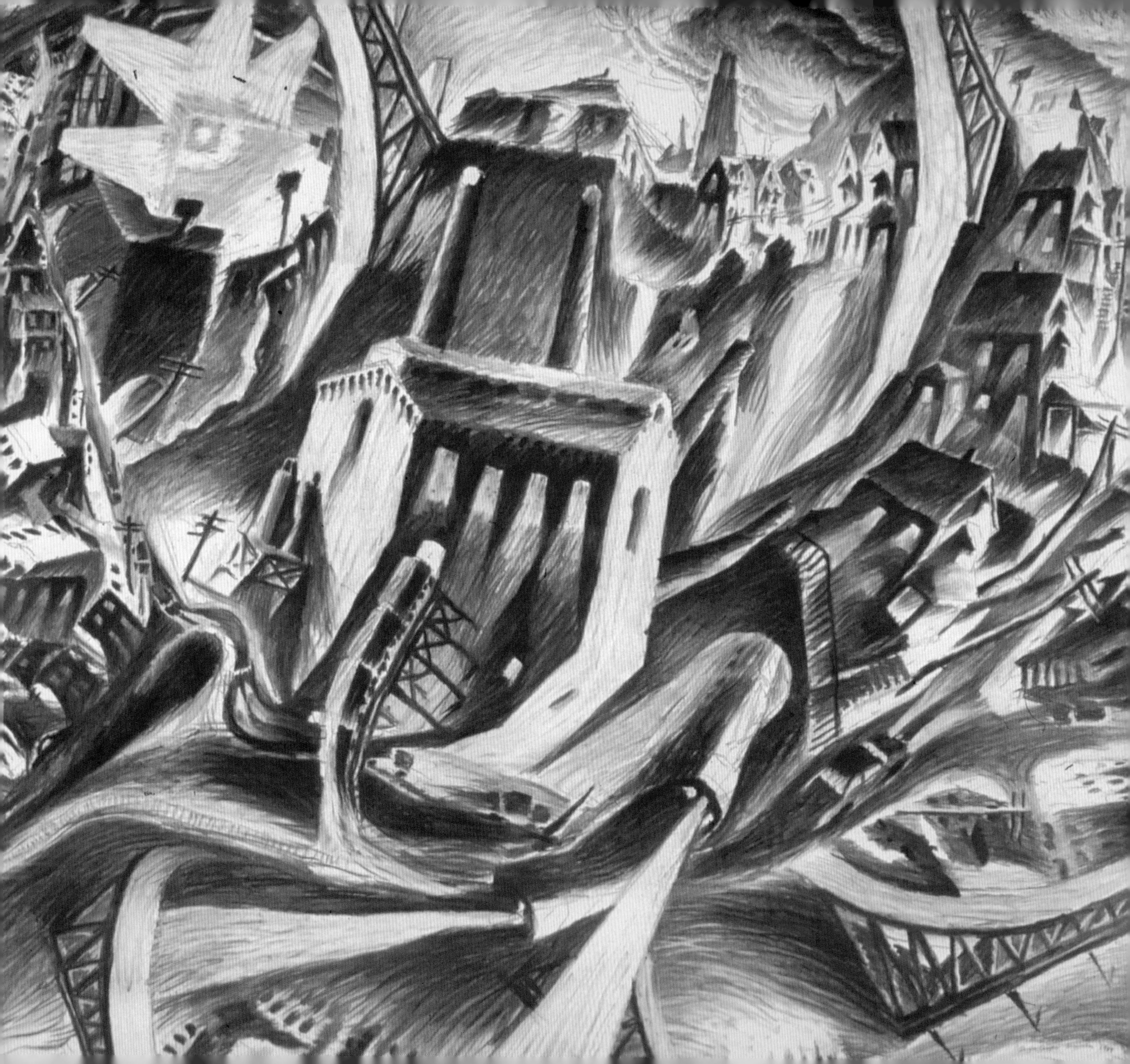

CHAPTER 3

THE KNOWING EYE

Washington DC, April 1989

It was spring 1989, and I had assembled works for a retrospective of my draw-ings at the American Institute of Architects (AIA) National Headquarters Gallery in Washington, DC. I had already had several exhibitions at the Rosenberg Gallery on 57th Street in New York, and this new show was a real coup for me. But underneath it all, I felt some misgivings about the direction of the work I was showing.

For almost fifteen years leading up to the exhibition, I had been working on highly detailed architectural fantasies drawn in carbon pencil. The origin of much of this work was a sketch I'd done years earlier in Siena, Italy, where I spent the winter of 1970–1971 (fig. 3.2). Across from the Campo (Siena's famous fan-shaped piazza), I'd found an intriguing pair of adjacent portals opening to two streets leading away from the Campo. The scene caught my attention because one of the streets led uphill to Piazza Tolomei, where all of Siena's banks are situated, and the other led downhill to the cemetery. I found this a nice irony in itself, but it was the character of the split visual field—one side looking up and the other down—that really intrigued me.

And so, for several years thereafter, I explored the nature of such split views, initially in a rendered version of my sketch in Siena (fig. 3.3), which I called "Due Porte," and then in a series of drawings where I sought to join upward- and downward-looking views into single images (fig. 3.4). These were perspectival anomalies, rendered in detail in the style of M. C. Escher, and they grew in size, eventually reaching eight feet square (fig. 3.5). As I was choosing works for the show at the AIA headquarters, I still found strength in these drawings because of their origin in authentic visual experience.

But I did not feel as positive about other works in the show. Many were bizarre architectural fantasies—floating rooms that hovered over deep can-yons. These used multiple viewing directions, upward, downward, left and right, but over the years, they became progressively less and less related to seeing itself; I had ceased drawing on site altogether. The rotated perspectives I had used in Kent Bloomer's class had arisen from my addressing Pittsburgh's singular landscape and its turning sightlines, but these more recent drawings had no equivalent source. Though they were technical marvels, they seemed lifeless to me (fig. 3.6). I was thinking that my fixation on perspective illusion was the source of the problem.

3.1. Detail, right side, *Panther Hollow*, Doug Cooper. Charcoal on paper, 56 × 80 inches. Collection of Laraine and Ulrich Flemming. Photo by David Aschkenas.

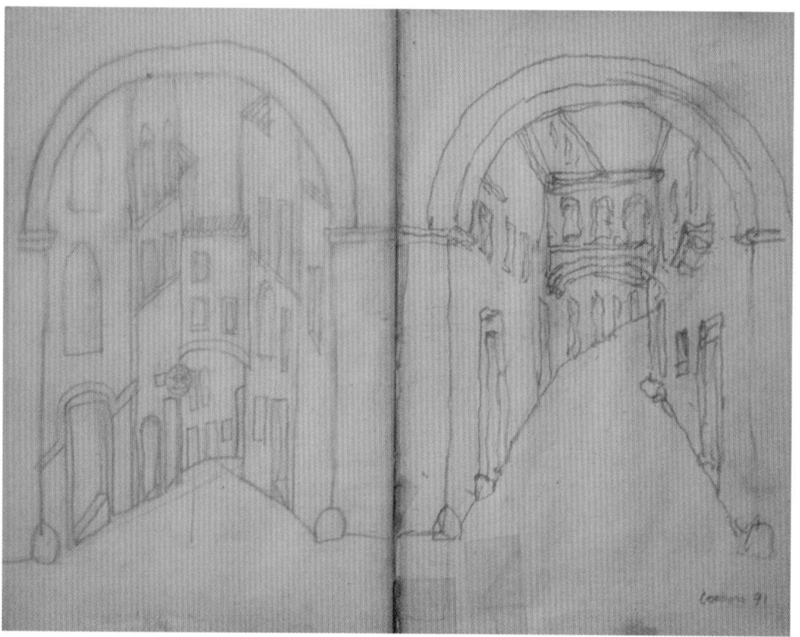

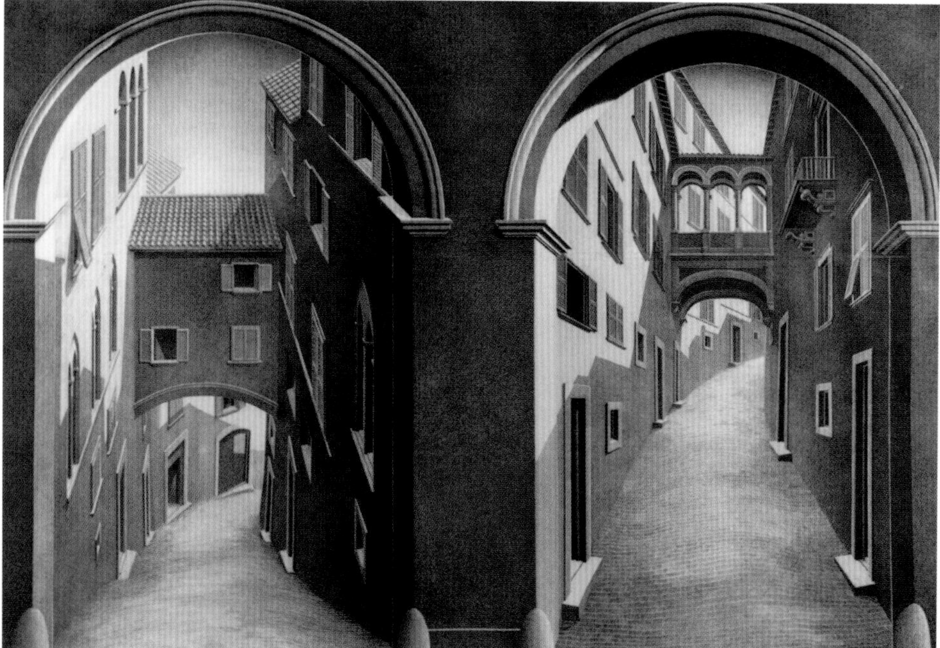

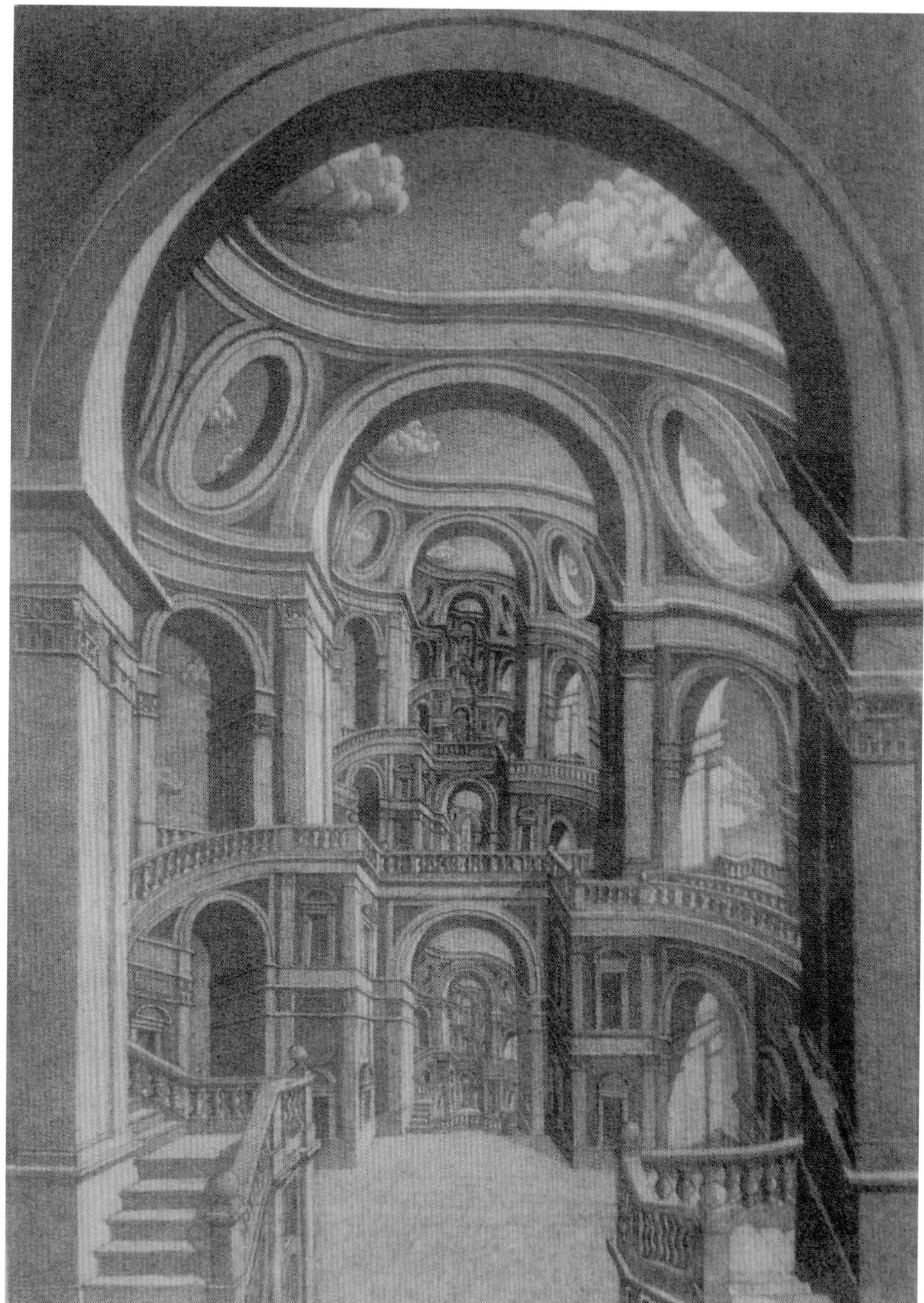

3.2 (*top left*). *Due Porte*, Doug Cooper, 1971. Pencil on paper, 8 × 10½ inches. Collection of the artist.
3.3 (*bottom left*). *Due Porte*, Doug Cooper, 1975, 1987. Carbon pencil on paper, 80 × 112 inches.
Private collection.

3.4. *Stairway to Above and Below*, Doug Cooper, 1978. Carbon pencil on paper, 14 × 9 ½ inches.
Collection of the artist.

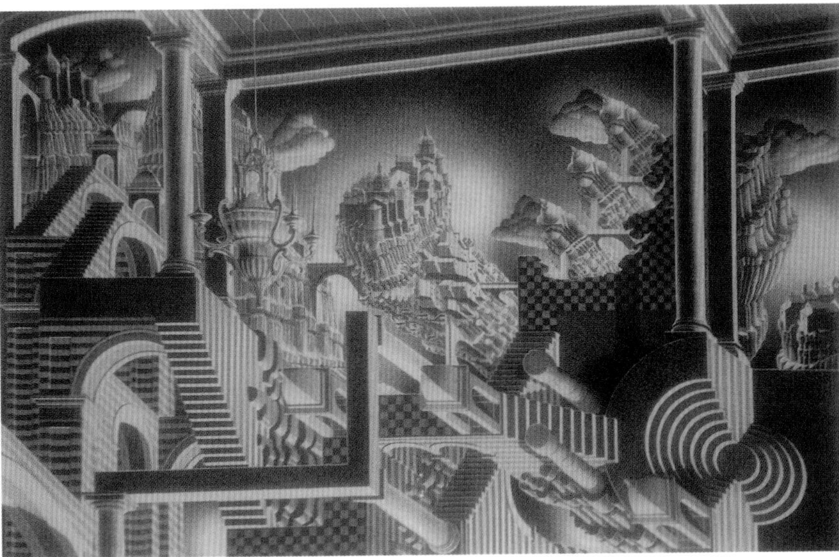

3.6. *Abovescape*, Doug Cooper, 1988. Carbon pencil on paper, 56 × 80 inches. Private collection. Photo by David Aschkenas.

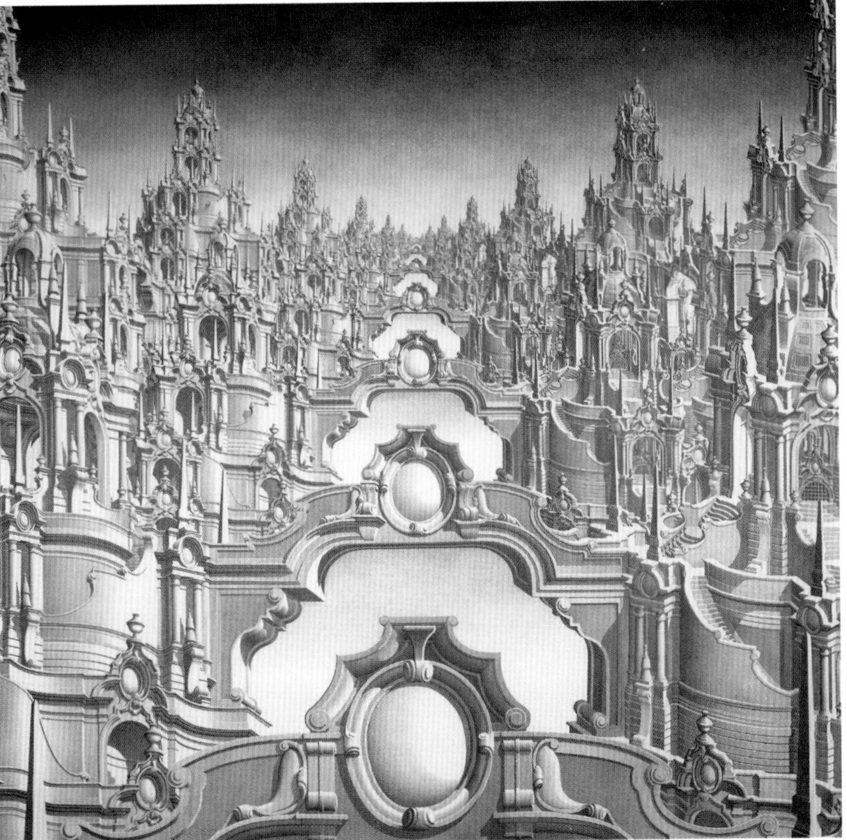

3.5. *The Approach*, Doug Cooper, 1979. Carbon pencil on paper, 96 × 96 inches. Collection of the artist.

Suspicions about Perspective

Distrust of perspective dates back to a passage in Plato's *Republic* on the topic of appearances. Greek artisans associated with the theater had developed considerable skill in perspective and pictorial illusion in general. The scene painter Agatharchos has been credited with inventing perspective during the fifth century BC, though he was most likely only one of many artisans who developed perspective for the theater. During this period, painting progressed from a more conceptual portrayal of the human form—figures with little or no use of modeling in light and foreshortening of limbs—to a more lifelike portrayal. The story was told that Zeuxis had painted grapes of such realistic appearance that even the birds tried to peck at them. This focus on creating appearances was anathema to Plato.

Plato considered working with concepts to be the highest form of thought, and, to the extent that they depended upon the senses, he distrusted other activities and illusionist painting most of all. Even the furniture maker, Plato allowed, at least needs to work with the *idea* of a chair in creating one instance. For him the work of the illusionist painters was yet one more step removed: amounting to an image of an image of an idea. Plato even called them deceivers of children!

Back in chapter 1, where we looked at Bloomer's assignment on insides and outsides, I noted his suspicions about perspective. I suggested that their source might have been his background as a sculptor, and I attributed them principally to differences between the visual activities involved—to the fact, that is, that sculptors see their work in three dimensions, where people drawing perspectives represent their subjects in two. But I think it goes deeper than that and can be understood in parallel to Plato's distinction between the furniture maker and the illusionist painters of ancient Greece—so long as we note the difference between making and depicting. Sculptors make things; painters make pictures of things.

On the strength of this, what if we were to take Plato's (and Bloomer's) critique of perspective as reason to consider drawing as an activity more like sculpting: more like the process of actually making something real rather than representing the appearance of a thing? The idea would be to upgrade drawing, so to speak, in Plato's estimation. If considered in this way, what might drawing become?

The cubists' effort to portray objects simultaneously from multiple viewpoints certainly did challenge perspective. Their effort to reconcile what is seen from one angle with what is seen from another is evident in their teacups with upturned tops and the like. But to me cubist imagery still presents more of a picture of a thing than a sense of the real thing itself. Here, we should remind ourselves: our search is for drawings that reflect something *real* about their subjects. Moreover, whatever their subjects, our drawings should be authentically *present* in themselves—more like things and less like pictures.

Drawing, Making, and Kimon Nicolaïdes

At this point, the work of teacher and author Kimon Nicolaïdes (1891–1938)—*The Natural Way to Draw* (1941)—becomes helpful. His pedagogy was directed squarely at the physical facts of subjects and drawings alike, and it offers an approach to drawing that is very nearly sculptural. Nicolaïdes taught drawing for twenty years at the Art Students League in New York during the 1920s and 1930s, a time of great experimentation in education generally. The ideas of Maria Montessori, Rudolf Steiner, and John Dewey were dominating educational reform at the time. One idea they all shared was a focus on learning by doing, and, for Nicolaïdes in teaching drawing, that meant a focus on the physical act itself: the hand in motion making a drawing. As a consequence, there is a compelling physicality to Nicolaïdes's pedagogy, which makes the act of drawing somewhat akin to the process of creating a two-dimensional sculptural relief. Principally, we find this characteristic in two of his exercises: cross contour and modeling. As with all of Nicolaïdes's exercises, these foster a haptic connection with subjects, one arising as much in touch and movement as in vision.

Cross contour focuses on a subject's surfaces, edges, and volume (fig. 3.7, left). We imagine we're touching these and use line to trace the path our eye might follow if it were to move like a fifth limb along and across them. Modeling addresses these attributes as well, but more as a sculptor might (fig. 3.7, right). First we build the subject's mass; then we shape it: depressing and releasing surfaces as we might if manipulating clay. Variation of the weight of the marks is a constant. Cross contour contributes more to a mark's expressive spatial movement, modeling more to its expression of mass.

So here we have a way of drawing that we can consider in the same vein

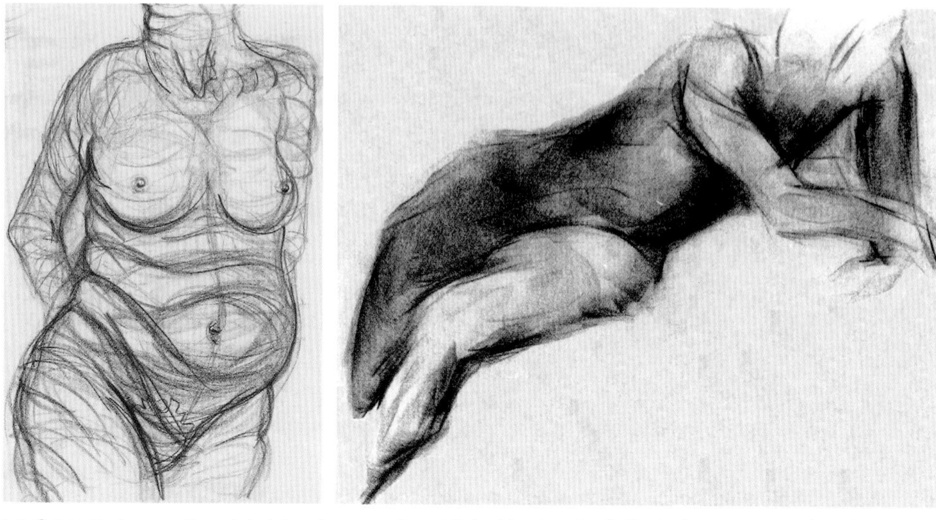

3.7. Cross contour and modeled drawing exercises. Misha Varshavsky (*left*), Andreas Petrusak (*right*).

as sculpting—something is being made. With no particular interest in creating the illusion of the third dimension, Nicolaïdes's approach is directed at the real facts of a subject: is it heavy or light, thick or thin, etc.? A drawing, in his eyes, is not just a picture of something external to itself; it is a thing in its own right. Plato might not have fully approved—after all, he didn't really approve of the furniture maker either—but even he would have to admit, I believe, that Nicolaïdes's pedagogy brought drawing somewhat back from the abyss into which he, Plato, had consigned all illusionists.

Nicolaïdes and Me: Taking My Own Medicine

Nicolaïdes's unique approach to drawing led me to adopt it for my own teaching. I teach drawing to architecture students at Carnegie Mellon University in Pittsburgh, and I've adapted his figure drawing exercises for architectonic exercises for more than thirty years now (fig. 3.8). I find that their gritty physicality makes them ideal for teaching students who in the end must be responsible for making real, physical things in the world—not just pictures of them.

Yet strangely, until my show at the AIA headquarters in Washington, DC, I had not incorporated any measure of Nicolaïdes's approach into my own work. But as I packed up the show, my displeasure with my own work led me to change course. The first thing I did was to start drawing from life again.

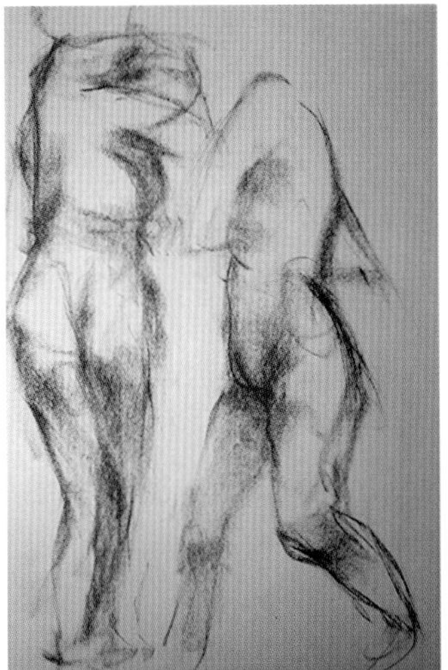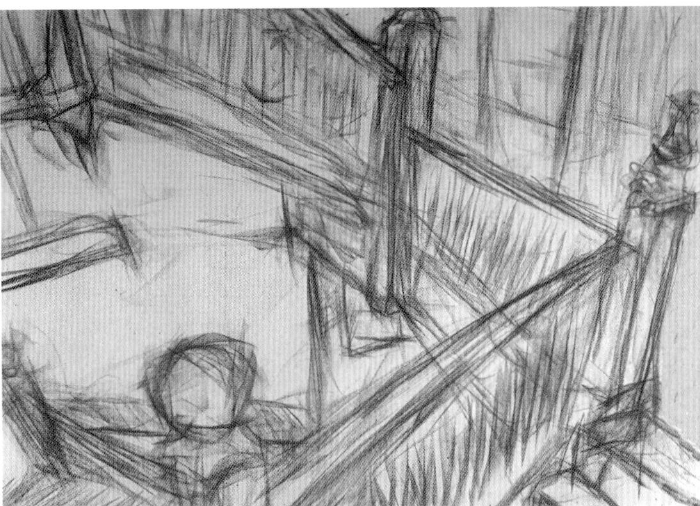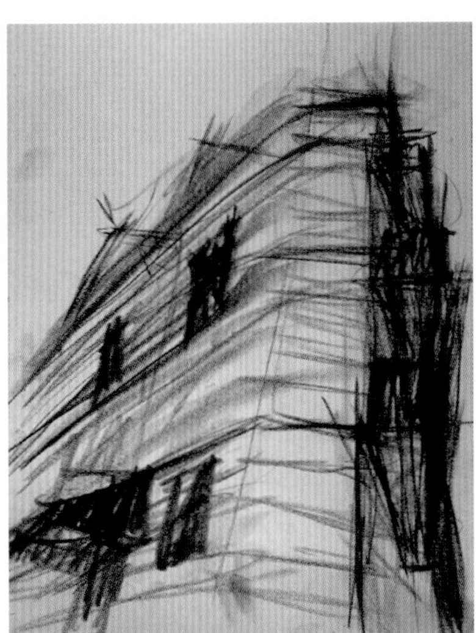

3.8. From figure drawings to architectural studies.
Misha Varshavsky (*left*), Brian Leet (*middle*), Vincent Chew (*right*).

I arranged to take a sketching trip to Bryce Canyon in southern Utah, where I camped out for a week and drew rock formations. I'd been there twice before on family trips, and I knew the landscape well from the numerous hikes we'd taken far down into the valley. But with the focus on family, I'd not found any time to draw the canyon. It's a bizarre setting, a walk-through Rorschach test of eroded forms.

Nicolaïdes's sculptural understanding of drawing was obviously well suited to the eroded shapes of the canyon's sedimentary rock formations. It took a while, but in Bryce, I started using contour lines to describe the downward rush of its slopes. I remember all the while thinking of the path the water once followed in eroding the slopes, and over the week, in thoughts such as that, drawing came to life for me again (fig. 3.9).

I flew back home to Pittsburgh elated with what I had accomplished during my trip and fully expecting to do a series of drawings about Bryce Canyon. But then something unexpected happened. No sooner was I off the plane than I saw Pittsburgh with renewed eyes. The city I had ignored for so many years—really since 1965—seemed suddenly alive. The trigger for this sudden reappearance of my muse was surely Bryce Canyon, but it came fully to life as I applied Nicolaïdes's techniques to the twisting steep slopes and gritty postindustrial landscape of Pittsburgh.

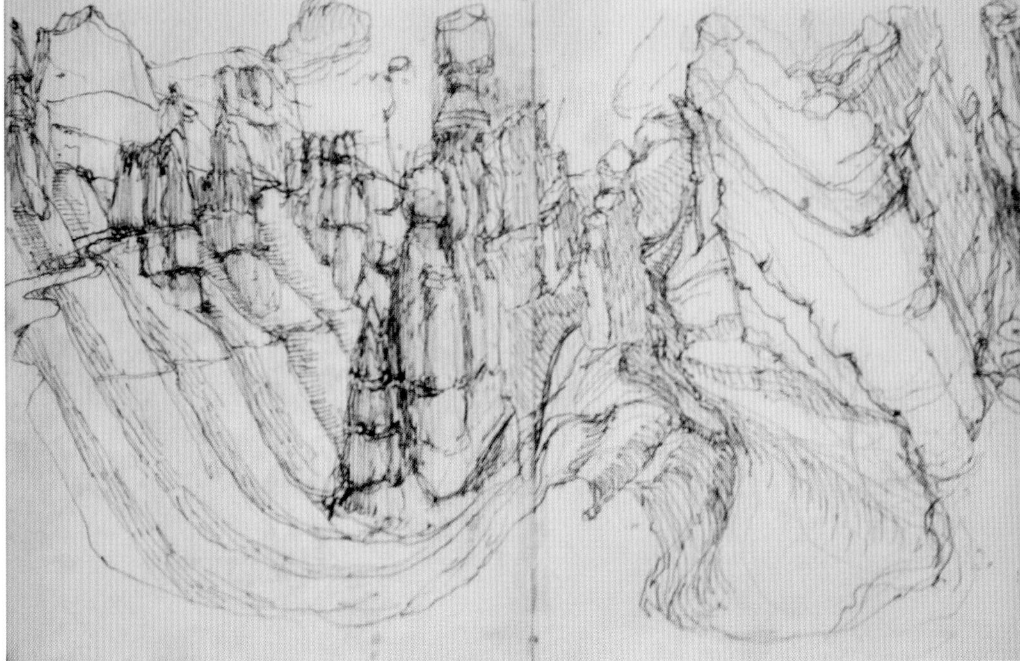

3.9. *Bryce Canyon Sketch*, Doug Cooper, 1990. Felt-tip pen on paper, 10 × 14 inches. Collection of the artist.

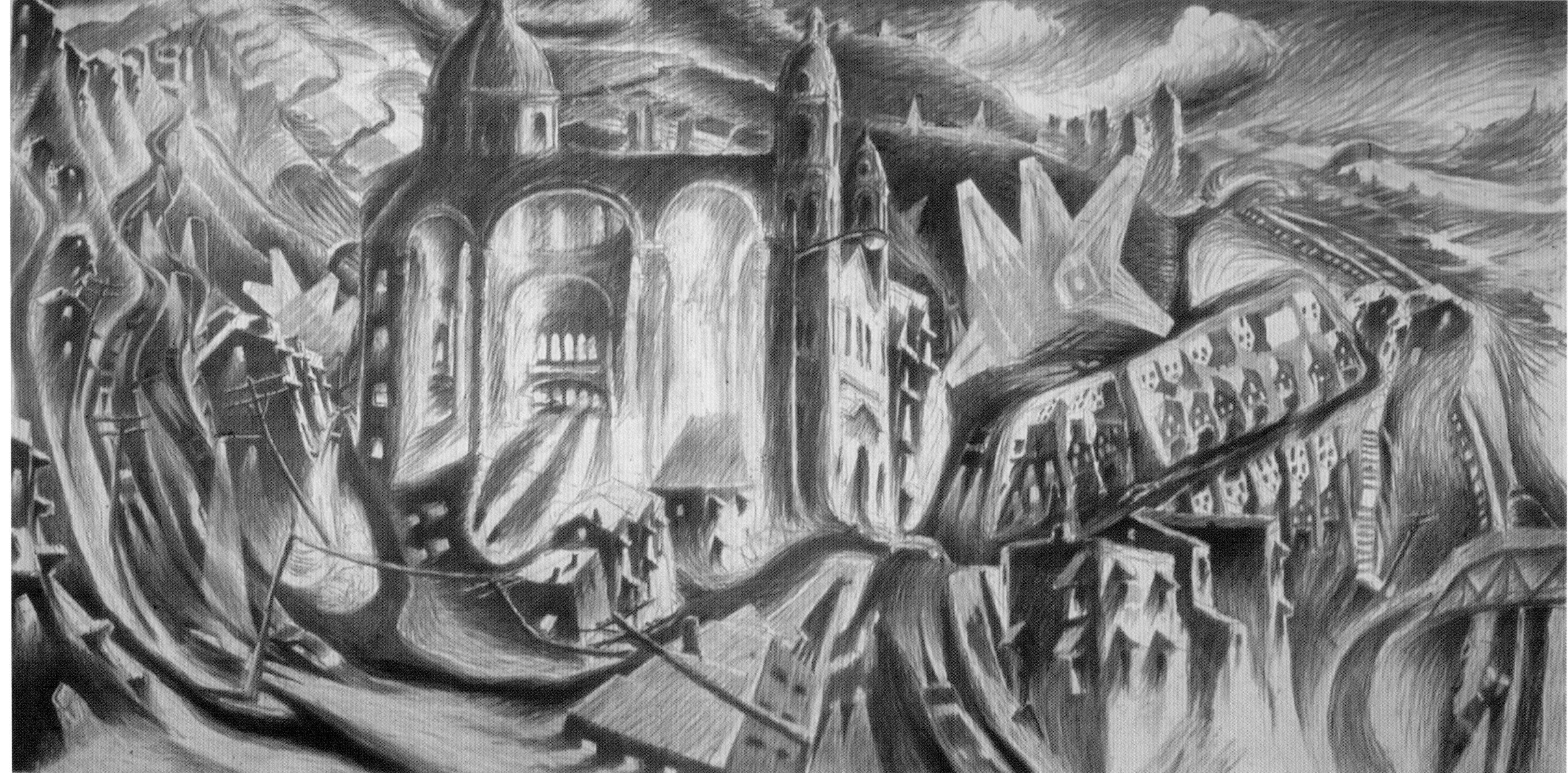

3.10. *Polish Hill*, Doug Cooper, 1999. Charcoal on paper, 56 × 112 inches. Carnegie Museum of Art, Pittsburgh. Photo by David Aschkenas.

I felt that landscape as I never had before. Sites I had not noticed now interested me. Drawings came swiftly throughout the summer of 1989, one after another. In their exaggerated registration of the steepness of Pittsburgh, these works took on an expressionist feel (figs. 3.10, 3.11, 3.12). I felt the movement of light and surface with new intensity. In a real sense, it was my hand moving on the surface of the land, more than any identifiable intention, that drove my work.

One drawing took on the sense of moving through the landscape because of my use of photography as a way of documenting my subject. I'd always loved the experience of descending P. J. McArdle Roadway from Liberty Bridge down across a steel truss over an old line of the Pennsylvania Railroad, and past Saint John the Baptist Church. What had drawn me to this roadway was its destination, the South Side high school football field below—that and the views along the way of the church seen through the steel members of the bridge truss. I took photos of both conditions, and laid them out as an assembled collage of photos—in the manner of works I'd seen by David Hockney (fig. 3.13). Then I recreated the assemblage of views as a tonal drawing (fig. 3.14).

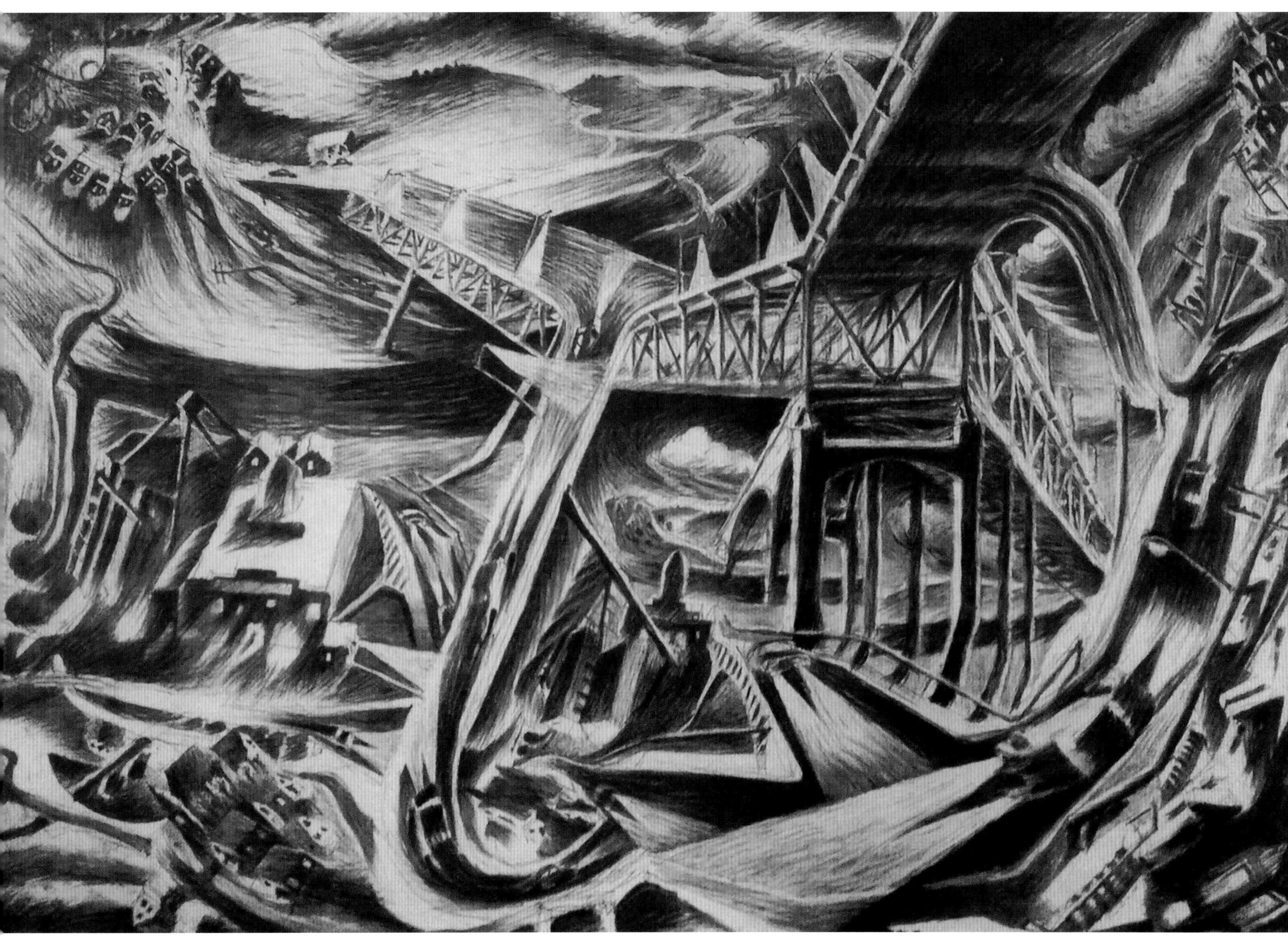

3.11. *Under Rankin Bridge*, Doug Cooper, 1989. Charcoal on paper, 56 × 80 inches. Collection of the artist. Photo by David Aschkenas.

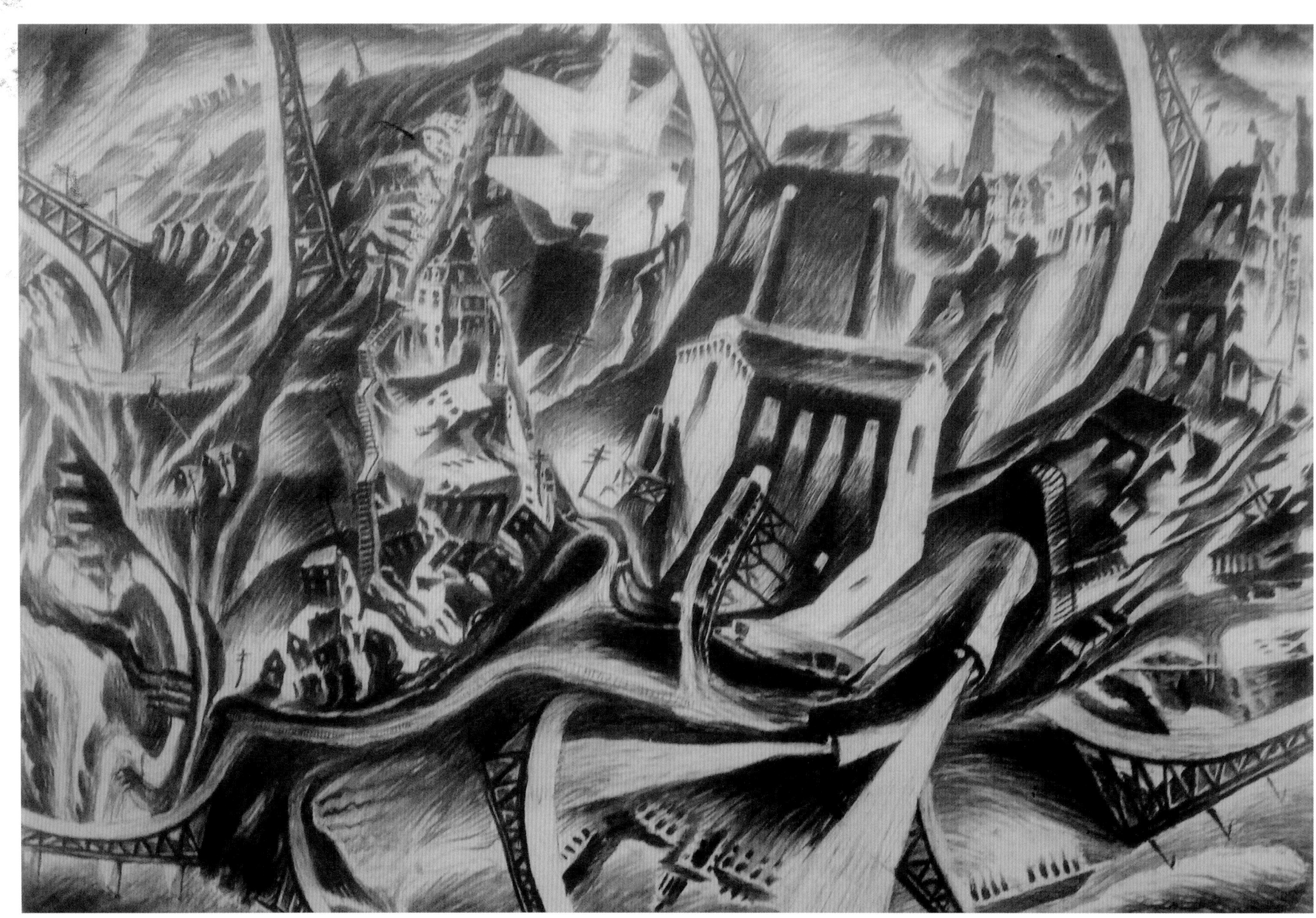

3.12. *Panther Hollow*, Doug Cooper, 1989. Charcoal on paper, 56 × 80 inches. Collection of Laraine and Ulrich Flemming. Photo by David Aschkenas.

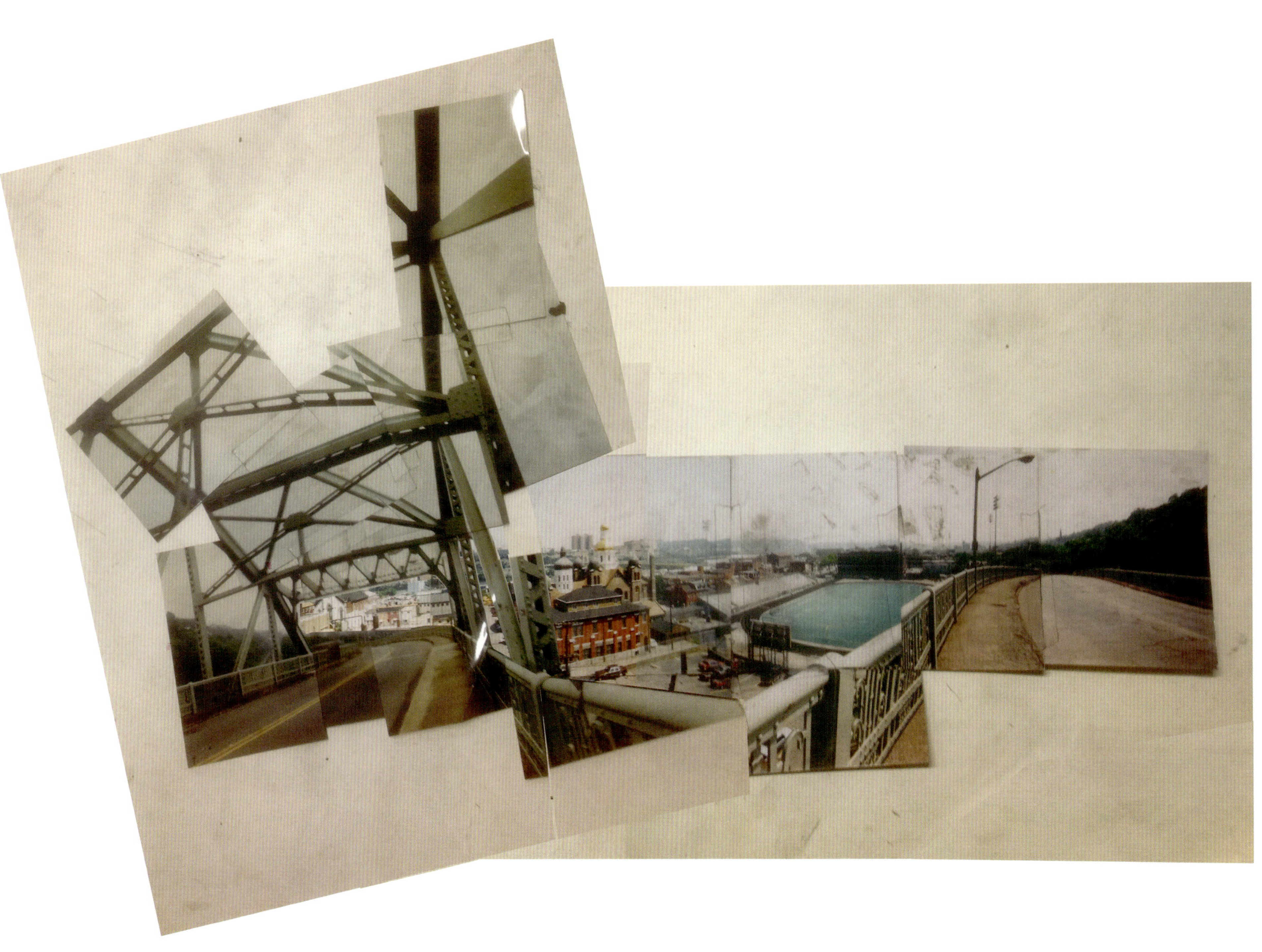

3.13 (*above*). Photo collage for *McArdle Roadway*, Doug Cooper, 1989. Collection of the artist.

3.14 (*following spread*). *McArdle Roadway*, Doug Cooper, 1999. Charcoal on paper, 56 × 112 inches. Senator John Heinz History Center, Pittsburgh. Photo by David Aschkenas.

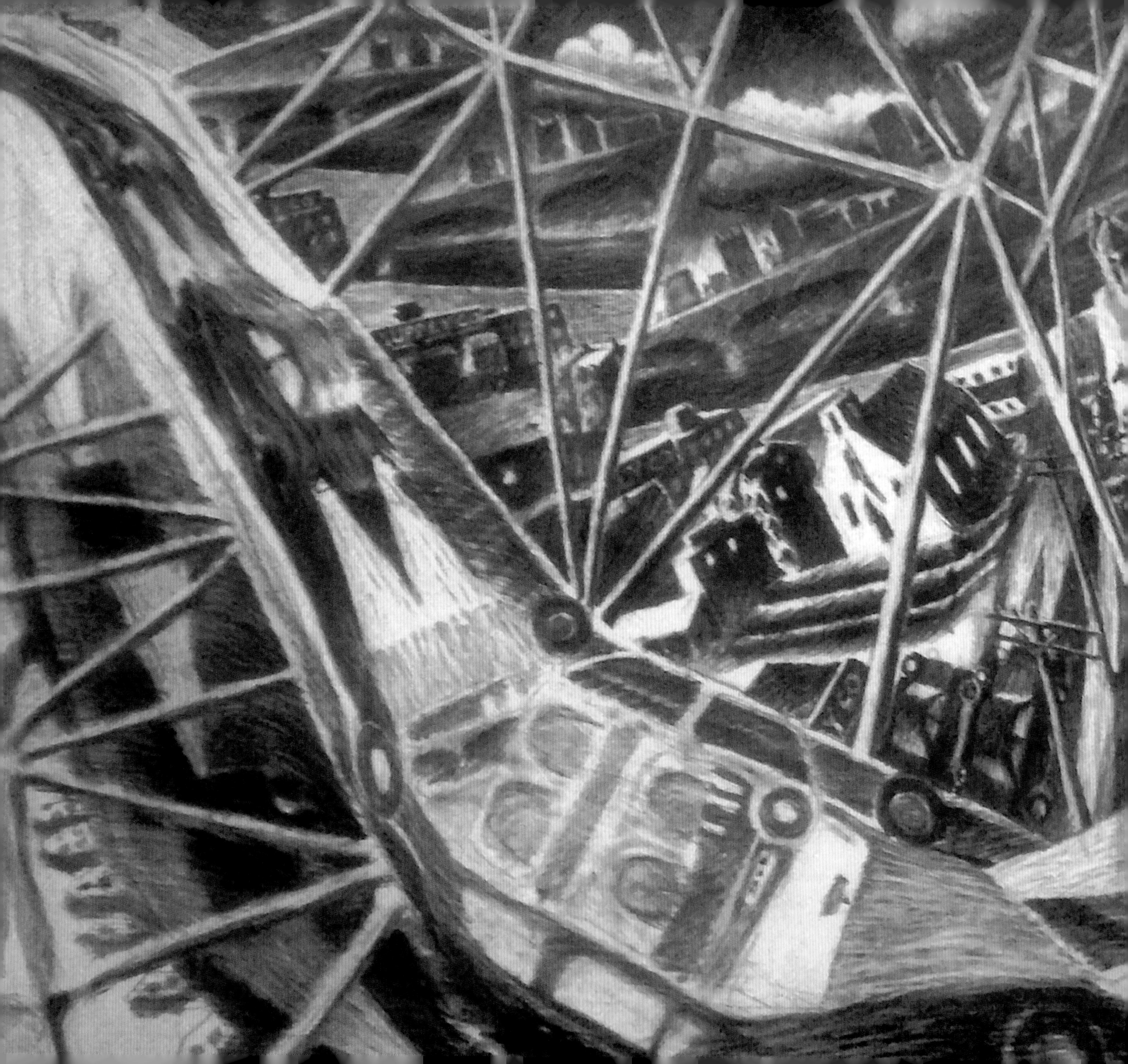

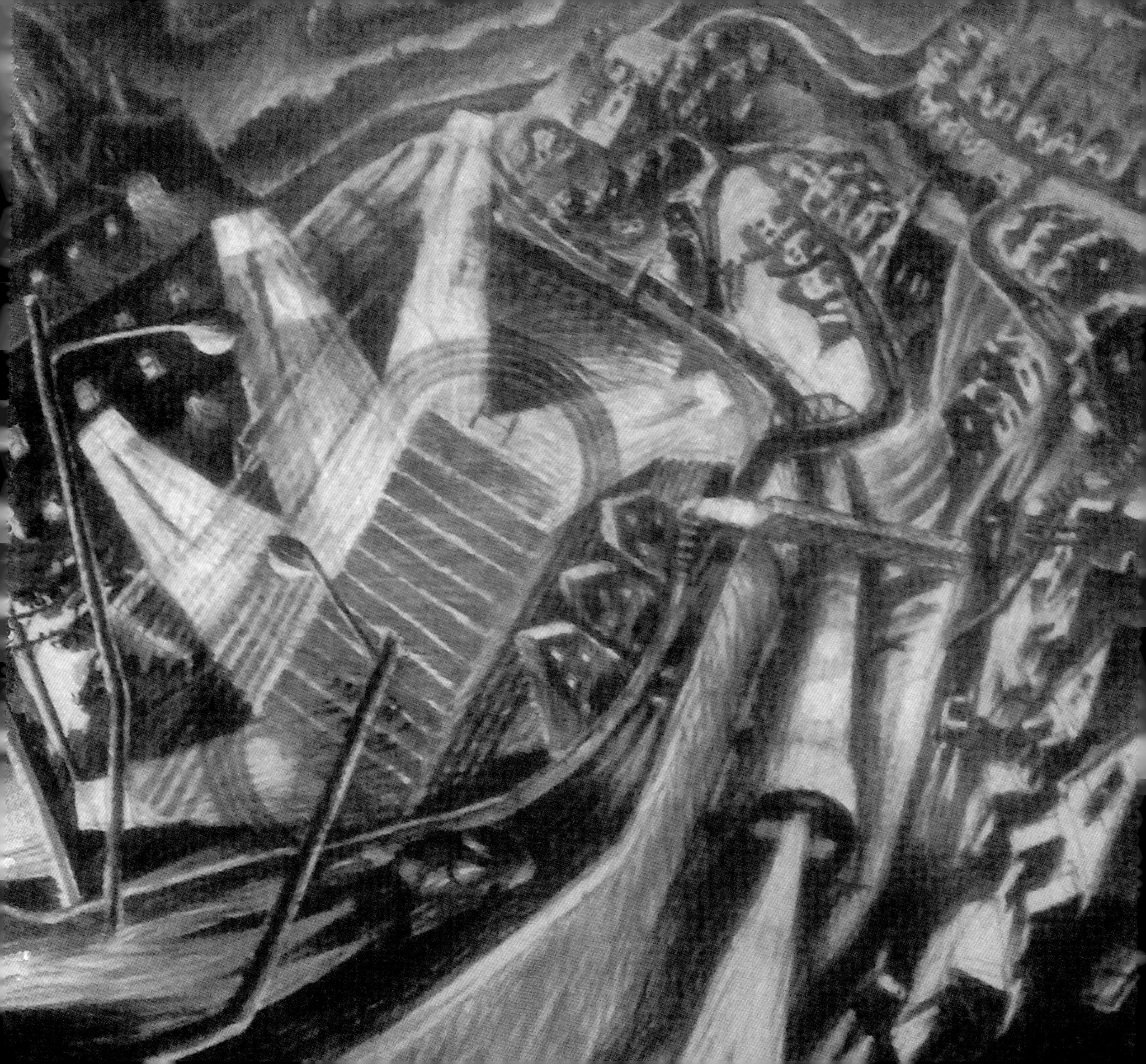

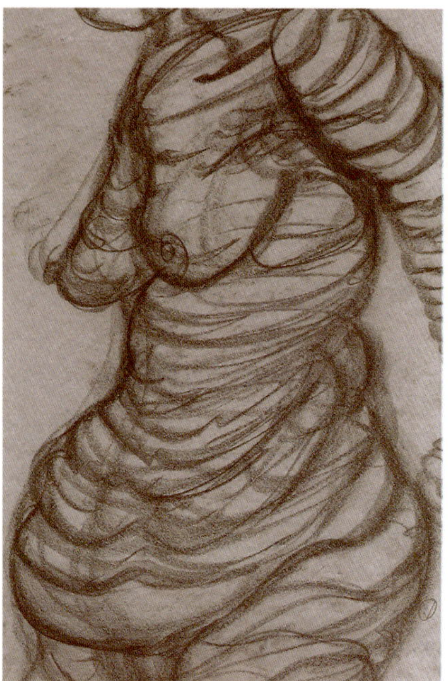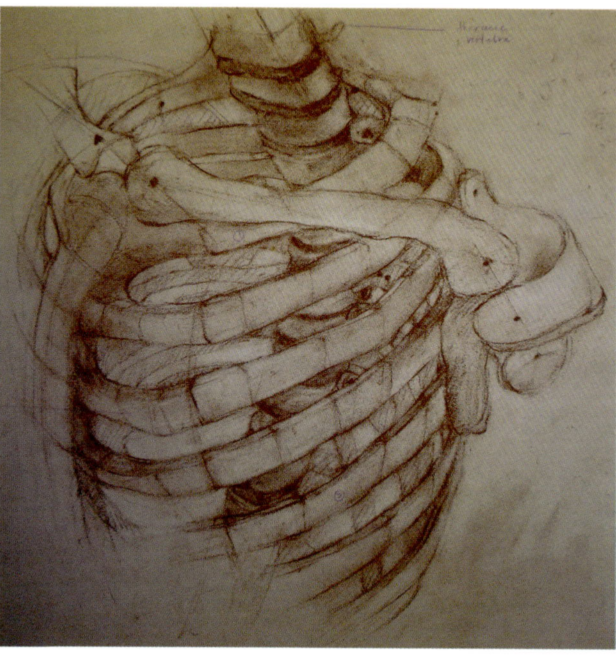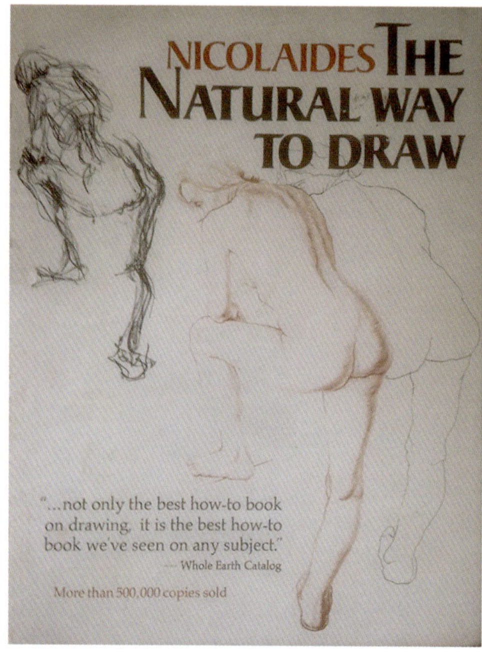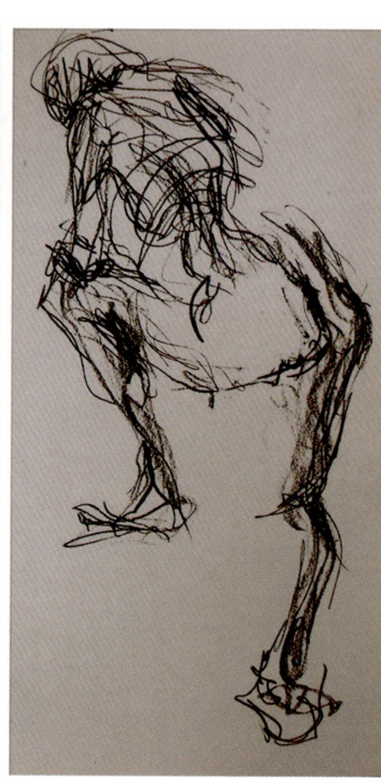

3.15. Full cross contour to volume, Allison Lukasky (*left*); drawing of the thorax, Ji Hee Hwang (*right*).

3.16. Cover image and detail from *The Natural Way to Draw*, by Kimon Nicolaïdes (Boston: Houghton Mifflin Harcourt, 1961). Used by permission of Houghton Mifflin Harcourt Publishing Company. All rights reserved.

Nicolaïdes and Embodied Cognition

What does Nicolaïdes's pedagogy bring to drawing that made it so transformative for me at this point in my career? I've talked about the objective realness with which he asks us to consider any subject we're drawing. But we should also note the transformation of our state of mind (and body) regarding what we're drawing when we draw it. When he introduces the exercise he calls "cross contour," for example, he does not ask that we draw only the visible side; he asks that we draw the back side as well (fig. 3.15). He asks that our marks literally surround any form we're drawing in a three-dimensional embrace. He asks that we *know* form, not just or even primarily with our eyes, but with our hands and arms too. There is, in other words, a connection between mind and body, between *knowing* and *seeing*, that his pedagogy fosters. This connection is best understood by taking an in-depth look at the exercise he called *gesture*.

Gesture was the central exercise of Nicolaïdes's teaching, and it has long been featured on the cover of his book (fig. 3.16). Although it builds on the techniques of contour and modeled drawing I already described, its purpose is different. With a gesture drawing, we seek the *essence* of the model's pose—the direction and resolution of forces in an athletic stance, for example. With his gestural exercise, Nicolaïdes took expressiveness to a new level. He instructs us to use our mark making to empathize with our subjects. If we are drawing a boxer throwing a jab, he wants us to feel the force and sting of that fighter's punch while we draw.

Empathy is discussed at length in Bloomer's *Body, Memory and Architecture*, a book he wrote well after I was in his class. There he reports the word's origination in German: *Einfühlung*. It was first used by the philosopher Robert Vischer, and literally, it means "feeling into." So, in essence, Nicolaïdes is asking us to *live within* or to *inhabit* what we might draw. Through the activity of drawing, he was seeking no less than a foundational connection between the activity of the mind and the experience of the body in understanding and depicting objects in space. He wanted drawing to be a vehicle for making something not just appear to be present, but to truly *be* present.

To my knowledge, the relationship of Nicolaïdes's pedagogy to current

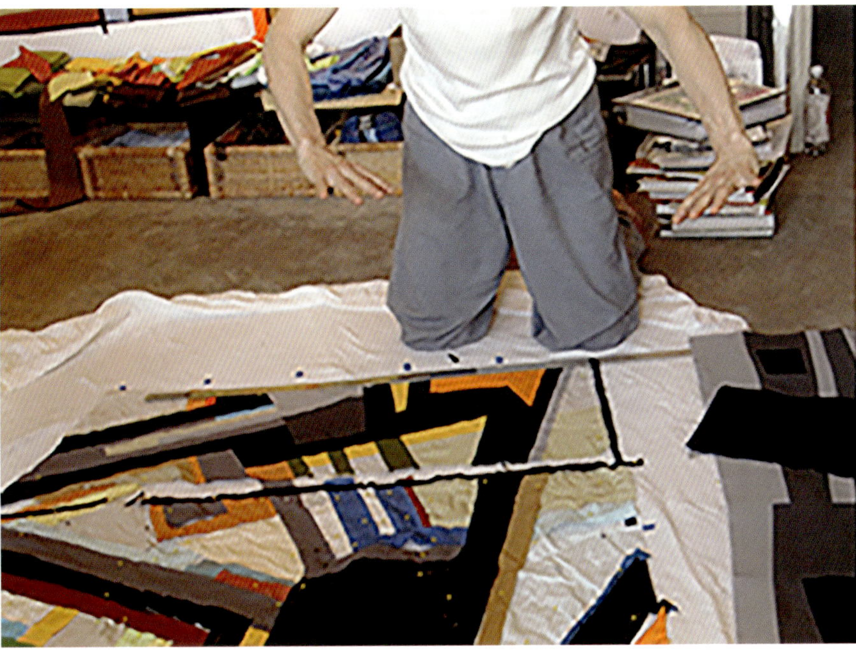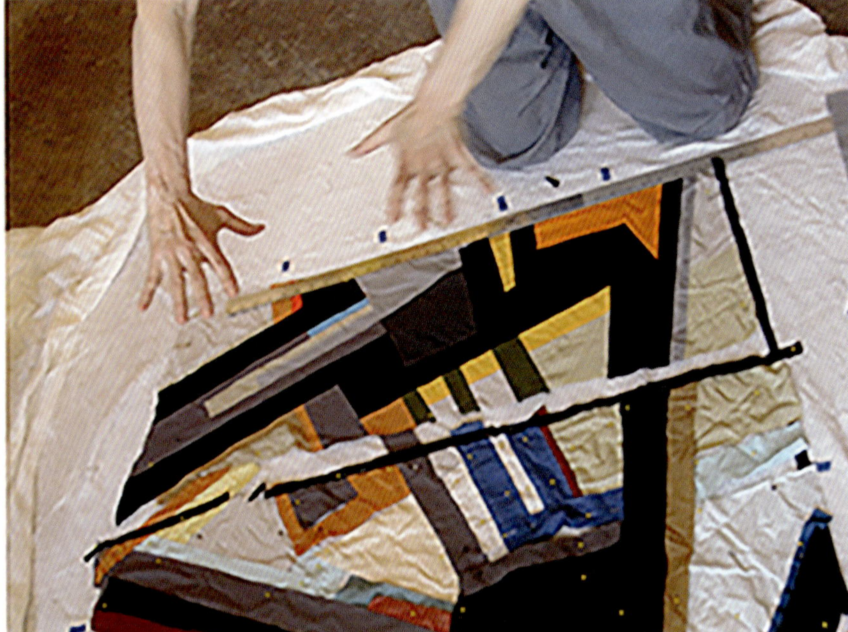

3.17. Suddenly, Stefani began moving her hands in mimicry of the shapes in the quilt.

thinking within a recent direction in cognitive psychology, called embodied cognition, has never been examined. But there is reason to consider it here because both seem to be pointing at the same foundational insight into spatial visualization. As a theory, embodied cognition recognizes no fundamental division between body and mind, considering each an extension of the other. Further, many of its researchers have pointed to a connection between hand gestures and spatial thinking. Given that Nicolaïdes placed such emphasis on gesture in drawing, this parallel may shed light on our effort to understand how *seeing* and *knowing* might relate through drawing.

Multiple researchers in embodied cognition have offered compelling evidence that the hand gestures we routinely use in describing spatial subjects—giving directions to a stranger in a city, for example—also assist our spatial visualization of these subjects. Further, they have found that the more complex the subjects are, the more we tend to gesture about them. Their research is relevant for us here because it points to a connection between drawing and conceptual thinking through the agency of the hand.

I have two examples from my own observation of what they were referring to in their research. Both appeared to use hand gestures to assist spatial thought. In the first, my wife Stefani and I were looking at a quilt she was working on. She had laid it out on the floor so we could discuss potential reorientations of some of its shapes. Suddenly, in the moment she began speaking about those options, her hands and fingers began to move in mimicry of those potential new placements (fig. 3.17). In the second, my daughter Sarah (then six) was eating a breakfast of pancakes and maple syrup, and she was talking about a rollercoaster. We were rushing to get her to the school bus on time, so, while she was describing the coaster (and eating), I was under the table tying her shoes. Over the preceding weeks, she had been making drawings of rollercoasters one after the other. For her it was a kind of design exercise; she knew my discomfort with riding rollercoasters and had been using these drawings to discover one we might ride together. Once, I happened to look up from beneath the table, and I could see from the movement of her elbow that she was drawing the rollercoaster in the maple syrup with her fork while she talked about it.

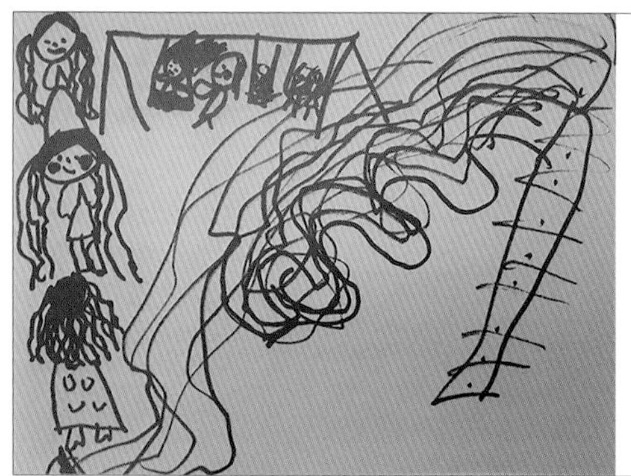

3.18. Sarah's slide and text, ca. 1980.

The abruptness with which Stefani began moving her hands in the moment she started talking about alternative compositions suggests an integral connection between the movement of her hands and her spatial thinking. And in Sarah's case, drawing the rollercoaster in maple syrup was for her own spatial thinking, not mine. After all, I was under the table and could not have seen her hand move. So, what do gestures do for the one who gestures? The conclusion of researchers is that gestures help our thinking about spatial subjects—Stefani's about alternative designs and Sarah's about imagined rollercoasters—by sustaining them in working memory. They refresh it.

Creating and Enacting

What were the essential properties that Nicolaïdes brought to my drawing when I resumed drawing Pittsburgh during summer 1989 after my trip to Bryce Canyon? Part of it was surely tied to the underlying sculptural character of the mark making involved in his approach. And, by looking at his pedagogy from the perspective of embodied cognition, we've seen that Nicolaïdes did indeed find a way to tap into deep connections between conceptual thought and sensory experience. But I've also said that his exercises helped bring *life* back into my drawing, and I want to be more specific about what I mean by that.

In making a drawing, it seems to me there are two capacities that a freely gesturing hand brings to spatial thought: (1) Through its ability to mimic shapes we have experienced before, it has a capacity to generate new ones; muscle memories of prior experiences are replayed and transformed. (2)

Through its ability to move through a drawing, it brings the opportunity to also experience what we've just shaped. That is, in a manner that relates back to the concept of empathy, it pairs creation and enactment: we make a spatial drawing and then we act within it—and vice versa.

Here's an example of what I mean. About the same time Sarah was drawing all those rollercoasters, I found the opportunity to watch and record her while she drew a playground slide (fig. 3.18). She started the drawing by making a curling sliding board. Then, with her marker, she climbed the ladder and repeatedly traveled up and down the slide. Her speech and her marks—note the repeated curling marks and dots on the ladder—establish the pairing of the two: creating and using. First she made the slide, and then she slid on it.

In empathizing with the subjects we draw, by being present in our subjects through the agency of our hands, we both bring them to life and relive our experience with them—both at once. As I think back, it was that character of presence—my hand rushing down the slopes of Pittsburgh and the fall of the land to its rivers—that brought the city back to life for me in 1989. And I would also note that this foundational understanding of drawing was independent of perspective. I could have used it or not used it. What mattered most in the end was that my hand also knew and felt what I was seeing. This was not-knowing in the sense that Plato might have meant it—concept versus percept. Here knowledge came from unifying haptic with visual perception.

Three-Dimensional Drawing

Muses come and muses go. That period of work, 1989–1993, remains for me that time in which I felt most completely in a zone. Like a batter in baseball on a hot streak, my hand felt guided. I only had to pick up a charcoal stick, and a strong drawing would magically come to me—or so it seemed at the time. What has remained from that Nicolaïdes-inspired phase of my work has been a sense of gesture and movement as the principal organizing element of my work—in both smaller works and murals in the public realm. Most are organized around some major path following a roadway or a bridge or a river valley from foreground into background (figs. 3.19, 3.20). But in recent years, the sense of the *realness* of the representation itself—Nicolaïdes's preference for a sculptural rather than an illusionist foundation for drawing—has found expression in other ways. And one of these has explored making the works themselves three-dimensional.

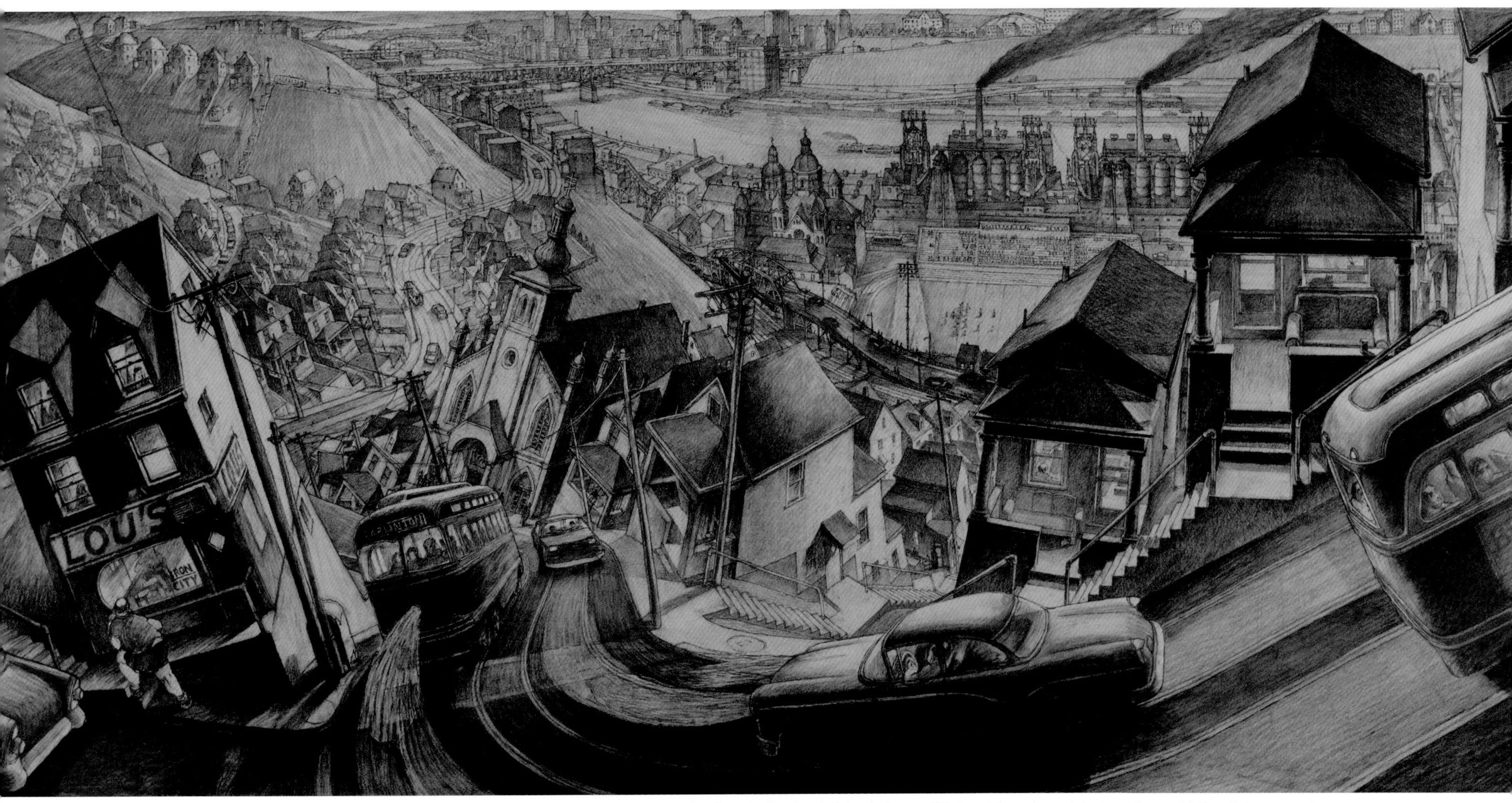

3.19. Scene from "Pinburgh," Doug Cooper, 2012. Charcoal on paper on board, 48 × 72 inches. Collection of Volker Hartkopf and Vivian Loftness. "Pinburgh" can be watched on Vimeo at https://vimeo.com/15749259.

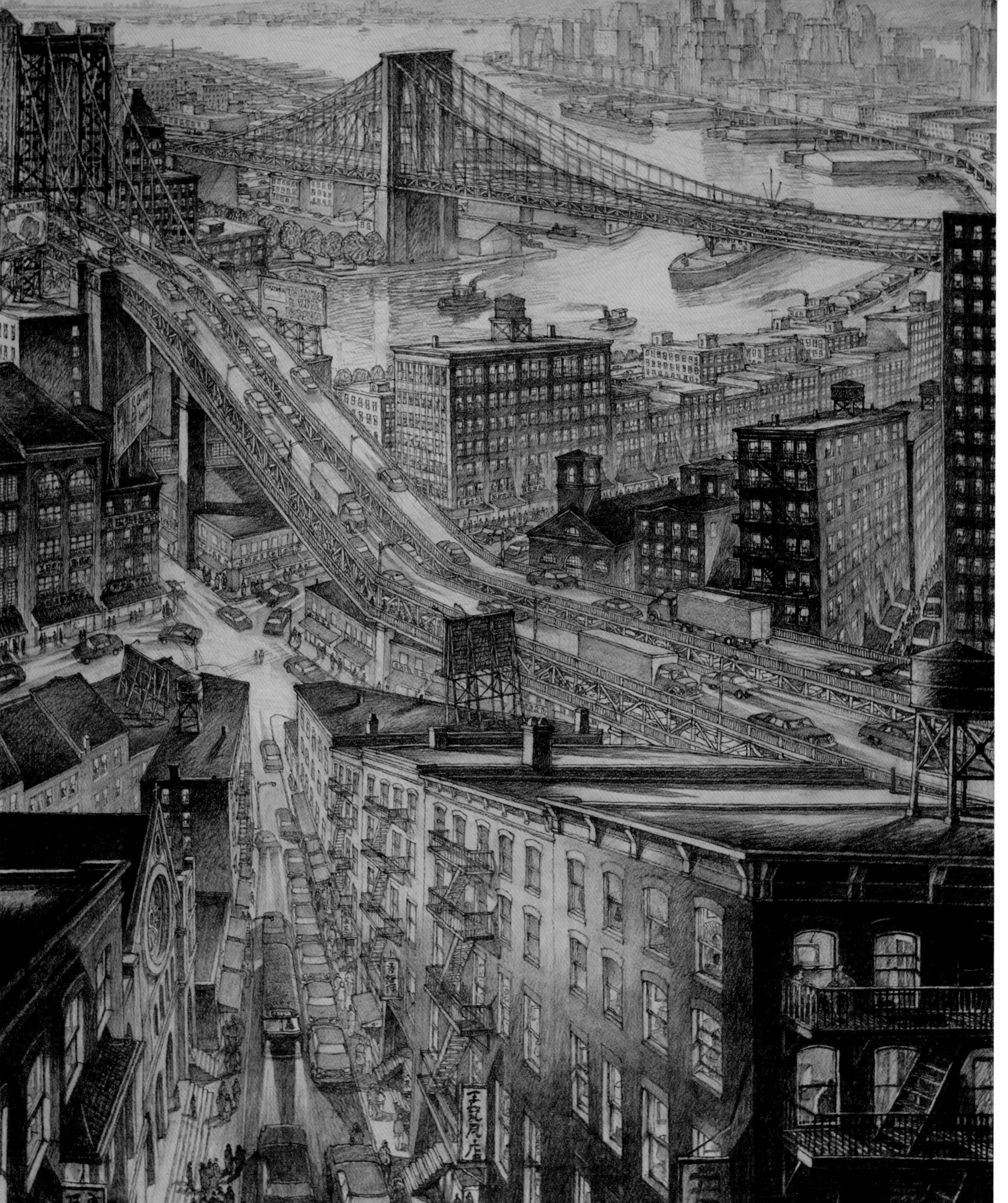

3.20. *Eldridge Street*, Doug Cooper, 2015. Charcoal on paper on board, 60 × 48 inches. Private collection.

The masterpiece for which the early Renaissance goldsmith and sculptor Lorenzo Ghiberti (1378–1455) is best known is the set of doors for the Baptistery of Florence, called the *Gates of Paradise* (fig. 3.21). A mere glance reveals the degree to which the third dimension has already been collapsed in each panel of this work. They represent scenes with great depth, yet they have collapsed that to a matter of a few inches.

Over the years of introducing Nicolaïdes's modeling exercise to my students, I have found it useful to compare what they are about to undertake to Ghiberti's low-relief sculptural work. I've found it a small step to transfer the students' understanding from the one to the other. I point out that they've only reduced the depth of their architectural subjects a bit further than Ghiberti—that their sense of depth is fundamentally the same as his. They press background elements into the background and release foreground elements forward; they establish edges by varying hand pressure, just as Ghiberti might have done in carving the originals from which his molds were cast centuries before (fig. 3.22).

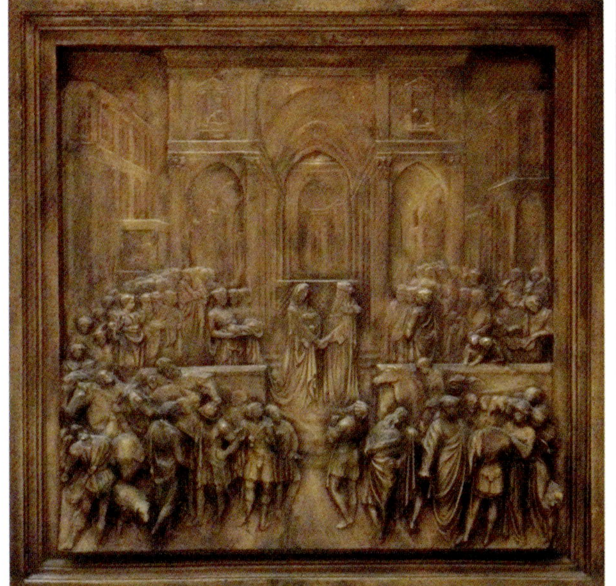
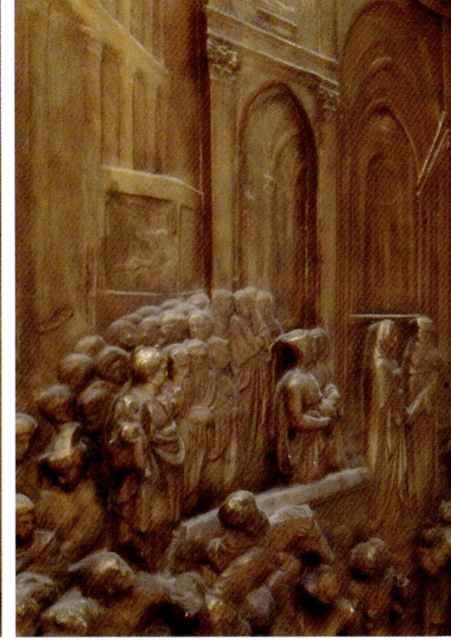

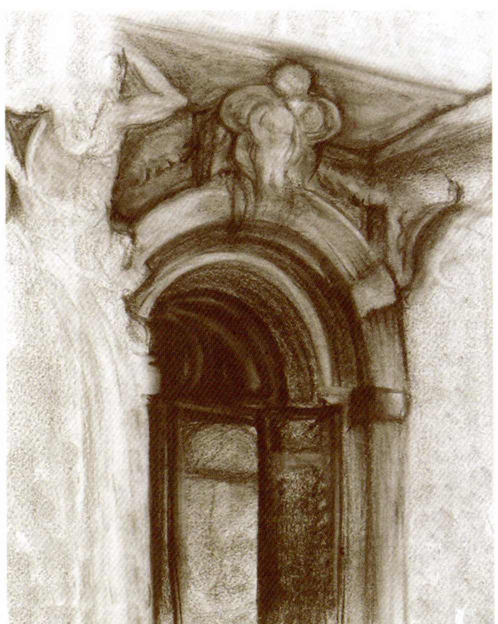
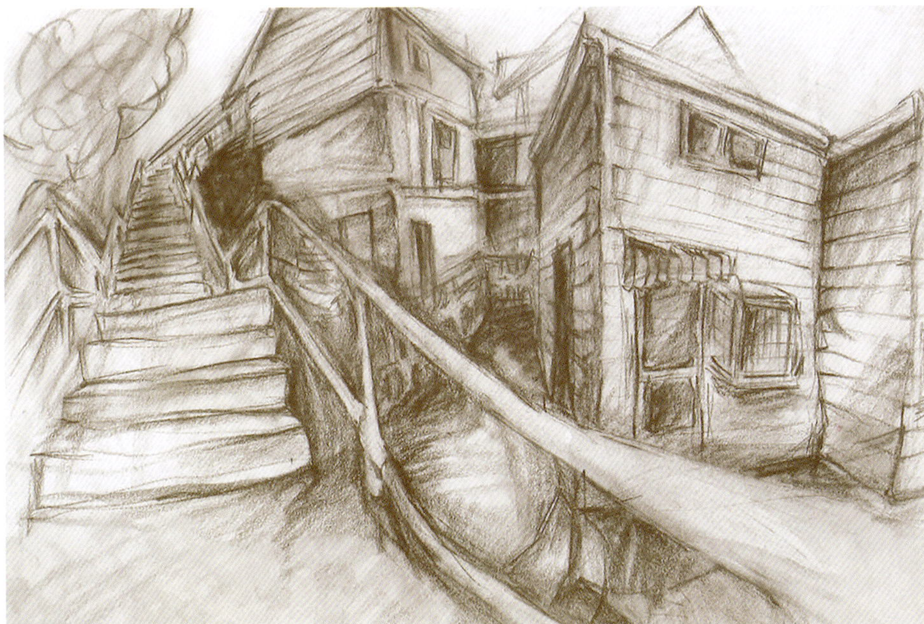
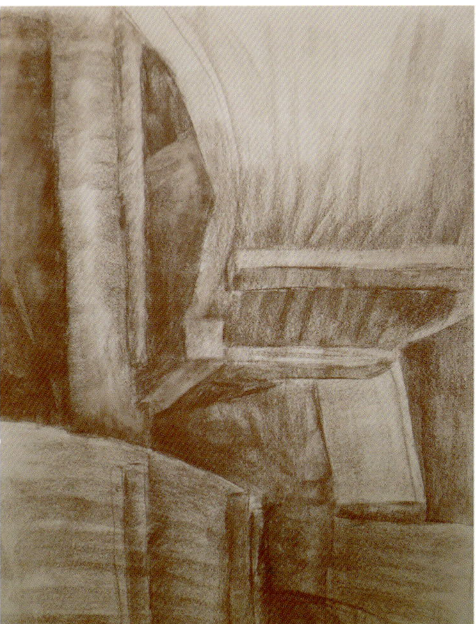

3.21 (*top right*). *Gates of Paradise*, Lorenzo Ghiberti. Eastern door of the Baptistery of Saint John in Florence, from a facsimile version. Carnegie Museum of Art, Pittsburgh. Photo by the author.

3.22 (*above*). Modeled drawings, Frederique Turnier (*left*), Yoosung Yang (*middle*), unknown student (*right*).

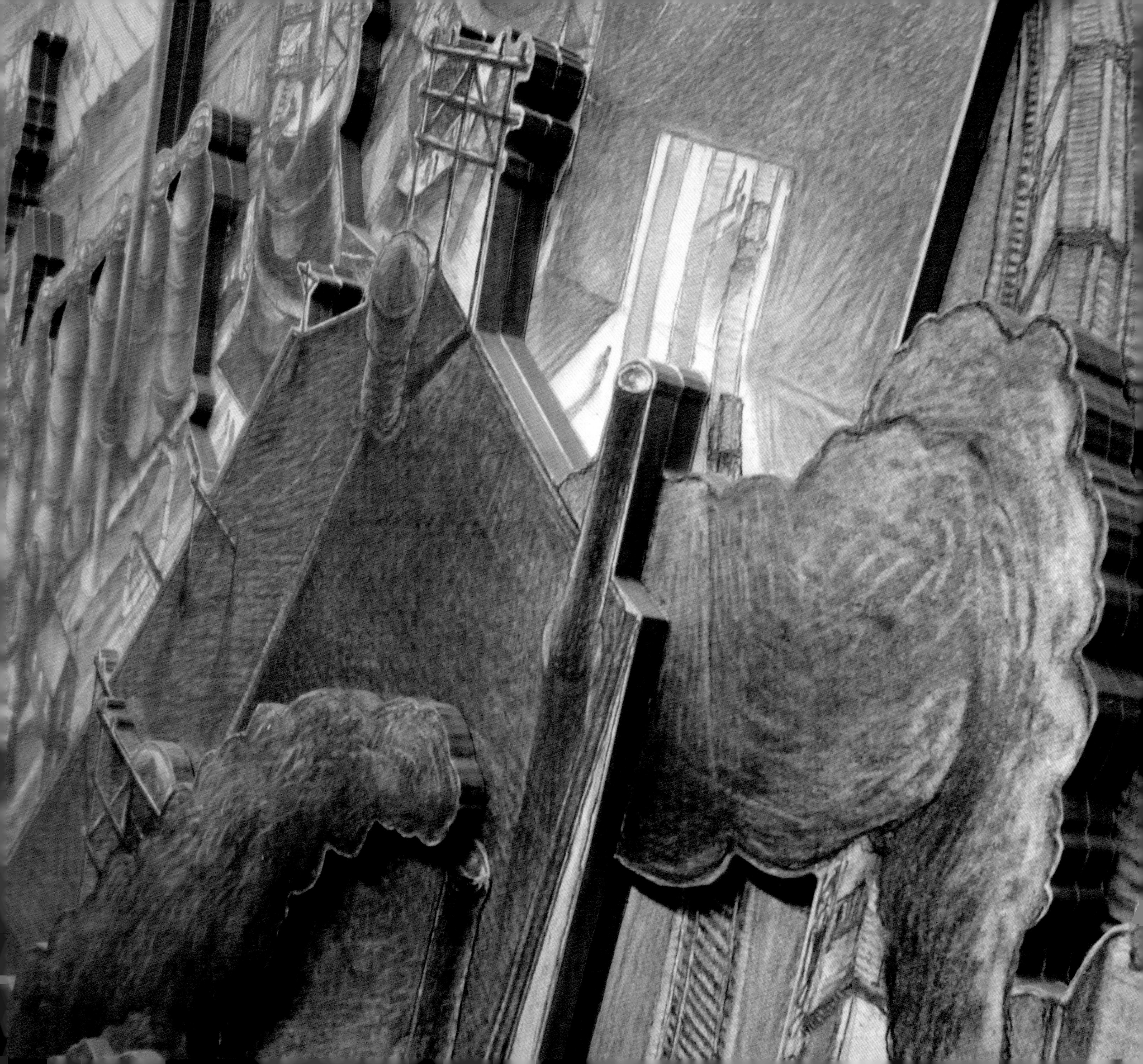

It was out of thoughts such as these that my interest in low-relief sculpture and its relationship to my own drawing first arose. After describing the equivalence of the two year after year for my students, eventually, I found myself applying the analogy in reverse: going from drawing to a kind of low-relief sculpture—layered drawings that had a true, if reduced, three-dimensionality (fig. 3.23).

Parallax, 2009–2011

Since arriving at my studio earlier that morning, I'd heard a general commotion outside and was vaguely aware that 3rd Street was being used as the setting for a film. This was not all that unusual an occurrence; with the concrete factory across the way, Liberty Bridge overhead, and the loading crane down by the tracks, this was a popular site for photo shoots needing a gritty industrial look in the background.

Then there was a knock on my studio door, and, when I opened the door, a man introduced himself as TJ, the film's director. He wanted to know if I knew how to reach the building's supervisor. I told him I did and invited him in while I searched for the contact information.

No sooner was he in the door than TJ started looking admiringly at the many drawings that were around my studio in various levels of completion for my next show. After I gave him the supervisor's contact information, we talked for a while about my work; it was obvious that he liked it, and he asked me lots of questions.

I also asked him about his film. It would be called *A New York Heartbeat*. It was being shot in Pittsburgh, but the story's location was Brooklyn in 1957—and that got me thinking. I'd gotten to know Brooklyn well when I lived near New York until I was fourteen. I'd crossed the Brooklyn Bridge many times, and I'd heard much about the city from my grandmother who'd lived there as a child. I'd known Ebbets Field in the 1950s in the days of the Jackie Robinson–era Dodgers. And, with all that as background, I was wondering how they could possibly make the time and setting of the film convincing for the viewer while filming it in a city that didn't look remotely like the Brooklyn I remembered.

And so I made an offer to TJ: what if I would create a drawing of Brooklyn circa 1957—one they could use for an animation for their opening credit sequence? I imagined the drawing as a multilayered image—like a collapsed

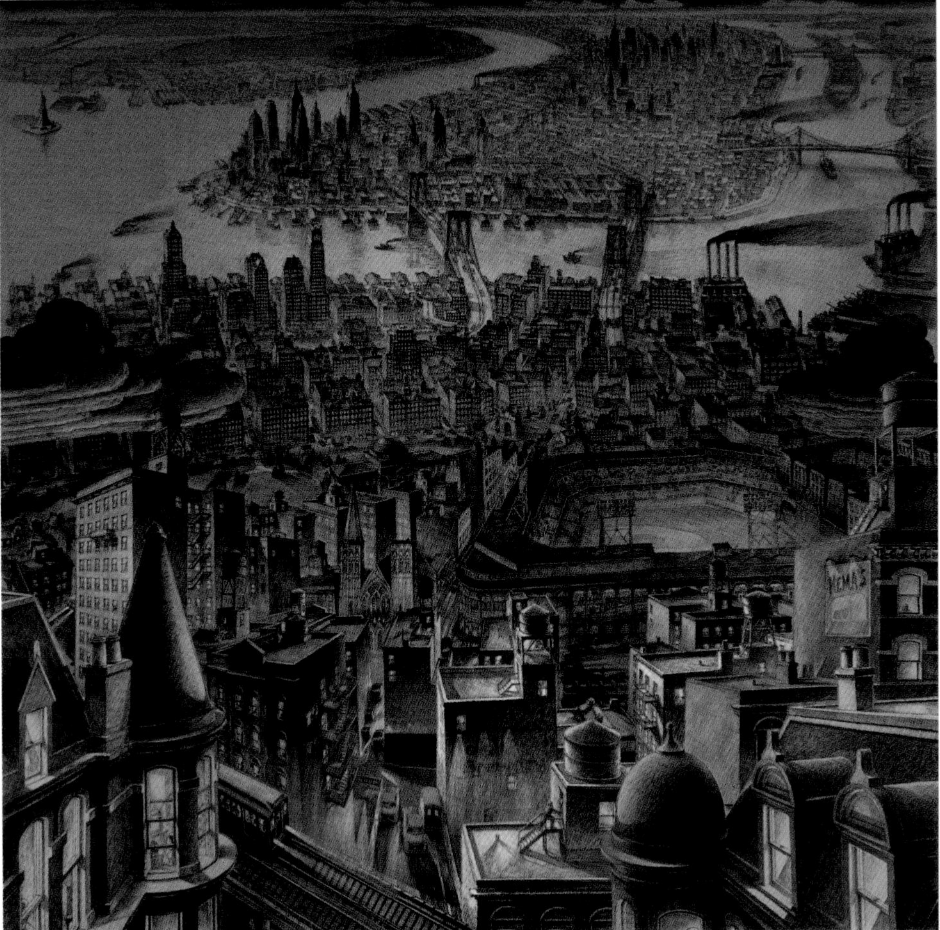

3.23 (*facing page*). Detail of *Mill from Above*, Doug Cooper, 2010. Charcoal on paper on board, 96 × 96 × 5 inches. Collection of Reed Smith, Pittsburgh. Detail from set for the video "Pinburgh," available at: https://vimeo.com/15749259.

3.24 (*above*). *Brooklyn 1957*, Doug Cooper, 2014. Proposed opening credits sequence for *A New York Heartbeat*. Relief assembly. Charcoal on paper on boards, 96 × 96 × 5 inches. Collection of David Tener. Sequence can be viewed at https://vimeo.com/56111201 (password: dougcooper).

model of a series of flats on a proscenium stage. I imagined an animation following the flight path of a descending airplane. The camera would drop gradually to street level accompanied by a good piece of period music—they chose "Shimmy, Shimmy, Ko-Ko-Bop"—buildings would part due to visual parallax, and viewers would feel they were entering a real Brooklyn (fig. 3.24).

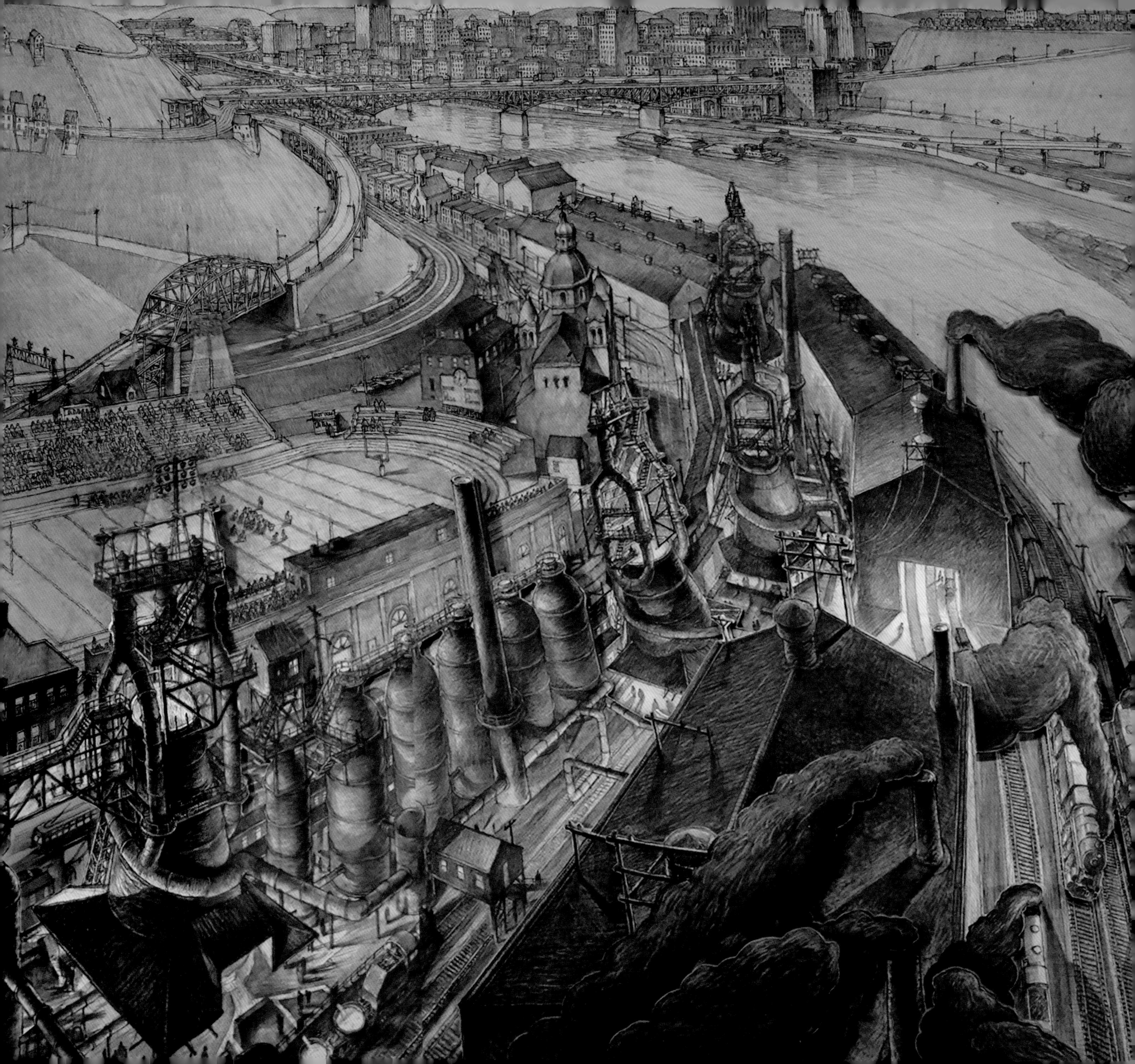

CHAPTER 4

THE PLACE OF PITTSBURGH

I still see the slag that was poured out on the land in fiery streams and flowing two thousand degrees hot down the sloping banks of the slag pits by the Mon River. People have told me that was the most dangerous job at the Jones & Laughlin Mill—dumping the slag. Even a thin coating of soft rain could super-heat and make the slag blow up in your face. That city of blast furnaces, open hearths, and a savaged landscape is still there with me in memory—most of all at night, when the danger was masked.

For years now I've drawn Pittsburgh with vine charcoal sticks. Charcoal is burned wood, a fire that used to be, and I use it for the shadows. I use the white of the paper for light. I darken the faces of buildings to heighten the drama of light's approach, letting the light slide along their sides as it does in film noir. I seek to combine night and day into one expression and to recreate the moment that still thrills me to remember: as the slag was poured tumbling down into the dark valleys below, as the Bessemers were turned, and as the light flared outward to bathe the houses and slopes in pulsing afterglow (fig. 4.1).

Why Pittsburgh Is the Way It Is

I spoke words like the ones above a number of years ago in introducing my Pittsburgh murals during a lecture, and I still feel the memory of the city as it once was. But how did Pittsburgh become what it is today, and more broadly, what is our sense of it as place—partly as a result of but also beyond its horrific industrial past?

There is a long line of American painters who have vividly captured the places they've experienced over their lifetimes. Grant Wood's (1891–1942) rolling Iowa hills, Thomas Hart Benton's (1889–1975) Midwest prairie, Ross Dickinson's (1903–1878) southern California, and Wayne Thiebaud's (1920–) upturned views of San Francisco all speak to us out of the past, not in a way that reflects how these places looked—no hills look like Dickinson's or Wood's—but in a way that seems to capture the essence of the land itself and our *idea* of it: of hills, of a coming storm, of a fertile landscape, and of steep slopes. They are directed more at what we know than what we see: more at conception than perception (figs. 4.2, 4.3, 4.4, 4.5).

The first thing to say about Pittsburgh is this: the true story of why the city looks the way it does is one that can surprise even longtime residents. It originates in the city's geologic history. Pittsburgh was once part of a vast swamp at the eastern edge of an epicontinental sea that occupied much of the North American continent some four hundred million years ago (fig. 4.6). Subsequently, these lowland beds were raised to their present height of approximately 1,200 feet above sea level by one of several collisions between North America and Africa, and the level line of that original basin and swamp-land has remained as the ever-present tops of Pittsburgh's present-day high-land plateaus.

These Pittsburgh plateaus have multiple levels, the result of erosion. Approximately one million years ago, the rivers of the Pittsburgh region (the Allegheny, Monongahela, and Ohio) flowed differently than they do today, draining northward in the direction of what is now Lake Erie. But when the most recent advance of polar ice reached the region (forty miles north of Pittsburgh) nine hundred thousand years ago, the ice sheet blocked these rivers and pooled a general body of water over the entire region, an area geologists have called Lake Monongahela.

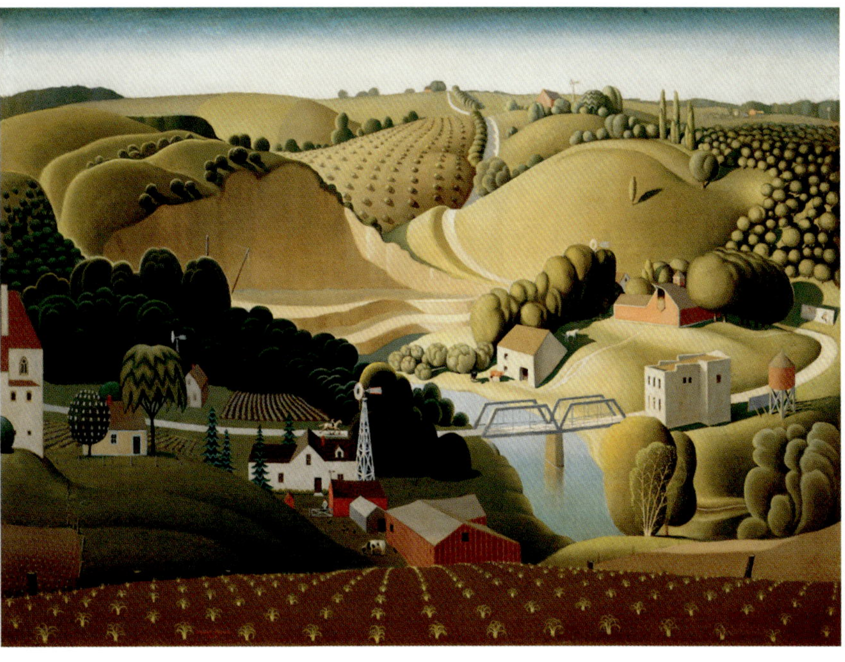

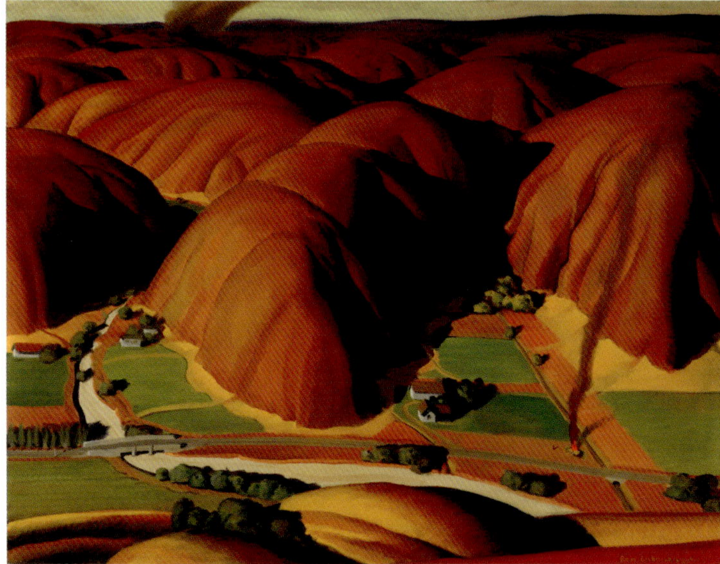

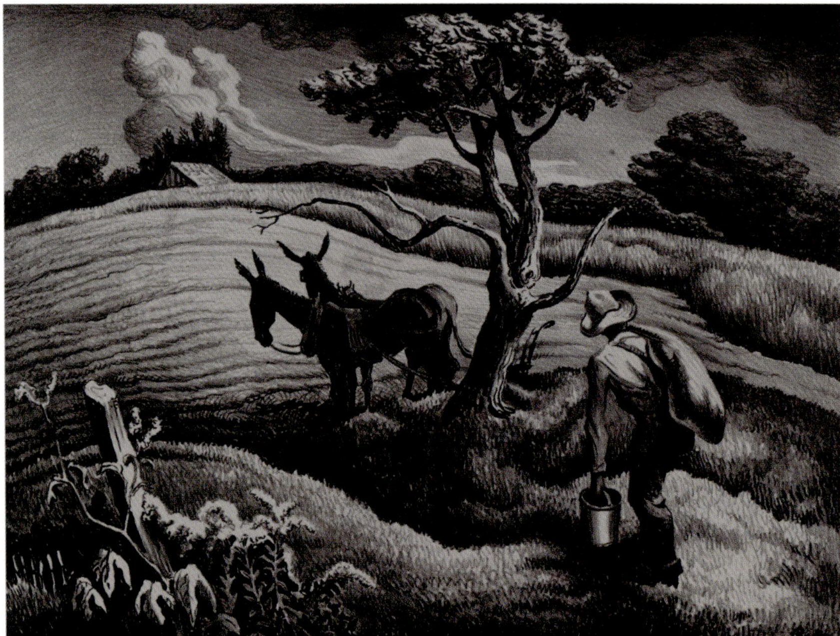

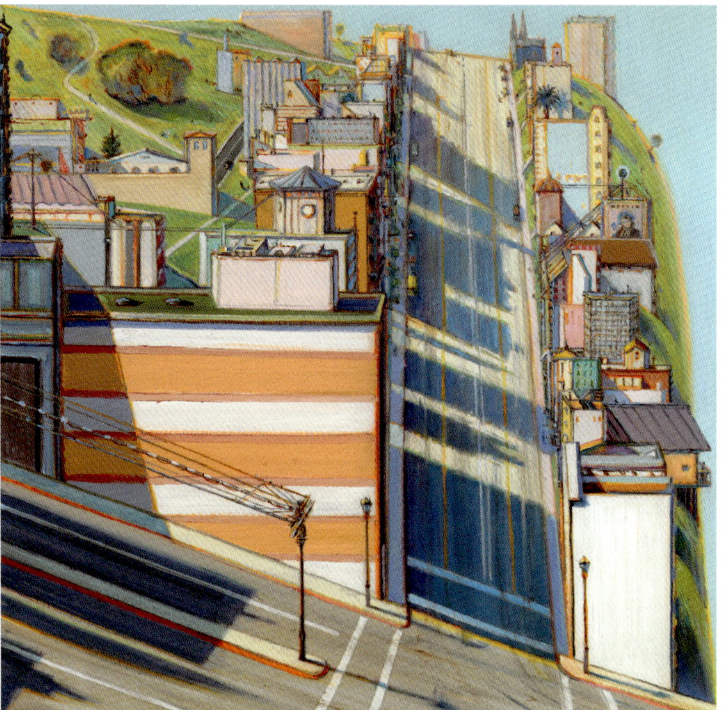

4.2 (*top left*). *Stone City, Iowa*, Grant Wood, 1930. Oil on wood panel, 30 ¼ × 40. Joslyn Art Museum, Omaha, Nebraska. Gift of the Art Institute of Omaha.

4.3 (*bottom left*). *Approaching Storm*, Thomas Hart Benton, 1939. Lithograph on paper, 9 ¾ × 12 ⅞ inches. Smithsonian American Art Museum, Washington, DC. Gift of Maltby Sykes.

4.4 (*top right*). *Valley Farms*, Ross Dickinson, 1934. Oil on canvas, 37 ⅞ × 50 ⅛ inches. Smithsonian American Art Museum, Washington, DC. Transfer from the US Department of Labor.

4.5 (*bottom right*). *San Francisco West Side Ridge*, Wayne Thiebaud, 2001. Oil on canvas, 36 × 36 inches. Smithsonian American Art Museum, Washington, DC. Gift of Sam Rose and Julie Walters.

Then, as this water gradually drained away, it did so following the earlier river beds. Except that along major parts of the Allegheny and Ohio, it flowed in an opposite direction. Eventually, the region's entire watershed drained westward and southward into the Mississippi. During this time the Monongahela also followed a wider and higher course across the future city at about nine hundred feet above sea level (fig. 4.7). This wider and higher Monongahela followed two branches, one following its present path, more or less, and the other taking a more northerly route from Braddock through East Liberty, past Bloomfield, Shadyside, and Oakland, and finally across Troy Hill and the northern edge of Polish Hill to rejoin its southern sister near the present-day Point. The relative flatness of these shelf neighborhoods that once formed the bottom of that earlier river is an inheritance of that prior route of the Monongahela. Over time this ancient river alignment cut yet deeper valleys and eventually reached its present level of seven hundred feet above sea level. Junction Hollow, Panther Hollow, Nine Mile Run, and the hollow between Bloomfield and Oakland and Polish Hill are the results.

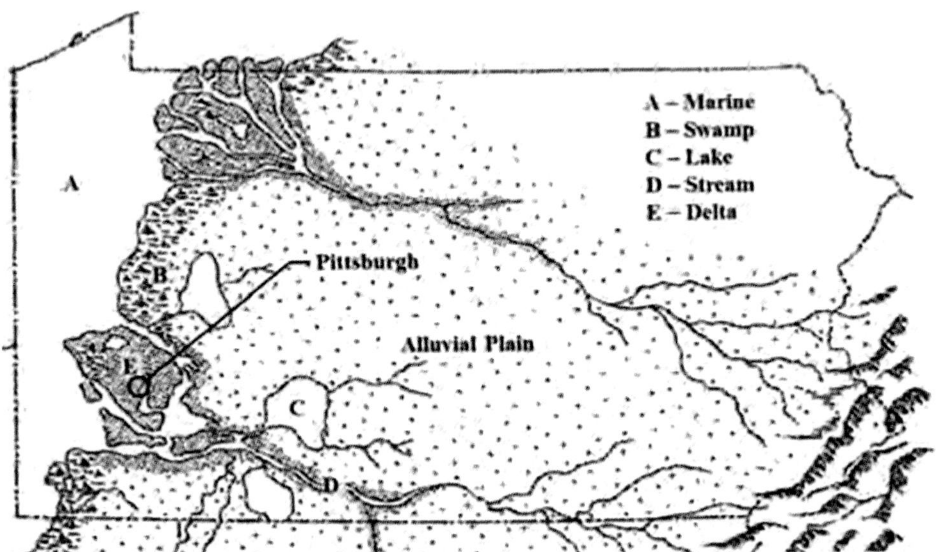

4.6. "Epicontinental Sea. Inferred Paleography of Pennsylvania during the Late Pennsylvanian when the rocks of Pittsburgh were being deposited." From Wagner et al., General Geology Report G59, Pittsburgh Geological Survey, Fourth Series, Harrisburg, PA, 1970.

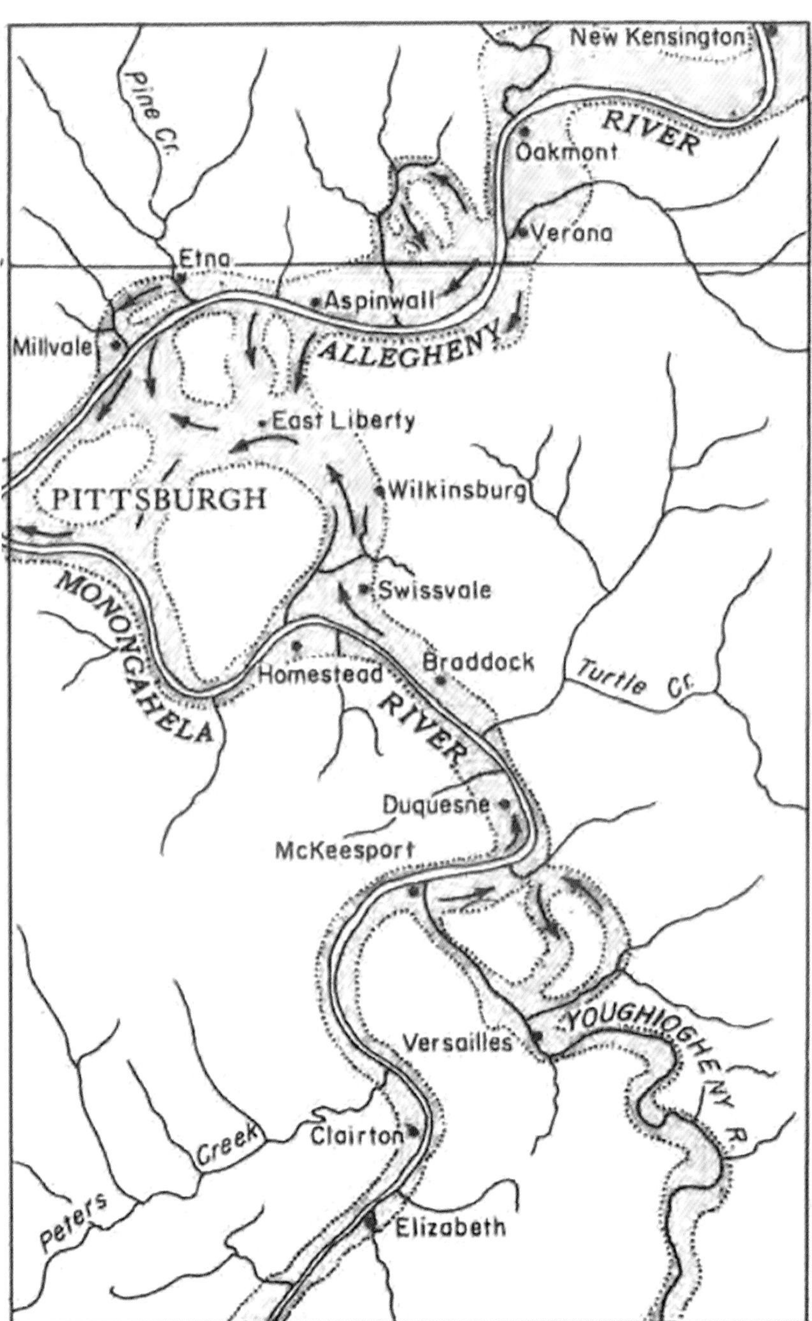

4.7. "Early Rivers. Abandoned Channels and High Level Terraces in Immediate Vicinity of Pittsburgh." From Heyman, General Geology Report G59, Pittsburgh Geological Survey, Fourth Series, Harrisburg, PA, 1970.

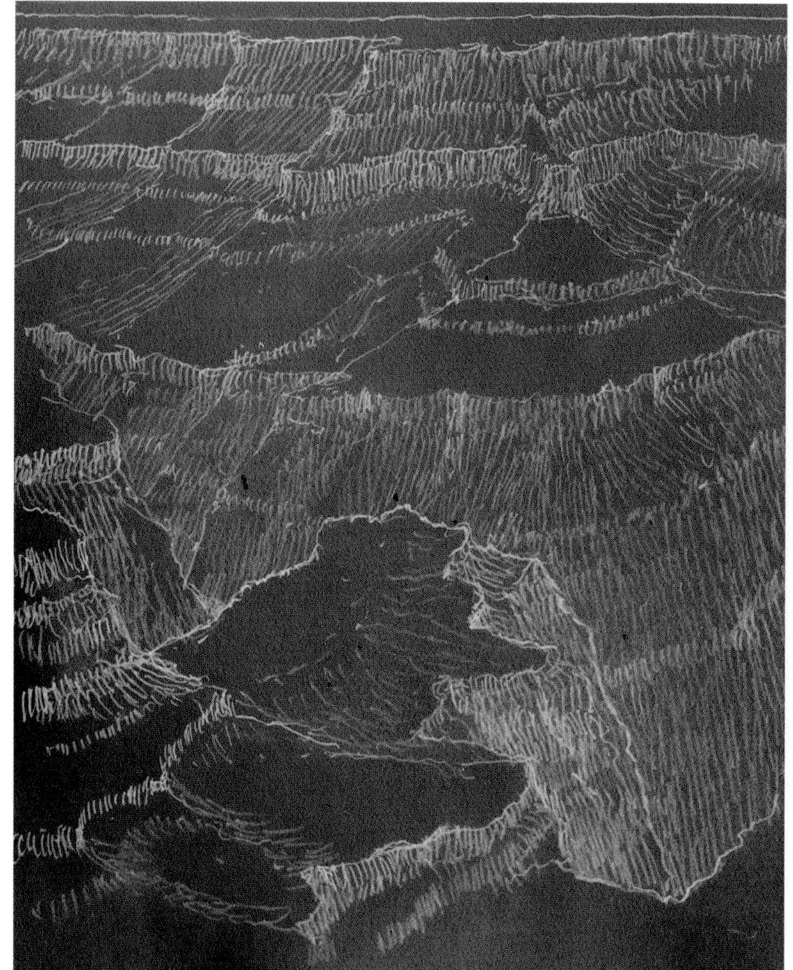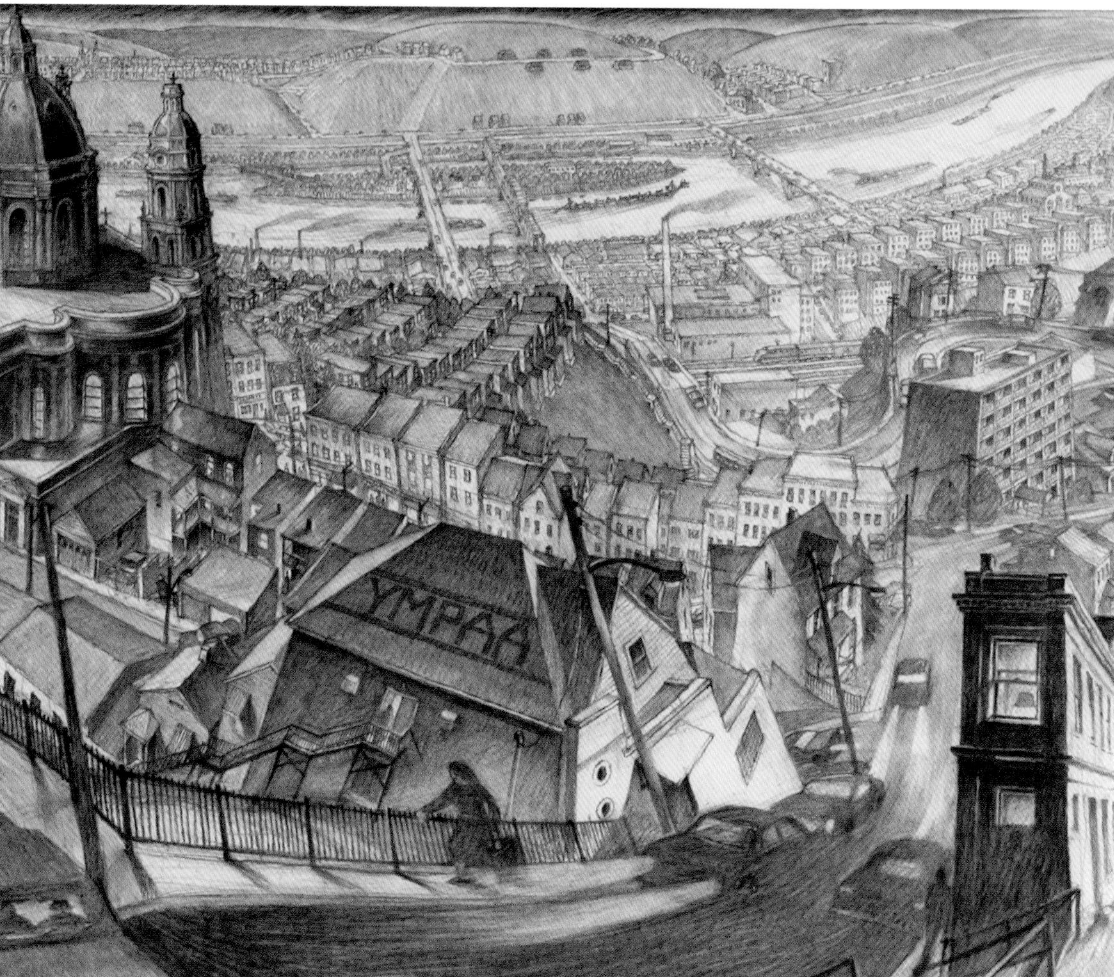

4.8. Comparison of Grand Canyon and detail of *Polish Hill from Herron Hill Intersection*, Doug Cooper, 2007. Charcoal on paper on board, 48 × 72 inches. Private collection.

So, contrary to what most of its residents think, Pittsburgh doesn't actually have hills at all. Rather, it has eroded plateaus with three distinct levels: (1) plateau tops approximately 1,200 feet above sea level—the original epicontinental seabed; (2) eroded intermediate-level plateau shelves—the bed of the higher river alignment of the Monongahela River described above—at about 900 feet; and (3) lowland rivers with more recent floodplains along their banks approximately 700 feet above sea level.

Despite their obvious differences, it is fair to compare Pittsburgh's multiple plateaus to the Grand Canyon, which also has three levels. I say that because this comparison is often in the back of my mind when I draw Pittsburgh's plateaus. In the background I tend to flatten their tops—making them look like the variegated cliffs that make up the canyon's north rim. In the middle ground, I tend to lift up midshelf areas to show the eroded plan-like shapes of their edges—much as I remember seeing similar shapes when looking down into the Grand Canyon years ago (fig. 4.8).

Industrial Expansion and the Rivers

Now that we have a sense of the legacy of the land, what patterns do we find in the ways people have inhabited that landscape, and how have these influenced the way I've drawn it? Since 1800, from the confluence where the Allegheny and Monongahela Rivers now join to form the Ohio, the city has grown in stages related to the three plateau levels I just described. Initially, the region's glass and iron industries grew out along the level flats bordering the three rivers. This expansion was driven by a need for water for industrial cooling; broad, flat, buildable sites; and barge and then rail access. Early increases of housing stock initially shadowed the industrial growth along these flats. The neighborhoods of Lawrenceville along the Allegheny River and Birmingham along the Monongahela, both east of the Point, were pre–Civil War expansions.

With the growth of the steel industry following that war, mills were built and expanded upriver into Hazelwood, Homestead, Braddock, and Rankin (and countless other towns along the Monongahela) to take full advantage of their proximity to the abundant coalfields of Fayette County and West Virginia. The largest plants and associated flats communities tended to be on the insides of river bends, where spring thaws had found shorter routes by broadening the floodplain and where sediment deposits tended to be made (fig. 4.9).

Each town had its own grid, and sometimes several, that turned with each river bend. By the time the United States entered the First World War, there was an almost continuous stretch of steel and steel-related plants (one side of the river or the other and sometimes both) stretching up the Monongahela River valley as far as Monessen some thirty miles upriver (fig. 4.10).

When I draw these bending rivers and the flats that border them, I tend to rotate them upward, viewing them more in plan in order to show how the mills and railroads lined their banks and how the neighborhoods turned in gridded segments with each bend of the river. And I draw the slopes that face the rivers in the same treeless state that I remember from my childhood (fig. 4.11)

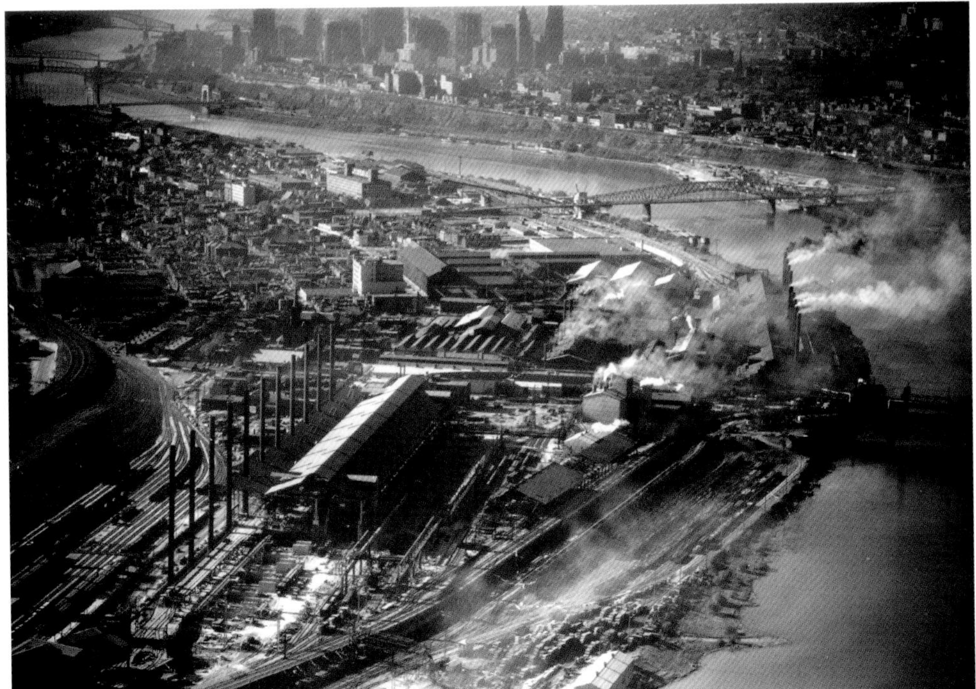

4.9. Aerial view of Jones & Laughlin Pittsburgh Works, unknown photographer, ca. 1950. Jones & Laughlin Corporation Photographs, Detre Library and Archives, Senator John Heinz History Center, Pittsburgh.

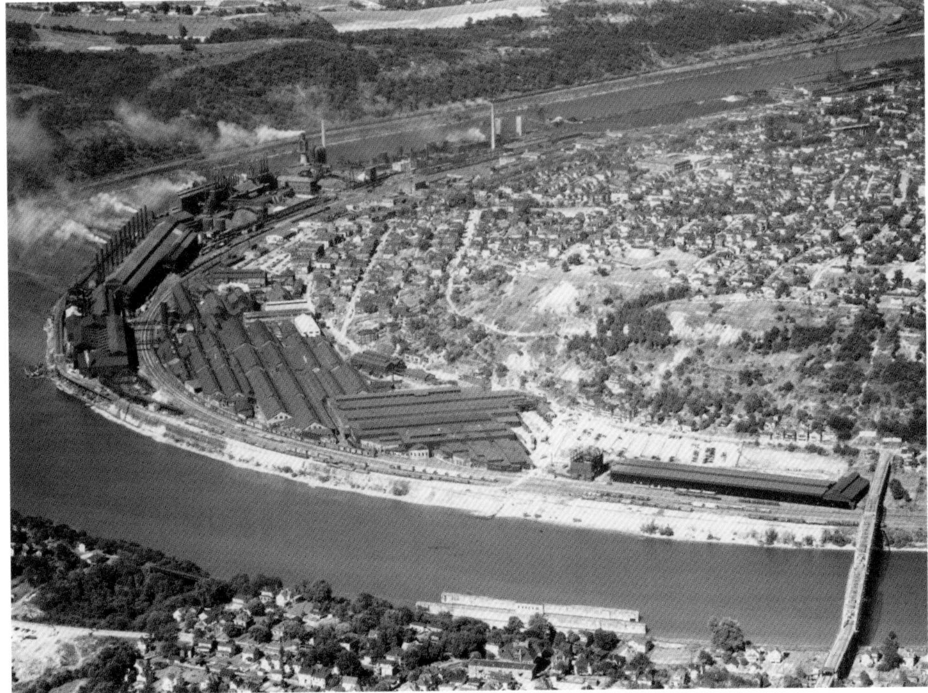

4.10. Aerial view of the Pittsburgh Steel Company Monessen Plant. O'Neil Photo Service, Allegheny Conference on Community Development Photographs, Detre Library and Archives, Senator John Heinz History Center, Pittsburgh.

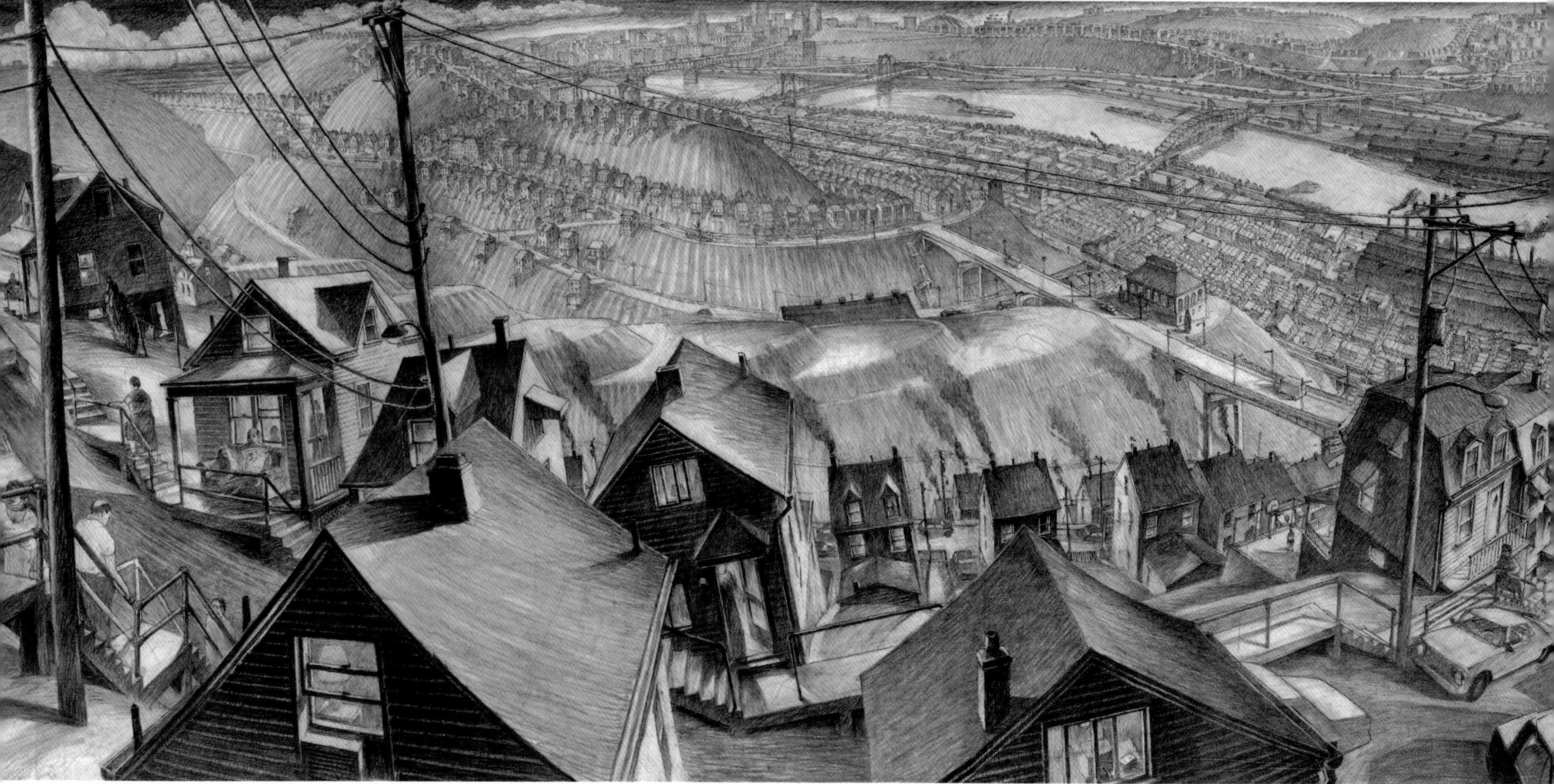

4.11. Detail, *Arrivals on Sterling*, Doug Cooper, 2006. Charcoal on paper on board, 48 × 108 inches. Private collection.

Flats, Slopes, Plateaus, and Hollows

With the expanded industrial plant, there was need for more housing near mills than could fit in adjacent flats, and so the housing was extended up into nearby hollows. These were one- and two-street-wide linear neighborhoods that followed meandering streambeds. The one that fills Four Mile Run near the Jones & Laughlin South Oakland blast furnaces is emblematic of this community type, with people's lives conducted around two centers: the mill at the hollow's mouth and the church midway up the length of the valley floor (fig. 4.12). When there was no hollow available nearby, houses were simply built up the slopes above the flats. Much of the housing on the South Side Slopes above the Jones & Laughlin Steelworks was built on sites that would be considered too unstable for building today.

Midshelf plateau communities at about nine hundred feet above sea level were populated somewhat later than the sloping land adjacent to industrial sites down in the flats. If they were close to industrial sites, as in Bloomfield, Polish Hill, Troy Hill, South Oakland, and Soho, these areas housed workers. Both the midshelf and slope communities were connected to the mills in the flats below with numerous city steps, some of which were legendary in length (fig. 4.13). The connection between house and mill with a zigzag line of city steps has been a constant theme in my work (fig. 4.14).

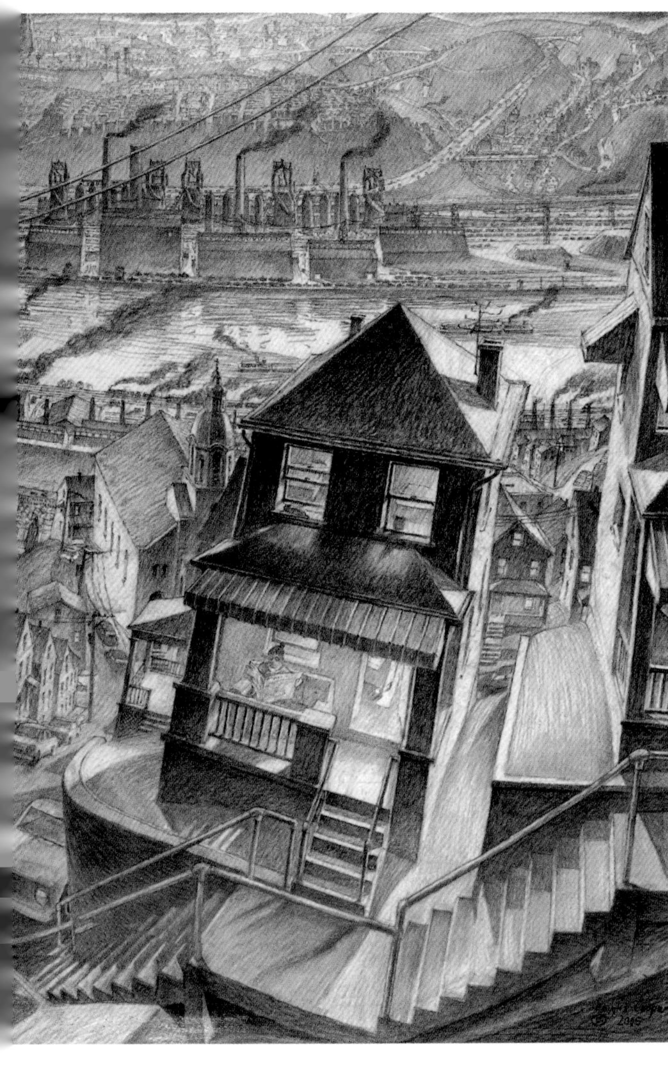

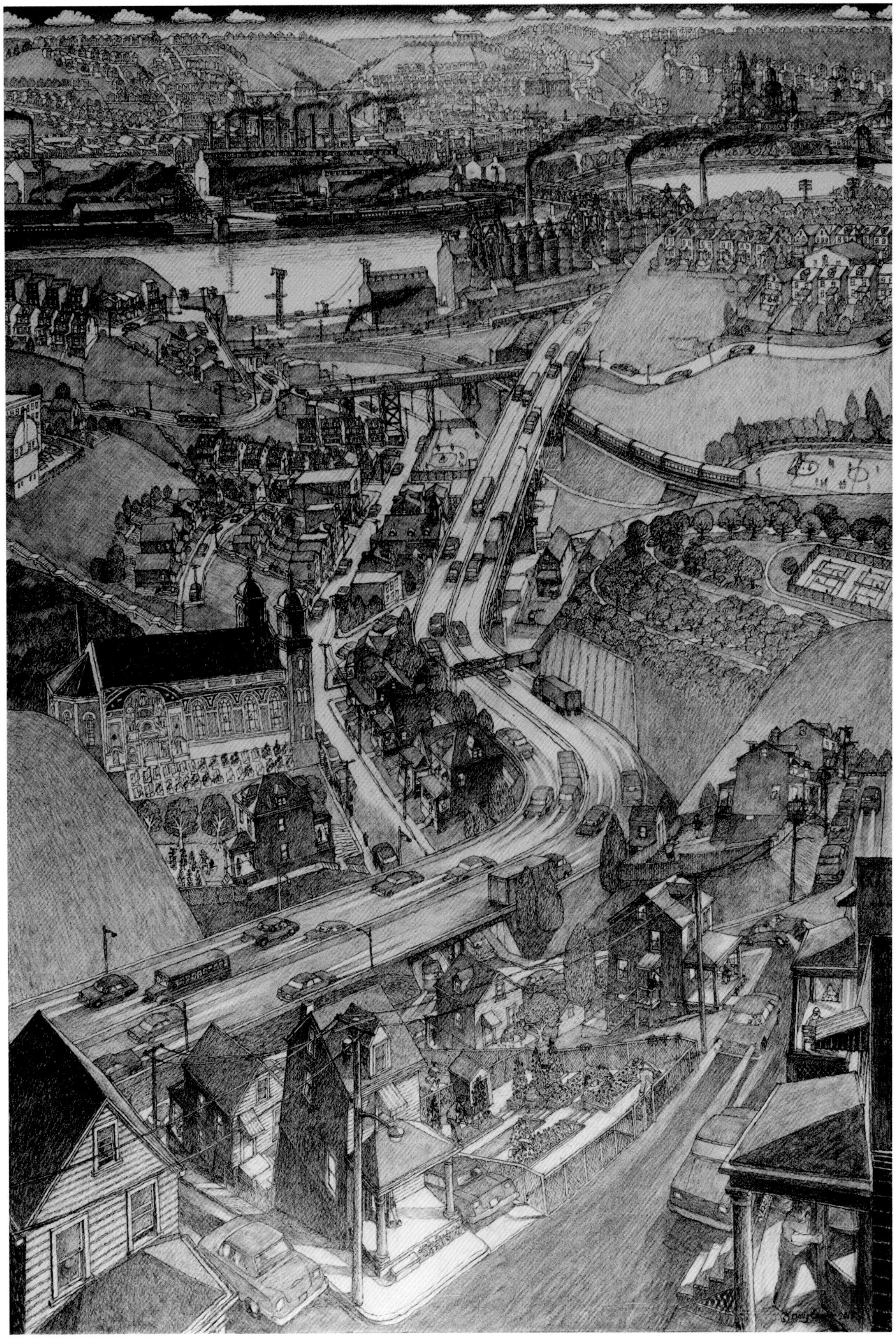

4.12 (*right*). *Saint Johns in the Run*, Doug Cooper, 2018. Charcoal on paper on board, 72 × 48 inches. Collection of the artist.

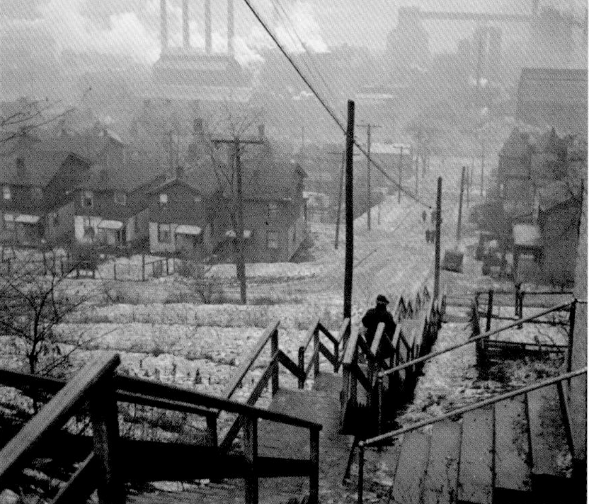

4.13 (*left*). *Long Stairway in Mill District of Pittsburgh, Pennsylvania*, Jack Delano, 1940.
1 negative: nitrate, 3 ¼ × 4 ½ inches or smaller. Library of Congress Prints and Photographs Division.
4.14 (*below*). *Steps Down from Mission*, Doug Cooper, 2006. Charcoal on paper on board, 36 × 48 inches.
Westmoreland Museum of American Art, Greensburg, PA. Gift of the William W. Jamison II Art Acquisition Fund.

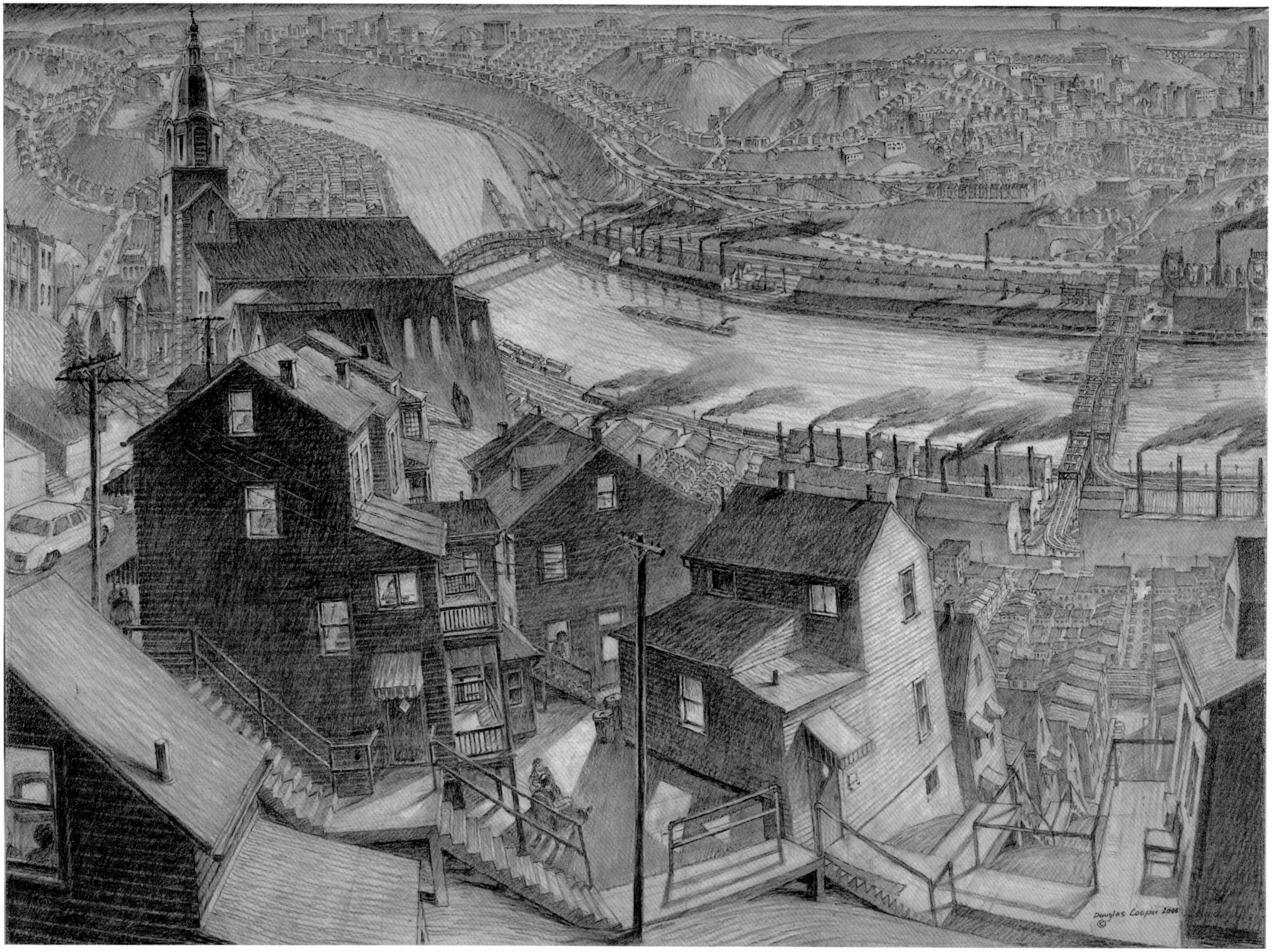

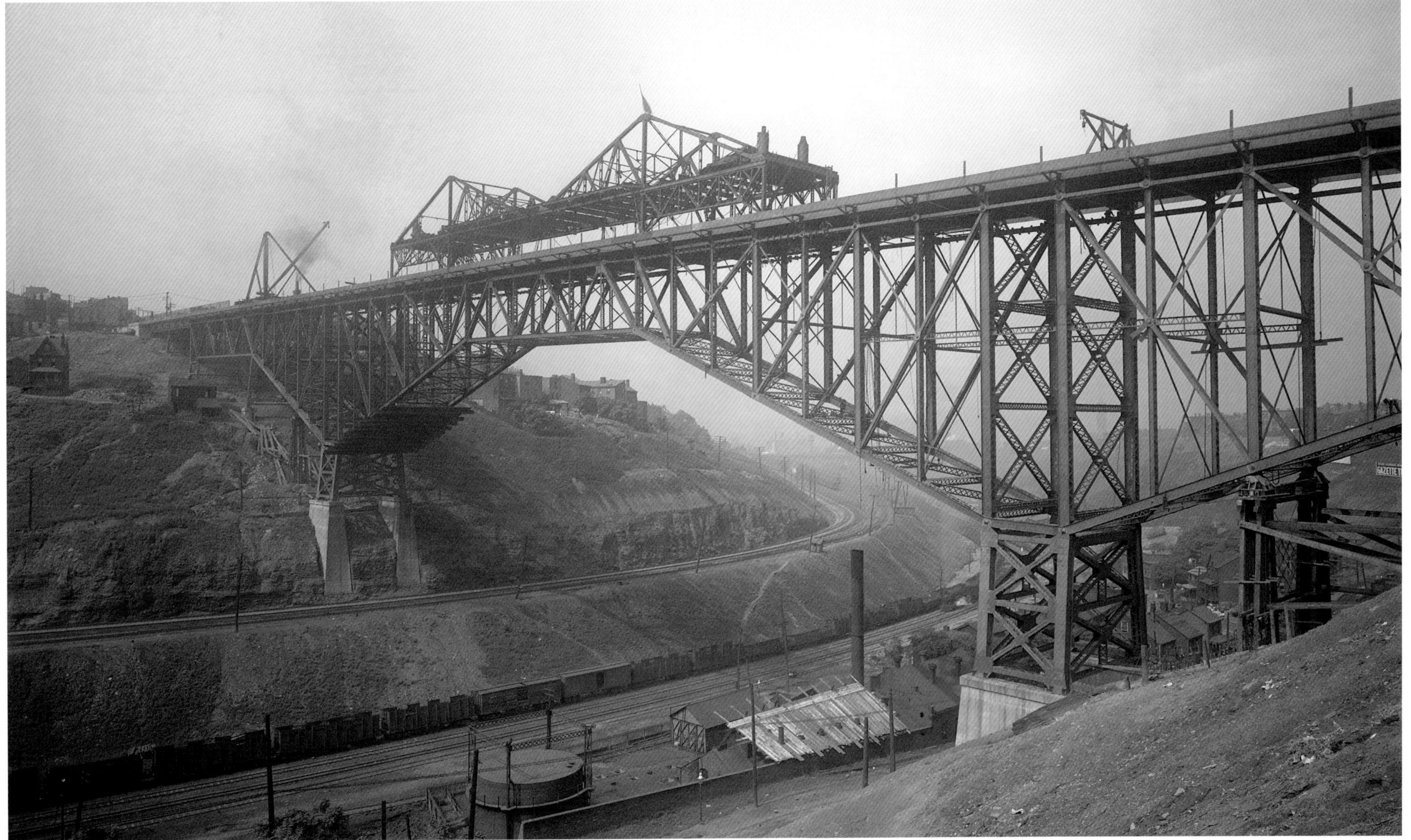

4.15. *Bloomfield Bridge Construction*, Pittsburgh city photographer, 1914. Pittsburgh City Photography Collection, University of Pittsburgh.

The hollows that were cut through Pittsburgh's midlevel plateau shelves have profoundly impacted the way people perceive the boundaries of their neighborhoods. With their steep, unbuildable slopes, they serve as interruptions in the urban fabric and have contributed to strong neighborhood and even ethnic divisions throughout the city, giving a clear edge to Bloomfield's distinctly Italian character to this day and reflected in names such as Polish Hill. Because of these hollows, travel between adjacent plateaus is often only possible by way of connecting bridges (figs. 4.15, 4.16).

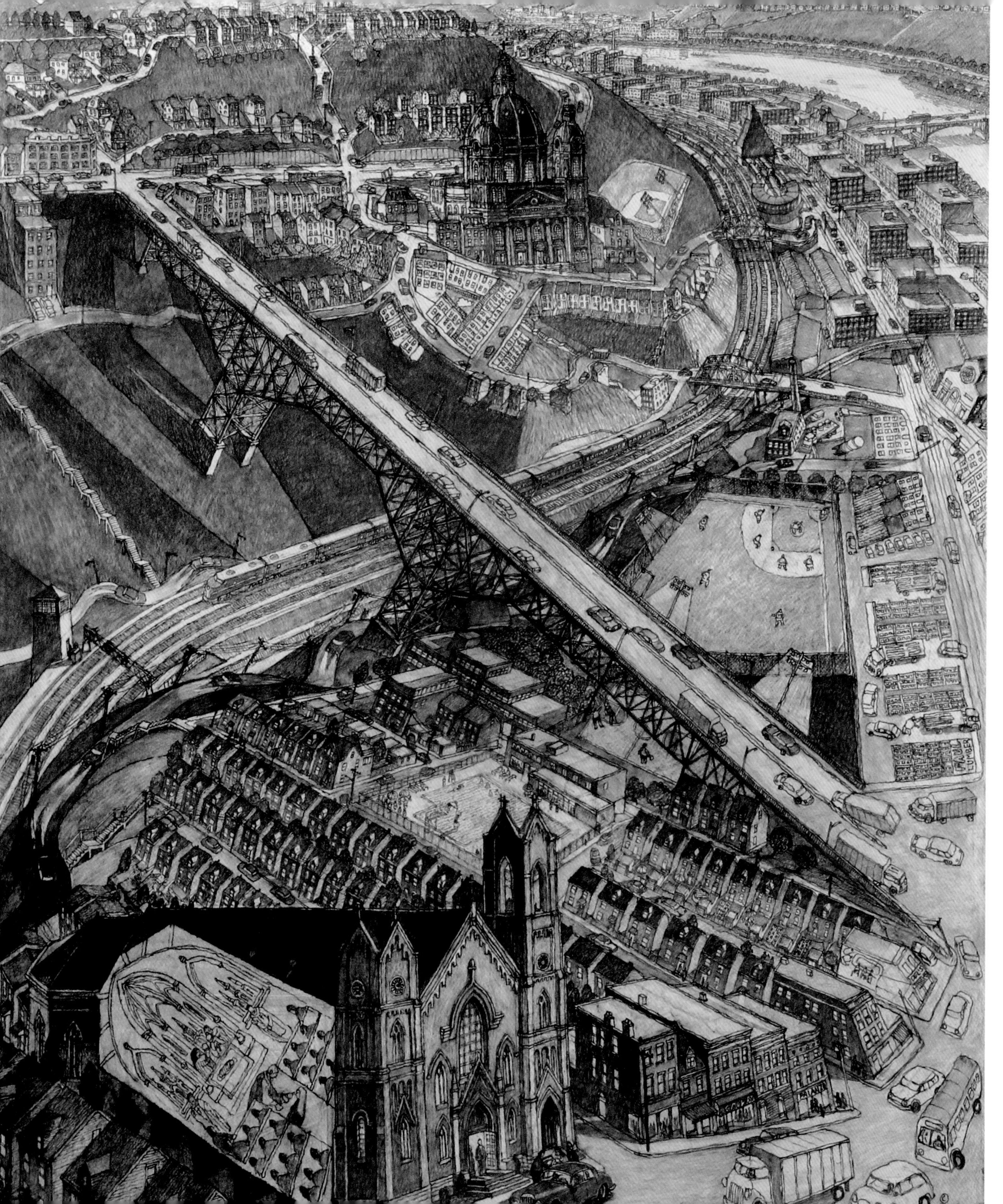

4.16 (*left*). *From Saint Joseph's to Immaculate Mother of Mary*, Doug Cooper, 2018. Charcoal on paper on board, 60 × 48 inches. Collection of the artist.

4.17 (*right*). North wall detail, 18th Street Valley. Jared L. Cohon University Center mural, Doug Cooper, 1996. Charcoal on paper on board, approx. 10 × 150 feet, Carnegie Mellon University, Pittsburgh.

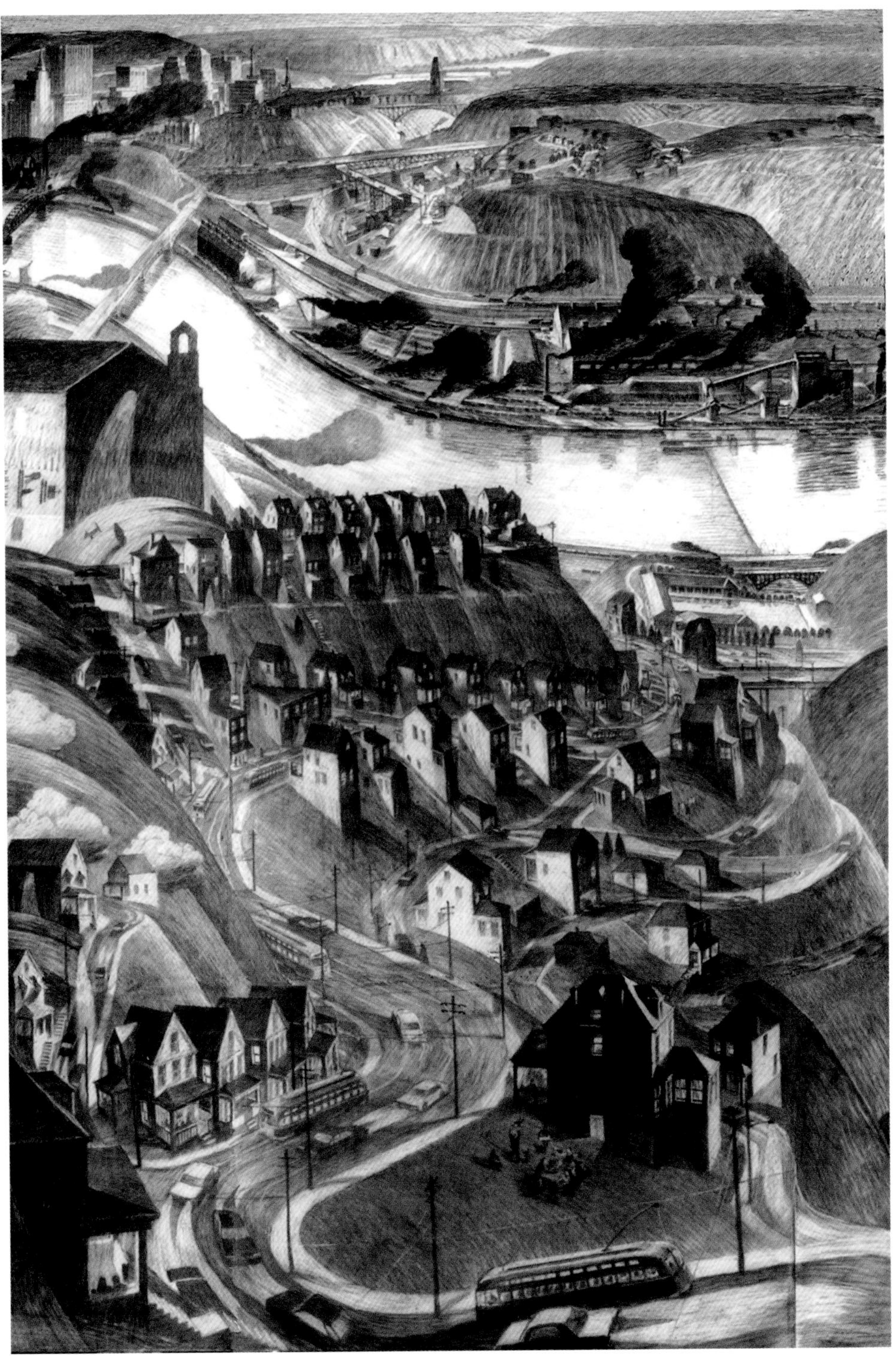

Their sides have also provided convenient routes for roadways to connect hilltop neighborhoods above 1,200 feet with midshelf plateaus at 900 and the flats below at 700. Where most streets in Pittsburgh are straight, as parts of the grids that parallel the river bends, these ravine connectors follow contours and twist and turn as they descend to the flats. One of my favorites to draw has been the 18th Street valley (fig. 4.17).

The fascination I've long held for Pittsburgh's hollows stems from their spatial definition: their boundaries. With their steeply sloping faces and streambed spines, they are experienced as neighborhood "rooms." And those that are crossed by bridges and those that are particularly narrow have an additional common experience: a shared window to the sky.

Pittsburgh's geologic heritage has played out for me in several compositional tendencies. Usually I begin at the top of a drawing, with the straight top of the plateaus across a river: the original seabed floor. Below that horizon, my marks follow the lines our eyes tend to follow when we look down into valleys from above—the bending rivers and streams that follow the valley floors and vanish behind the turning slopes at either end of the view—left and right (fig. 4.18).

I tend to deal with the vertical axes of drawings in a different way: I'll often start with some foreground scene of houses, one with steep roads and city steps, and with telephone wires vanishing behind houses further down a slope—all of them coursing together along routes the water once followed in eroding the land ages before. These paths have generated the perspective angles turned every which way that dominate the foregrounds and middle grounds of my drawings (fig. 4.19).

I have come to favor a near 1 × 2 landscape format in drawing the city's terrain. Partly, this is due to the proportion of the visual field—with the side-by-side placement of our eyes, roughly a 1 × 2 oval. In combining what I *see*—the lines my eyes follow—with what I *know*—the midplateau neighborhoods and the industrial neighborhoods in the flats—my drawings have tended to have a common underlying compositional structure: a placid horizontal at the top, a wiggly *U* following the rivers and edges of intermediate shelves, and paths that follow the hollows and connect foreground and middle ground to background (fig. 4.20).

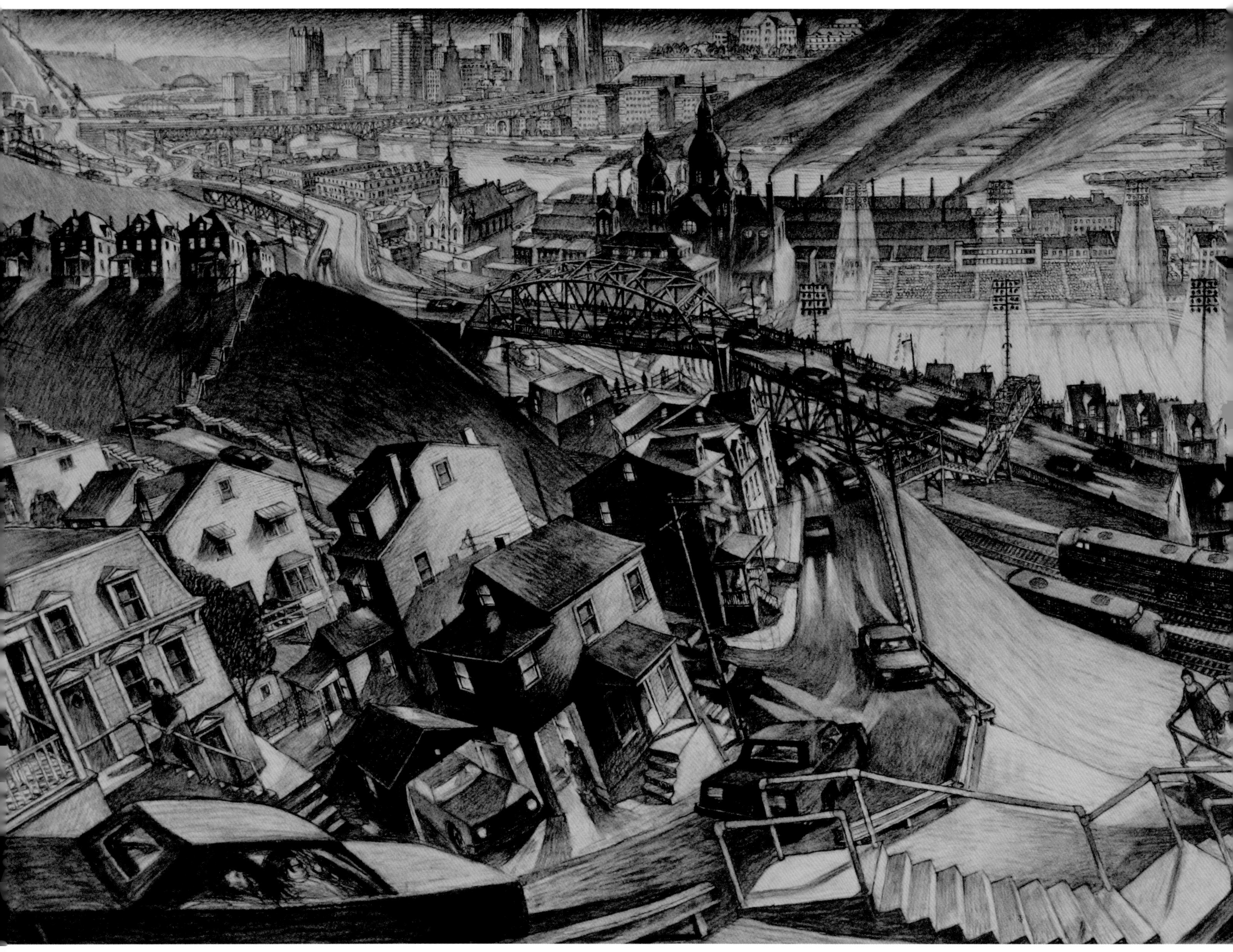

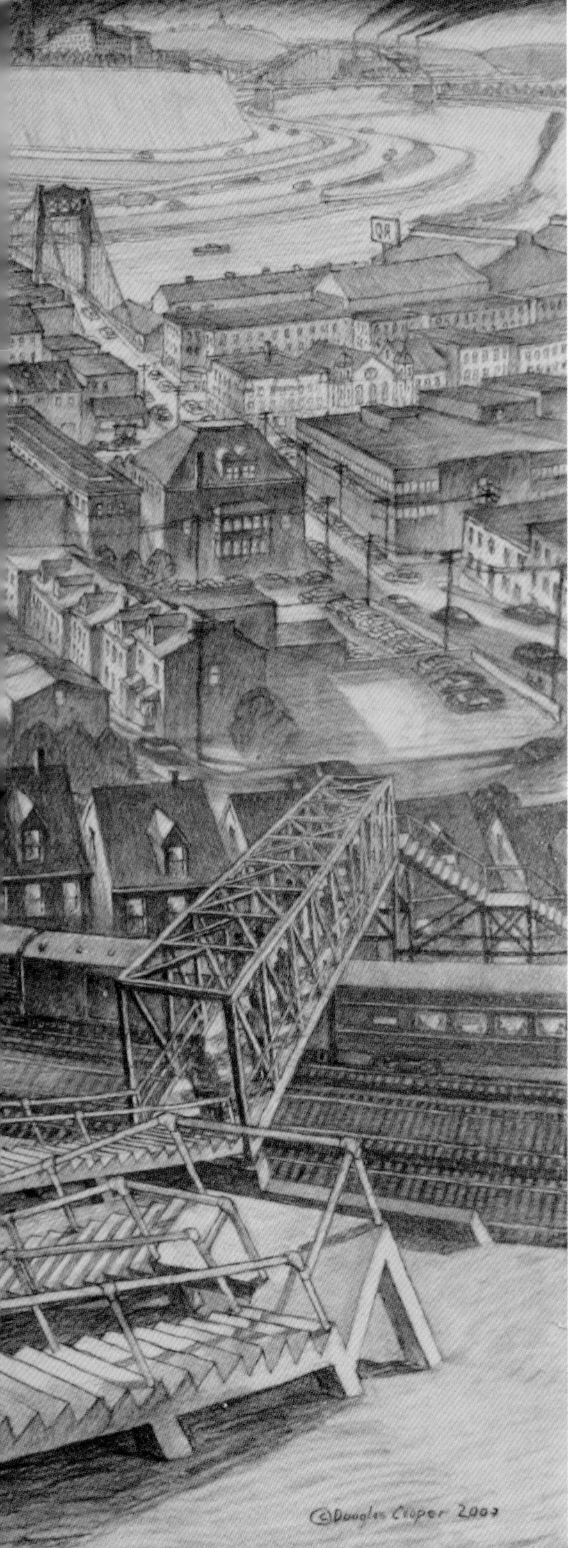

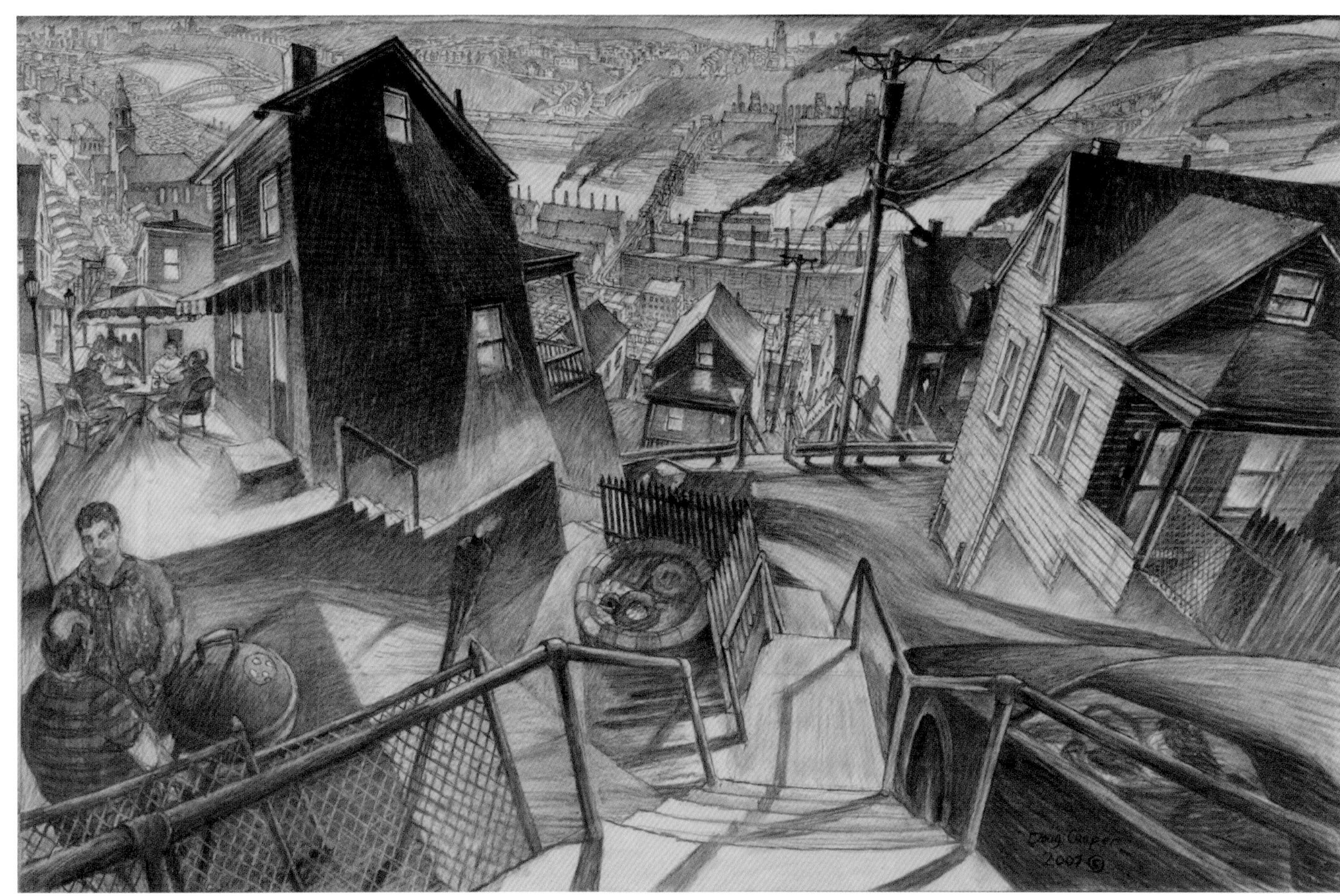

4.19. *Tiki Party*, Doug Cooper, 2007. Charcoal on paper on board, 36 × 48 inches. Private collection.

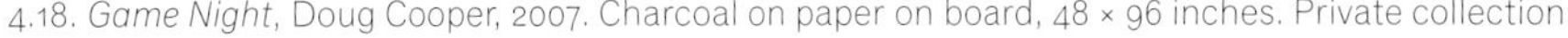

4.18. *Game Night*, Doug Cooper, 2007. Charcoal on paper on board, 48 × 96 inches. Private collection.

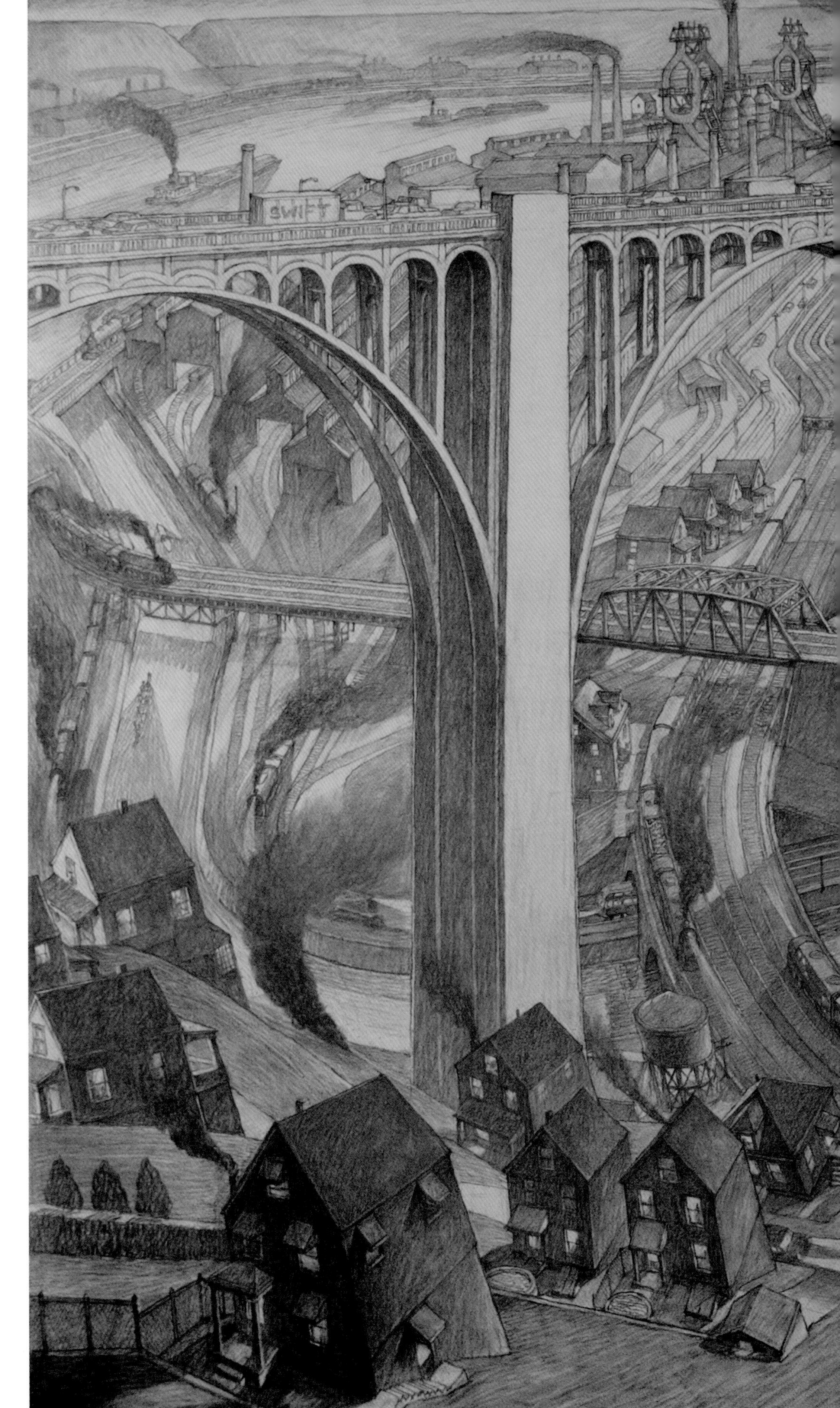

4.20. *Above Lower Street*, Doug Cooper, 2015. Charcoal on paper on board, 48 × 80 inches. Private collection.

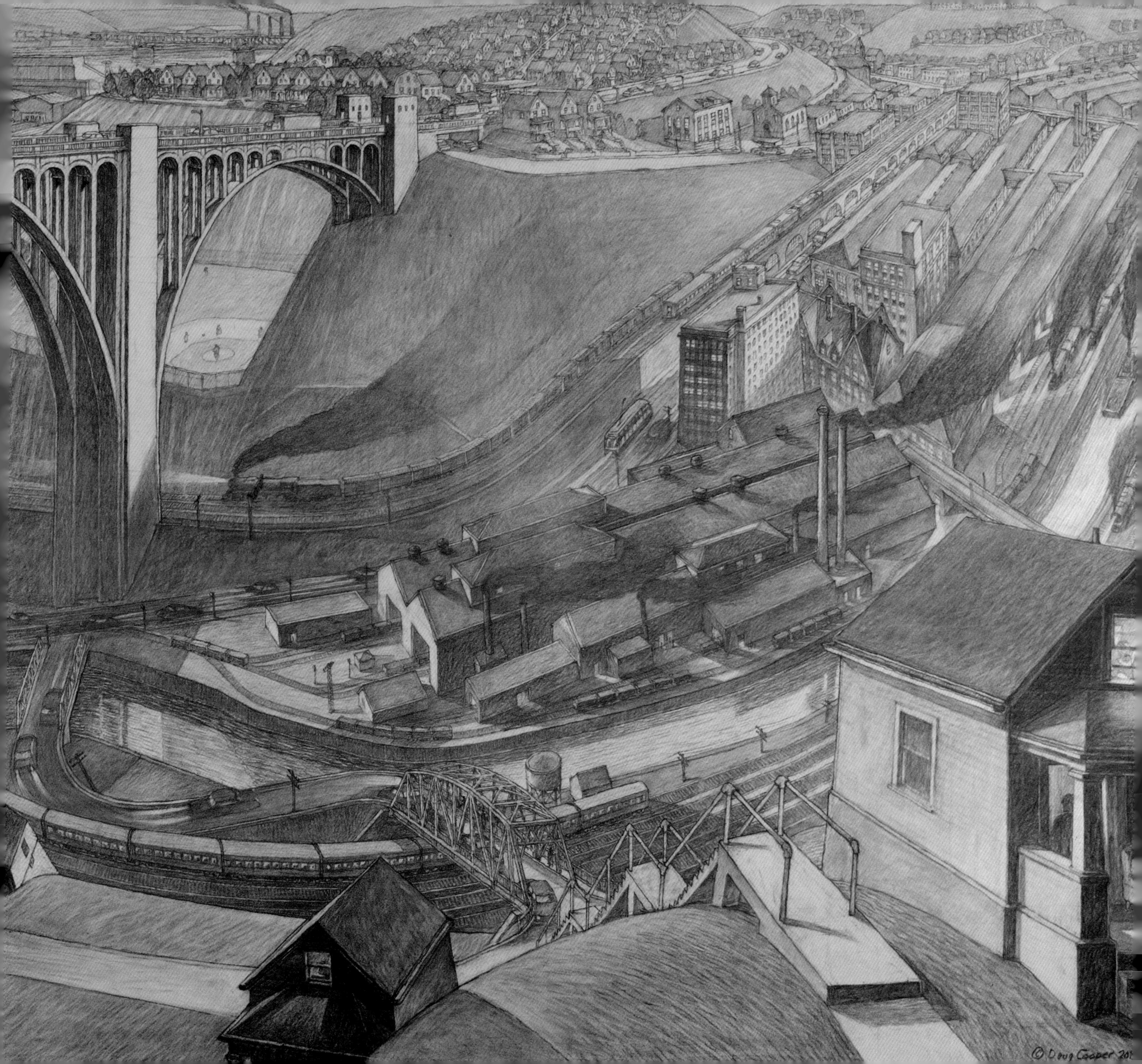
© Doug Cooper 201

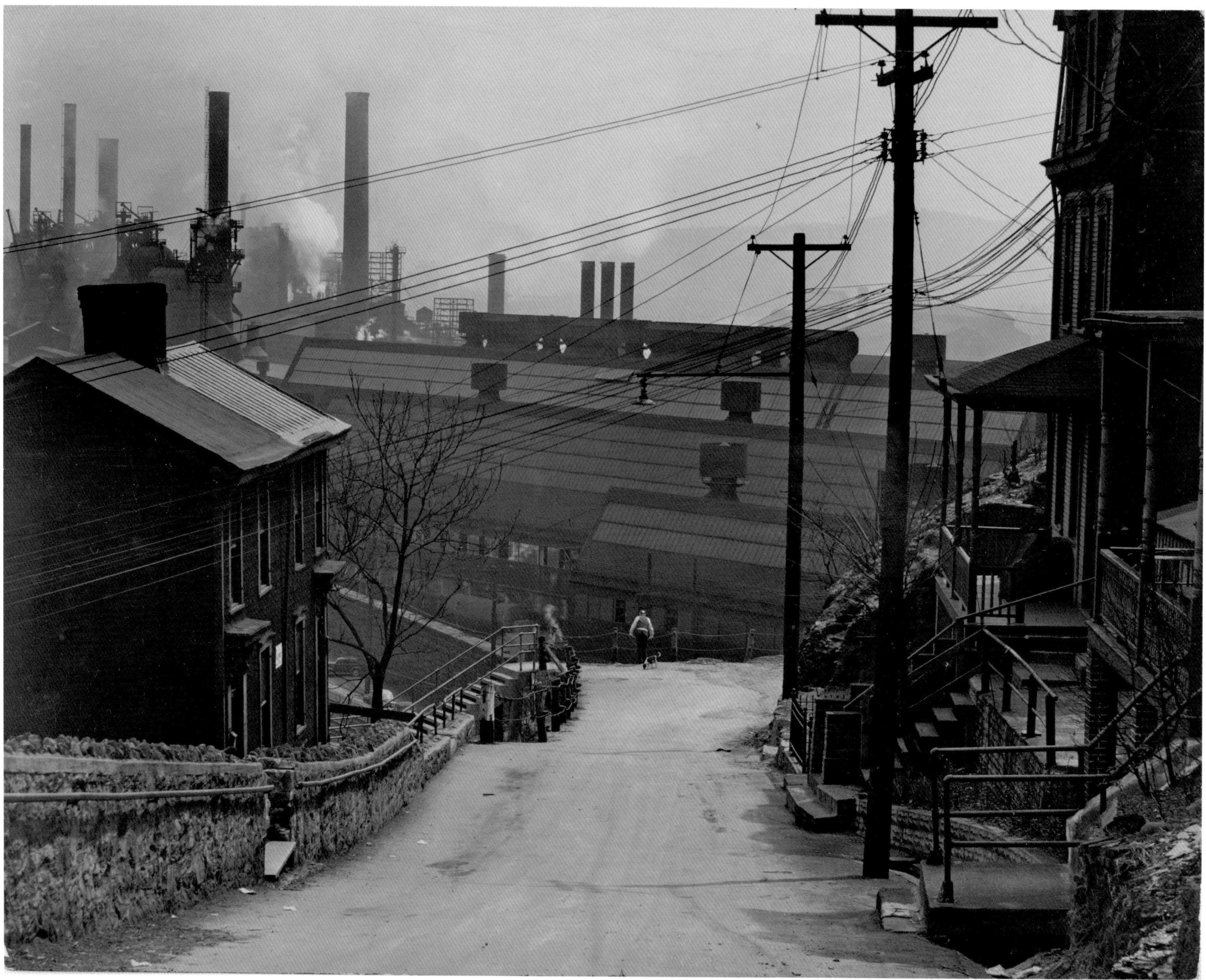

Pittsburgh through the Eyes of Photographers

Pittsburgh has attracted and inspired numerous photographers to come to the city and then stay to document it. It is one of the world's more photogenic cities, most of all in black and white. W. Eugene Smith (1918–1978), famed for his photojournalism with *Life* magazine, came here originally on a three-week-long assignment from Stefan Lorant to provide photographs for his book on the city's history, and then remained, photographing the city over three years, from 1955 to 1957. Luke Swank (1890–1944) grew up in nearby Johnstown. He became a professional photographer almost by accident when he began taking photographs of the Bethlehem Steel Works in his native Johnstown and found that people wanted to buy them. His career as a photographer was short (1930–1944), but recognized—his work was shown several times at the Museum of Modern Art in New York. He spent most of his professional career

in Pittsburgh. Todd Webb (1905–2000) is better known for his photographs of places other than Pittsburgh, but he spent time in the city during the early 1950s. Harold Corsini (1919–2008), Teenie Harris (1908–1998), Charlee Brodsky (1950–), and Clyde Hare (1927–2009) spent their careers in Pittsburgh, the latter commissioned for numerous industrial photographs for annual reports.

Taken as a collective body of work, their photographs have distilled perceptual truths about the city that resonate for those who know it well. Some of these are small details such as the way foundation walls form triangular shapes when they meet the sloping ground, or the way electrical wires and overlapping porch roofs all cascade down slopes with the descending streets they parallel (fig. 4.21). But some have also seemed larger than life. The sizes of industrial plants (compared to dwellings) and their scaleless construction have made for jarring shifts between human and industrial scales (fig. 4.22).

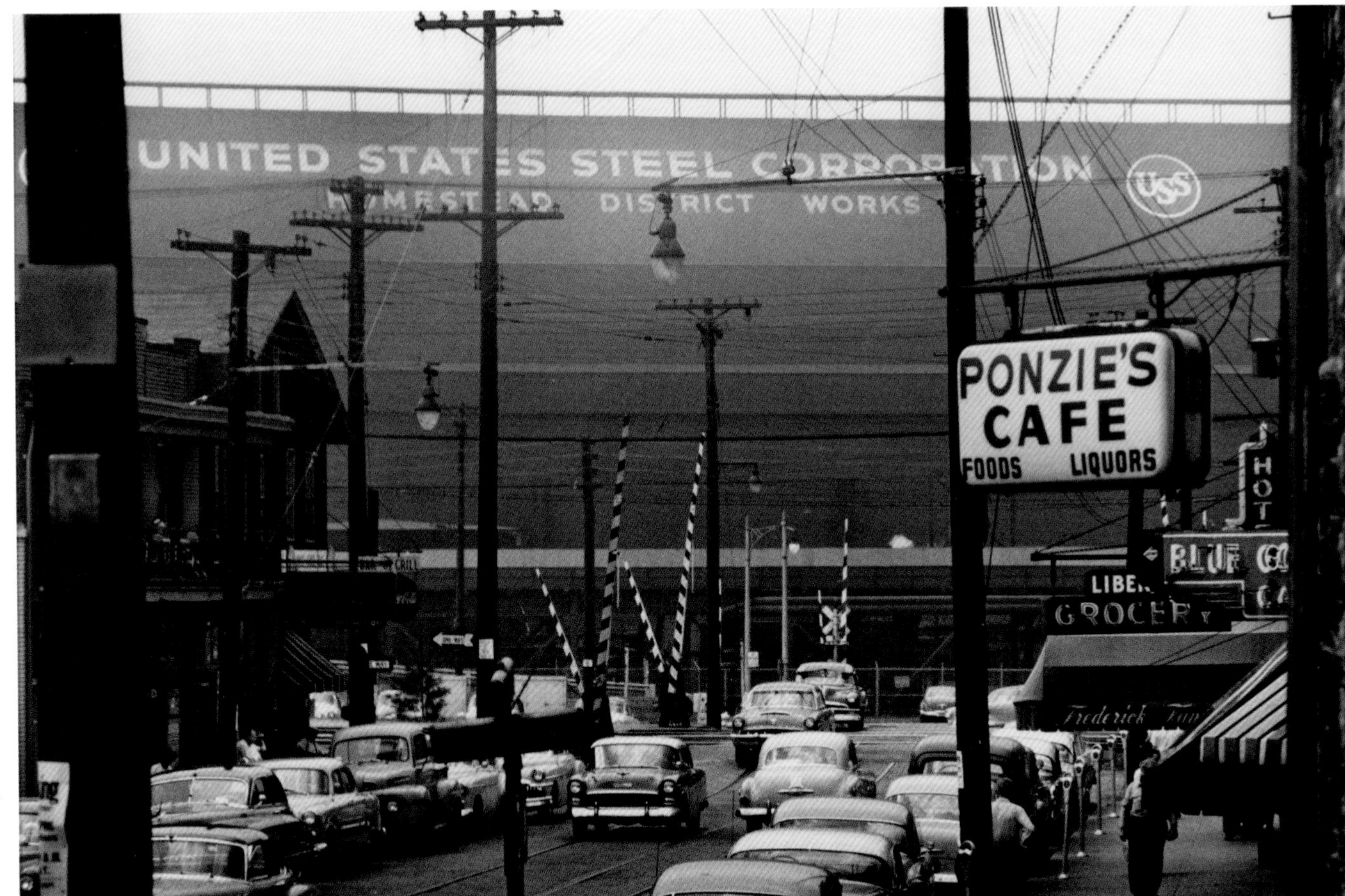

4.21 (*left*). *Jones and Laughlin Steel Mill*, Todd Webb, 1948. Gelatin silver print, 7⅝ × 9 7/16 inches. Carnegie Museum of Art, Pittsburgh. Gift of the Carnegie Library of Pittsburgh.

4.22 (*right*). Untitled, photo of United States Steel Company, Homestead Works, W. Eugene Smith, 1955–1956. Gelatin silver print, 9 × 13⅝ inches. Carnegie Museum of Art, Pittsburgh. Gift of the Carnegie Library of Pittsburgh, Lorant Collection.

Responding to Pittsburgh as Kevin Lynch Might

Given what the photographers have documented, what is our *conception* of Pittsburgh: our *image* of the city? As I described in chapter 1, Kevin Lynch clarified much about the ways in which people understand the underlying order of cities where they live. His research in several diverse cities identified five elements that people use in forming their understanding of their city and neighborhood. Recalling them, these are: paths, edges, nodes, landmarks, and neighborhoods/districts. If these are the elements out of which we form our image of any city, then, how are they evident in Pittsburgh—are some more important or even exaggerated than others?—and how do they contribute to our sense of Pittsburgh: *the place?* We'll start with the first two on Lynch's list, the linear elements: edges—that is, boundaries—and paths.

Clear boundaries are among the most important characteristics of Pittsburgh. These are the legacy of its geologic past, for it is from its vertical dimension, its plateau tops and intermediate shelves, that Pittsburgh gains its well-defined edges. As we've seen, stream courses and earlier river alignments have cut deep valleys through Pittsburgh's plateaus, and these draw clear boundaries around its neighborhoods: Polish Hill, Bloomfield, Shadyside, Troy Hill, Spring Hill, etc. It is rare in Pittsburgh that we have difficulty sensing when we have left one neighborhood and are entering another, whether by crossing a bridge, descending suddenly down a slope, or crossing over a ridgeline. Pittsburgh does not sprawl continuously in the way that a city like Cleveland or Detroit does.

Those are elements of plan, but because the dropoffs at the edges of the shelves are so steep, the boundaries of Pittsburgh have an elevational character as well. We can face them. They are visible as the defining walls of the river-centered valley rooms, and the runs and hollows we find throughout the city. And the tops of these walls have a vivid physical presence about them—felt when we lift a foot off an accelerator at the top of a slope or as we gasp for air at the top landing of a steep climb of stairs (fig. 4.23).

These steep valley walls have left the city with a distinctive set of paths—whether meandering roads (one of the reasons so many get lost in the city), or city steps (one of them climbed continuously almost four hundred feet from base to top), or funiculars (there are now only two, but there were once seventeen!). Pittsburgh is also a city of bridges: a 2006 study counted 466 of them.

They serve as thresholds between neighborhoods throughout the city. Whether we are crossing a river or a ravine, they provide clear signals we have left one district and are in route to another. (fig. 4.24).

If Pittsburgh is a city with distinctive boundaries and paths, concerning Lynch's point elements, its nodes and landmarks, Pittsburgh shares much with other nineteenth-century immigrant cities that grew with unskilled labor recruited out of Eastern and Southern Europe. Many of its neighborhoods grew up around Catholic and Orthodox parish churches that remain today as the landmarks people use in their perceptual maps to locate themselves. And Pittsburgh had one additional monumental landmark in abundance: the huge sheds and blast furnaces that filled the flats along its river edges. These were so large that even with their passing they remain as landmarks even as missing large pieces of a changed puzzle. Unique about Pittsburgh's nodes and landmarks is how visible they are—whether seen from above at the center of a neighborhood or at the edge of a river below, or seen from below against the sky at the rim of a slope.

As I look back over my decades of drawing Pittsburgh, it interests me to observe how I have abstracted and revealed—largely through exaggeration of shape and scale—those same elements that Lynch has listed, but without having ever particularly intended their inclusion. In a way, this may be Lynch's point. They are unavoidable once one begins the process of distillation that drawing naturally brings. But once I've found them, I have sought to give form to the way I experience them, by exaggerating the ways in which they are evident here in Pittsburgh.

The boundaries and paths that are the legacy of its steep slopes are the most obvious example. As I've already described, I tend to turn shelf plateaus upward so that their edges are more apparent and so I can show the stairs that descend them more readily. The slopes have also affected the way I draw the land itself. Taking a cue from the painter Sam Rosenberg (whom I mentioned earlier and will discuss later in this essay as well), I scour the surfaces of facing slopes with the strokes of my charcoal to emphasize their sheer verticality. And I always exaggerate the sizes of key landmarks: whether Forbes Field, the Cathedral of Learning, or Polish Hill's Immaculate Heart of Mary church. In figures 4.25, 4.26, 4.27, and 4.28, I have paired several of my images with Lynch-inspired diagrams of boundaries, paths, nodes, and landmarks to show the evidence of his thinking in my work.

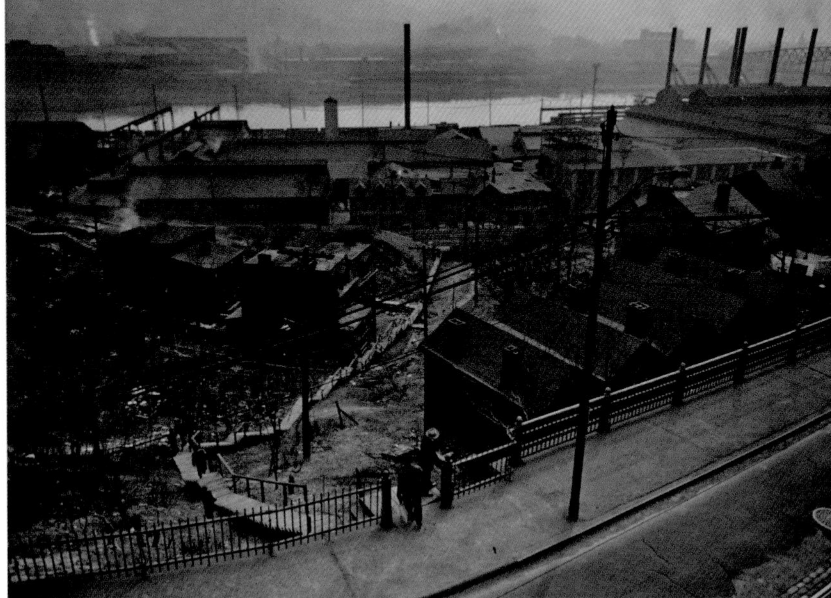

4.23 (*above*). *Forbes Avenue Taken from the Boulevard of the Allies, the C.C. Hussey Co in Soho*, Harold Corsini, 1952. Gelatin silver print, 11 × 13⅞ inches. Carnegie Museum of Art, Pittsburgh. Gift of the Carnegie Library of Pittsburgh.
4.24 (*right*). Detail, *Backyards along Greenfield Avenue*, Doug Cooper, 2015. Charcoal on paper on board, 36 × 48 inches. Private collection.

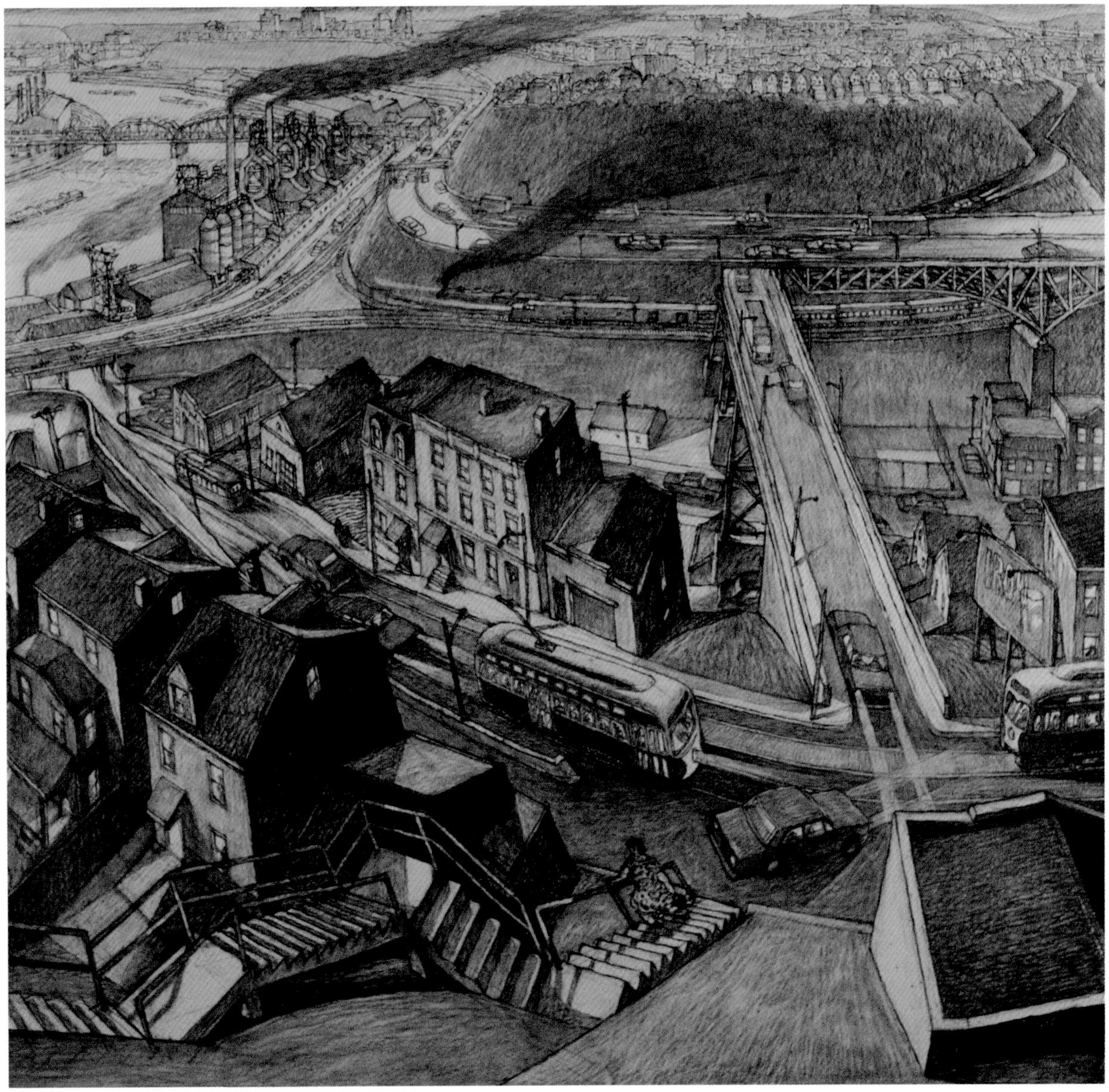

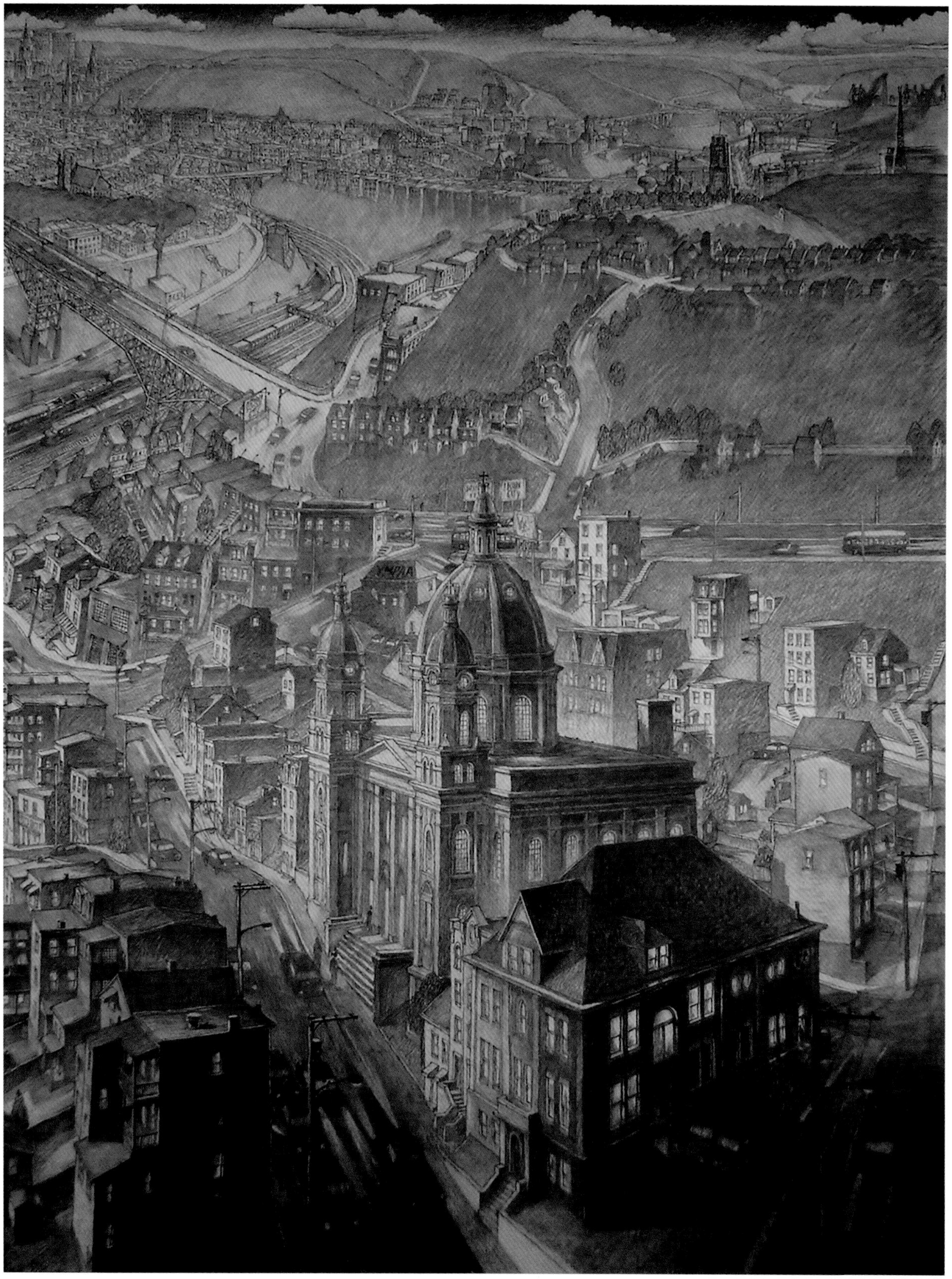

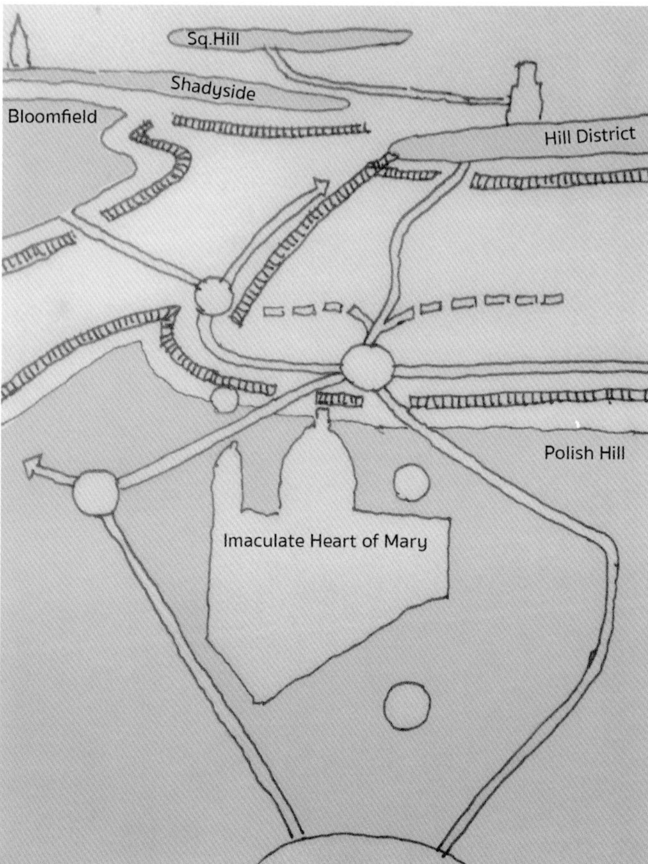

4.25 (*left*). *Immaculate Heart of Mary*, Doug Cooper, 2012.
Charcoal on paper on board, 64 × 48 inches. Private collection.
4.26 (*above*). Lynch-inspired diagram of Immaculate Heart of Mary.

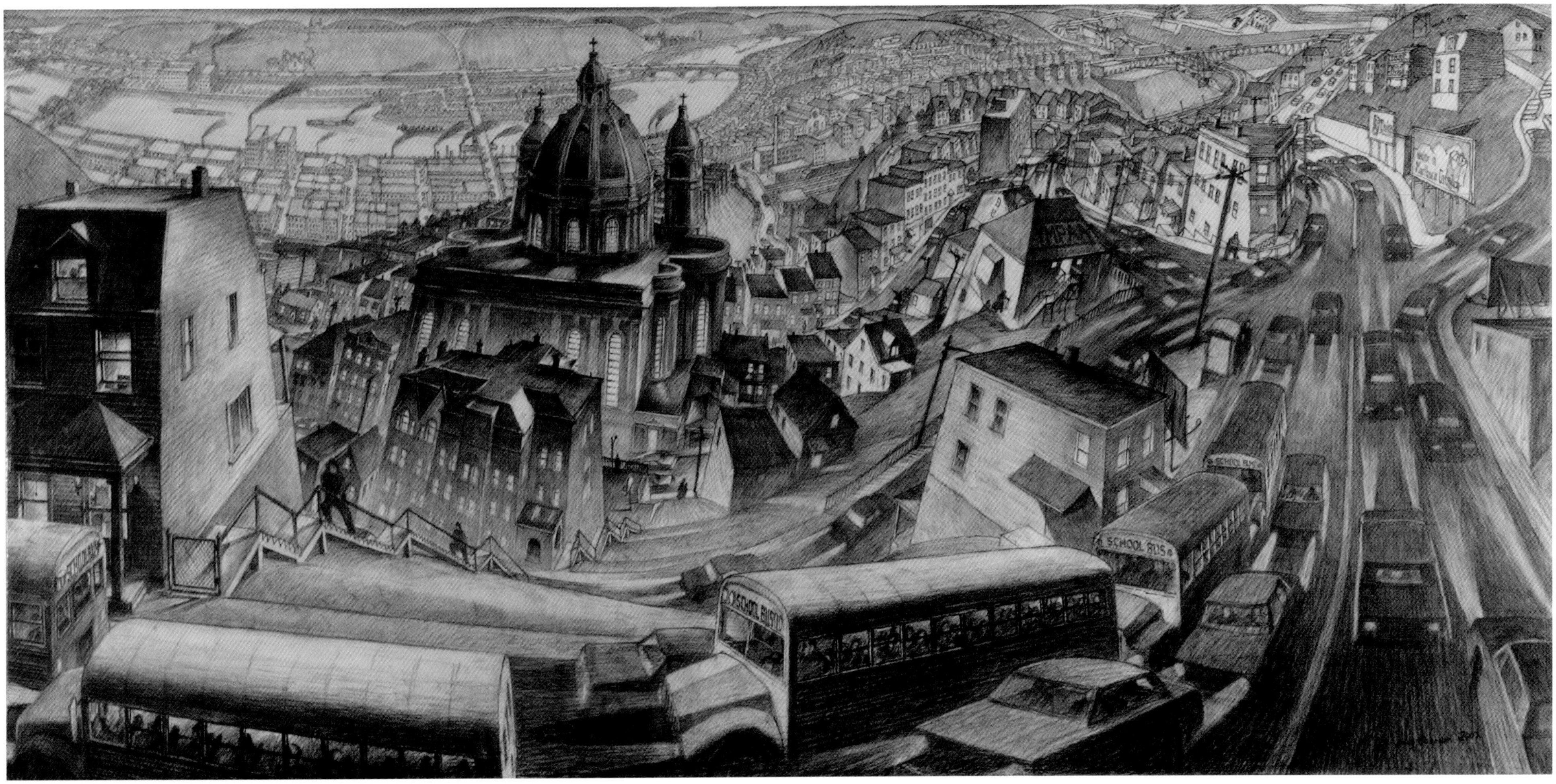

4.27 (*above*). *School Outing*, Doug Cooper, 2007. Charcoal on paper
on board, 48 × 72 inches. Private collection.
4.28 (*right*). Lynch-inspired diagram of school outing.

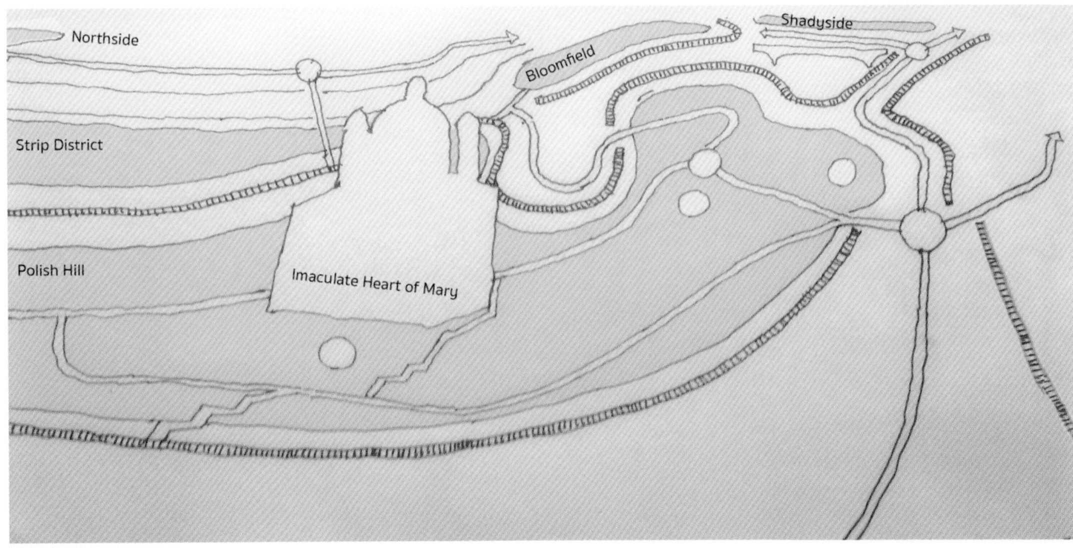

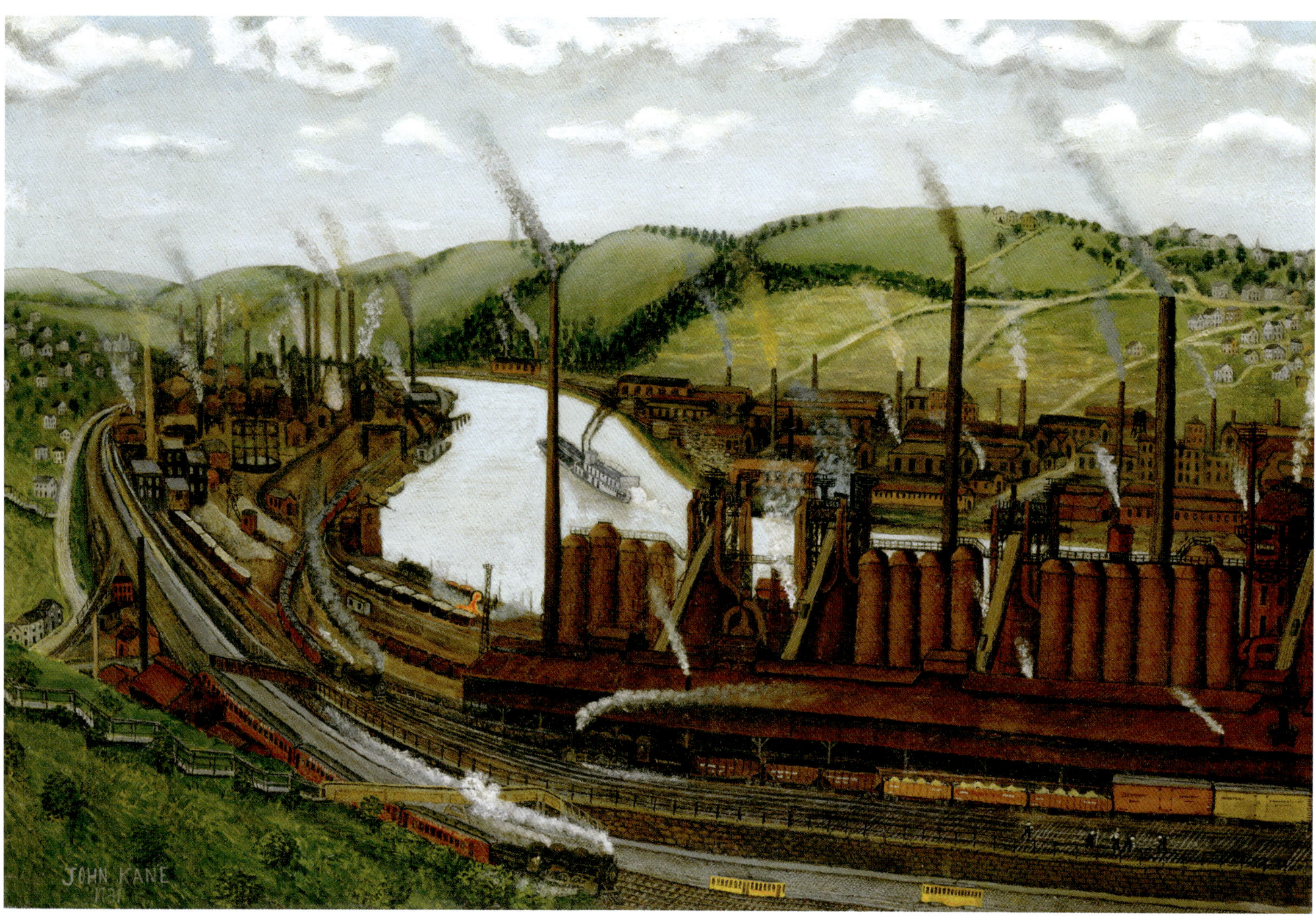

4.29. *The Monongahela River Valley*, John Kane, 1931. Metropolitan Museum of Art, New York, NY. Bequest of Miss Adelaide Milton de Groot. Image source: Art Resource, NY.

John Kane and Sam Rosenberg

In bringing the work of the photographers who have documented Pittsburgh together with the work of Lynch, there is something of the notion of joining the perceptual with the conceptual. And in relating my work to both, I've tried to discern what aspects of the landscape I've found most telling in communicating its essence as a place. Another way of understanding this process is to look back at the work of those landscape painters who have had the greatest impact on my work. There are two: John Kane (1860–1934) and Samuel Rosenberg (1896–1972).

I first learned of Kane in the late 1960s from Leon Arkus, then director of the Carnegie Museum of Art. In 1966 Leon had curated a show of the paintings of three self-taught western Pennsylvania artists, one of them being Kane, whom he had written much about. Kane's work had been discovered shortly before he had died in 1934, and so by the time of this show he was widely known.

What has always stood out in Kane's paintings is the relationship of his experience of Pittsburgh—largely through his lifetime as a laborer who took great pride in his work—and his representation of that in depicting the cityscape. He painted most of his works in the last decade of his life, after working various jobs during the great industrial expansion of the city in 1880–1920 (fig. 4.29).

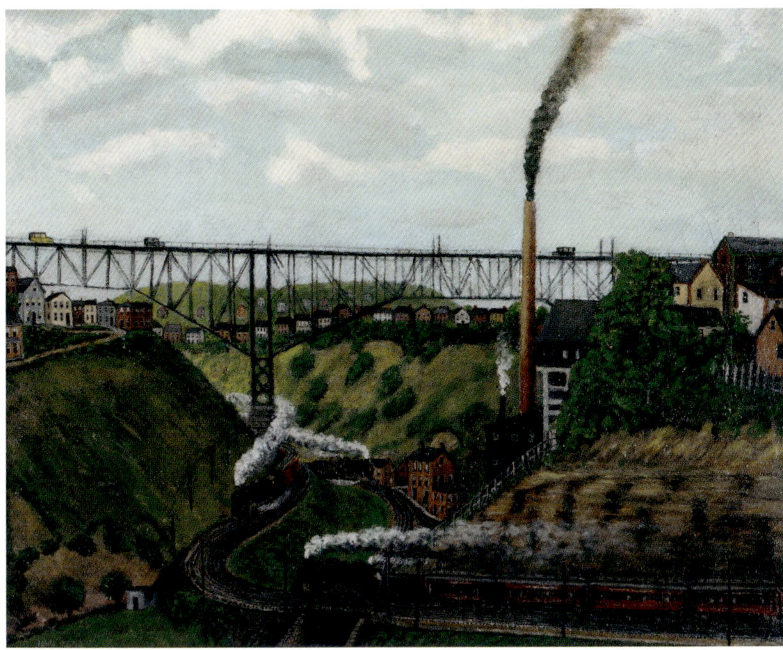

4.30. *Bloomfield Bridge*, John Kane, ca. 1930. Oil on canvas, 19 ⅜ × 23 ⅜ inches. Carnegie Museum of Art, Pittsburgh. Gift of Mr. and Mrs. James H. Beal.

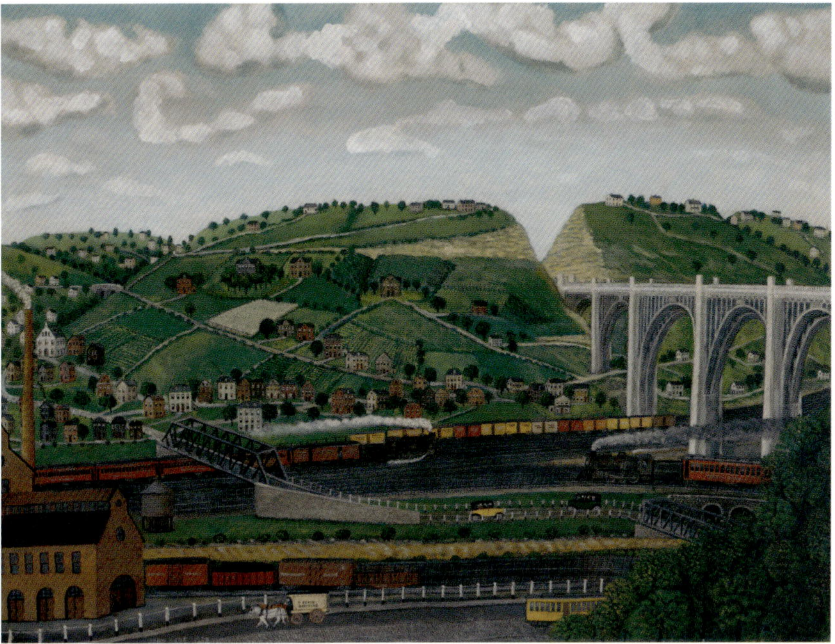

4.31. *Turtle Creek Valley, No 2*, John Kane, 1932. Oil on canvas, 34 ⅛ × 44 ⅛ inches. Roland P. Murdock Collection, Wichita Art Museum, Wichita, KS.

His first job was as a gandy dancer, tamping down the ballast between railroad ties on the Baltimore & Ohio Railroad. While working with the B&O, he was struck by a train running without lights at night and lost his left leg below the knee. But he learned to wear an artificial limb and worked in Braddock laying the foundations of the Edgar Thomson Steel Mill and later worked seven days a week there in its Bessemer blast furnaces. In the 1890s he worked as a street paver in Pittsburgh and McKeesport. Years later he would point to the detailed paving patterns of streets he included in his paintings and describe how he had painted those streets exactly how he had paved them. In the early 1900s, Kane worked as a railroad car painter at the Pressed Steel Car Company in McKees Rocks. It was in that job that he began painting images of the city on the sides of railcars during his lunch breaks and painting them over each afternoon.

One of the most telling summaries of the relationship of Kane's experience of the city and his landscapes appears in his own words in his autobiography, *Sky Hooks*. Kane wrote, "It has been said that that I am able to apply a technical knowledge to my industrial scenes, my paintings of steel mills, furnaces, pipe factories and of buildings of all sorts. Another man might paint a plant that could never stand up. But, not I. I know how the building was erected for I have worked on every part of it, from digging the foundations to the entire structure. Floor by floor, I know how it goes up." Elsewhere, Kane spoke of his knowledge of the many railroad cars he had painted. In his painting of the valley beneath the Bloomfield Bridge, we see each freight car in a detailed manner that only one who had once painted the real thing would know (fig. 4.30).

I have always wondered about Kane's backgrounds. They seem to ignore the degradation of the natural environment that photographers of the city clearly documented. They almost seem like the verdant pastures he might have remembered from his native Scotland where he lived until age nineteen. Perhaps they capture some sense (unrecognizable at the time Kane was painting) of the natural beauty the region once had in abundance. At the very least, they offer a counterpoint to what Kane's paintings celebrate: the assembled knowledge of the city gained from a lifetime of hard work (fig. 4.31).

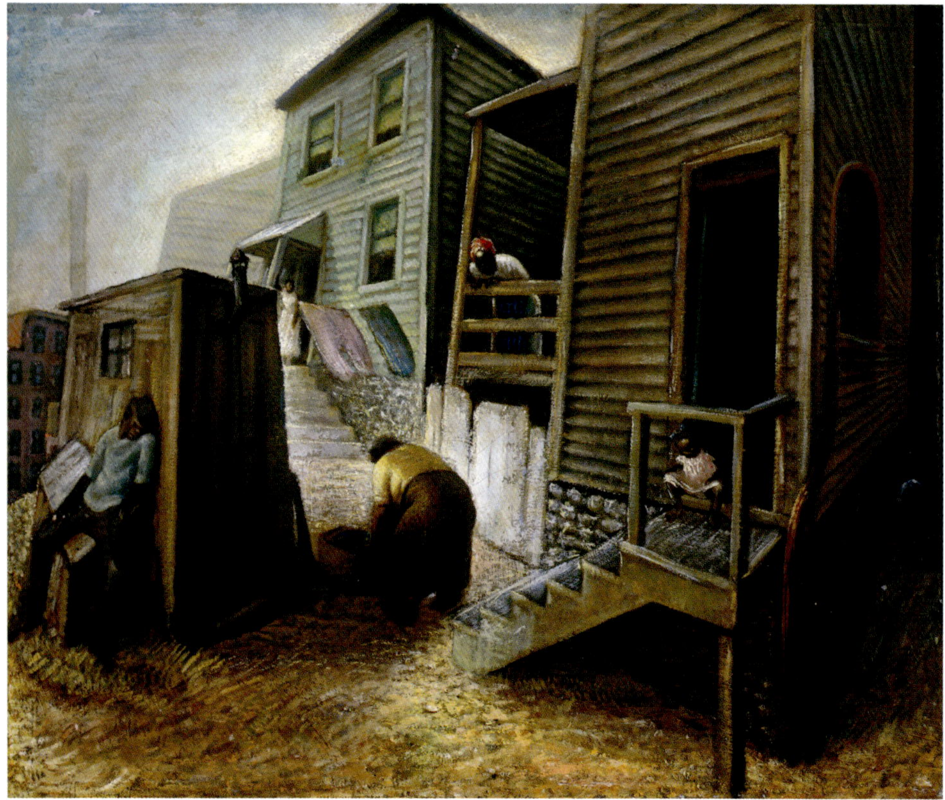

4.32. *Monday Morning (After the Night Shift)*, Samuel Rosenberg, 1935. Oil on canvas, 30 × 36 inches. Courtesy of Arline Rosenberg.

Unlike Kane, Rosenberg received ample formal training in art, and his experience of the city through his painting reflects that past. His mother recognized his talent at an early age and he attended the Columbian Council School in the Hill (the forerunner of the Irene Kaufmann Settlement house). After growing up in the city's Oakland district, he attended Carnegie Tech in Pittsburgh and then the National Academy of Design in New York in 1917.

According to a recent biography by Barbara Jones, *Samuel Rosenberg: Portrait of an American Painter*, a lecture by George Bellows at the Art Students League was a profound influence on Rosenberg from his time in New York. The League was at the center of the Ash Can school, whose leaders—Bellows, Robert Henri, and John Sloan—advocated focusing on distinctly American themes such as the lives of ordinary people in the inner city. Indeed, more than a decade later,

after concentrating on portraiture throughout the 1920s, Rosenberg did just that: working almost exclusively on landscape subjects close to home in Pittsburgh's Hill District and Soho neighborhoods. His landscapes have the same gritty character we see in the work of others from the Ash Can school.

I knew Rosenberg's Pittsburgh paintings from an early age because they were featured (along with Kane's) in Stefan Lorant's *Pittsburgh: The Story of an American City*, published in 1958. Where Kane was interested in endowing his paintings with things in the city that held meaning for him because he had made them, Rosenberg was interested in depicting how he *sensed* the city through painting it: its inhabitants, its spaces, and its terrain. For him it was largely a matter of surfaces and edges, whether accelerating the perspective of the siding and splaying the perspective of verticals in *Monday Morning*, or using cross contour to model the city's sloping and deeply eroded terrain in the background of *Greenfield Hill* (figs. 4.32, 4.33). Value contrast plays a role, to be sure, but his brushstrokes and their movement along surfaces are the most important element in his work. His work is tactile—something he may have picked up from Kimon Nicolaïdes, one of the most prominent teachers at the Art Students League, and it is that quality that I have sought to bring into my own work in drawing the city.

Bringing Knowing and Seeing Together

If my techniques share something with Rosenberg's, I have brought something of Kane's focus on *knowing* into my landscapes as well, albeit with a knowledge of the city that is different from his. I cannot describe mills in my drawings with any knowledge of their inner workings or construction. I have never worked in a mill or been part of building one. I know them from the outside, only, and can only show them as they appear to an outsider.

But what I do know is the layout of the city from years of walking through it and drawing it. This has amounted to two kinds of knowledge: one, a knowledge of the appearance of what I see—how houses and city steps appear on slopes when I look down at them; and two, a more cartographic knowledge of the layout of the city, a knowledge of what I cannot see because it is out of sight, hidden by a corner or below the rim of the slope.

I'd relate what I've done with Pittsburgh to those who have come before me in this way: The foregrounds build on the features the photographers and

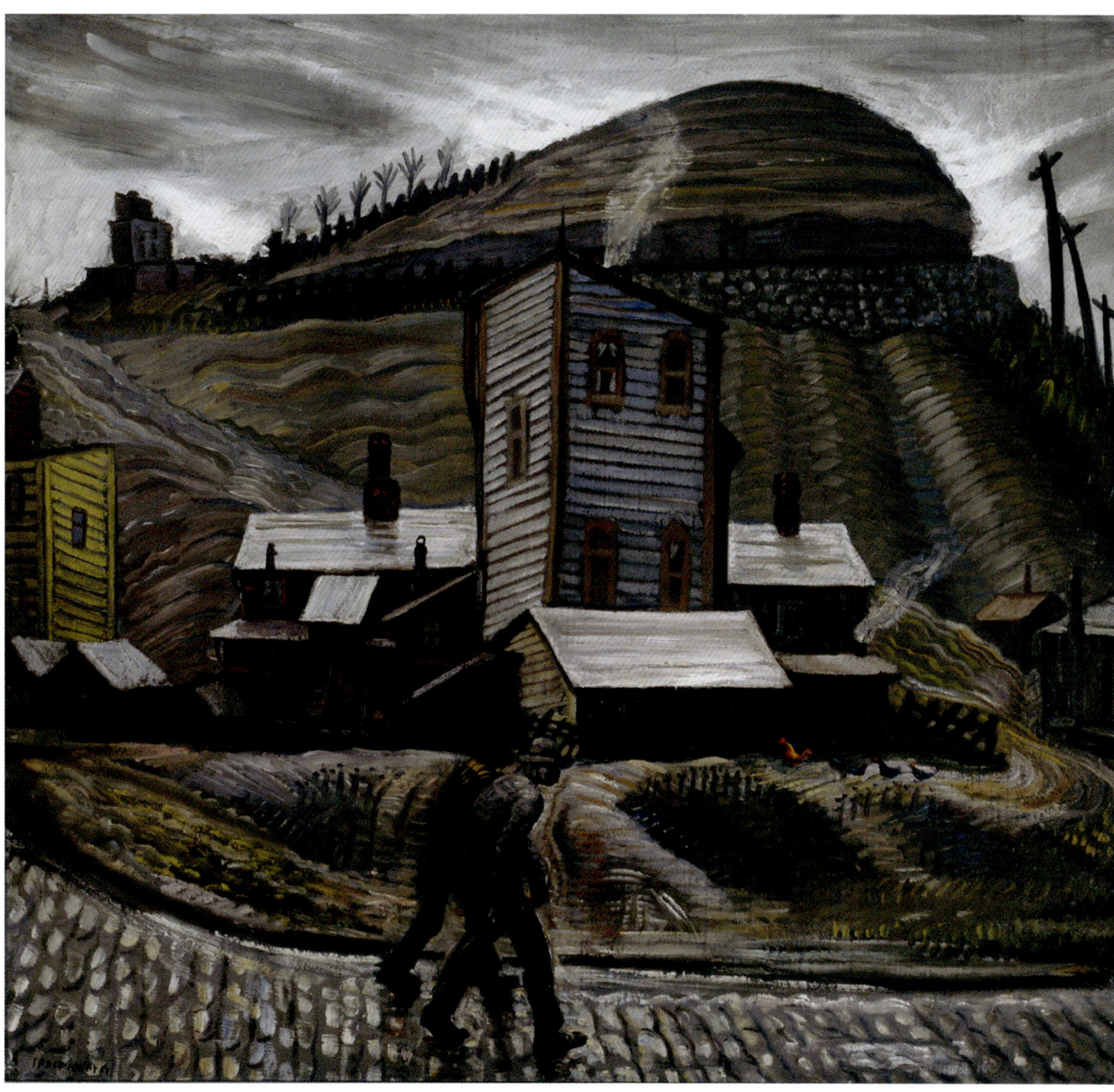

4.33. *Greenfield Hill (Gazzam's Hill)*, Samuel Rosenberg, 1932. Oil on masonite, 39 ⅛ × 40 ½ inches, Carnegie Museum of Art, Pittsburgh. Patrons Art Fund: Gift of A. W. Mellon Educational and Charitable Trust.

Rosenberg have captured and exaggerated. I am drawn to sites with city steps and porches and exposed foundation walls on slopes simply because they reveal the land in a manner that resonates with a sense of the city that I share with them. But the backgrounds and middle grounds build on Kane.

As I'm looking at it today, I can best describe the union between Kane and Rosenberg that I've sought by looking at one of my favorite paintings by Rosenberg, *Sunday Morning* (fig. 4.34), and imagining how I might have addressed the same scene, but in a manner that also builds on Kane. The church still exists, though, sadly, it is completely disconnected from the neighborhood that surrounded it in Rosenberg's time. Were the scene in my hands, I would have raised the stoops and porch roofs further down the street, and shown the layout of the Soho neighborhood below and its connection to the Brady Street Bridge and the Southside beyond. In short, I would have sought to connect the foreground subject to its context and to a second center: the view's destination and possibly other centers along the way (fig. 4.35). And in that I would have been bringing a sense of the city that is more like Kane's, having less to do with how it looks and more to do with what I know it to be.

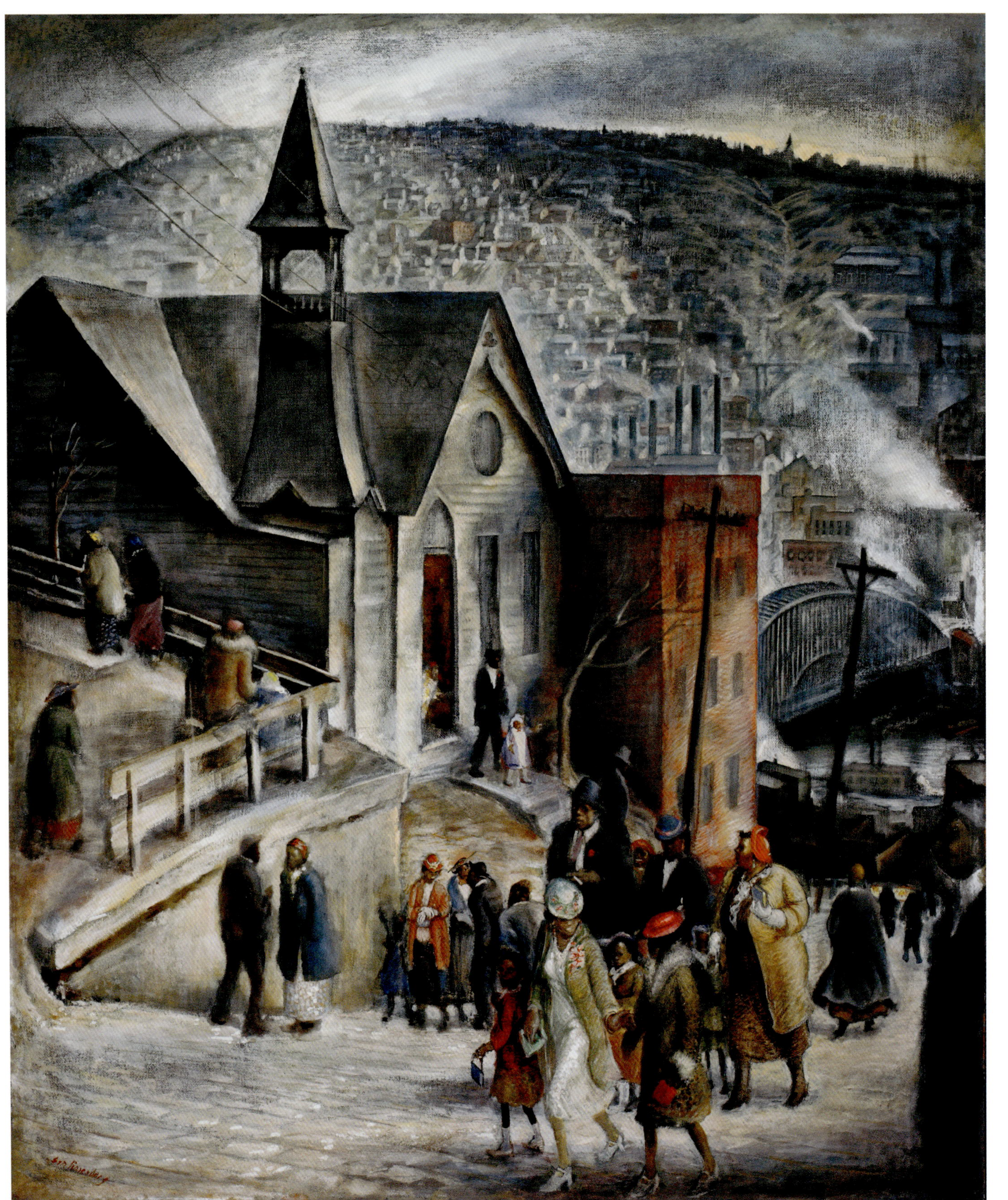

4.34 (*left*). *Sunday Morning*, Samuel Rosenberg, 1937. Oil on masonite, 56 × 46 inches. Westmoreland Museum of American Art, Greensburg, PA. Gift of Arline Rosenberg. 4.35 (*right*). *Sunday Morning (Sketch after Sam Rosenberg's painting)*, Doug Cooper, 2018. Pencil on paper, 14 × 11 inches. Collection of the artist.

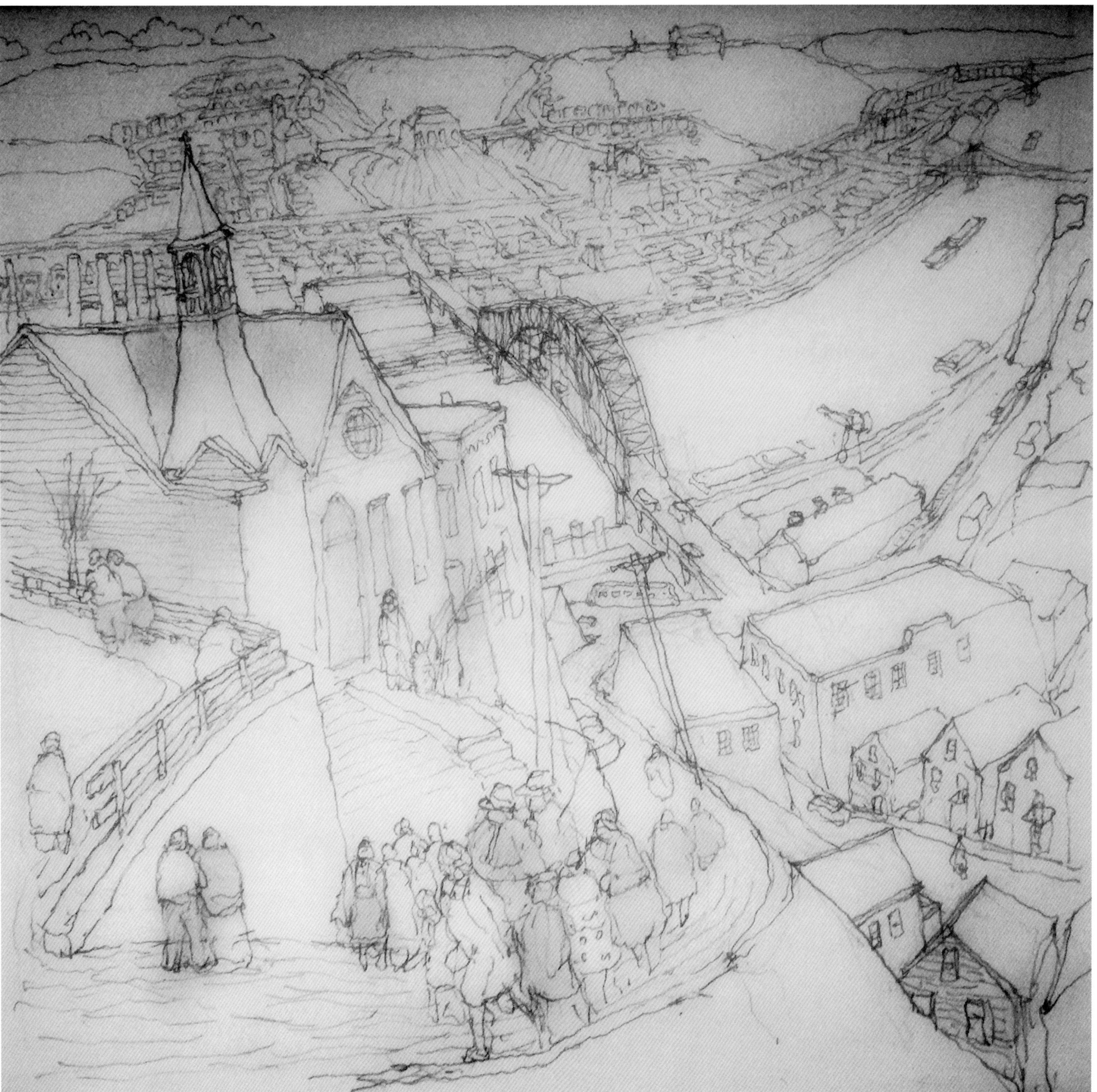

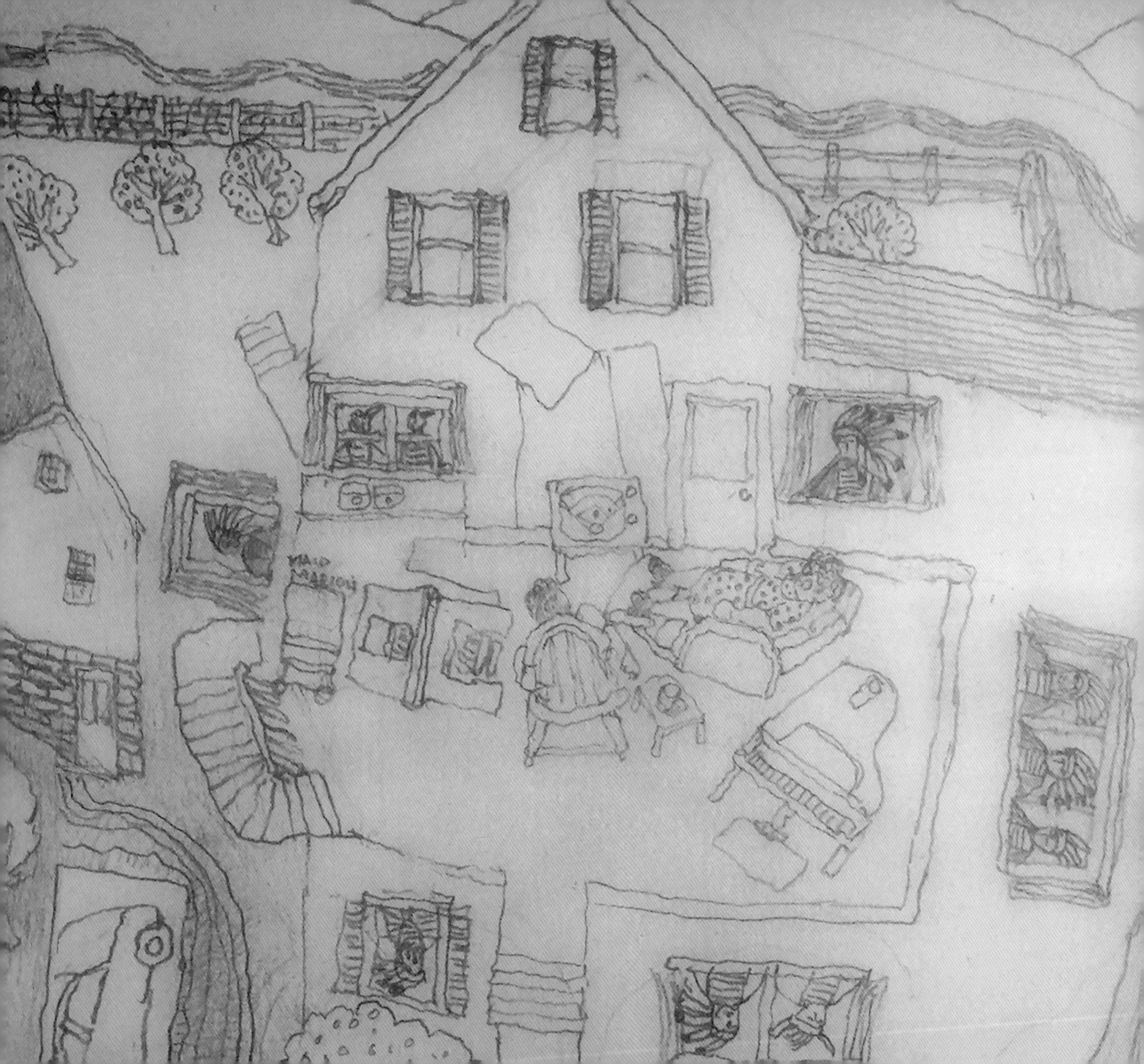

MAID
MARION

CHAPTER 5

PLACE AND MEMORY

One summer, my former wife, Meg, and I were visiting her two maiden great-aunts who lived in an old farmhouse in Cornwall, Connecticut, where they had retired from teaching in the New York City public schools (fig. 5.1). Their names fit them perfectly—Alma was ninety and Blanche was in her mid-eighties—and there was something of an *Arsenic and Old Lace* mischievousness about them. Their father had served under General Philip Sheridan during the Civil War (he had been awarded the Congressional Medal of Honor) and had remained with Sheridan after the war, during the years of fighting the Sioux. Blanche and Alma had spent the first years of their lives at Fort Custer in Montana. Years later, it was still a family mystery why Alma, every evening at sundown, went to each window in their Cornwall house and pulled the curtains shut tight. To the extent anyone could understand it at all, her behavior seemed driven by modesty taken to an extreme.

One evening Blanche and Meg wanted to go to the movies. By this time in her life, Alma was suffering some cognitive problems, so I agreed to babysit. Alma was quite childlike in her perceptions of the world around her, and her reactions to it were often funny. Among other things, she thought people on the TV set in their living room were visitors in their home, so if her sister entered the room wearing just a nightie, Alma would admonish her to dress more modestly in front of their guests.

But Alma also loved baseball, and on this evening, after Meg and Blanche had gone, we settled down to watch the Mets on TV as dusk fell. She was seated in her favorite chair, a large leather Barcalounger. After a while, she began rocking herself rhythmically, all the while humming and whistling. It was a kind of sucking whistling that produced sound whether she inhaled or exhaled. This was a habit of hers at the time, and I had noticed that it seemed to comfort her. But this time it went on longer and grew more insistent. Eventually it took on a metered cadence and seemed to cast a nearly hypnotic spell over her.

Then suddenly, she began speaking in an unusual voice and commenced describing events as if they were taking place there in the room around us. It was as if she was speaking in tongues—taking dictation right out of the past.

"It is dusk.
"We're in our home at Fort Custer.
"There are small windows along two walls.
"Father is away, chasing down a horse thief.
"We are sitting at our table, and mother is bringing us dinner
   from the stove.
"And now I see them again, they're all peering in at us—the Sioux.
"One face at every window.
"And their faces are ghoulishly lit from the oil lamps on our table.
"The curtains, the curtains!"

And then in Cornwall, ninety years after the incident, Alma leapt up from her Barcalounger and raced from window to window, pulling the curtains shut tight.

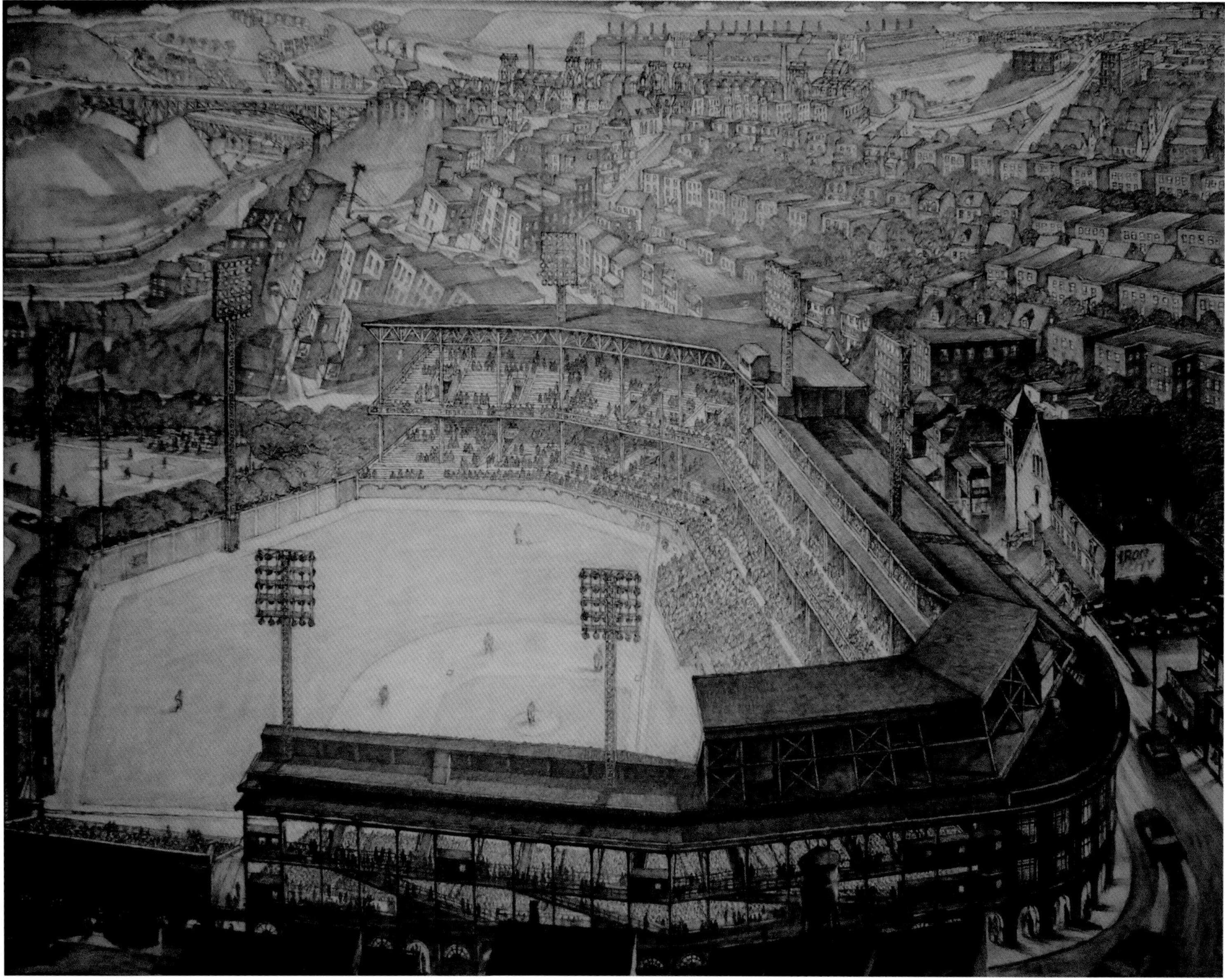

Knowing the Past, Seeing the Present

How do the meanings of places in our towns and cities vary from person to person? Forbes Field was where the Pittsburgh Pirates used to play baseball (fig. 5.2). Their field was torn down in the early 1970s to make way for a new quadrangle for the University of Pittsburgh. In its day it would have been one of the city's most important landmarks (by Kevin Lynch's use of the term), and its former location is still known by most. But its meaning varies widely among people. For nearby neighbors in Oakland, it was a place that glowed on the horizon on summer evenings (fig. 5.3). For some it was a place they visited several times a summer with their dads; for some it remains the nearly sacred ground where Bill Mazeroski hit his ninth-inning home run to win the 1960 World Series against the Yankees; for still others it was the place where traffic used to snarl when the games let out. For me, it was once the center of my life; Meg and I used to live across the street from it, and it was where our first daughter, Laura, was born (fig. 5.4).

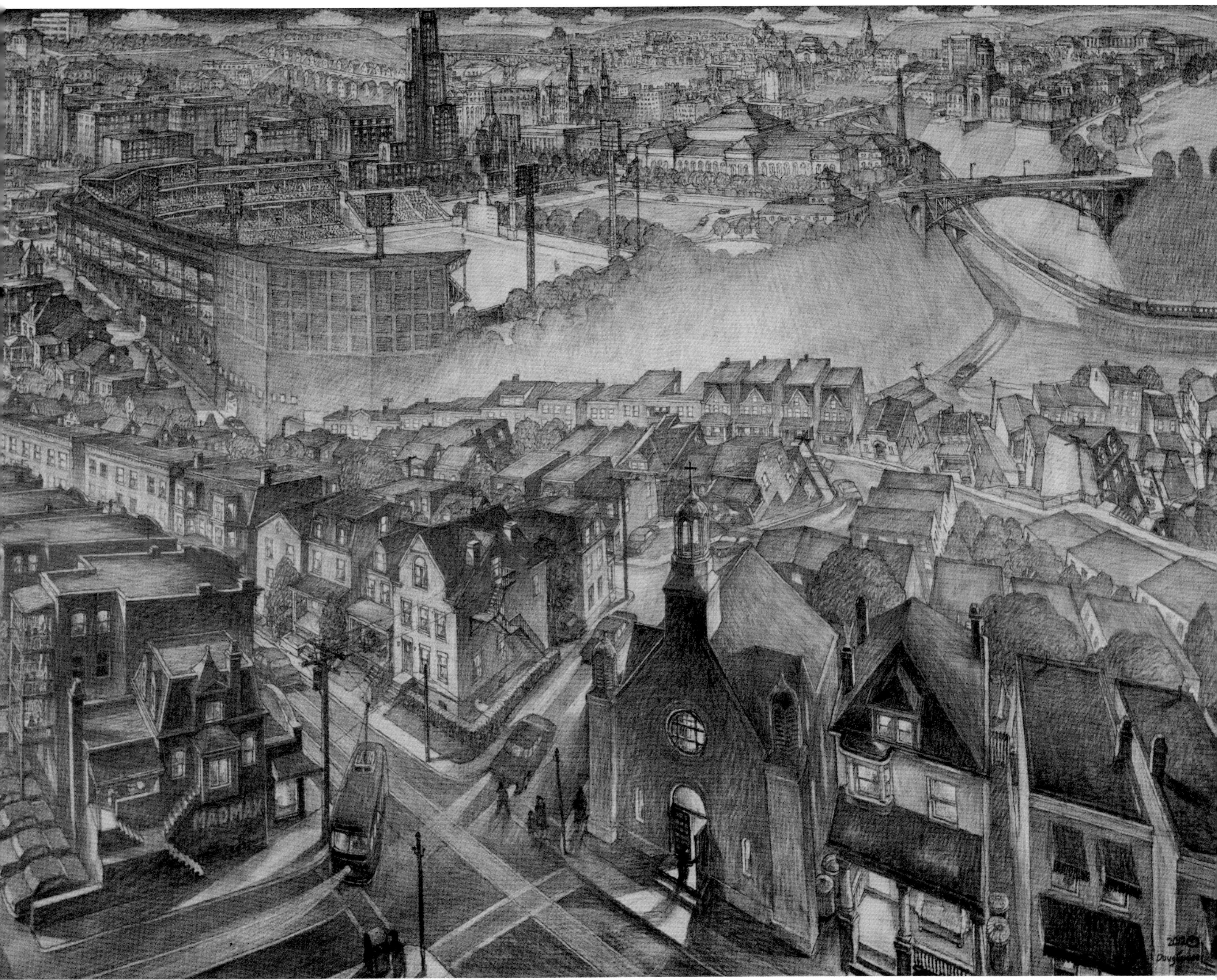

5.2 (*facing page*). *Forbes Field*, Doug Cooper, 2013. Charcoal on paper on board, 36 × 48 inches. Private collection.

5.3 (*above*). *Corner of Atwood and Bates*, Doug Cooper, 2012. Charcoal on paper on board, 36 × 48 inches. Private collection.

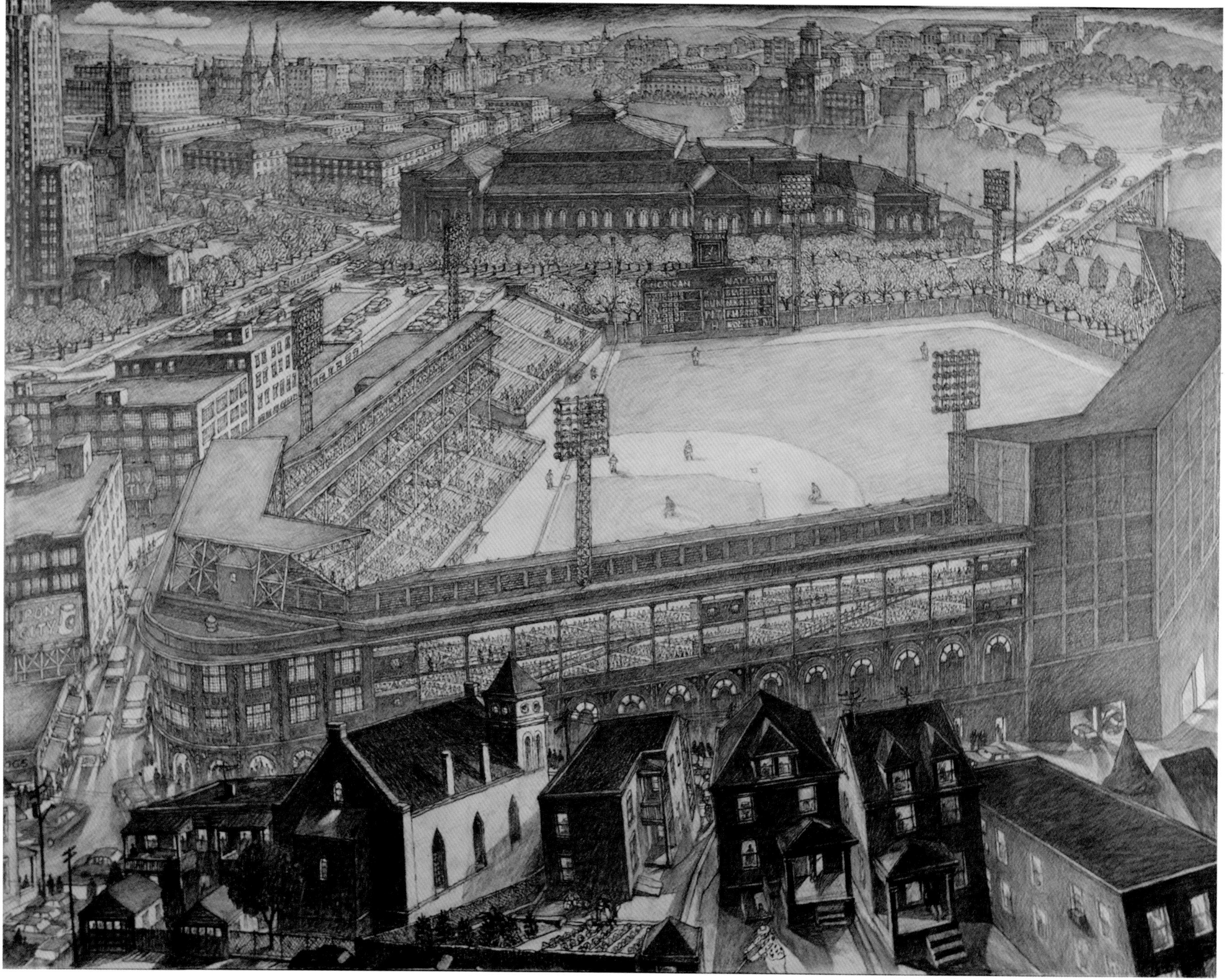

The interplay around this issue—what is shared meaning, what is unique meaning, and what is the role of time in both—really struck me one day when I was driving with a friend who was visiting the city along the street that now travels through what would have been the outfield of Forbes Field and arrived at the intersection with South Bouquet Street directly across from where our former house once stood. I could have talked with my friend for hours about all I had experienced there, and yet that location could have never meant for him what it had for me. He had not been there—then.

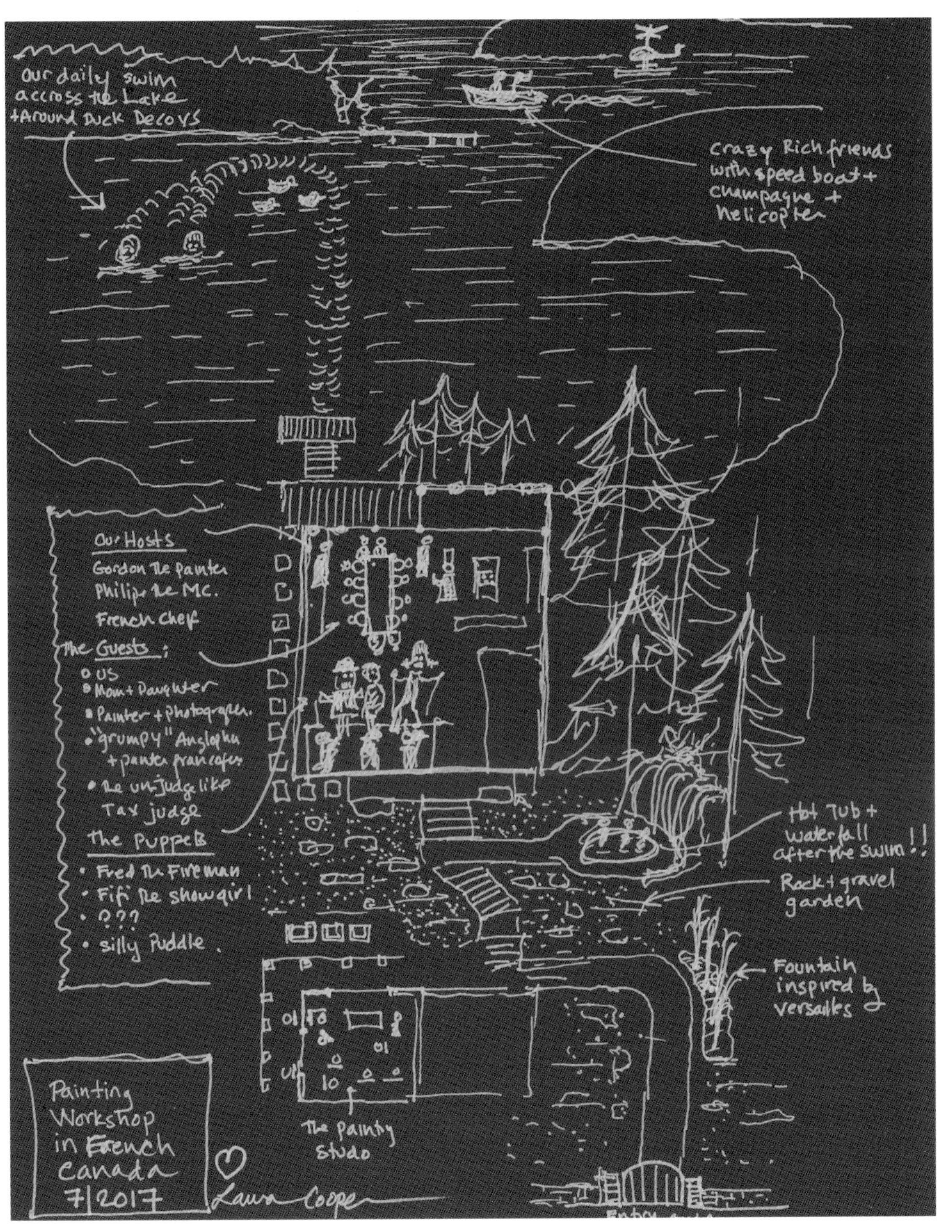

5.4. (facing page) *Backyards Opposite Forbes Field*, Doug Cooper, 2015. Charcoal on paper on board, 48 × 60 inches. Private collection.

5.5 (above). *Vacation in the Laurentians*, Laura Cooper, 2017. Felt-tipped pen on paper (reverse print), 11 × 8 ½ inches. Collection of the artist.

The story that I related at the beginning of this chapter about Alma's curious habit also points out how forcefully the playback from remembered surroundings can project into later life. In Alma's case just the fading light of dusk was a sufficient trigger. It is a truism that the meanings of places are forever bound up with what we have once experienced there.

When I first began thinking about doing public murals of cities, it was out of experiences such as these that I sensed it would be important for the broader meaning of the works to include the memories and perceptions of others. Over the years, I've also found that drawing can provide a powerful prod to memory—witness a delightful drawing my daughter Laura recently made of a vacation she took with me and my wife Stefani to Canada's Laurentian Mountains (fig. 5.5).

So, in 1992 when I began planning the first mural I did in Pittsburgh, a work that grew to 12 feet high by 120 feet long and is now in Pittsburgh's Heinz History Center, I approached a social center for seniors called Vintage, in the city's East End, where I was able to work with people whose memories of the city dated back as far as the First World War.

Working with Others at Vintage in Pittsburgh

My work at Vintage was early in the process of developing the mural's composition. We worked in groups organized around the city's neighborhoods and focused on places that no longer existed. Wherever possible, I got people to draw—I planned to collage their drawings into the mural—and I was startled by what that process dredged up from out of the past.

Part of it was the detail. Josephine Zielinski remembered a long-forgotten oval-framed picture of her father and the exact shape of the brackets that supported the kitchen sink when she drew her childhood home in South Oakland (fig. 5.6). Gertrude Diskin drew the boathouse by the lake in Panther Hollow and remembered how in winter she and her friends used to descend the long steps by the Adams Bridge to go skating. They always carried potatoes to roast in the great stone fireplaces at either end of the boathouse. Both Gertrude and Josephine spoke often about a little island with a single tree that was out in the middle of the lake. It had been important to them because it was something to skate to. Today Panther Hollow Lake has no island, but several weeks later I saw an old photograph of the lake. It showed a little island with a lone tree (fig. 5.7).

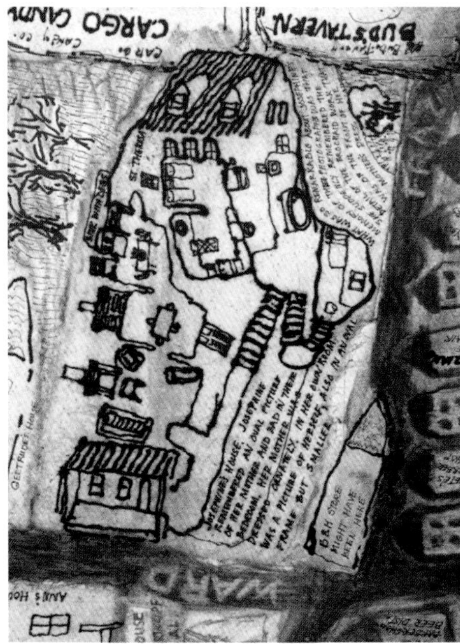

5.6. "Remembered House," Josephine Zielinski, 1992. Drawing done at Vintage Senior Center. Detail, Senator John Heinz History Center mural, Pittsburgh.

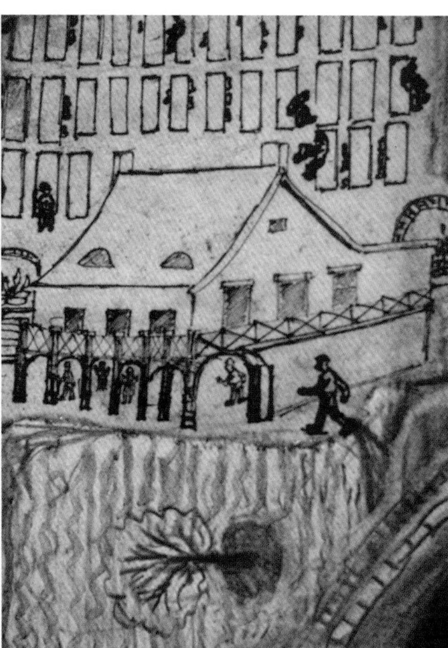

5.7. "Panther Hollow Lake Boathouse," Gertrude Diskin, 1992. Drawing done at Vintage Senior Center. Detail, Senator John Heinz History Center mural, Pittsburgh.

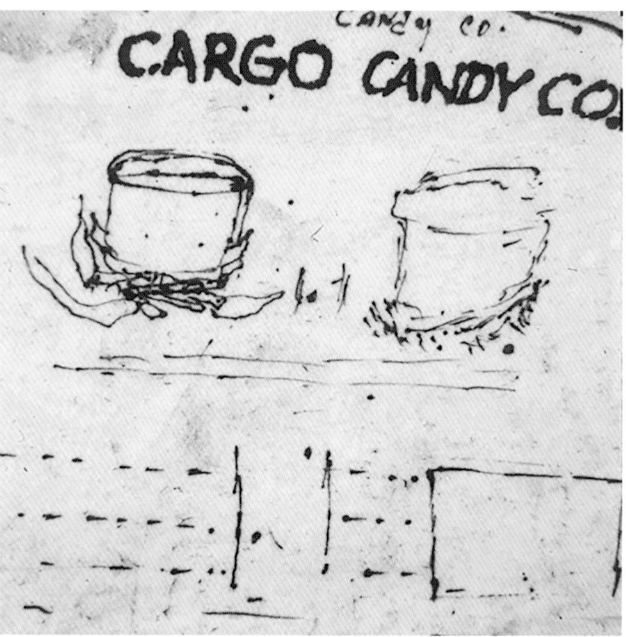

5.8. "Cargo Candy Company," Anna Edmondson, 1992. Drawing done at Vintage Senior Center. Detail, Senator John Heinz History Center mural, Pittsburgh.

Anna and the Saint Patrick's Day Flood, 1936

One woman, Anna M. Edmondson, developed an unusually abstract technique, which I began calling "Morse code drawing" because of its many dots and dashes. She usually worked alone with a kind of silent intensity. When I sat next to her and had her explain her drawings, their abstraction became clear. The dots and the dashes were shorthand. When she drew the Cargo Candy Company (a factory/store in South Oakland that no longer exists), she used dots and dashes to represent the candy she remembered seeing in the cases at the front of the store at Eastertime (fig. 5.8).

Because it tells an entire story, her drawing of the 1936 Saint Patrick's Day flood stands out most of all (fig. 5.9). She lived in Lawrenceville at the time. On the seventeenth of March, she came home from her job as an elevator operator at the Fort Pitt Hotel just as the water was reaching the curb. Later that night, the water continued to rise, and she had to be rescued the next day from her second-story window.

I sat next to her as she drew and talked. First she drew a kind of house shape. When I asked her how high up the water had risen, she drew the water rising to her second-story window. Then she drew events. She remembered that as the waters rose through the night, her downstairs neighbor had torn the front door off its hinges, put his family on it, and then, using the door as a kind of kickboard, floated his family to safety. This event she drew at the base of the house. Later, a casket from a nearby casket factory had floated by. In the early morning she had looked down into the back yard and seen terrified cattle from the nearby stockyards being swept through by the rushing water. They were driven against the picket fence, where their hooves became shackled, and there they were drowned. By later that day the water had reached the second floor and Anna, terrified, ran from window to window looking for help. In the distance she saw boats looking for trapped residents. Prisoners had been let out of jail to man them. She called one over to her and was rescued. Anna could not swim.

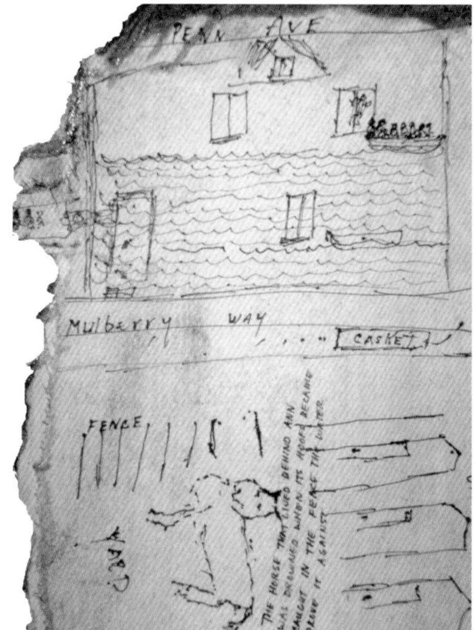

5.9. "House in Saint Patrick's Day Flood," Anna Edmondson, 1992. Drawing done at Vintage Senior Center, 1992. Detail, Senator John Heinz History Center mural, Pittsburgh.

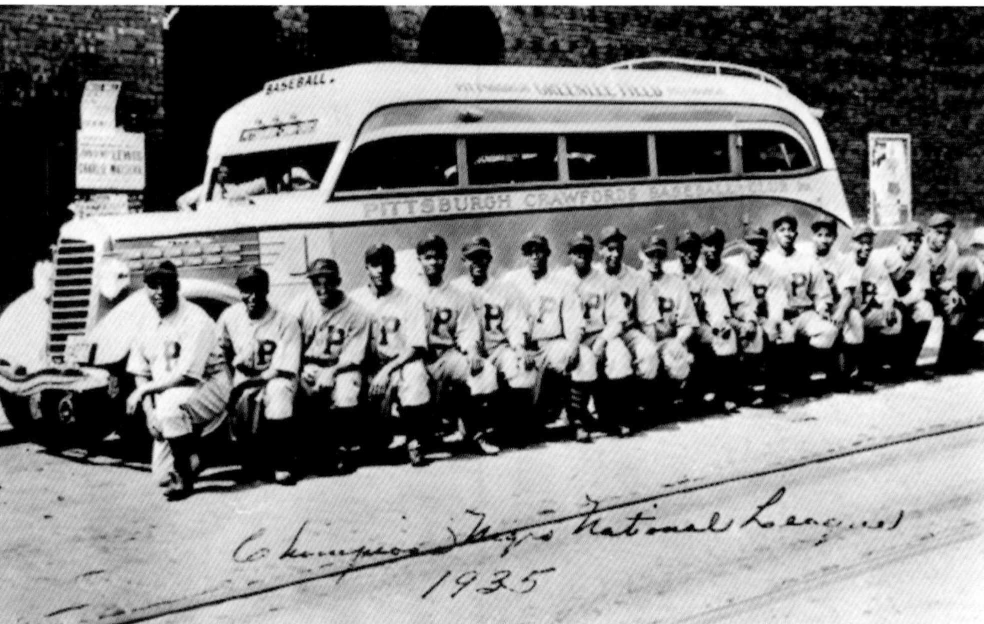

5.10. *Pittsburgh Crawfords*, anonymous, with Judy Johnson, Josh Gibson, Cool Papa Bell, Satchel Paige, Oscar Charleston, 1935. Courtesy of Associated Press.

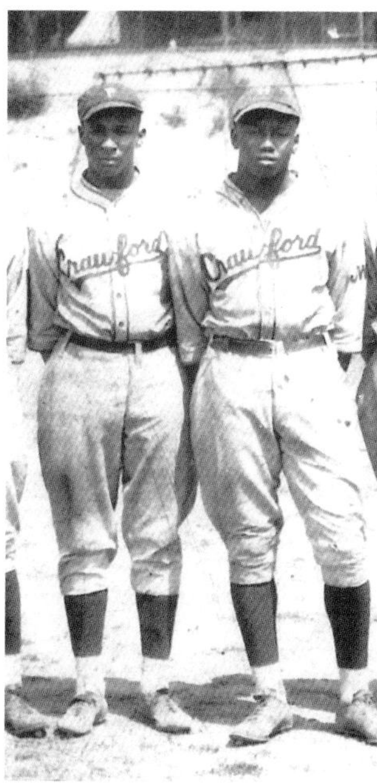

5.11. Harold Tinker (*left*) with Josh Gibson (*right*), ca. 1929. Photo courtesy of Harold Tinker Jr.

Reverend Tinker: Forbes Field, 1930s

At Vintage I met the former center fielder of the Pittsburgh Crawfords, one of the legendary teams of the Negro Baseball League (fig. 5.10). Almost ninety years old by this time, Reverend Harold Tinker had retained his full height. He was wearing a clerical collar and had a narrow face with prominent cheekbones. When he stood up to greet me, I noticed how bowed his legs were, and then I noticed his hands, which were huge. And in the center of his left hand was a baseball-size pocket worn into his palm by thirty years of catching fly balls.

Reverend Tinker's father had brought his family to Pittsburgh from Birmingham, Alabama, in 1916 during the World War I production boom. The next year, 1917, was the last that Honus Wagner played for the Pirates, and Tinker remembered sneaking into Forbes Field several times through the board fence behind the bleachers to see him play. Being African American and given the segregation of the time, he had never expected to play there himself.

Tinker first joined the Crawfords in the mid-1920s, when they were still a semipro team. They were just one of several teams he joined on top of his regular job with RKO Pictures. But in the late 1920s, with the addition of players such as Josh Gibson, the team grew stronger. Gibson would go on to a legendary career with the Crawfords and later the Homestead Grays, Pittsburgh's nationally known black team—he was called the "Black Babe Ruth"—but it was Harold Tinker who originally discovered him hitting monstrous home runs at a field on Spring Hill and brought him to the Crawfords (fig. 5.11). By the summer of 1930 the Crawfords were ready to challenge the Grays. The game was not played at the Crawfords' home field on the Hill. It was played on August 25 in Forbes Field, where Tinker had assumed he would never play.

Tinker described the game while I acted as scribe. The Crawfords were not favored—Gibson had jumped to the Grays several days before—but the game remained close. Grays pitcher Oscar Owens held the Crawfords hitless through five innings until Tinker hit safely in the sixth. Though the Crawfords

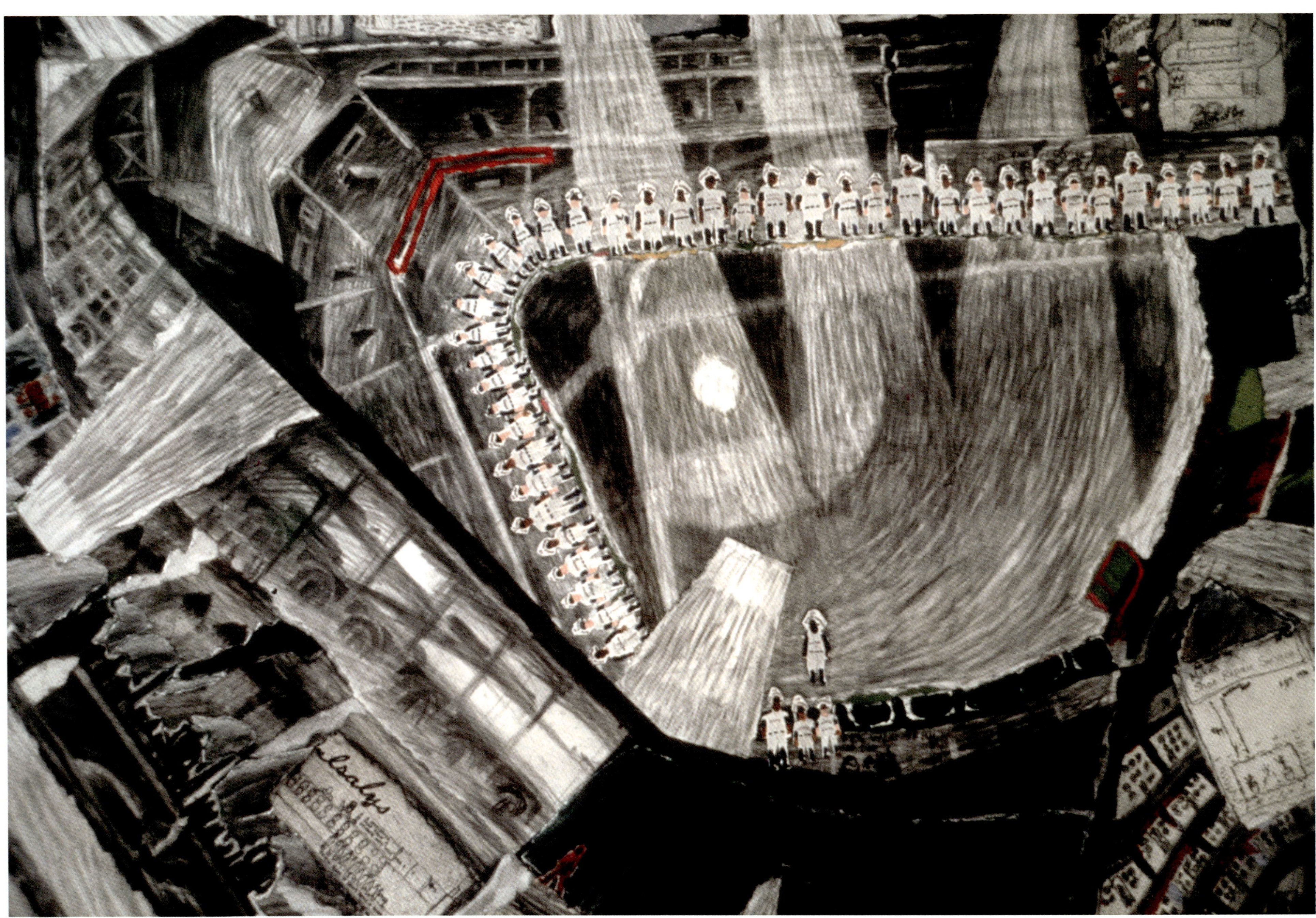

5.12. "Forbes Field," Doug Cooper, 1992. Acrylic and charcoal on paper on board. Based on Harold Tinker's description of a game played between the Pittsburgh Crawfords and the Homestead Grays in 1930. Detail, Senator John Heinz History Center mural, Pittsburgh.

scored two runs that inning, they entered the ninth inning still down by a run. They finally lost by a 3–2 margin when Bill Harris made a running catch of Charlie Hughes's line drive with two outs and two runners on base.

After Reverend Tinker finished describing the game, I drew a baseball diamond on a sheet of paper and asked him to list the players at each position. He named all but one. On the field that day were three future Hall of Fame players: Judy Johnson, Oscar Charleston, and Josh Gibson (fig. 5.12).

Later in 1930, Gus Greenlee, the Hill District's well-known numbers racketeer, bought the team. Greenlee also owned the Crawford Grill, the center of Pittsburgh's jazz scene. Greenlee put the players on full salaries and pointed the team in a direction that would make it the premier team in the Negro League by 1935. Reverend Tinker knew he would eventually have to quit the team because, with a large family to support, he would have to maintain his regular job. But he did not quit until the Crawfords finally did beat the Grays in the summer of 1931.

Philadelphia, Frankfurt, Doha, and Rome

I found the experience of working with people in Pittsburgh so inspiring and rewarding that when I completed public murals in other cities I engaged local residents and included the stories they told me. In Philadelphia I worked with Debbie Zwetsch and people at the Center in the Park and the Marconi Center to produce a mural for the Philadelphia Courthouse. Professor Stephen Brockmann and I brought students with backgrounds in the German language to my former hometown, Frankfurt, Germany, to work with me at various senior centers and produce a mural for the city's central food market. In Rome, Professor Jan Vairo and I engaged students with capabilities in Italian to work with centers in the neighborhood known as Esquilino (fig. 5.13). In Doha, Qatar, I worked with my daughter Sarah and her fellow photographer Nina Gorfer. Here, then, are some of their stories.

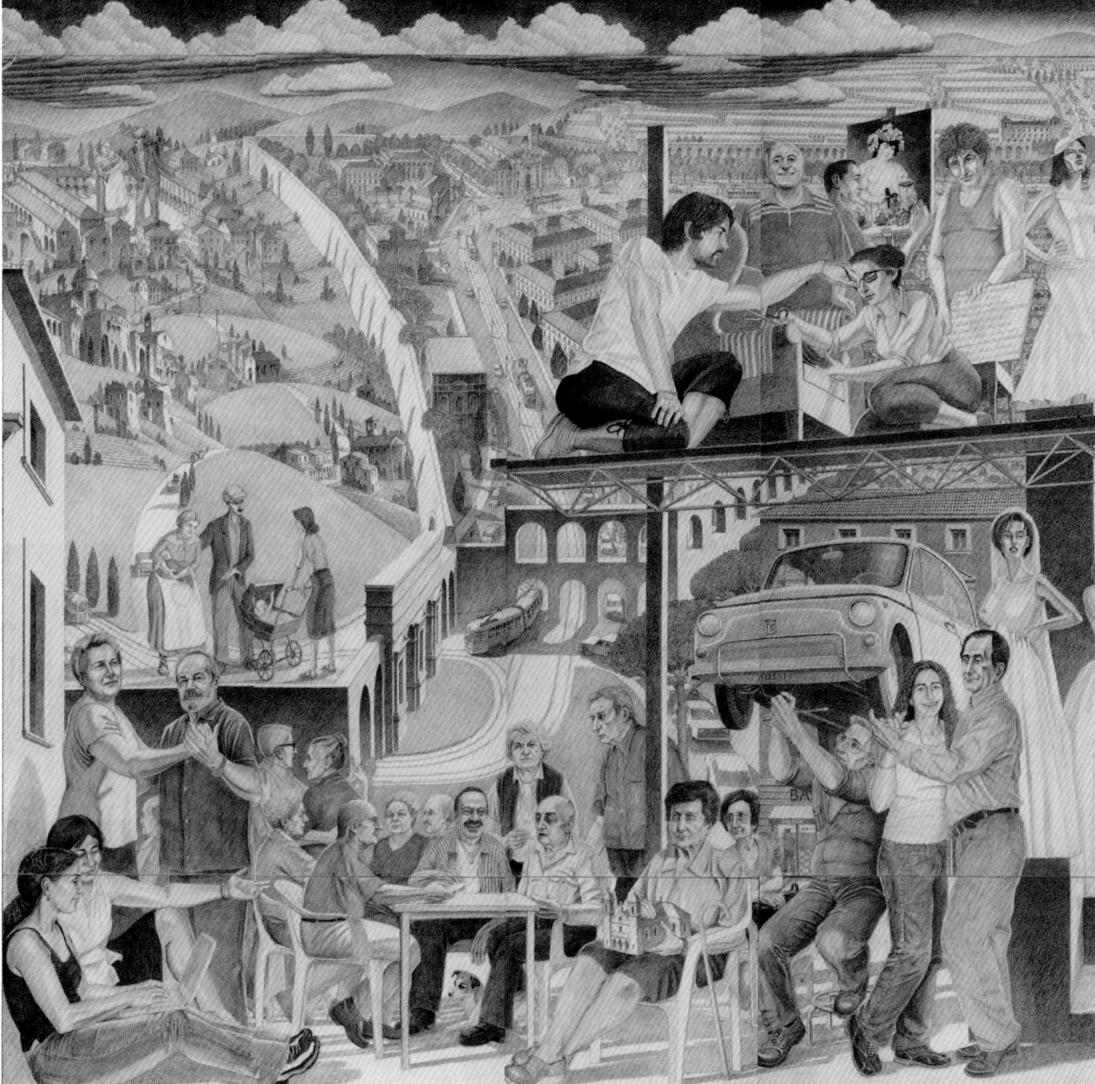

5.13. Detail, Rome south wall, Aula Magna, Ex Caserma Sani mural, Doug Cooper with Grégoire Picher and Patty Culley, assisted by Ross Christy, Carla Collada, Lara Hoke, Ashok Kanagasundram, and Jan Vairo, 2005. Università Roma Tre, Rome.

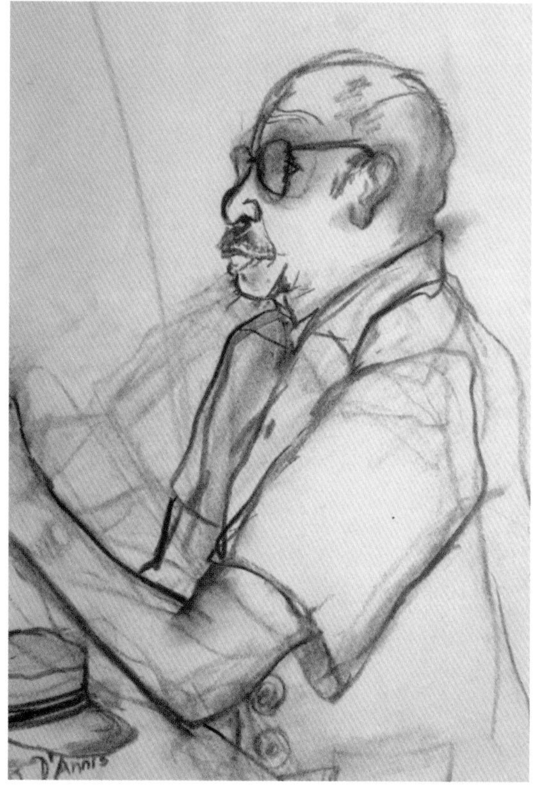

5.14. "Jim DeAnnis," Debbie Zwetsch, 1994. Drawing done at Center in the Park. Detail, Philadelphia County Courthouse mural, Philadelphia.

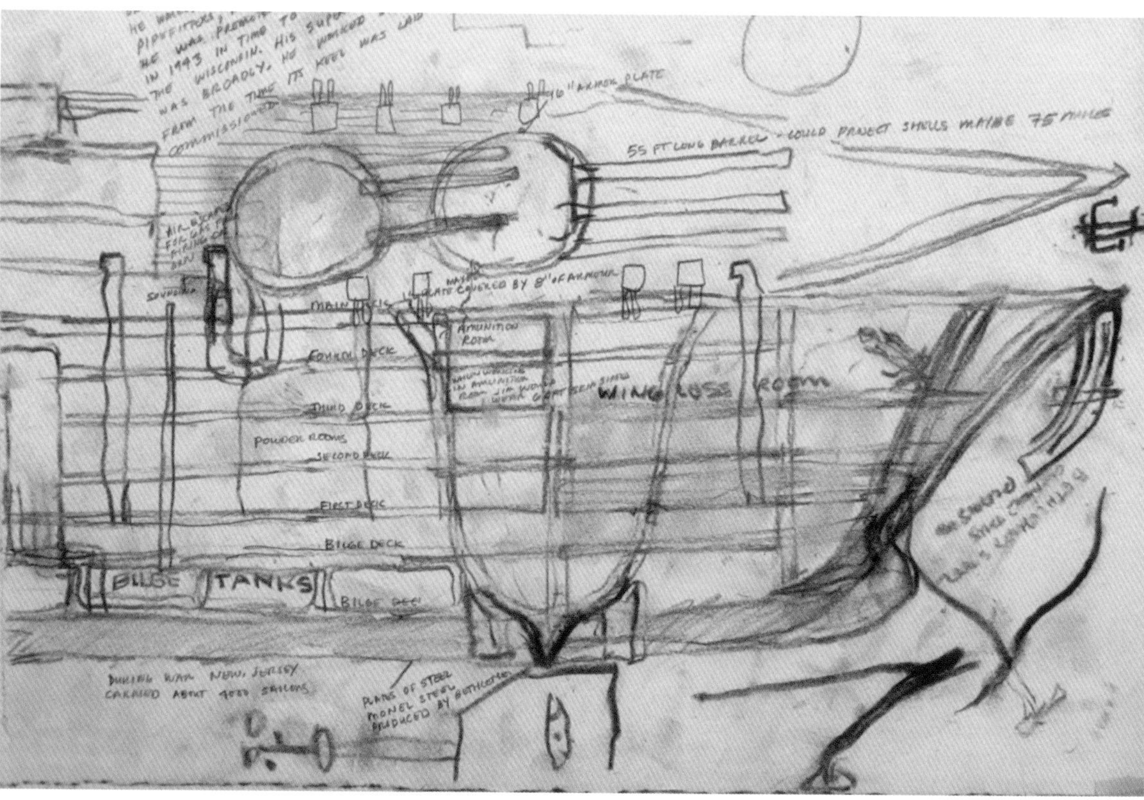

5.15. "USS *Wisconsin*," Jim DeAnnis, 1994. Drawing done at Center in the Park. Detail, Philadelphia County Courthouse mural, Philadelphia.

The Navy Yard, Philadelphia, 1941

Jim was a tall strapping black man about seventy-five years old originally from Jamaica. The first thing he told us was that he was a Jamaican Maroon. That is, he was descended from the escaped slaves and Colley Indians who had lived in the mountainous interior of the island and had fought the British to a standstill in the eighteenth century. He told us this in describing the two personal characteristics that dominated the arc of his life: his confident independence and his fierce temper—both of which he traced back to his Maroon ancestry (fig. 5.14).

His confidence was the first of these traits to play a role in his story. Before emigrating from Jamaica, Jim had been trained as a pipefitter. Arriving in Philadelphia in 1941, he contrasted himself to others of African descent he got to know in Philadelphia at that time. "I was not cowed like they were. I knew what I could do as a pipefitter and intended to do it," was how he put it. So Jim sent a letter to President Franklin Roosevelt asking him for a job as a pipefitter at the Philadelphia Navy Yard. And amazingly, it worked! Several weeks later, Jim received a letter back from the secretary of the navy, telling him to report to the navy yard to begin work. That was how Jim became the first African American skilled worker at the Philadelphia Navy Yard.

Jim told us about the various ships he worked on. Hearing his pride as he spoke, it was as if he had built most of the navy's ships by himself (fig. 5.15). Though he didn't draw it, the most memorable was an Essex-class carrier he worked on late in the war. It was near the end of its construction that the other characteristic Jim had attributed to his Maroon heritage, his hot temper, played out in a way that proved deeply destructive for the rest of his life. The carrier was substantially complete, needing only a battery of final tests before sea trials. One involved testing the pipes that were to carry aviation fuel and those intended for water. Assurance that they had not been mixed with one another was needed. These tests were conducted by running liquids of multiple colors through both systems to verify that what went in at the supply end came out undiluted at the correct point of delivery. During the tests, it was an absolute rule that no one was to touch any of the valves, no one other than the one conducting the test—on that day, Jim.

Jim was belowdecks when he saw an officer fiddling with one of the valves. Jim called out to him to stop. The officer looked up, saw that the man who had shouted at him was black and called him a "nigger." In that moment Jim—who was by this time facing the officer some two feet away—became all Maroon warrior and punched the officer. Reeling from the blow, the officer fell over backward and down an open elevator shaft that would be used for raising the airplanes up to the flight deck. Luckily for the officer (and Jim), he was not killed. He landed in a pile of loose garbage that had been collecting at the base of the shaft and survived the fall. But Jim was immediately fired and was never able to work again at the level of technical expertise he had acquired while working at the navy yard. From then on he was a journeyman laborer.

Going Home, Philadelphia, 1994

The morning Mamie, eighty-seven, came into her session with Debbie and me, she was crying. When I asked her why, she told me that a very close friend's daughter had died and that she had just returned from the funeral. For some reason, I asked her if she believed in angels. She looked at me for a moment with a look of bewilderment, as if the answer were self-evident. "Of course I do," she said. "I've seen one."

Then she told me how six years before she had undergone an operation for a brain tumor. She remembered falling into a deep and dreamy sleep in the post-op recovery room, when suddenly an angel appeared and circled her bed, finally coming to rest at its foot. A choir of the most beautiful voices was singing. I asked her, which song? "Going Home," she said. Then she saw two beautiful white doors slowly open, and the music grew yet more beautiful. Then the angel spoke softly to her and told her that her time was not yet come; she must remain to help care for her daughter, who was leading a troubled life.

At that moment she awoke. Her daughter was sobbing at her bedside, begging her mother not to die and leave her alone. Later, her doctors who had been called to her bedside told her that her heart had suddenly stopped beating during post-op recovery, but then "miraculously" resumed beating again (fig. 5.16).

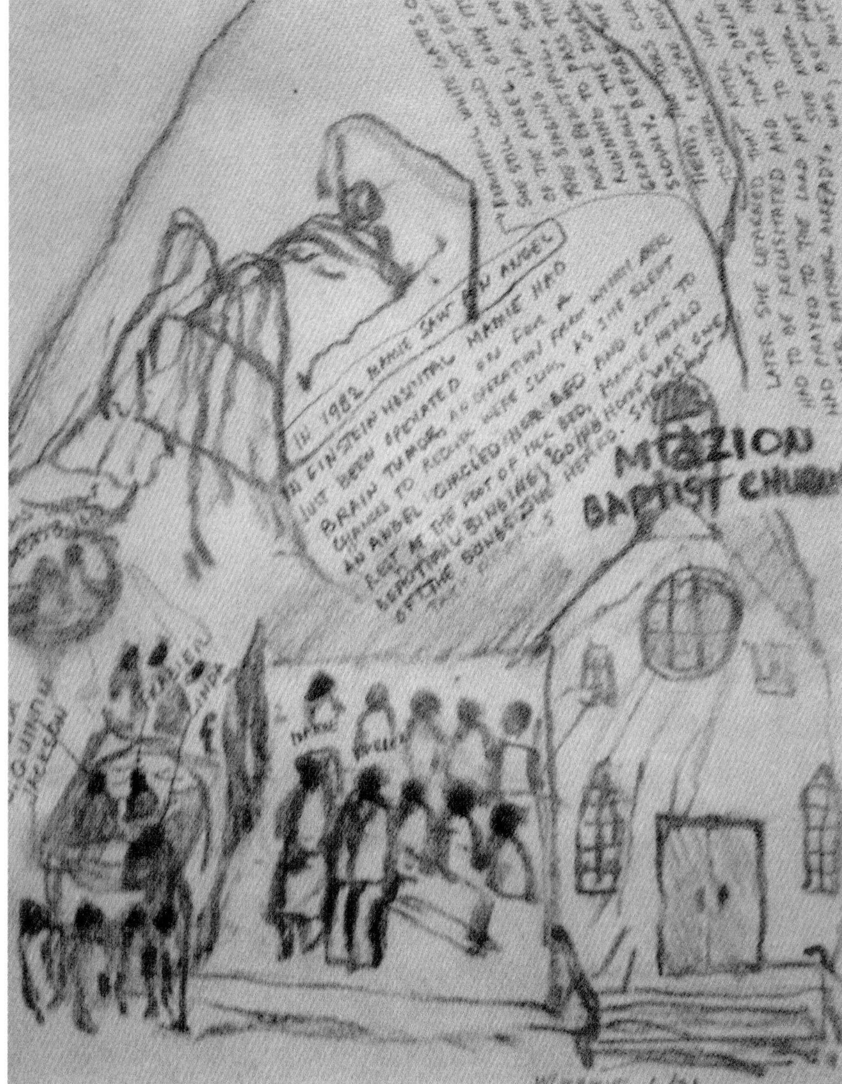

5.16. "Mamie's Dream," Doug Cooper and Debbie Zwetsch, assisted by Walter Tien. Drawing done at Center in the Park, 1994. Detail, Philadelphia County Courthouse mural, Philadelphia.

Hail to the Kaiser, Frankfurt, 1910

We got to know Frau Slotkewicz at the Jewish home for the elderly in Bornheim. She was more than ninety years old, and her father had originally brought the family to Frankfurt from Kraków in Poland. "We really wanted to become Germans," she said—her father had fought for Austria during World War I. Her mother was pious, but her father was not a particularly religious man.

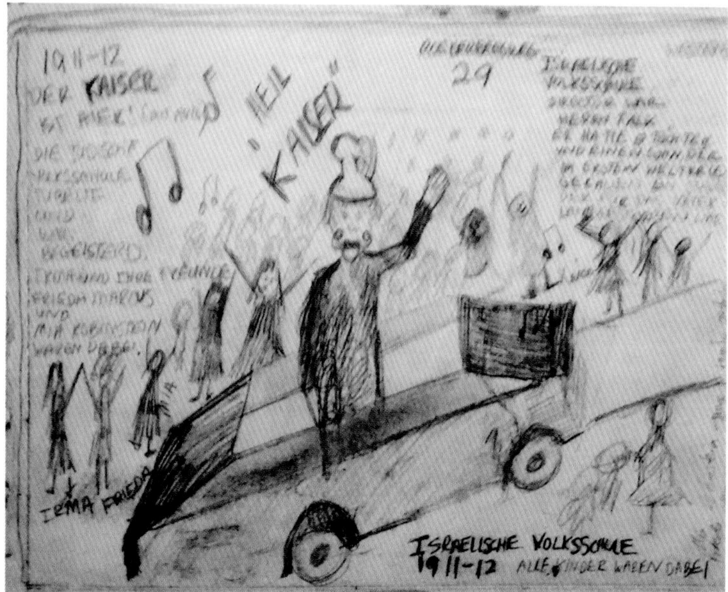

5.17. "Heil Kaiser," Doug Cooper with Annie Garibaldi, Amie Robinson, Rachel Schmeidler, Christa Sherwood, and Stephen Brockmann, 1996. Drawing done at the Zentrum für Sozialarbeit. Detail, Kleinmarkthalle mural, Frankfurt am Main.

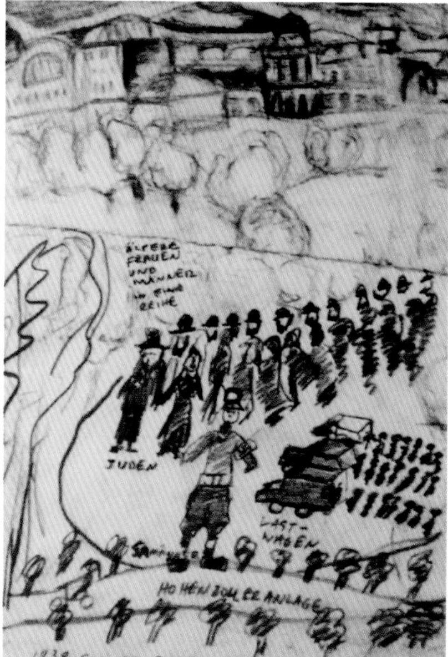

5.18. "Festhalle," Doug Cooper with Annie Garibaldi, Amie Robinson, Rachel Schmeidler, Christa Sherwood, and Stephen Brockmann. Drawing done at the Zentrum für Sozialarbeit, 1996. Detail, Kleinmarkthalle mural, Frankfurt am Main.

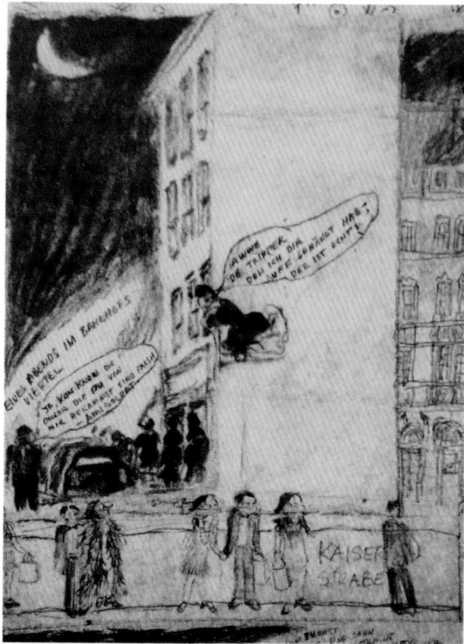

5.19. "Kaisersträße," Doug Cooper with Annie Garibaldi, Amie Robinson, Rachel Schmeidler, Christa Sherwood, and Stephen Brockmann, 1996. Drawing done at the Zentrum für Sozialarbeit. Detail, Kleinmarkthalle mural, Frankfurt am Main.

Frau Slotkewicz remembered her childhood in Frankfurt with fondness and the pride her family felt when they became German citizens. She also remembered how she and other children at the Volksschule der Israelitischen greeted the Kaiser by singing patriotic songs such as "Heil dir im Siegerkranz" (Hail you, in victor's crown). However, in 1938 her large family lost their citizenship and they were forced to leave for Poland. In 1939 they emigrated from Poland to England. Since 1976 she has lived once again in Germany, and is happy there (fig. 5.17).

Congress Center, Frankfurt, 1938

In the late 1930s Frau X had to go to work by bicycle. Every morning she had to pass near the Congress Center. One day in the summer of 1938 she was riding by as always, but this time she saw hundreds of older people being herded together by the SA troopers, men in one row and the women in another. The men were wearing black clothing and had long white beards. The people were Jews, and they were being deported by trucks. When Frau X got to work she described to her boss what she had just seen at the Congress Center. He knew all about it because he was a Nazi. He wanted nothing to do with people who were outside the Nazi party. Frau X described the event at the Congress Center to her father, and her father described it to his Jewish doctor. Two weeks later the doctor and his entire family, wife and twelve- and ten-year-old daughters, committed suicide. They did not have enough money to flee (fig. 5.18).

A Joke from the Postwar, Frankfurt, 1947

At the end of one day, Karlheinz Marowsky told us this joke from the postwar era: After leaving the brothel, the American solder called up to the prostitute who was still seated above by her open window, "You know, the dollars I paid you are fake." But then the prostitute called down to him, "Fine, but the clap I laid on you, that's real" (fig. 5.19).

The Store Window Mannequin, Frankfurt, 1946

Irma Penk told us how as a young woman during the postwar period, a very annoying man who owned a clothing store for women started wooing her. One evening when they went to visit his store, the man had to step out for a few minutes. Irma was wondering how she could get away from this guy.

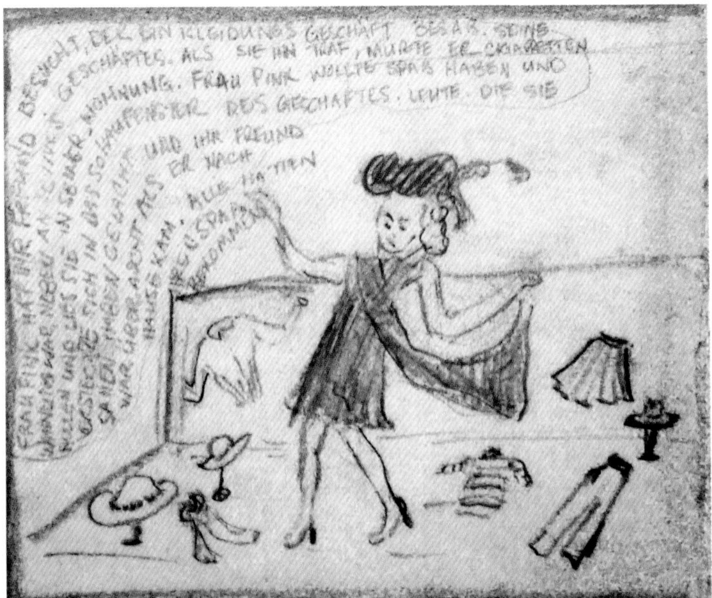

5.20. "Schaufensterpuppe," Doug Cooper with Annie Garabaldi, Amie Robinson, Rachel Schmeidler, Christa Sherwood, and Stephen Brockmann (drawing done at the Zentrum für Sozialarbeit), 1996. Detail, Kleinmarkthalle mural, Frankfurt am Main.

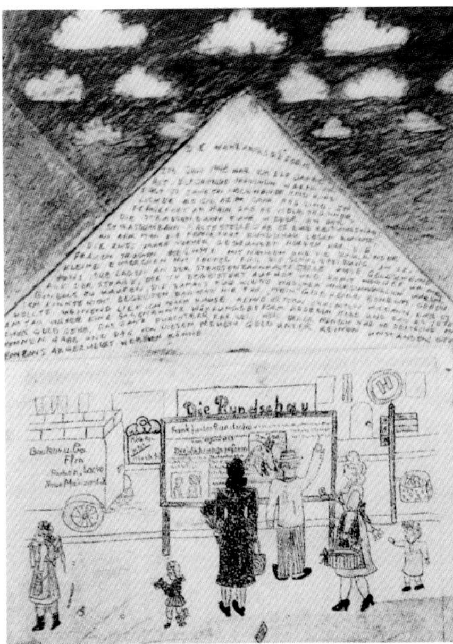

5.21. "Die Währungsreform," drawing from Ilse Werner. Drawing done at the Zentrum für Sozialarbeit, 1996. Detail, Kleinmarkthalle mural, Frankfurt am Main.

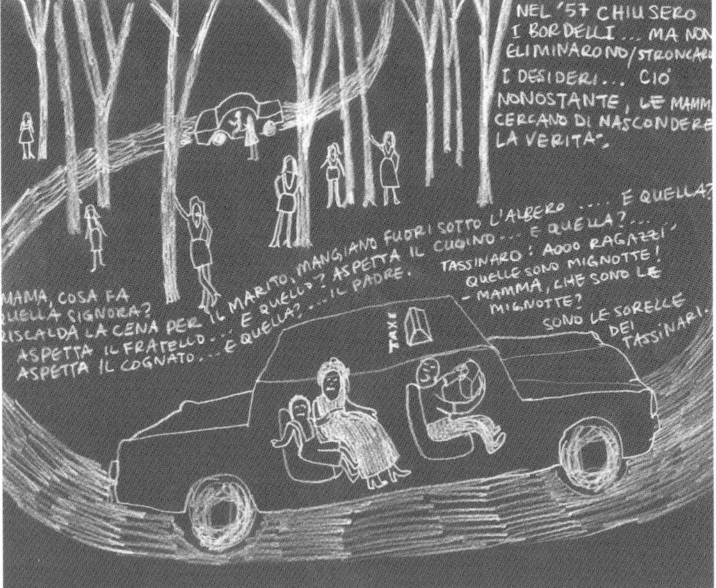

5.22. *Le Mignotte*," Doug Cooper with Grégoire Picher and Patty Clark, assisted by Ross Christy, Carla Collada, Lara Hoke, Ashok Kanagasundram, and Jan Vairo, 2005. Detail, Aula Magna, Ex Caserma Sani mural, Università Roma Tre, Rome.

Suddenly, the idea came to her that she might dress up as a show window mannequin. So she did it and stood stiff and motionless as people passed by in the street and gawked at her. When after a few minutes the man came back, he couldn't find the one he coveted. After a while, of course, he did find her, but now he knew that he had no romantic chance with her (fig. 5.20).

The Currency Reform, Frankfurt, 1948
Ilse Werner told us this story, also from the postwar: "In July 1948, I was eleven years old. Fifty years ago, eleven-year-old girls were more naïve and childish than they are in 1996. In Frankfurt am Main there was a lot of building wreckage. The streetcars were running again. At the streetcar stop there was a newspaper wall where one could read the *Frankfurter Rundschau*, which was founded two years before. Women wore stockings with seams and the school kids carried small lunchboxes with spoons for the school lunch. On the twenty-seventh of June 1948 all around the streetcar stop there was paper money lying in the street. I eagerly picked up the money and walked off with it to buy candies—something impossible for little girls to afford at the time. I couldn't understand, however, why no one wanted to take my money in exchange for candies, so I ran home crying. My parents then explained to me that on the day before the so-called currency reform had started, and so now there was new money, a money that was very rare because each person had gotten only forty Deutsche Marks and that from this new money something might be put away for candies" (fig. 5.21).

The Streetwalkers, Rome, 1957
One of the men at the senior center in Esquilino told us this joke from the postwar. In 1957, when they had closed the bordellos, there was a red-light district near the city where the prostitutes waited, each under her own tree. This conversation takes place between a mother and her daughter, passengers in a taxi.

"Mama, what's that woman doing?"

"She's warming dinner for her husband."

"And that one?"

"She's waiting for her brother."

And so on until the taxi driver cannot take any more of these excuses and says, "They're whores." And the child asks: "Mama, what are whores?"

"They are the sisters of the taxi driver" (fig. 5.22).

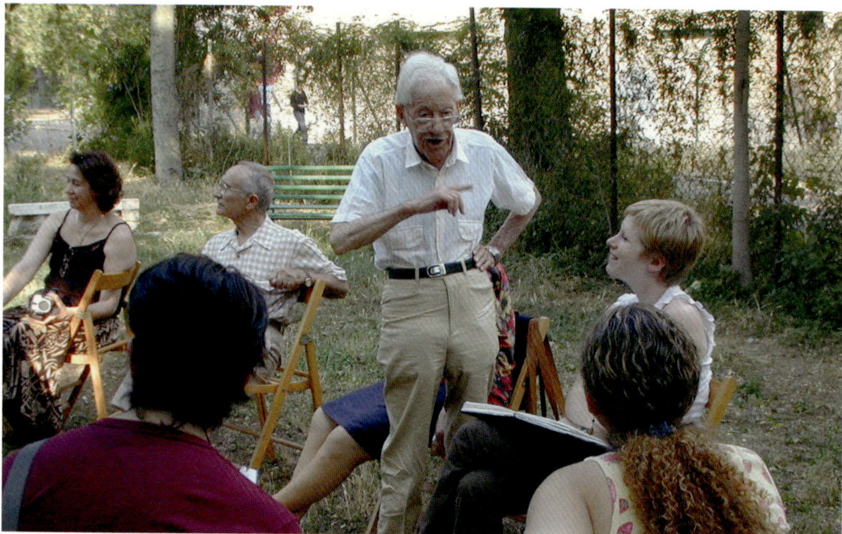

5.23. Renzo speaking with Ross, Carla, and Lara.

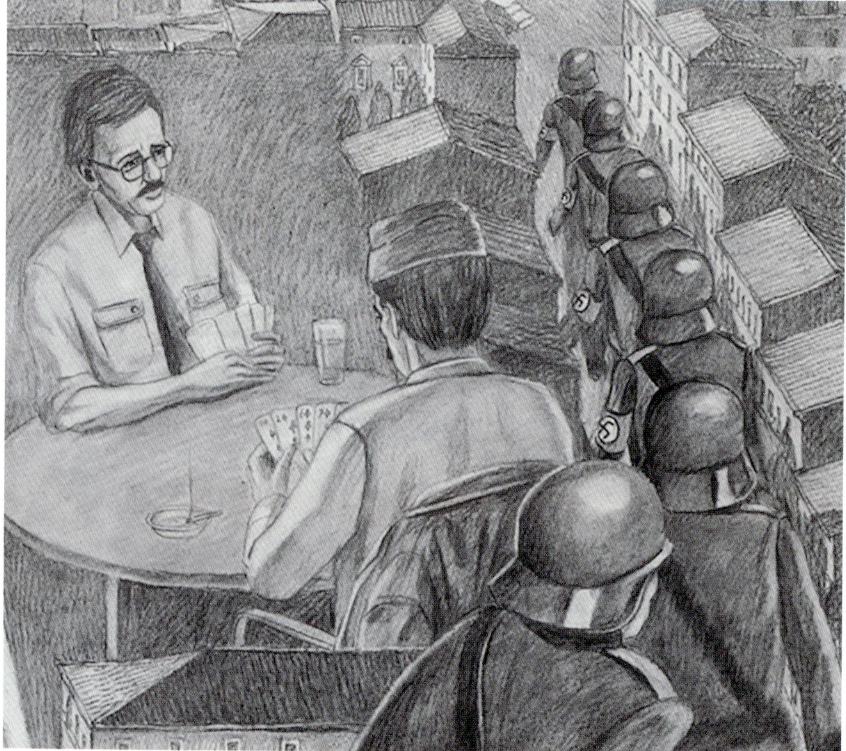

5.24. "Renzo's story," Doug Cooper with Grégoire Picher and Patty Clark, assisted by Ross Christy, Carla Collada, Lara Hoke, Ashok Kanagasundram, and Jan Vairo, 2005. Detail, Aula Magna, Ex Caserma Sani mural, Università Roma Tre, Rome.

The Survival, Rome, 1944

One day we had a visit from Renzo di Segni, the owner of one of the many bridal stores on the edge of the Piazza Vittorio (fig. 5.23). He was Jewish and had survived the war living more or less openly in the city. He had paid particular attention to maintaining the close friendships he had had from before the war with members of the local civil police. So it happened that on the day the Gestapo left their headquarters right next door to the local police barracks, his friends on the force tipped him off. All the while that the SS were ransacking his house and looking for him, he was there at the police headquarters right next door, playing cards (fig. 5.24).

Kayyali, Syria

Salma's family is originally from Iraq, but moved to Syria hundreds of years ago. This is the story she told of how her family got its name, Kayyali. Her great-great-grandfather had just moved to a new village with his wife. "It was a time of hardship and famine. There had been no rain for years and there was no wheat. He and his wife were living in a small hut on a small hill a little bit outside the village. One day, travelers came to the village, asking for food. It is a tradition to treat travelers as guests and provide them with a meal. But the villagers did not even have food for themselves and so they must have thought, 'Let's send the travelers over to the strangers on the hill, and let them deal with it.'

"So the travelers came to my great-great-grandfather's house, saying that they were told he had wheat. My grandfather, bound to the rules of tradition, asked them to come inside and sit down and he would go get the wheat. Back then the wheat was stored in a separate room that was connected to the kitchen through a little bull's-eye opening in the wall. But the storage room was empty.

"So my great-great-grandfather prayed to Allah for wheat for his guests. And Allah granted his wish and from the opening in the wall wheat was flowing out like a stream of water. It was flowing and flowing, until it covered the whole kitchen floor. My great-great-grandfather called the travelers and said, 'Here is wheat, please, fill your bags with as much as you can carry.' The guest then asked if he could help them to scoop the wheat into their bags, but my great-great-grandfather replied, 'It will scoop itself,' and so it did. And so we got our family name: Kayyali, 'the scooper.' To this day people are coming to

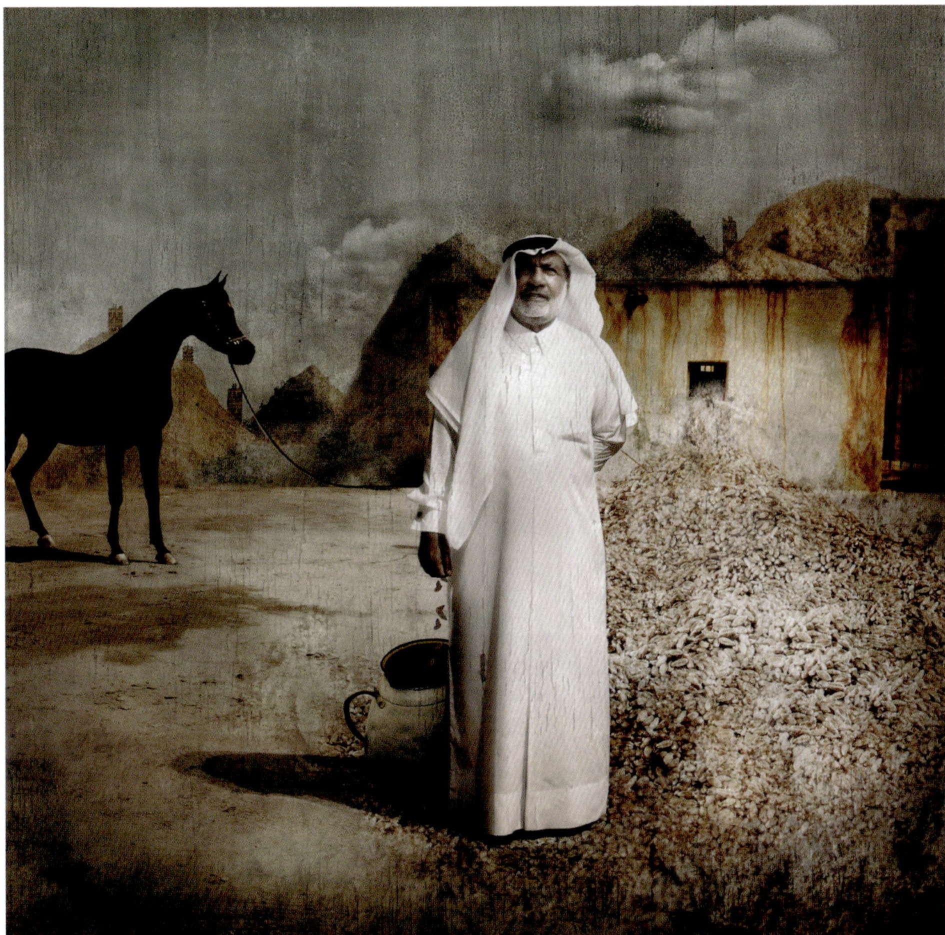

5.25. "Kayyali," Sarah Cooper and Nina Gorfer, SEEK, Gothenburg, Sweden, 2009. Photocollage detail, *Memory between Desert and Sea*. Carnegie Mellon University at Qatar, Doha.

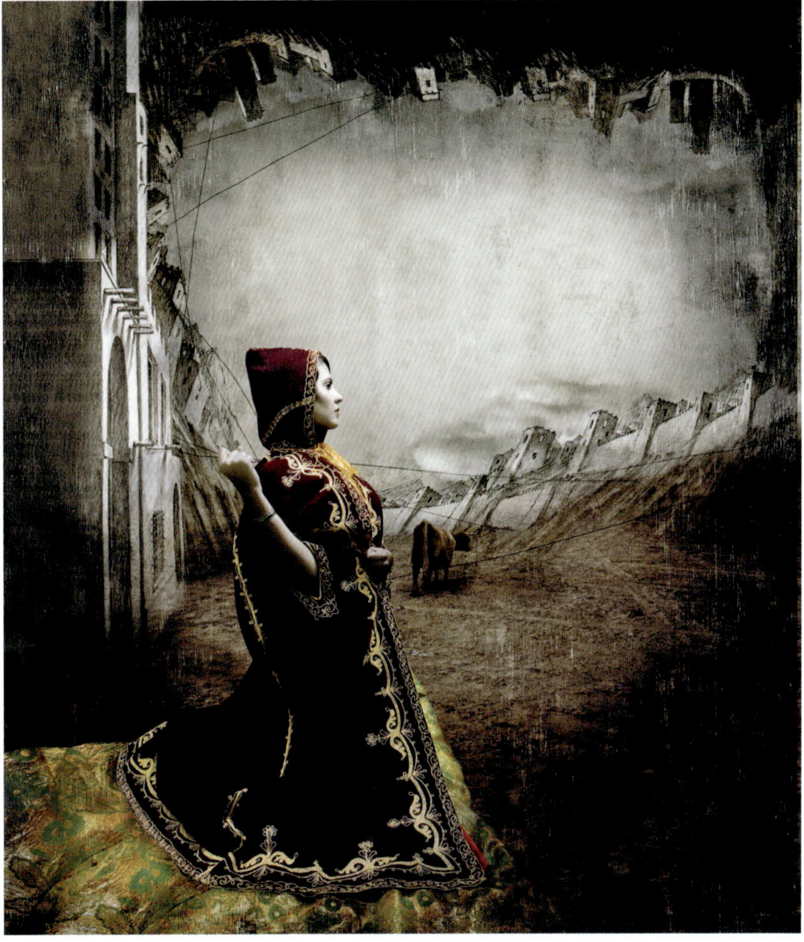

5.26. "Alissa," with Sarah Cooper and Nina Gorfer, SEEK, Gothenburg, Sweden 2009. Photocollage detail, *Memory between Desert and Sea*, Carnegie Mellon University at Qatar, Doha.

my family for help. They believe we have a gift. *Barake*, we call it; it means 'blessing from God'" (fig. 5.25).

Alissa, Lebanon

The king of the Phoenicians' daughter Alissa was constantly pestering her father about what kingdom she might inherit when her brother would inherit Phoenicia. In exasperation, her father one day offered her a bull's pelt. "Here," he said, "you may have this, and I will garrison whatever you can surround with it!" Alissa then took the pelt. Thinking he was finally done with her ambitious pestering, the king was more than a little worried and perplexed when she seemed so happy to accept what he assumed was a meager and dismissive offer. Alissa cut the pelt into strips and eventually braided these into a rope of great length. Then she returned to her father, saying to him that he must provision a ship and sail for the African coast, where she would land and lay out the rope to surround what would become the great city of Carthage. Thus was Carthage founded (fig. 5.26).

So what does all of this work with others finally add up to? Do I feel any closer to an understanding of what is shared and what is unique memory of place? Or, to put it in terms that parallel a central theme of this book, what is outside and common memory and what is private inside memory, and what might the one have to do with the other?

I think it comes down to the degree to which others can also empathize with the experience of an individual. This might be felt even with small details, as in the memories of the boathouse at Panther Hollow Lake, where people I met at Vintage had all gone to skate as children and where they had roasted potatoes to keep warm. Ilse Werner's story of the 1948 currency reform in West Germany, though unique in its details for her, had great resonance for others across Frankfurt with whom I shared her story because it was a nationwide experience, and others could attach their own experiences to it. Or there can be a broader theme involved. The story of Jim DeAnnis at the Philadelphia navy yard strikes a chord with nearly everyone for its relationship to the struggle for integration in the workplace more generally. In that same vein, another story in the Philadelphia Courthouse mural has had a similar impact.

The Integration of Girard College

As my colleague Debbie Zwetsch and I gathered stories for eventual inclusion in the Philadelphia Courthouse mural, one emerged as particularly important; we heard about it from multiple residents of North Philadelphia. It was the story of the effort to end the segregation of Girard College. It's a story of a long and complicated struggle—lasting more than a decade at high intensity, 1953–1968, a story set in motion by events from a century before.

In 1830 banker Stephen Girard had willed Girard College to the city of Philadelphia. According to his will, it was to be a school for "poor white orphan boys." And that it had remained in the intervening years while the neighborhood around it gradually changed to become predominantly African American. As the years went by, its presence, a neoclassical edifice occupying the high ground in North Philadelphia, coupled with its policy of racial exclusion, caused the institution to be deeply resented by the surrounding community. Even after the Supreme Court's 1954 *Brown vs. Board of Education* decision, Girard College remained segregated.

Demonstrations attempting to change Girard's policy began almost immediately. But the administration of the board of directors of city trusts of Philadelphia claimed that it could not be integrated because of the provision of Girard's will. Then, through various maneuvers by the college's defenders, it came to be treated as a private institution and therefore outside the jurisdiction of the Supreme Court's ruling. Demonstrations became more and more intense and then violent as the 1960s progressed. Finally, in 1968, Girard was integrated.

This was the story Debbie and I heard from multiple residents of North Philadelphia, and this was the story we drew. It was a simple drawing: just a classical building ringed by demonstrators and with nearby text (fig. 5.27).

It was more than ten years after we had installed the Philadelphia Courthouse mural when I received an email from a woman in Philadelphia regarding the story about Girard. The woman described her experience as a jurist serving at the Philadelphia Courthouse. The jury meeting rooms are right down the hall from the mural. When the jury first met, she felt excluded from the others on the jury—not because of anything anyone said to her; for her it was simply a matter of race. She was the only white member of a jury that, outside of herself, was all African American. The first meeting of the jury after it was impaneled also left her with a feeling of being an outsider and wondering if she might ever find common ground with her colleagues.

At some point during the second meeting, the jury agreed to take a small break and took a stroll down the corridor outside the jury room, a walk that took them past the mural. The mural seemed to gain the attention of many among the jurors, and so they paused to look at it. The conversation starter was the story about the integration of Girard College. The author of the email had also followed that story as it unfolded in the 1960s and was supportive of the final outcome. She and the other members of the jury talked about it in great depth that day in the corridor, and it was through sharing that story and then others along the wall that she was able to become one of twelve.

To me this woman's experience points to the central reason to work with others in creating civic works. It's not just or even primarily the uniqueness of any individual's story of urban life that matters. What does matter is the shared sense of experience that comes through such stories. To this day, I regard her note as the highest personal compliment I have ever received for my role in public art.

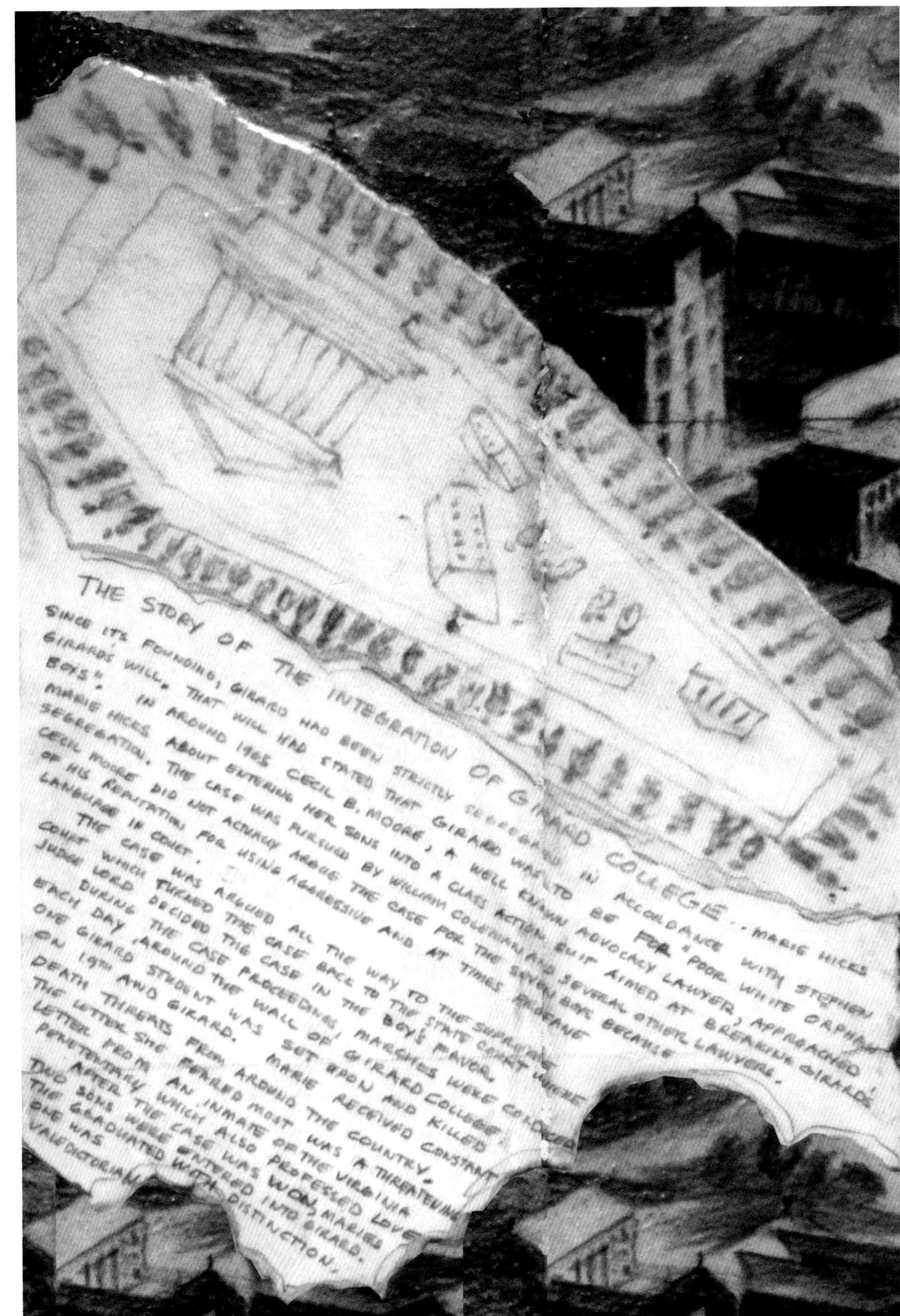

5.27. "Integration of Girard College," Doug Cooper and Debbie Zwetsch, assisted by Walter Tien. Drawing done at Center in the Park, 1994. Philadelphia County Courthouse mural, Philadelphia.

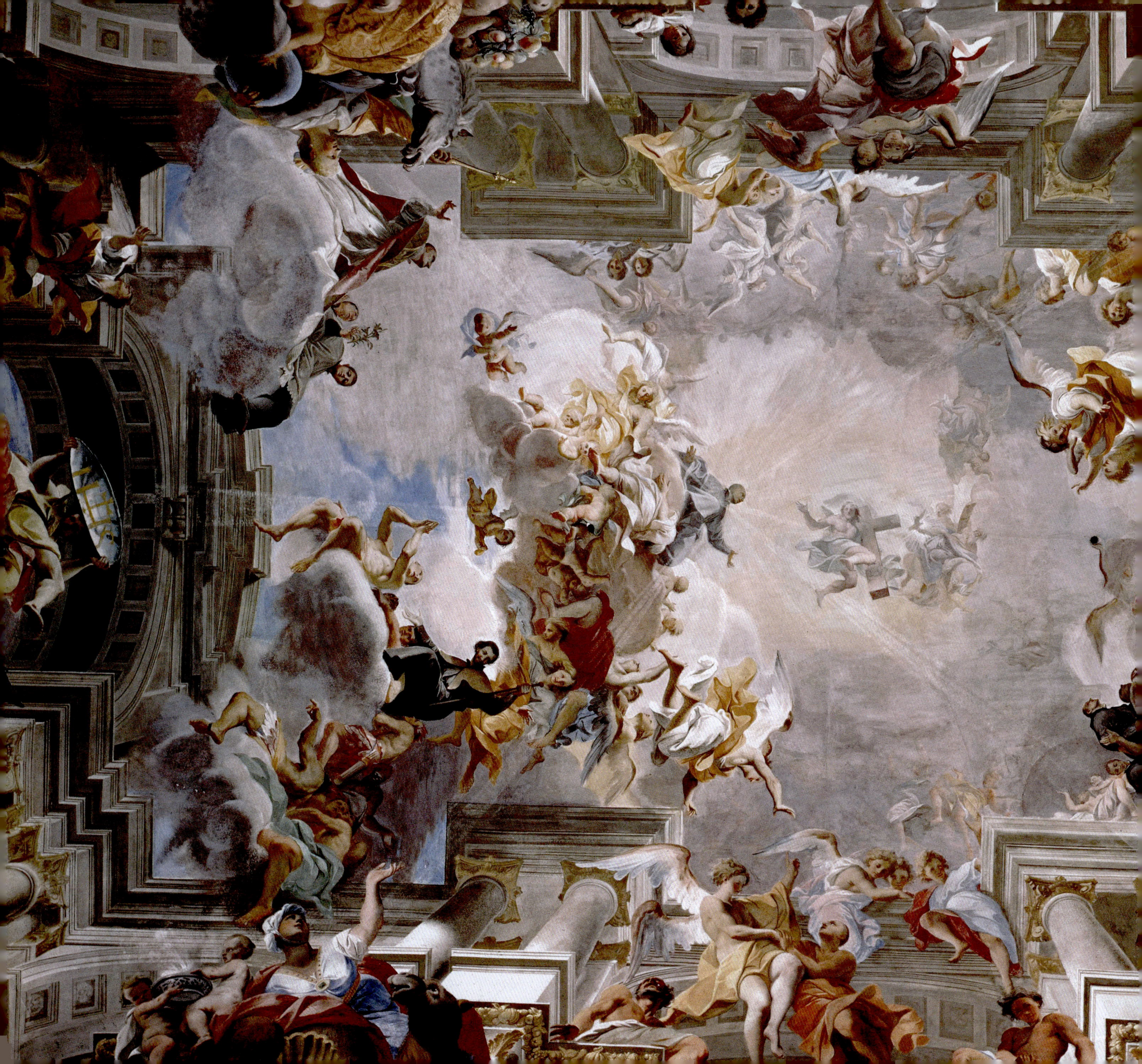

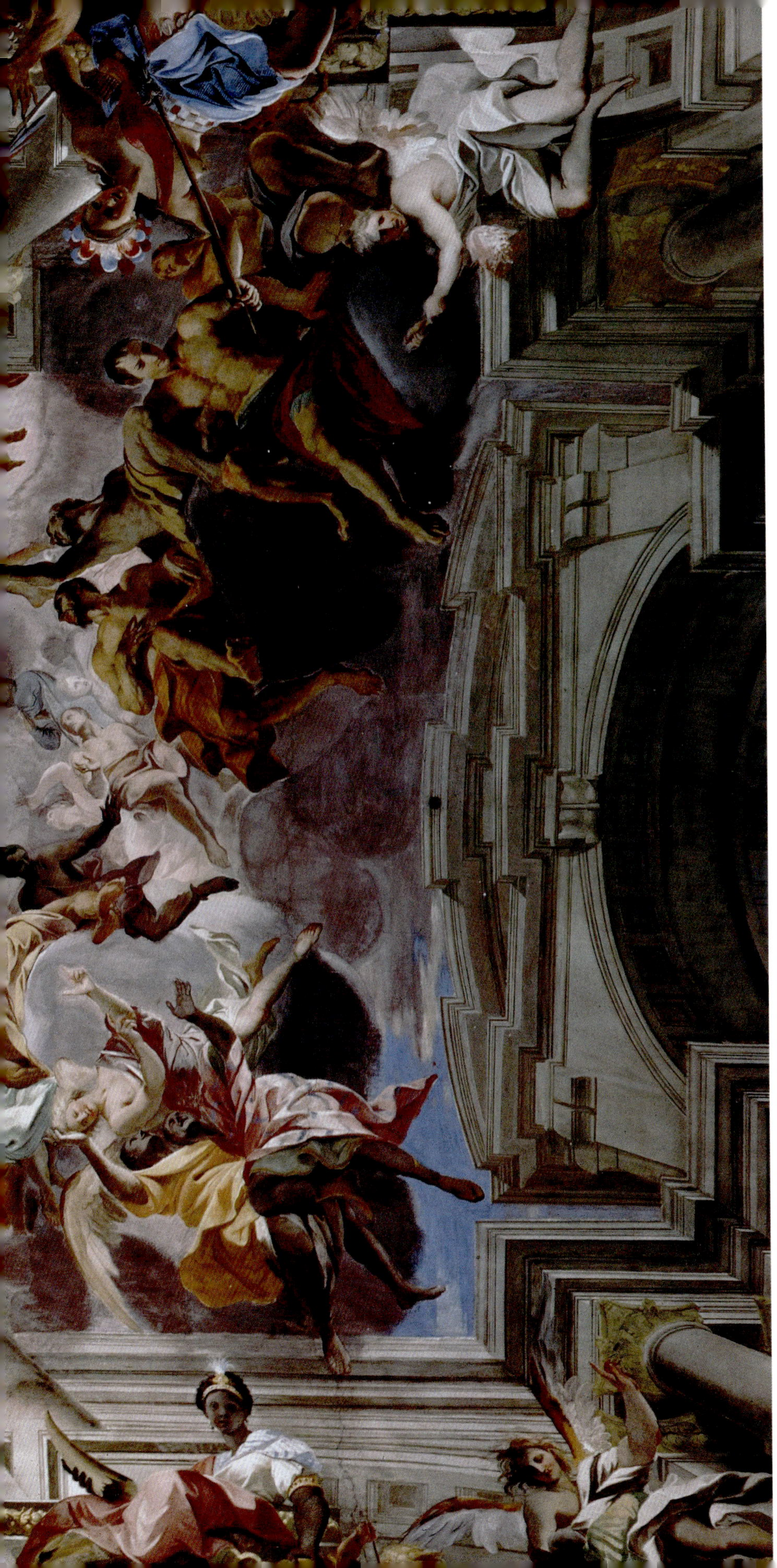

CHAPTER 6

WORKING IN THE MURAL TRADITION

My CMU design professor Ray Gindroz had told us not to miss it when we got to Rome. So, when Meg, Laura, and I got to Sant'Ignazio late one afternoon, we walked to the center of the nave where a small disc embedded in the floor marks the spot, and looked up—looked up, that is, to a ceiling fresco that runs the length of the nave and shows the ascension of Saint Ignatius into heaven, where he is welcomed by Christ and the Virgin Mary. Painted by Andrea Pozzo (1685–1694), it is an astonishing illusion that seems to extend forever heavenward, in the process dissolving the barrel vault above the nave. This was my first real view into the pictorial space of a mural (fig. 6.1).

We were living in Siena for the winter of 1970–1971, but our daughter Laura's bout of pneumonia left me needing to find a job, so we moved to Frankfurt, Germany, where I found work with the architect Herbert Ohl. The apartment where we would live for five years in Frankfurt had a large expanse of blank wall. And that first summer, in my spare time, I tried to extend our truncated time in Italy by making a large drawing to recreate our experience in Siena. I had a few snapshots to work from, but it was largely a work from memory.

I drew it on sheets of paper that I tacked up piece by piece on the wall. As the drawing grew, maplike, outward from the Piazza del Campo (Siena's famous fan-shaped plaza), it took on the shape of the room: following walls, turning corners, going over the tops of doors, extending out over part of the ceiling, and finally going around the radiator and its pipes.

This was my first mural, and it brought an interesting mix of plan and elevation into play. Because Laura was often at home due to her lingering

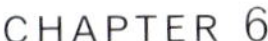

6.1. *Saint Ignatius in Glory*, Andrea Pozzo, ca. 1685. Ceiling fresco in the nave of San Ignazio. Sant'Ignazio Church, Rome, Italy. Alinari/Art Resource, NY.

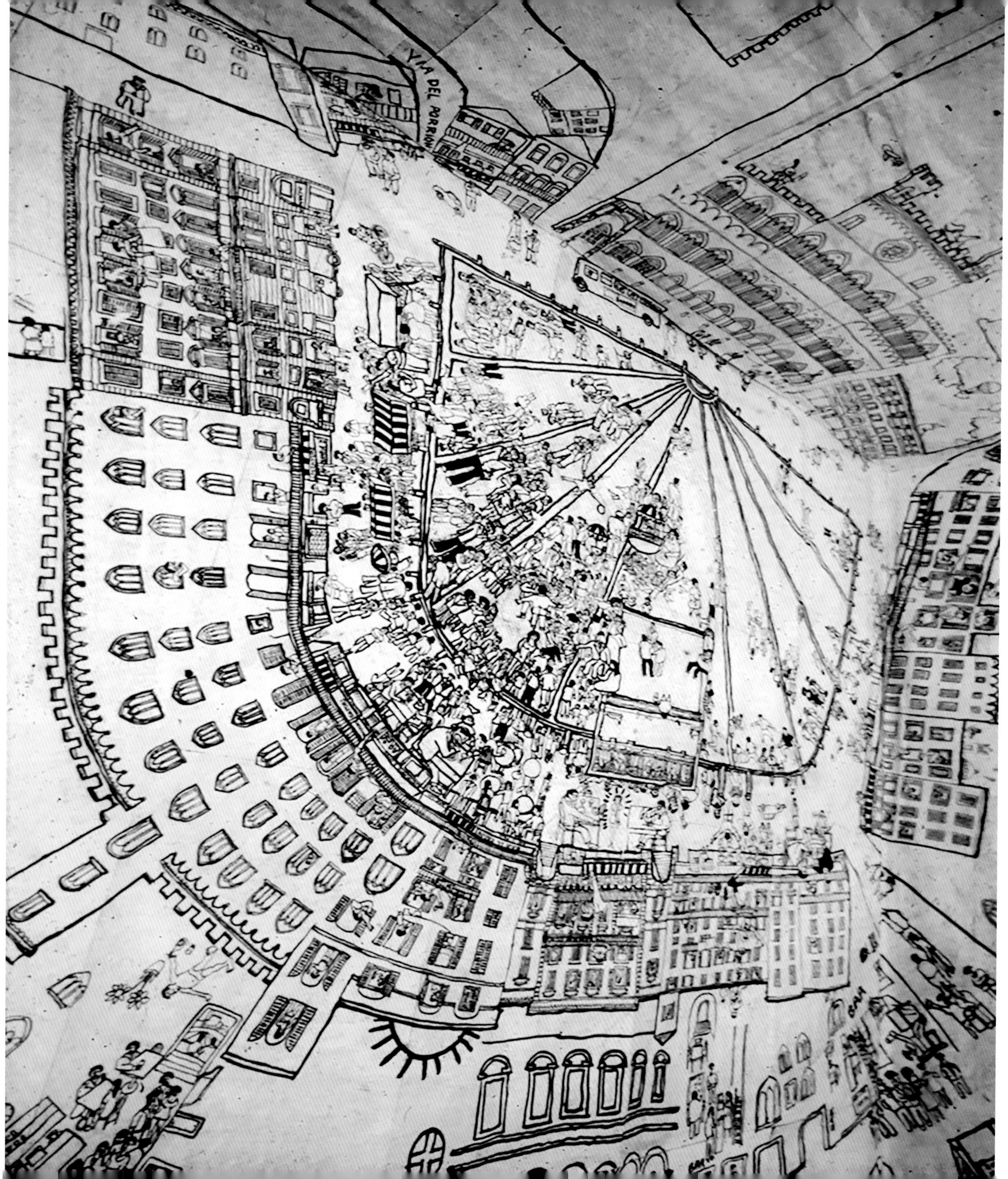

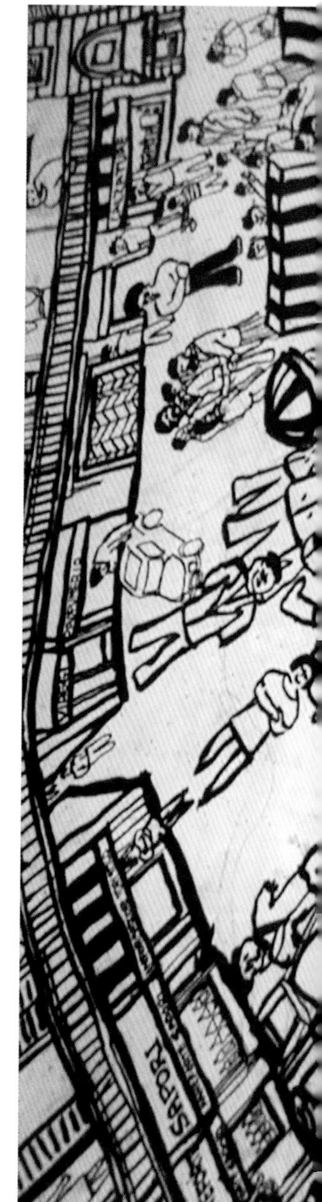

VIA DEL PORRIONE
SAPORI

pneumonia, I often laid the mural out on the floor so she could drive her toy cars along its streets. That brought elements of path and map into the work. But along those streets, I also drew in major facades and the interiors of the stores I used to frequent: a kind of picture and map all in one (figs. 6.2, 6.3).

Murals and Their Intentions

Our English word *mural* comes from the Latin for *wall*. Beginning with the earliest murals we know from the caves of southwestern France and continuing to the present day, we have always considered murals to be integral parts of the spaces whose walls they cover. They are not artifacts, which might one day be transported from building to building like framed portraits; they are part of the architecture itself. What ultimately is their purpose with respect to the buildings they occupy?

In early mural traditions in the hands of the Egyptian, Greek, Roman, and Byzantine craftsmen, we find several intentions regarding inside and outside space. One brings an outer world inside. The stylized figures painted on the walls of Egyptian tombs were present in those spaces to ensure the power of the one entombed through the afterlife. Another intention seems unrelated to the world outside and is directed at enhancing the qualities of the interior. In early Christian churches built throughout the Roman Empire following the Edict of Milan (313 AD), and particularly in the eastern empire, artists covered walls with mosaics to intensify the candlelight within and to give a luminous figurative presence to liturgical practice (figs. 6.4, 6.5).

A third seeks to extend interior space outward by creating views onto a world outside. And some murals even seem to make the walls disappear in the process. The illusionist paintings we find in frescos at Pompeii or the Room of the Masks in the House of Augustus in Rome used a faux architecture to bring a compelling sense of both frame and depth to these views. Further, they show the great skill and knowledge in the use of perspective achieved by Greek and Roman craftsmen—capabilities not seen again until the early Renaissance. Because most of my mural work has been directed at this last goal, seeking to expand an interior space beyond its walls, we'll look at several of the visual implications of that intention before considering the larger issue of the purpose(s) of murals relative to the architecture of their settings

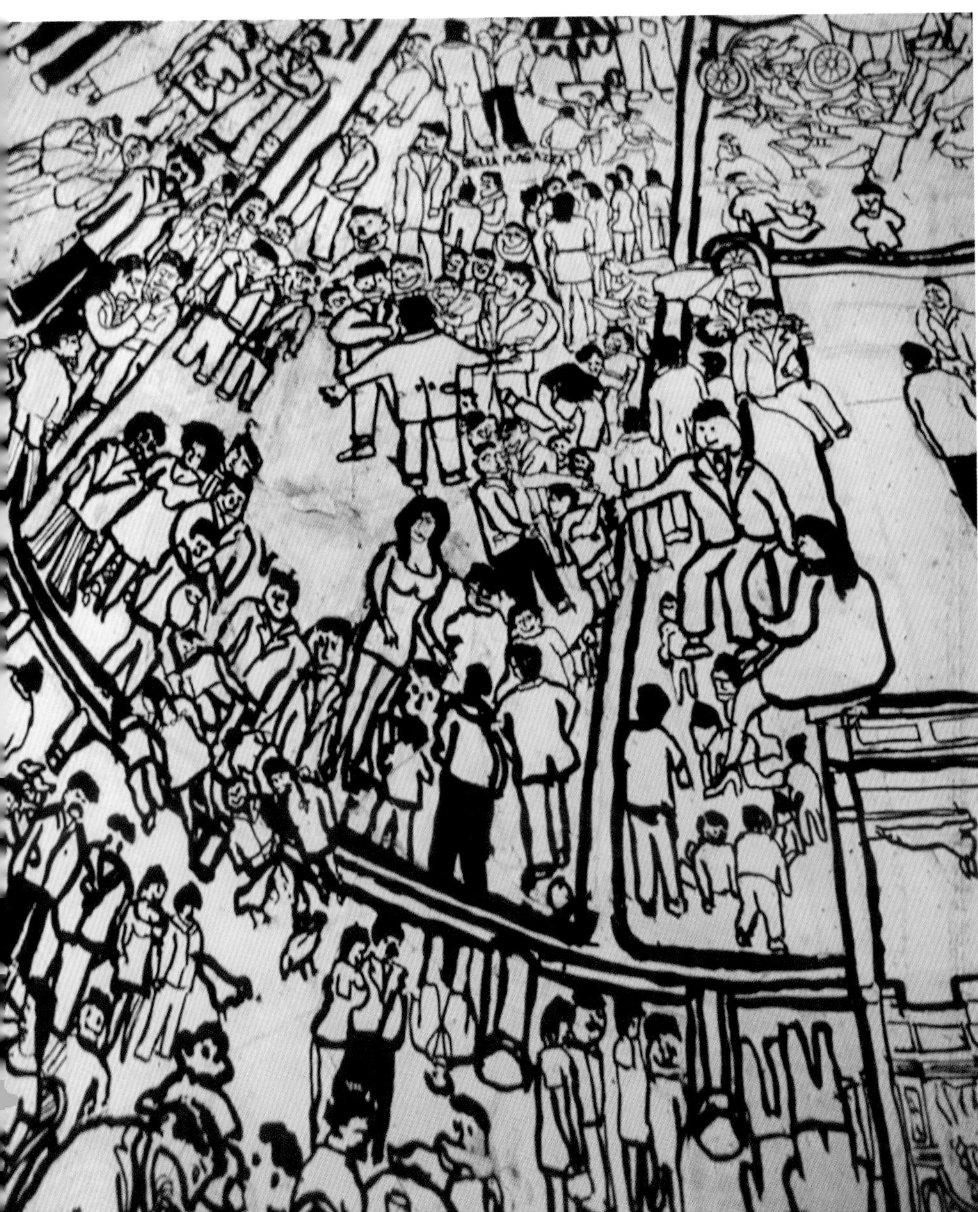

6.2 (*left*). Detail showing Piazza del Campo, mural of Siena in Cooper's Frankfurt apartment, Doug Cooper, 1961–1962. Tempera on paper, approx. 3 × 10 meters. Collection of the artist.

6.3 (*above*). Detail, mural of Siena in Cooper's Frankfurt apartment, Doug Cooper, 1961–1962. Tempera on paper, approx. 3 × 10 meters. Collection of the artist.

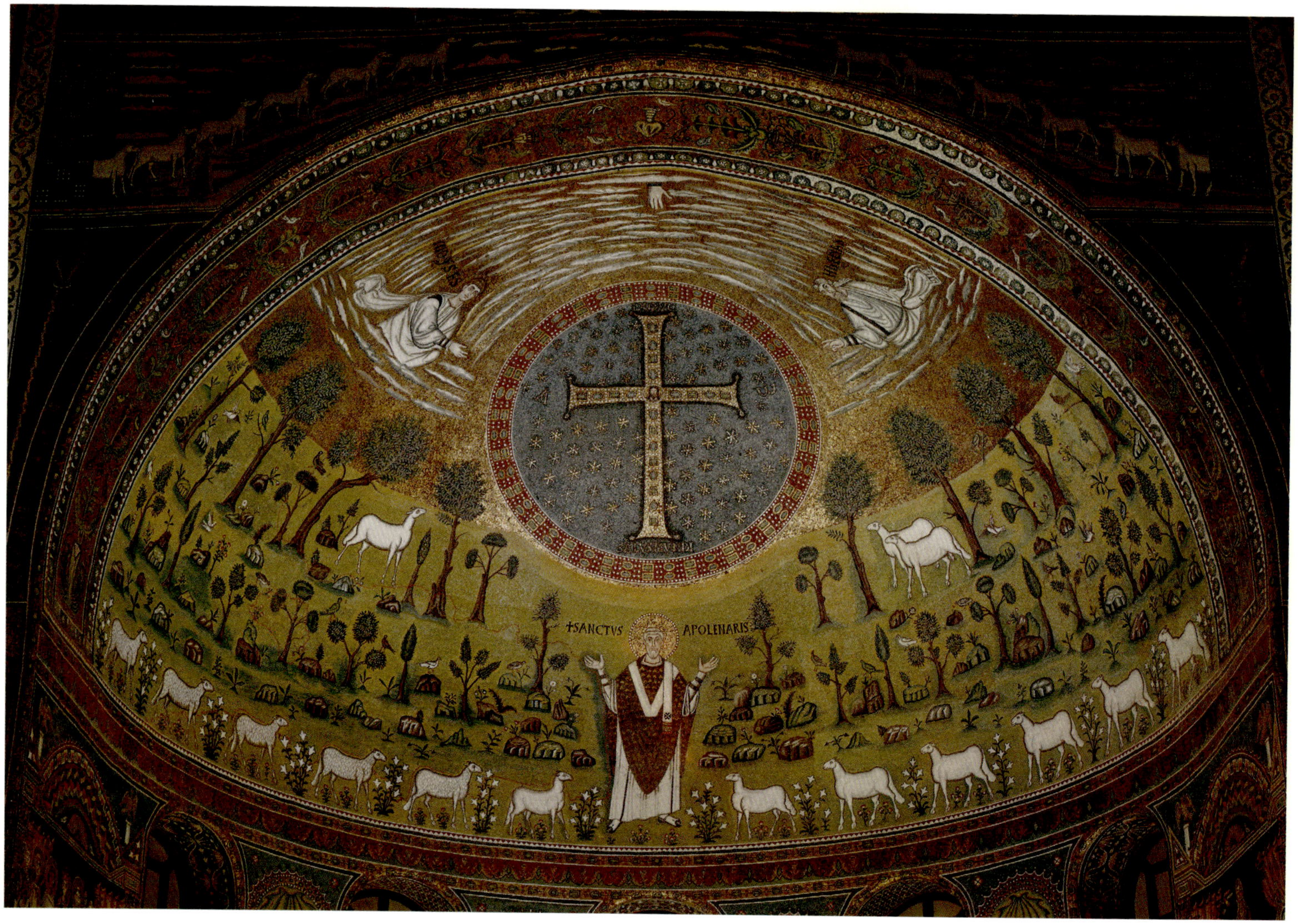

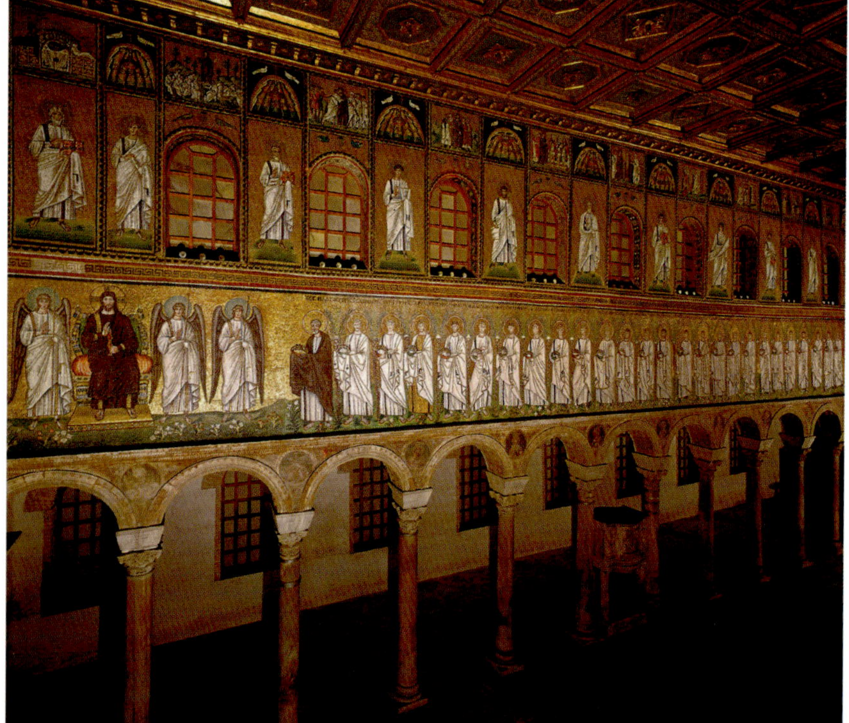

6.4 (*left*). View of the wall with Christ and series of martyrs ca. 500. Basilica di Sant'Apollinare Nuovo, Ravenna, Italy. Scala/Art Resource, NY.

6.5 (*above*). Apsidal vault. Byzantine mosaic ca. 500. Basilica di Sant'Apollinare in Classe, Ravenna, Italy. Scala/Art Resource, NY.

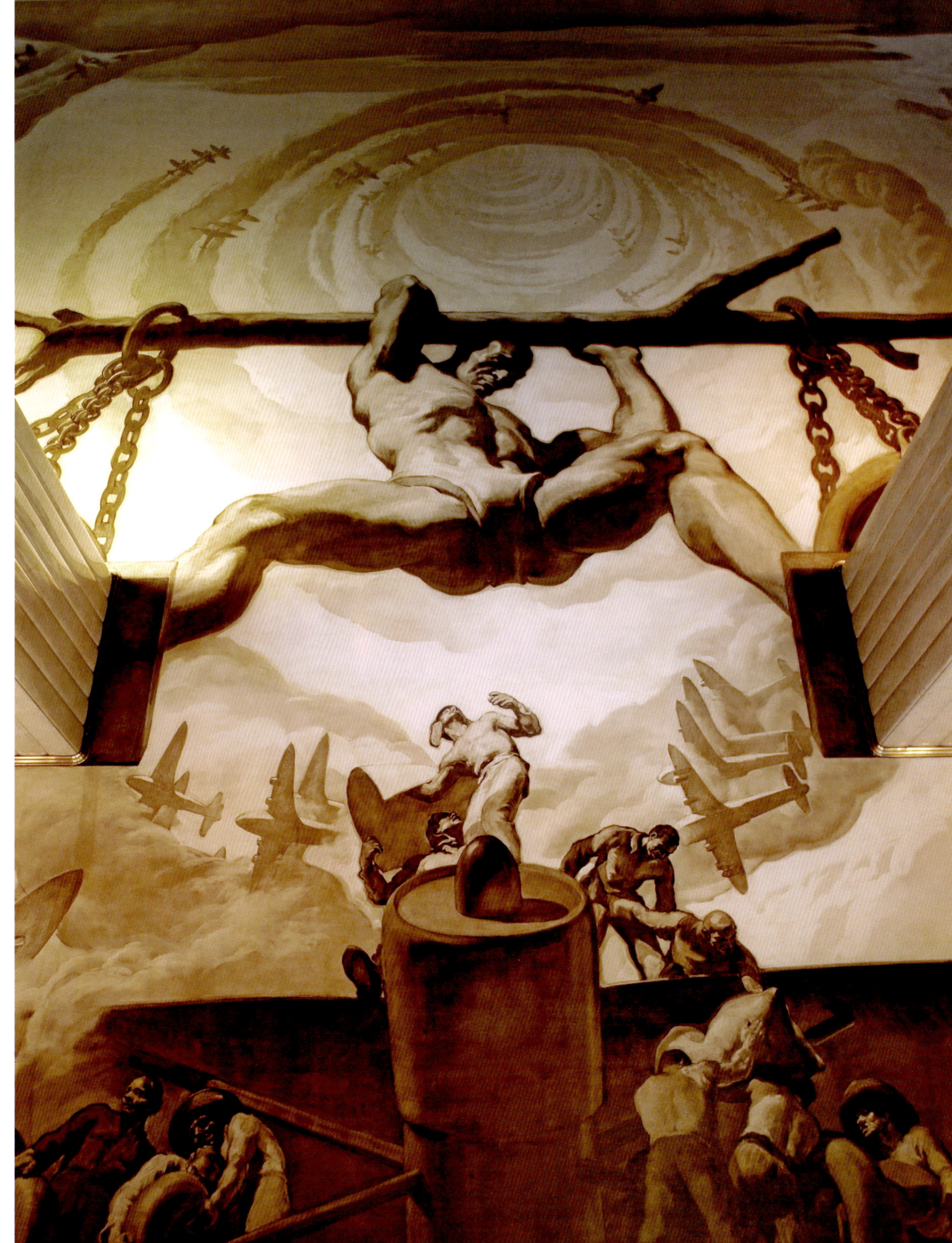

6.6. *American Progress*, Josep Maria Sert, 1937. Fresco. 30 Rockefeller Plaza, New York, NY. Photo by Anna Nielsson.

In my experience the highest achievement in using a mural to extend an interior space is Andrea Pozzo's high baroque tour de force ceiling fresco at Sant'Ignazio in Rome described at the beginning of this chapter (fig. 6.1). Pozzo went to extraordinary lengths to get its perspective to work. He started by stringing a grid at the level of the cornice. Then in a kind of mechanical version of a slide projector, he used a taut wire to project that grid point by point upward onto the barrel vaulted ceiling overhead so he could correctly map out the distortions of the figures and surrounding architecture that would be necessary for the illusion. Beyond that, the work is executed with such skill at the boundary between what is real and what is painted that it's actually hard to differentiate the true cornices from the painted ones: where the architecture stops and the illusion begins. And yet, while all of this perspective technique was important, Pozzo's nave fresco transcends it. Its airy composition lifts us upward into the heavenbound space above, and makes that space present for us as an extension of the one we inhabit below.

It is the relationship of Pozzo's mural to its setting that I want to build upon now in looking at the tradition of murals and then my own mural work: the fact that Pozzo used the architecture of the space—its cornice, lunettes, vault, and height—and then ultimately transformed that architecture. So, what are some of the ways in which a muralist's response to a setting and the setting itself contribute to the impact of a mural? Here are four:

(1) Using parts of a setting. In 1940 Catalan muralist Josep Maria Sert (1874–1945) created a ceiling mural, *American Progress*, for the lobby of 30 Rockefeller Plaza in New York City. The mural celebrates the achievements of American industry, and, to emphasize the contributions of workers, Sert used the lobby's columns as platforms on which to set colossal figures astride the space between them. These figures run the length of the lobby. To activate the space above them, he set airplanes to circle about and weave clouds of dense smoke in their wakes. The entire skyscape is beautifully lit. Warm light washes it from below the column capitals, and serves to bridge the boundary between what is real and what has been painted (fig. 6.6).

(2) Extending the space of the setting. We've already seen how Andrea Pozzo lifted the nave space at Sant'Ignazio upward into heaven. Diego Rivera (1886–1957) achieved something similar in a horizontal direction with his mural at the San Francisco College of Art, *The Making of a Fresco* (1931; fig. 6.7). It's really a mural about the making of a mural—artists are shown at work painting a mural about building the city of San Francisco, and Rivera painted a scaffold for them as a kind of foreground screen. This resonates in material with the wood truss that spans the room. But more importantly, it obscures the corners of the space (between the end wall and the ceiling and side walls) and thereby allows the mural to take the light walls of the room and believably extend them back into the space behind the scaffold and the figures seated on it.

(3) Echoing the circulation pattern of a space. People move through the spaces where murals are installed, and muralists sometimes build their compositions around the routes they follow. Such is the case with Ezra Winter's (1886–1949) mural, *Fountain of Youth* (1932), for the stairway at New York's Radio City Music Hall. The mural follows a long processional stair, gentle in its rise for the well-dressed people headed up to their seats to view stage shows. And the mural moves with them both in path and spirit. It's shaped like a great cavalcade of youthful people ascending to the sky, presented with a graphic intensity typical of art deco. The rich red in the mural matches the red of the lobby's walls and strengthens the profiles of the mural's silvery figures as they climb the wall (fig. 6.8).

(4) Responding to a viewer's sightline. Some murals are designed to be viewed from a single location and direction, a technique called anamorphic perspective. It's a trompe-l'oeil technique intended to fool the eye into perceiving the painted image in place of the true wall or ceiling surface—its orientation and shape—on which the image has been painted. We've already seen how Pozzo created his fresco on the barrel-vaulted ceiling at Sant'Ignazio to be viewed from the center of the nave. But impressively, the mural works no matter where we stand in the nave, and this fact brings up an important qualification about anamorphic projection.

At the same church Pozzo also painted the illusion of a cupola on the flat disc ceiling over the crossing. It was designed to look like a real cupola when viewed from the nave near the crossing, and it is effective from there (fig. 6.9). And yet in the moment we move left or right the fake cupola appears weirdly distorted. Unlike the nave mural, which is convincing no matter where we are in the space below, the illusory cupola is distracting the moment we move away from its designated viewing location.

6.7. *The Making of a Fresco Showing the Building of the City*, Diego Rivera, 1931.
Image copyright © San Francisco Art Institute.

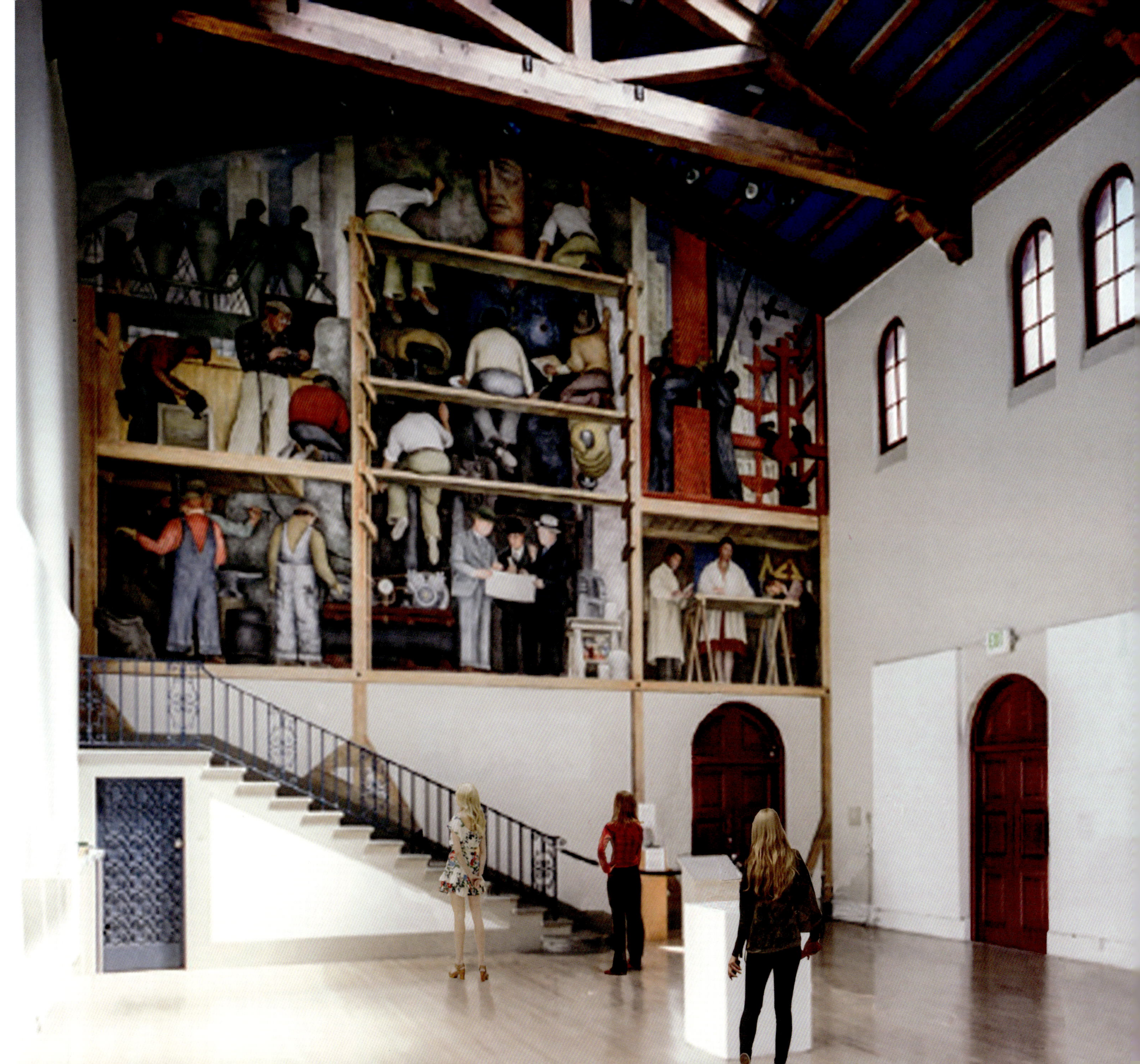

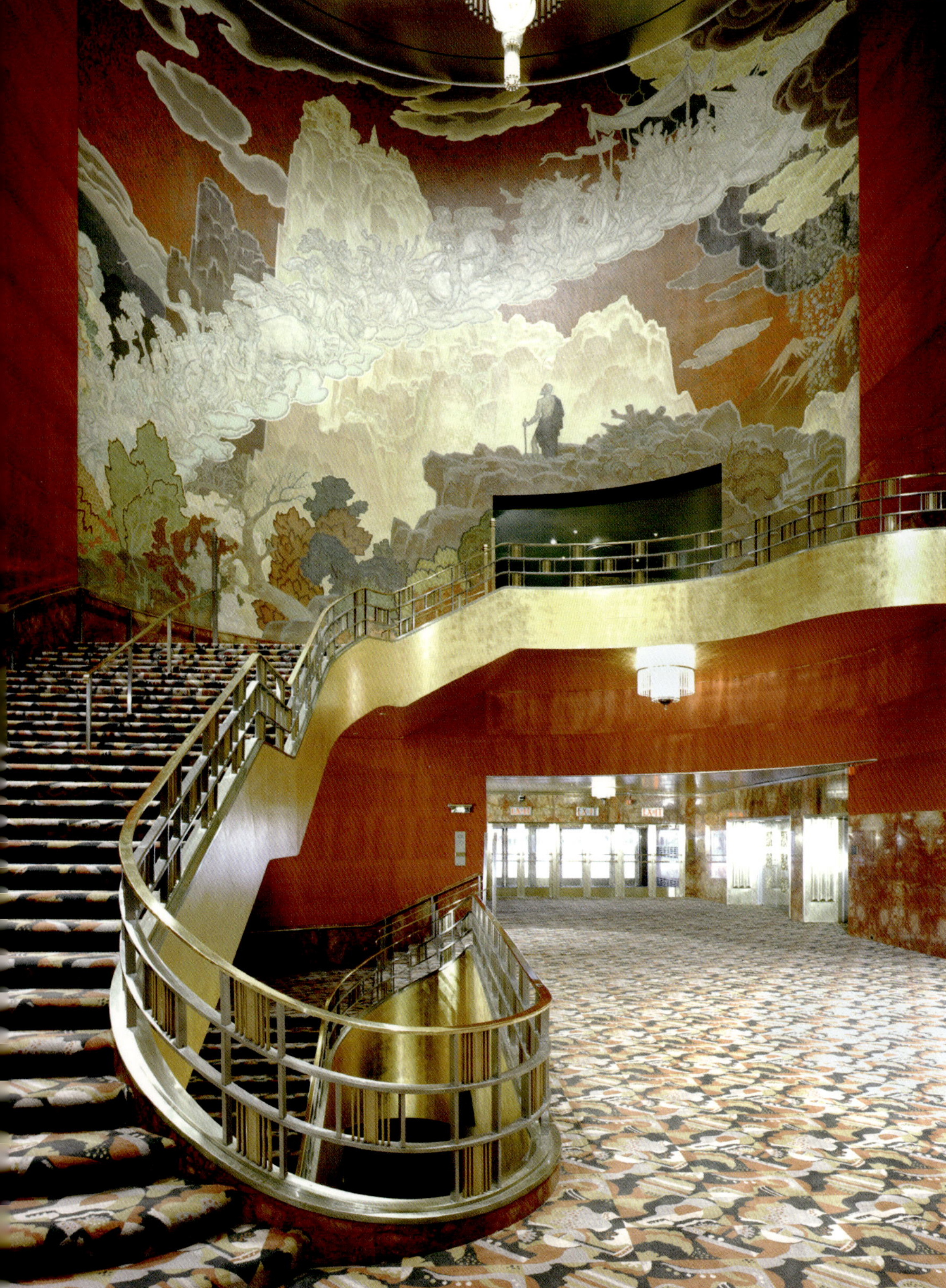

6.8. *Fountain of Youth*, Ezra Winter, 1932. Radio City Music Hall Foyer, New York, NY. Photo by Whitney Cox.

My sense of illusionist works of this character is that they are far more successful when they are not only architectural in content and when their composition is not too tied to the single position from which the perspective illusion has been projected. A looser fit is better. This is the case with one of the best-known murals of the high Renaissance, *The School of Athens* (1509–1511), by Raphael (1483–1520). It's a one-point perspective, with Plato, it is believed, at its central vanishing point, and perspective does play a role in the painting's pull on the viewer (fig. 6.10). But importantly, the painting works no matter where the viewer stands—witness the angular view showing the mural in its full context (fig. 6.11). Its success when seen from various locations is due mostly to the arrangement of figures around the mural's central space and the strong longitudinal shapes in the floor that are revealed by the absence of people covering them. This distinction—tight fit versus loose fit—is what explains to me the limited success of Pozzo's false cupola and the power of his nave ceiling.

With these four examples, we've seen ways in which muralists might work responsively with the settings of their murals. It has been my experience that this kind of fit between mural and setting arises not only in finding the possibilities of a space—what the space might want to become, as architect Lou Kahn might say—but equally in finding ways of taking a problematic quirk (every space will have one) and finding a way to use that as an opportunity. Here are several examples of both from my practice as a muralist.

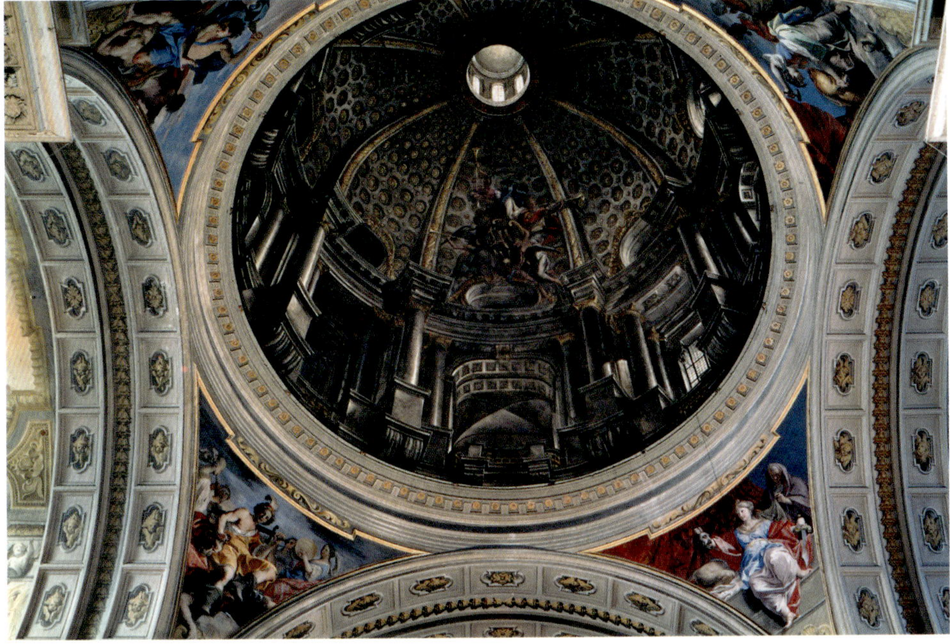

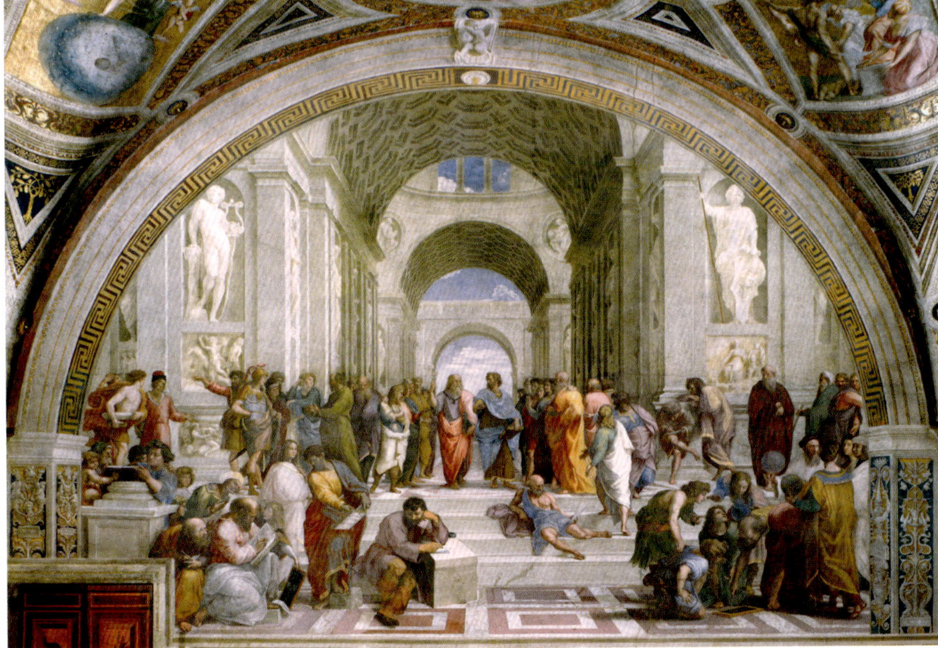

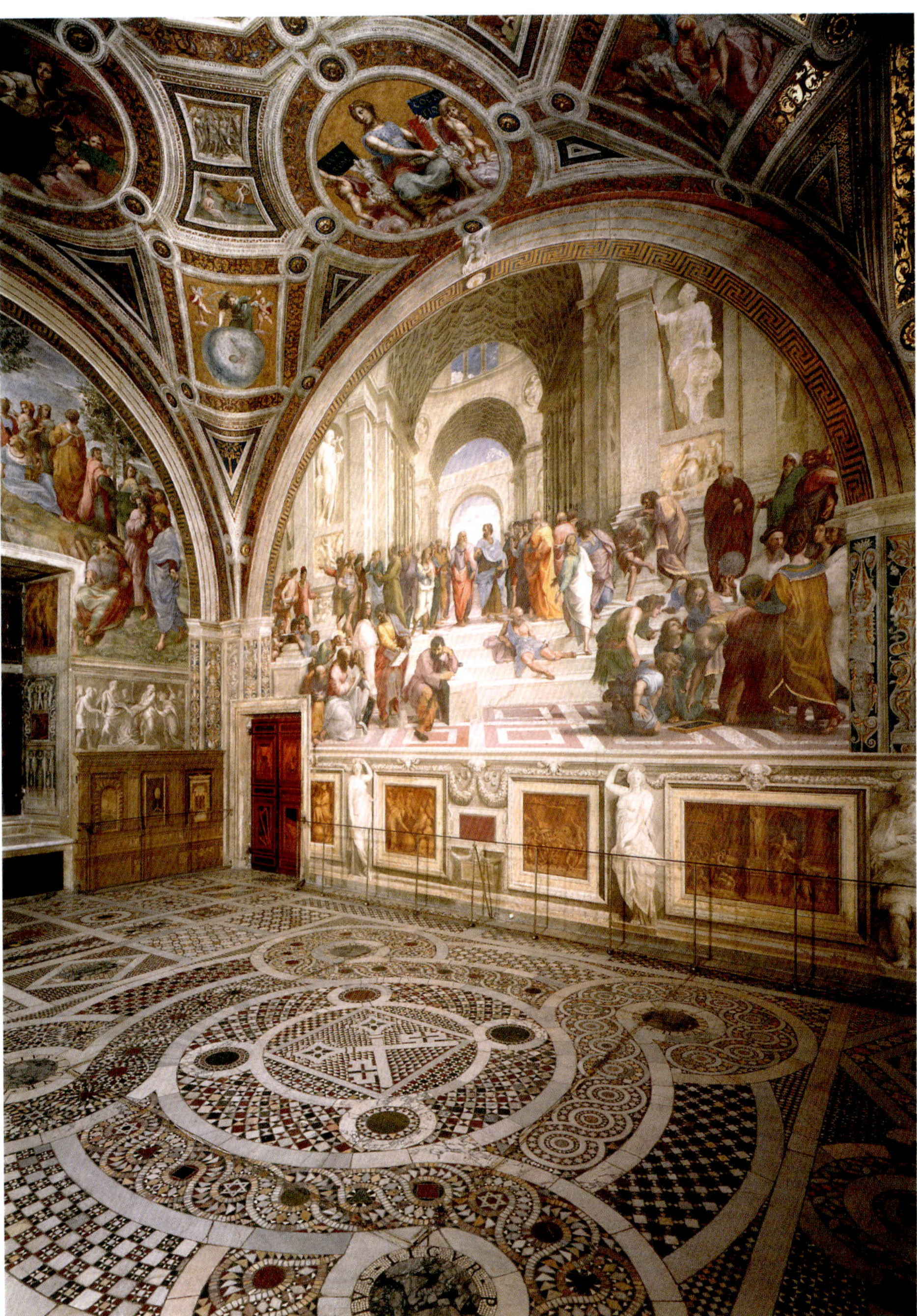

6.9 (*top left*). *Cupola in Perspective*, Andrea Pozzo (1642–1709). Sant'Ignazio Church, Rome. Scala/Art Resource, NY.

6.10 (*bottom left*). *School of Athens*, Raphael (Raffaello Sanzio), ca. 1510–1512. Fresco. Stanza della Segnatura, Stanze di Raffaello, Vatican Palace, Rome. Scala/Art Resource, NY.

6.11. View of the Stanza della Segnatura, with the *School of Athens* to the right. Vatican Palace, Rome. Scala/Art Resource, NY.

Using and Extending a Part: Michael Baker (2003)

The ground floor lobby at the headquarters of Michael Baker International Inc. had a quirk: the *L*-shaped receptionist's desk abutting the wall where the mural would go. At its base the mural would have to go around and over the top of this desk. It seemed to me I had to find a way to connect that desk to the content of the mural, one that would show a fictitious landscape of Michael Baker's works of civic infrastructure (fig. 6.12). Eventually, I found two. First, I used it as a base for a column that would rise up through the second floor and carry an extension of the mezzanine. Secondly, I extended the desktop's work surface into the mural by transforming it into a busy roadway in front of the hotel where the Michael Baker Company had been founded years before. So in a real sense the desk became the generator of the mural (fig. 6.13).

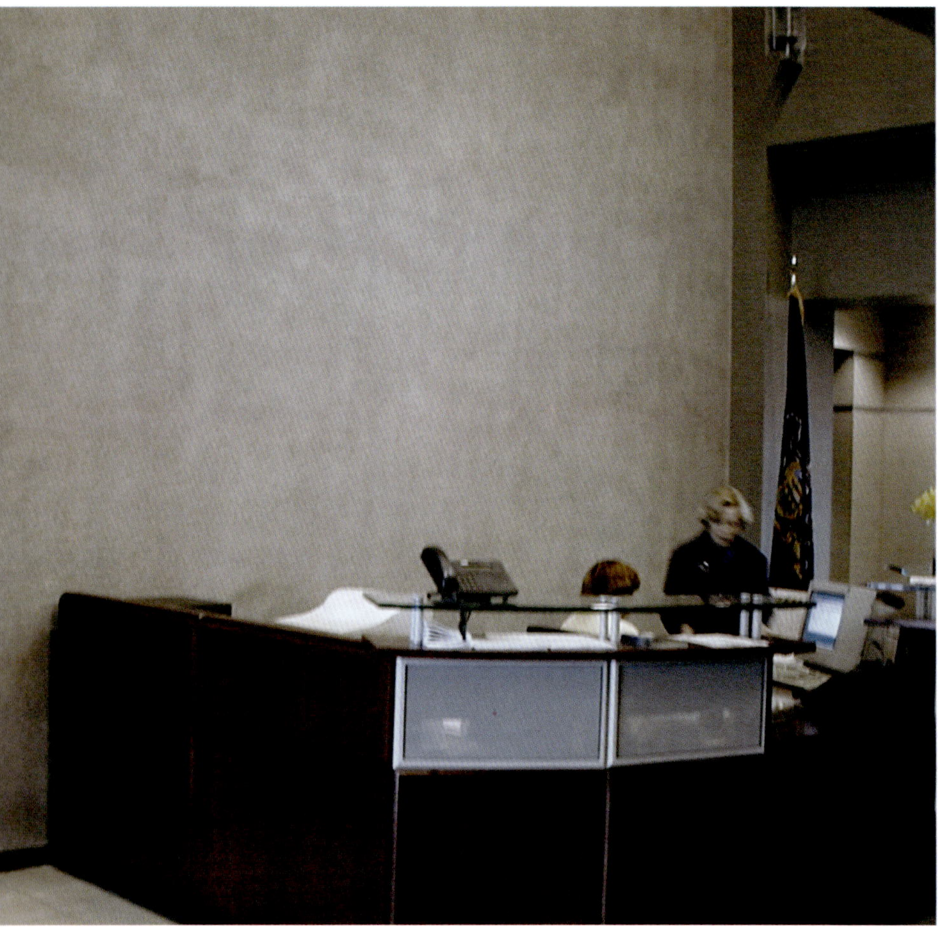
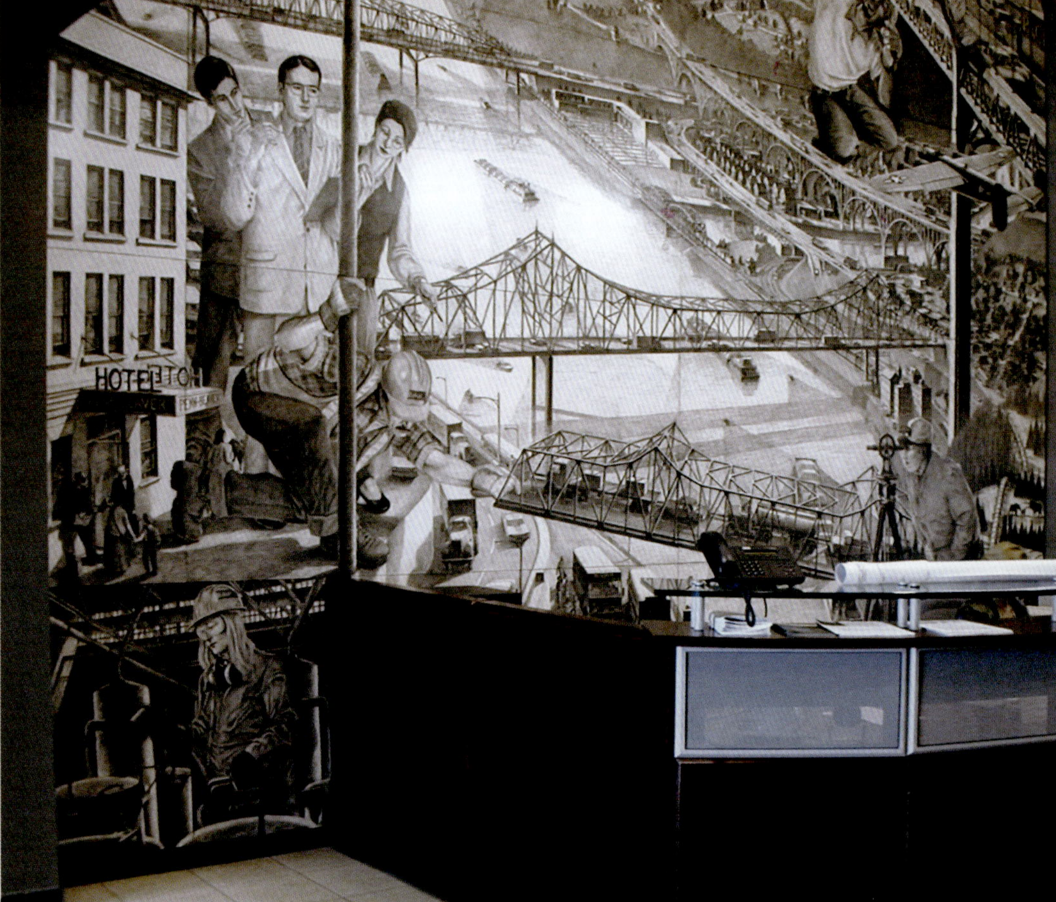

6.12. Detail showing desk before and after. Michael Baker lobby mural, Doug Cooper with Grégoire Picher, 2003. Charcoal on paper on board, 24 × 21 feet. Pittsburgh.

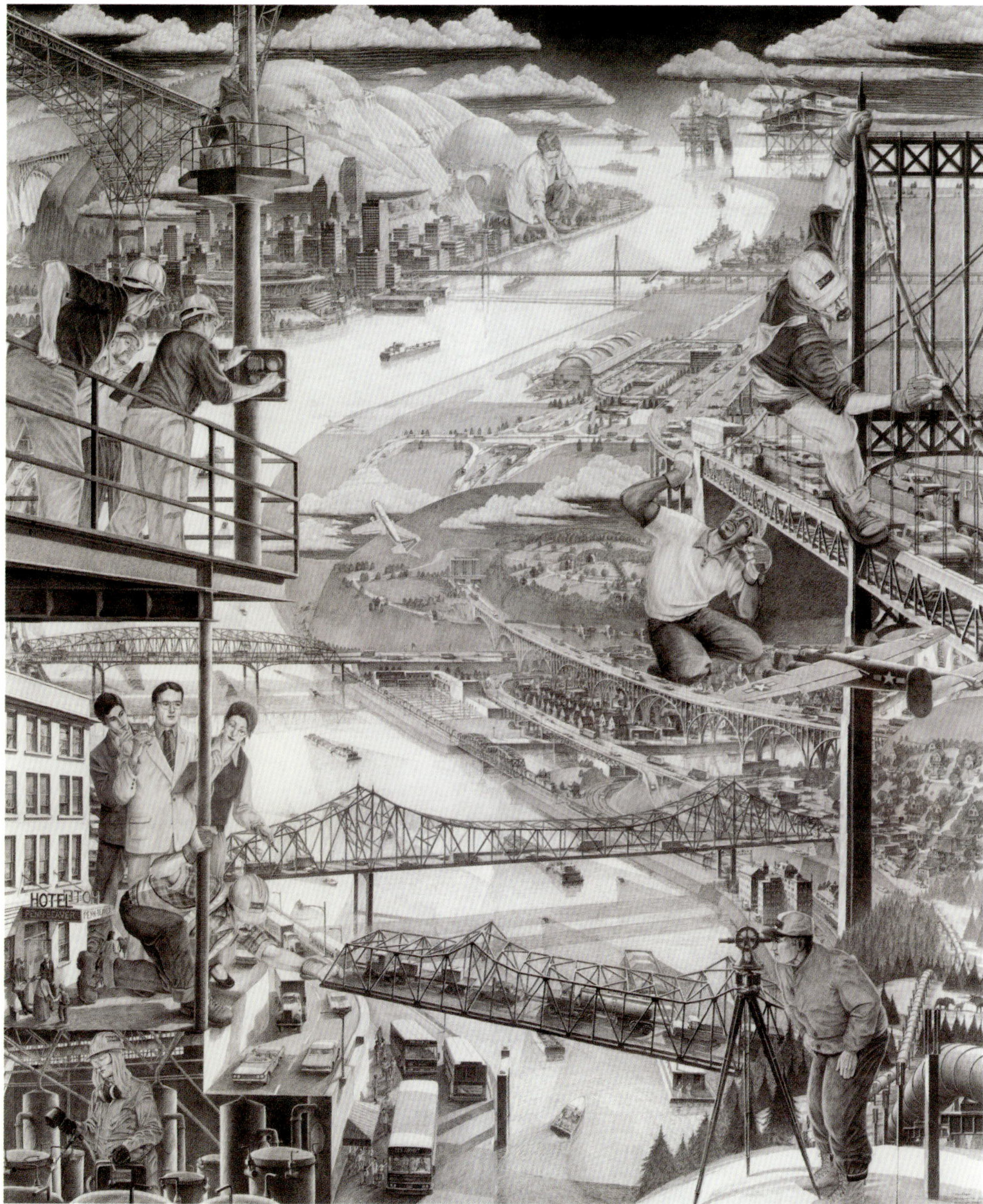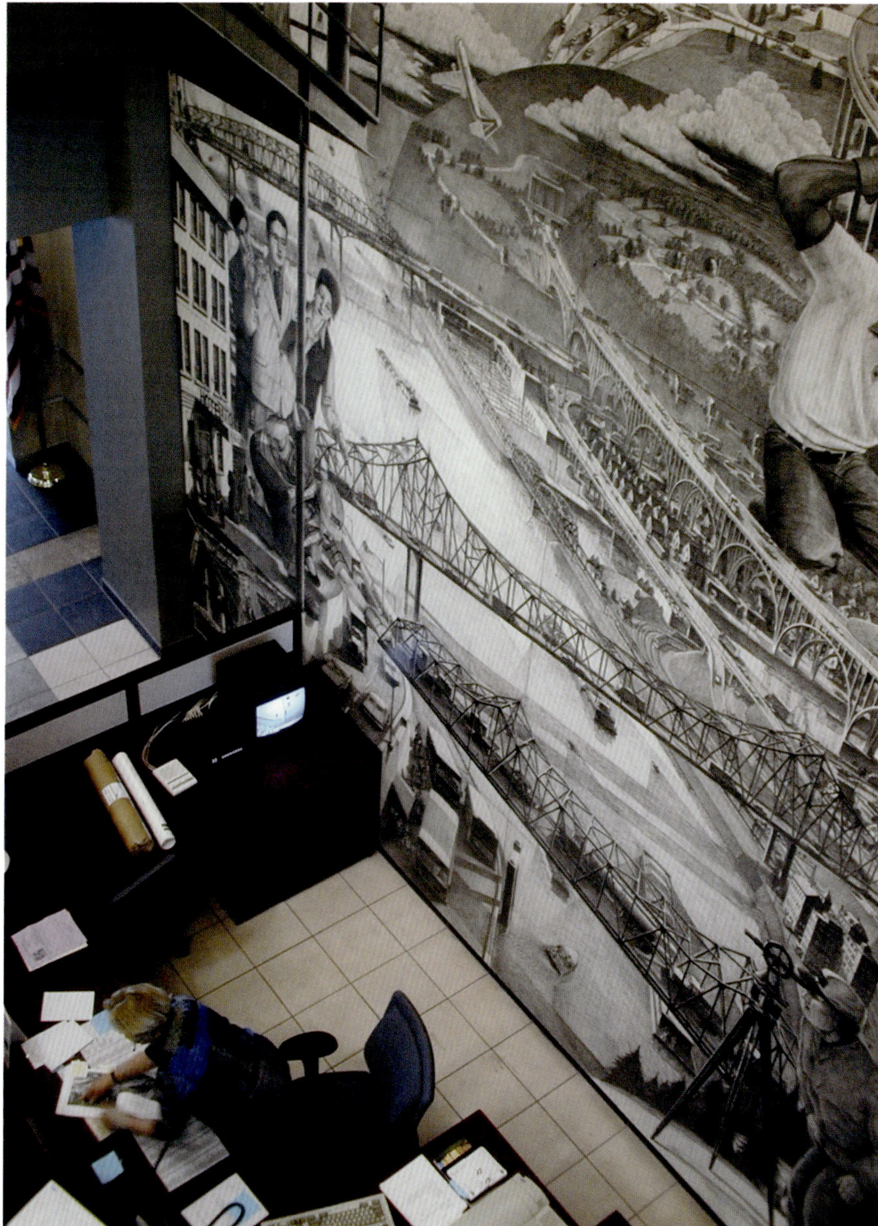

6.13. View of overall mural and details from second-floor mezzanine. Michael Baker lobby mural, Doug Cooper with Grégoire Picher, 2003. Charcoal on paper on board, 24 × 21 feet. Pittsburgh.

Using the Ugliest Part:
University of Rome, (2003–2005)

Originally, the mural I did for the *aula magna* (lecture hall) at the Ex Caserma Sani in Rome's Esquilino neighborhood was for the Sapienza University of Rome. But the building is now used by Rome's other major university, Roma Tre. The mural goes all the way around the hall at a height of sixteen feet and a length of two hundred feet (fig. 6.14). But when I began planning the mural, I couldn't help noticing the four large, ugly ventilator grates on either side of the lectern along the end wall, the lecture hall's most important wall. And there was no getting rid of them. So I decided to make them part of the mural.

One of Esquilino's most important landmarks, Piazza Vittorio, provided the opportunity. That piazza is surrounded by arcades, and so, with my assistants, Grégoire Picher and Patty Culley, I developed two anamorphic elements that would extend the lecture hall's sidewalls as two arcaded porticos flanking the lectern. It was a theatrical approach, more like a set of flats in a stage set than a view into a virtual scene. We made them trapezoidal and gave them real physical edges, and in that context the realness of the grates didn't seem to matter much at all. Indeed, the visual texture of their slats and strong expression of frontality made them serve very well as faux panels in the arcades' piers (figs. 6.15, 6.16).

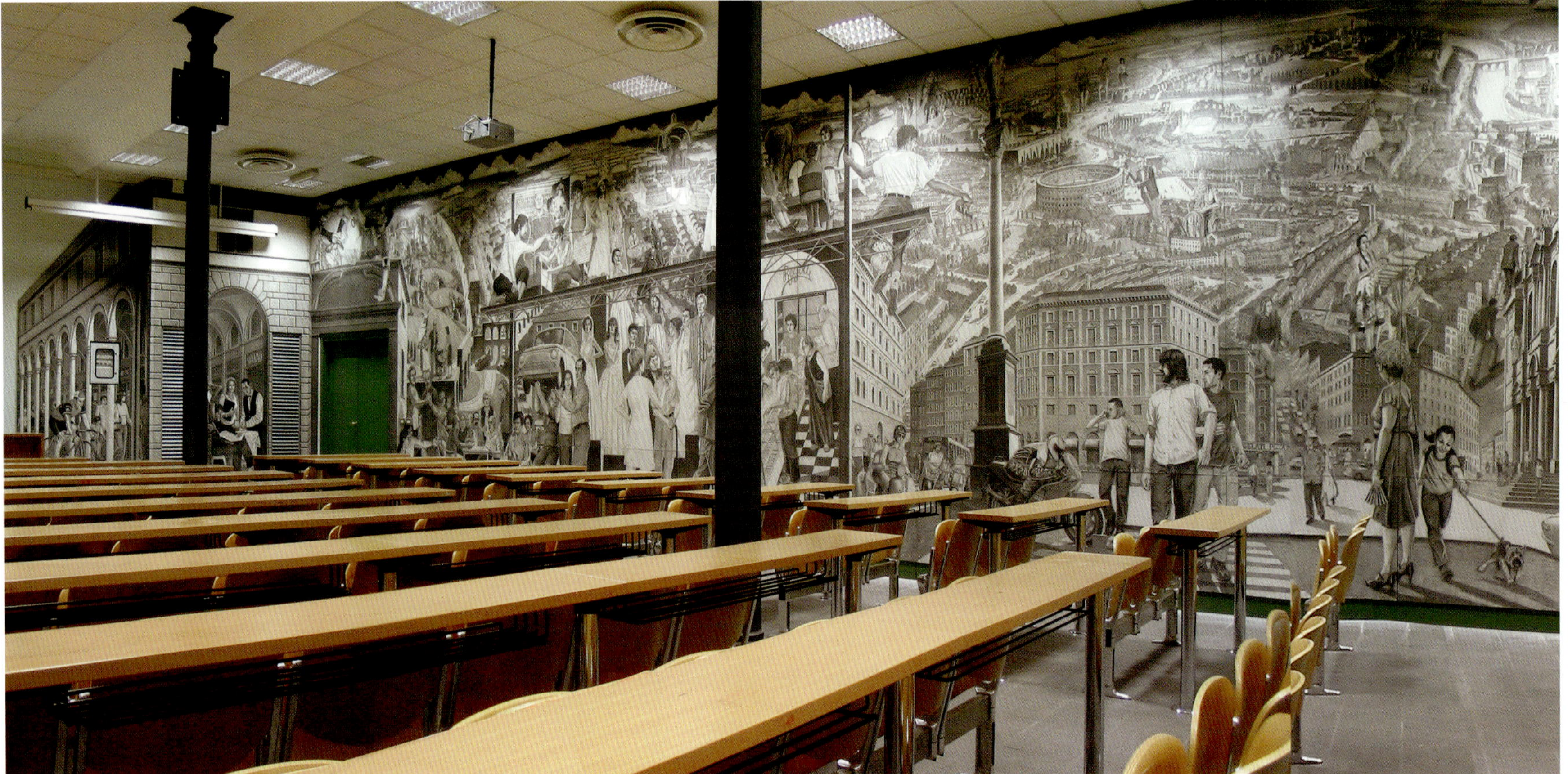

6.14 (*above*). South wall detail looking toward Saint Peter's. Aula Magna, Ex Caserma Sani mural, Doug Cooper with Grégoire Picher and Patty Culley, 2005. Charcoal on paper on board, approx. 16 × 200 feet. Università Roma Tre, Rome.

6.15 (*facing page, inset*). Southeast corner detail showing grates before and after. Aula Magna, Ex Caserma Sani mural, Doug Cooper with Grégoire Picher and Patty Culley, 2005. Charcoal on paper on board, approx. 16 × 200 feet. Università Roma Tre, Rome.

6.16 (*facing page*). Detail of southeast corner showing arcade extending south wall. Aula Magna, Ex Caserma Sani mural , Doug Cooper with Grégoire Picher and Patty Culley, 2005. Charcoal on paper on board, approx. 16 × 200 feet. Università Roma Tre, Rome.

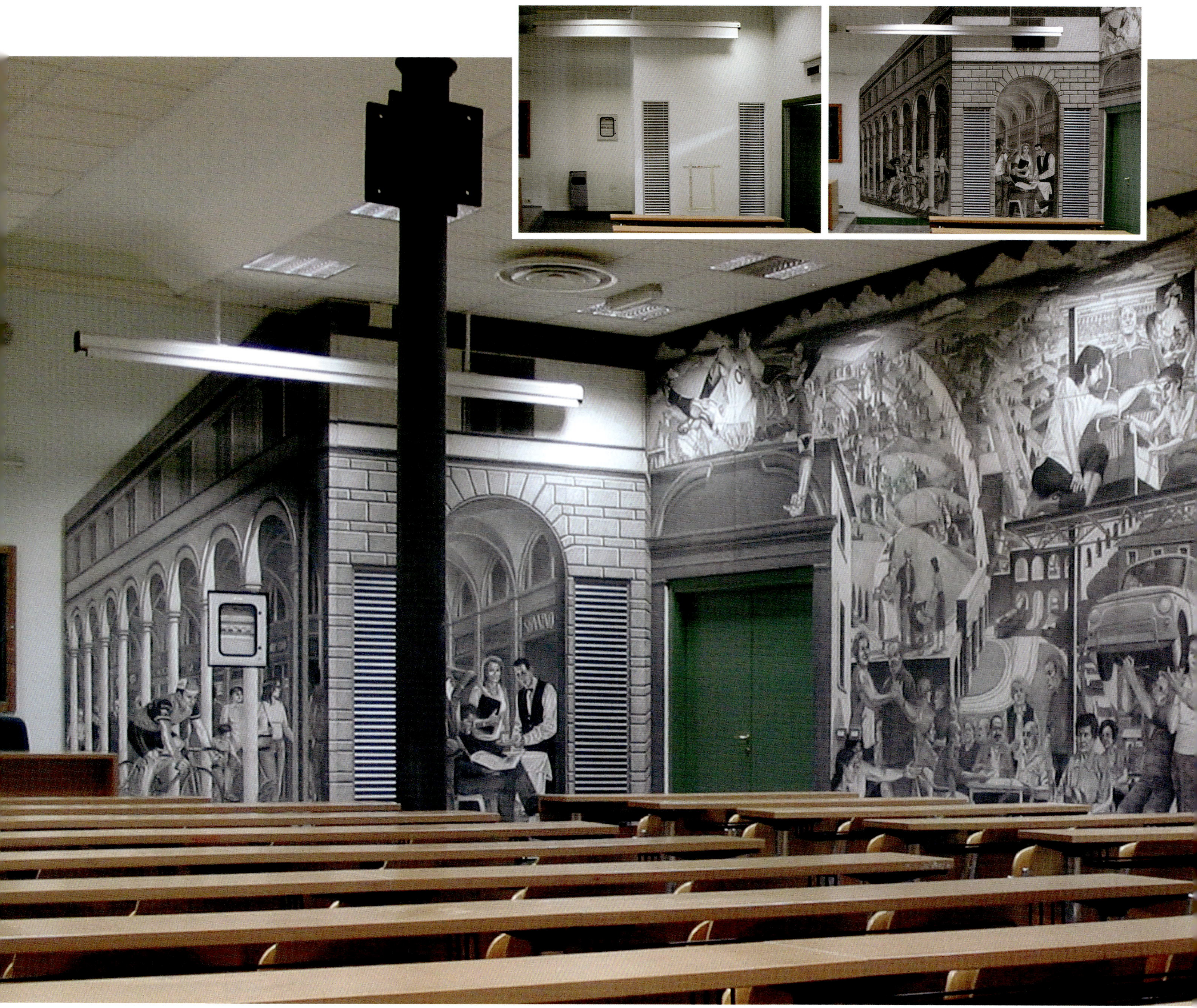

Responding to Movement:
Cohon Center Mural (1996)

With the Carnegie Mellon Jared L. Cohon University Center mural, I found a way to respond to the circulation pattern in the space by using a loose-fit anamorphic perspective. The mural is located along three walls of a mezzanine surrounding a rotunda. Because the center was still under construction while I was drawing the mural in my off-campus studio, I had to anticipate sightlines from the architect's plans and model them in my studio. In those plans I saw an opportunity along the west-wall mezzanine, leading to the main dining hall. As viewers would move along it, they would view the mural diagonally as they approached it at the mezzanine's more open end, but more frontally where it narrowed.

These conditions helped solve a political/visual problem for me. I wanted to use this part of the mural to show the central quadrangles of the CMU campus, Henry Hornbostel's original campus design and the recent additions by architect Michael Dennis. But I wanted to show these in a way that would not privilege one part of the campus over another—the School of Engineering versus the College of Fine Arts, etc. At the same time, I wanted this part of the mural to lead the eye along a diagonal path leading to the dining hall.

Experimenting in my studio, I found that if I slowed the rate of convergence for the view over the campus, the mural would work well for both directions of view. Seen frontally, the axonometric portrayal of the buildings would allow the viewer to float over all the buildings more or less equally (fig. 6.17). Seen diagonally the same area would show the campus as a deep space convergent perspective (fig. 6.18).

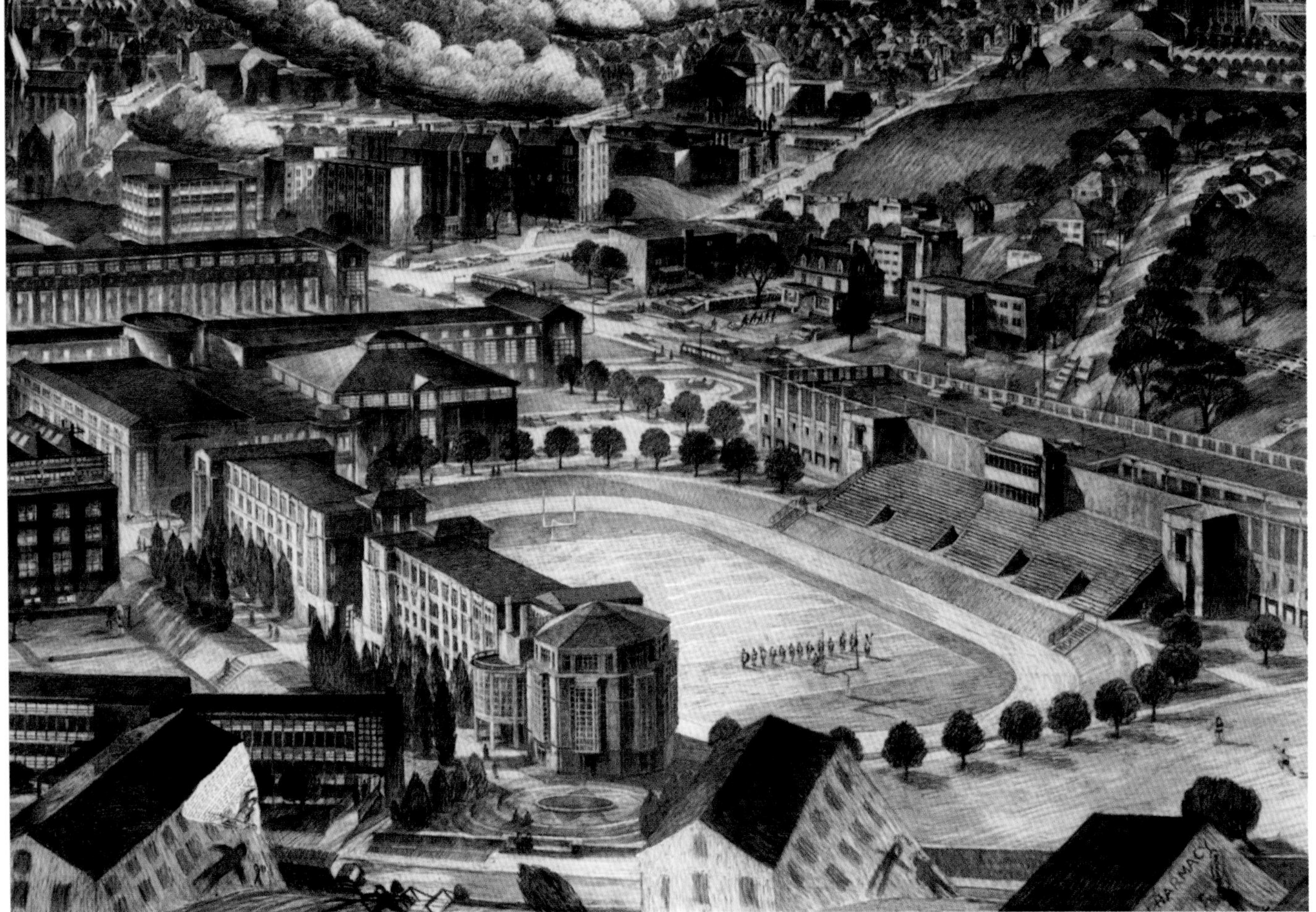

6.17 (*left*). West wall detail showing campus from a frontal view. Jared L. Cohon University Center mural, Doug Cooper with John Trivelli and Jonathan Kline, 1996. Charcoal on paper on board, approx. 10 × 150 feet. Carnegie Mellon University, Pittsburgh.

6.18 (*right*). West wall detail showing campus from a diagonal view. Jared L. Cohon University Center mural, Doug Cooper with John Trivelli and Jonathan Kline, 1996. Charcoal on paper on board, approx. 10 × 150 feet. Carnegie Mellon University, Pittsburgh.

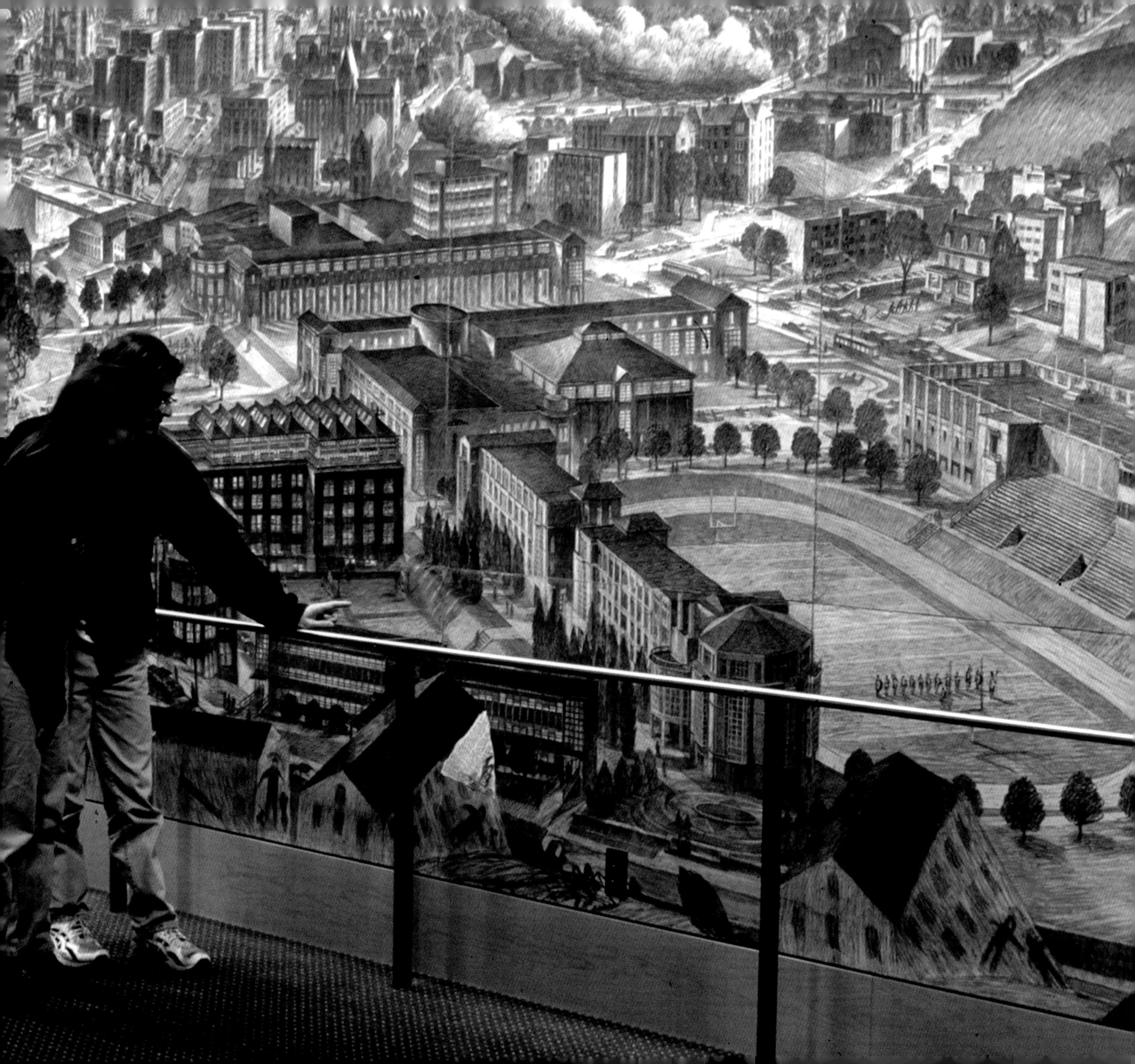

Using the Height of a Space: Mascaro (1999)

I created a composite mural in the two-floor-high entrance lobby of the headquarters of Mascaro Construction Company in Pittsburgh. At ground level, I used views of the city featuring many of Mascaro's signature projects, such as the then new Heinz Stadium, where the Pittsburgh Steelers play. But the upper areas of the mural at the mezzanine level were a different matter. I wanted them to lead the viewer's eye upward in a way that would also personalize Mascaro's primary activity: construction. So, up there I built an "abovescape" of upwardly viewed columns, beams, scaffolding, and construction riggers (expertly drawn by my assistant John Trivelli) guiding beams up into place (fig. 6.19).

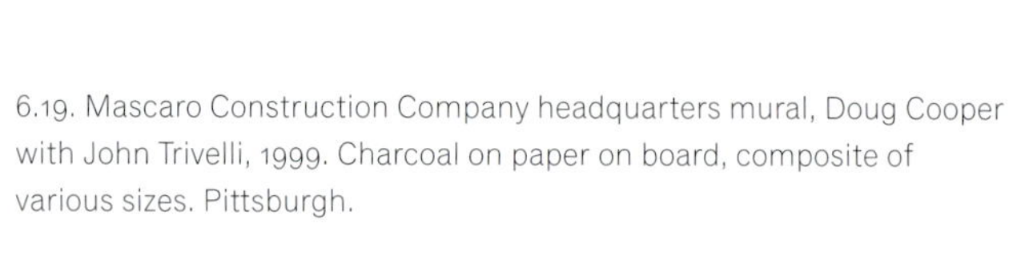

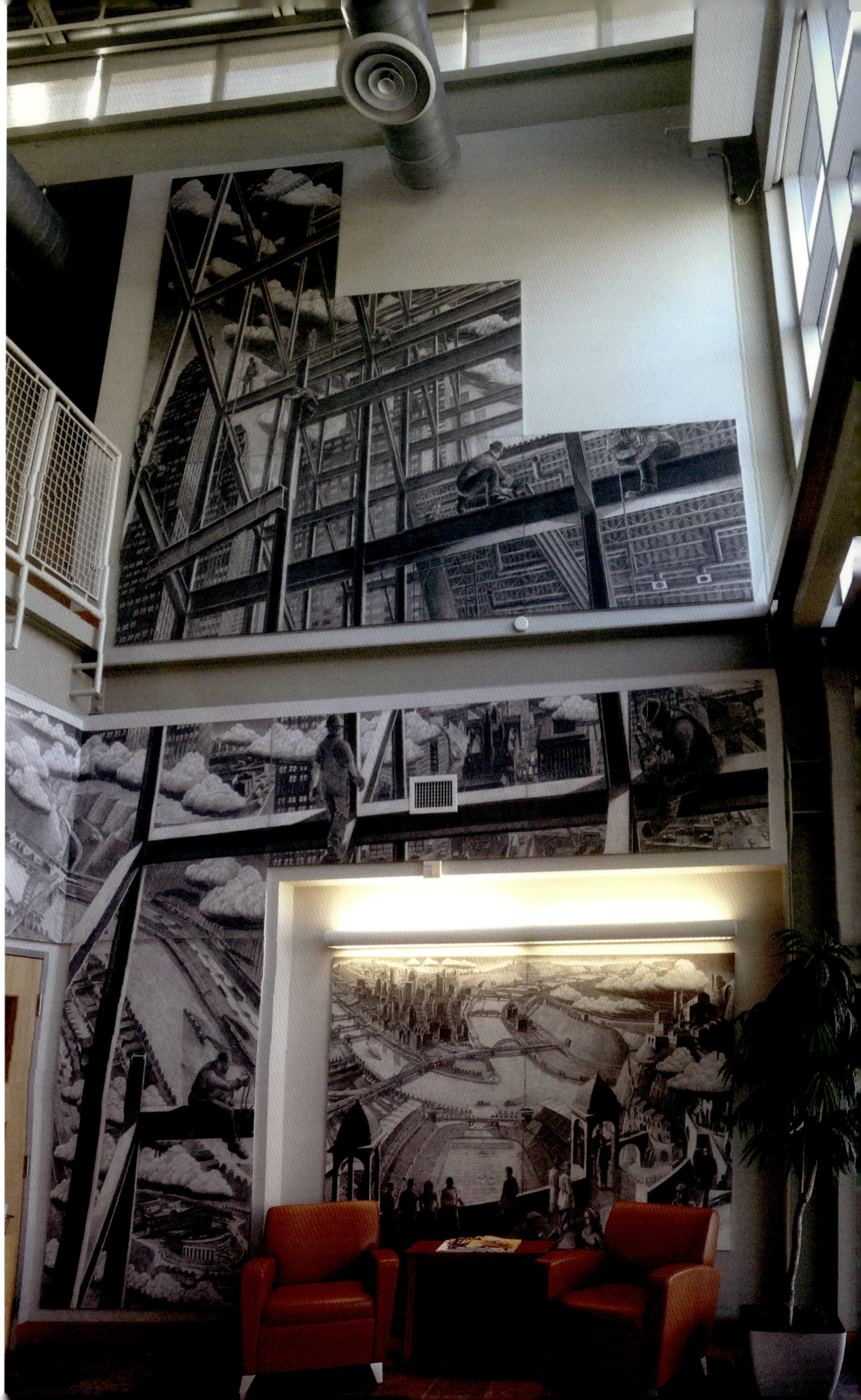

6.19. Mascaro Construction Company headquarters mural, Doug Cooper with John Trivelli, 1999. Charcoal on paper on board, composite of various sizes. Pittsburgh.

Responding to Movement 2:
CMUQ, Doha (2008–2009)

The central part of the Carnegie Mellon University in Qatar (CMUQ) mural would be installed on a forty-foot-long gently curving wall along a corridor. During a trip to Doha during March 2008 I visited the eventual mural site. The building was still under construction, but the wall was already roughed in, and I slowly walked its length several times to get a sense of its visual impact.

Sometime during that trip, the image of a freight train slowly rounding a bend suddenly came to mind. In my imagination the train was unfolding serially, car by car and edge by edge, as it passed by me. This momentary reverie really caught my attention because it seemed to offer a solution to a vexing problem. I would be working with two photographers on the project, my daughter Sarah and her business partner, Nina Gorfer. The mural would combine their photographic imagery with my drawing, and I was wondering how to combine the two.

Out of this image of the moving train, the idea of building this mural in multiple layers eventually emerged. It would permit us to join our two materials one over the top of the other (drawings over photos), a solution that would resolve the two roles we were in the midst of defining for ourselves as the mural's content developed: my drawings would represent a present in front eclipsing a past represented photographically behind. And it gave me insight into how to compose the mural in a way that would dynamically respond to the condition of a viewer moving close to the wall and viewing the mural at a steep oblique angle.

After the mural was up in Doha, I was able to assess the mural as a whole (fig. 6.21) and particularly the curving wall. The layers really did seem to unfold serially as I walked past. Even with intervals of depth measured in the increments of ¾-inch-thick panels, there was enough of a discrepancy in the parallax between nearer and deeper panels for the eye to read depth in the image—not the actual depth the mural represents, of course, but enough for the image to be believably three-dimensional (fig. 6.20).

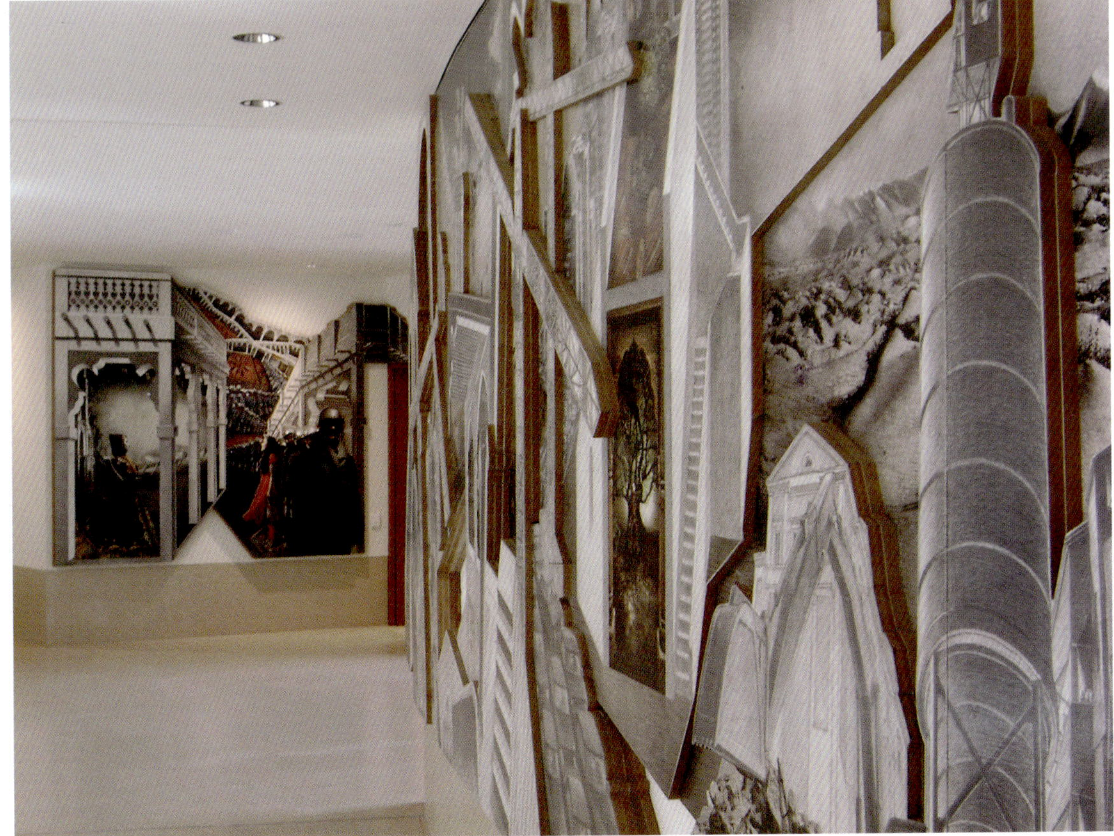

6.20 (*left*). Details showing layered treatments. *Memory between Desert and Sea*, Doug Cooper, Sarah Cooper, and Nina Gorfer with David Kennedy, 2009. Charcoal and photoprint on paper on board, approx. 9 × 50 feet. Carnegie Mellon University in Qatar, Doha.
6.21 (*following spread*). *Memory between Desert and Sea*, Doug Cooper, Sarah Cooper, and Nina Gorfer with David Kennedy, 2009. Charcoal and photoprint on paper on board, approx. 9 × 50 feet. Carnegie Mellon University in Qatar, Doha.

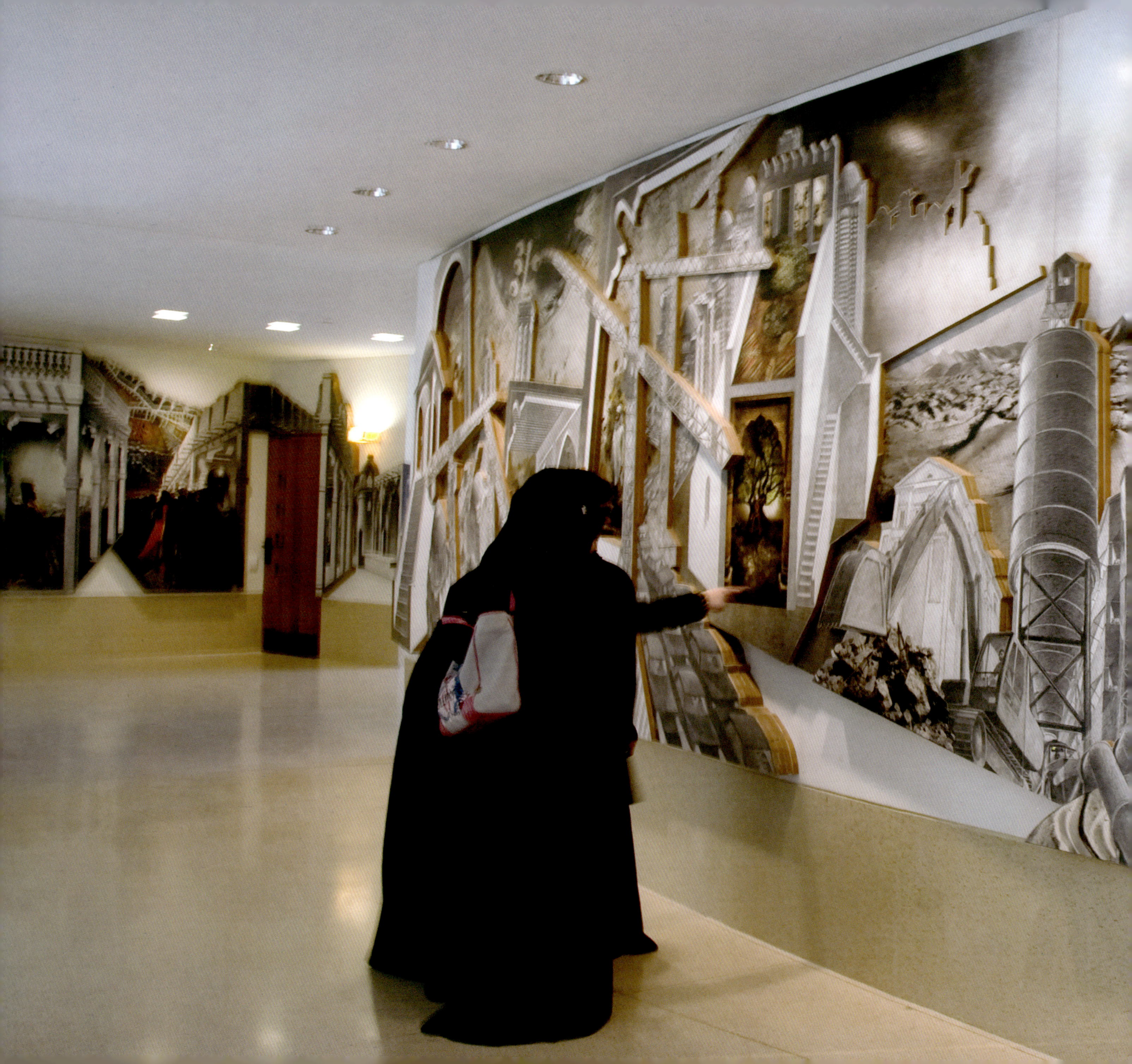

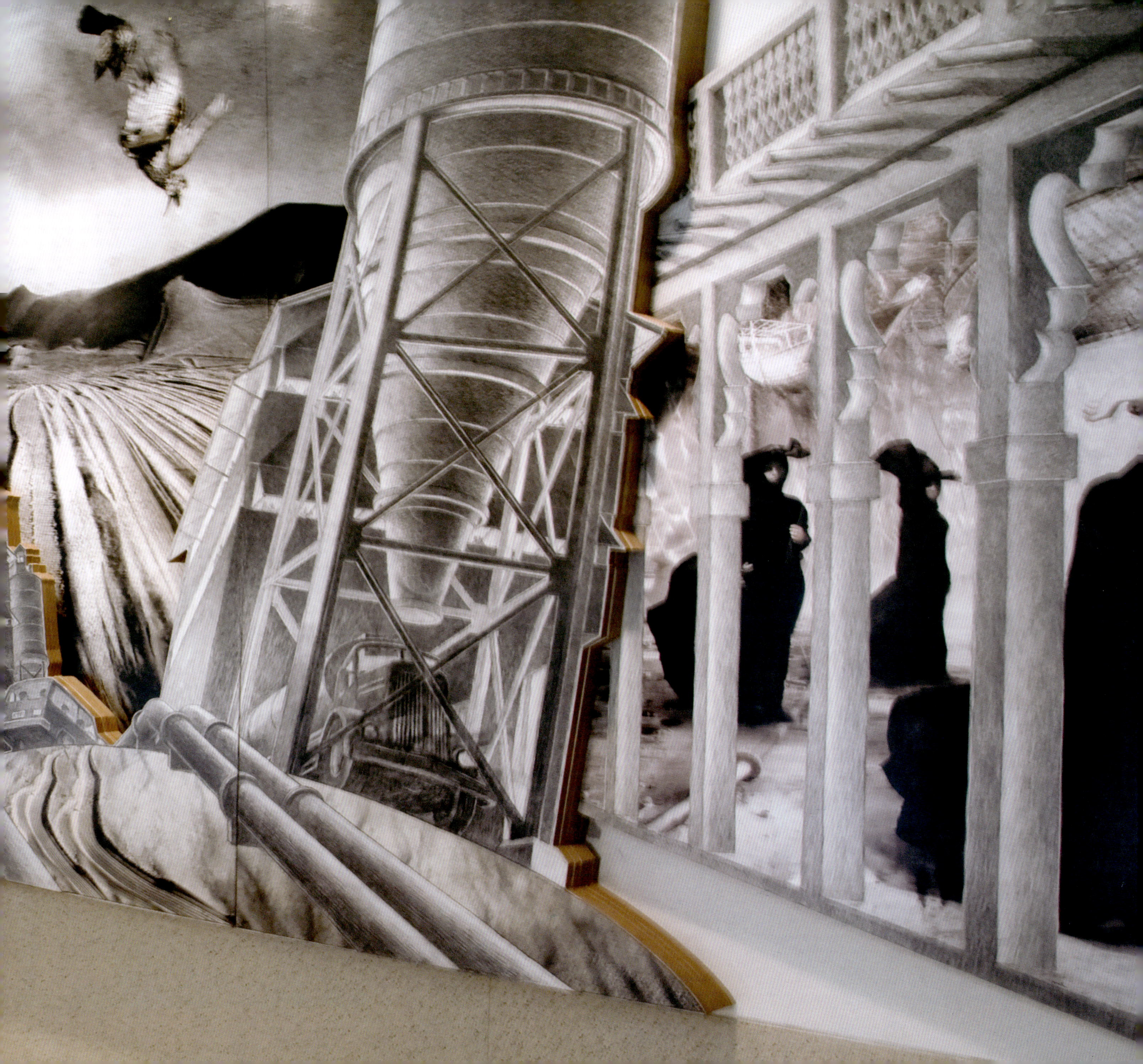

The Place of Murals

What can these several examples tell us about why murals matter for their settings? In the cases of the Michael Baker and Rome murals, we've seen how a mural can take ordinary or even unsightly conditions and make them parts of greater wholes. And at Qatar we've seen how an otherwise banal curving wall can be made into a dynamic condition to walk past. But there's more to murals than just visual upgrades. The central contribution of murals to their settings is tied to the idea of place-making itself.

One of the most unfortunate impacts of contemporary architectural practice has been a loss of a sense of place in interiors. With its stripped-down architecture and its reductionist principles, the modernist project has often led to a kind of sterile neutrality in which all locations within buildings tend to become equal or at least equally unmemorable. There is a loss of a sense of spatial hierarchy. It is that sorry state that murals address by making the settings where they are placed more important. They do so by resonating in fundamental ways with people's sense of the larger world around them or the civic importance of the building in which they are located.

They may address the social forces at work in the larger society, as we find in so many of Diego Rivera's works, or its civic aspirations, as we see in numerous WPA-era courthouse murals. They may reflect the land itself and the stories and legends that people may attach to it, as we find in Thomas Hart Benton's and Grant Wood's regionally focused murals. In a word, a mural on a wall or set of walls can take an otherwise mute and anonymous room or corridor and give it meaning.

David A. Tepper Business School, January 2019

The corridor outside of the Sullivan Auditorium in Carnegie Mellon's new David A. Tepper School of Business would have been indistinguishable from other similar corridors throughout the building. But this particular location, which is also directly adjacent to the reception office for all of the university's prospective students, is part of people's first impression of the university. The mural we placed there was a joint effort with my wife Stefani (6.22). We call it *The Collaborative Campus*, and it explores the cooperative work that has long been a hallmark of Carnegie Mellon University—really since its founding.

Out of our preliminary sketches, an approach emerged that created an alternating rhythm of fabric collage and charcoal drawing (figs. 6.23, 6.24). The four vignettes of familiar campus settings focus on the kinds of community building that is at the heart of collaborative work: students, faculty, staff, and other professionals in arts, technology, and decision sciences all working together. The four scenes are representative of four different modes of working together to create knowledge: the classic scientific/academic tradition, project-based teamwork, serendipitous discoveries by people who work independently, and events that create an evolving cultural context.

The mural extends the idea of cooperation to suggest diverse uses of physical space. It imagines cooperative activities that we would not normally expect to see in each of the four venues: for example, artificial intelligence and robotics are set in the College of Fine Arts, and a musical theater production of *The Magic Flute* is being performed in the atrium of the School of Computer Science (figs. 6.25, 6.26). To make the mural even more particular to its setting, it incorporates the Tepper building's architects' concept of crystal-like bays growing out of the building. And more broadly, the mural speaks of the university's history, culture, and aspirations and brings its own colorful and lively architecture to a setting that might otherwise be a lobby in any contemporary office building around the world.

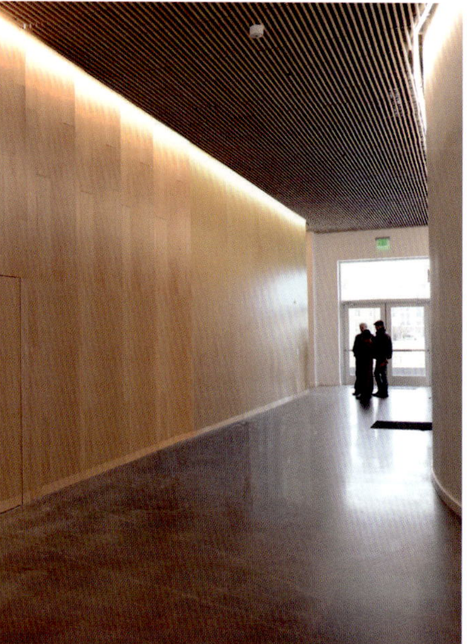
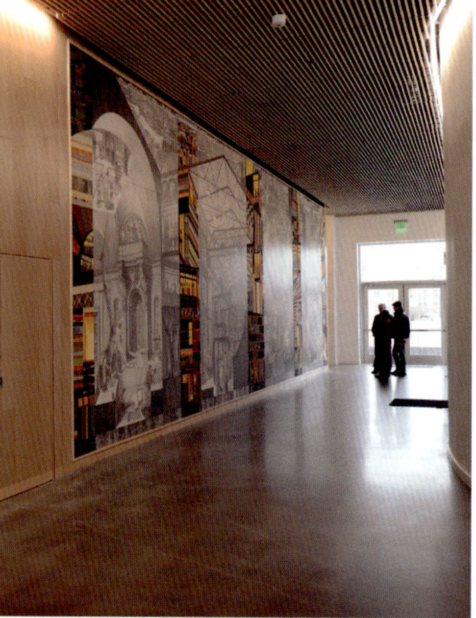

6.22 (*above*). Detail showing corridor before and after. *The Collaborative Campus*, Doug Cooper and Stefani Danes, Adryan Miller-Gorder assisting, 2019. Charcoal on paper on board, fabric mounted around board, 15 × 45 feet. Carnegie Mellon University, David A. Tepper School of Business.

6.23 (*right*). *The Collaborative Campus*, Doug Cooper and Stefani Danes, Adryan Miller-Gorder assisting, 2019. Charcoal on paper on board, fabric mounted around board, 15 × 45 feet. David A. Tepper School of Business, Carnegie Mellon University, Pittsburgh. Photo by Ben Speiser.

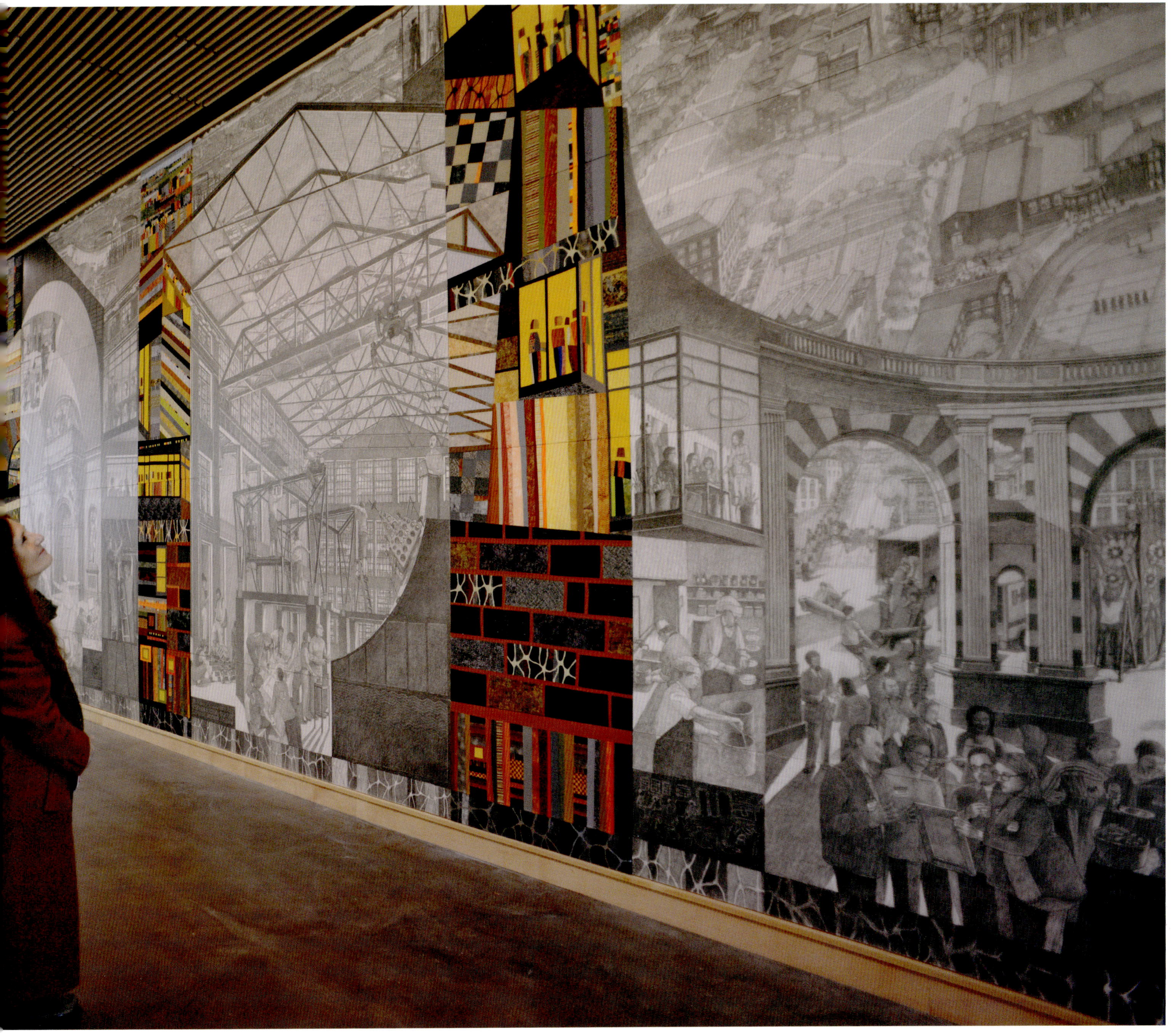

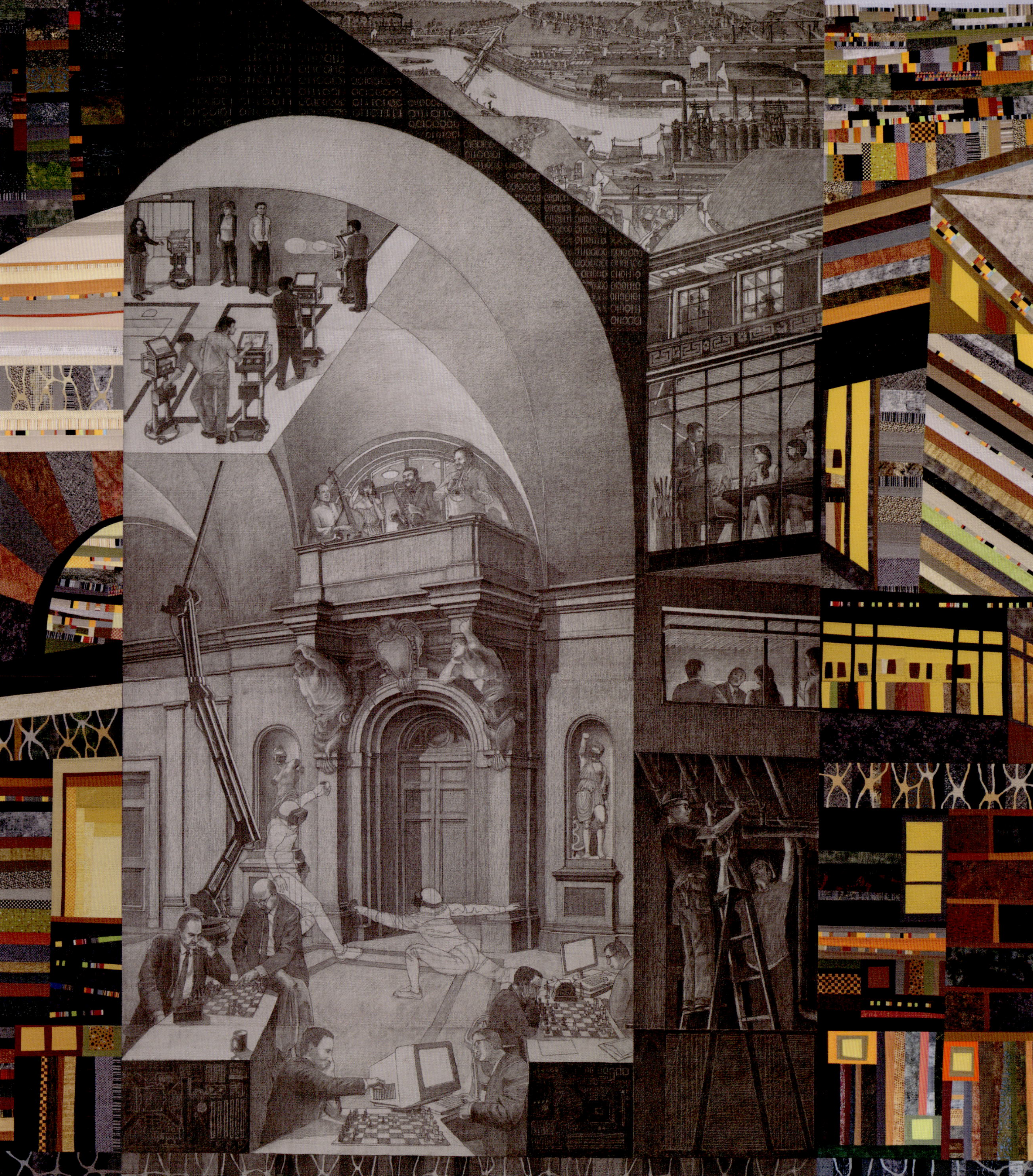

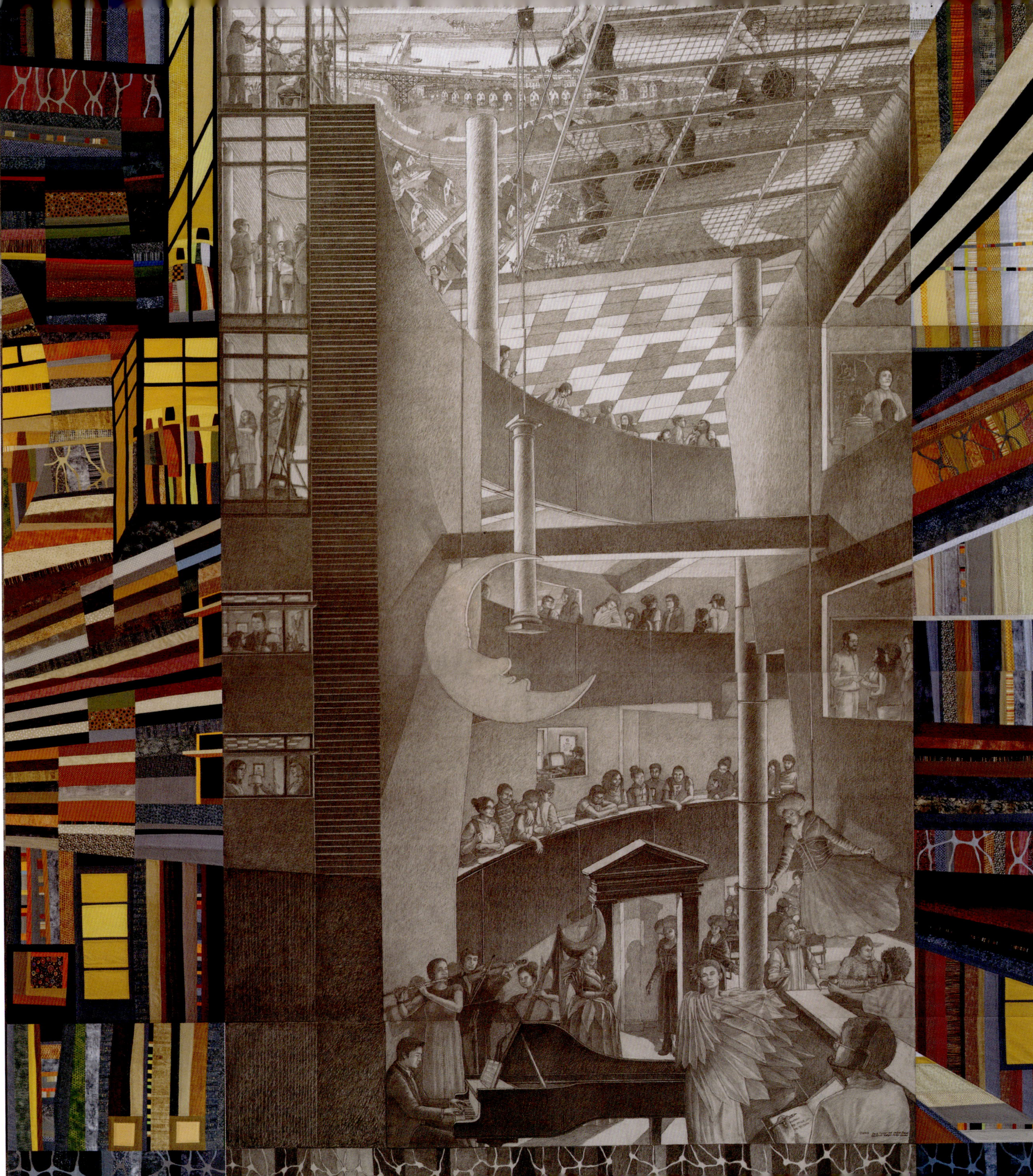

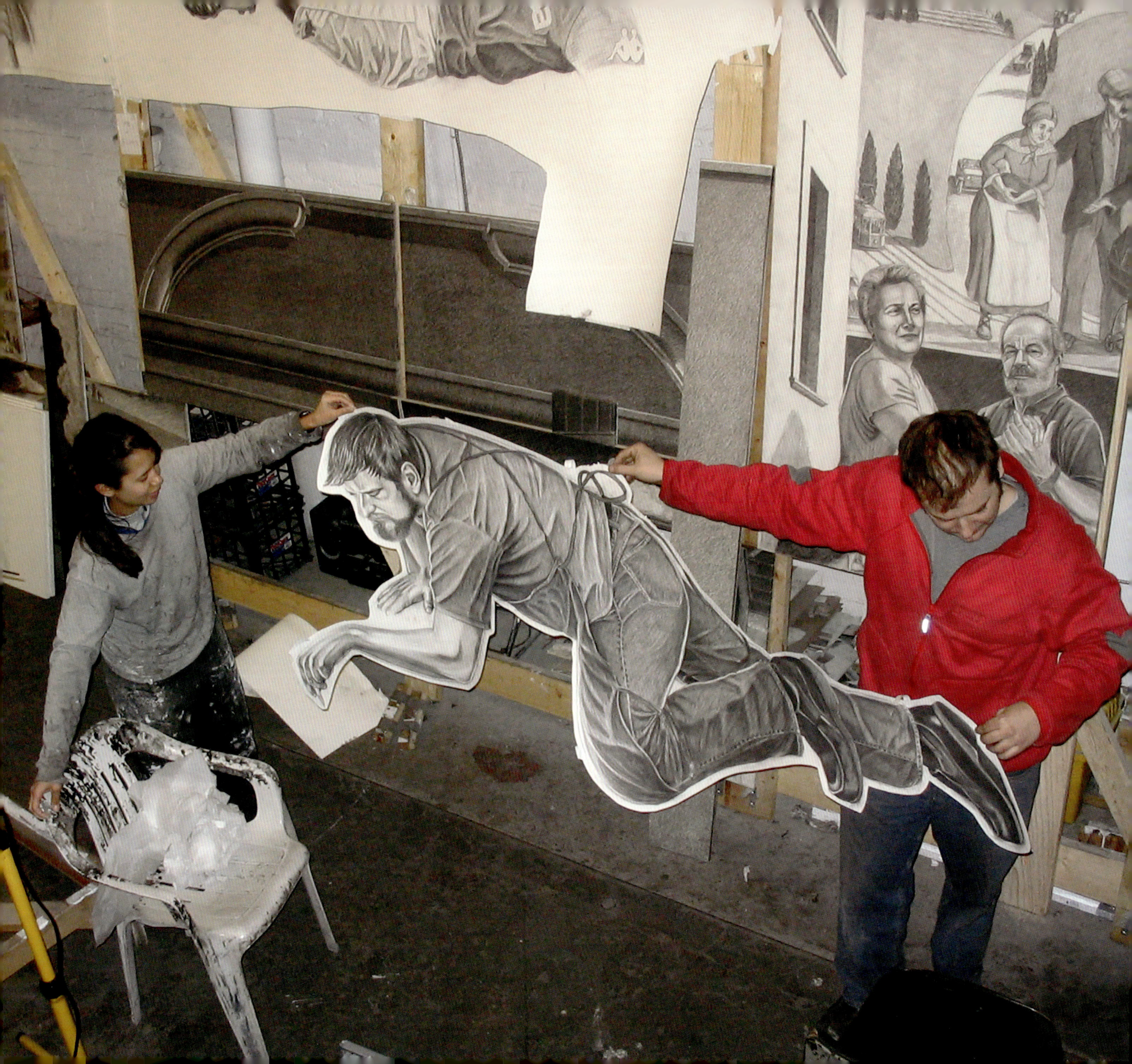

CHAPTER 7

MURALS AND COLLABORATION

We gathered to do research for the mural in Doha, Qatar, in February 2008, and I sensed from the start that I would need to work differently with Sarah and Nina than I had with earlier collaborators. Partly owing to the differences between our media—they are photographers—I knew I would have to give them a freer rein. I wasn't yet sure what that would mean, but I made a point of not sitting at the head of the table when we had dinner the first night together in our apartment.

Teamwork is a fact of making murals (fig. 7.1). With new or renovated spaces, there are discussions that must take place with architects and contractors about wall substrates, durability of surfaces, lighting, protective rails, and installation. For larger works, just the amount of time it takes to draw that much surface means I must work with others. But over the years my collaborative work has grown to become more than just a response to practical necessities. It has had a profound impact on the character and content of the work itself.

Practical issues first: my murals are drawn on panels off-site. We bring the panels to the mural site only at the very end, after all of the drawing has been completed and the panels coated. The panels are medium-density fiberboard (MDF) covered with paper on which the mural is then drawn. After cutting the panels to size and sealing them, we roll out acrylic glue over their faces and sides. Then while the glue is still wet we roll the paper over the top, press it down, and wrap it around the sides and back much as one would wrap a Christmas package. After the panels are dry, we set them in place on a scaffold to execute the drawing. On tall murals such as one Stefani and I did for Pittsburgh's East End Cooperative Ministry, this can be a high-wire act

(fig. 7.2). When the drawing is complete and after fixing the charcoal, we coat the panels with clear acrylic and finally an outer reversible varnish.

The installation is the most intensive part of my operation, and for large murals it can take up to a week. Over the years I've developed close working relationships with a small group of installers: Rob Johnson, Ross Kronenbitter, and more recently my stepson Ben Ledewitz and his small company. They have worked with me on multiple jobs, as far away as Doha, Rome, San Francisco, and Seattle. The consistency of these relationships and their input at early design stages has assured ease of installation at the end.

To hang the panels, I've used inch-wide aluminum tabs mounted on the backs of panels. In this way, with the hardware remaining out of sight, each panel is held tightly to a wall by its neighbor along one side and the bottom, and its weight is carried by the hardware affixed along its top and other side edge (these are visible along the edges in fig. 7.3). With this system we tile the wall. It has worked for tall murals—the tallest has been twenty-four feet (fig. 7.5). And there have been heavy ones. The multilayered panels for the Qatar mural were 48 × 96 × 7 inches of MDF and weighed up to 250 pounds! It took three and sometimes four men to lift them into place (fig. 7.4).

7.1. *Carrying Grégoire*, Patty Culley and Grégoire Picher, 2004.

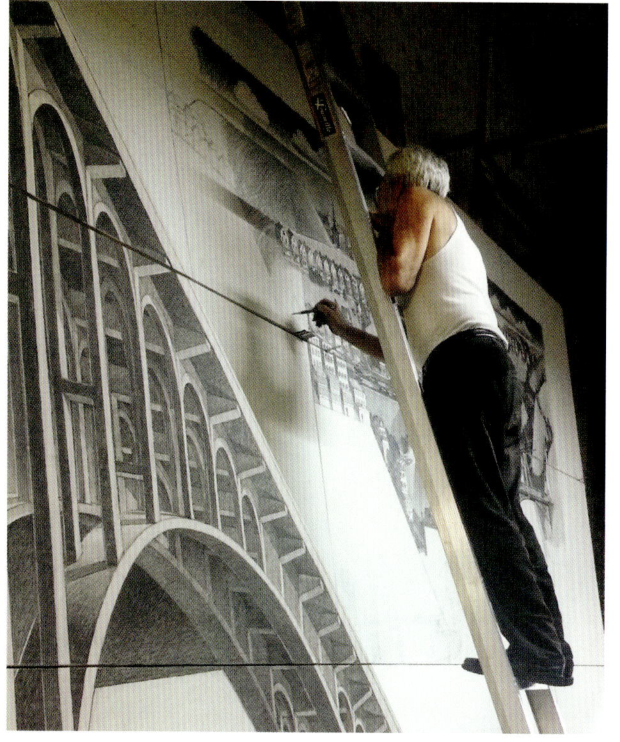

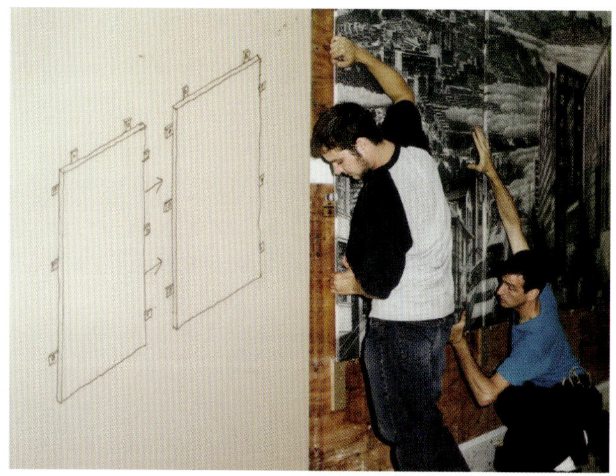

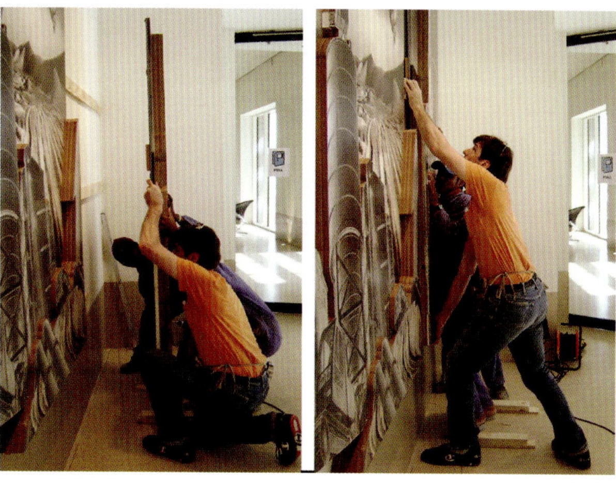

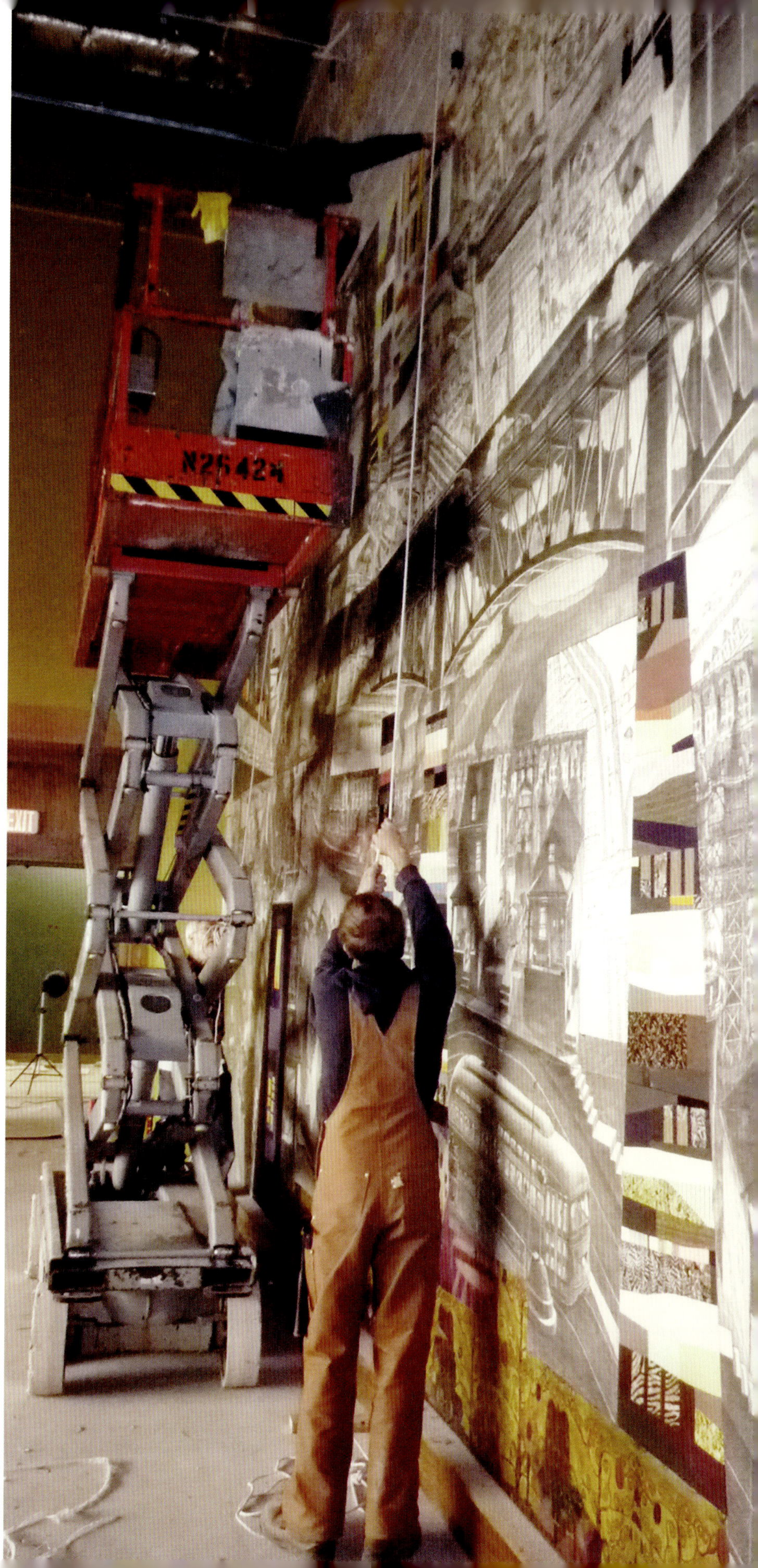

7.2 (*top left*). Doug working on the mural for East End Cooperative Ministry, 2013.

7.3 (*middle left*). Grégoire Picher and Ross Kronenbitter installing a panel at University of California San Francisco, 2002.

7.4 (*bottom left*). Ross Kronenbitter et al. lifting a panel at Carnegie Mellon University in Qatar, 2009.

7.5 (*far right*). Ben Ledewitz and Fourth River Guild installing at East End Cooperative Ministry, Pittsburgh, 2013.

Collaboration on Content

However, as I described earlier, my work with others has also influenced the content of my murals. It has involved several types of collaboration and has evolved significantly in recent years. One has been supplementary. I've felt the need to broaden and deepen my knowledge of the cities where I've placed murals. I've worked with local residents in Pittsburgh, Philadelphia, Frankfurt, Doha, Rome, San Francisco, and Seattle so they could bring their personal experience of each city's history to the murals. Sometimes my collaborators have done the drawing themselves—whenever possible, I've preferred that route. But often I've employed students to help with this work. Many of the drawings shown in chapter 5 were theirs.

The other type of collaboration has been more complementary, and has arisen from my need to bring skills and media into the work that were beyond my own experience and capabilities. Since 1997, I've worked with outstanding people in figure drawing, animation, photography, and quilting. They have allowed the works I've done in the interim to address content I could not have engaged otherwise.

My need for this kind of collaboration first became evident to me in 1997 when I was creating a mural series for John's, a pizzeria just west of Times Square in New York City. I'd gotten the job through my good friend Andrew Tesoro, the project's architect. The restaurant would occupy a former tabernacle church. With seating in an upstairs mezzanine, the main room was like a theater, and I was immediately taken with the idea of providing it with a panoramic overview of Manhattan. I imagined it bringing a cinematic presence to the room (fig. 7.6).

But there would be booth seating along the base of this panorama, and for that I needed a more intimate scale of imagery. I decided to give each booth an individual mural focused on one of Broadway's theatrical venues (fig. 7.7). One would show the CBS Theater, just a few blocks north of Times Square, from which the *Ed Sullivan Show* was broadcast live each Sunday evening during the 1950s and 60s. The panel would focus on the stage, and because the show had been so popular, it was important that the people on that stage be recognizable—Ed Sullivan and the many guests who appeared on his show during the 1960s: Liza Minnelli, Topo Gigio, the Beatles, and Jim Morrison of the Doors among them. Because I'm not strong with likenesses, I hired the

daughter of a good friend, Rebecca Schultz . Working with Rebecca and John Trivelli to develop likenesses of famous people for the John's front room mural was the first instance where my collaboration with others would bring capabilities to the work beyond my own (fig. 7.8).

When I look back at this and the many murals on which I have collaborated with others (work that approaches ten thousand square feet in area), I find myself searching for the right balance between unity and dialogue. With earlier collaborations, I sought unity in the manner that Peter Paul Rubens (1577–1640) did when creating his huge canvases. For those paintings, he engaged many specialists—one person did dogs, one person did hands, and so on—but the work after completion appears to have been created by one person. In this tradition, with my earlier murals I sought to mask the collaboration. With more recent murals, however, I've sought to create a dialogue between distinctly different makers and have welcomed the evidence of the multiple hands at work. Indeed, it has become part of the content of these works.

The accounts that follow will tell the stories of how four murals came to be. I'll provide a detailed picture of what is involved in creating large murals for public venues beyond the practical considerations of mounting and installing them. I'll address decisions I reached on their thematic content, the historical precedents I drew upon, and responses to what I learned about the history of each locale. But throughout these accounts, there will be an underlying theme tracing how the nature of my collaboration has shifted over time. In first two murals, for the University of California at San Francisco and King County Courthouse, Seattle, my collaboration was intentionally hidden. In the last two, Carnegie Mellon University at Qatar and East Liberty Presbyterian Church in Pittsburgh, my collaboration was obvious and a true generator of the works' content.

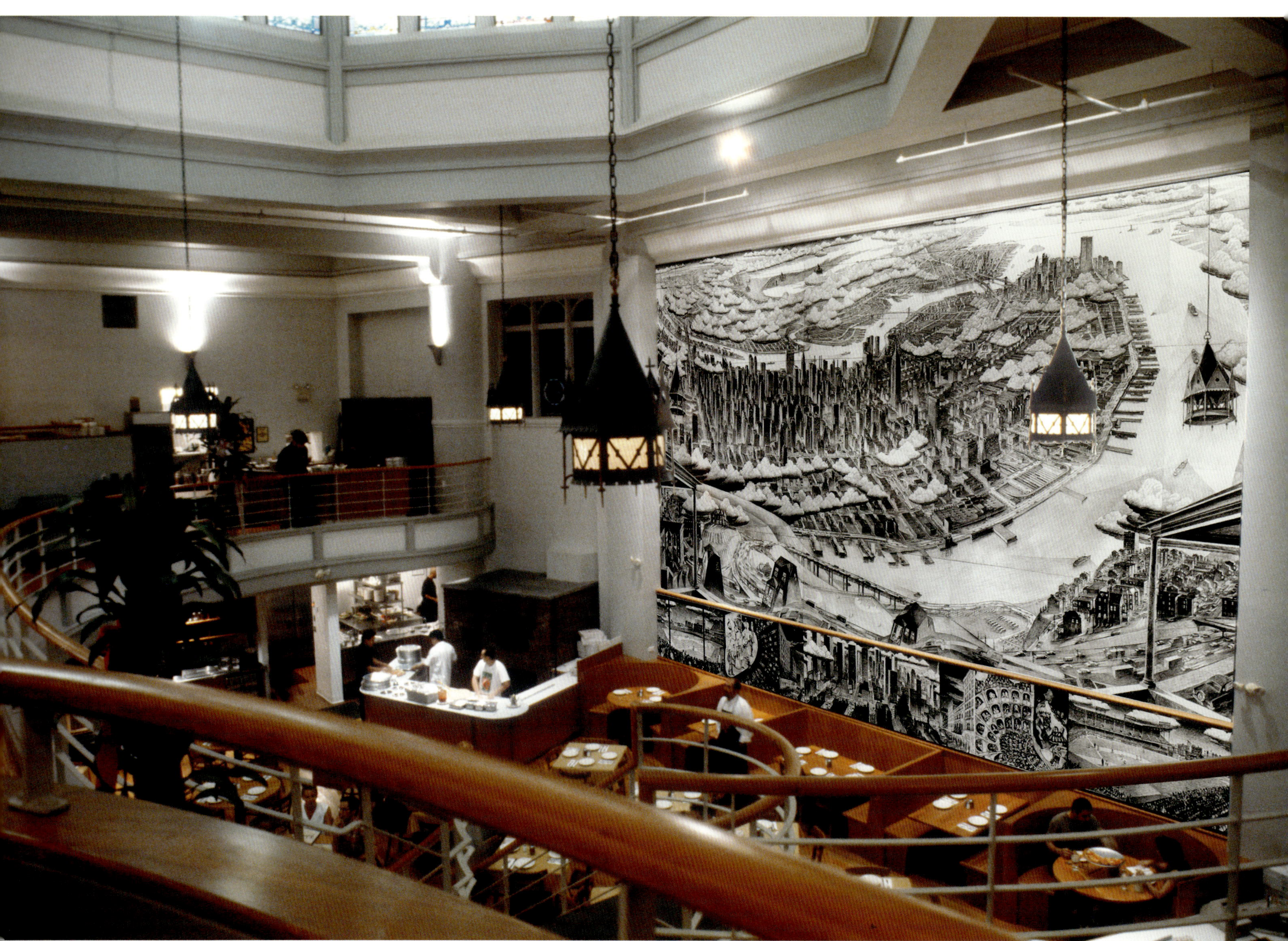

7.6. John's 44th Street mural, Doug Cooper with Sarah Cooper, Rebecca Schultz, and John Trivelli, 1997.
Charcoal on paper on board, 21 × 30 feet. New York

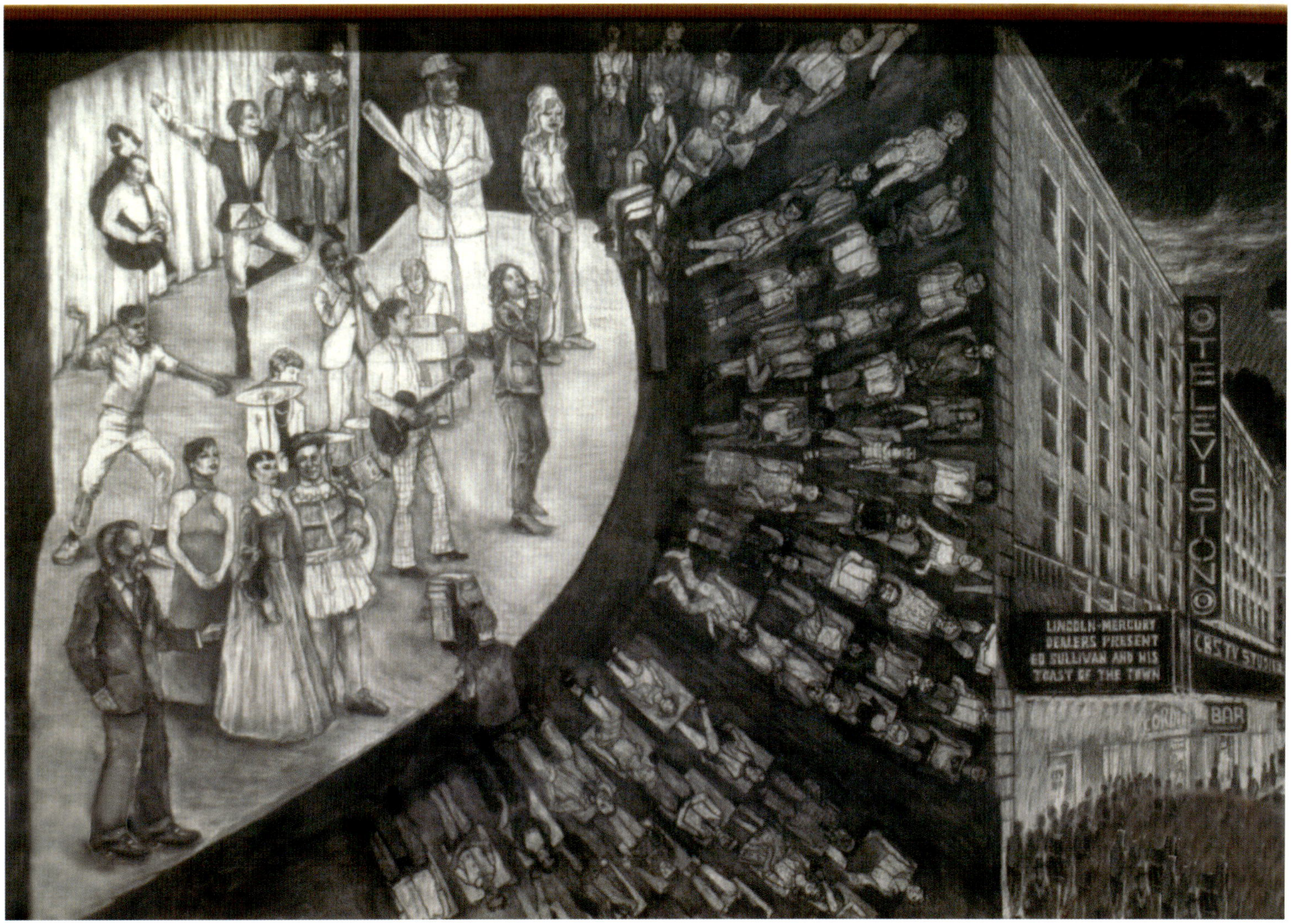

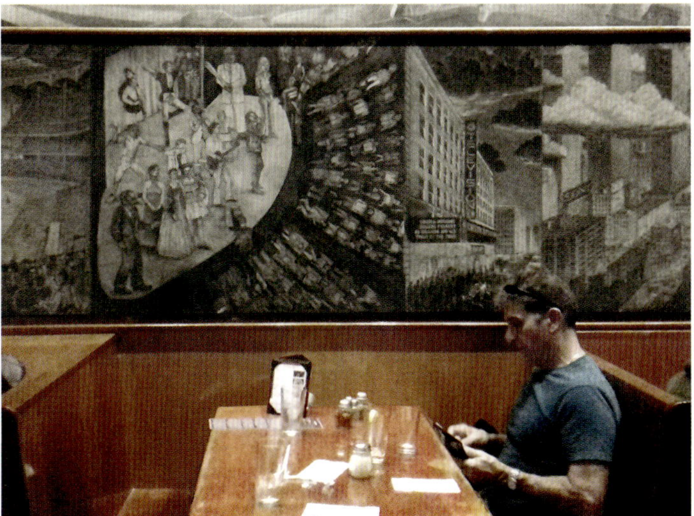

7.7 (*left*). Detail of booth seating, John's 44th Street mural, Doug Cooper with Sarah Cooper, Rebecca Schultz, and John Trivelli, 1997. Charcoal on paper on board, 21 × 30 feet. New York. Photo by Ken Lau.
7.8 (*above*). Detail of *Ed Sullivan Show*, John's 44th Street mural, Doug Cooper with Sarah Cooper, Rebecca Schultz, and John Trivelli, 1997. Charcoal on paper on board, 21 × 30 feet. New York. Photo by Ken Lau.

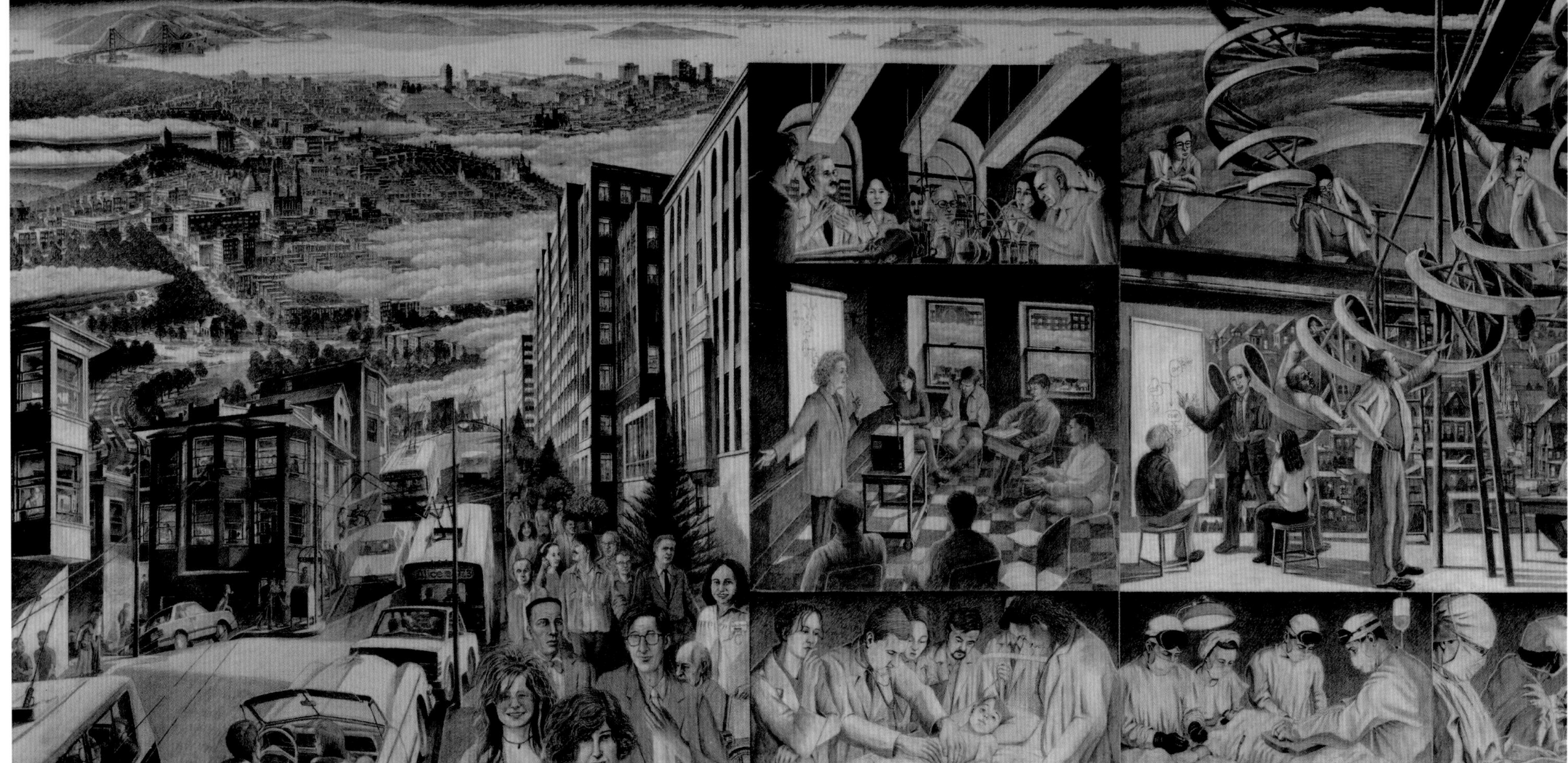

7.9. Medical Sciences Building mural at University of California, San Francisco, Doug Cooper and Grégoire Picher with Judith Schachter [Modell], Jessica Bollinger, Eric Lai, Melissa McMahon, and Henry Weinberg, 2002. Charcoal on paper on board. UCSF Parnassus Campus, San Francisco.

University of California at San Francisco: 2001–2002

I'd always wanted to do a mural in San Francisco (fig. 7.9). With its steep slopes and overlooks, the city shared something with Pittsburgh. But San Francisco held an additional attraction for me. Dating back to works by Diego Rivera, the city has a deep and continuing tradition of mural making. Then in 2001, through a personal connection, I arranged to create a work for the Medical Sciences Building at the University of California at San Francisco (UCSF), one of the world's premier medical schools.

I felt Rivera's influence almost immediately. On a first trip to San Francisco, I visited his mural at the San Francisco Art Institute (described briefly in the previous chapter). As with many of Rivera's murals, this one used larger-than-life figures of people (fig. 7.10). Inspired by it, I envisioned taking a similar approach to showing UCSF's mission as a teaching and research hospital—with scientists at work instructing students, treating patients, and constructing models of life processes. That was the reason I hired my nephew Grégoire Picher. With his background in figure drawing from studies in classical animation, he was far stronger with the figure than I. He ended up collaborating with me off and on for five years and influenced the character of the mural projects I undertook throughout that period. In all of them, I sought a seamless unity between Grégoire's figures and the architectural and landscape settings that I drew.

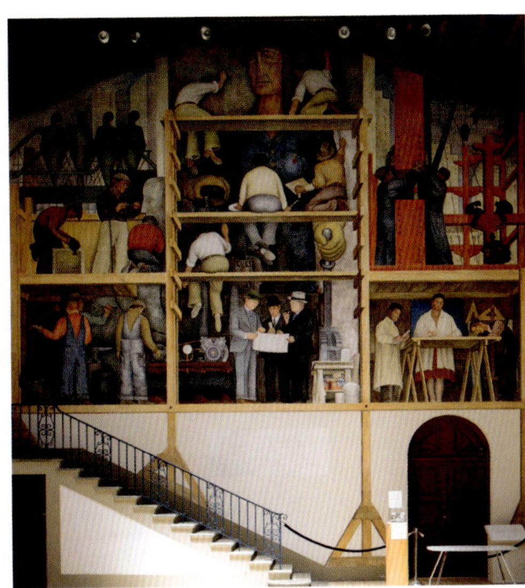

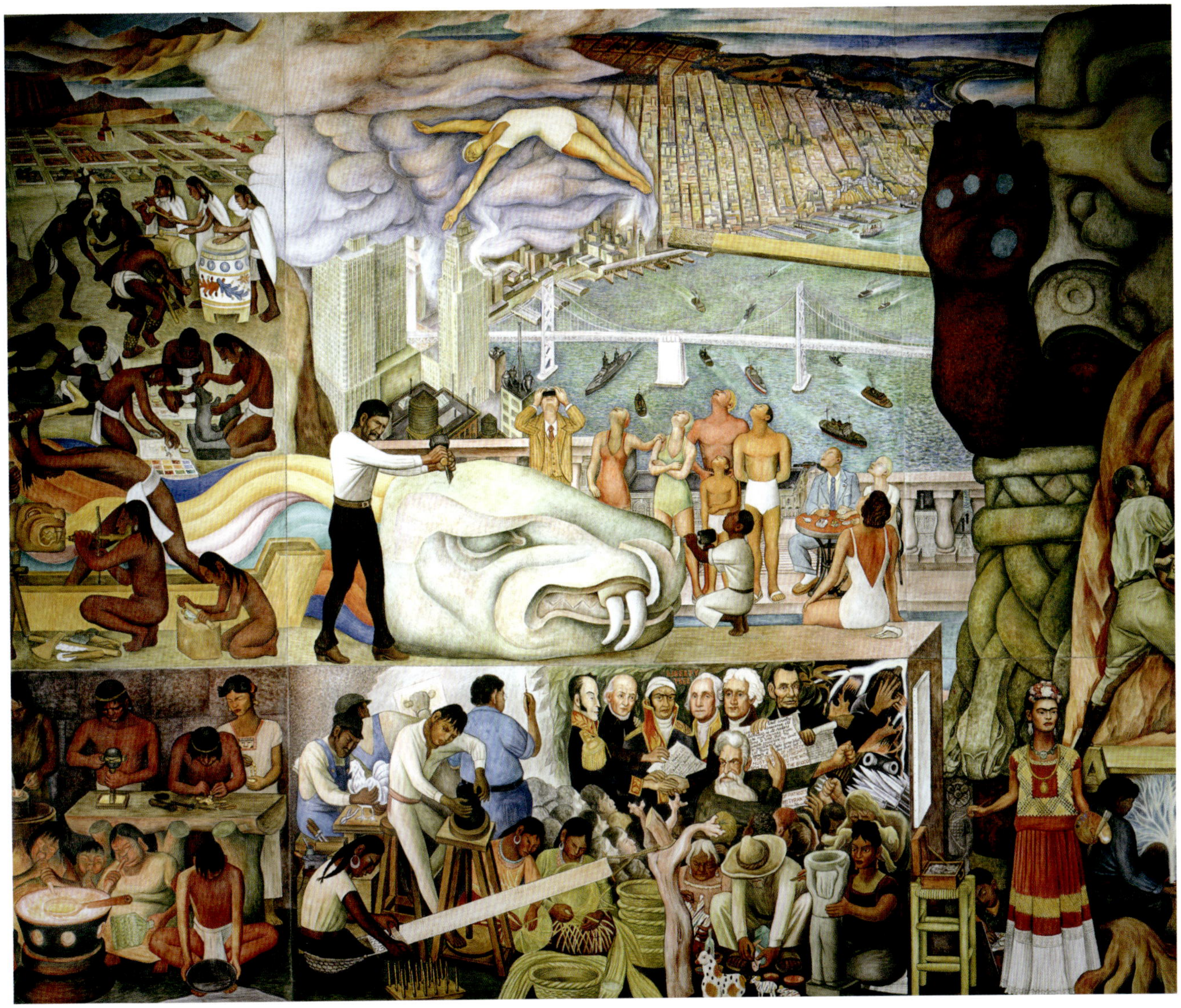

7.10 (*above*). *The Making of a Fresco Showing the Building of the City*, Diego Rivera, 1931. Image copyright © San Francisco Art Institute.
7.11 (*right*). *Pan American Unity*, Diego Rivera, 1940. City College of San Francisco.

To personalize UCSF's role as a teaching hospital, I borrowed again from Rivera—specifically from his *Pan American Unity.* Now housed at City College of San Francisco, the mural had been originally commissioned for the Pan American Exposition held on San Francisco Bay's Treasure Island in 1940. Rivera had composed the mural with a frieze of aedicules at its base, a device he used to present multiple narratives within the mural. It's a sort of doll house portrayal of space with cutaways into multiple spaces within one image—an approach I'd relate back to Kent Bloomer's assignment discussed in chapter 1 (fig. 7.11). Years earlier, when I lived in Italy, I had seen something quite similar by Giotto and others in the upper and lower chapels at the Basilica of Saint Francis of Assisi. There the device was used to present multiple biblical stories. I'm sure Rivera knew of these works as well, and by using the same technique at UCSF, I saw a way to show doctors and scientists engaged in multiple specialties in multiple settings (fig. 7.12).

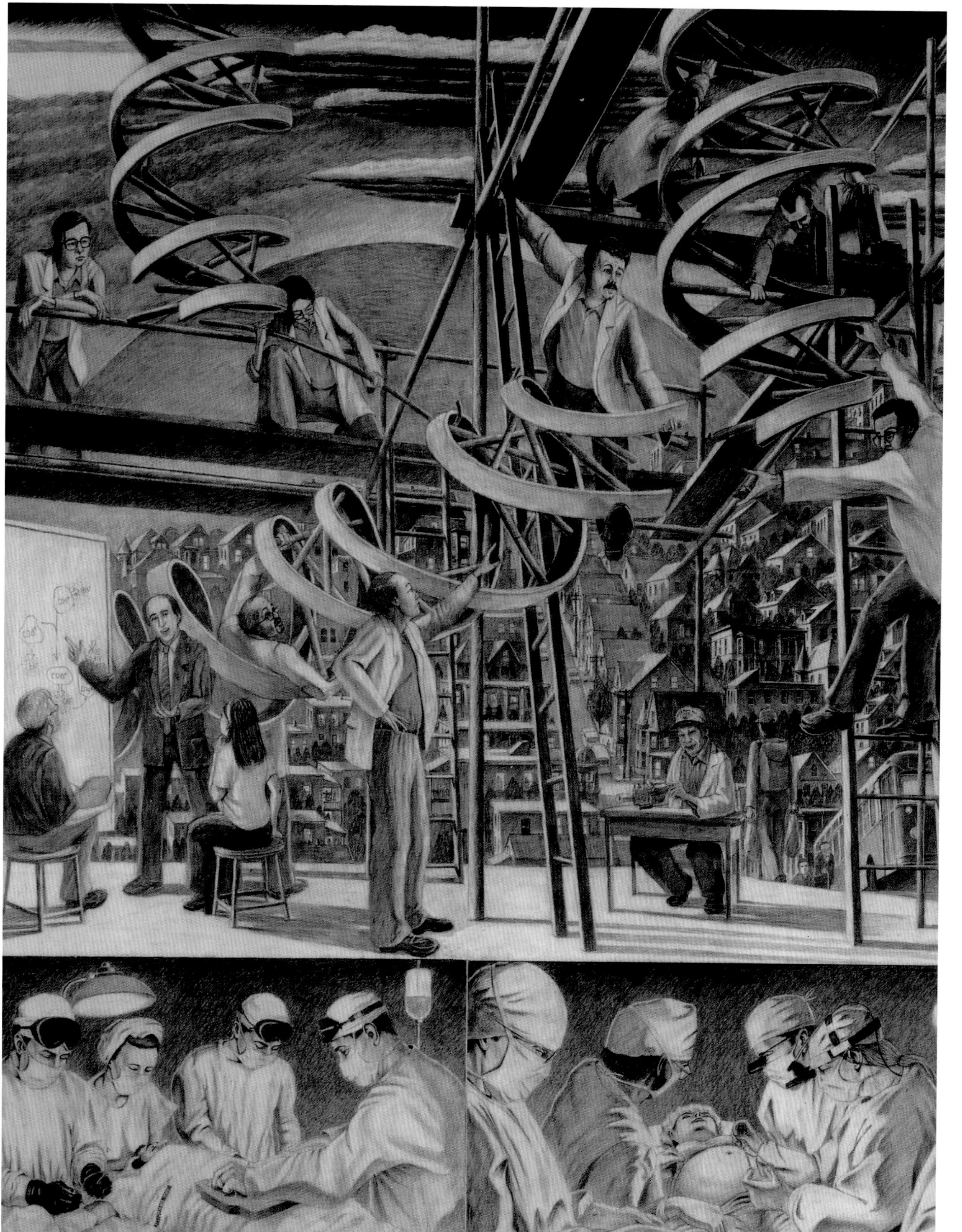

7.12. East wall, detail of aedicule. Medical Sciences Building mural at University of California, San Francisco, Doug Cooper and Grégoire Picher with Judith Schachter [Modell], Jessica Bollinger, Eric Lai, Melissa McMahon, and Henry Weinberg, 2002. Charcoal on paper on board. UCSF Parnassus Campus, San Francisco.

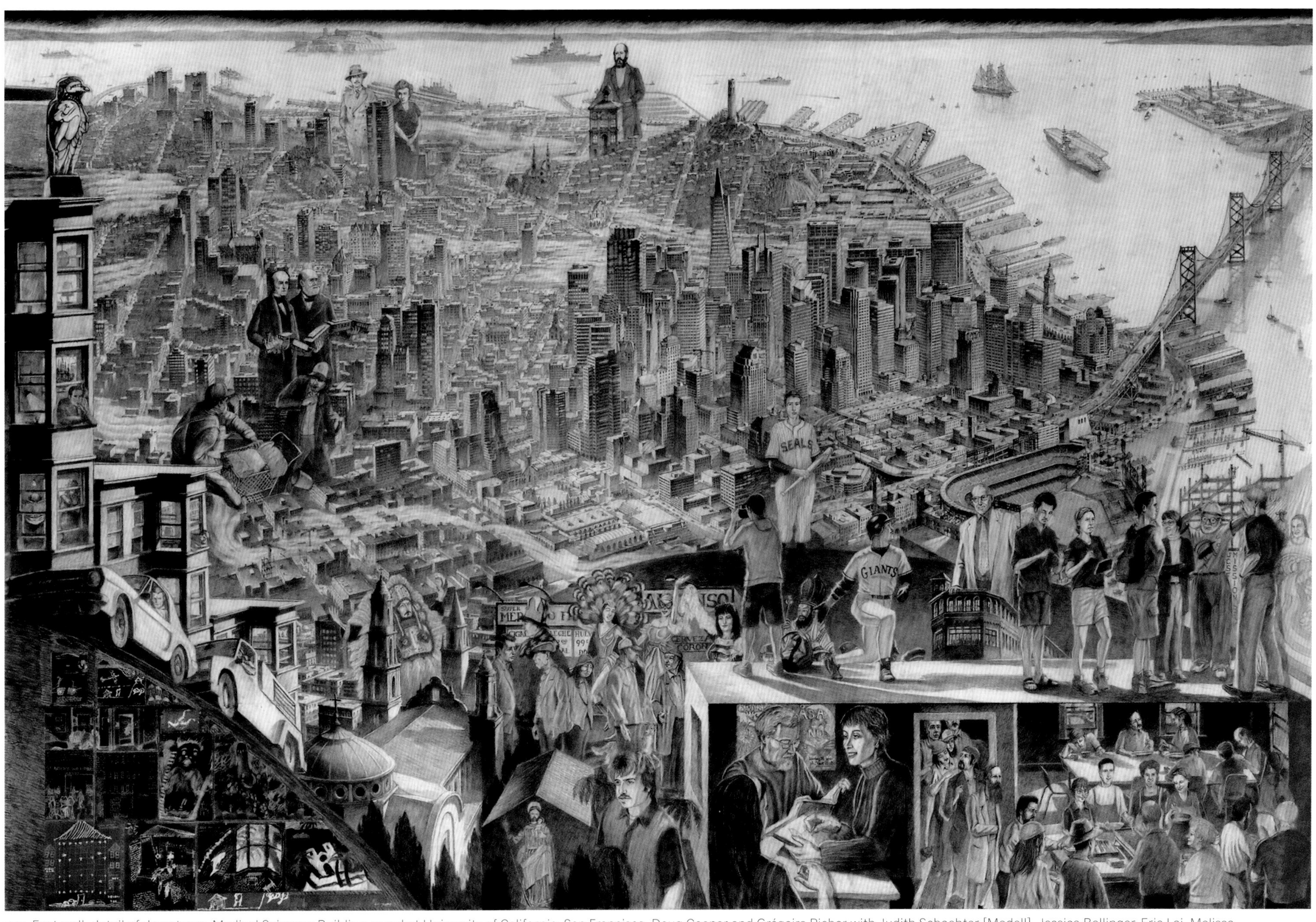

7.13. East wall, detail of downtown. Medical Sciences Building mural at University of California, San Francisco, Doug Cooper and Grégoire Picher with Judith Schachter [Modell], Jessica Bollinger, Eric Lai, Melissa McMahon, and Henry Weinberg, 2002. Charcoal on paper on board. UCSF Parnassus Campus, San Francisco.

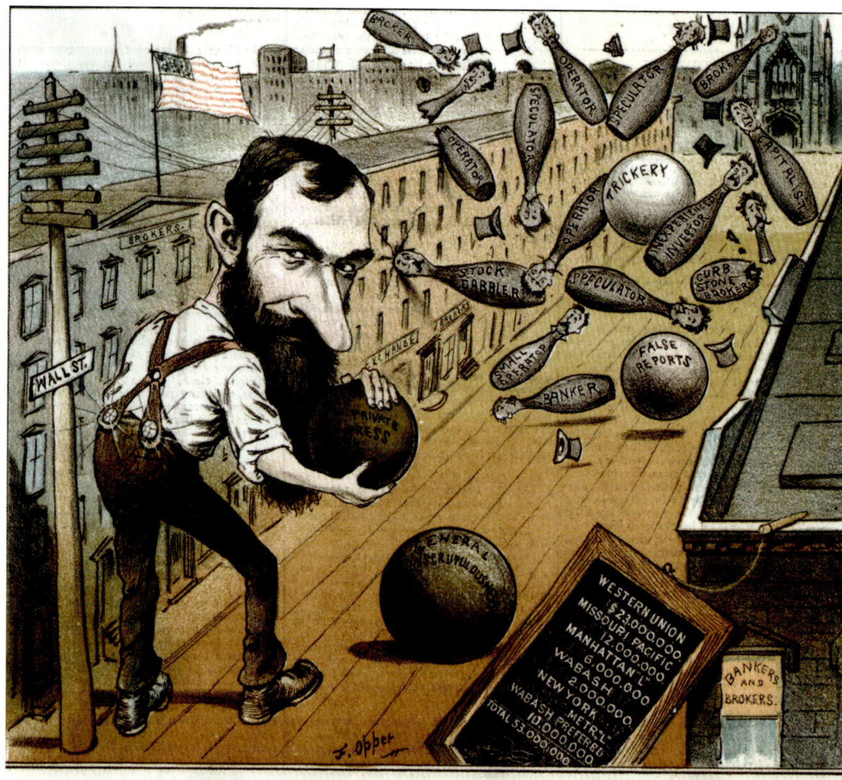

7.14. *Jay Gould's Private Bowling Alley*, Frederick Burr Opper, 1882. Appeared in *Puck*.

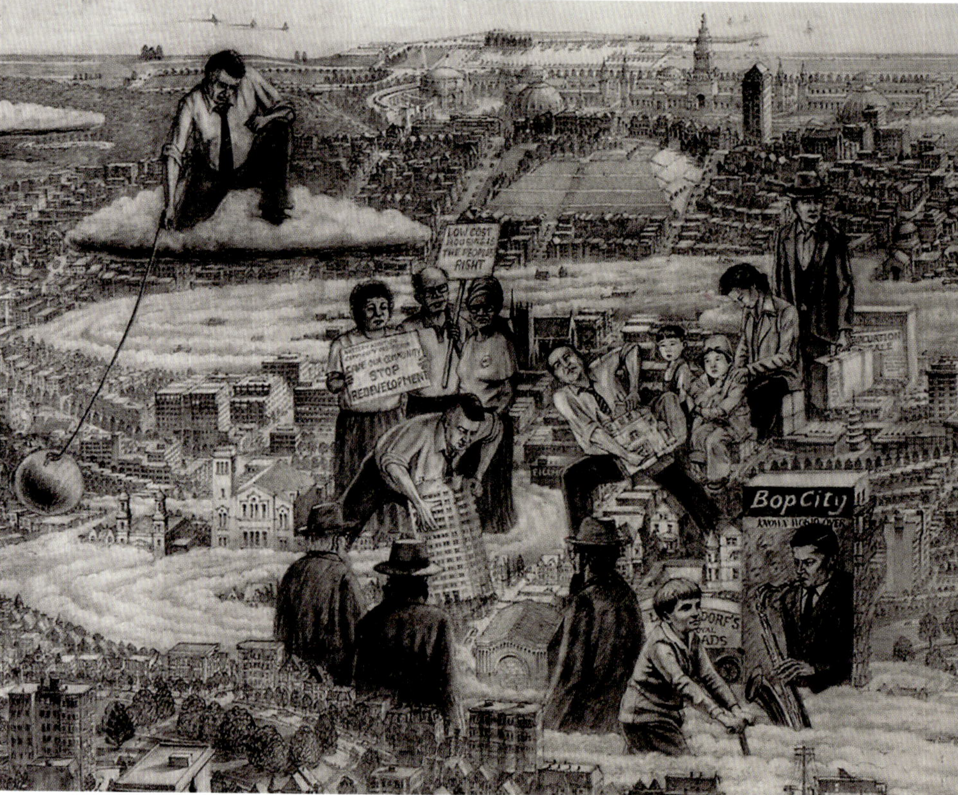

7.15. East wall, detail showing Justin Herman wielding a wrecking ball in the Western Addition, Medical Sciences Building mural at University of California, San Francisco, Doug Cooper and Grégoire Picher with Judith Schachter [Modell], Jessica Bollinger, Eric Lai, Melissa McMahon, and Henry Weinberg, 2002. Charcoal on paper on board. UCSF Parnassus Campus, San Francisco.

I also wanted the mural to include more about the city beyond the confines of UCSF, so I did a good amount of research prior to Grégoire's joining me (fig. 7.13). Throughout the first half of the summer 2001, I worked with anthropologist Judith Schachter [Modell] and a group of four CMU students interviewing people throughout the city. From this I had learned much about San Francisco's complex social and political history. One part of the history was particularly interesting—and controversial. It concerned the "renewal" of the Western Addition during the late 1960s. At the time, Justin Herman directed San Francisco's Redevelopment Agency (1959–1971). His wholesale clearing of the area for new housing resulted in the displacement of most of the neighborhood's African American community—up to ten thousand people.

I had always loved the tradition of late nineteenth-century political cartoons and the oversized figures they used to make their points. One such example is Frederick Burr Opper's cartoon from *Puck* in 1882, with Jay Gould treating Wall Street as his personal bowling alley (fig. 7.14). So, I asked Grégoire to develop an oversized image of Herman wielding a wrecking ball from a cloud above the neighborhood and then uprooting Victorians and replacing them with midrise apartment buildings on the ground below. And to Herman's right I had Grégoire show an earlier displacement: the deportation of the Japanese community from the Western Addition following the attack on Pearl Harbor (fig. 7.15).

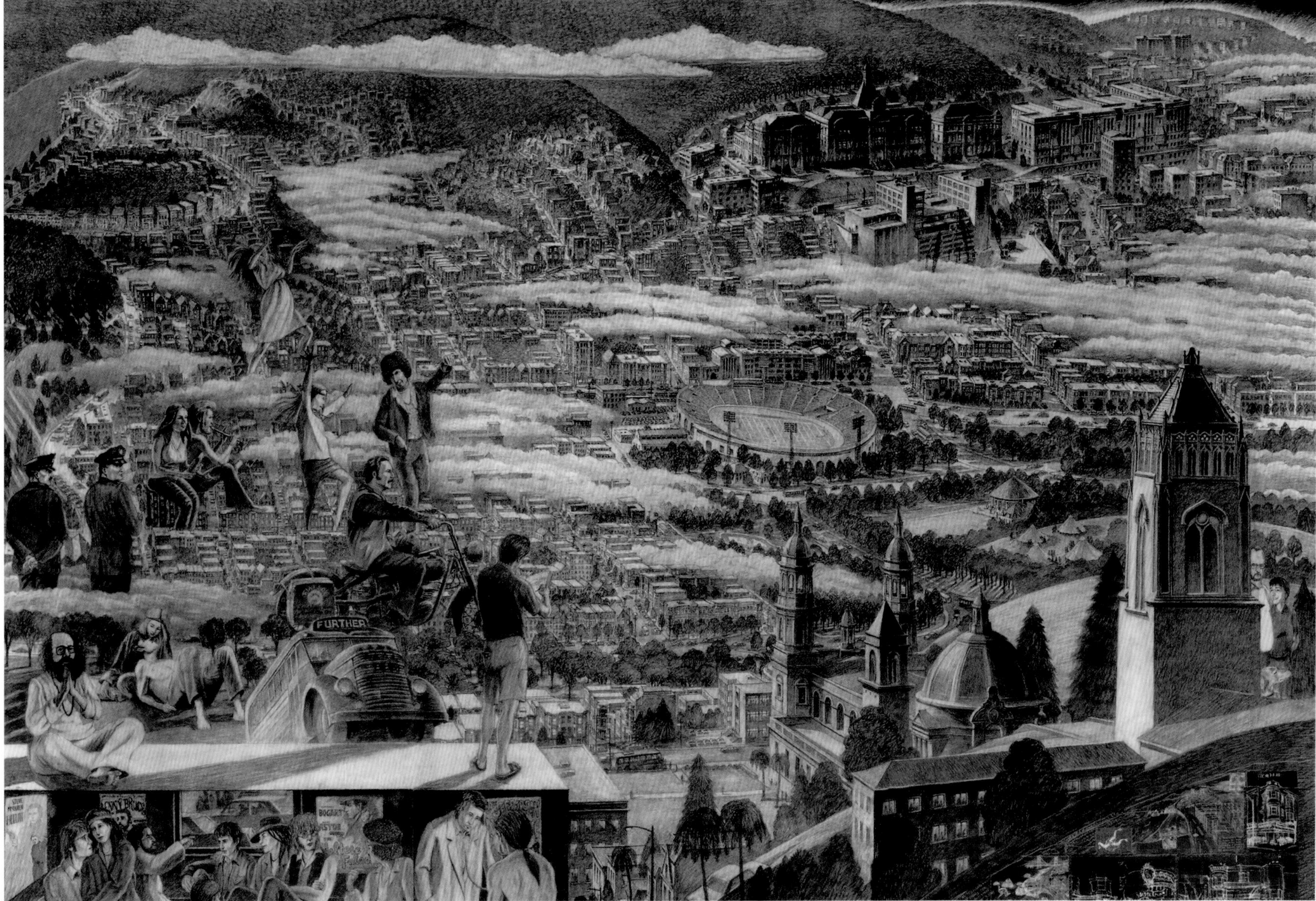

7.16. South wall, detail showing Haight-Ashbury, Merry Pranksters et al. Medical Sciences Building mural at University of California, San Francisco, Doug Cooper and Grégoire Picher with Judith Schachter [Modell], Jessica Bollinger, Eric Lai, Melissa McMahon, and Henry Weinberg, 2002. Charcoal on paper on board. UCSF Parnassus Campus, San Francisco.

On the mural's south wall we showed the UCSF Parnassus Campus overlooking Golden Gate Park and Haight-Ashbury in its full flower of excess during the late 1960s. At the base of the mural are two fixtures from the 1960s: the Merry Pranksters' Bus (Ken Kesey et al.) and the Haight-Ashbury Free Clinic. The clinic was founded by Dr. David Smith and continues to this day staffed by UCSF students; it is a model of effective public health practice. The south wall ends with San Francisco's weather: fog. Fog can quickly appear anywhere in the city, but it is a particular feature of the Parnassus and Sunset districts (fig. 7.16). Throughout these areas, Grégoire and I worked back and forth between figure development and architectural context—almost like two arms operating from one brain.

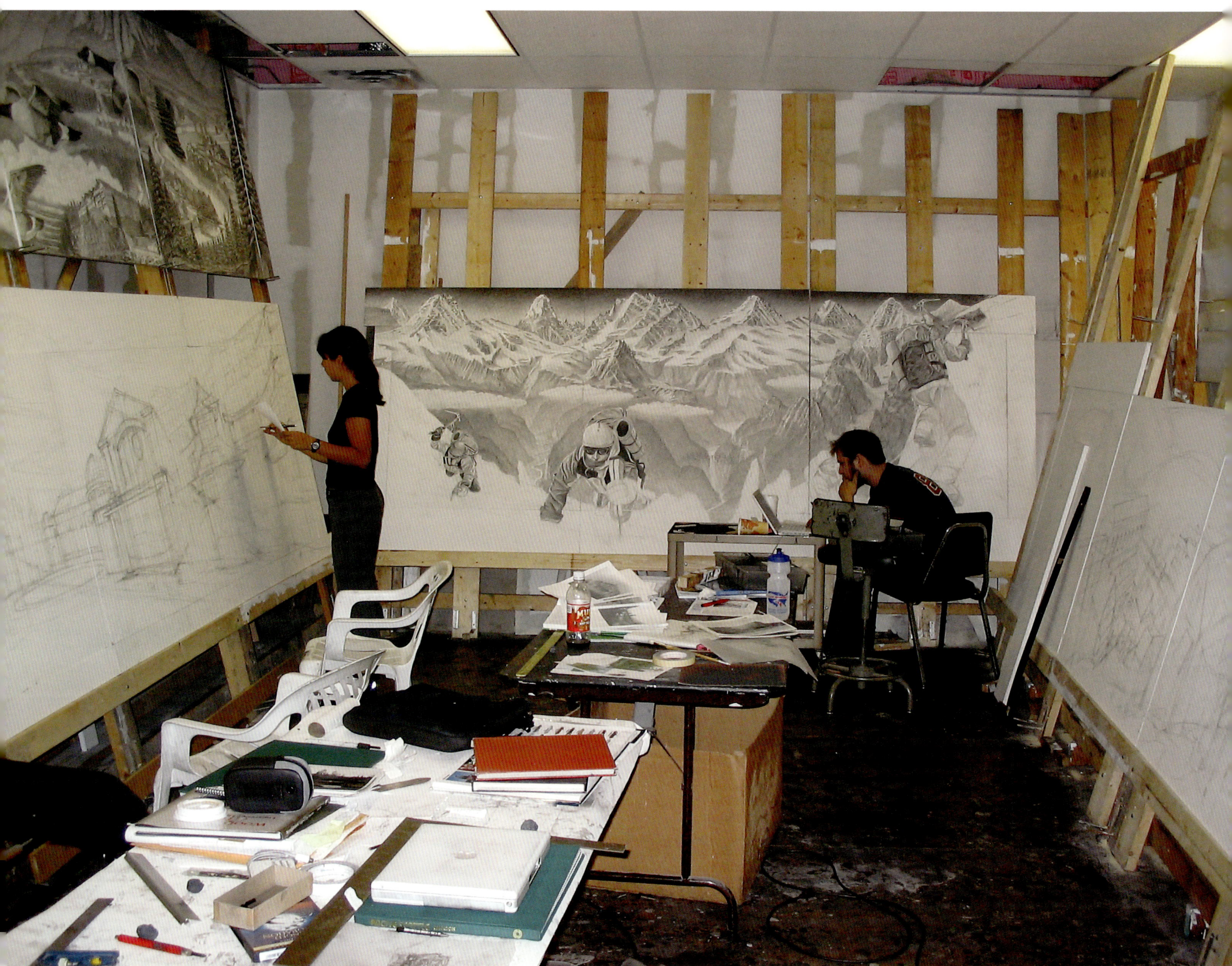

7.17. Patty and Grégoire at work on the King County Courthouse mural. Studio in the Run, 2005.

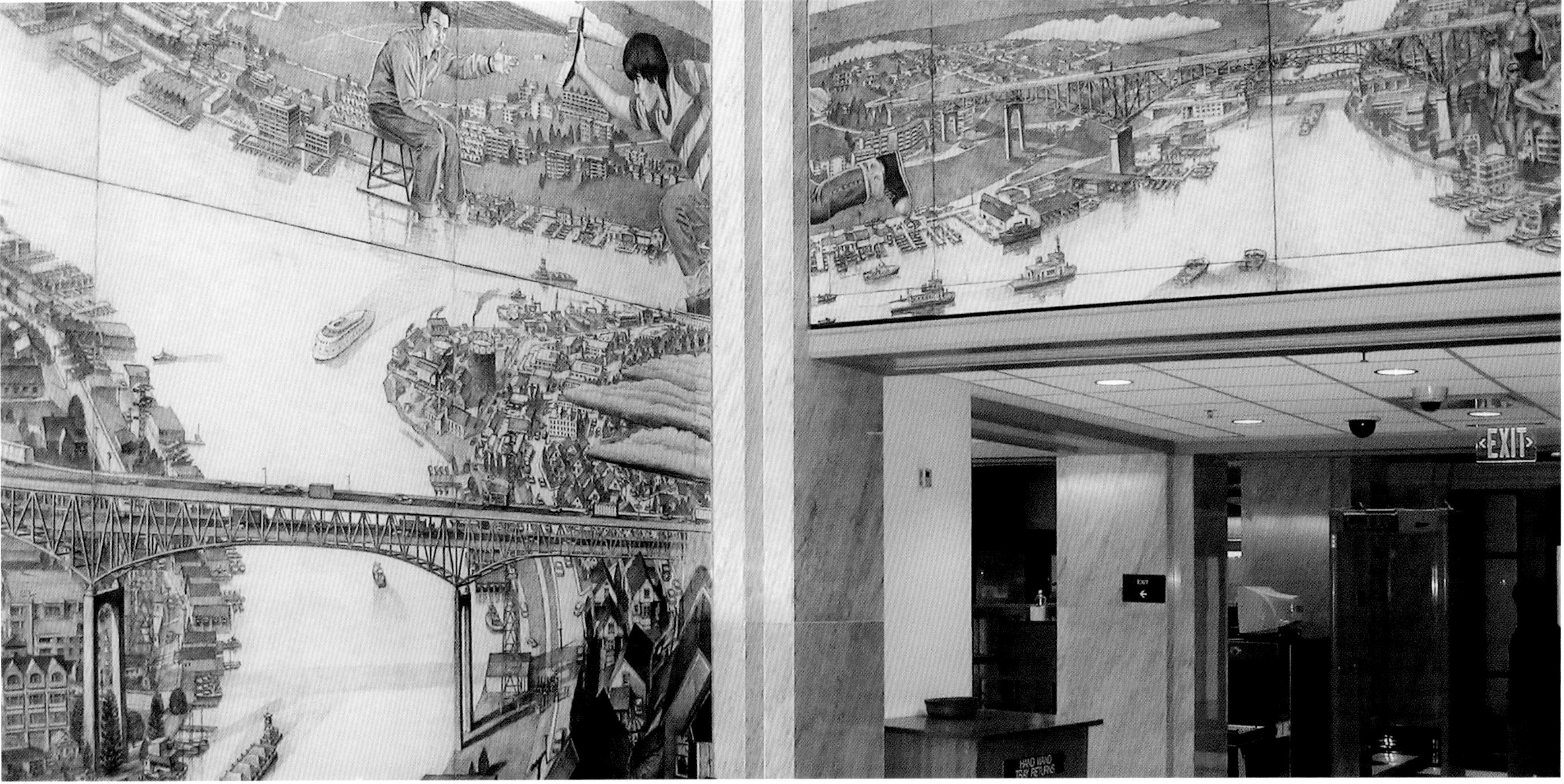

7.18. Detail showing transition over corners. *From these Hills, From these Valleys*, mural series, Doug Cooper with Grégoire Picher and Patty Culley, 2005. King County Courthouse, Seattle.

From these Hills, From these Valleys
King County Courthouse, Seattle, 2004–2005

Because it would be in a county courthouse, the King County Courthouse mural series would address an entire region: its rural as well as its urban areas. When I got the commission, Grégoire and I were already at work on a mural for the University of Rome. With the volume of work we had under way, I hired my former student Patty Culley to help us on both. Patty's role was different from Grégoire's—as one of the very best students from my drawing class at CMU's School of Architecture, she brought the same kind of skills in perspective drawing to the work that I did (fig. 7.17).

Given the architecture of its main floor corridor—a sequence of wall areas between pilasters—the work would be different from any I had composed before. It would be a set of discrete images, which we would have to unify in some way.

I developed a two-part strategy. Water is ubiquitous in the Seattle area, and I used its many lakes as big shapes crossing from one wall panel to another. In parallel, I used Grégoire's large figures. I asked him to set them partly behind where pilasters would be located so the figures would seem to leap from one panel into another (fig. 7.18).

My effort to tie the mural to the larger setting, its home in the Pacific Northwest, got a substantial boost from the rich documentation I found about the region's history. As much as any city in the United States, Seattle was founded during the age of photography, and at the archive of the University of Washington I found images of the city from its earliest days of settlement by immigrants from the Midwest. Through the work of anthropologist Hilary Stewart (1924–) and the renowned photographer Edward Curtis (1868–1952), I had access to information about Native American customs and practices—in the case of Curtis, from a time when these were

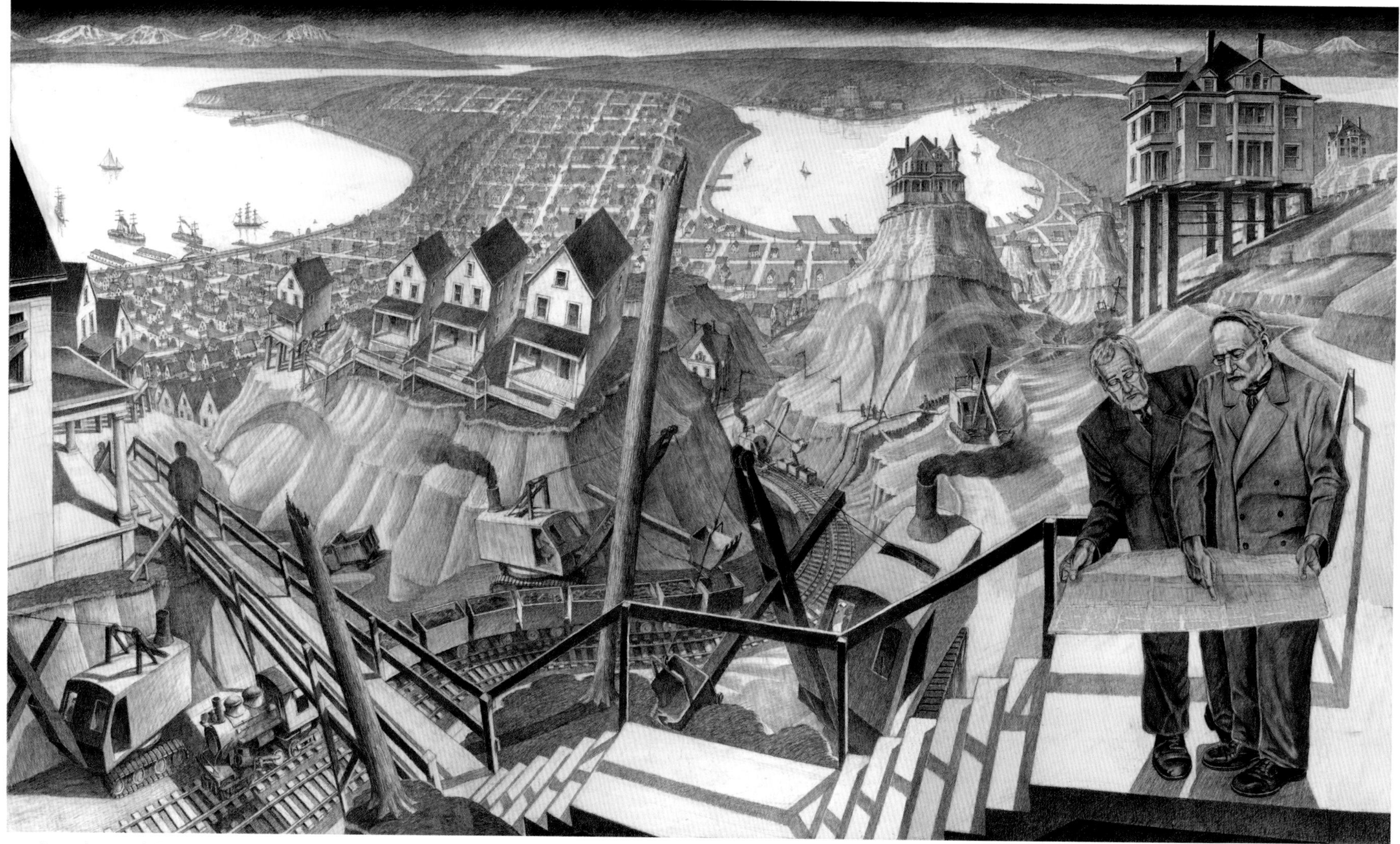

7.19. Regrades panel, *From these Hills, From these Valleys*, mural series, Doug Cooper with Grégoire Picher and Patty Culley, 2005. King County Courthouse, Seattle.

still part of daily life. Related to present-day Native American issues, I got to meet with Lois Sweet Dorman, tribal legal-counsel for the Snoqualmie Tribe for the disposition of Snoqualmie Falls. The panel we developed about the Falls is discussed at length in chapter 2, addressing maps. Through her, I gained insight into the multiple meanings people sometimes attach to the same place.

Ambiguity of meaning became something of an overall theme for the work. Notwithstanding its commitment to environmental stewardship today, the region had come of age during what I might call the "heroic age of engineering," 1880–1910, a period that saw the completion of the Brooklyn Bridge, the building of the Panama Canal, and other great civic works. I found ample photographic documentation of Seattle's own versions of the hubris of the age: the lowering of Lake Washington so it could share a continuous shipping channel through Lake Union to Puget Sound, and the wholesale removal of the hills that seemed to block the city's expansion northward from Elliot Bay. They were simply sluiced into Puget Sound in what came to be known as the "great regrade" (fig. 7.19).

With all of this background material, I found we could respond to the region in ways that would resonate with its broader heritage. In the end, each wall section took on an individual theme. Here are several:

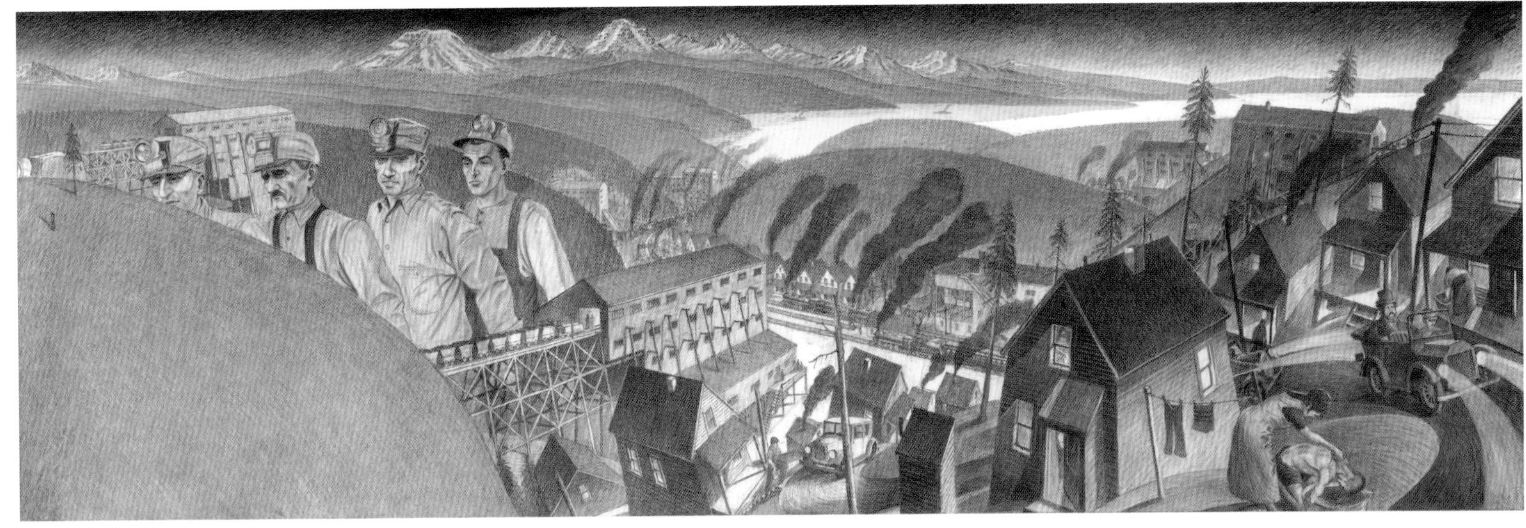

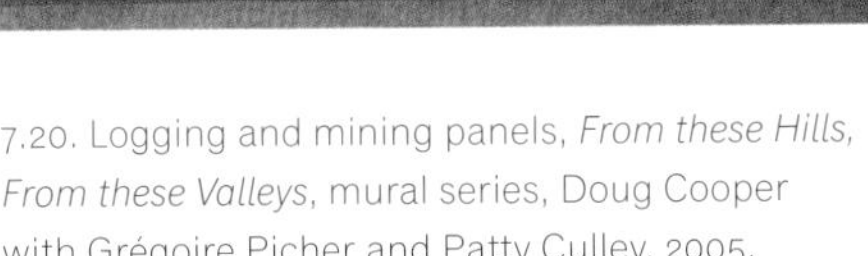

7.20. Logging and mining panels, *From these Hills, From these Valleys*, mural series, Doug Cooper with Grégoire Picher and Patty Culley, 2005. King County Courthouse, Seattle.

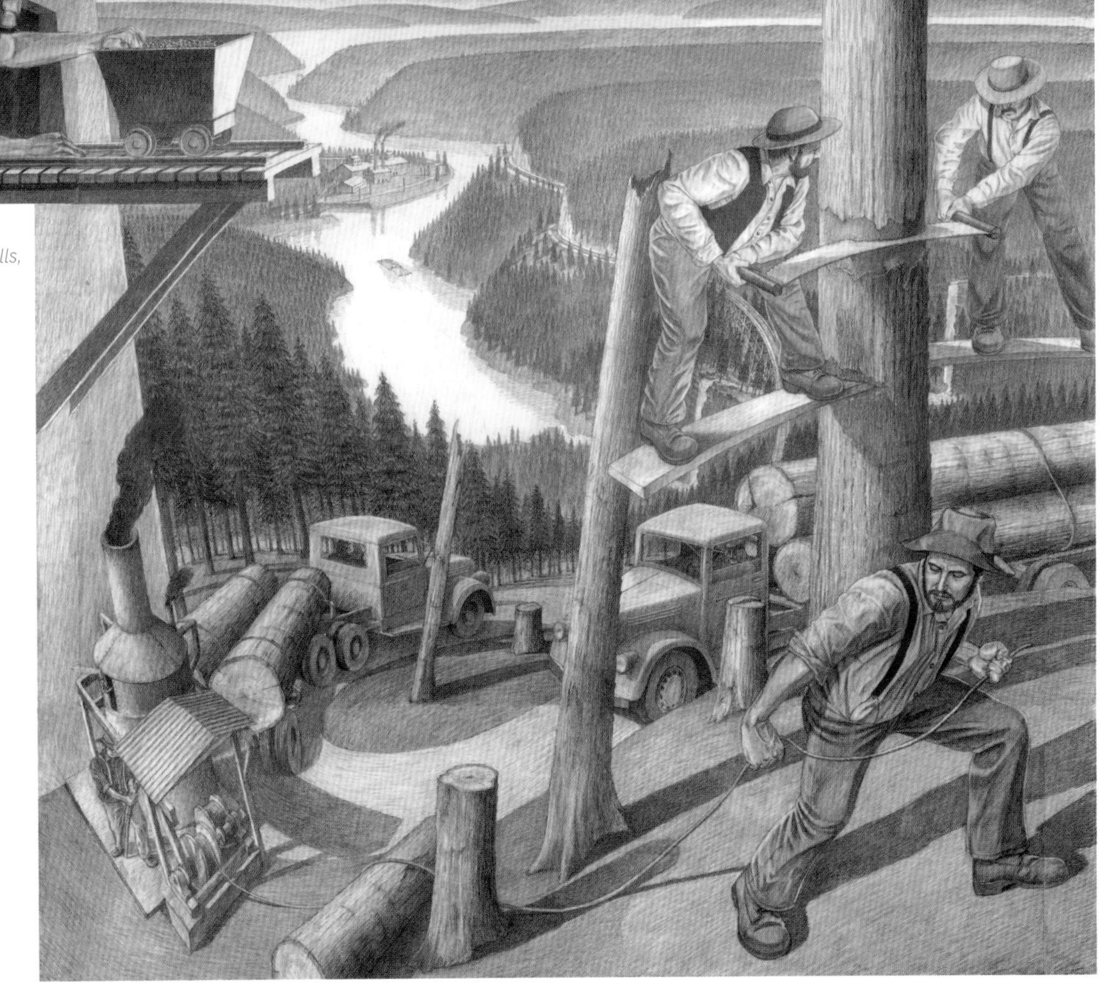

(1) Logging and mining (fig. 7.20). I threaded this mural over the entrance to the lobby's convenience shop and across a horizontal spandrel above. The upper panel depicts a fictitious coal town in the early part of the twentieth century. Miners are grimly entering the hill where they will spend their next shift underground. In the right foreground a woman is scrubbing her husband's head after his return from the mines. I based the coal-washing facility and the miners' housing on photographs from the Black Diamond Area. The lower panel shows logging practices in the Tiger Mountain area over multiple periods of time. Two men stand on what were called "springboards" as they use a crosscut saw to cut and fell a tree. A choker setter, one of the most dangerous jobs in logging, is pulling a line from a steam donkey to the cut logs so they can be dragged to an awaiting truck. Grégoire used himself as the model.

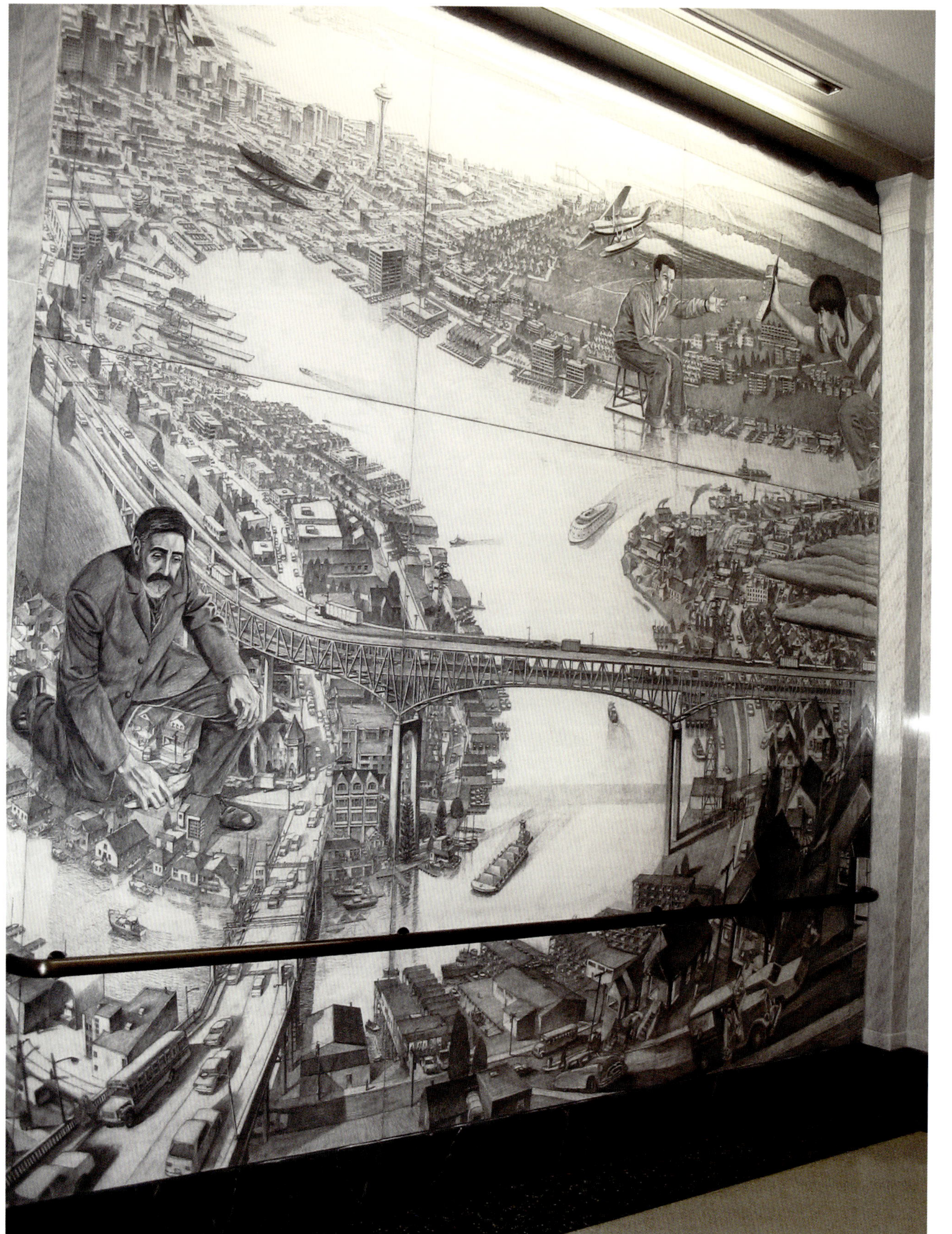

7.21. Panel showing Lake Union, *From these Hills, From these Valleys*, mural series, Doug Cooper with Grégoire Picher and Patty Culley, 2005. King County Courthouse, Seattle.

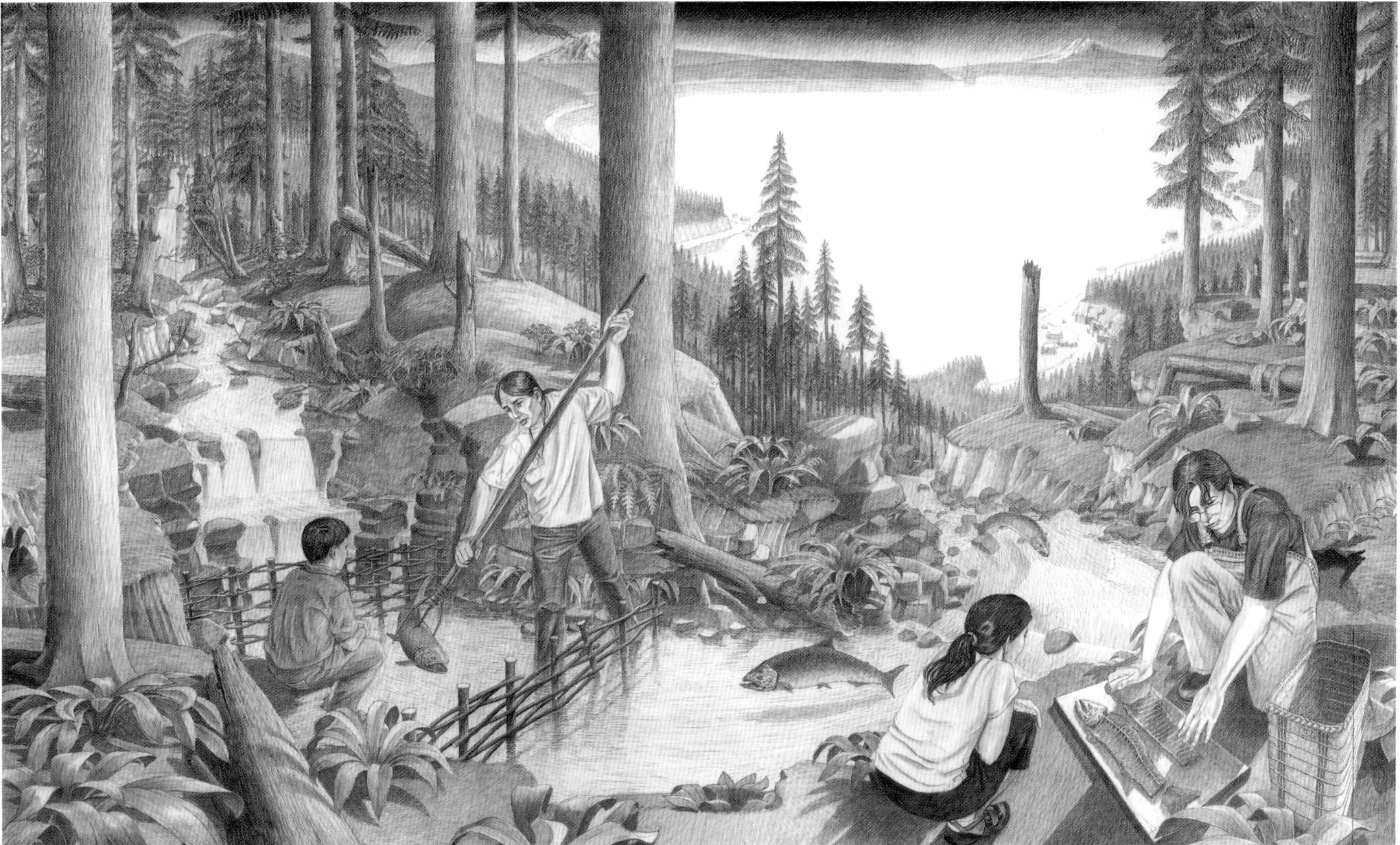

7.22. Fishing panel, *From these Hills, From these Valleys*, mural series, Doug Cooper with Grégoire Picher and Patty Culley, 2005. King County Courthouse, Seattle.

(2) Lake Union (fig. 7.21). The subject of this panel is water: the ways people live on it, the bridges that cross it, and the engineered waterways that transformed it. In the foreground are University Bridge and Wallingford. The drawing's perspective exaggerates the steepness of the streets. In this panel I really took advantage of Grégoire's skill at showing recognizable historical figures in their historical roles. One is Hiram Chittenden, who is shown by the edge of Lake Union, boat in hand, and further downstream at the Chittenden Locks. He was chief engineer of the project that joined Lake Washington to Lake Union and constructed the locks in 1911–1917 to allow lake traffic access all the way to Puget Sound.

(3) Fishing (fig. 7.22). This mural looks out to a bay similar to what might have been the original state of Elliot Bay. It shows Native American fishing techniques used on inland streams during salmon runs. Parents are shown in modern dress showing their children how they used weirs to trap and spear salmon and the implements they used to prepare fillets for smoking. The man is using a leister spear. There are cedar plank houses below at the shore of the distant bay. In the distance the *Exact* is arriving off Alki Point in November 1851 with the Denny party aboard, the first white settlers to the area. Details of the Native American tools and methods shown were based on Stewart's work.

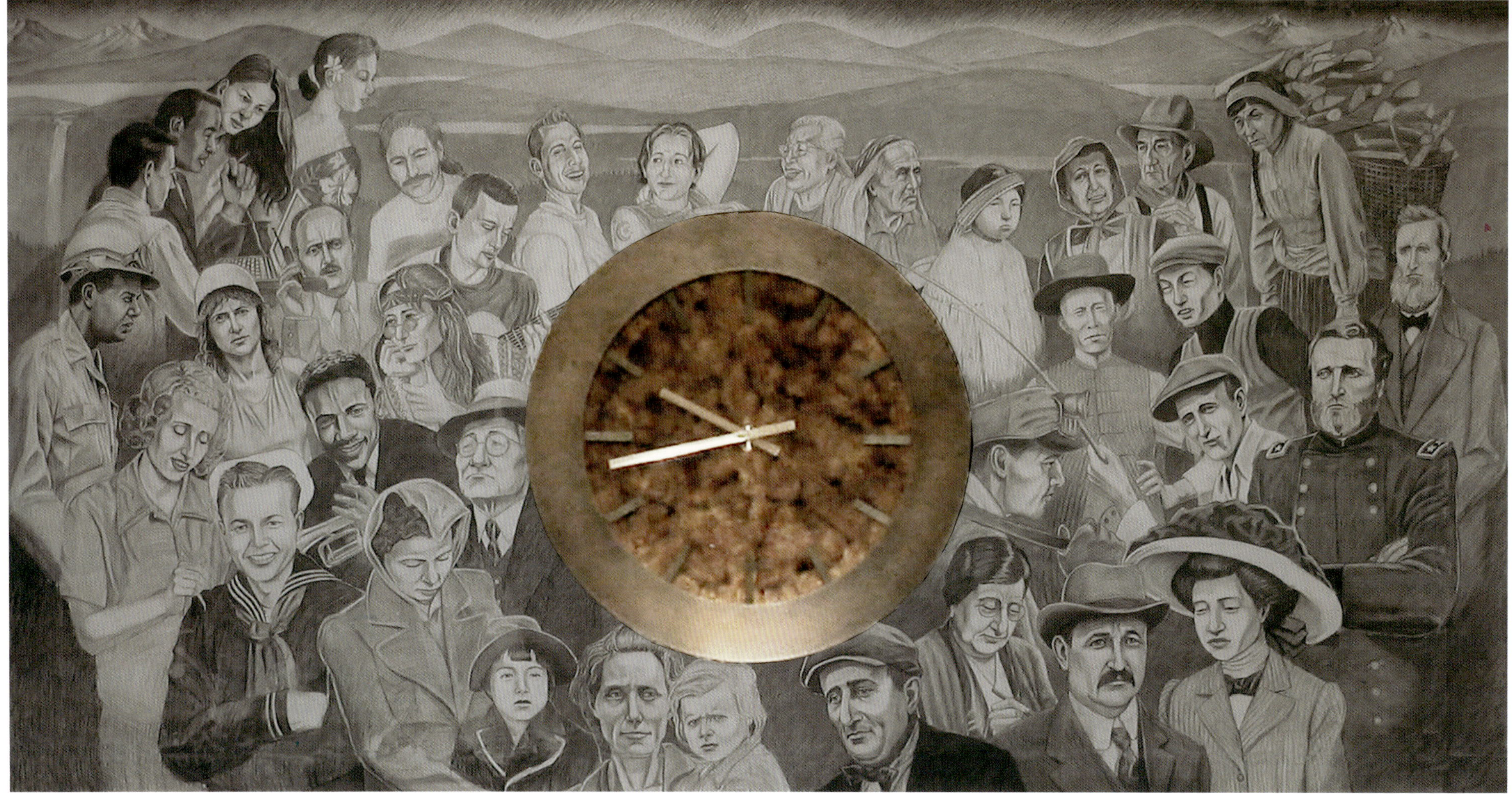

7.23. Clock wall panel with Linda Beaumont, *From these Hills, From these Valleys*, mural series, Doug Cooper with Grégoire Picher and Patty Culley, 2005. King County Courthouse, Seattle.

(4) Clock wall (fig. 7.23). For our mural surrounding the rotunda's clock, we worked in concert with fellow King County Courthouse artist Linda Beaumont. I wanted to use the clock as a prop to depict the passage of time, so I asked Grégoire to create a cyclical image showing the arrival of people to the region over time. It begins with Native Americans at twelve o'clock and moves clockwise. Along the way some faces to recognize are General George Thomas, one of the most successful commanders of the Civil War, who commanded the military division of the Pacific after the war; John Henry Smith wearing a cap as a member of the "Wobblies" (International Workers of the World), who were prominent in the region in the 1920s; Mayor Bertha Knight Landes, who in 1926 became the first female mayor of a major US city; and a young Quincy Jones, who got his start playing the clubs near Jackson Street before moving on to become one of popular music's best-known producers.

This last panel, the clock-wall mural, was the one where I let Grégoire work very nearly independently of me, and the quality of that image shows up well. It's an indicator, if only a small one, of what might have happened had I taken a different approach to our work together, one that might have contrasted what he did with what Patty and I did. In any event, the entire nature of my work with others was about to change.

Memory between Desert and Sea
Carnegie Mellon, Doha, Qatar, 2007–2009

Initially, I was ambivalent when associate dean Kevin Lamb first called me in June 2007 with the idea of making a mural for Carnegie Mellon University's new building at Education City in Doha, Qatar's capital city. I thought charcoal would be an ill-suited medium to represent a coastal desert Arab country.

But at the same time, I had a vague sense that the project might work if I found a way to combine drawing with photography (fig. 7.24). I imagined a rich tableau of sand, geometry, eclectic architecture, and carpets. So, I called my daughter Sarah, who lives in Gothenburg, Sweden. She and an Austrian, Nina Gorfer, had formed a photo/graphics firm and were engaged in large-sized combinations of landscape and portraiture. That was how our collaboration came to be.

The next March, we gathered in Doha to begin research for the mural. Nothing could have prepared us for the number of construction cranes and the long lines of blue-suited construction workers we found throughout the city on our first day of fieldwork (fig. 7.25). This was a city in a state of hyperchange: a place hell-bent on rebuilding itself overnight, and in the process erasing its past.

As we learned more about the city (and the country), and as we spoke to Qatari students at the school, it seemed many of their memories were about places that no longer existed. We heard about a flash flood along a road that passed through a wadi that had been recently covered over by an expanse of apartments. As we talked about our day's experiences each evening, I found myself wondering what it would be like to live out a life in such a place—in a world that was changing so rapidly around me. Familiar landmarks fill a mnemonic role in the lives of people everywhere. They help maintain the stability of our sense of place in the world. I wondered, what would be the end result of such rapid change? Would memory itself be at risk?

The rate of Doha's change can be best appreciated by juxtaposing two photographs showing the same location in Doha from points in time spanning a mere twenty years. (Note the one building common to both images: fig. 7.26.) It was our observation of a present at odds with a past—a past being rapidly obscured before our eyes—that helped us understand how to use our two very different media as a response. We would create a mural with multiple

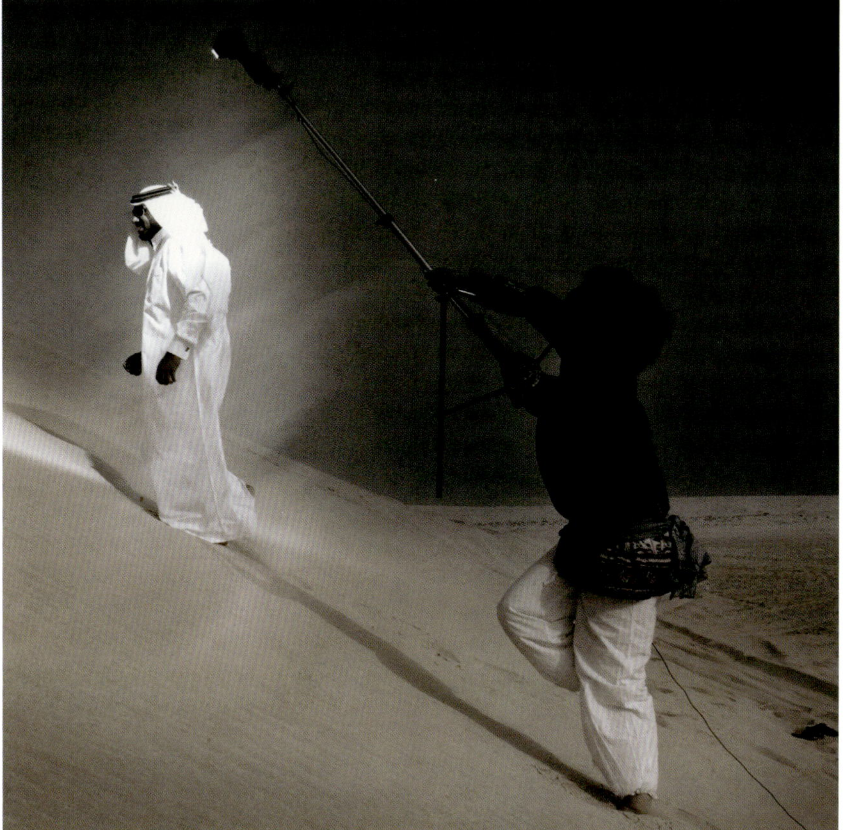

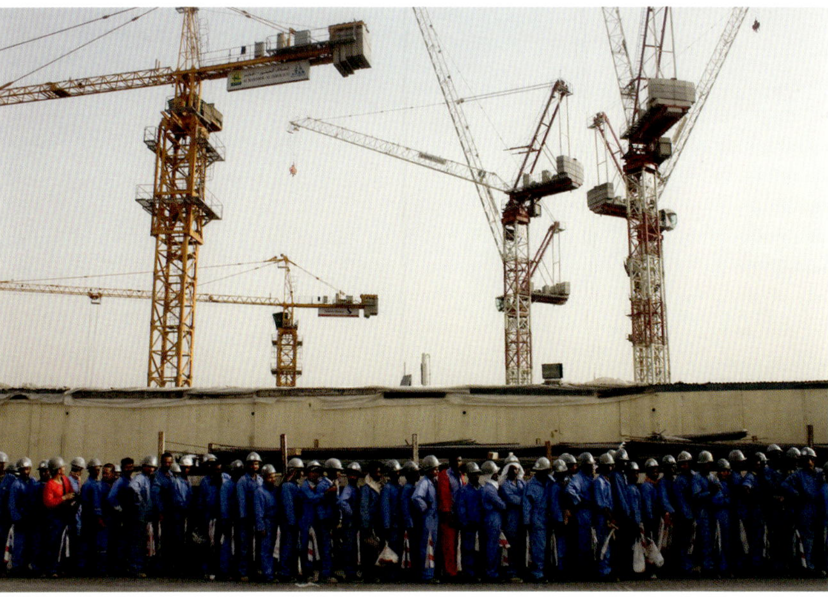

7.24 (*top*). The desert of Qatar, 2008. Photo: Cooper/Gorfer.
7.25 (*bottom*). Nothing could have prepared us for the number of cranes and construction workers. Photo: Cooper/Gorfer.

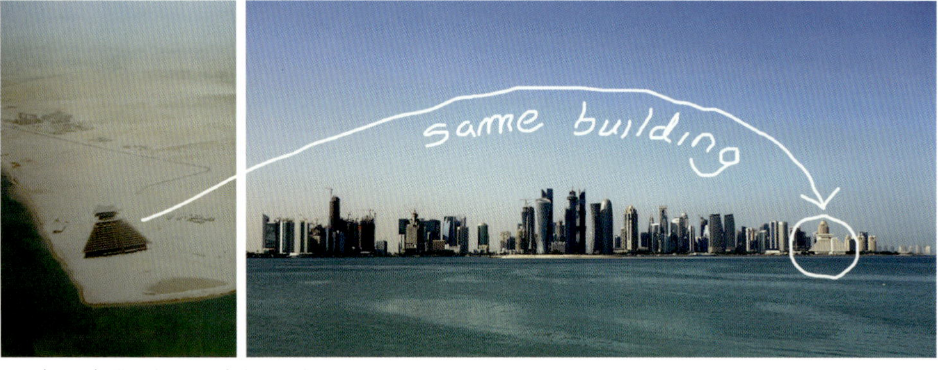

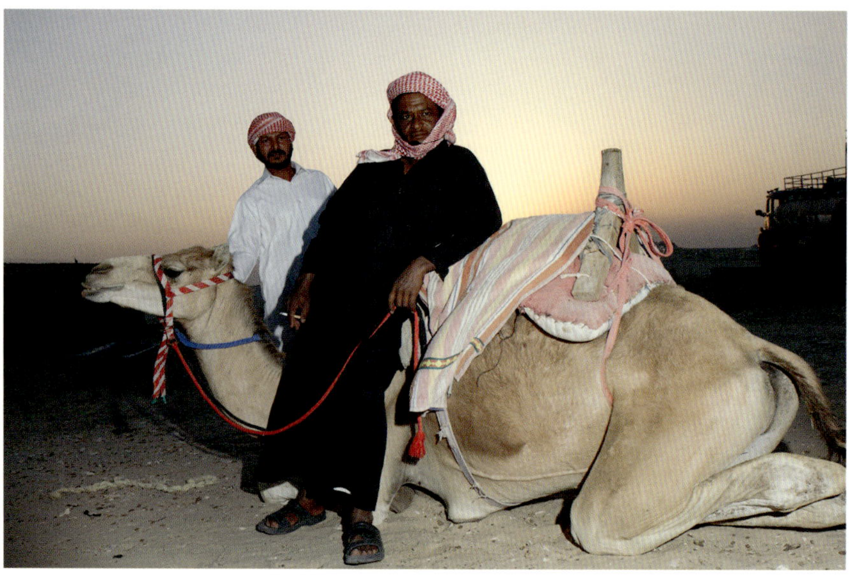

7.26 (*above*). The degree of change in Doha.
7.27 (*right*). We found a desert of startling beauty and traditional practices. Photo: Cooper/Gorfer.
7.28 (*below*). Over the summer, Sarah and Nina began producing landscapes of startling beauty.
Photocollage: Cooper/Gorfer

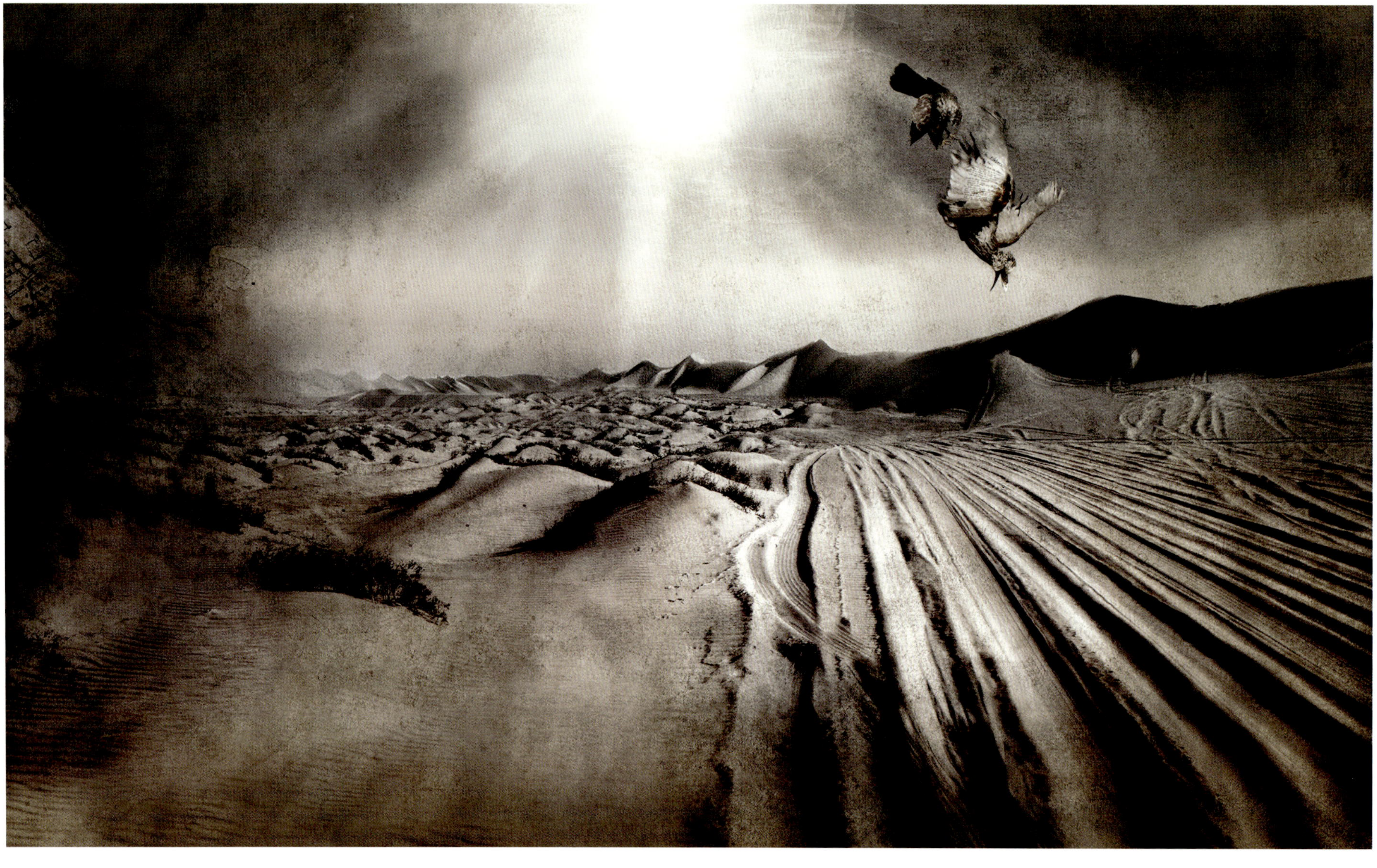

layers, in which my drawings depicting Qatar's building boom would be set over Sarah and Nina's photos of the past and seem to eclipse them. The buildings and cranes, as profiled shapes all akimbo, would be actively displacing the memory of the past.

Additional themes emerged as Sarah and Nina began developing friendships with the Arab women who were students at CMUQ. It was a role that only they could take on, since as a man in an Arab country I could not possibly interview women. Sarah and Nina were able to hear out their family stories and convince them to bring in the traditional garments that would allow them to photograph material for some of the stories that appear in chapter 5. These contacts allowed us to represent a changing role for women in Qatari society.

During our visit, Sarah and Nina took over two thousand photographs of people and landscape. We made sure to go outside the city before we left. There we found a desert of startling beauty, with camels, falcons, traditional dress, and stories arising from the past (fig. 7.27). It was that material that allowed us to represent the past that present-day Qatar was busily erasing.

Working in Sweden over the summer of 2008, Sarah and Nina began producing the series of arrestingly beautiful landscapes that would form the background layers of the mural's long wall (fig. 7.28). Worked over in Photoshop, pixel by pixel, these images possessed a dreamlike character of light that would contrast with the drawings of cranes constructing skyscrapers that I was developing back in Pittsburgh.

In Pittsburgh I had hired an assistant, a former student of mine, David Kennedy, who was an expert in the use of the School of Architecture's new computer numerical control (CNC) router, and soon we had the panels all cut out and the mural fully mocked up (figs. 7.29, 7.30). Had it not been for the presence of that tool and David's knowledge of how to use it, we could not have taken the layered approach we did for the mural. David and I then drew the foreground layers in pencil and then charcoal with a general knowledge of what Sarah and Nina were developing to go underneath.

At the end of the summer I began printing their Photoshop files and gluing them onto the back panels. Finally the mural had taken shape, and we could see it all assembled in our studio prior to shipping it out to Qatar via container ship (fig. 7.31).

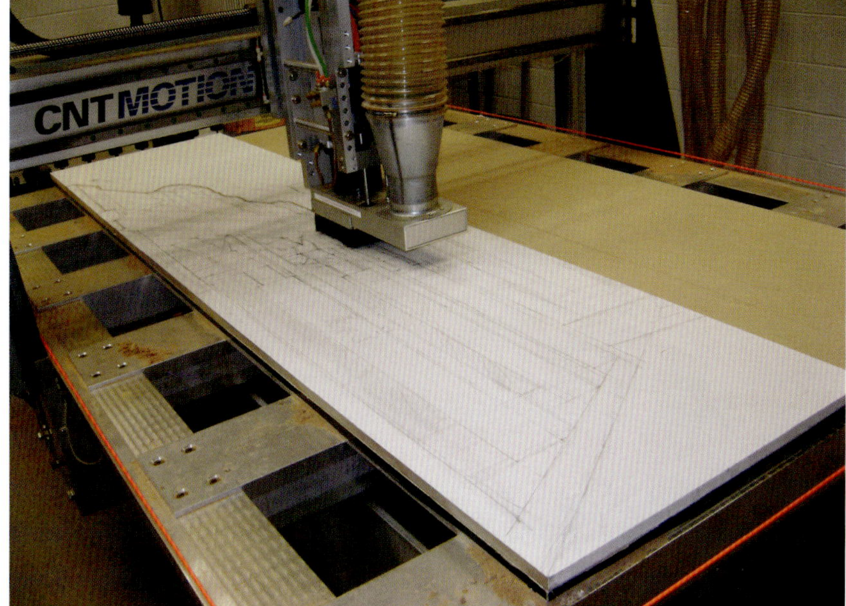

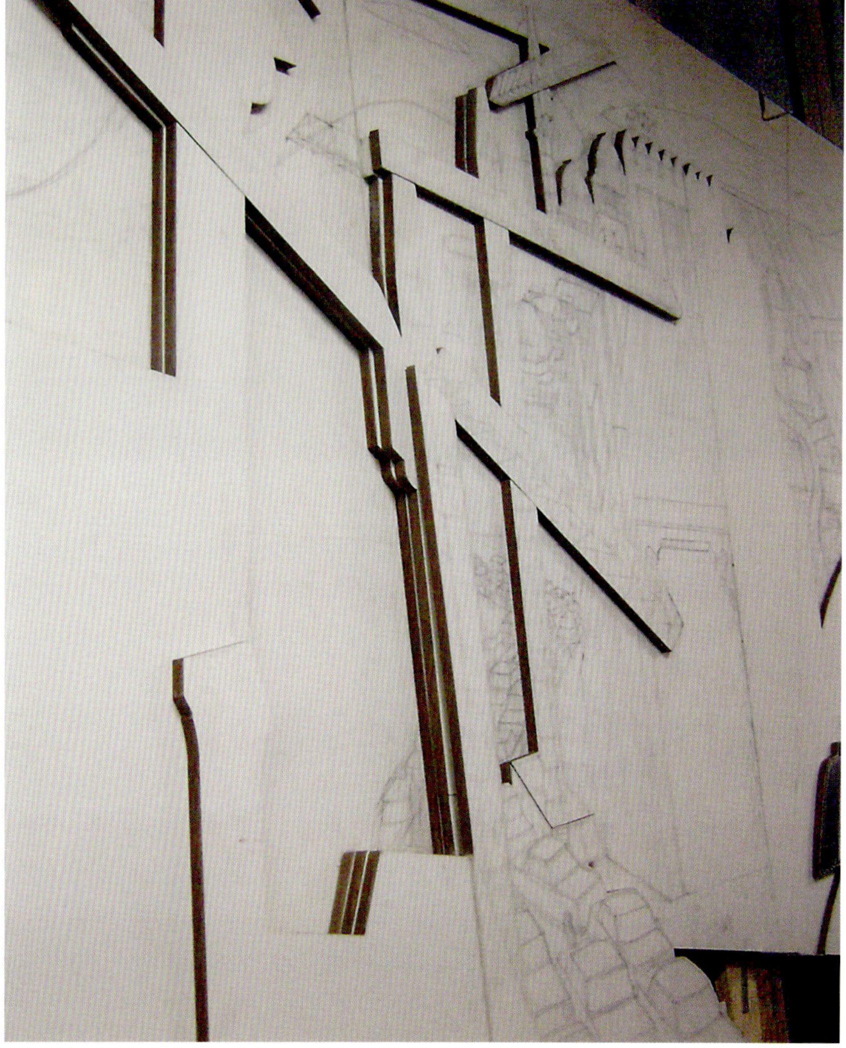

7.29 (*top right*). Cutting the panels on the CNC router.
7.30 (*bottom right*). Mocking up the panels in our studio.

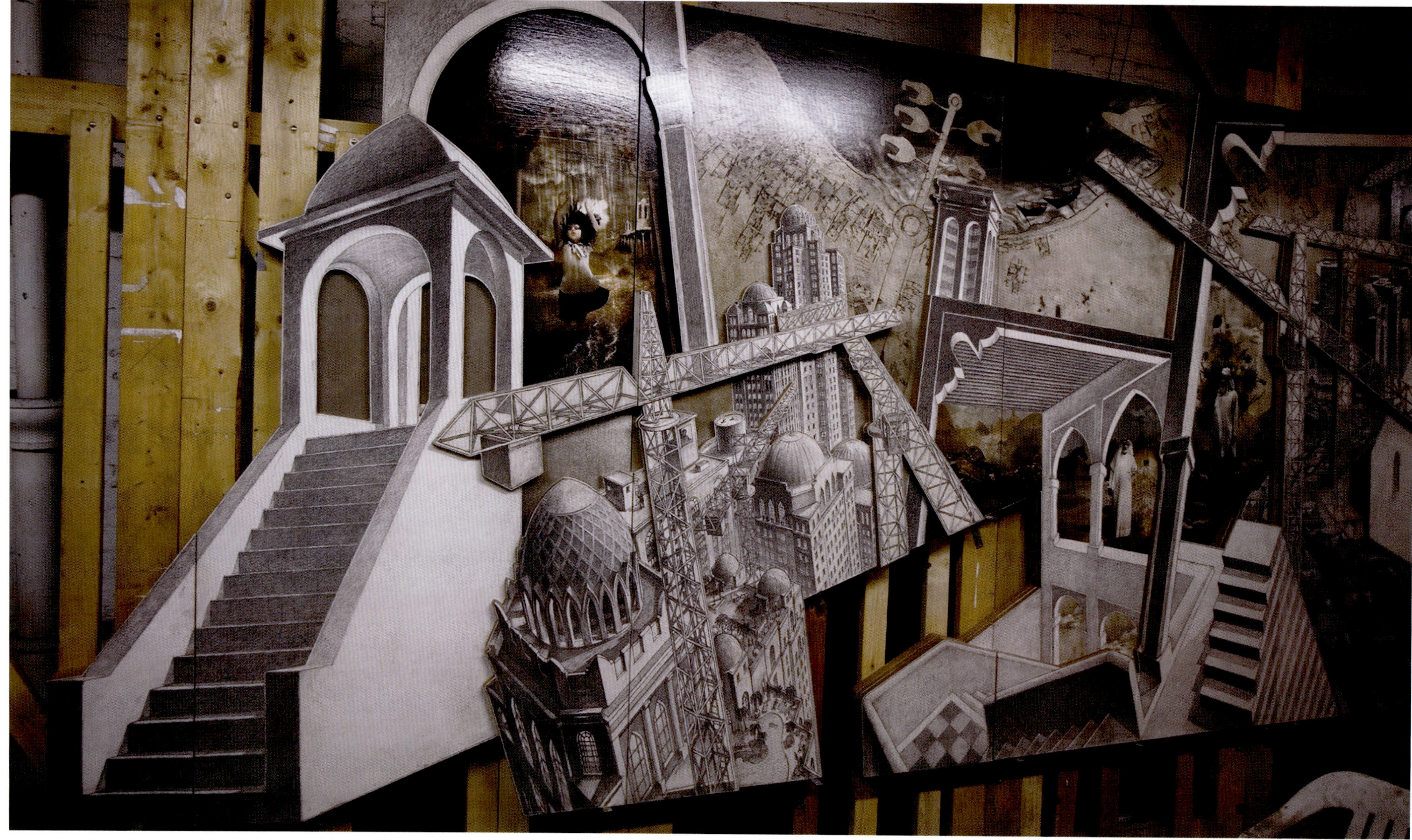

7.31. Finally we could see the mural all assembled in our studio.

Once the mural was up in Doha, we had a chance to see the contribution it made to the corridor (fig. 7.32). We were pleased by how active the drawn shapes appeared over top of the photographs of the traditional life of Qatar (fig. 7.33).

We also had a first chance to gauge the public's reaction to the more controversial parts of the work, and we learned how important ambiguity can sometimes be for public works. Sarah and Nina had shown women in traditional dress in dancelike poses in the aedicules I had built at the mural's right end, and our treatment could have touched a nerve. The scenes seem to be underwater, and they show women dancing with dhows floating overhead (fig. 7.34). We saw that treatment as a way to imply the numerous mermaid stories that are such a strong tradition of Persian Gulf culture.

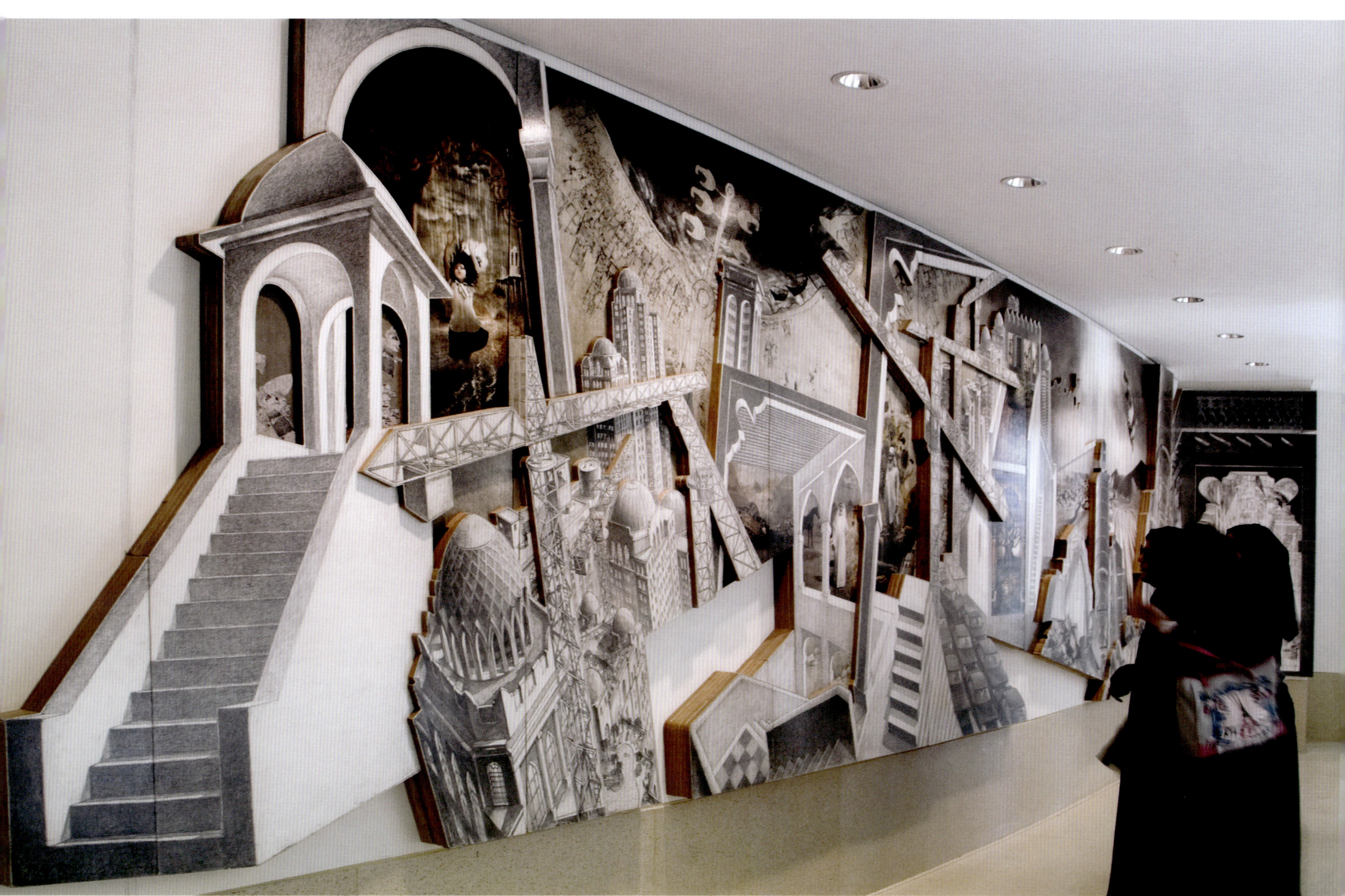

7.32. View of west wall, *Memory between Desert and Sea*, Doug Cooper, Sarah Cooper, and Nina Gorfer with David Kennedy, 2009. Charcoal and photoprint on paper on board, approx. 9 × 50 feet. Carnegie Mellon University Qatar, Doha.

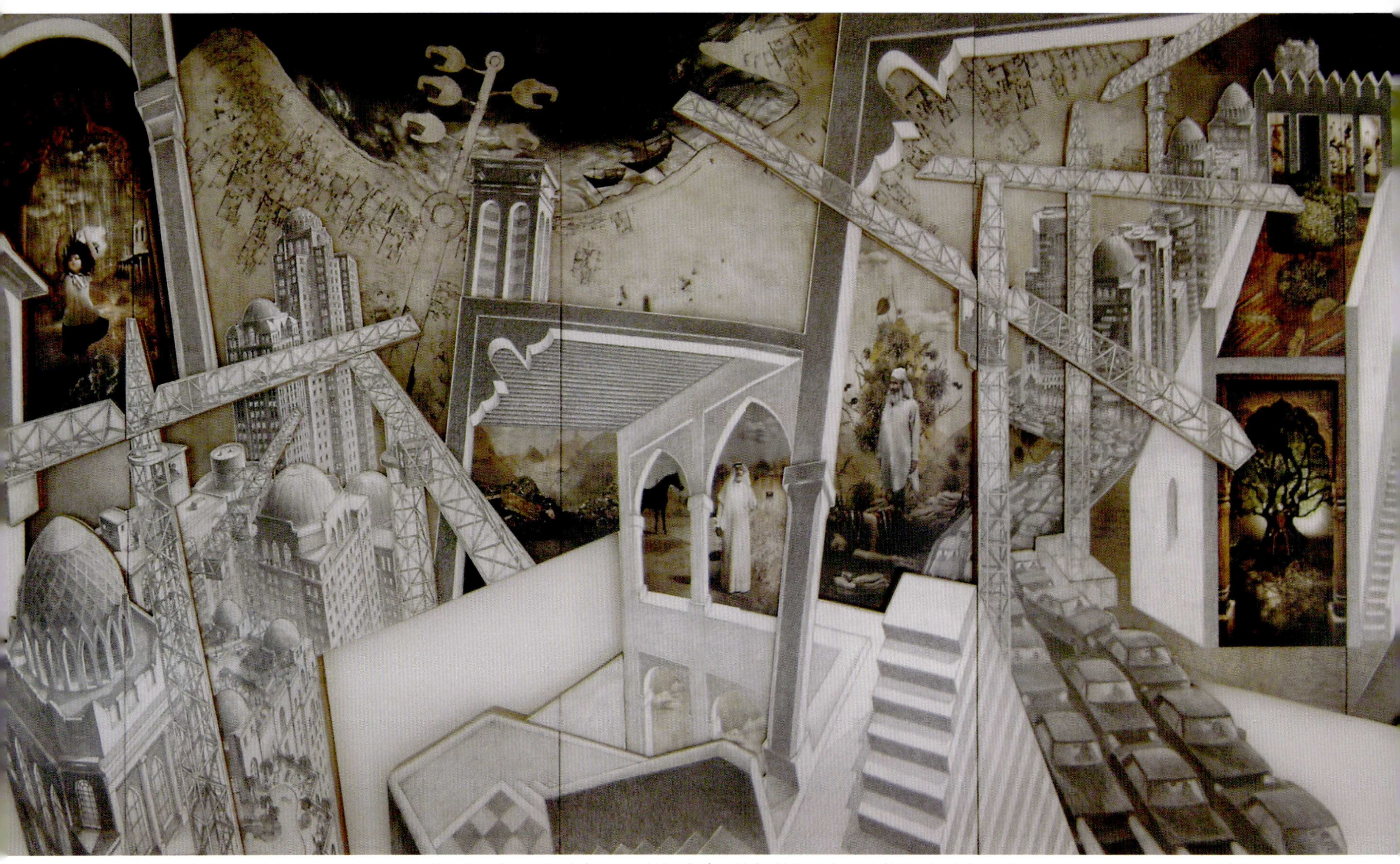

7.33. Detail of west wall, *Memory between Desert and Sea*, Doug Cooper, Sarah Cooper, and Nina Gorfer with David Kennedy, 2009. Charcoal and photoprint on paper on board, approx. 9 × 50 feet. Carnegie Mellon University Qatar, Doha.

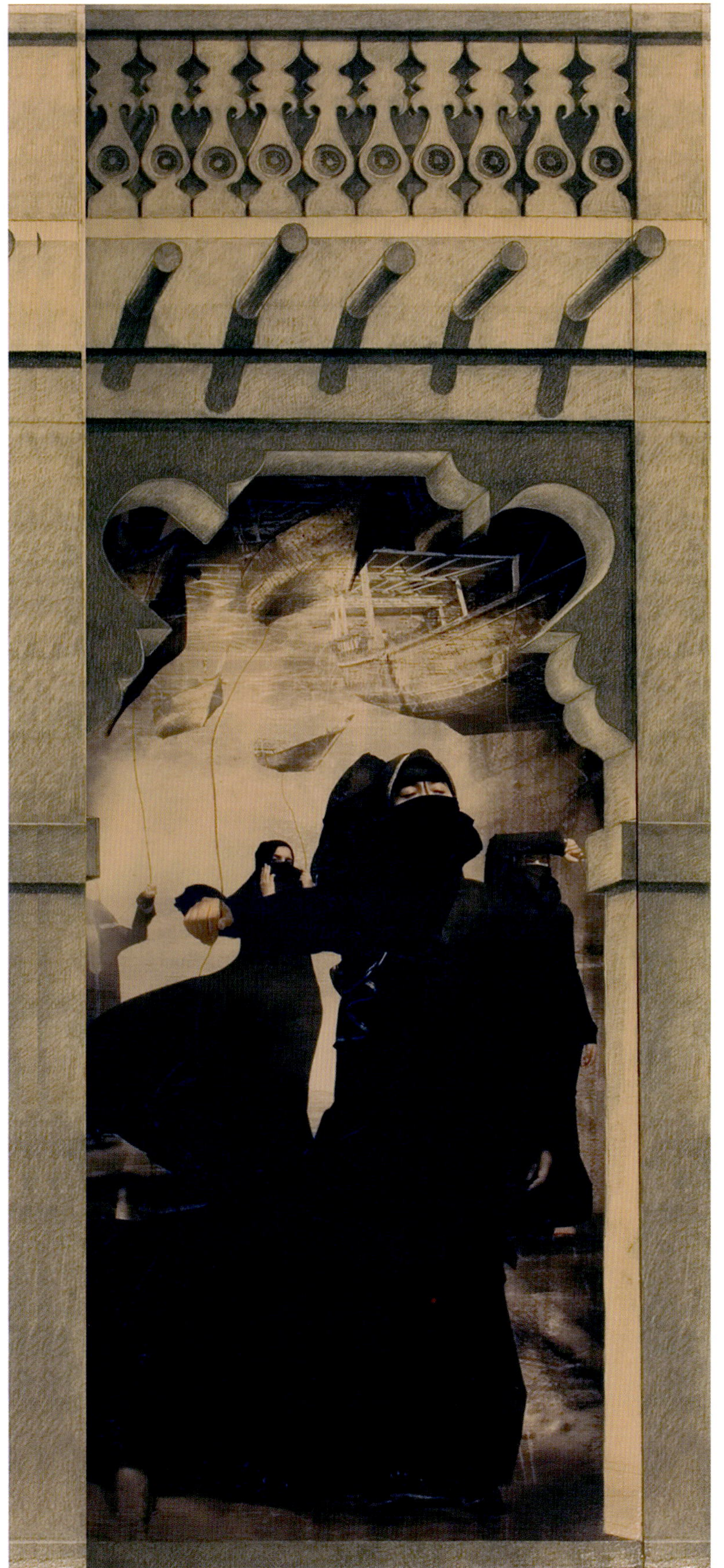

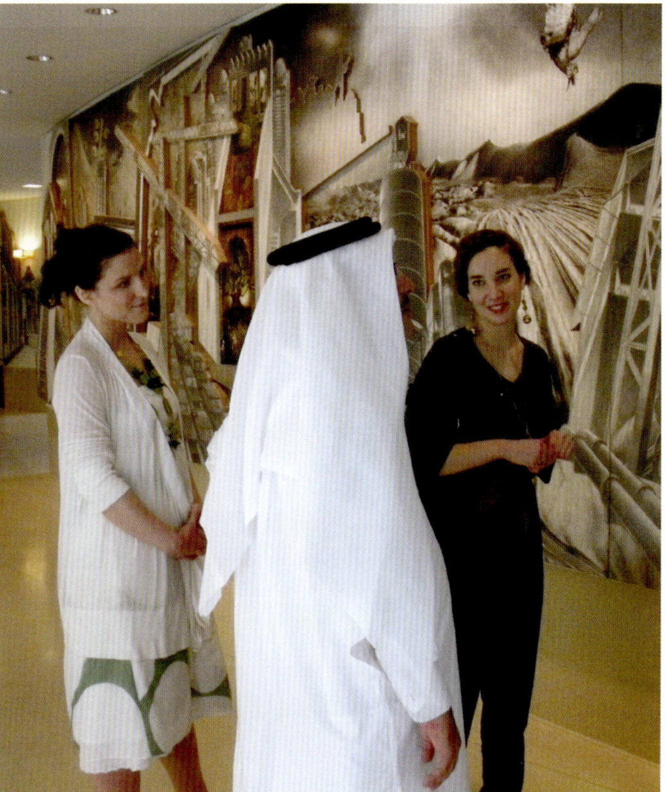

7.34 (*far left*). One area seemed almost underwater.
7.35 (*left*). For him, that was the meaning of the strings.

The women are also holding strings that are attached to the dhows. The strings came from the stories of kite flying we had heard from women, and that was our way of incorporating them in the work. We felt they were important for a mural in a coastal nation with a good deal of seasonal wind. Wisely, as it turned out, Sarah and Nina had used great foresight by maintaining a high level of ambiguity in the relationships of the figures to each other and to men. They had implied relationships, but had left the precise nature of those relationships for the individual viewers to formulate.

Then one day an older, traditionally dressed Qatari gentleman came by, and he asked us about the area (fig. 7.35). I found a way of asking him what he thought the strings meant, and he told us. During long fishing voyages out on the dangerous waters of the Persian Gulf, he said there was a tradition of singing that bound the men in the boats to the women left back home. From far out at sea, the men would sing to their wives and their families. The women in turn would sing to their absent men to protect them in their dangerous work. For this man, that was the meaning of the strings: the connecting tethers maintained during long absences through the medium of song.

Sanctuary and Sacred Space: *City Church, City,*
East Liberty Presbyterian Church (2018)

After a long career as an architect, my wife, Stefani Danes, began a new one making "art quilts," and over time the idea arose between us that we might collaborate on a mural one day (fig. 7.36). Our first opportunity came in 2013 with a mural for Pittsburgh's East End Cooperative Ministry. It was a large mural (24 × 44 feet), for which we developed a "jigsaw" technique of puzzling fabric-covered panels together with my panels drawn in charcoal (fig. 7.37).

This decision to join two different materials, fabric and charcoal drawing, in one layer was the outcome of lengthy discussion between us. I had initially favored using multiple layers, as I had done in Qatar with Sarah and Nina. But Stefani eventually convinced me that using a single layer made of multiple pieces joined edge to edge would allow us to create continuous readings of shape crossing the boundaries between her abstraction in fabric and my figurative drawing (fig. 7.38).

We were sufficiently encouraged by what we had achieved with this mural that we decided to collaborate once again when the opportunity arose to create a mural for our church in Pittsburgh, East Liberty Presbyterian. We developed it as a part of a larger body of individually produced works: quilts and drawings all focused on the theme of sanctuary, or sacred space in a secular world. We showed these at Pittsburgh's Concept Gallery throughout the summer of 2018 prior to installing the mural at the church in August. We used the individual works as a way to help us better understand the ideas that would guide the design of the mural.

The idea of sanctuary—holy or sacred space—has a long history, with roots far deeper than even its etymology suggests. As Stefani and I prepared for the show, our readings took us back through the history of the three Abrahamic religions, Celtic ideas about geography, Greek and Aboriginal myths, and Eastern iconography.

Traditionally the word *sanctuary* is associated with a dwelling place of the divine. Sacred places are exceptional. They stand out from the everyday secular world. They might be known through a miracle or a connection to a divine power, a disruption in the everyday order of the world. A sanctuary is also a place that is set apart from everyday fears and anxieties. A sanctuary is a quiet and calm center of transcendent beauty.

But sanctuary is not synonymous with a religious place of worship. People may experience a connection with the divine in a sunset, on a city street, or in a child's face. For one person, a sacred space may be a clearing in the woods; for another, a stretch of quiet beach or a quiet bedroom with a cradle and a rocking chair. *Sanctuary* is a word that resonates deeply in our current political

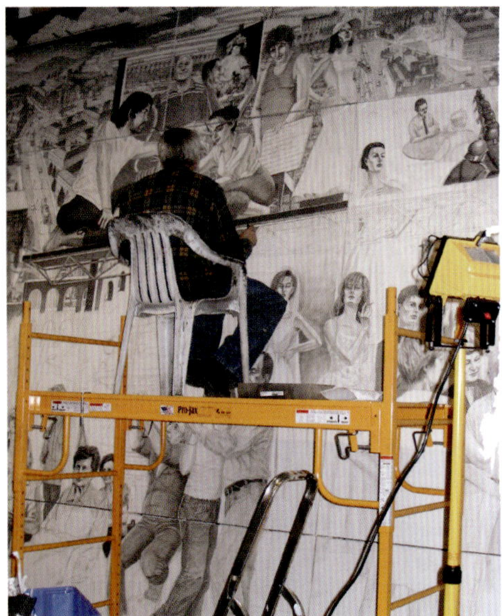

7.36. Doug at work in his studio, Stefani in hers.

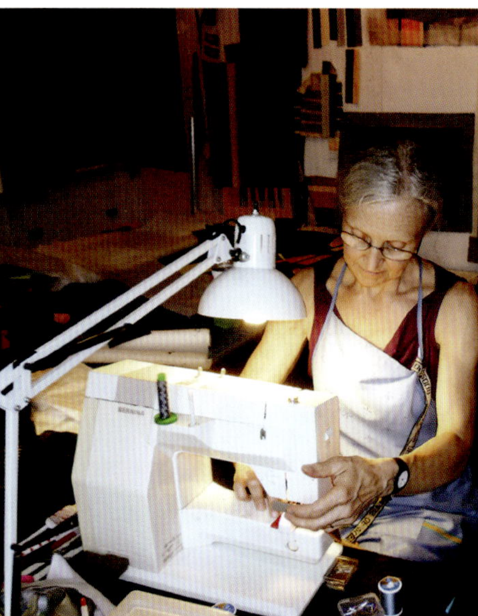

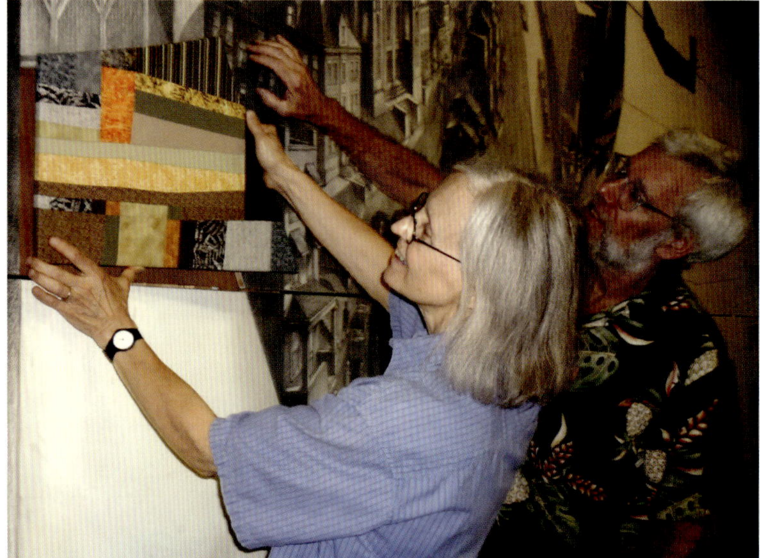

7.37. Fitting the panels. Photo by Pam Picher.

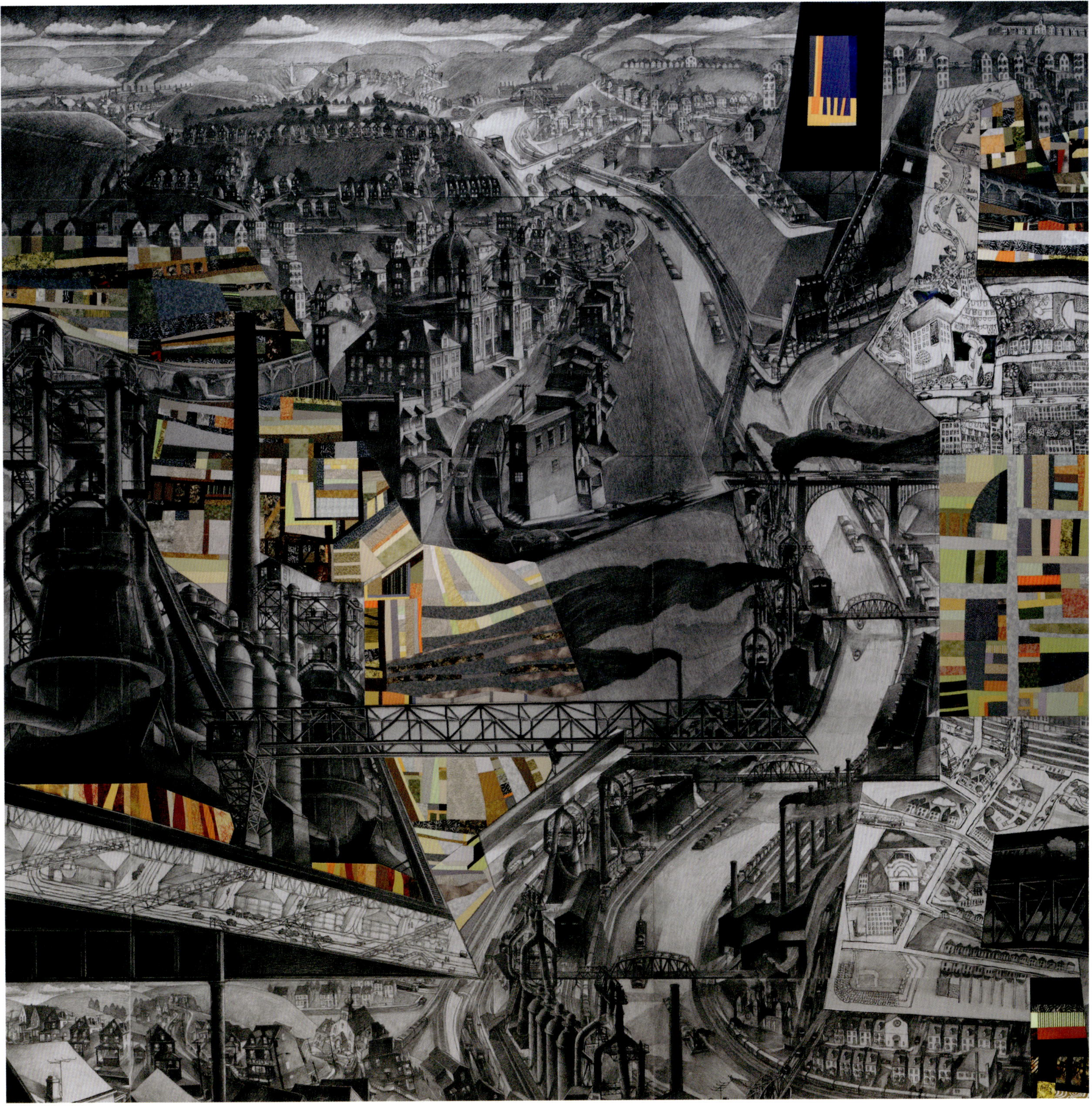

7.38. Detail of upper left corner, *The Greening of the City*, Doug Cooper and Stefani Danes with Samantha Gao, 2015. Charcoal on paper on board, fabric mounted around board, 23 × 44 feet. East End Cooperative Ministry, Pittsburgh.

life in ways that reflect its meaning as a place of refuge. That idea has a long history. In a place where divine order is manifested, human rules are supplanted by divine justice. Since the 1300s, our secular legal codes have recognized that, once within sanctuaries, people seeking safety (except traditionally murderers and heretics) are outside the domain of secular laws.

So when we asked, "What makes a space sacred?" we knew there would be no one answer. People may recognize a sacred space by a steeple or dome and its carved stone or stained glass, but those are not its essential elements. From our backgrounds in architecture, we were curious about what makes space sacred and looked to find its essential elements. What tells us this place is a sanctuary? What among our diverse personal experiences and memories are the meanings we share, the expectations we hold in common, or archetypal images that are wired into our brains? These are some of the characteristics we found:

(1) Sacred space is centered, a cosmos: an ordered universe. Secular space is empty: a chaos.

(2) Sacred space can be experienced as light or darkness. As in the example of Byzantine interiors covered with mosaics, it may be luminescent. But sacred space can be a place of darkness, as in the ancient oracular caves that emitted mist and knowledge of the future.

(3) Sacred space offers a model of the cosmos. Mandalas and labyrinths make our relationship to a center visible. It can be seen in a transepted nave, a cloister garden, or the orientation of an apse.

(4) Finding sacred space requires effort, crossing thresholds, and overcoming obstacles along the way. Finding it requires courage and perseverance. As in labyrinths we find in churches and gardens to this day and as in medieval pilgrimage maps, a spiritual path is a journey to a center that is both a known and an unknown destination.

(5) Sacred space is both found and made: In religious traditions around the world, altars are erected to make visible a place of divine presence. The Norse arriving in Iceland tilled the land to consecrate the soil. The Greeks erected the Temple of Delphi at the spring that was the source of oracular wisdom. In England, visitors since the Iron Age have sought the healing powers of the white and red spring waters at Glastonbury, symbols of purity and sacrifice. Aboriginal Australians place poles at encampments during journeys to reestablish sacred apertures.

My Drawings

Pittsburgh is a city rich with the sacred spaces of many faiths. Sacred buildings were constructed as the centers of neighborhood communities; some still exist today; others have dissolved into a (secular) urban scene. Yet the buildings still have the power to take us away from the everyday. As I drew them, sometimes I emphasized their inner light, sometimes their paths toward a center, and sometimes their disappearance.

East Liberty Presbyterian Church contrasts inside and outside. Inside there is order, calm, and refuge in contrast to the world outside where streets race every which way. The drawing styles emphasize the differences. The outside is linear and maplike; the inside tonal and evocative. At the center of the entire composition is the garth (courtyard): glowing, fertile, and filled with trees. Whirling about the outside are streets filled with rushing people and vehicles. The city outside spins with a rotational energy, but the inside and its center are calm (fig. 7.39).

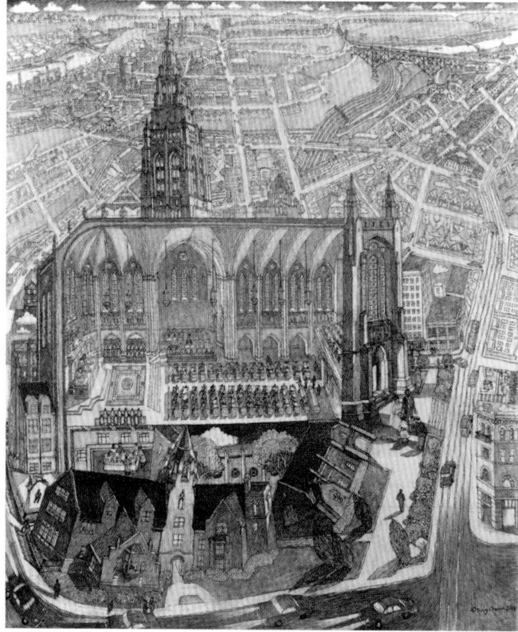

7.39. *East Liberty Presbyterian Church*, Doug Cooper, 2018. Charcoal on paper on board, 60 × 48 inches.

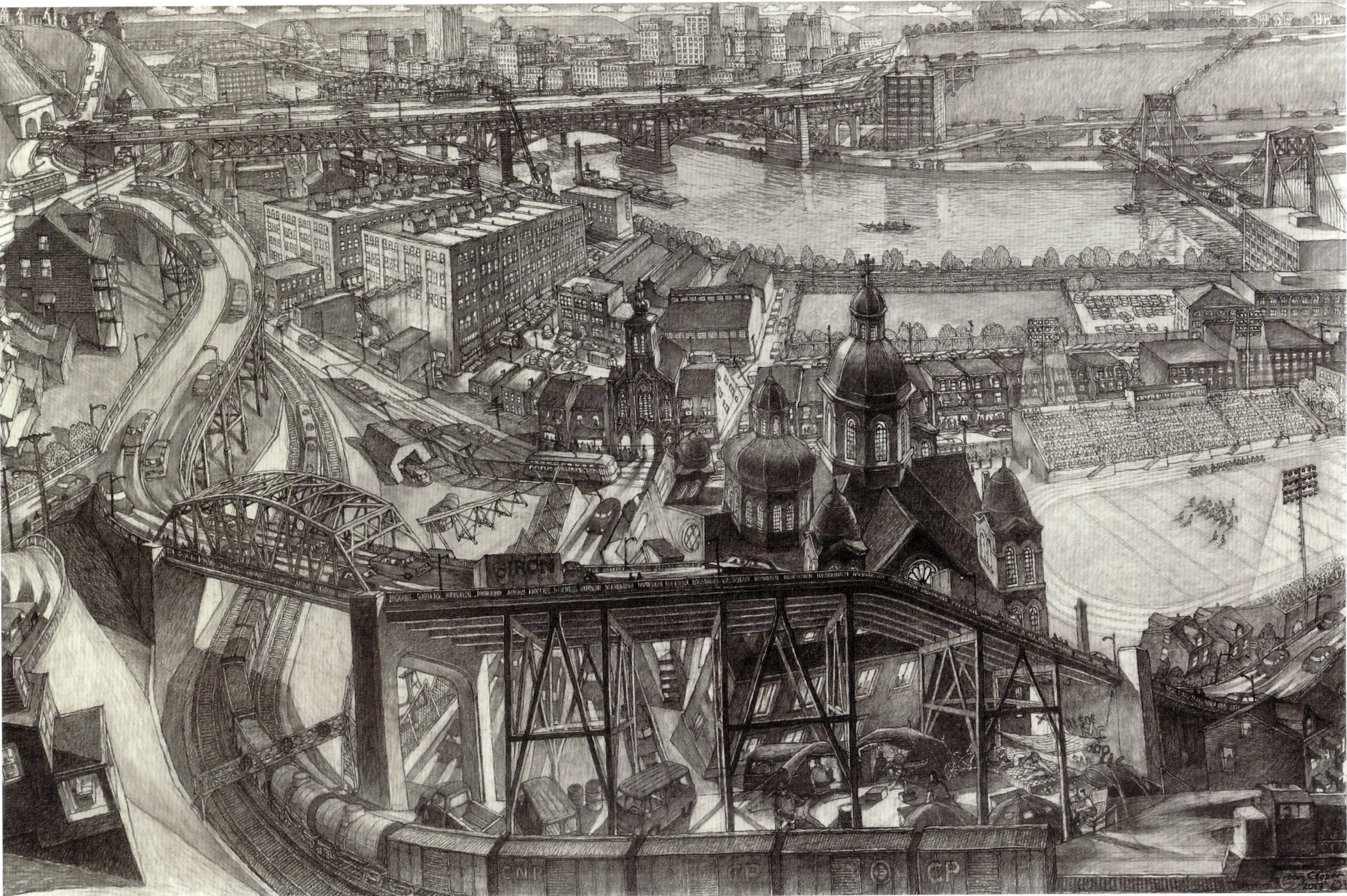

7.40. *Under McArdle Roadway*, Doug Cooper, 2017. Charcoal on paper on board, 48 × 72 inches. Collection of Ben Speiser and Valentina Vavasis.

Under McArdle Roadway shows the creation and maintenance of a temporary sanctuary by a small community of homeless people under the McArdle Bridge. This is set against the view of the Ukrainian Catholic church, Saint John the Baptist, beyond (fig. 7.40).

Sacred Places of the Bottoms points to the enduring significance of a location over time. There are three distinctive churches visible to motorists crossing the long viaduct leading to the McKees Rocks Bridge over the Ohio River. But that site had long before been consecrated by local Native Americans who erected the mound there some ten thousand years ago, which is visible in the background (fig. 7.41). The importance of these churches to their contexts is underscored by the contrast provided by two other drawings: *Three Downtown Churches* and *Epiphany Church of the Crosstown*, where the once prominent profiles of these churches are overshadowed by city development around, beside, and above them (figs. 7.42, 7.43).

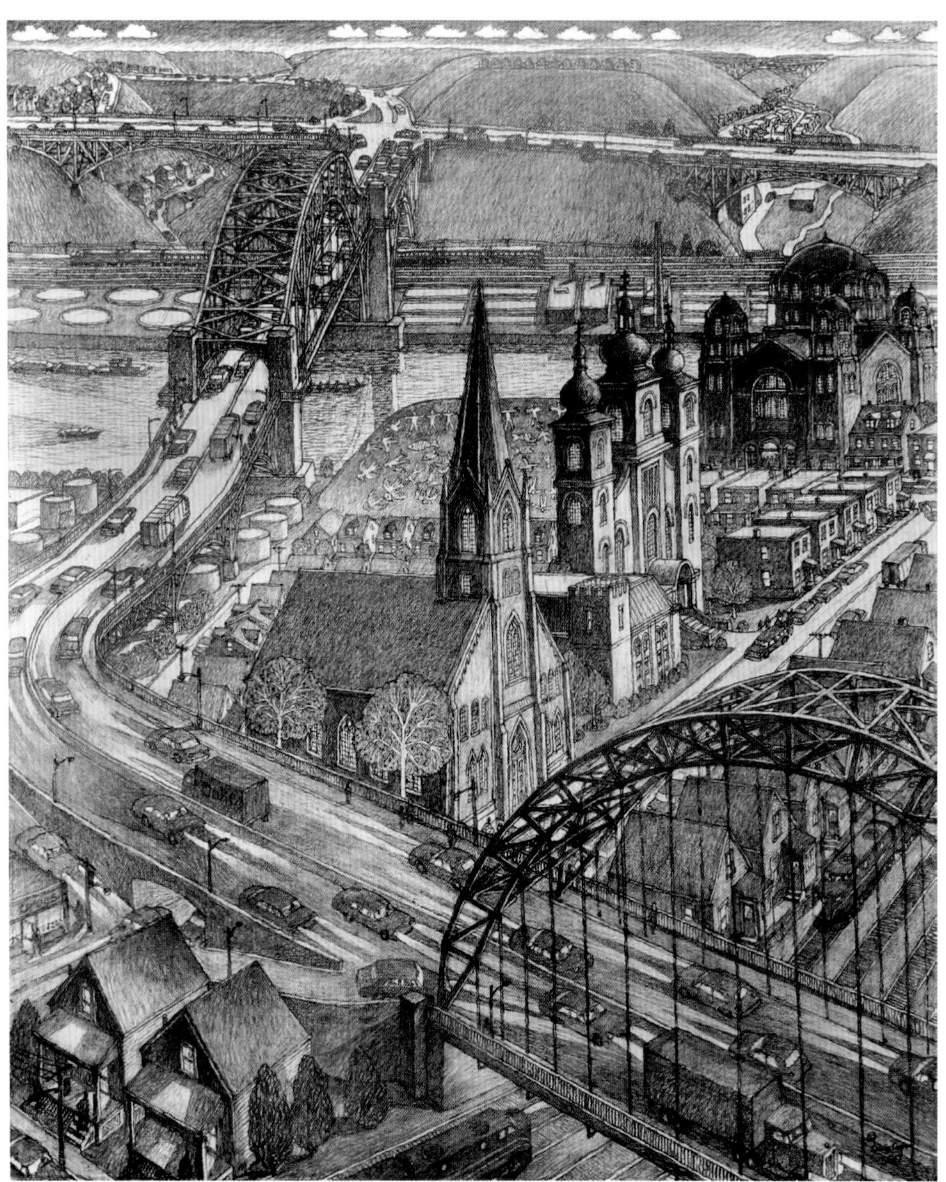

7.41. *Sacred Places of the Bottoms*, Doug Cooper, 2018. Charcoal on paper on board, 48 × 36 inches.

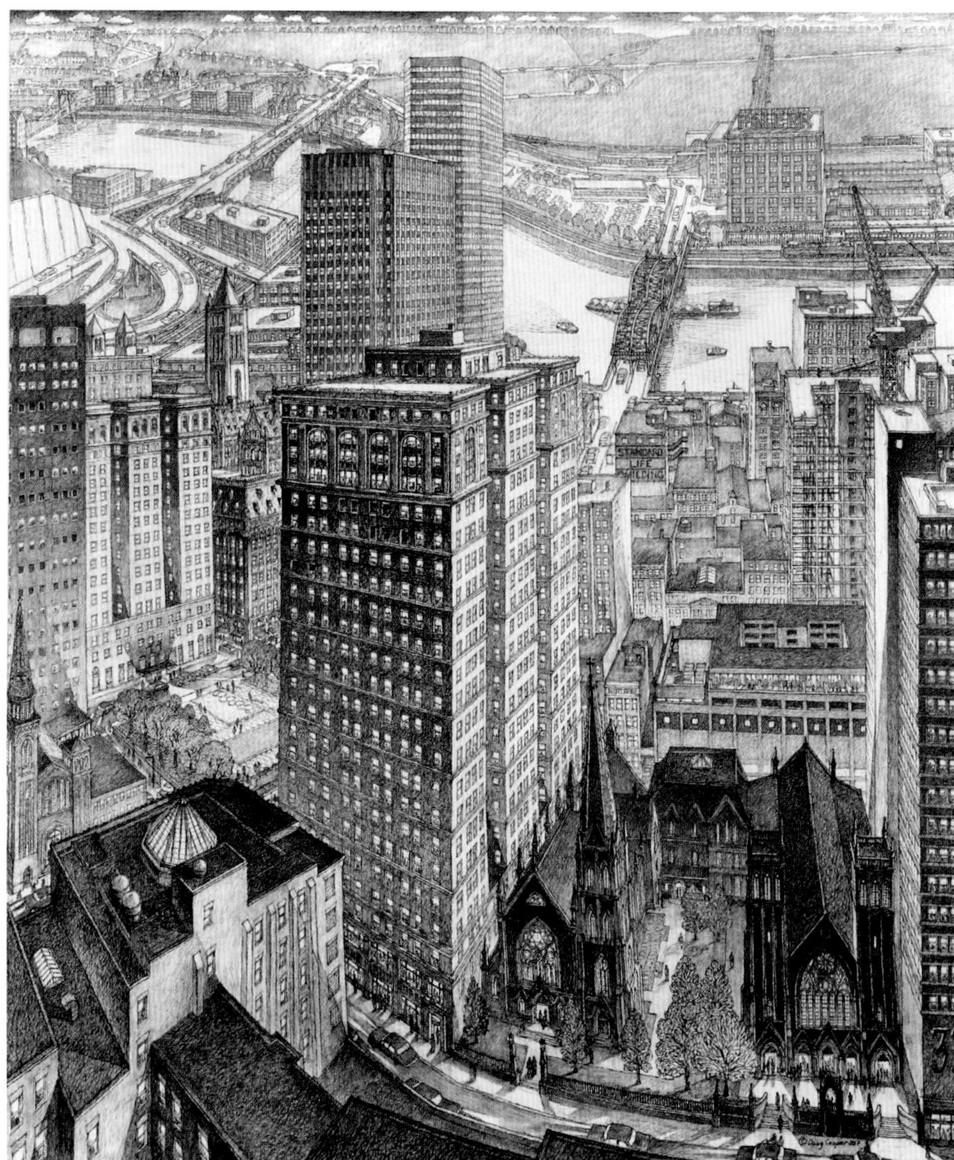

7.42. *Three Downtown Churches*, Doug Cooper, 2018. Charcoal on paper on board, 60 × 48 inches.

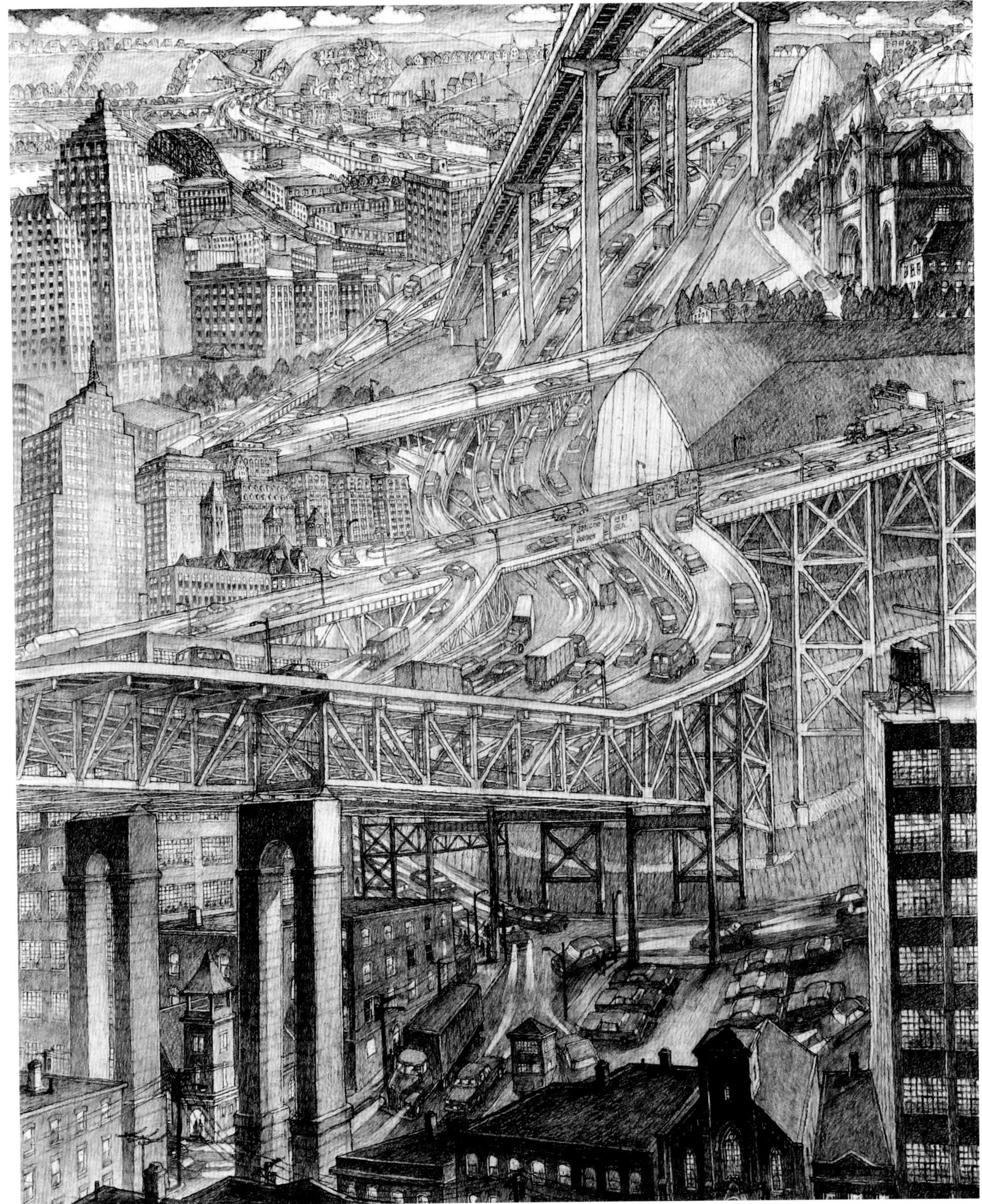

7.43. *Epiphany Church on the Crosstown*, Doug Cooper, 2018. Charcoal on paper on board, 60 × 48 inches.

Stefani's Quilts

Stefani focused on the underlying nature of sanctuary, its relationship to the world, and its role in our lives: the sacred center, the path toward the center, and the many thresholds along the way. Perhaps the most fundamental attribute of sanctuary is its ambiguity, its multifold and paradoxical nature. Path and destination are sometimes indistinguishable from each other. Place and context are reciprocal. Sacred space may exist at multiple scales, from garden to city and beyond.

A story that our minister, Dr. Bush, told in a sermon early during our work touched on themes of being a sanctuary for each other, the hazardous journey, linking across boundaries, and gathering at the table or altar. In its bare outlines, it was the story of a couple who lived in a house on the border of Germany and a nonoccupied neighboring country during World War II. At their front door, which was on German soil, they welcomed people desperate to leave Germany into their home. They always invited them to gather to share a meal, then led them out the back door into safety. Perhaps that moment was a threshold to refuge, perhaps the only sanctuary in a dangerous world.

Stefani's quilts explored these questions, and responded to the challenge of understanding the enigmatic quality of sacred space through color, shape, and line. *Toward Dawn* and *Into the Night* are composed around a sacred center, one a glowing light and the other a deep darkness. Paths of light pass through layers of space, converging at the center or extending out into the world. (figs. 7.44, 7.45).

We Gather Together and *One Great Fellowship* interpret the experience of the sacred center at different scales: as a communal table, as an architectural structure, and as a place that brings order to a city (figs. 7.46, 7.47). *In a Great Procession* describes journeys from the secular to the sacred, ambiguous boundaries, and choices (fig. 7.48). *A Joyful Noise* celebrates the spirit and uncertainty of the journey. *Between* is dynamic balance between opposites. (fig. 7.49).

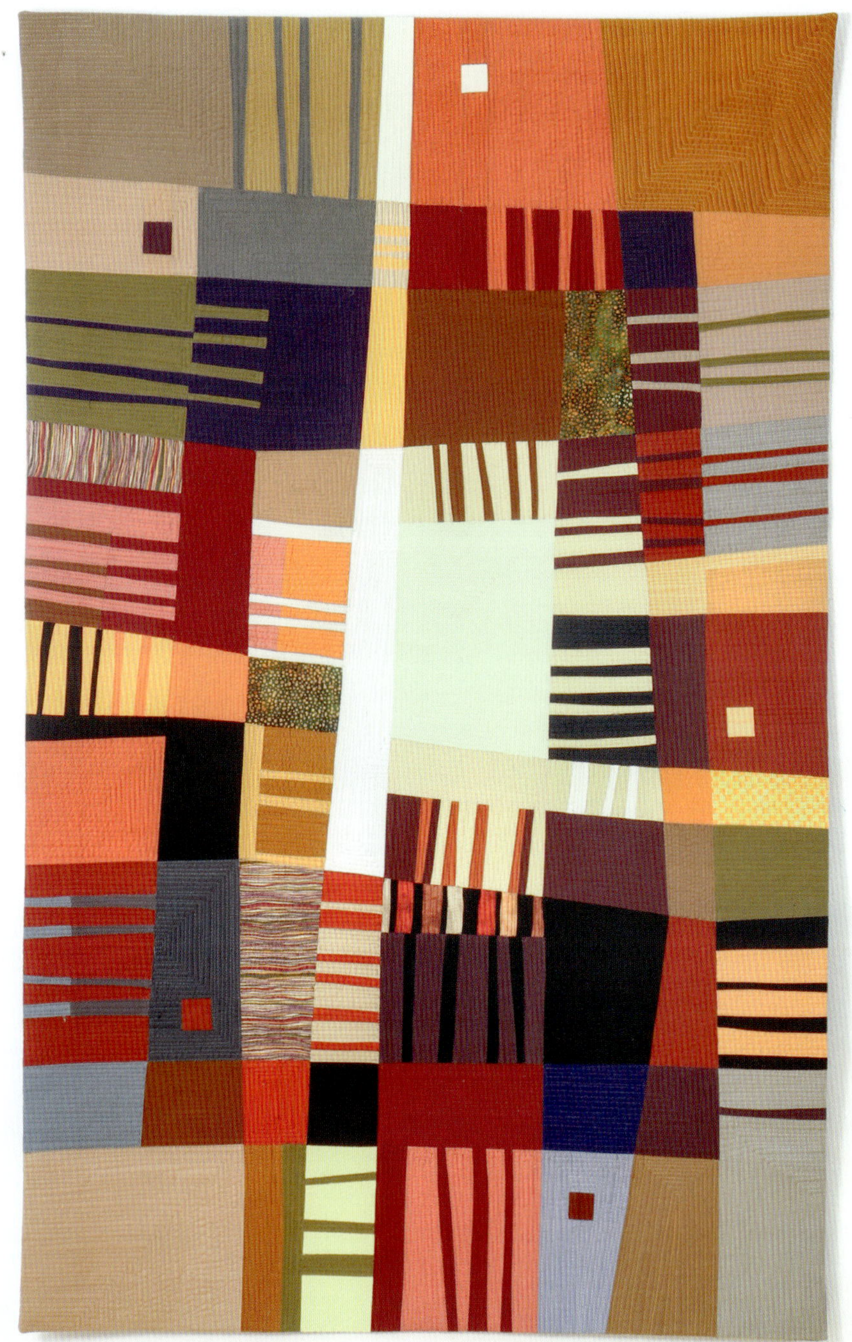

7.44. *Toward Dawn*, Stefani Danes, 2018. Quilted fabric, 50 × 31 inches.

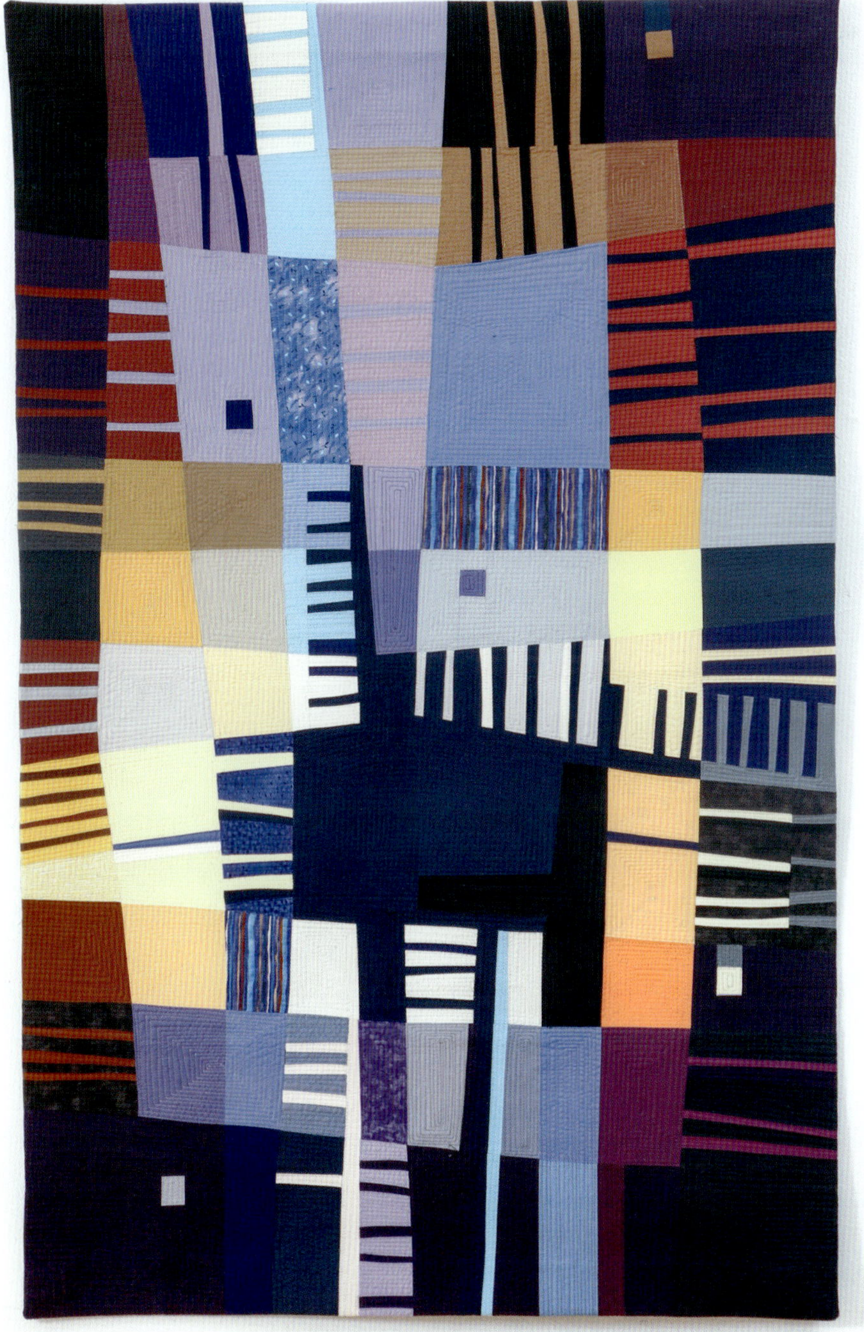

7.45. *Into the Night*, Stefani Danes, 2018. Quilted fabric, 50 × 31 inches.

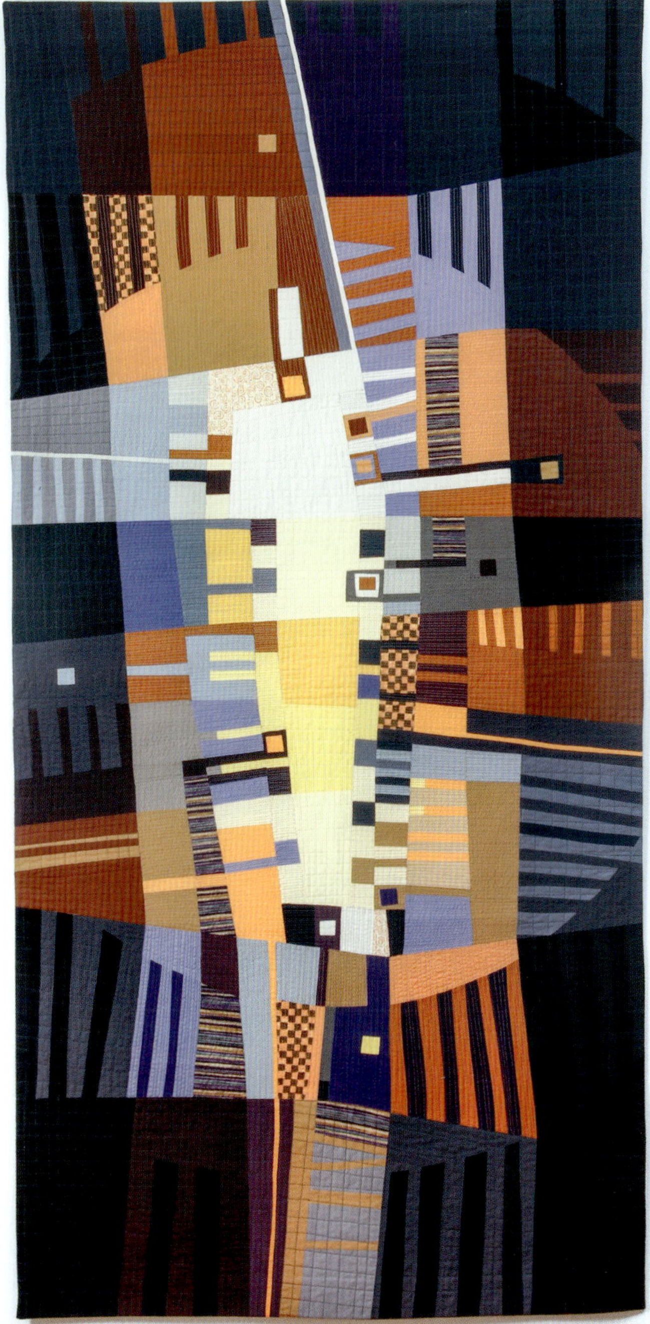

7.46. *We Gather Together*, Stefani Danes, 2018. Quilted fabric, 81 × 39 inches.

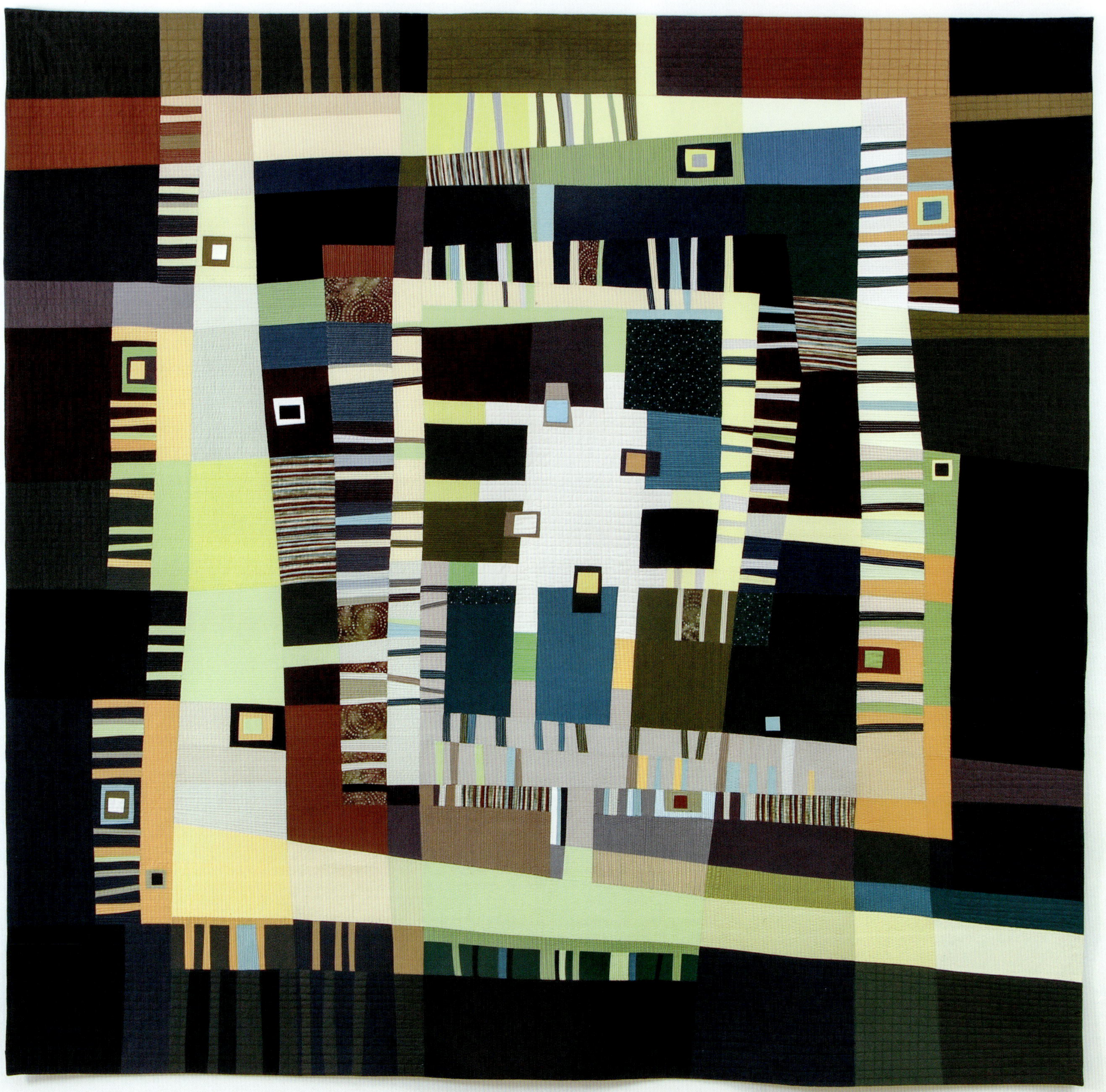

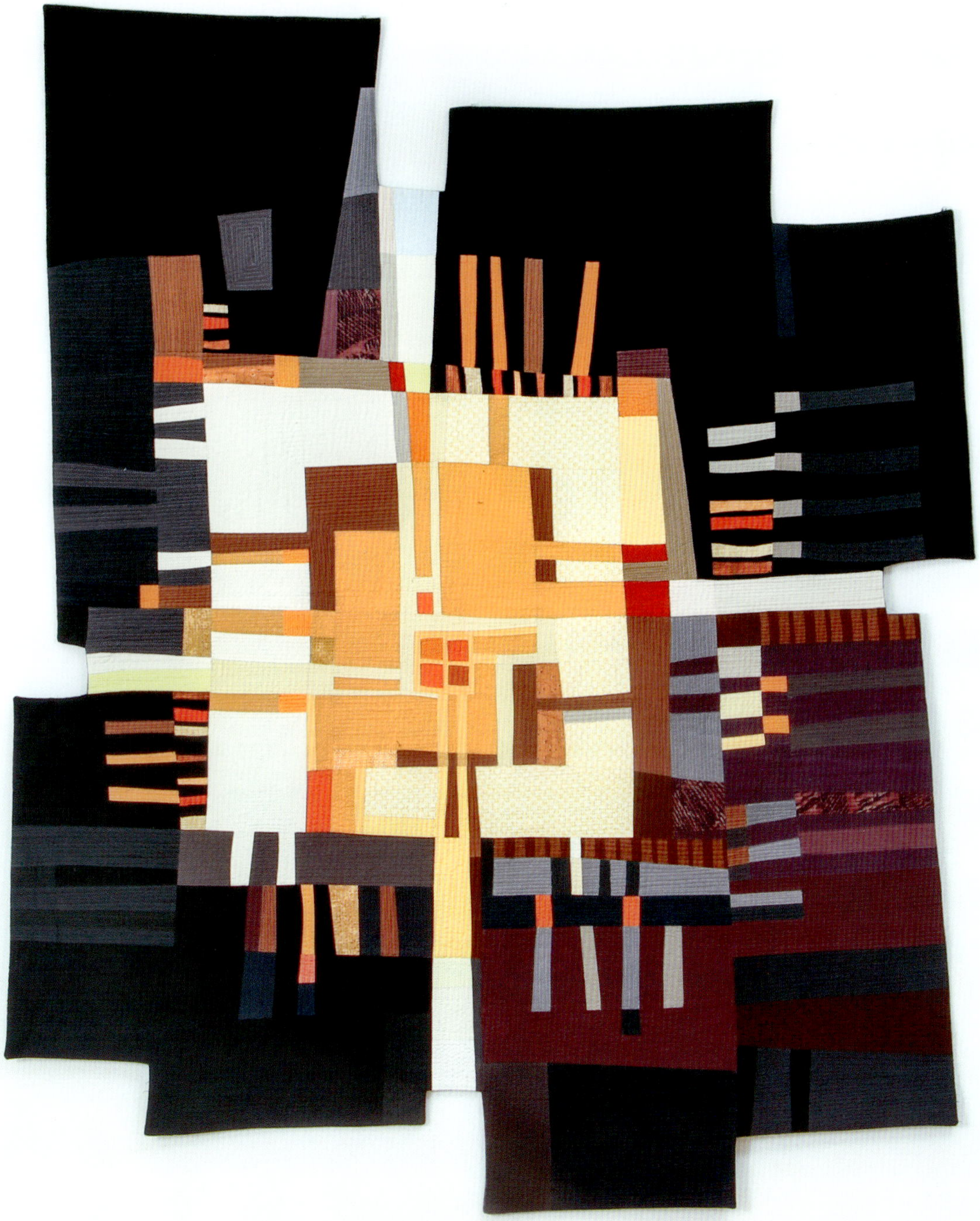

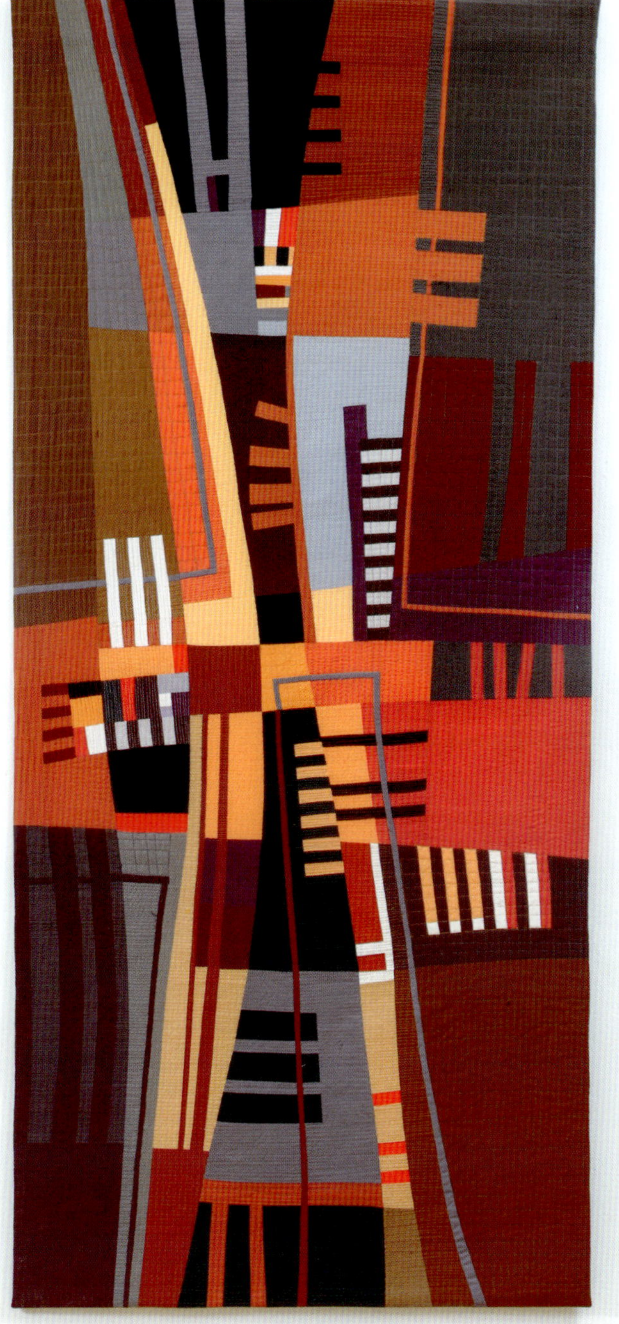

7.49. *A Joyful Noise*, Stefani Danes, 2018. Quilted fabric, 78 × 35 inches.

7.48 (*left*). *In a Great Procession*, Stefani Danes, 2018. Quilted fabric, 85 × 83 inches.

7.47 (*above*). *One Great Fellowship*, Stefani Danes, 2018. Quilted fabric 46 × 56 inches.

City Church City

The individual works served as preparation for *City Church City,* the mural we installed at East Liberty Presbyterian Church at the exhibition's conclusion. We started our work together with a series of sketches over a two-day period in January 2018 that developed from some early compositions that Stefani had drawn. These reinforced a strong center with a series of concentric curves and captured the early stages of the set of long radiating shapes that would remain in the finished work (fig. 7.50). In retrospect the most critical sketches were two that joined Stefani's ideas for the composition of *We Gather Together* and some of the cross-sectional studies I had developed for my drawing of the church. Joining the two had the beneficial effect of asserting the focus on a center that her fabric and my drawing could share. Until then, my figurative work had been directed more at the restless and agitated city outside than on the calm center within. In concept, the mural is ordered by a map or plan of the church at its center, which frames the views of church and city life, linking what we know and what we see. In the progression of sketches, the next one retains the circular elements of the earlier sketch (fig. 7.51). The following one brought that focus on the garth and dispensed with the curves (fig. 7.52), and then a final one got us fairly close to the final composition (fig. 7.53).

Some of Stefani's thoughts about the reciprocal relationship between the church's inner life and the city at large gave me much help in giving the inside of the church a more specific life. The church, after all, is a part of the city—working with neighbors toward justice and vitality—and the church brings the city inside by hosting community organizations and events, educating children in the arts, and welcoming those who feel marginalized or forgotten. The church is indeed many sacred spaces. It is an urban mosaic of spaces for gathering, worship, fellowship, meditation and prayer, singing, bowling, and square dancing. This sense of the outside being welcomed in and the inside radiating outward is what ultimately gave our mural its name.

At the heart of the church is the garth, which in the mural is represented as the Garden, the center that connects all people north, south, east, and west. As people from all directions are welcome in the Garden, so the fabric tree of life grows from the Garden in all directions to connect all people of all cultures as part of God's family (fig 7.54).

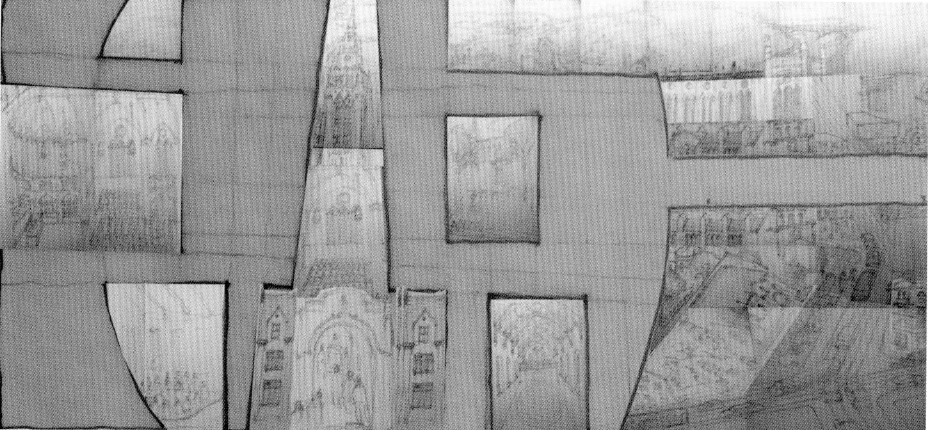

7.50 (*top*). Sketch 1, January 2018.
7.51 (*bottom*). Sketch 2, January 2018.

7.52 (*facing page, top*). Sketch 3, January 2018.
7.53 (*facing page, bottom*). Sketch 4, January 2018.
7.54 (*following spread*). *City Church City,* Doug Cooper and Stefani Danes, 2018. Charcoal on paper on board, fabric mounted around board, 80 × 216 inches. East Liberty Presbyterian Church, Pittsburgh.

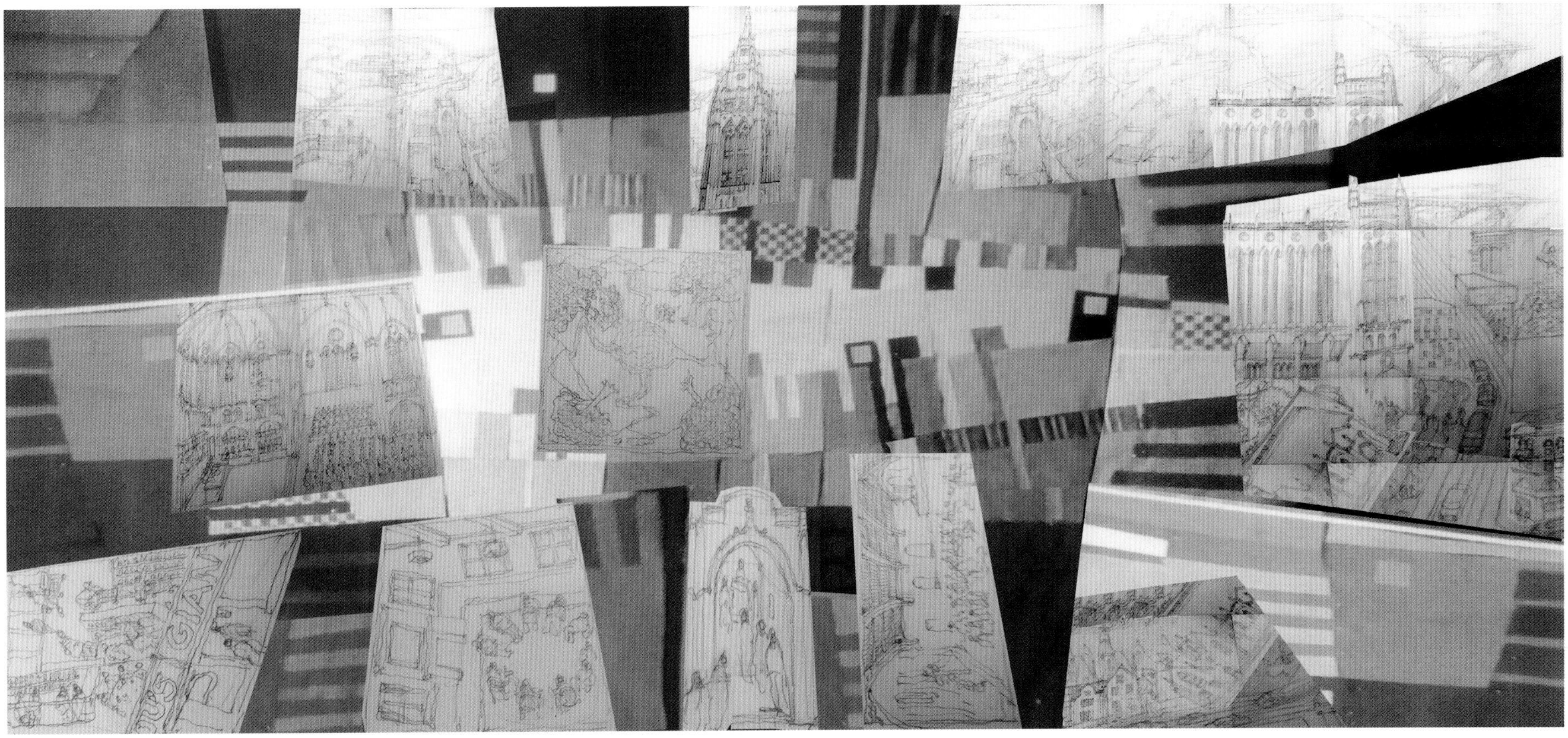

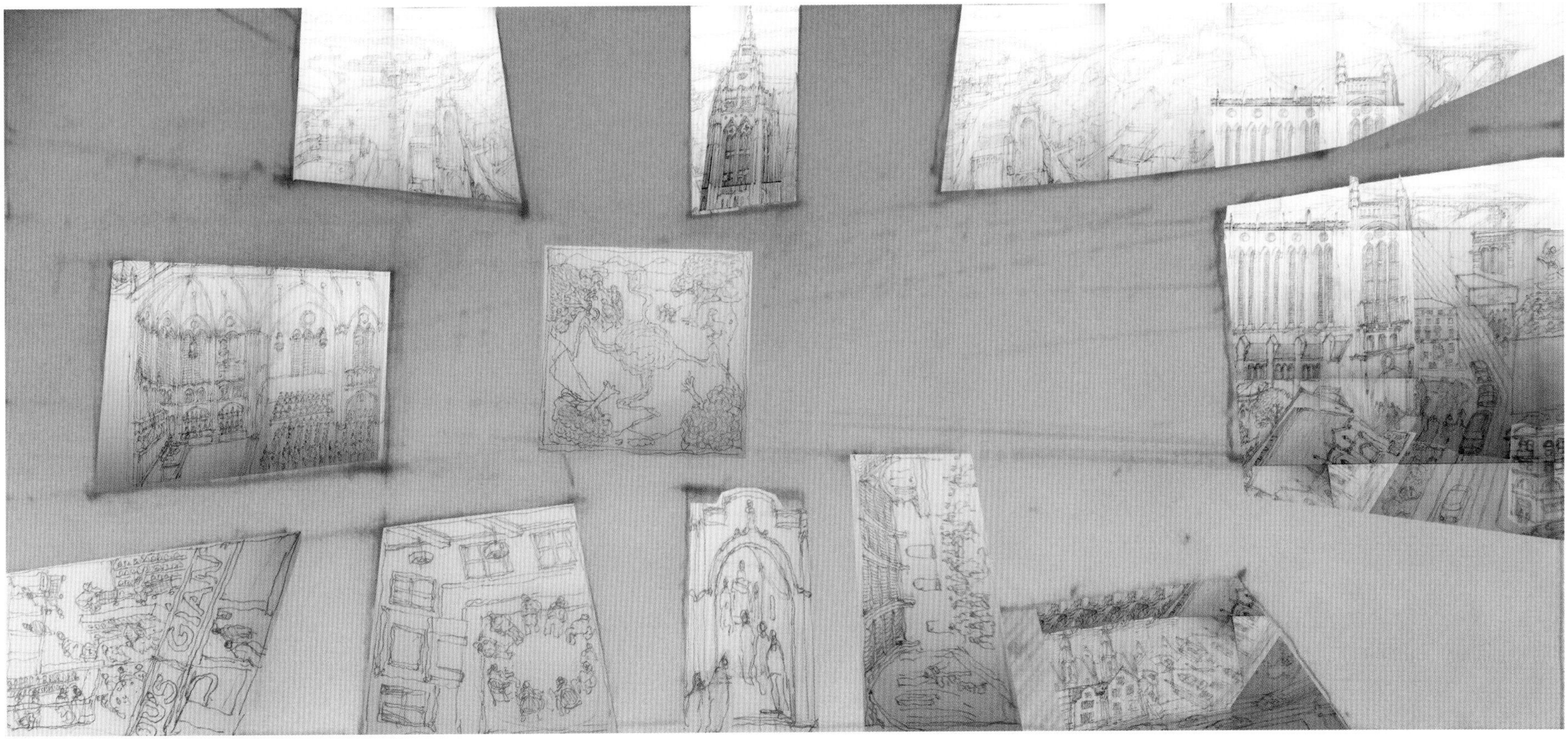

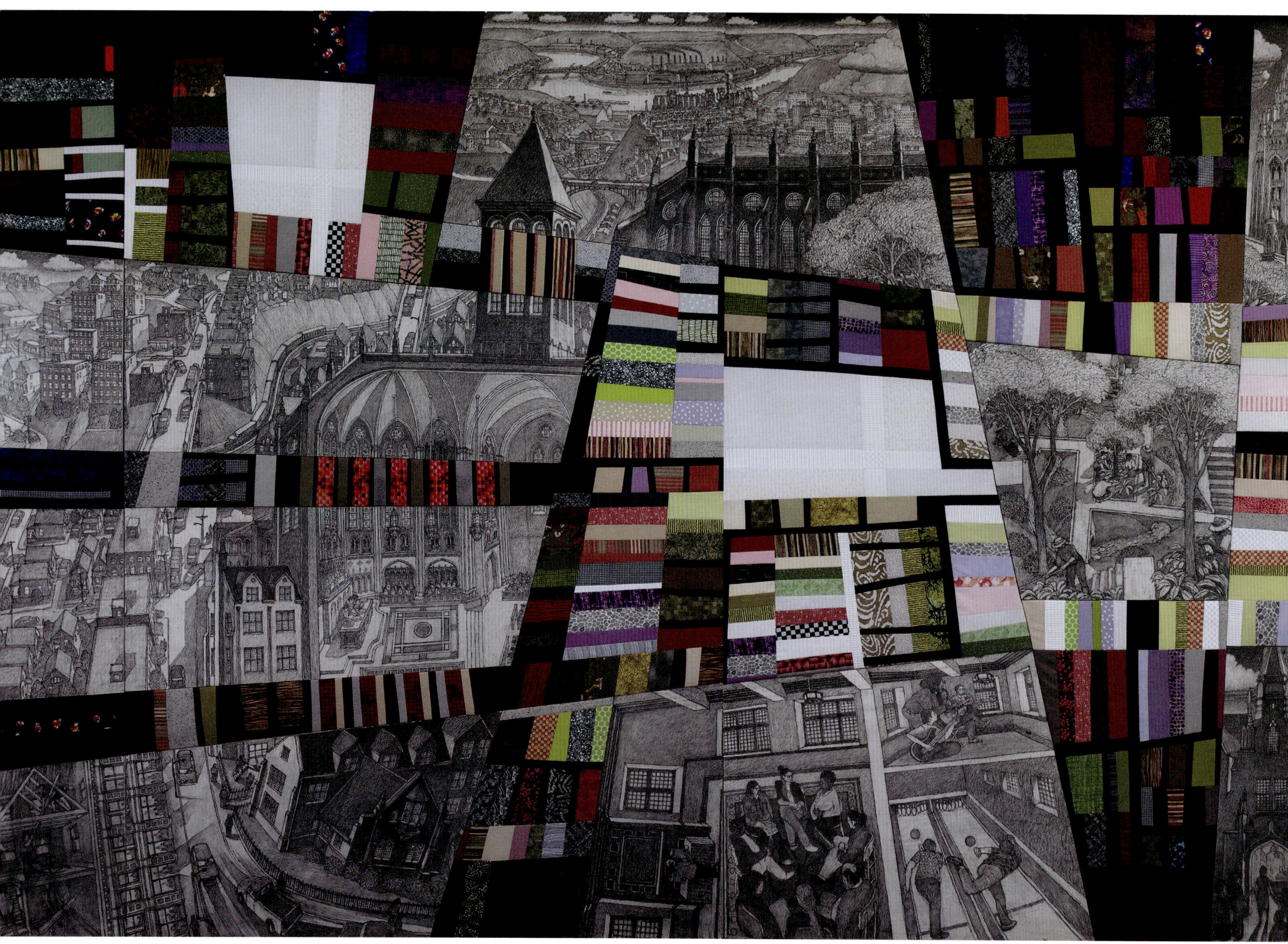

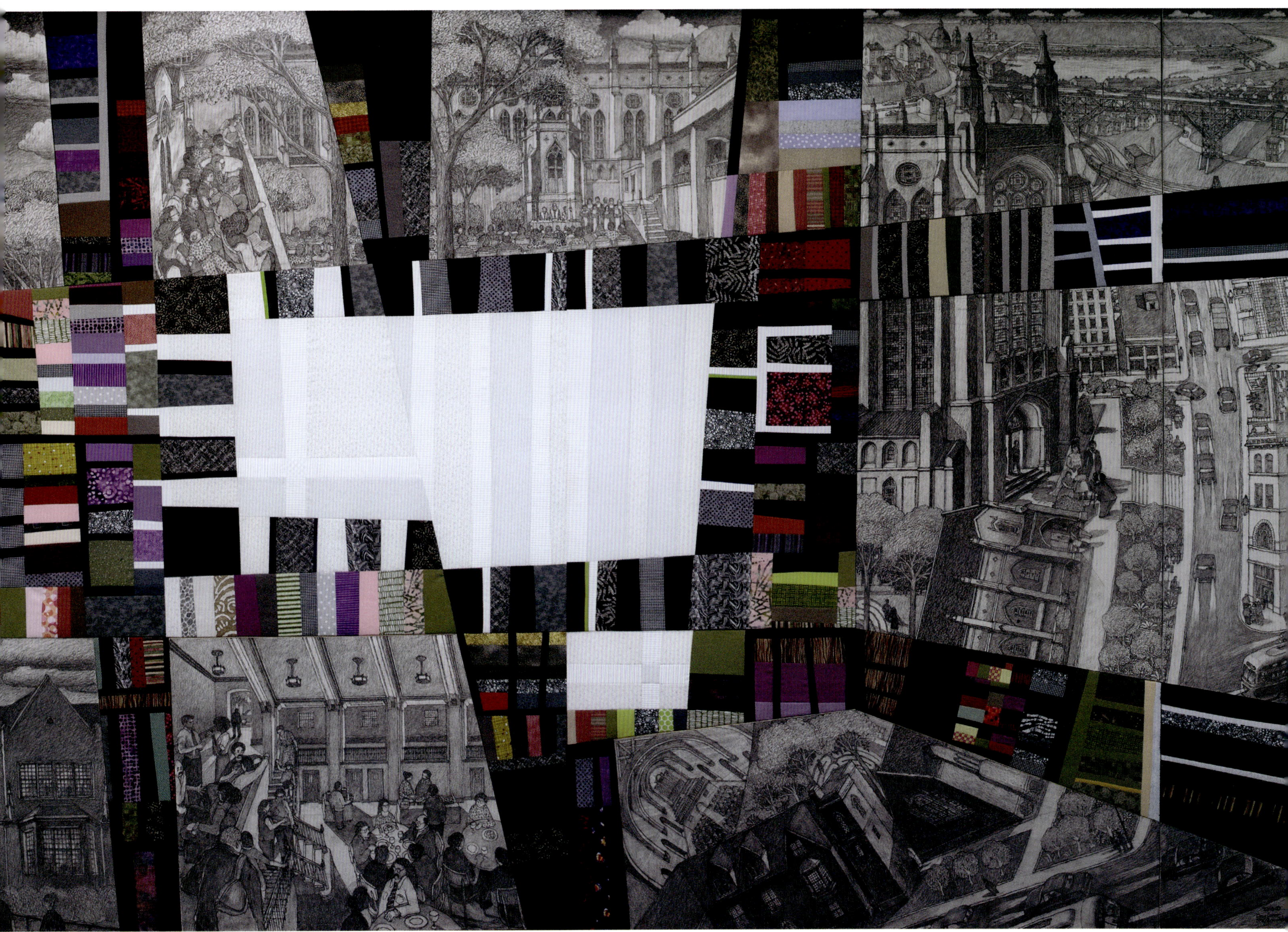

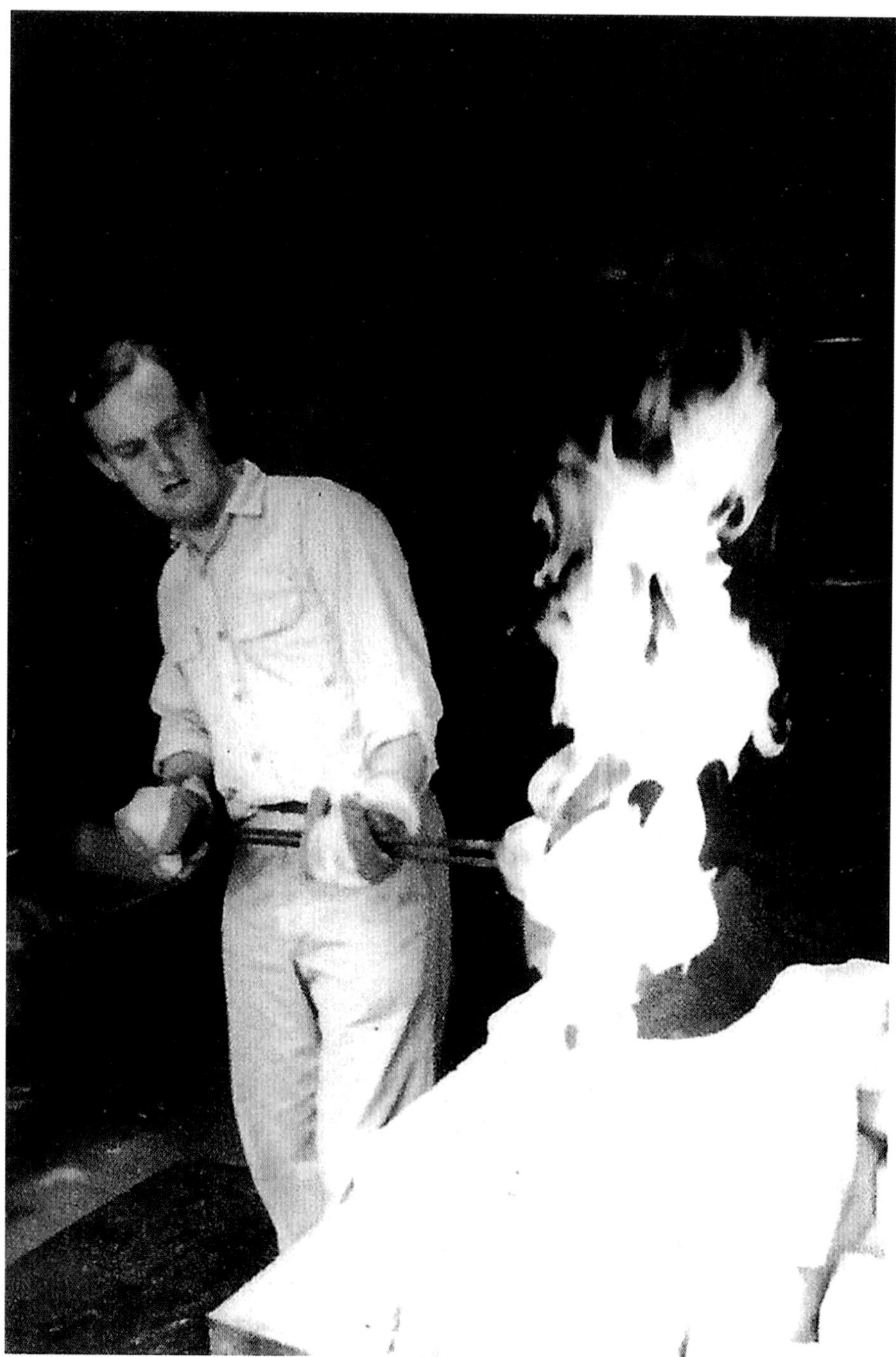

A.1. Kent Bloomer in his studio, circa 1965.

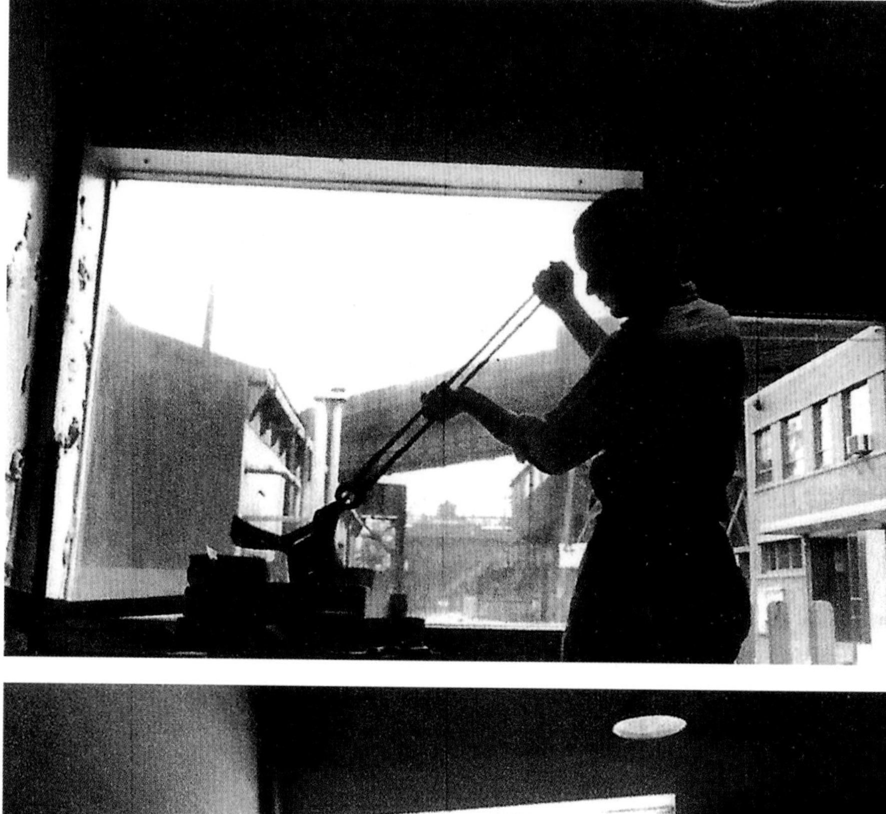

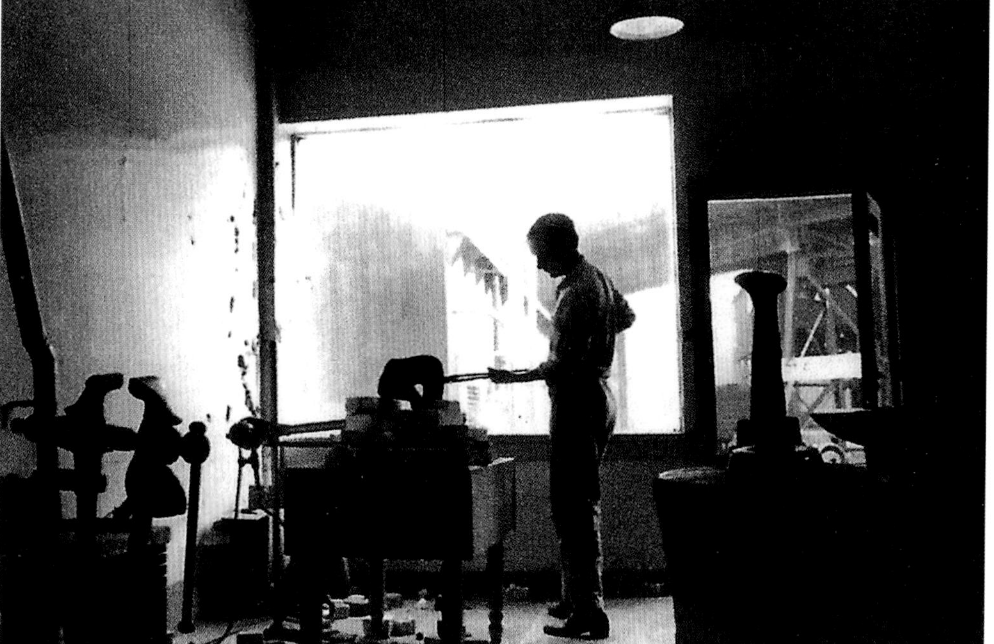

AFTERWORD

By the time you read these few words of mine you will surely have turned the pages of this visually stimulating book. Cooper's drawings don't move; your thoughts do. Every drawing is about movement. You travel through streets, buildings, hills, and valleys. You climb steps, walk along alleys, soar over highways, and cross bridges. You travel through space, time, light, shadow, up, down, inside, outside—very often all at once. Most of the drawings are of one city—Pittsburgh. Other drawings are of other cities—New York, Seattle, London, Frankfurt. Does it matter? Not at all. Cooper's drawings are really about ourselves. The somewhere of these drawings is you.

My own somewhere is in 1962. I am new from England and I'm at the wheel of the rusty old Dodge that I had rescued from a scrap dealer in Connecticut. I'm booked to give a talk to architecture students at the Carnegie Institute of Technology in Pittsburgh, and I'm coming to the city for the first time. It is late in the afternoon and dusk is settling in. I have left the turnpike and I have followed the Penn Lincoln Parkway as it weaves between gentle hills before entering a long twilit tunnel, and I have country music twanging softly on the car radio.

Emerging from the tunnel was like an explosion. Wham! Ahead was a huge steel mill with flames leaping into an orange blanket of smoke overhead. At first the parkway seemed to aim straight into the flaming stacks of the blast furnace. But then it veered like a python around a steep hillside with small houses and flights of steps and a broad silent river the color of lead. All in a matter of seconds.

Why am I concluding Doug's book with this account of entering the city? Because my first memory of Pittsburgh—the city to which Doug has dedicated most of his life—is one of split-second motion, an instant of unfolding drama, of hills, tunnel, flames, chimneys, river, clouds, small houses clinging to steep hillsides, terraces, steps, river—behind the wheel of an old car. If you asked me to draw it—how could I draw motion? I can't—but Cooper can. I'm reminded of Paul Klee's description of drawing as going for a walk with a line. How about in an old rattletrap car at fifty miles an hour?

The morning after my lecture I am in the School of Architecture, in Kent Bloomer's studio for first-year students. The room is full of young men and women, and huge empty cardboard boxes, and it's loud with nervous uncertainty and laughter. Kent plunges me into the problem he has set. Demonstrate inside and outside; enclosure and openness; static and motion; simultaneous and sequence—all in a single drawing! He is young, excitable, voluble. He isn't an architect; he's a sculptor. On an anvil he hammers red-hot sheets of metal into curvilinear shapes and hollows. When he revolves his sculptures on a turntable, they become continuously flowing movement in light and shadow, space and time, inside and outside. Excitement reigns. I'm telling you this because Cooper went through that first year of study. In a way he seems to have never left it.

Odd, isn't it, how our lives play out? My lecture meant something to Kent because I'd described movement in urban and architectural spaces. I'd showed slides of 1930s buildings by Le Corbusier and Mies van der Rohe alongside constructivist sculptures by Naum Gabo and Antoine Pevsner. Outside, inside, light, shadow, movement through. Let's go, Kent said. I'll drive you through constructivist spaces!

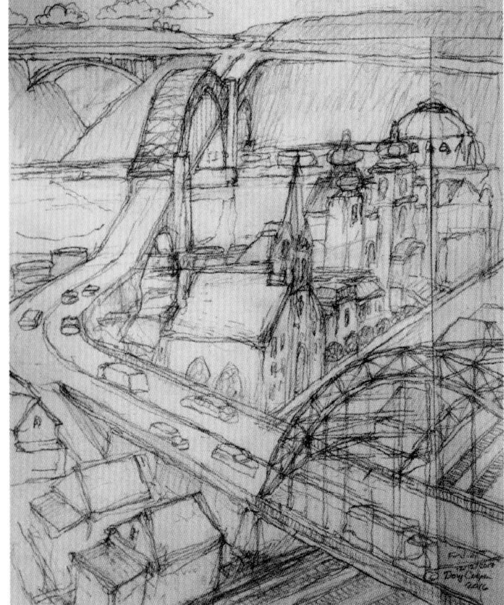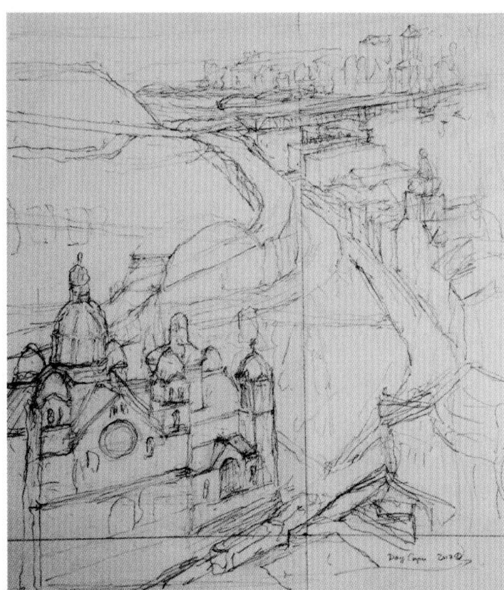

A.2 (*above left*). Sketch, *Sacred Places of the Bottoms*, Doug Cooper, 2018. Pencil on paper, 13 × 10 inches. Collection of David Lewis and Judi Tener.

A.3 (*above right*). Sketch, *City of God*, Doug Cooper, 2018. Pencil on paper, 13 × 12 inches. Collection of David Lewis and Judi Tener.

He put me in the front seat of a jeep and we rattled up and down urban streets and through neighborhoods and around hills and across steel bridges over rivers and into tunnels and along narrow hillside lanes at perilous angles, and we came to a stop at the South Side gates of the vast Jones & Laughlin blast furnace, and through the gates we could see the soaring black interior of the mill and the intense red glow of molten steel, and across the street was Kent's studio, a little narrow room with a firebox worked with a foot pedal and an anvil and hammers (fig. A.1). The steelworkers loved Kent. He was, as the saying goes, something else. In the tavern two doors from Kent's studio I experienced for the first time "a shot and an iron"—bourbon and Iron City beer—while workers in hard hats and big boots clamored around Kent.

My lecture must also have appealed to the faculty at the architecture school too. I was urged to return and to teach urban design—and now, half a century later, I am still in Pittsburgh. From that first day with Kent the city has fascinated me. Its topography had been formed by centuries of erosion. Millions of years of streams and rivers had carved a landscape of shale into hilltops and valleys. The city's three arterial rivers, the Allegheny, the Monongahela, and the Ohio, became lined with railroad lines, steel mills, and related industries, responding to cheap coal and coke. Small towns with narrow streets and cheap frame houses grew up around the industries and became magnets for immigrants—German, Polish, Irish, Italian, Greek, Serbian, African American—who in turn generated local cultures, schools, churches and shopping streets. More affluent neighborhoods were built on the hilltops to escape the pollution. They too had their own churches, synagogues, schools, and shopping streets. The result is a city that is an aggregation of small towns and neighborhoods—each with its own physical, racial, and cultural identity, and each responding to a maverick topography. And this is the city to which Doug has devoted his cultural and artistic life.

Within my first few months in Pittsburgh I opened an office in the attic of an old house. dedicated to keeping the traditions of urban neighborhoods alive—a practice that continues to this day. We occupied an attic in an old house and we employed young architects. One of these was—you've guessed it—Douglas Cooper. Fast forward. A couple of months ago Doug invited me to accompany him to the studio he works in now. He drove me up and down and this way and that through a variety of Pittsburgh neighborhoods until we parked on a side street in what seemed like a cluster of old buildings on a hilltop, and we walked along a narrow sidewalk to a flight of broad stone steps and through a huge front door and into a hallway with another tall flight of steps, and up and up we climbed until at the top we reached his studio room. Another attic! Some things never change.

I have here in my workroom two of Doug's pencil sketches that I acquired that day to share with my wife, Judi (figs. A.2, A.3). Both could have been drawn from the windows of that high-up studio. The smaller drawing looks down on a four-lane highway and on the roofs of automobiles swinging through a riverfront town and across a river that enters a ravine through a faraway hill. Pencil lines nervously explore—as an inquisitive sparrow might—the triangular roofs and church spires of the town, and the intricate girders of two bridges, one crossing railroads and the other crossing the river. The larger drawing also looks down, this time on a multidomed church, possibly Russian, or maybe Serbian, around which a highway arcs across a bridge over a broad river to a highway and town on the other side.

These drawings are not descriptive. Like so many of the drawings in this book they are explorations. They tell us about a mind exploring and experiencing actual cities, not only visually but intellectually too. They are at once firm—yet tentative and exploratory. Through Doug's mind we explore our own. This is important because this sensitive, intelligent draftsman is now America's premier muralist. His huge drawings are in many public buildings in European cities and in the United States. They are portraits of the cities and places in which they are located. He invites us to explore streets and places that we recognize, but in ways we've not experienced before. At one level, as I've already said, they are portraits of cities and places we know. But at the most important level they are portraits of ourselves.

In Pittsburgh there are three huge Cooper murals. Two of them are in buildings at Carnegie Mellon University. In these pages Doug has illustrated and described the mural in the student union building, and the only point I would like to add here is that it has a significant ambassadorial role. To students from many countries it illustrates how our city of today continues to evolve from an industrial past into a technological future in which many nations and many cultures play dynamic roles.

Recently Doug and his wife, Stefani Danes, invited Judi and me to see the latest mural they have both made in the new Tepper Building at Carnegie Mellon University. We entered the reception area and walked down a ramp, and there, along a broad corridor, their giant mural soared, with Stefani's bright fabricwork panels, tall and slender, integrated into it and framing its structure. Maybe I'm just being me, but this latest mural was a lot like going home. It reminded me of the way CMU was in the 1960s—an intimate place called Carnegie Institute of Technology, where everyone, it seemed, including its president, knew everyone else by their first name.

How did Doug and Stefani do this? By drawing iconic places and spaces, such as the cupola of Margaret Morrison, or the "cut," and by placing familiar and characteristic activities in them. Here are students rehearsing a play, eating lunch in the commons, and experimenting in labs. And because the campus is a small world—we run across people who are at one level international figures in the arts or in science or in economics, and yet who are, at another level, simply colleagues. Here are Herb Simon and Alan Newell, with the early computer they called artificial intelligence; the origin of those pocket computers we all carry around with us and which rule not only our everyday lives but the lives of our children.

Today CMU is recognized worldwide as one of the great intellectual hubs of computer research and robotics, and foreign countries send their brightest young men and women to study here. But Doug makes sure that we get glimpses, as though through windows to the past, of the old Andrew Carnegie steel mill stacks and the smoke and the pollution of air and rivers, and the immigrant neighborhoods clinging to the hillsides, and that we remember the immigrant parents from many countries melding their ethnic cultures into the contemporary city.

As I've said, Stefani's fabricwork columns give the mural its structure. Passengers in her vividly colored elevators are invited to access, floor by floor, the rich inventory of activities in the panels Doug has drawn. Doug brought me a chair. Sitting there, listening to both of them describe the activities of each panel, my memory took me back to a train ride through Tuscany half a century ago. By mistake I had boarded a local train. It stopped at every town and village as it clanked around the Tuscan hills. The train's conductor, seeing me alone and staring out of the window, sensed that I was a foreigner. He sat down next to me and described with pride not only the history of every church in every village but the altars and frescos and doorways too, and he described the vineyards and the cemeteries with a sense of the past being today and a sense of complexity that was also unity.

I am reminded of Doug's description in these pages of Lorenzetti's fourteenth-century fresco in Siena in which the inside spaces of the city and the countryside outside its walls are shown simultaneously, telling us of a unity that he wants us to know—all of which takes me back to Doug's first year studio and Kent Bloomer's cardboard boxes. Inside and outside, enclosure and openness, the flow of tradition and the collapse of time—all at once in one drawing.

David Lewis
March 28, 2019

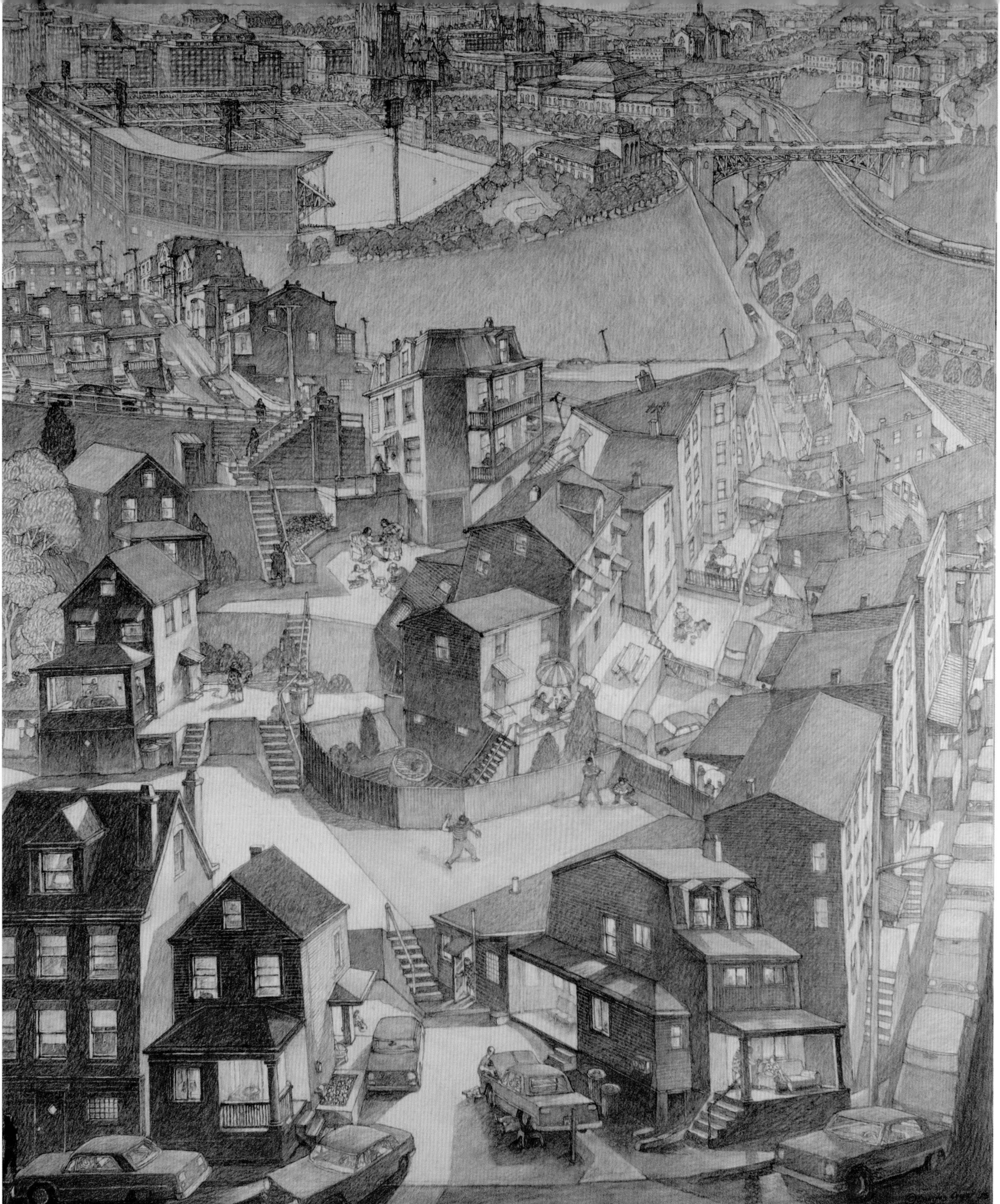

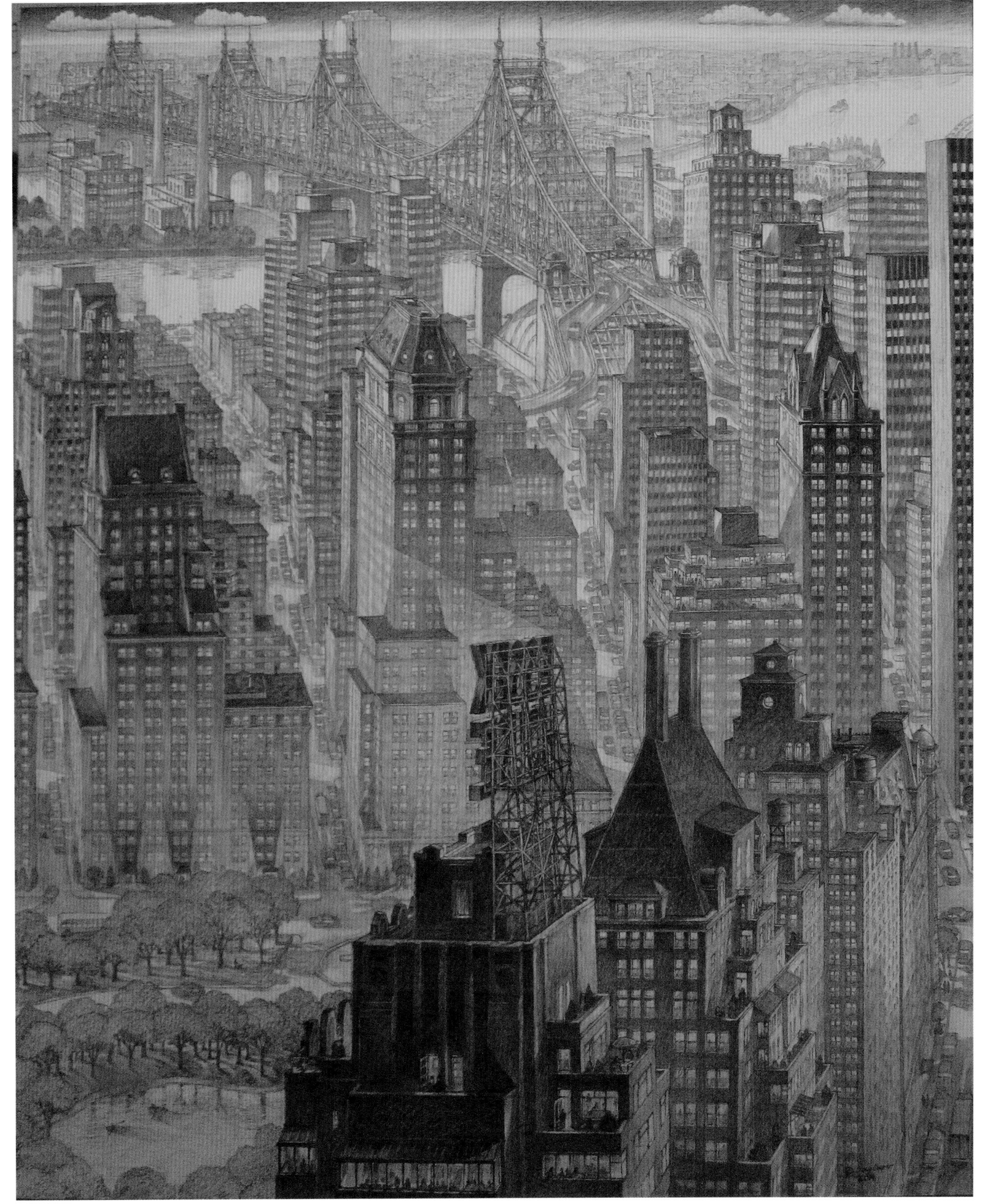

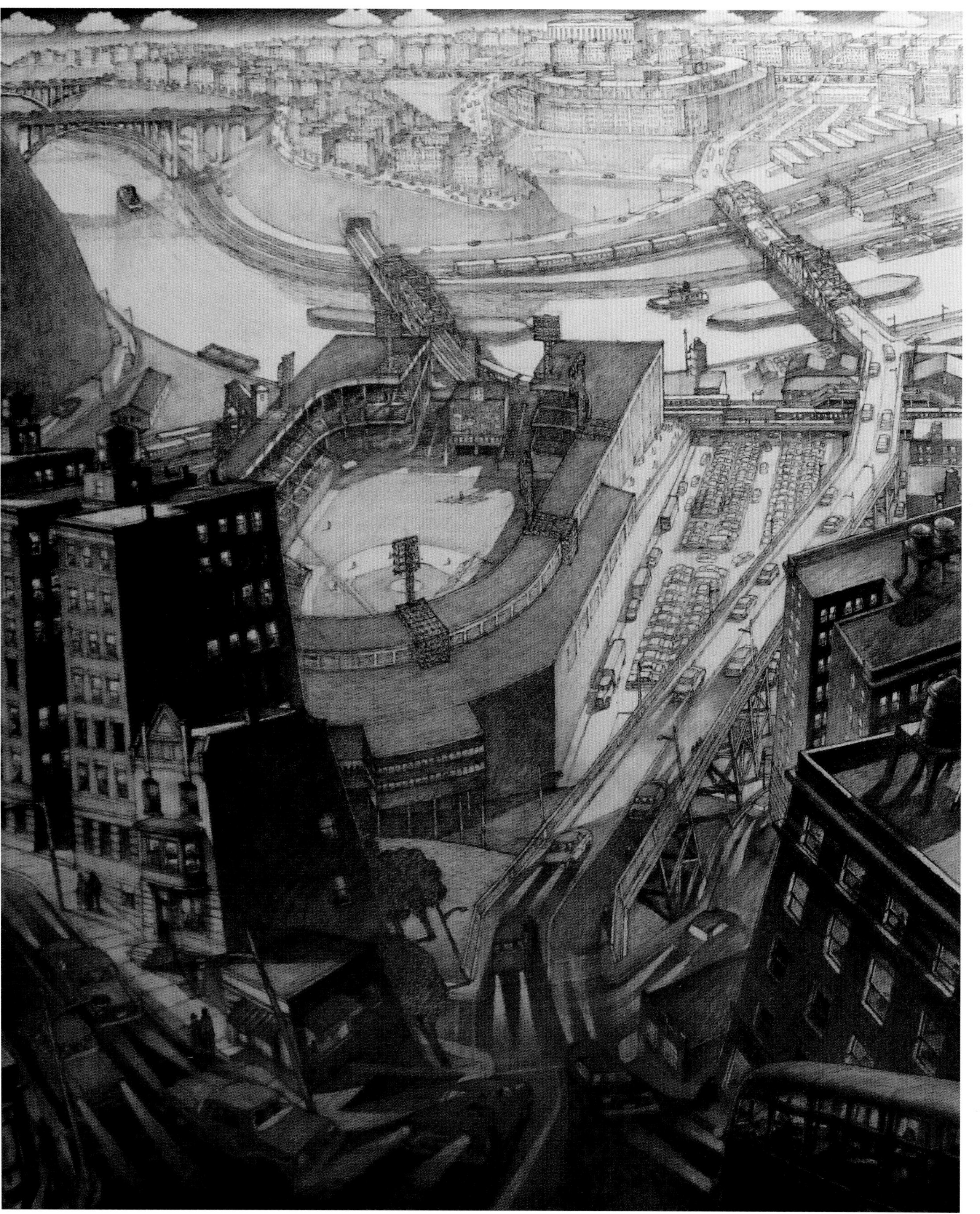

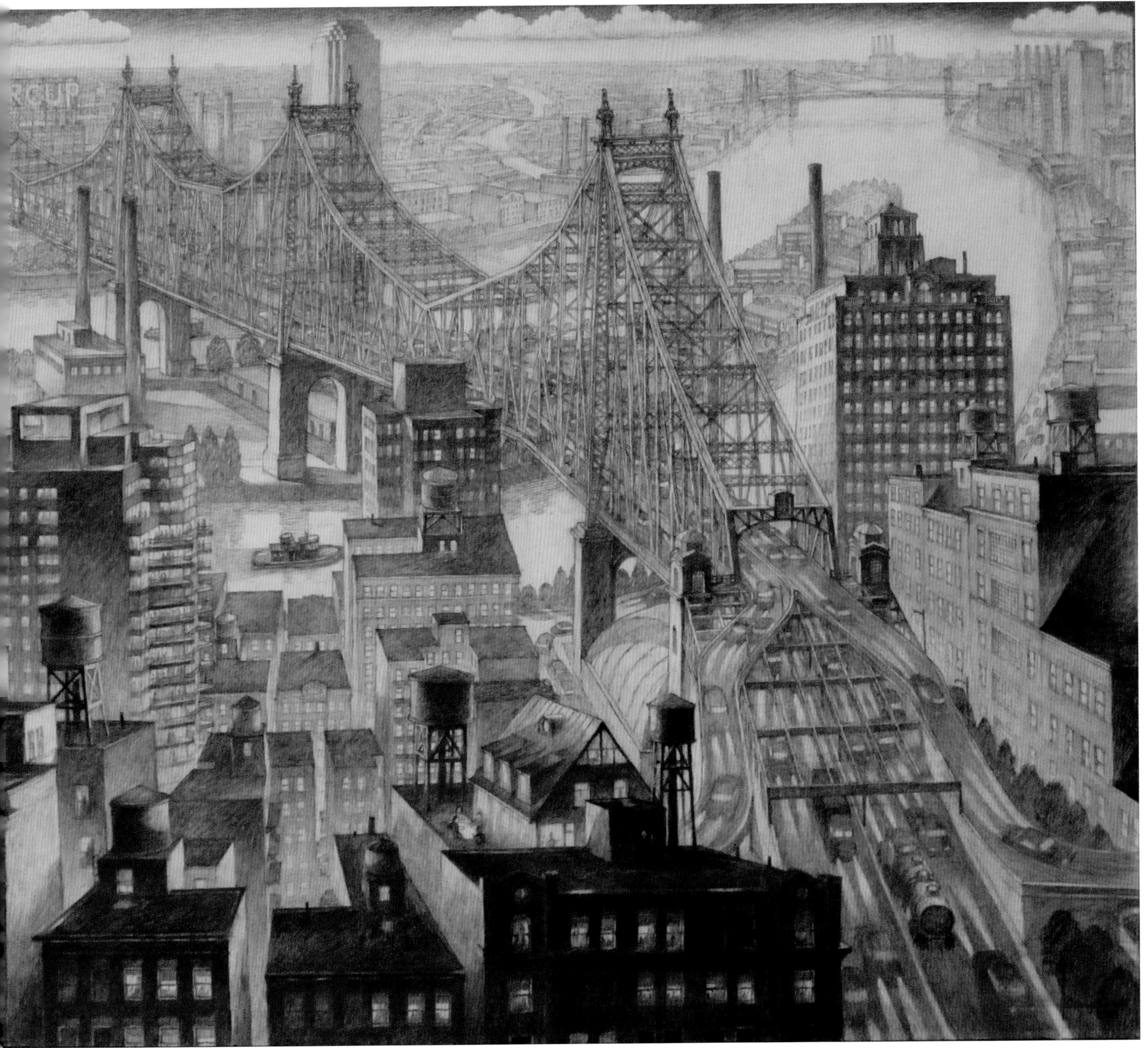

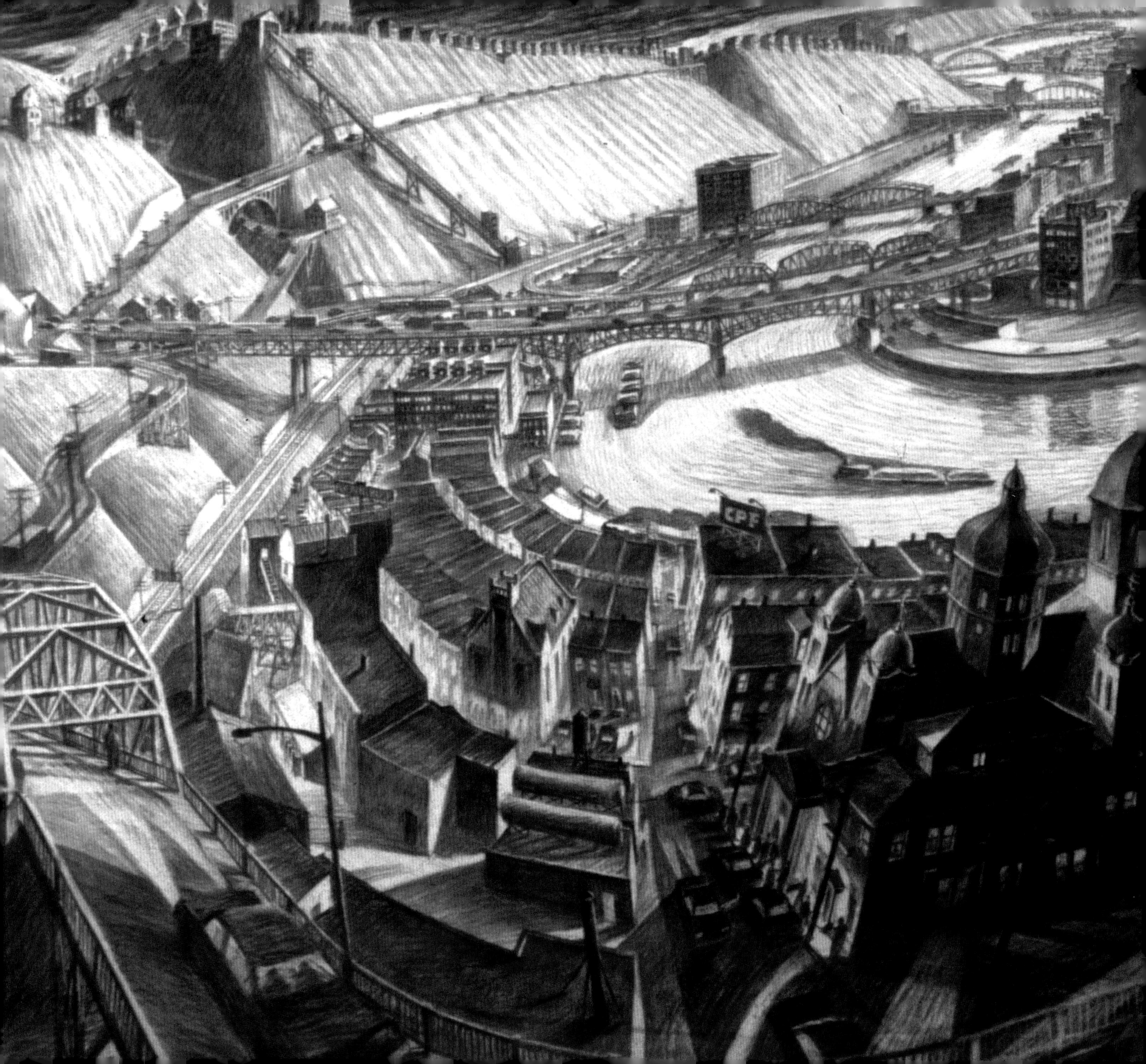
CPR

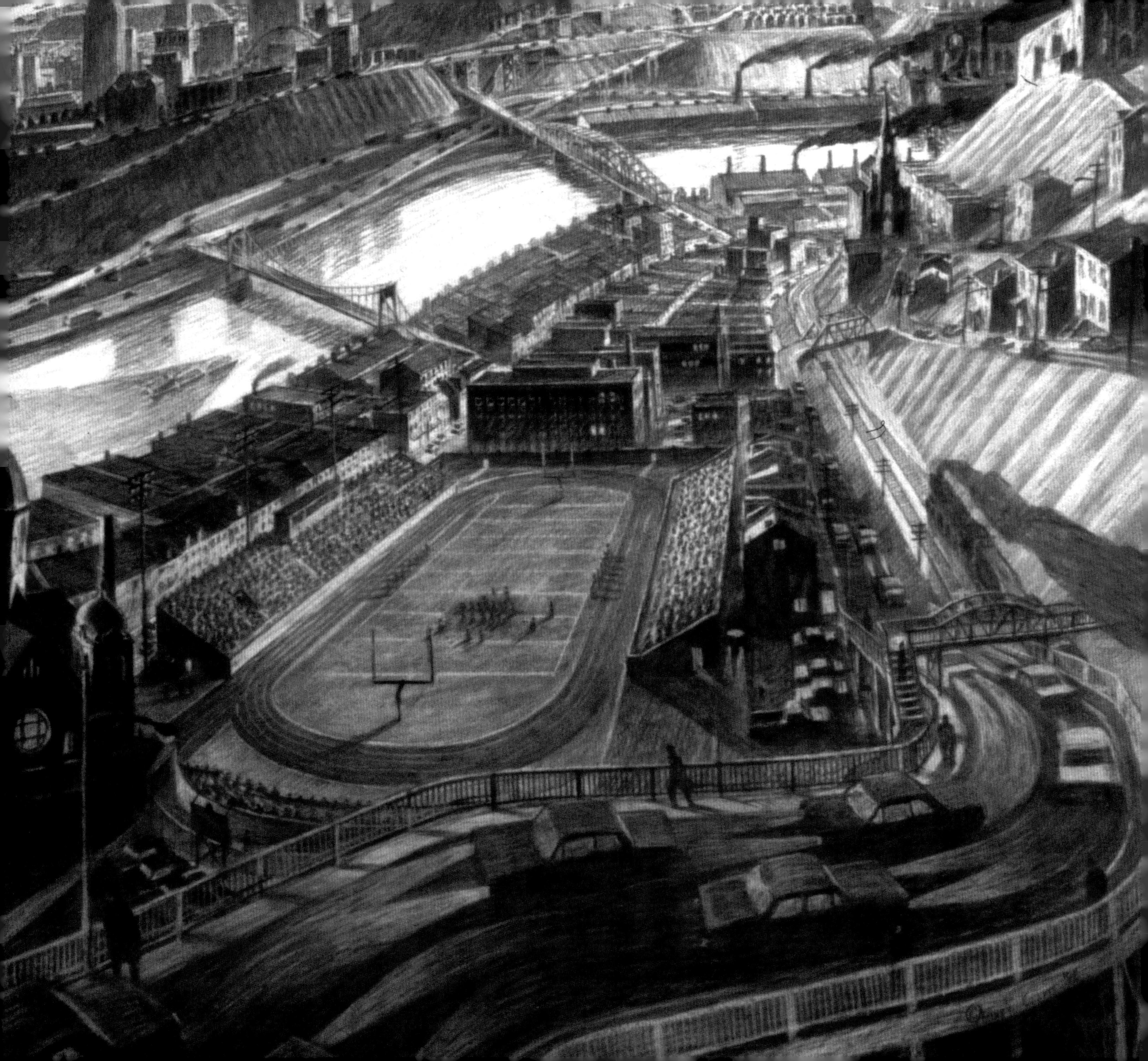

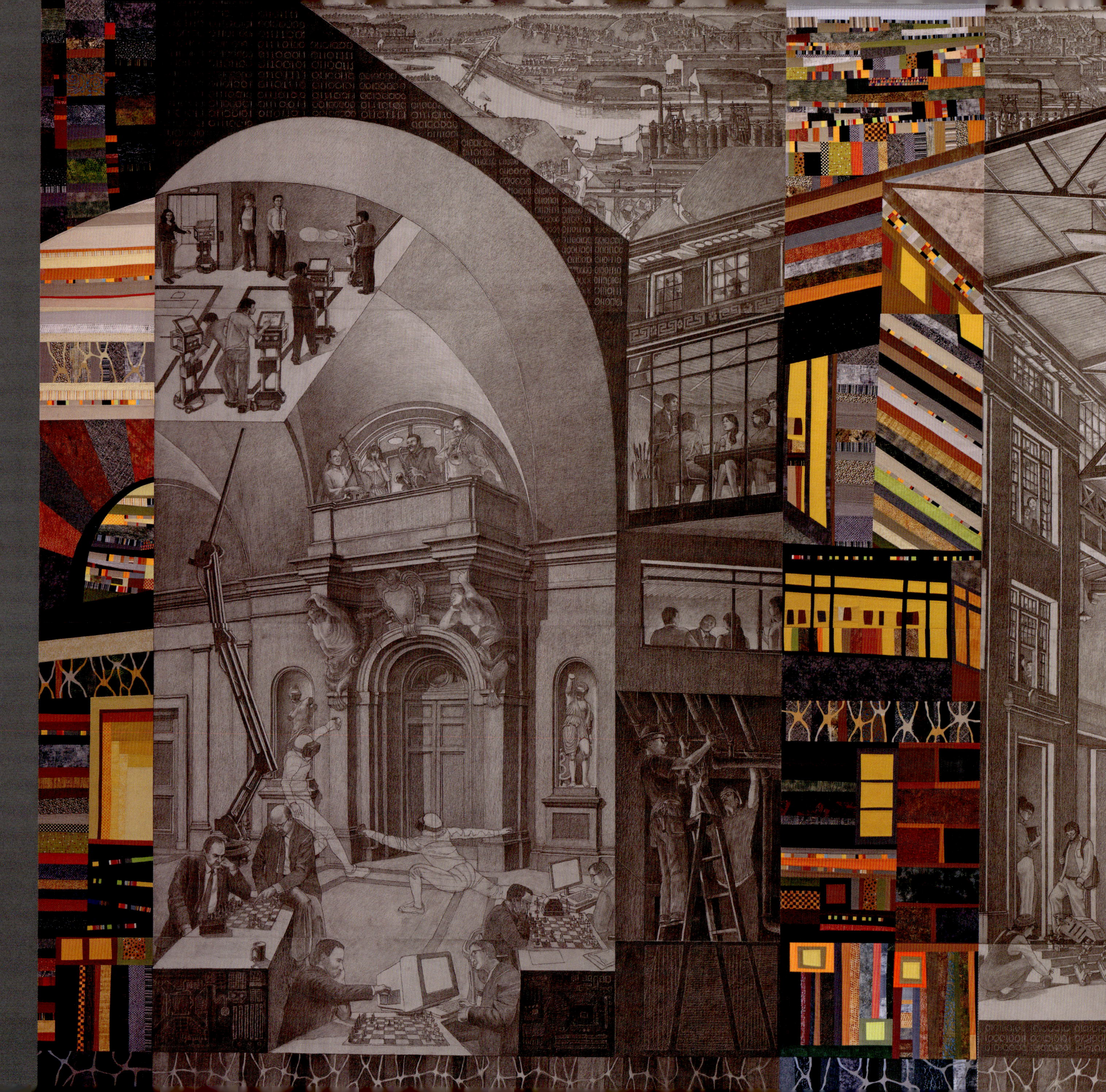

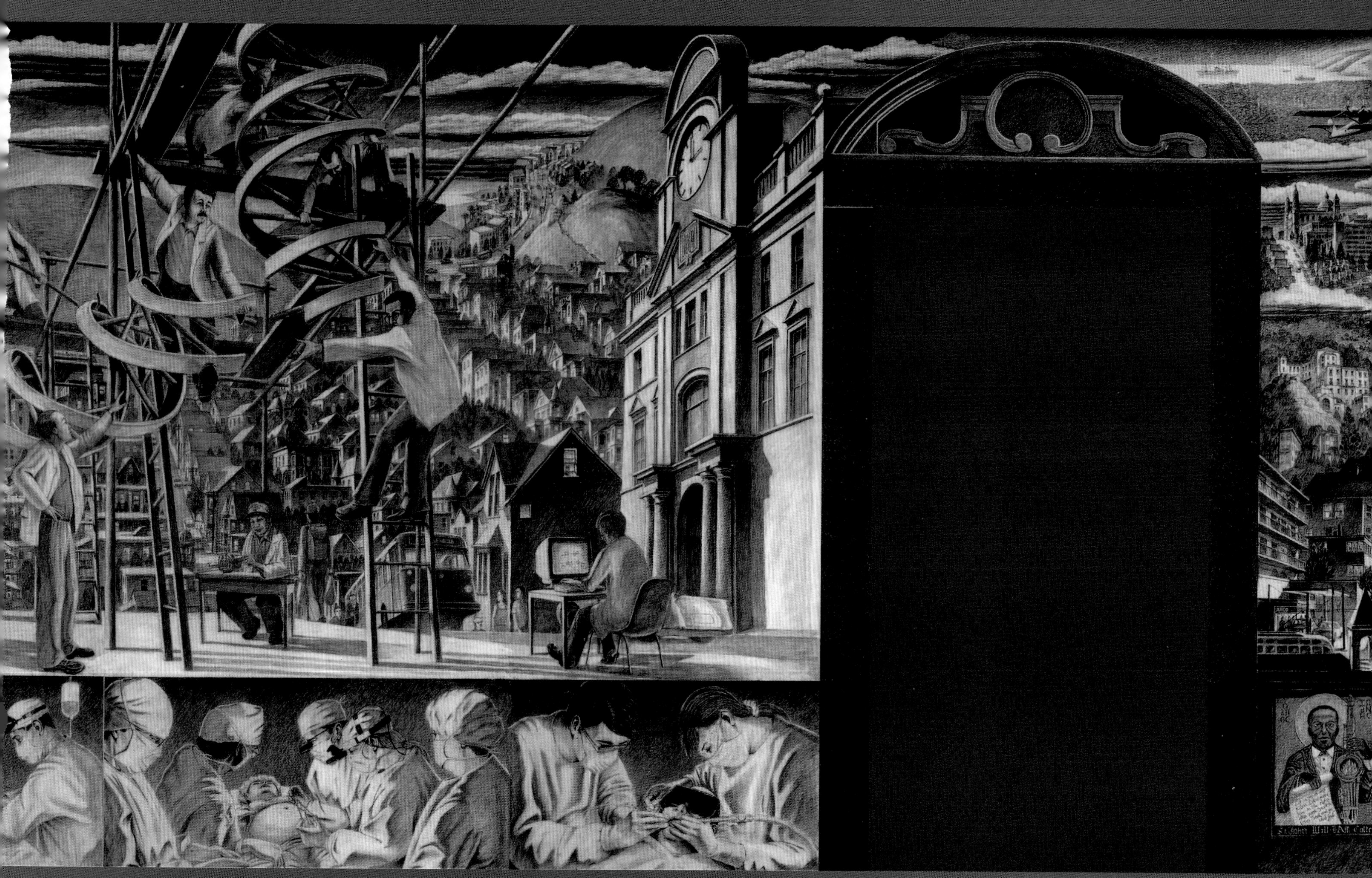

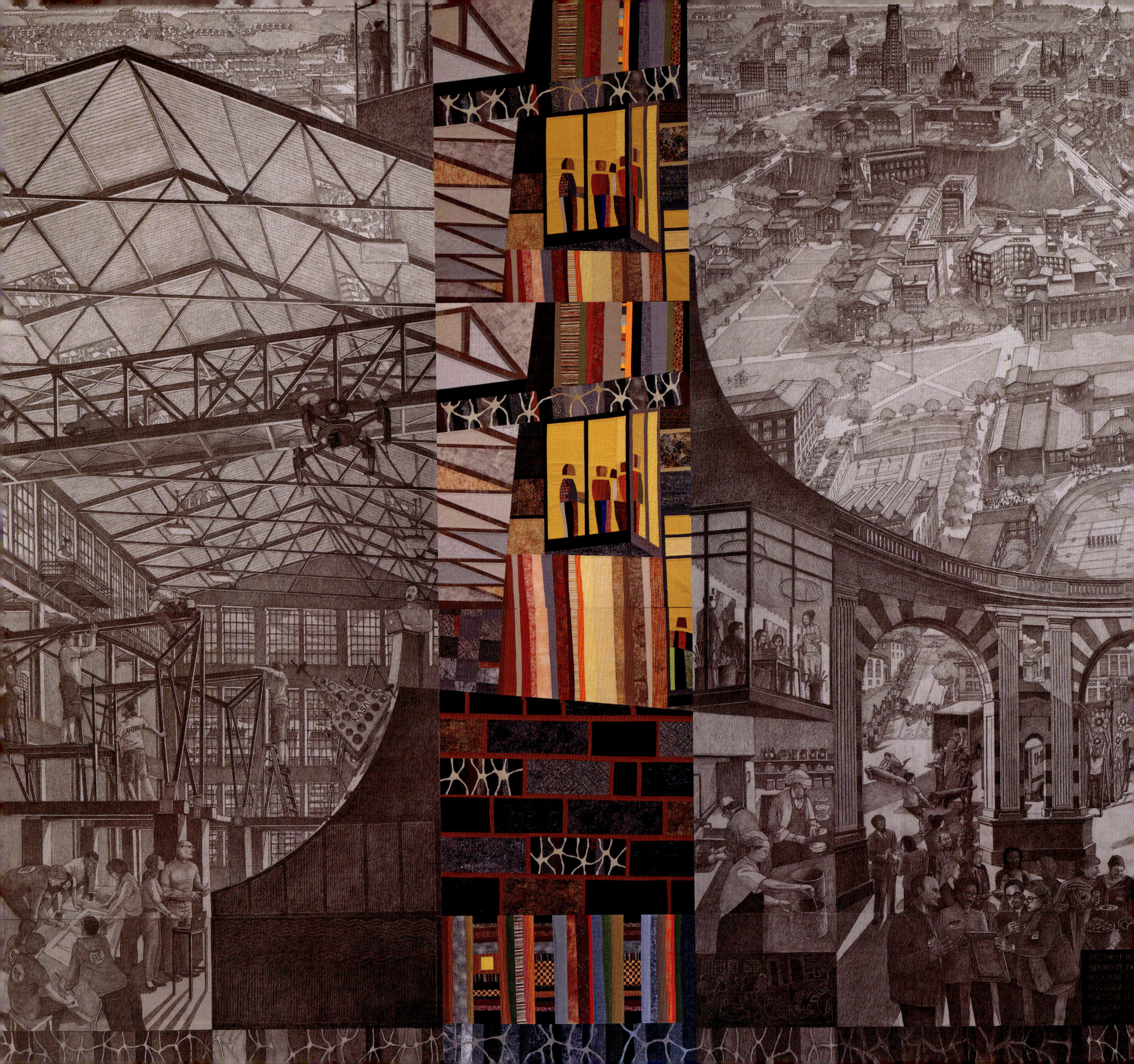

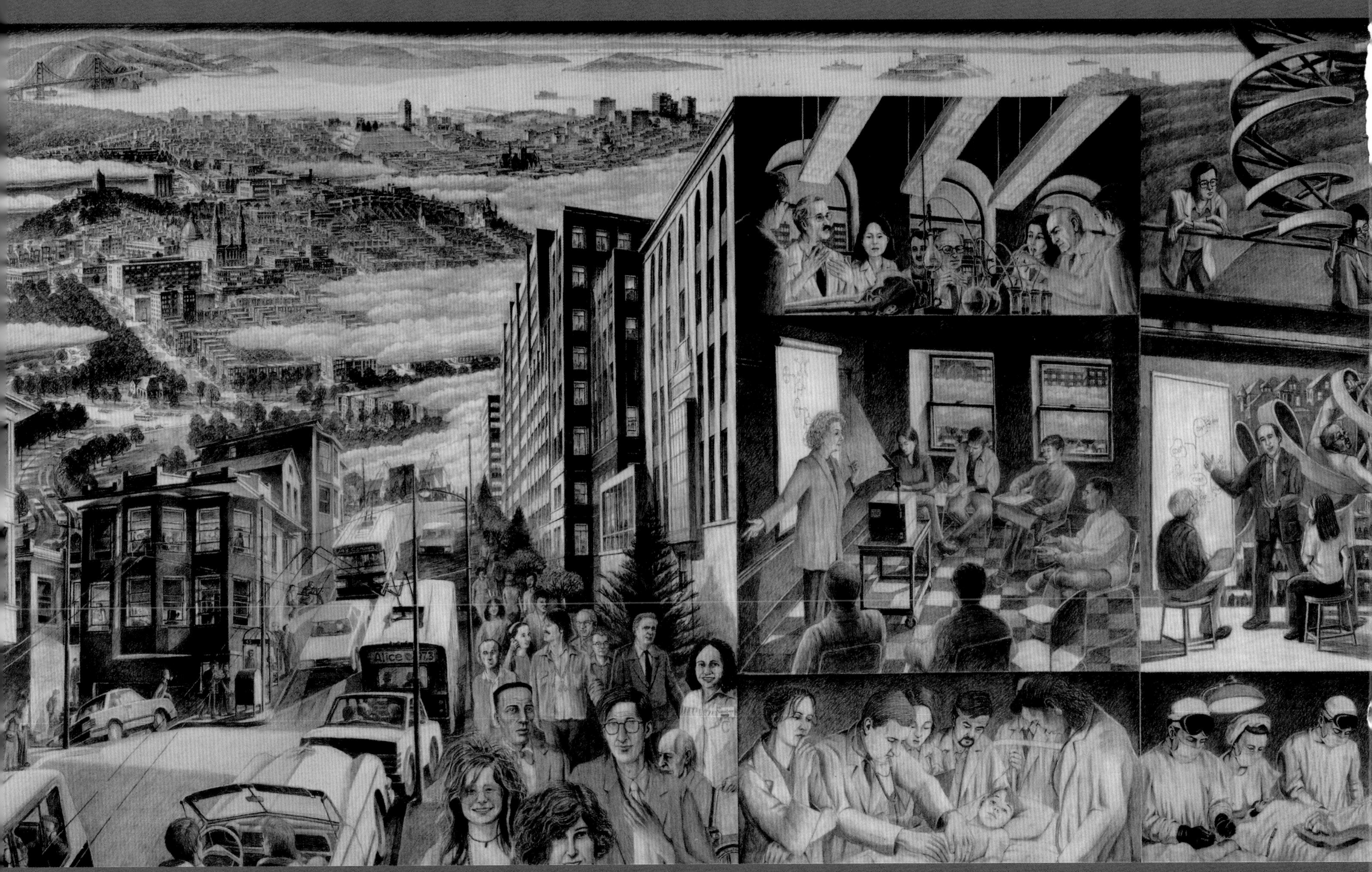

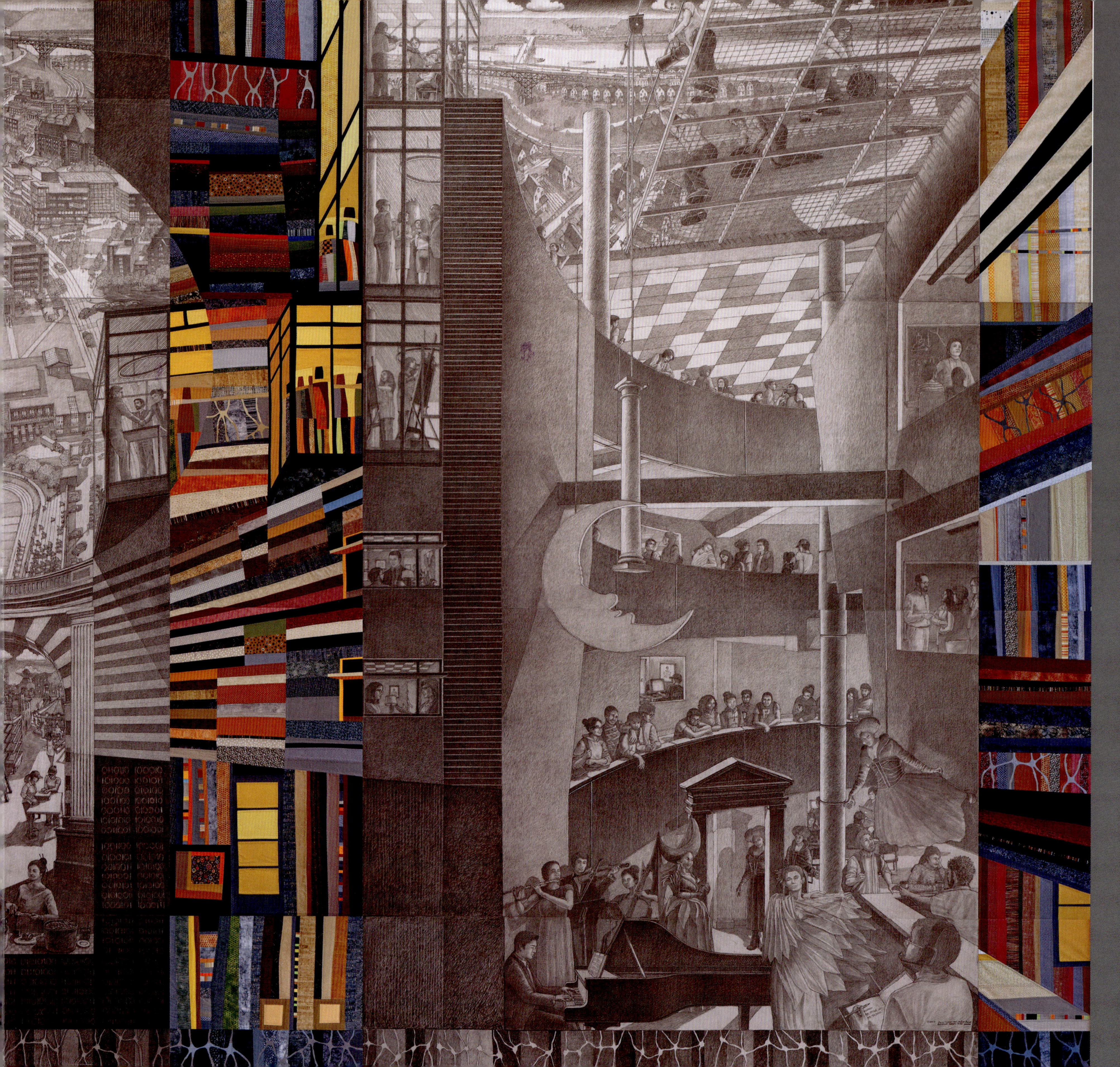

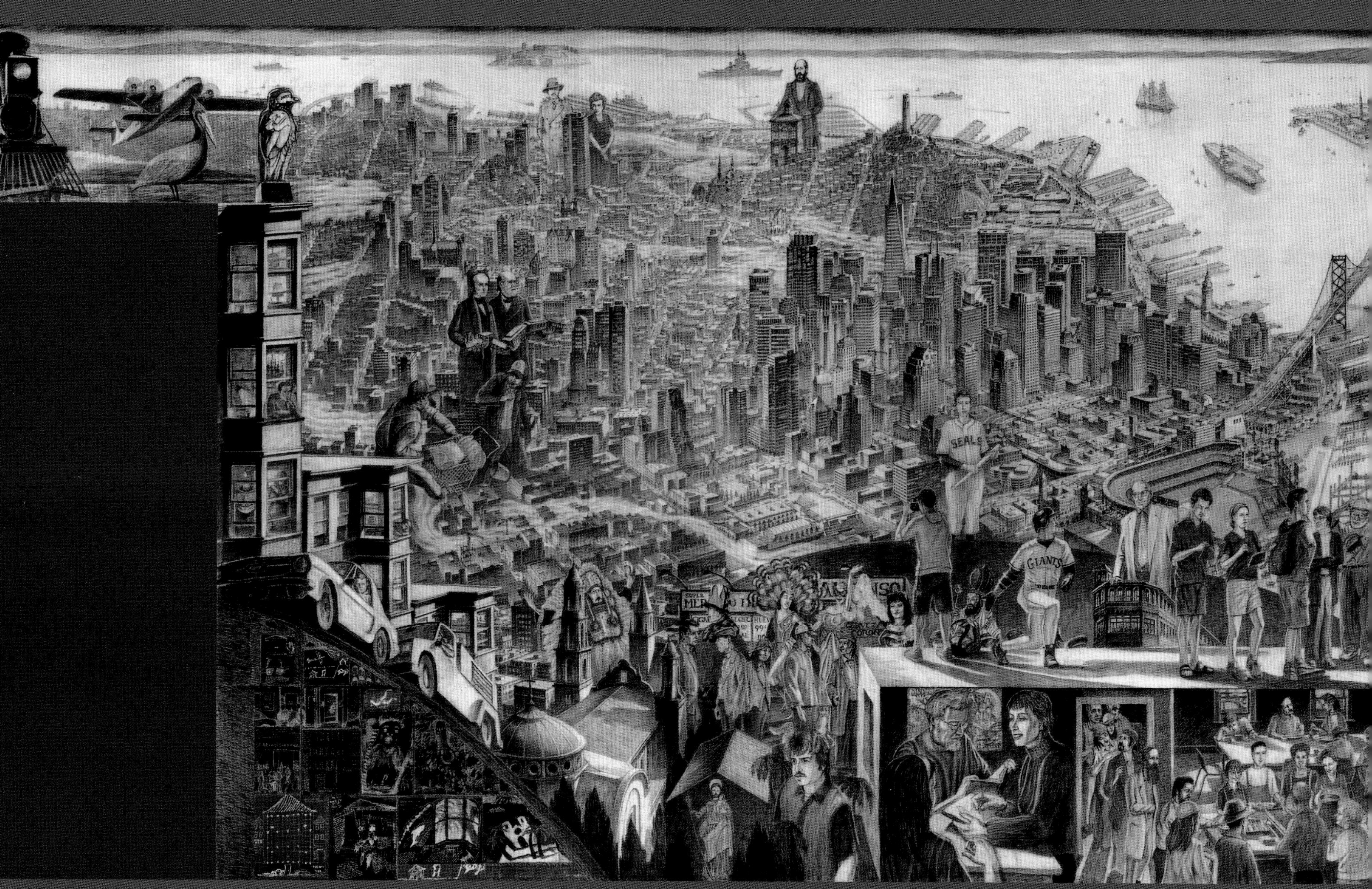
SEALS
GIANTS

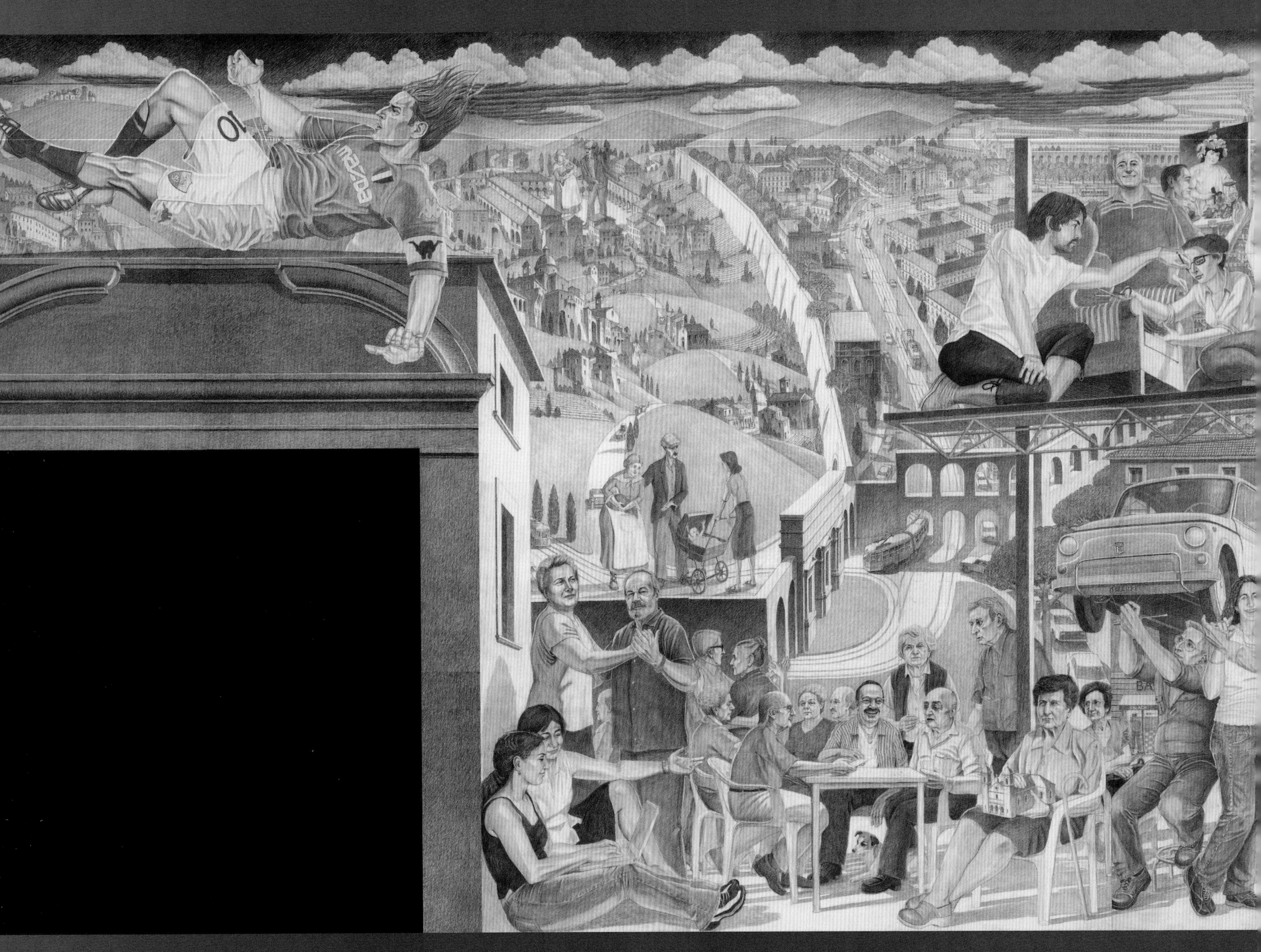

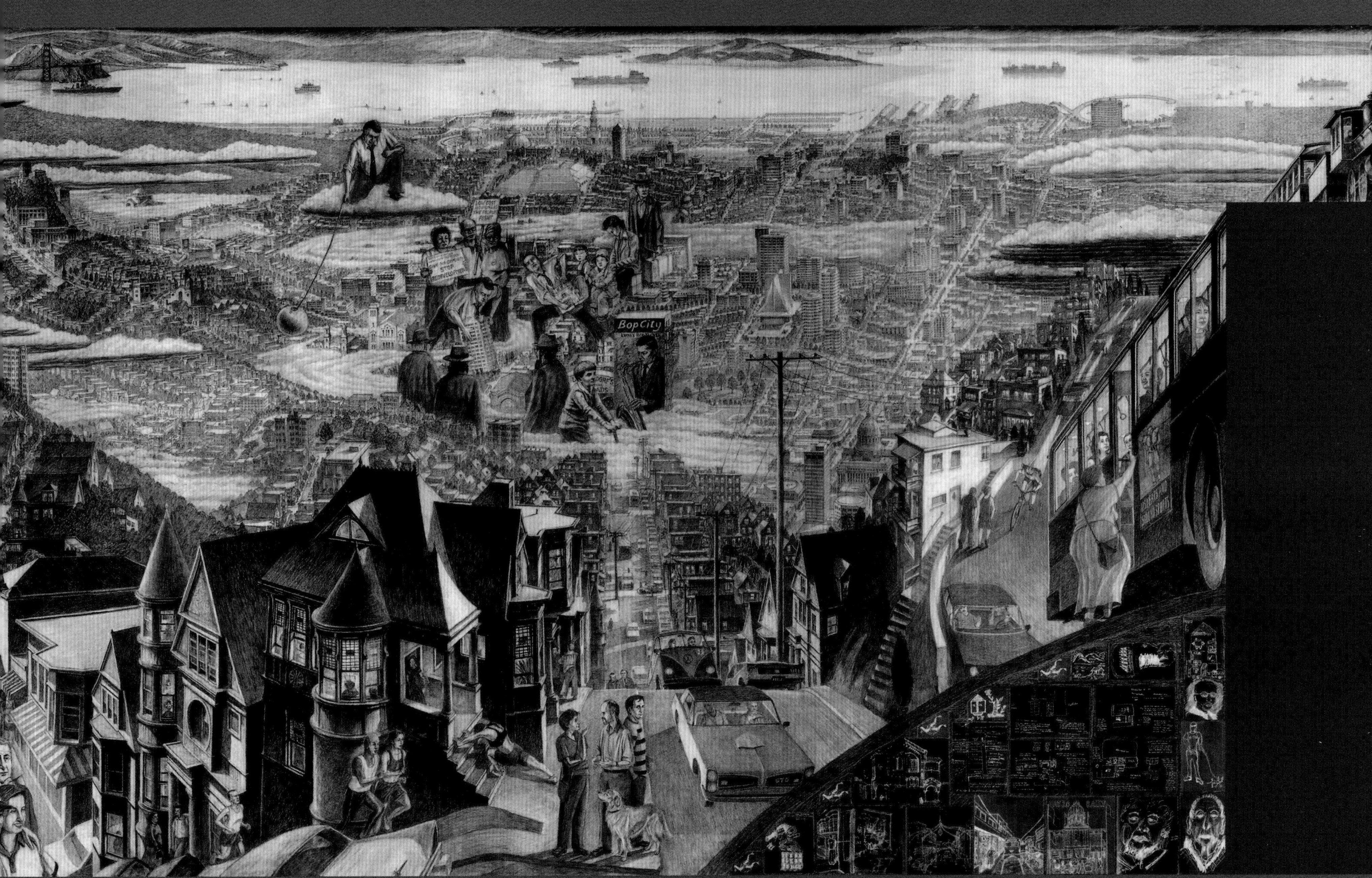
BopCity

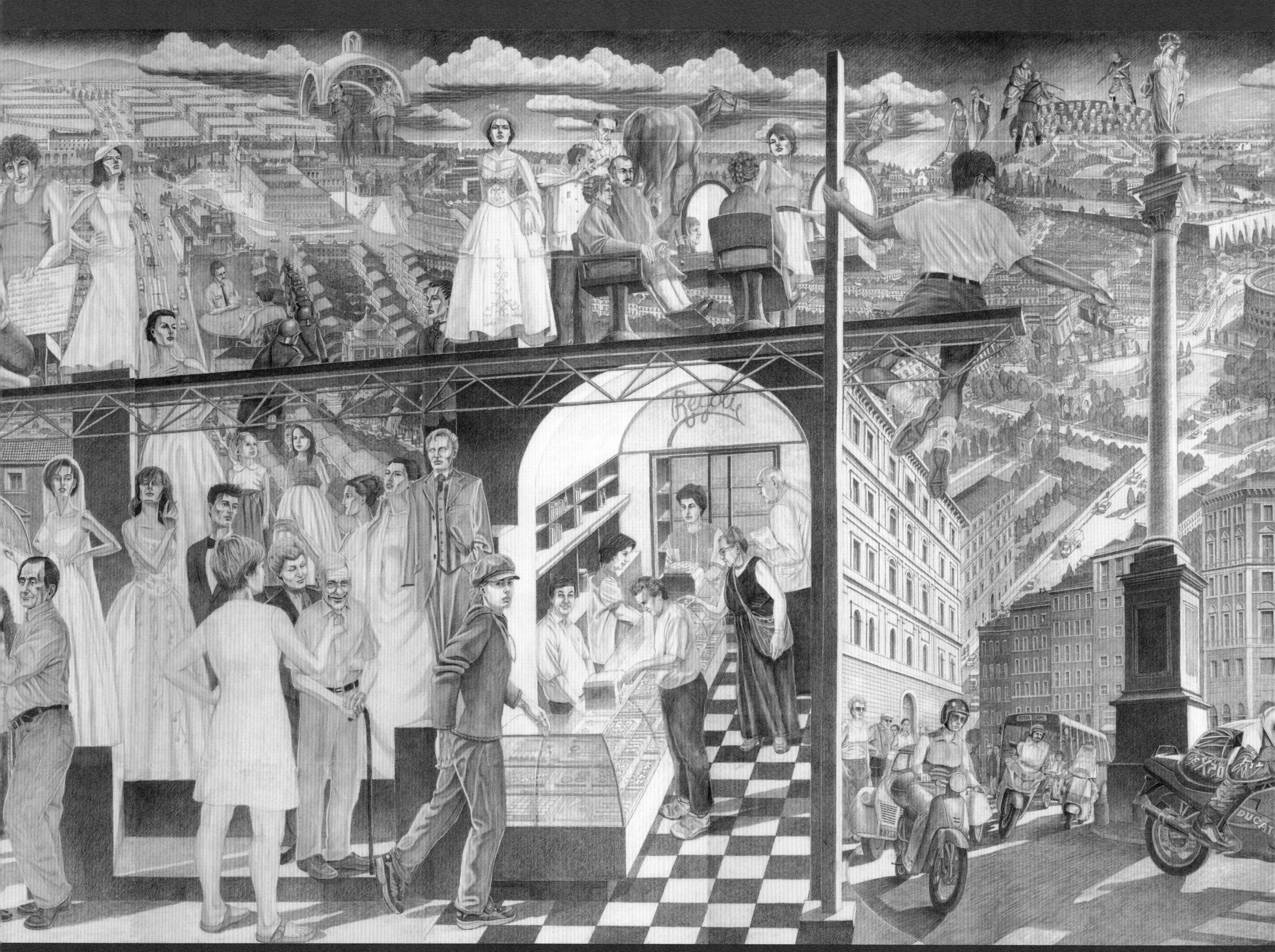

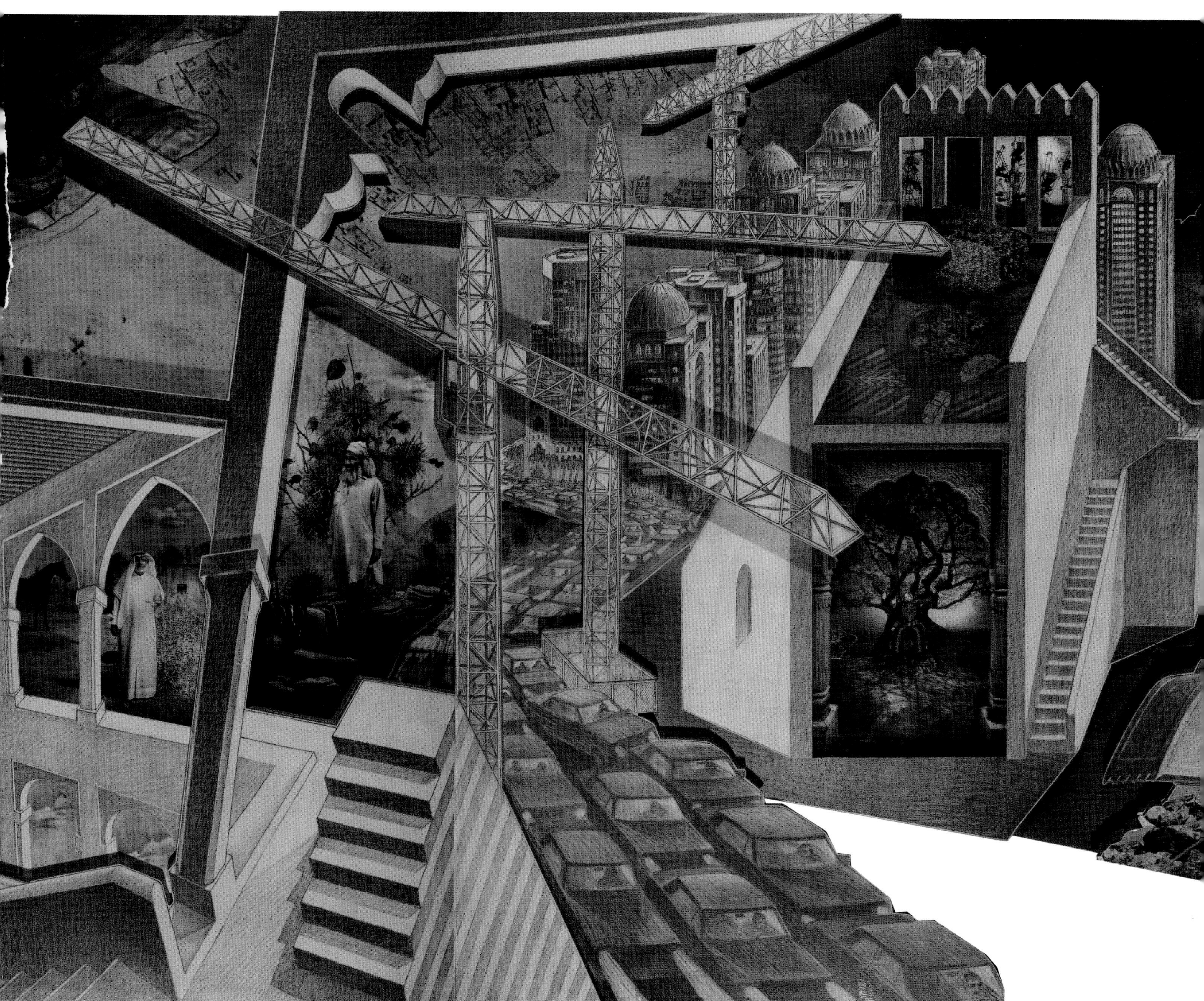

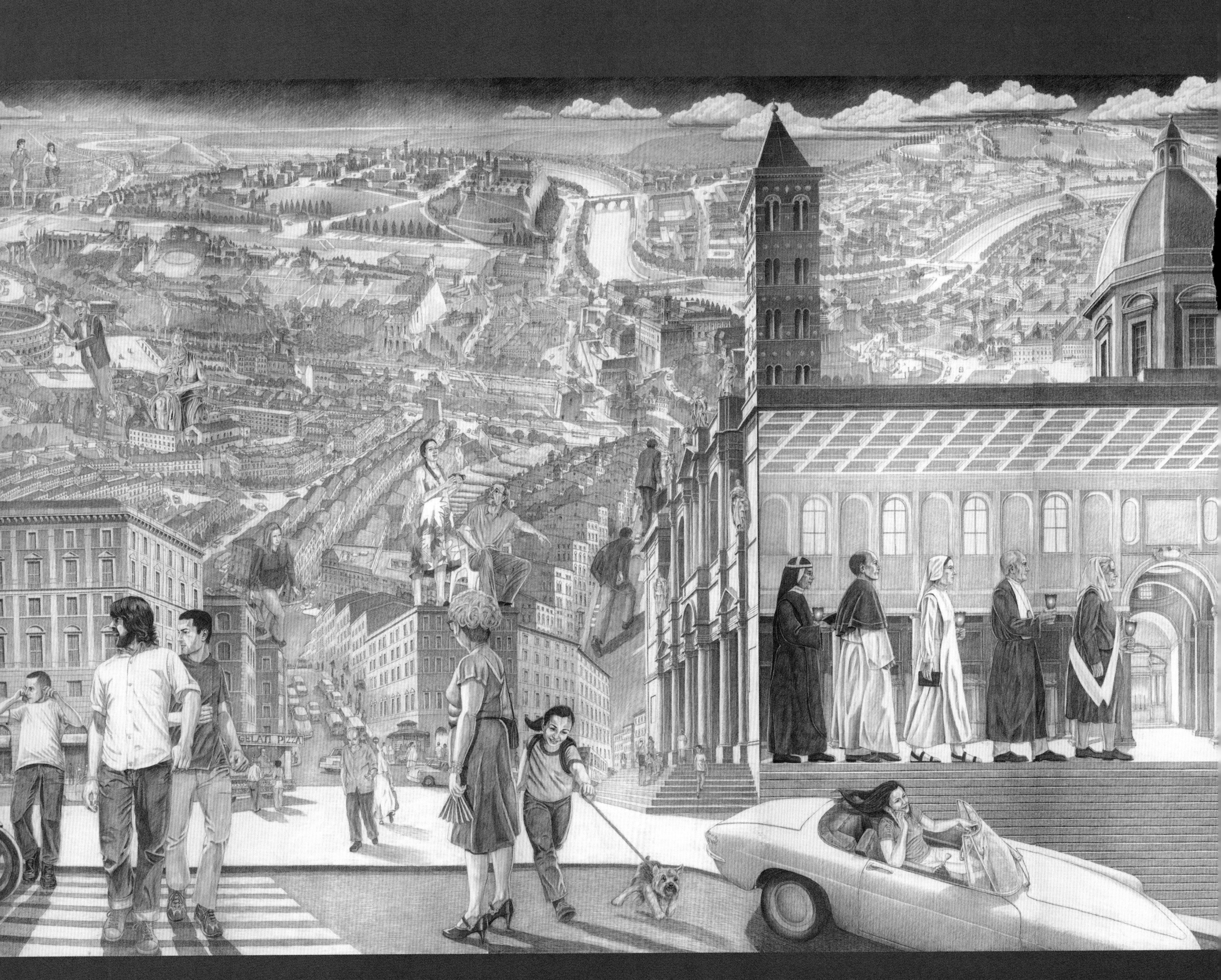

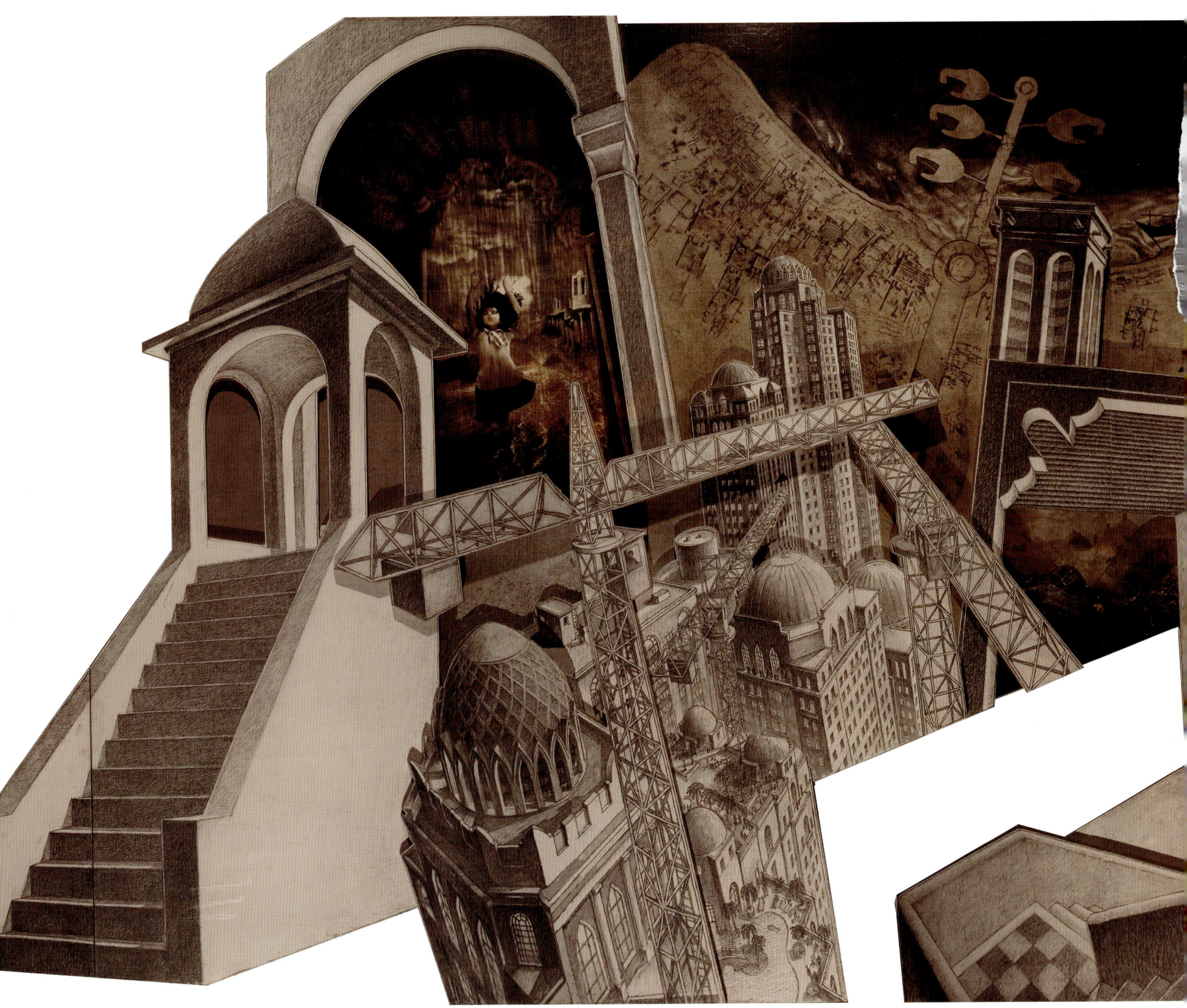

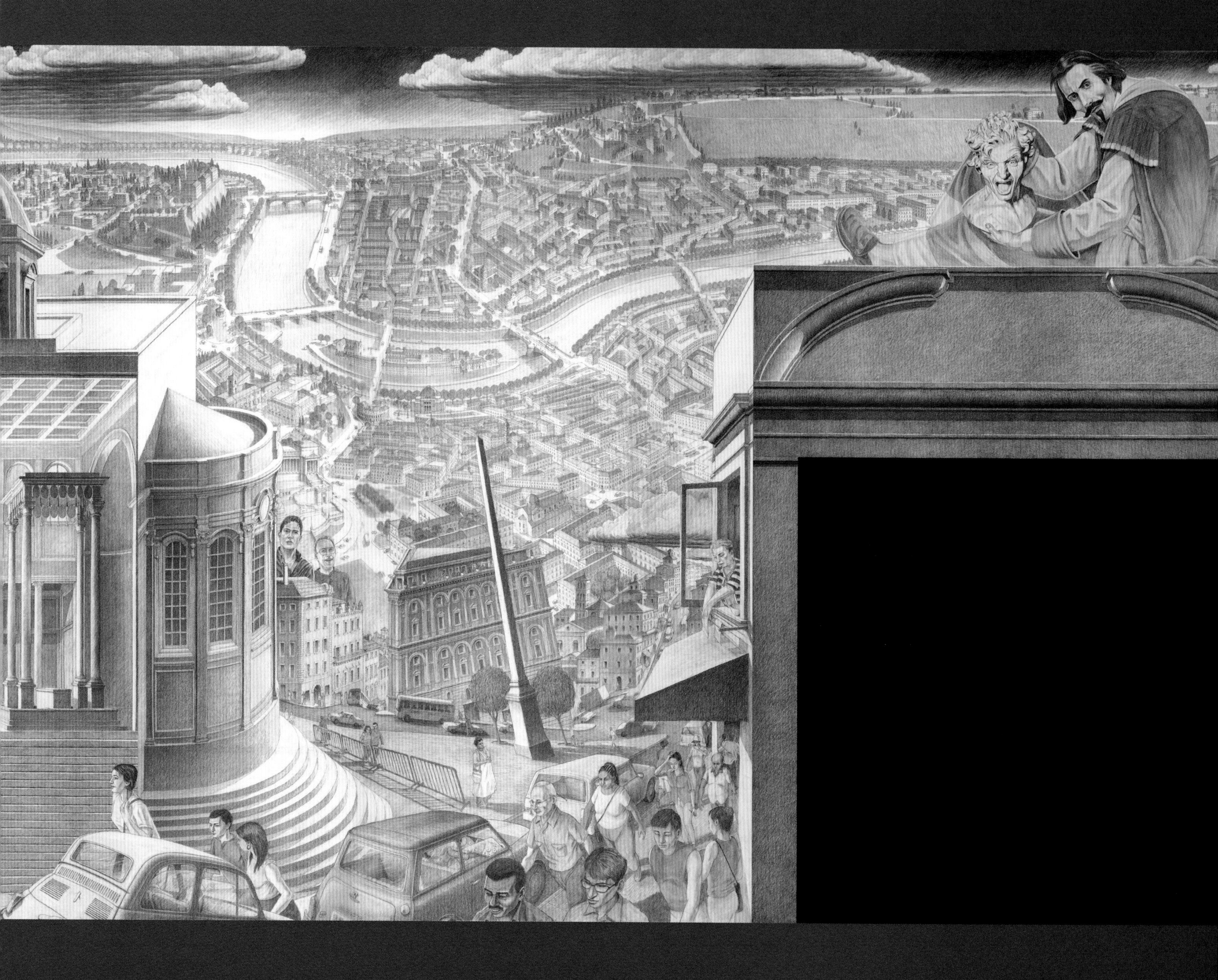

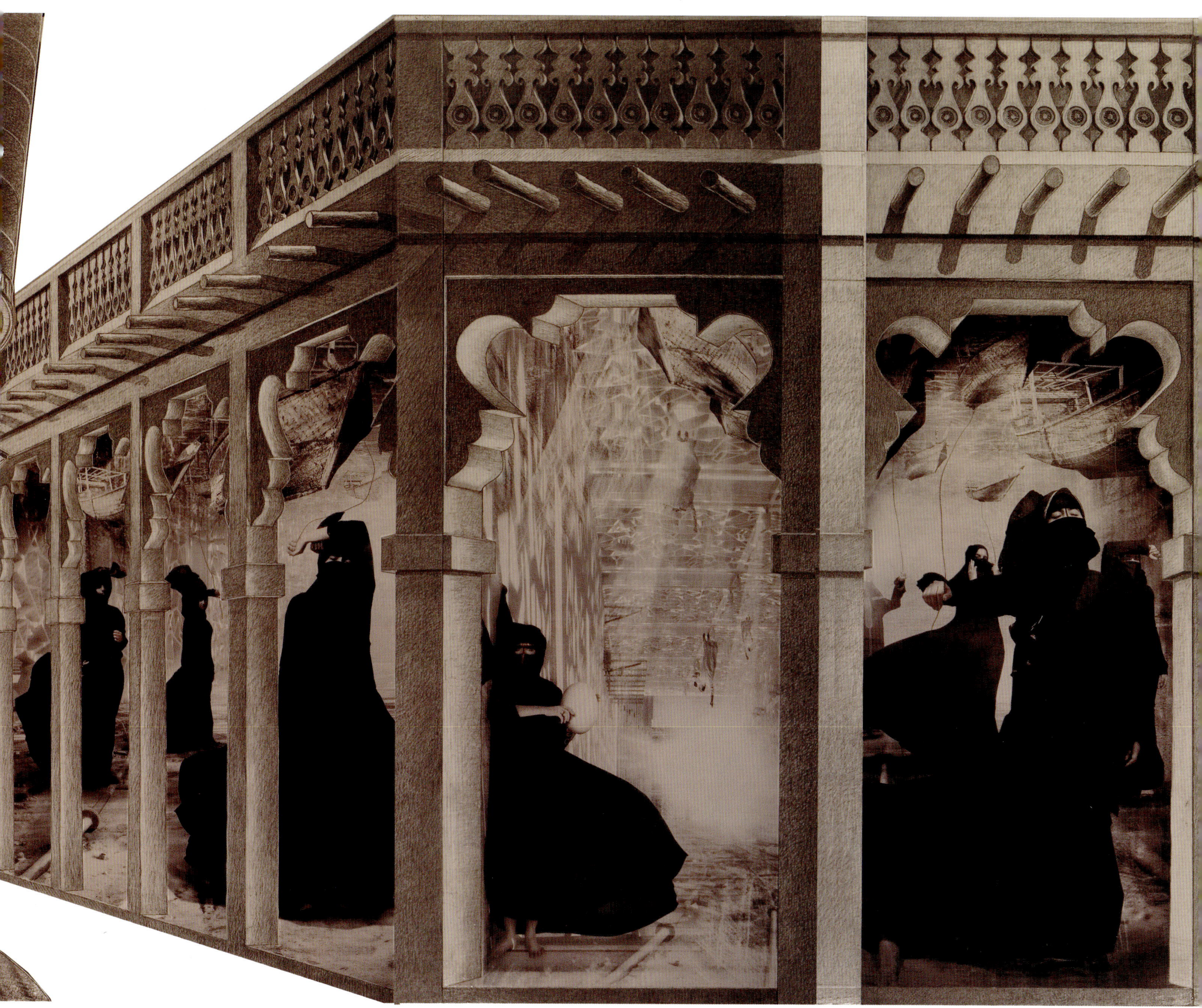

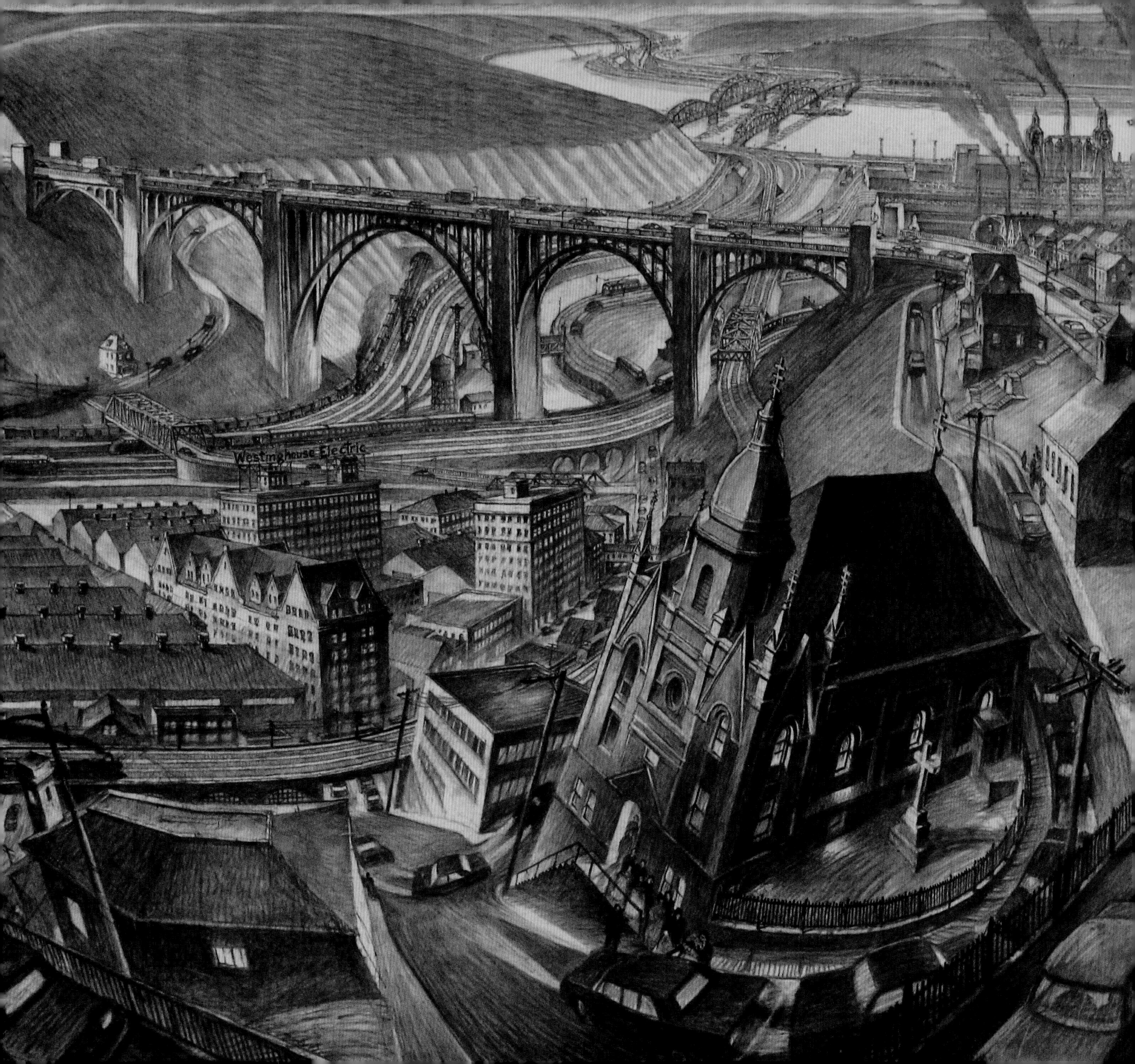

Westinghouse Electric

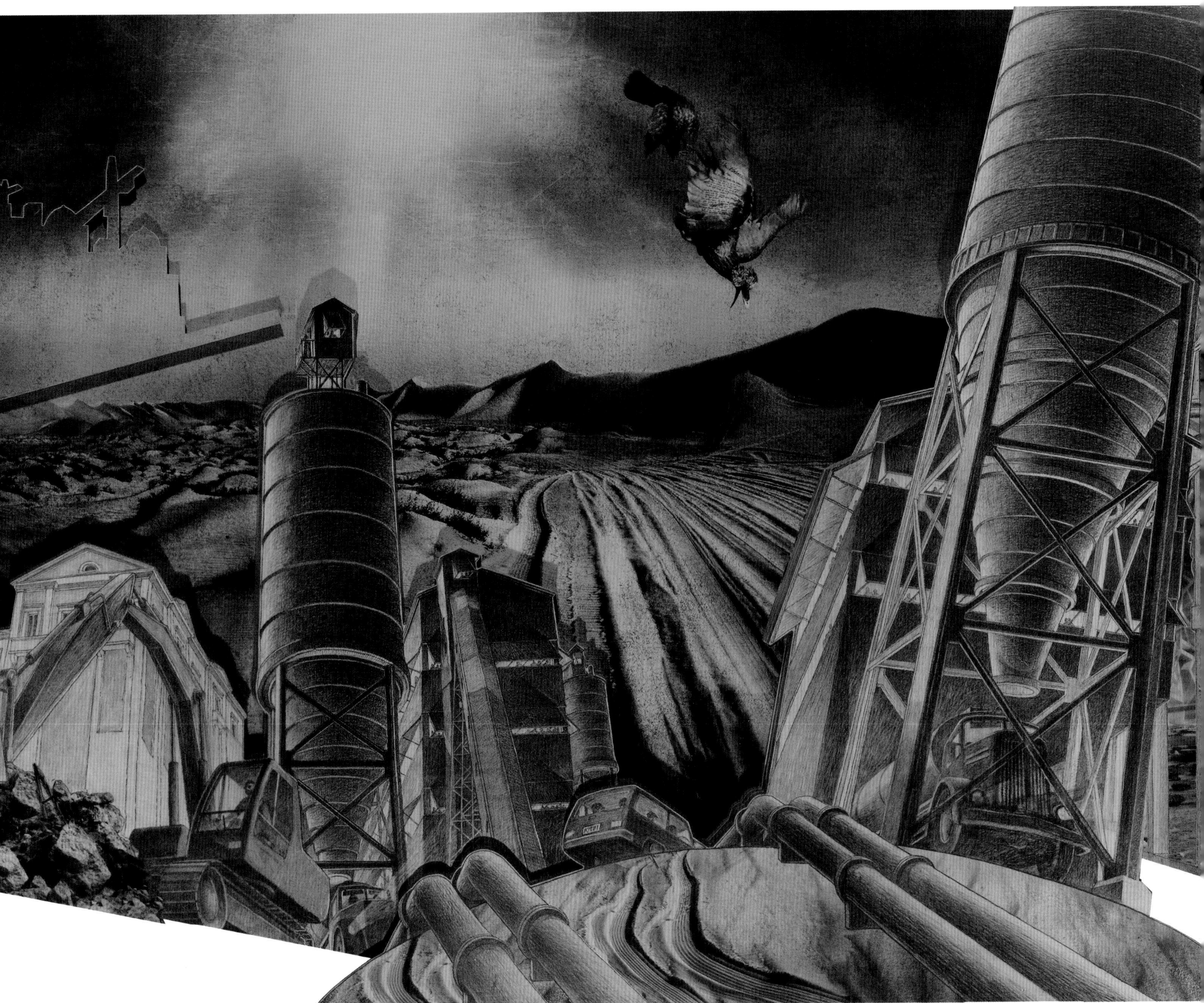

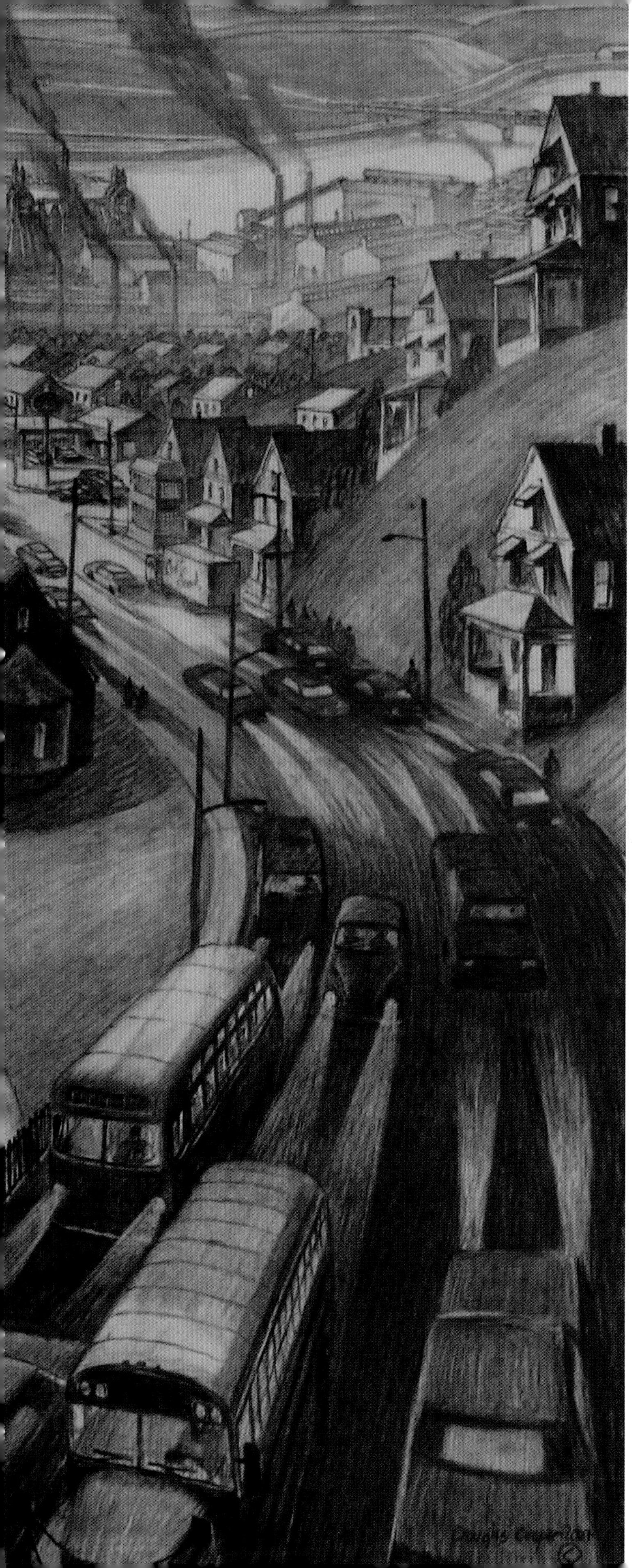

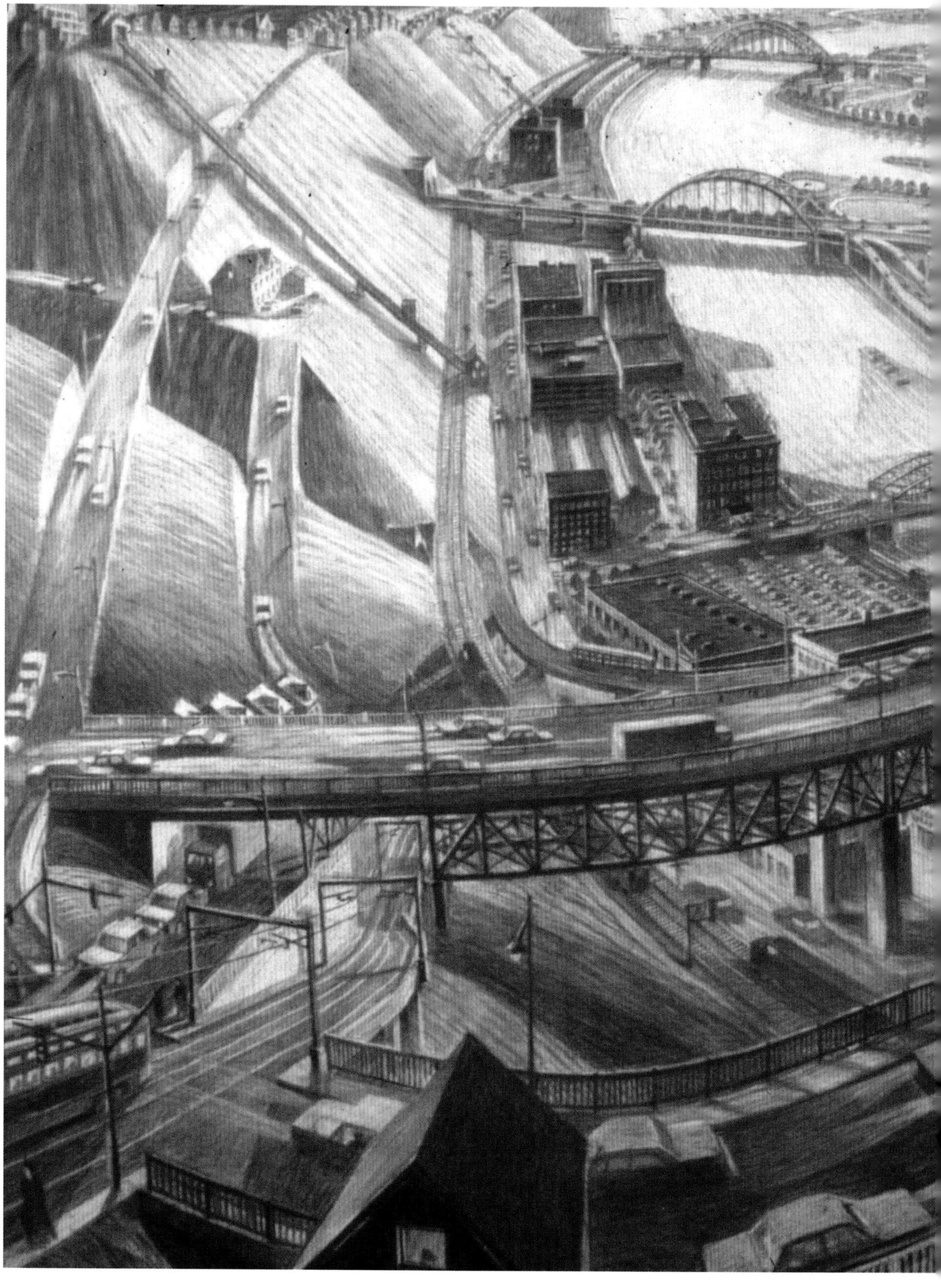

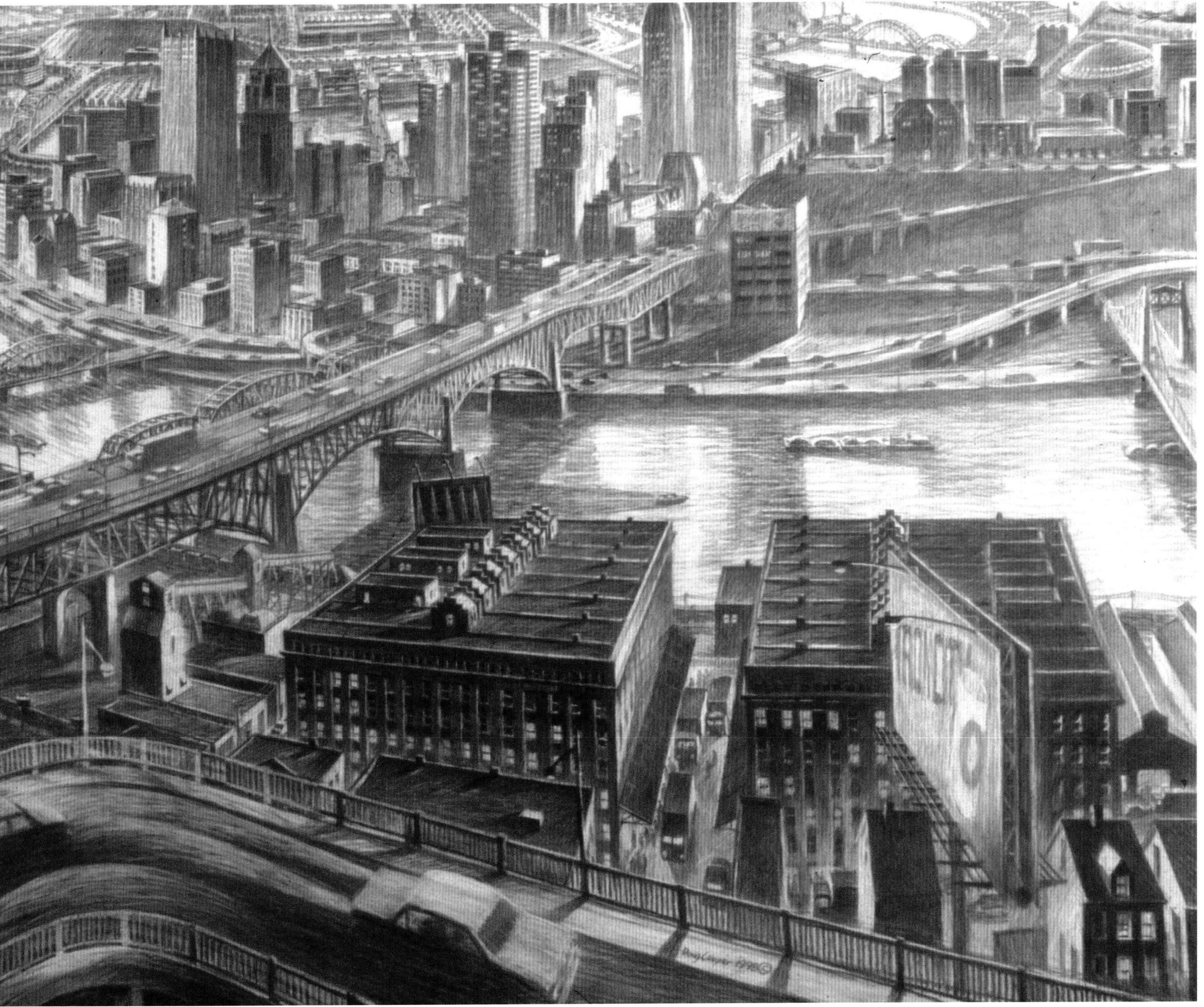

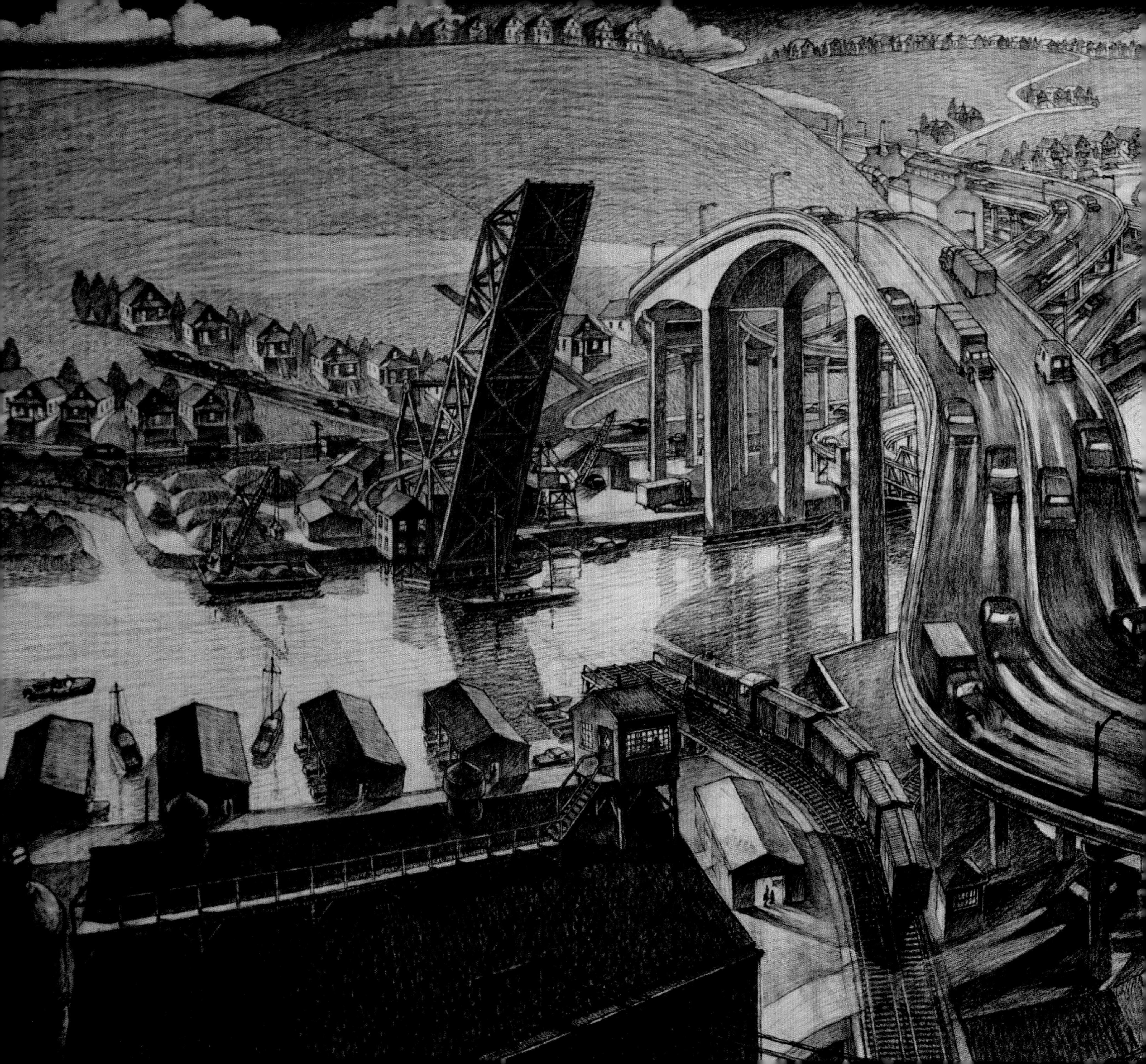

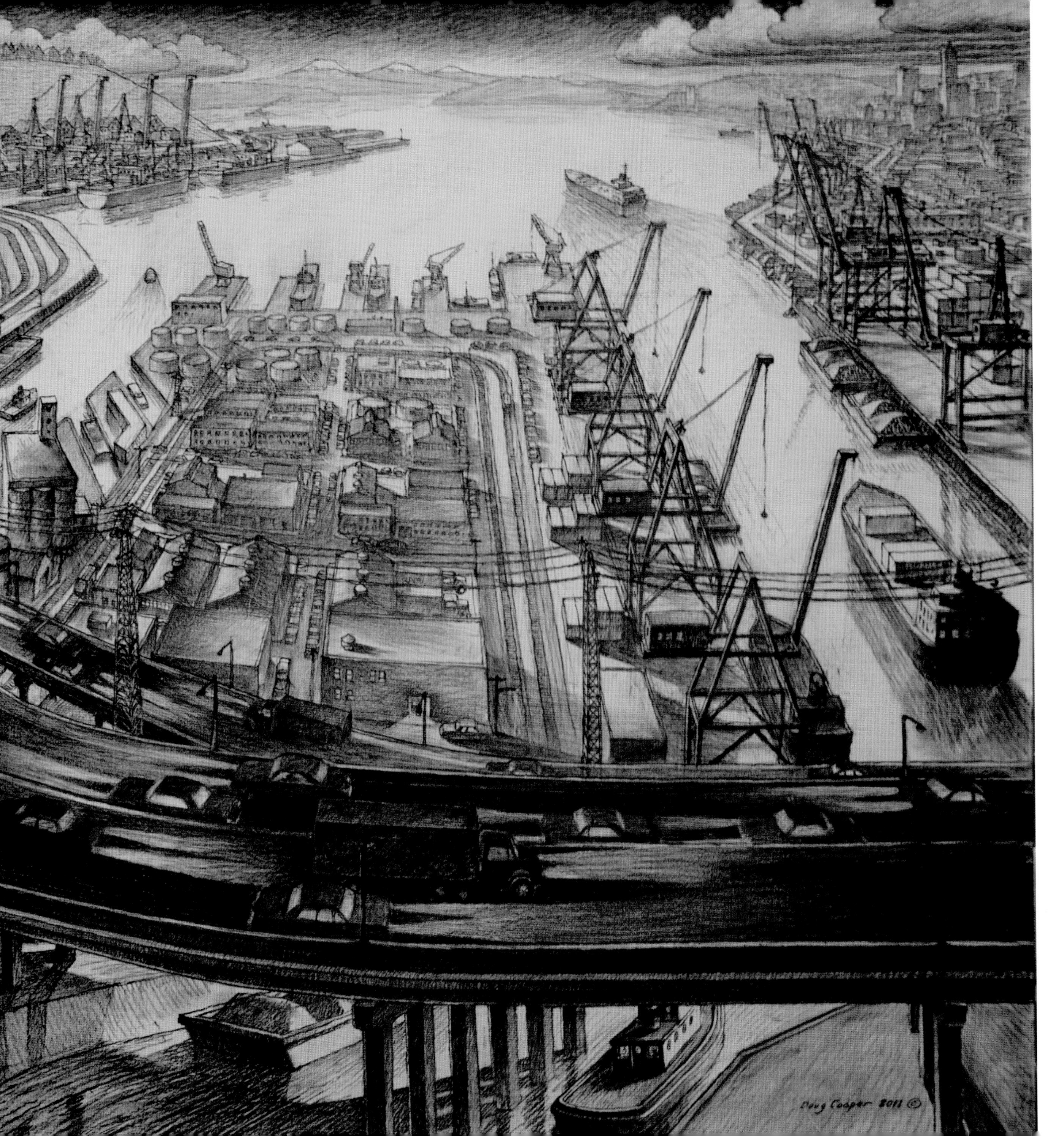

Doug Cooper 2011

ILLUSTRATION CAPTIONS FOR GATEFOLDS AND PLATES

First Gatefold

Page xiv–xv: *Steve's Corner*, Doug Cooper, 2007. Charcoal on paper on board,
48 × 72 inches. Private collection.

Page xvi–xviii: *Arrivals on Sterling*, 2006. Charcoal on paper on board, 48 × 144 inches

Page xix–xxii: East wall, *Jared L. Cohon University Center mural*, Doug Cooper with Sarah
Cooper, Jonathan Kline, and John Trivelli, 1996. Charcoal on paper on board, approx.
10 × 150 feet. Carnegie Mellon University, Pittsburgh.

Page xxiii–xxiv: *McKees Rocks Bridge*, Doug Cooper, 1999. Charcoal on paper on board,
48 × 96 inches. Collection of the Duquesne Club, Pittsburgh, PA.

Page xxv: *Backyard Auto Repair*, Doug Cooper, 2011. Charcoal on paper on board,
96 × 96 × 5 inches. Private collection.

Page xxvi–xxvii: *Jones and Laughlin Mill*, Doug Cooper, 2013. Charcoal on paper on board,
48 × 96 inches. Private collection.

Plates

Page 198: *Along Diulus Way*, 2015. Charcoal on paper on board, 60 × 48 inches.
Private collection of Geoffrey Kurland and Kristen Kurland.

Page 199: *Essex House*, Doug Cooper, 2014. Charcoal on paper on board, 60 × 48 inches.
Private collection.

Page 200: *Coogan's Bluff*, Doug Cooper, 2014. Charcoal on paper on board, 60 × 48 inches.
Private collection.

Page 200–201: *Rooftops over the Queensboro Bridge*, Doug Cooper, 2015. Charcoal on paper
on board, 48 × 60 inches. Private collection.

Page 202–3: *McArdle Roadway*, Doug Cooper, 2008. Charcoal on paper on board,
48 × 96 inches. Private collection.

Second and Third Gatefolds

Page 204–6: *The Collaborative Campus*, Doug Cooper and Stefani Danes with Adryan
Miller-Gorder, 2019. Charcoal on paper on board, fabric mounted around board,
15 × 45 feet. Carnegie Mellon University, David A. Tepper School of Business.

Page 207–10: East wall, *Medical Sciences Building Mural*, University of California, San
Francisco, Doug Cooper with Grégoire Picher, 2002. Charcoal on paper on board,
9 × 100 feet. Parnassus Campus, University of California, San Francisco.

Page 211–14: South wall, *Ex Caserma Sani mural*, Universitá Roma Tre, Doug Cooper with
Grégoire Picher and Patty Culley, 2005. Charcoal on paper on board, approx.
16 × 200 feet. Rome, Italy.

Page 215–18: West wall, *Memory between Desert and Sea*, Doug Cooper, Sarah Cooper,
and Nina Gorfer with David Kennedy, 2009. Charcoal on paper on board, approx.
9 × 50 feet. Carnegie Mellon University Qatar, Doha.

Page 219–20: *Late Afternoon Wedding*, Doug Cooper, 2011. Charcoal on paper on board,
48 × 96 inches. Private collection.

Page 220–21: *McArdle to Liberty*, Doug Cooper, 2008. Charcoal on paper on board,
48 × 72 inches. Private collection.

Page 222–23: *Harbor Island*, Doug Cooper, 2013. Charcoal on paper on board,
48 × 96 inches. Private collection.

ANNOTATED LIST OF WORKS AND EXHIBITIONS BY DOUG COOPER

Civic Murals

The Collaborative Campus, David Tepper School, Carnegie Mellon University (CMU), Pittsburgh, with Stefani Danes, assisted by Adryan Miller-Gorder (2019)

15' high × 45' wide. Collaboration with quilter Stefani Danes. Mural combines fabric and charcoal drawing. Focuses on the theme of people working together.

City Church City, East Liberty Presbyterian Church, Pittsburgh, with Stefani Danes (2018)

7' high × 19' wide. Collaboration with quilter Stefani Danes. Mural combines fabric and charcoal drawing. Focuses on themes of sanctuary and sacred space.

East End Cooperative Ministries, Pittsburgh (2013)

23' high × 44' wide. Collaboration with quilter Stefani Danes and students at Crossroads Church. Depicts the benefits of cooperation in bettering the physical environment of the city of Pittsburgh.

Memory between Desert and Sea, Education City Campus, CMU Qatar, Doha, with Sarah Cooper and Nina Gorfer (2009)

Mural series various heights and lengths. Collaboration with photographers Sarah Cooper and Nina Gorfer. Combines drawing and photography in a layered presentation. Depicts Qatar in its present state of frenzied development against a background of traditional settings and stories.

Ex-Caserma Sani mural, Università Roma Tre, Rome, Italy, with Grégoire Picher, Patty Culley, et al. (2005)

Approximately 14' high × 160' long. Created for the *aula magna* at the university's Esquilino facility, Ex Caserma Sani. Depicts the topography and personal stories of the Esquilino district of Rome. Developed jointly with Jan Vairo, Department of Modern Languages at CMU, and four CMU undergraduates. Project supported by Roy A. Hunt, Olivetti, and Bitner Foundations and CMU.

From These Hills, From These Valleys, King County Courthouse, Seattle, with Grégoire Picher and Patty Culley (2005)

Mural series with various heights and widths for lobby spaces of the King County Courthouse in Seattle. Murals depict regional history.

Michael Baker Corporation, Pittsburgh, with Grégoire Picher and Laura Cooper (2003)

20' × 24'. Mural for corporate headquarters depicts history and traditions of Michael Baker Corporation.

Medical Sciences Building mural, University of California at San Francisco, with Grégoire Picher (2002)

Approximately 9' high × 120' wide. Depicts history of San Francisco and University of California at San Francisco (UCSF). Developed with UCSF staff, patients, and neighboring residents. Work assisted by CMU anthropologist Judith Schachter [Modell] and four CMU undergraduates. Project supported by Bitner and Emma Eastman Foundations and CMU.

Pennsylvania Turnpike Commission Headquarters, Harrisburg, Pennsylvania, with Sarah Cooper (2001)

8' × 13' and 8' × 16'. Pair of murals depicting the history of the turnpike for the commission's boardroom.

Pittsburgh Ballet Theatre, "Indigo in Motion," show curtain, with John Trivelli (2000)

Design and implementation oversight for production of show curtain for "Indigo in Motion," a performance of dances to the music of Pittsburgh jazz legends.

Mascaro Construction Company, Pittsburgh, with John Trivelli (1999)

Approximately 25' high × 30' wide. Set of murals going around a narrow entrance hall of Mascaro's headquarters. Depicts buildings under construction with image of Pittsburgh in background.

Deloitte Consulting, Pittsburgh, with John Trivelli (1998)

9' × 22'. Entrance hall mural showing Pittsburgh viewed from the North Side and buildings associated with various public sector clients of Deloitte Consulting.

John's New York, New York City, with Sarah Cooper, Rebecca Schultz, and John Trivelli (1997)

Set of murals on the themes of Manhattan (20' × 30'), Times Square (8' × 24'), and the Theater District (2' × 24') for John's, a restaurant on West 44th Street just west of Times Square.

Kleinmarkthalle, Frankfurt, Germany (1996)

> 6 × 9 meters. Mural for central market (die Kleinmarkthalle) of Frankfurt am Main, Germany. Developed jointly with various senior centers around the city of Frankfurt and assisted by Professor Stephen Brockmann, of Department of Modern Languages, CMU, and four CMU students. Project supported with grants from the National Endowment for the Arts, Roy Hunt Foundation, Bosch Corporation, Deutsche Bank Bauspar AG.

Jared L. Cohon University Center, Carnegie Mellon University, Pittsburgh, with Jonathan Kline and John Trivelli (1995–1996)

> 9' high × 200' long. For permanent installation along three walls around the rotunda of CMU's university center.

Philadelphia Courthouse, Philadelphia, with Debbie Zwetsch and Walter Tien (1993–1995)

> 9' high × 96' long. Composite mural of Philadelphia. Work developed jointly with the Center in the Park, Philadelphia center for the elderly.

Senator John Heinz Regional History Center, Pittsburgh, with Sarah Cooper (1991–1993)

> 15' high × 120' long composite mural. Depicts Pittsburgh personal histories. Developed jointly with elderly at Vintage, a Pittsburgh activities center for senior citizens. Work supported by grants from the Pennsylvania Council on the Arts and the National Endowment for the Arts. Work has been purchased by Senator John Heinz History Center for its new Strip District facility. Installation 1996. Work was subject of PBS half-hour-long feature "A Map of Memories."

John's New York, New York City, with Sarah Cooper (1993)

> 40' long. Mural depicting New York City installed in John's, a restaurant on West 65th Street, near Lincoln Center.

Exhibitions

Concept Art Gallery, with Stefani Danes, Pittsburgh, 2018

Hirschl & Adler, New York, 2015

Concept Art Gallery, Pittsburgh, 2015

Concept Art Gallery, Pittsburgh, 2013

Davidson Galleries, Seattle, 2012

Concept Art Gallery, Pittsburgh, 2011

Concept Art Gallery, Pittsburgh, 2006

Concept Art Gallery, Pittsburgh, 1999

Concept Art Gallery, Pittsburgh, 1997

Institut für Stadtgeschichte, Karmeliterkloster, Frankfurt am Main, Germany, 1997

Carnegie Museum of Art, Forum Gallery, Pittsburgh, 1993

Carnegie Museum of Art, Pittsburgh, 1992

Galerie Der Spiegel, Cologne, Germany, 1990

Galerie Der Spiegel, Cologne, Germany, 1989

American Institute of Architects National Headquarters, Washington, DC, 1989

Alex Rosenberg Gallery, New York, 1985

Open Atelier of Design, New York, 1983

Carnegie Museum of Art, Pittsburgh, 1978

Galerie Der Spiegel, Cologne, Germany, 1975

Videos

"Pinburgh" (2011)

> A short fantasy (4:56) set in panoramic Pittsburgh industrial landscapes. A man on a street car sees a dancer on city steps who then enters a bar where someone is playing pinball, and the game is joined with the entire city activated in a citywide game. The film features CMU School of Drama's PigPen Theatre as actors and as the creators of the score. Ryan Woodring led the postproduction effort. Three-dimensional modeling by Shawn Cencer and Greg Tanski. Green screen filming at Pittsburgh Filmmakers. http://vimeo.com/15749259

Articles

"Imagination's Hand: The Role of Gesture in Design Drawing." *Design Studies* 54 (January 2018): 120–39.

Books

Drawing and Perceiving, 4th ed. (New York: John Wiley and Sons, 2007)

Steel Shadows (Pittsburgh: University of Pittsburgh Press, 2000)

Frankfurt Panorama (Frankfurt am Main: Deutsche Bank Bauspar AG, 1997)

BIBLIOGRAPHY

Appleton, Jay. *The Experience of Landscape*. West Sussex: John Wiley and Sons, 1996.

Arkus, Leon Anthony, comp. *John Kane, Painter*. Pittsburgh: University of Pittsburgh Press, 1971.

Bloomer, Kent C., and Charles W. Moore. *Body, Memory, and Architecture*. New Haven, CT: Yale University Press, 1977.

Edgerton, Samuel Y., Jr. *The Renaissance Rediscovery of Linear Perspective*. New York: Basic Books, 1975.

Harvey, P. D. A. *The History of Topographical Maps: Symbols, Pictures and Surveys*. New York: Thames and Hudson, 1980.

Jones, Barbara. *Samuel Rosenberg: Portrait of a Painter*. Pittsburgh: University of Pittsburgh Press with Carnegie Museum of Art, 2003.

Kane, John, and Marie McSwigan. *Sky Hooks: The Autobiography of John Kane*. Philadelphia: J. B. Lippincott, 1938.

Lorant, Stefan. *Pittsburgh: The Story of an American City*. Garden City, NY: Doubleday, 1964.

Lynch, Kevin. *The Image of the City*. Cambridge, MA: MIT Press, 1960.

McCullough, David. *The Great Bridge*. New York: Simon and Schuster, 1972.

Nicolaïdes, Kimon. *The Natural Way to Draw: A Working Plan for Art Study*. New York: Houghton Mifflin, 1941.

Plato. *The Republic*. In *The Dialogues of Plato*, translated by B. Jovett. New York: Random House, 1937.

Norberg-Schulz, Christian. *Genius Loci: Towards a Phenomenology of Architecture*. New York: Rizzoli, 1979.

Stewart, Hilary. *Cedar: Tree of Life to the Northwest Coast Indians*. Vancouver, BC: Douglas and McIntyre, 1984.

Stewart, Hilary. *Indian Fishing: Early Methods on the Northwest Coast*. Vancouver, BC: Douglas and McIntyre, 1977.